SOCIAL PROBLEMS

Why should there be one empty belly in the world when the work of one man can feed a hundred? What if my brother be not as strong as I? He has not sinned. Wherefore should he hunger—he and his sinless little ones? Down with the old law. There is food and shelter for all, therefore let all receive food and shelter.

—JACK LONDON, "Wanted: A New Law of Development"

SOCIAL PROBLEMS
A World at Risk

MICHAEL P. SOROKA
University of San Diego

GEORGE J. BRYJAK
University of San Diego

ALLYN AND BACON
Boston / London / Toronto / Sydney / Tokyo / Singapore

THIS BOOK IS DEDICATED TO OUR PARENTS:

Joseph and Alvina Soroka
Joseph and Sophie Bryjak

Executive Editor: Karen Hanson
Vice-President, Publisher: Susan Badger
Editorial Assistant: Sarah L. Dunbar
Marketing Manager: Joyce Nilsen
Production Administrator: Annette Joseph
Editorial-Production Service: Communicáto, Ltd.
Text Designer: Karen Mason
Composition/Prepress Buyer: Linda Cox
Photo Researcher: Susan Duane
Manufacturing Buyer: Megan Cochran
Cover Administrator: Linda Knowles
Cover Designer: Susan Paradise

This book is printed on
recycled, acid-free paper.

Library of Congress Cataloging-in-Publication Data

Soroka, Michael P.
Social problems : a world at risk / Michael P. Soroka, George J. Bryjak.
p. cm.
Includes bibliographical references and indexes.
ISBN 0-205-14128-5
1. United States—Social conditions—1980– 2. Social problems. 3. Social problems—Cross-cultural studies. I. Bryjak, George J. II. Title.
HN65.S587 1994
306'.0973—dc20 94-31405
CIP

Printed in the United States of America

10 9 8 7 6 5 4 3 2 1 99 98 97 96 95 94

PHOTO CREDITS

(Listed on page 461, which constitutes a continuation of this copyright page)

CONTENTS

CHAPTER 6

CHAPTER 7

CHAPTER 8

CHAPTER 9

CHAPTER 12 Health and Health Care: Paying the Price 364

PREFACE

THEMES AND RATIONALE

When we first decided to write a social problems text, we were surprised to discover that the majority of existing texts focused almost exclusively on the United States, offering little analysis of other societies, and that the presentations of these texts were rather mechanical and stilted. In addition, many of the books we looked through followed an "inventory" format, in which specific problems were discussed serially, without much regard for their connections to other social problems. Finally, since we both lean toward a macrolevel approach, we were dismayed to find that global-level issues (if discussed at all in conventional texts) were usually relegated to the last few chapters (the ones that, in a 13- to 16-week semester, are never covered).

Inasmuch as existing texts did not suit our particular needs, we finally selected a main text for our course and, in effect, redesigned it. We told students to read the book as background material, but we structured and presented our classroom lectures according to *our* vision of what a social problems course ought to cover. This arrangement probably added to our students' angst over impending course examinations ("What should we study—the book or the notes?"), but it also convinced us of the need for another social problems text.

Our ultimate goal in writing this text was to create a book that would examine contemporary social problems from a macrolevel and somewhat historical perspective. Like most other texts in the field, *Social Problems: A World at Risk* centers on the major social problems in the United States. However, unlike many other texts, we have tried to provide students with a sound basis for assessing both the dimensions and the prognoses for social problems in their own society by examining similar problems in other societies. We have accomplished this objective in several different ways.

ORGANIZATION OF THIS TEXT

A GLOBAL PERSPECTIVE

First, this text begins, rather than ends, with an analysis of the "global village" nature of contemporary life—namely, that events and policies unfolding in one part of the planet typically have repercussions for people and societies half a world away. Following an extended discussion in Chapter 1 of the sociological orientation to the study of social problems, Chapters 2 through 4 examine those "three aspects of the current human predicament" that, as economist Robert L. Heilbroner (1980) noted in *An Inquiry into the Human Prospect,* pose the most serious threats to humankind at large—war, population pressures, and environmental destruction. Localized "dirty little wars" being fought in many countries around the globe as well as the destruction of local environments through overpopulation and overuse have created a flood of international refugees. As these tens of millions of people have fled military or environmental catastrophes in their homelands, they have put tremendous strains on the societies in which they have settled. These societies, which are generally more affluent, are expected to respond with financial and other material support, but quite often, they respond with hostility instead.

By the time students have completed Part One, "Global-Level Problems," they should have a greater appreciation of the larger context within which the problems of their own society exist. Students should also have developed the sense that, as one senior administrator for the United Nations Development Program recently stated, "In the age of global interdependence, human crisis anywhere is a human threat everywhere."

The remainder of the book is strongly rooted in this global, cross-cultural perspective. Part Two, "Societal-Level Problems," includes chapters on urban problems (5); inequality and poverty (6); race and ethnicity (7); sex and gender (8); and crime, violence, and criminal justice (9). The chapters in Part Three, "Individual- and Family-Level Problems," address family disorganization and sexuality (10); drugs, alcohol, and gambling (11); and health and health care (12). The Epilogue contains our final comment on contemporary social problems, offering some hope for change in the future based on what has been accomplished in the past.

FEATURES OF THE TEXT

Maintaining the global perspective, each of the topical chapters (2 through 12) contains a "Focus On" section in which a society other than the United States is singled out for detailed analysis of the topic at hand. For example, in Chapter 3, the focus is on population problems in Nigeria, one of the fastest-growing and poorest nations in Africa. In Chapter 6, the focus is on inequality and poverty in Brazil, a country once hailed as the model for economic development in Latin America but now recognized as one of the most economically inegalitarian societies in the Western world. In addition to the "Focus On" segments, these topical chapters also contain a wealth of cross-cultural examples, offering students a solid foundation for comparing and contrasting social problems in developing nations with those in the developed world.

To help students make the needed geographical associations, each "Focus On" section includes a small map of the country under analysis, showing its location within the world. A large world map, highlighting all the countries identified in "Focus On" sections, follows this Preface.

Finally, in an effort to acquaint students with the enormous complexities of the world in which they live, each chapter also contains a section called "Connections," which explores some of the many linkages among problems within and across societies. For example, the problems of excessive population growth found in many developing societies are, to a large extent, the result of traditional gender stereotypes that define masculinity in terms of sexual conquest and continue to relegate women and girls to subordinate positions (including being denied control over reproduction). Similar gender stereotypes consign women in many developed societies to so-called pink-collar occupations that are undervalued and underpaid. In both instances, one major consequence has been increasing poverty for a growing portion of the population in both the developing and the developed worlds. Efforts to stem increasing poverty and population growth have been thwarted by entrenched resistance to the redefinition of both male and female roles that would be required to make such efforts successful.

Ordinarily, social problems are much more complicated than they first appear, and students need to realize that simple solutions are not likely to solve complex problems. In the course of our analyses, we introduce students to some of the strategies that have been proposed or implemented toward solving or at least alleviating particular problems. We also comment on why these interventions have succeeded or failed—wholly or in part—and on the prospects for future success or failure in addressing social problems in the United States and in other societies.

We have tried to make *Social Problems: A World at Risk* as readable and stimulating as possible so that students will want to read each chapter in its entirety. But the facts are that a textbook cannot be written exactly like an adventure story and the subject matter of a social problems text, in particular, will not make for lighthearted reading. It is equally true, however, that even grim factual material written in a lively style will more likely be read than the same grim material written in a dry or pedantic manner. We think our presentation of the many facts in this book has succeeded in achieving an overall coherency within and among chapters—a quality that is missing from many texts. Students may not relish learning about all the harsh realities of human social life, but they will at least find the presentation of this information interesting.

Social Problems: A World at Risk reflects our attempt to provide comprehensive, coherent, and contemporary coverage of the world's social problems in a format that will appeal to students' interests and financial resources. This is not an exhaustive text, given the impossibility of addressing every social problem facing the world today in a 12-chapter format. It is nonetheless a thorough text, in that it examines a set of specific social problems and also provides a framework for analyzing other problems. We believe that an adequate understanding of contemporary social problems requires a global, cross-cultural perspective that takes into account both the similarities and the differences that mark individual societies of the modern world. This book represents not the final word but rather a first step toward achieving that understanding.

SUPPLEMENTS FOR STUDENTS AND INSTRUCTORS

STUDY GUIDE Prepared by Dale Hoffman-Barger, the student study guide contains learning objectives, chapter overviews, chapter outlines, and self-test questions. (The latter are divided into matching, multiple-choice, true-false, and essay/short-answer questions.)

SOCIETY IN CRISIS: THE WASHINGTON POST SOCIAL PROBLEMS COMPANION By exclusive arrangement with the *Washington Post,* Allyn and Bacon has published an integrated collection of over 80 articles that explore social problems in the United States and around the world, as illustrated by real-world events. Studying social problems in the United States as well as in societies other than their own will help readers gain a sense of the strong interdependence among societies.

ALLYN AND BACON/CNN VIDEO III In keeping with the focus on the global nature of social problems, a fully integrated, 60-minute video program accompanies this text, presenting segments from recent CNN programming from the United States and around the world. These video segments address timely and important topics that illustrate key text issues or concepts. The segments are introduced by a narrator, who alerts students to what they are about to see and discusses the relevance of the film clips to concepts discussed in various chapters. The segments focus on issues in four major areas: conflict and war, environmental destruction, race/ethnicity and immigration, and crime. An accompanying video guide provides a description of each segment and keys it to the appropriate text section.

A wide variety of other videos are also available from the Allyn and Bacon Video Library.

INSTRUCTOR'S MANUAL/TEST BANK Also prepared by Dale Hoffman-Barger, the instructor's manual includes a variety of teaching aids: chapter overviews, learning objectives, chapter outlines, and video resources as well as a comprehensive set of tests (again, consisting of a variety of question formats and all cross-referenced to pages in the text).

COMPUTERIZED TEST BANKS Allyn and Bacon offers computerized test banks for both IBM and Macintosh formats, allowing instructors the options to edit questions already in the test banks, to add their own questions, and to create multiple versions of a test. Full customer support is available.

CALL-IN AND FAX TESTING SERVICES The Allyn and Bacon testing center can process and send a finished test, ready for duplication, within 48 hours of request. Fax service of hard copy is available on a same-day basis.

CUSTOM-PUBLISHED ANCILLARIES Allyn and Bacon can customize packages of supplements to meet instructors' specific needs. For example, an instructor may wish to add a course syllabus or additional study and test questions.

For more information on custom publishing or any of the supplemental materials described here, please contact your local Allyn and Bacon representative.

ACKNOWLEDGMENTS

Once again, we have had the good fortune of working with many talented people who have made significant contributions in the preparation of this book. We are especially grateful to Executive Editor Karen Hanson, who prompted us to write this text and gave us the opportunity to present our interpretation of social problems. Developmental Editor Sylvia Shepard did a superb job in shaping our rough outlines and lengthy chapters. We thank Sylvia for her thoroughness and professionalism during the many weeks we worked together and also for the benefit of her considerable knowledge of the social sciences.

Production Administrator Annette Joseph kept all the pieces of this multifaceted project together. Other members of the Allyn and Bacon staff, including Sarah Dunbar, were most helpful. Susan Freese of Communicáto, Ltd., did a great job keeping things running smoothly during the final, sometimes hectic days of rewriting and proofreading, when chapters were flying back and forth through the mail. We would also like to thank copyeditor Karen Stone, who helped make sense out of our sometimes garbled prose.

Many reviewers made important comments during the development of this manuscript, and we thank them for their assistance: H. David Allen, University of New Orleans;

Tom Arcaro, Elon College; Chet Ballard, Valdosta State University; Patrick Donnelly, The University of Dayton; Jane Foraker-Thompson, Boise State University; Michael C. Hoover, Missouri Western State College; and Kathleen Tiemann, University of North Dakota.

Colleagues at the University of San Diego also read portions of this manuscript and gave us valuable insights. We would like to thank Judy Liu, Anne Hendershott, Gene Labovitz, Kathy Grove, Alberto Restrepo, Jim Gump, Gary Macy, and Allen Wittenborn for their time and expertise. Special thanks to the library staff at USD—especially Tony Harvell, Steve Staninger, and Marjo Gray—who helped track down a good deal of hard-to-find information that we always needed "as soon as possible." Pat Drinan, Dean of the College of Arts and Sciences at USD, provided us with research minigrants for copying and duplicating.

Departmental secretary Jan Fain did most of the copying after numerous chapter revisions and gave us encouragement when it seemed as though this project would never end. Shelley Heffernan spent countless hours searching out articles and bringing back piles of books from the university library—thanks, Shelley. Departmental work/study students cut and pasted the hundreds of newspaper articles we reviewed for this text. Without the efforts of all these people, this book would not have been possible.

Finally, we acknowledge our significant others—Gaye Soroka and Diane Kulstad—who endured yet another long-term project. Their understanding, love, and support during those especially difficult periods when we had two full-time jobs—teaching and writing—is deeply appreciated. Now it's time to relax awhile.

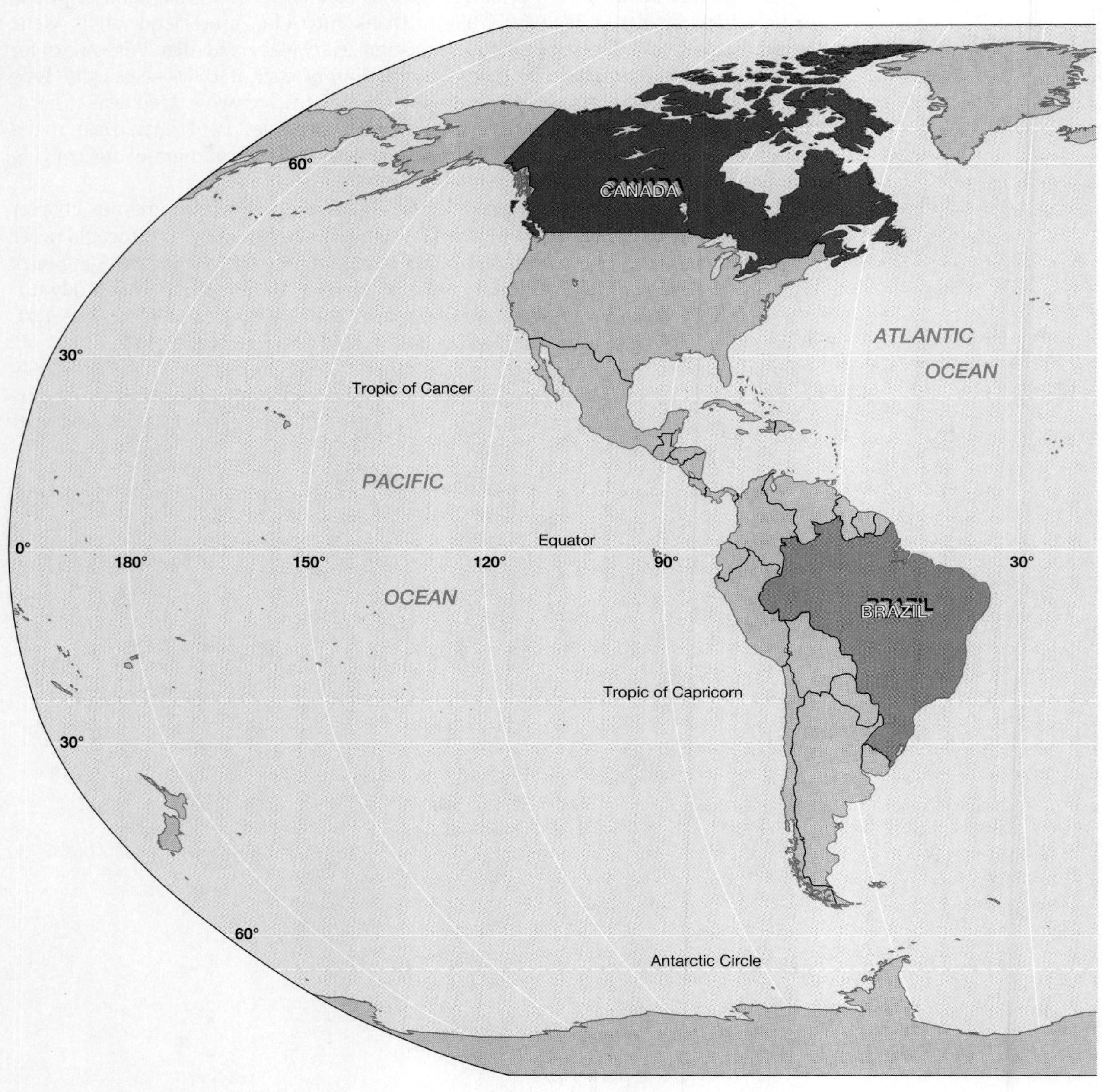
60°
CANADA
ATLANTIC
OCEAN
30°
Tropic of Cancer
PACIFIC
0°
Equator
180°
150°
120°
90°
30°
OCEAN
BRAZIL
Tropic of Capricorn
30°
60°
Antarctic Circle

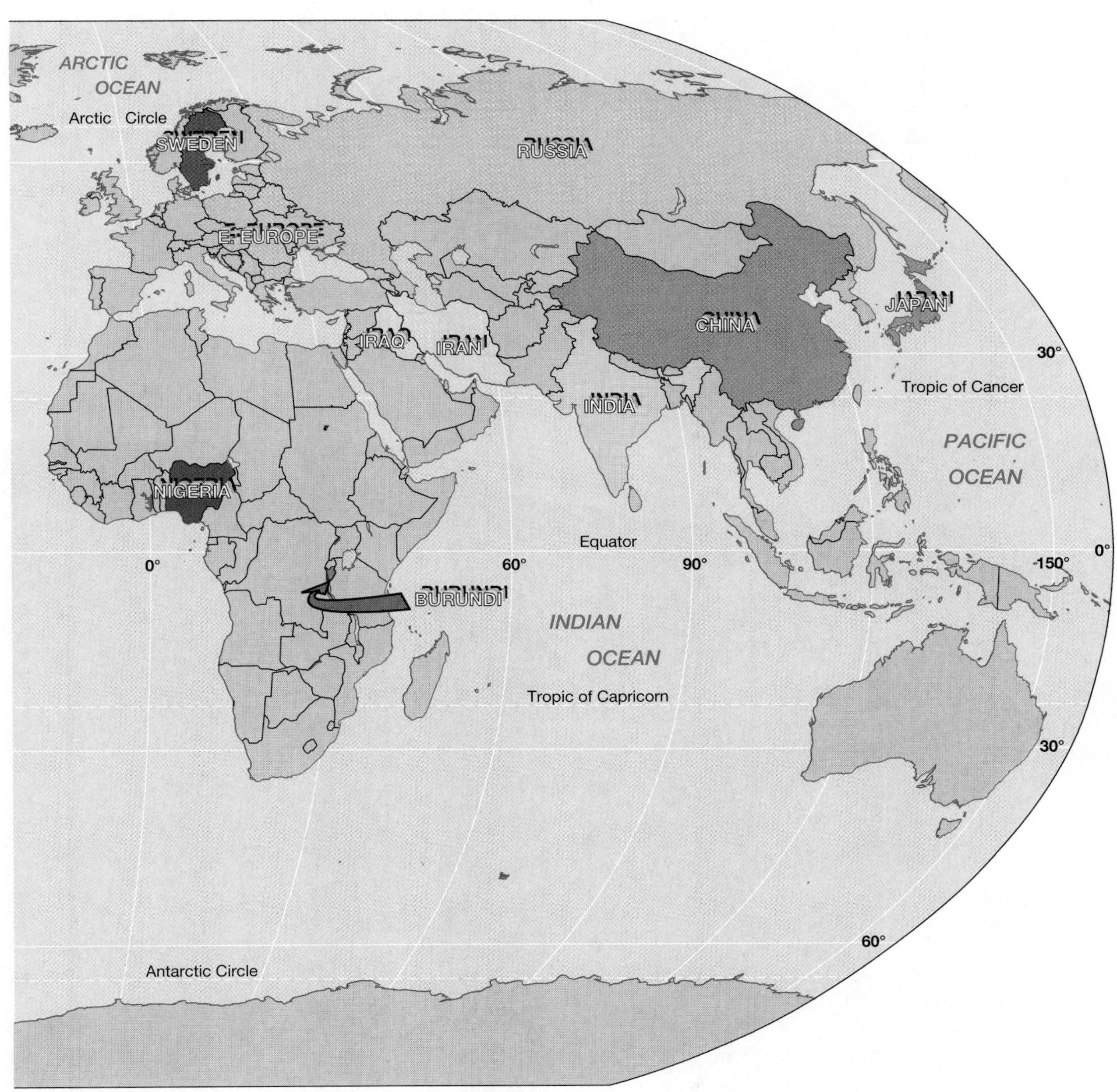

Countries highlighted are featured in the "Focus on" sections appearing in chapters 2–12.

CHAPTER ONE

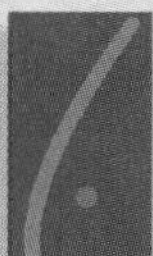

THE SOCIOLOGY OF SOCIAL PROBLEMS

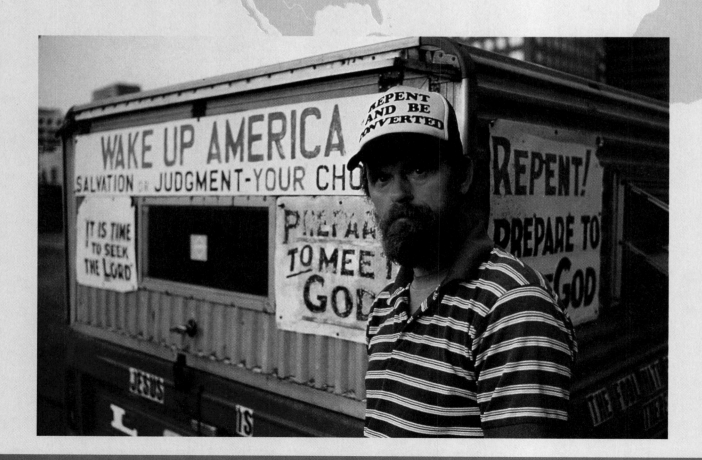

"In the old days, books and movies were clean, decent entertainment. People then wouldn't dream of writing about or showing the things they do nowadays."

"When I was your age, people didn't drink and use drugs the way they do today. We had better things to keep us occupied."

"In the old days, it was safe to be on the streets. You could walk anywhere in town, any time of the day or night, and never worry about being robbed or killed while you were out."

"The old days" lecture certainly is not an institutionalized or formal part of the child-rearing process in American society. Nevertheless, it is a very familiar—though seldom cherished—memory of the passage from childhood to adulthood for tens of millions of people in the United States. Also known as the "when I was your age" speech, this ritual follows a classic pattern: An adult speaker bombards a young (and usually unwilling) listener with supposedly incontrovertible proof of how good things were in "the old days," when the speaker was the listener's age. These little vignettes then are followed by the speaker's analysis of just how and why things have fallen apart since that better and happier time. Often, the young listener is given the distinct impression that his or her own generation somehow is personally responsible for the terrible mess the country and the world have fallen into during these not-so-good modern times. If only young people today were more respectful and weren't so drug, sex, power, money, music, and hedonism crazed, the world just might be a halfway decent place.

However, an examination of the factual details of these "good old days" would reveal a reality quite different from that depicted by the tellers of tales. Entertainment may have been more "decent" in years past, but most people had little time or money to spend on leisure activities. They worked jobs for which the hours were much longer, the wages far lower, and the working conditions considerably more difficult and dangerous than they are today. Illegal drug abuse may not have been so rampant one or two generations ago. But many over-the-counter medicines were laced with addictive substances, and thousands of

people died each year from illnesses now considered minor or routine. Rates of violent street crime certainly were lower in the past. But millions of people were victimized by the dangerous products and practices of companies driven by pure profit and unrestrained by any public-interest regulatory agencies.

The kinds of past-perfect times portrayed so often in these "good old days" stories never really existed, although generations of parents and grandparents have tried to convince their young charges that they once did. And many people who have been the captive audiences of these morality tales in the past may well become the nostalgic spinners of the same kinds of stories to their own children and grandchildren in the future. For them, *these* may be the good old days.

Considering the apparent state of our society and our world today, it may be hard to imagine that people someday may actually look back on the present time as "the good old days." Widespread environmental destruction, poverty, hunger, injustice, substance abuse, crime, genocide, and AIDS are not the usual ingredients for nostalgic reflections, and these conditions seem to be persistent elements of the contemporary social world. To speak of the present as future "good old days," then, implies that the actual consequences of these conditions are not nearly as serious or dramatic as their outward appearances would suggest. Alternatively, it might imply that future societal and world conditions will become so bad that contemporary problems will pale by comparison and that one day, the present will seem like a far better time than it actually was.

In this text, we are going to explore systematically, from a sociological perspective, a number of the most serious problems facing our society and our world today. First, we will discuss the sociological orientation and examine a number of different ways that sociologists have conceptualized and studied the major social problems of their times. Then we will turn to an analysis of those conditions that make many people's lives far different and lesser experiences than they otherwise could be. We also will consider various attempts to solve these problems in the United States and in other societies.

As we hope to make clear, it often is very difficult to identify and isolate the exact causes of a given social problem. It is even more difficult to develop policies and programs that will effectively put an end to the problem. The history of this particular facet of human social life has been one in which attempted solutions to existing problems frequently have themselves become the causes of later and more serious social problems. And yet, our continued existence as a species may require that we make the best effort possible to understand and to rectify those conditions that so dramatically limit the lives of millions of our fellow human beings.

QUESTIONS TO CONSIDER

- 1. How did social problems affect the development of the field of sociology?
- 2. What is the difference between a *natural problem* and a *social problem?*
- 3. In what sense are all social problems subjective in nature?
- 4. Why is it impossible to engage in a completely scientific study of social problems?
- 5. What was the social pathology interpretation of social problems?
- 6. What is a *cultural lag?*
- 7. What is the difference between a *manifest dysfunction* and a *latent dysfunction?*

- 8. From the Marxist conflict perspective, what is the underlying cause of social problems in any society?
- 9. How do non-Marxist conflict theorists explain social problems in modern societies?
- 10. What is the main argument of the social constructionist interpretation of social problems?
- 11. From the labeling theory perspective, what is the difference between *primary deviance* and *secondary deviance?*

SOCIOLOGY AND SOCIAL PROBLEMS

As an academic field devoted to the examination and understanding of human social arrangements, sociology has had a long-standing historical association with the study of social problems. In a very real sense, the discipline of sociology itself was created in response to a series of problems plaguing the Western European countries during the late eighteenth and early nineteenth centuries.

August Comte (1798–1857) is generally credited as being the founder of sociology. As a scholar, Comte was intrigued and concerned by the destruction of a traditional way of life and the massive dislocation of people that had resulted from the Industrial Revolution. Millions of individuals and families in Comte's native France and across Western Europe had been displaced from a well-established rural, agrarian life and pushed into an unfamiliar factory-based, urbanized existence, often with tragic results. Comte saw his new "science of society" as a perfect vehicle for deciphering the massive forces of change at work in his world and undertook the development of sociology in that direction.

The great German social thinker Karl Marx (1818–1883) also significantly influenced the interest of sociologists in the study of social problems. Like Comte, Marx focused his attention on the profoundly negative effects of industrialization on the lives of the population masses. However, unlike Comte, Marx did not view the movement from traditional, agrarian societies to modern, industrial systems as part of some natural, progressive, evolutionary process. Rather, he saw this new factory- and city-based way of life as the most recent facet of an age-old struggle between the "haves" and the "have-nots" in all human societies. For Marx, the excesses and the miseries of the modern age were simply contemporary manifestations of social problems inherent in any economic and social system based upon private property ownership. As Marx saw it, the fundamental problem was the nature of private property itself.

Another crucial figure in the early history of sociology, Emile Durkheim (1858–1917), also directed many of his studies toward an analysis of the social problems of his times. Originally published in 1897, his landmark work, *Suicide,* was a pivotal effort to establish a sociological perspective for comprehending a significant and otherwise perplexing social problem. According to Durkheim, even the seemingly private and desperate act of taking one's own life was a "social fact" that could be understood only through an examination of other social facts—in this case, the web of relations among individuals and groups of various kinds. Durkheim's classic analysis of the growing problem of suicide in his native France offered a practical answer to a specific social problem. More importantly, it helped to establish the parameters and operating principles of the sociological orientation.

Like their European counterparts, the early pioneers in American (that is, U.S.) sociology also had a fundamental and abiding interest in the social problems of their day. During the last quarter of the nineteenth century, the United States began to experience many of the same problematic consequences of massive, rapid industrialization and urbanization that Western Europe had encountered nearly a century earlier. In addition, these problems were compounded by the waves of foreign-born immigrants who were descending upon the United States in record numbers and clustering in cities that were already overcrowded and poorly prepared to accommodate them (Pfohl, 1985). The resulting skyrocketing rates of crime and social decay were a matter of great concern to those academicians who became the founding generation of U.S. sociologists.

Centered around large urban areas (in particular, the city of Chicago) that served as "living laboratories," scholars such as William Isaac Thomas (1863–1947) and Florian Znaniecki (1882–1958) devoted their attention and skills to the formulation of a sociological interpretation of the most pressing problems of their times. Their monumental study, *The Polish Peasant in Europe and America* (published, in five volumes, between 1918 and 1920), was perhaps the most famous of the works undertaken by what has since become known as "the Chicago school" of sociology. But it was only one among hundreds of such efforts by U.S. sociologists to examine and understand social problems in the early decades of this century.

The involvement of sociologists with the study of the major social problems of this society perhaps reached its peak during the 1960s. In colleges and universities around the country, the ranks of the discipline were filled by activist-oriented students seeking "relevant" knowledge that they could use to change the world. Professional sociologists increasingly became involved in government-sponsored studies of social problems and in government offices themselves. A sociological view of the world and a host of sociological

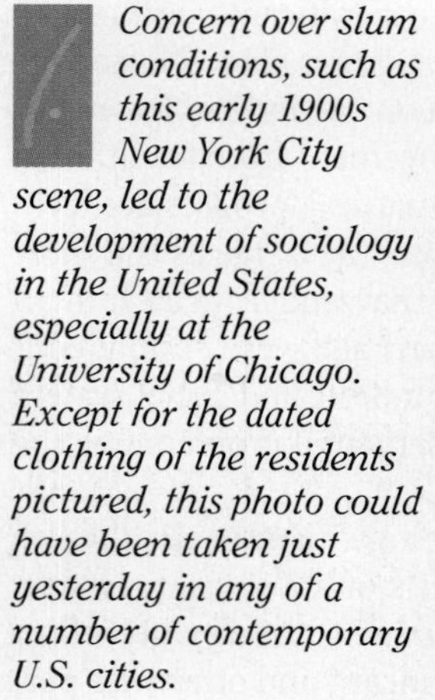

Concern over slum conditions, such as this early 1900s New York City scene, led to the development of sociology in the United States, especially at the University of Chicago. Except for the dated clothing of the residents pictured, this photo could have been taken just yesterday in any of a number of contemporary U.S. cities.

research findings often became incorporated into social policies designed to eliminate or at least mitigate poverty, hunger, racial injustice, and other obstacles to the great society.

Though this strong activist orientation declined somewhat during the succeeding three decades, the discipline of sociology remains committed to an attempt to understand contemporary social problems. Various schools or factions within the field continue to disagree on the question of whether or not sociologists should act as agents of social change in dealing with the significant problems of the 1990s. But no sociologist would question the involvement of the discipline with the scientific study of contemporary problems. This goal of examining and understanding societal problems remains a central or core focus of the field.

STUDYING PROBLEMS SOCIOLOGICALLY

On first thought, it might seem that the study of social problems in one's own society (or in any other society) would be a relatively simple and straightforward process: First, identify the most significant problems affecting the society in question. Second, apply the proven techniques of the scientific method—careful observation and controlled empirical testing—to arrive at a basic understanding of the contributing causes and major consequences of existing social problems. Finally, on the basis of the completed scientific investigation, develop a program for resolving these unfortunate social situations.

However, the real human social world seldom works as simply or as straightforwardly as one might imagine. If it did, there would be no need for therapists, psychologists, sociologists, and a host of other professionals. These groups' existence rests upon what seems to be an inevitable discrepancy between the way human affairs might logically be expected to work and the way they actually do work, and it appears that their continued survival is assured for the foreseeable future. This gap between the logical and the actual is nowhere more evident than in the area of social problems and their attempted solutions.

COMPLICATIONS IN STUDYING SOCIAL PROBLEMS

NATURAL VERSUS SOCIAL CAUSES

The first issue complicating the study of social problems revolves around the fact that not all the serious problems confronting the members of a given society are *social,* even though they may involve a number of important social consequences or implications. For example, in August 1992, Hurricane Andrew ripped through the southern tip of Florida and into southern Louisiana. The storm destroyed over 85,000 homes, caused property damage in excess of $30 billion, and shattered the lives of tens of thousands of people. Earlier that summer, southern California had been rattled by two substantial earthquakes that also caused great property damage and disrupted the lives of thousands of people. But even though both of these events led to the fragmentation of normal social patterns and the interruption of many individual lives, neither event could properly be classified as a social problem. Rather, these two "acts of God," as insurance companies would term them, constituted natural problems—*natural* in the sense that they were part of and were generated by the operations of the natural physical environment. Hurricanes and earthquakes happen to be integral and recurring (though hardly welcomed) parts of the respective physical settings of the Gulf Coast and of California. For all practical purposes, these phenomena remain beyond the control of human efforts to eliminate them.

More recently, torrential rainfall throughout the midwestern states caused devastating flooding as the Mississippi, the Ohio, the Missouri, and many other rivers in the region overran their banks. Farms, towns, and some major cities across the heartland of America suffered billions of dollars' worth of damage as they were literally washed away by the raging waters. The everyday lives and livelihoods of hundreds of thousands of residents of the area also were devastated as they were figuratively washed away in the floods. Again, however, there was little or nothing that could be done to keep this "natural" event from occurring.

In contrast, the Los Angeles riots of April and May 1992, whose fires resulted in close to 1 billion dollars in property damage and the disintegration of established social patterns in that city, would be regarded as part of a social problem. They were not "acts of God" but rather acts of members of social groupings in response to existing social conditions. In this respect, they were part of and were generated by the operations of the human-created social environment rather than the natural physical world. These fires, and the riots that spawned them, were and are amenable to human control efforts. Presumably, if specific social factors, including the economic living conditions of African Americans and the treatment of racial and ethnic minorities by police, were altered, the problem (riots and their related property destruction) could be eliminated. From a sociological viewpoint, then, the designation *social problem* is reserved for certain conditions or situations that reflect the consequences of specific structures or processes in a given society.

OBJECTIVE AND SUBJECTIVE FACTORS

Second, to speak of identifying the major social problems of a given society implies the existence of some objective criteria or standards to assess whether a condition or event constituted a real problem. Specific situations or conditions that met the relevant criteria would be defined and treated as social problems; those that did not would not be so regarded. For example, an unemployment rate of 7 percent of the available workforce might be the prevailing, accepted indicator of problems in the occupational sector. At the point that the number of people out of work rose above this level, the government would recognize unemployment as a genuine social problem and begin to take some appropriate action to deal with the situation. Similarly, a traffic accident death toll of 25,000 people per year might define the threshold or boundary at which highway safety became defined as a serious social problem requiring public (that is, governmental) response.

But why 7 percent unemployment and 25,000 deaths? Why not 6 percent (or 3 or 2 or 1 percent) out of work and 15,000 (or 5,000 or even 500) lives lost? What is so inherently significant or magical about one set of numbers rather than some other?

The answer to this last question is Nothing. In point of fact, the "objective" indicators defining what are and what are not social problems in a given society at a given time are as much subjective as they are anything else. Objectively, the fact may be that, in this society in a particular year, 12,500 people were killed in vehicular traffic accidents. However, in and of itself, this objective fact might not be enough to trigger a widespread perception that highway deaths are a serious social problem and a public outcry to "do something" about it. Highway safety will become a societal issue only if and when enough people become concerned about the situation to make it an issue. In the final analysis, whether these 12,500 deaths are sufficient proof of a significant traffic safety problem depends upon the subjective perceptions and responses of concerned members of the society.

And just how many members of the society have to become concerned about a situation before it becomes regarded as a social problem? Once again, there is no clear-cut, objective answer. In large part, the critical mass is as much a matter of the social identities and social positions of the concerned individuals as it is their sheer numbers. For example, assume that all the surviving families of the 12,500 traffic accident victims in the above example happened to be of average or below-average socioeconomic status group backgrounds. A great deal of research (as summarized, for example, in Conway, 1991; Marger, 1987) indicates that, in the United States, these groups are only moderately or occasionally involved in political affairs. In this case, the overall number of deaths may not be enough to trigger an official or serious government response to the traffic safety question, since the affected families are not very likely to effectively pressure or push political leaders for action.

But imagine what might happen if some of the surviving families of these 12,500 accident victims happened to be well-heeled, well-connected people—wealthy corporate executives or community leaders, for example. In this second case, given the documented tendency of members of higher socioeconomic status groups in modern societies to be more aware of how political processes work and more heavily involved in those processes, there is every reason to predict some sort of likely government response. Outraged survivors of traffic accident victims could and probably would use their knowledge and their connections to bring effective pressure on political leaders for appropriate action. In short, a situation will become defined and treated as a social problem in need of public response when a sufficient number of influential societal members decide that such a response is warranted and take action to make it happen.

The bottom line here is that although social problems involve events or situations that have an objective component (the specific number of people killed in traffic accidents each year, for example), they have a fundamental subjective component, as well (the perception by a critical mass of influential people that the situation is unacceptable and in need of appropriate public response). Each component—the situation itself and the perception of the situation—is a necessary condition that must be present for a social problem situation to exist. But neither component is a sufficient condition that, by itself, can cause a social problem situation to exist. Both components must be present before any given phenomenon can be sociologically regarded as a social problem.

Keeping these issues in mind, we might offer the following working definition. For the purposes of sociological examination and analysis, **social problems** can be conceptualized as conditions arising from the operation of the social order that are perceived as unacceptable by an influential segment of the population and that become the targets of attempted corrective social action. This is a far from perfect formulation and no doubt would be challenged by some sociologists. But it does provide a reasonable starting point for a systematic and realistic analysis of some of the most pressing social problems facing people in the world today.

Having at last arrived at a working definition that takes into account these conceptual complexities, are we now in a good position to begin a straightforward scientific investigation of social problems and their possible resolutions? Unfortunately, we are not.

RESEARCH LIMITATIONS

ETHICAL FACTORS

As is the case with virtually every other area of sociological inquiry, the ultimate subject matter of social problems research is human beings—in this case, humans whose lives are being disrupted or harmed by some aspect of their surrounding social world. And as is also true with other areas of sociological research, our ability to study human subjects scien-

tifically is limited by ethical and legal constraints. As social scientists, we simply cannot manipulate and control human subjects experimentally in the same way that may be possible with nonliving or nonhuman subjects, and this fact may seriously compromise the integrity of our research findings. For example, the logic of the scientific method may require that we test the effects of severe economic deprivation on family violence (a topic examined in Chapter Ten) by carefully and systematically subjecting a randomly selected group of families to increasing poverty. We would then observe their rates of spousal, parental, and child physical abuse relative to a comparable control group whose members have not been so deprived. But even assuming that the technical and mechanical difficulties in conducting such a project could be resolved, we would find ourselves in very serious legal trouble. Human lives cannot be endangered, nor basic human rights violated, in the name of science or for any other supposed worthwhile cause, and these restrictions can substantially cramp the sociologist's research style.

In conducting social problems research, sociologists often must compromise scientific integrity and rely on data gathered under less than rigorous circumstances. Consequently, the conclusions drawn from that research often are more suggestive than definitive. This may not be the most desirable of all possible research worlds, but it is at least a viable one. The point remains, however, that much of what sociologists know (or think they know) about the causes, patterns, and consequences of social problems is the result of analyses that may suffer from a lack of scientific purity. But this does not necessarily mean that the integrity of these findings has been fatally wounded. As we hope to show in the chapters that follow, even research that may be flawed has given us many important and useful insights about the problematic aspects of human social life.

POLITICAL FACTORS

The mere existence of a body of valid, reliable information does not automatically guarantee that this knowledge actually will be employed to help solve a particular problem. Governmental decisions as to how (and whether) to deal with a given issue often are based as much on *political* considerations as on *mechanical* grounds. For example, raising the levels of welfare payments to the poor may be a technically sound strategy for eliminating some of the most damaging effects of economic deprivation. However, if these increases were to necessitate additional taxation of the middle and upper classes, they well may be rejected by public officials more concerned (especially during an election year) about a taxpayers' revolt than the plight of poverty-stricken but politically inert population segments. When it comes to developing and implementing programs for treating various social problems, issues of technological possibility typically are tempered, and are often overruled, by questions of political feasibility.

THEORETICAL INTERPRETATIONS OF SOCIAL PROBLEMS

Over the course of the discipline's long involvement with social problems, sociologists have approached the study of these phenomena in a wide variety of ways. (For an extended discussion of some of these approaches, see Skolnick & Currie, 1994.) To some extent, their research has directly mirrored the prevailing popular ideas of the specific time and place. However, in large measure, the influence of public opinion on sociological analysis has been more indirect. It has been mediated through the various theoretical paradigms that at different times have dominated the field and guided sociological thinking and practice in general. Much like other population members, sociologists are shaped by the social and cultural factors that constitute their immediate world. These shared beliefs, values, and practices create an environment that favors one particular interpretation of social events over others. The underlying, often unstated, assumptions that sociologists make about human beings and their societies may be as much a product of accepted (but untested) cultural beliefs as of scientifically validated investigation.

STRUCTURAL-FUNCTIONALIST PERSPECTIVES

Structural functionalism (or, more simply, *functionalism*) was the earliest sociological paradigm. This approach was borrowed from the biological sciences and first articulated by Auguste Comte, Herbert Spencer, Emile Durkheim, and other pioneer sociologists. Sometimes referred to as "the organic analogy," it views human societies as being similar in many ways to living organisms. Like other entities, societies represent an intricate system of interrelated parts (*social structures*) whose activities have consequences (*social functions*) for the continued survival of the organism. These consequences may promote system survival (they are *functional*) or lessen it (they are *dysfunctional*). Functionalist theorists assume that human beings are intelligent, goal-directed creatures who form social groupings and engage in organized activities to enhance their collective well-being. They further assume that the individual members of these groupings share a set of common beliefs and values (*consensus*) that helps create the feelings of solidarity and cohesiveness that make organized social life possible.

From the functionalist standpoint, established social patterns found in particular societies must be explained and understood in terms of their effects upon the long-term survival of those social systems. The social institutions of marriage and the family, for example, are found in all human societies because in all societies, people who die or otherwise leave the system must be replaced. In turn, these new or replacement members must be cared for and taught the proper rules of conduct for that society. By granting both reproductive rights and parental responsibilities to specific groups of people, marriage and family structures help insure a steady supply of new societal members and, thus, the continuity of the society over time. The particular structural forms that marriage and family take in a given society (for example, monogamous marriage and a nuclear family pattern in the contemporary United States) can be examined in terms of their efficiency in fulfilling their intended functions. They can also be compared to the efficiency levels of different arrangements found in other societies (the polygynous marriage and extended family patterns found in some African societies, for example).

SOCIAL PATHOLOGY

Classical functionalist theory offered two interpretations for the existence of social problems in a given society. According to the **social pathology** explanation, social problems were the result of deliberate or inadvertent actions of morally evil or misguided individuals. Just as individual humans could be infected and made ill by viruses or germs from outside the body or by diseased cells from the inside, human societies could be infected and made ill by pathological agents from outside or inside the system. Just as fevers and chills were symptoms of bodily illness, problems such as poverty and crime were symptoms of societal illnesses. And just as bodily disease or illness necessitated the treatment or the removal of the pathological agent, social problem solution required the rehabilitation or the removal of the offending individuals or groups.

For example, poverty could be eliminated by teaching ambition and a work ethic to those people whose laziness and lack of ambition were responsible for their own economic failures. Crime was to be controlled by locking up those individuals caught in the act. Incarceration in jails or prisons was viewed as an opportunity for both the moral reeducation of offenders and their at least temporary removal from the law-abiding society. In the worst-case scenario, hardened or unrepentent criminals could be jailed for life or even executed for the protection of the society. The continued health of that larger system was a higher good that legitimized and offset whatever lesser evils might be created by the amputation of infected societal parts.

SOCIAL DISORGANIZATION

According to the **social disorganization** interpretation, social problems were the result of a disturbance in the state of balance and harmony (*equilibrium*) that normally existed within and among the structural components of society. Whether brought about by external or by internal forces, the disruption of one or more structural units generated changes that might travel throughout the entire system, creating disturbances in other sectors, as well. Social problems thus were signs that the system, or some part of it, was malfunctioning and out of balance. From this perspective, problem solutions involved restoring the affected structure to its previous state of equilibrium. If that proved impossible, problems might be resolved by establishing a new and different level or type of structural balance.

CULTURAL LAG

One famous example of the social disorganization approach involves what has been called **cultural lag** (Ogburn, 1950, 1957). According to this perspective, every organized society is built upon a cultural system that provides its population members a coherent world view. Through the medium of technology, material culture gives people opportunities for social interactions of different kinds. And through the medium of norms and values, nonmaterial culture offers moral guidelines defining when and how (and if) these opportunities should be utilized. Social problems result when rapid technological changes create new behavioral possibilities at a rate that outstrips the ability of existing norms and values to provide relevant behavioral guidelines. People who now find it possible to act in ways they could not act before also find themselves without any clear-cut, culturally approved set of rules to guide these actions. Until such time as appropriate guidelines are established to regulate the new behaviors, a moral vacuum, or cultural lag, will exist, during which a variety of serious problems may ensue. By the time new norms and values are established to cover the new situations, technological changes once again likely will have created even newer behavior possibilities and a new set of dilemmas. Modern, complex societies thus will experience almost perpetual cultural lag and resulting social problems.

For example, as a result of startling advances in medical and drug technologies in this society, people who in the past would have died now can be kept alive through the use of machines and chemicals that assist breathing and other vital human functions. But the life these people face often is that of a persistent vegetative state, in which they are incapable of virtually all normal human activities. To avoid the grim prospect of such an existence, many individuals have begun to establish living wills, giving instructions that they be allowed to die rather than having extraordinary measures taken to save their lives. However, these living wills have been legally challenged by opponents who see dangerous precedents and possibilities involved in giving medical practitioners the right to withhold vital medical care from selected patients.

Some of the opponents' worst fears perhaps were realized in 1992, when voters in California were confronted with Proposition 161, the physician-assisted-death or so-called death with dignity initiative. Under the provisions of this legislation, patients would be given the right to opt out of potentially long, painful, and ultimately fatal degenerative illnesses that threatened to rob them of their human dignity before finally killing them. After first consulting with the patients, physicians could assist those who were so inclined to end their own lives. For legal, insurance, and other purposes, these acts would not be considered suicide.

Proponents of the measure saw it as a mechanism enabling individuals to end their lives as humans while still truly human. Opponents saw it as a dangerous foot in the doorway that opened the possibility of government or other agencies unilaterally deciding that certain kinds of people (the sick, the disabled, the aged, and the mentally impaired, for example) should not be permitted to continue life, since they are not fully human. In either event, this very controversial moral and legal issue could not and did not exist prior to the advent of modern life-support technology. As medical breakthroughs have made it more and more possible to cheat death, they have also raised serious questions and concerns about both the right to life and the right to death.

CRITICISMS OF THE FUNCTIONALIST APPROACH

These early functionalist interpretations of social problems have been criticized for their somewhat naive assumption that given social practices have consequences for survival that are clearly and uniformly either positive or negative. They also have been charged with being inherently conservative—that is, of favoring the status quo as the best of all possible social worlds. These criticisms led to substantial modifications in the classical functionalist model, in particular, from Robert K. Merton, a modern functionalist whose concepts of *manifest* and *latent* functions offered a more complete look at the complexities of contemporary social systems.

MANIFEST AND LATENT FUNCTIONS AND DYSFUNCTIONS

According to Merton (1968), social structures and their operations produce any number of survival-related consequences. Some of these effects represent intended outcomes, or at least those recognized as occurring (*manifest* functions). Other effects are neither intended nor recognized as they occur (*latent* functions). Some of these consequences may be functional for overall system survival, whereas others are dysfunctional for the system at large. Specific consequences may be functional for the survival of one or more particular population subgroups but dysfunctional for other subgroups. Given these complexities, it may be just about impossible to arrive at an objective assessment of the overall net survival consequences of a particular social structure or pattern.

For example, consider the heated debate that surrounded NAFTA, the North American Free Trade Agreement. Under the terms of this agreement, Canada, the United States, and Mexico have formed a North American economic community, similar to that already found in Europe and to others developing in Asia and elsewhere around the world. In the interest of promoting mutually beneficial trade, NAFTA has eliminated or substantially reduced many import and export tariffs, quotas, and other barriers on goods and services among its member nations.

On the positive side, NAFTA could be regarded as functional for the United States in a variety of ways. First, it could make the United States better able to compete successfully with Japan, the European Community, and other emerging international economic superpowers. Second, it could lower prices on a wide variety of products for U.S. consumers, thereby raising living standards for a substantial number of people. Finally, by creating more job opportunities for Mexicans in their own country, NAFTA could help reduce the large number of illegal immigrants currently flooding into the United States to seek work. Substantial reductions in the number of these immigrants would relieve border states such as California and Texas of much of the tremendous financial burden they now face in providing health care and other social welfare benefits for these people. (Some of the problems surrounding the rising tide of Mexican and Latin American immigration to the United States are discussed in Chapter Seven.) Additionally, with many jobs no longer being filled by illegal workers, more employment opportunities would be created for U.S. citizens.

On the negative side, opponents point to the significant dysfunctional consequences of NAFTA for the United States. First, it is likely that a large number of manufacturing jobs would be lost in this country, as companies would move their operations south of the

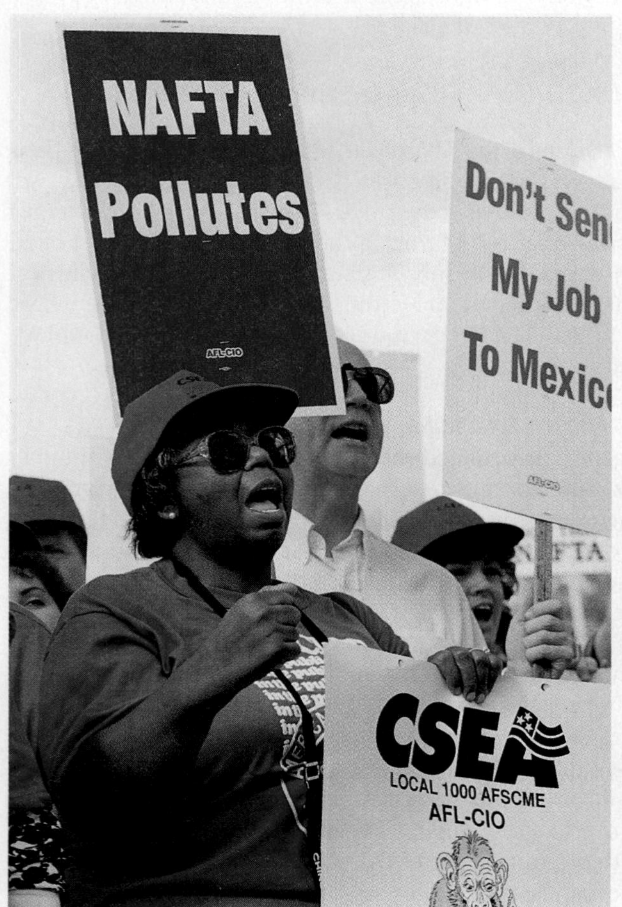

Although touted by President Clinton as a boon to the U.S. economy, the North American Free Trade Agreement (NAFTA) was bitterly opposed by trade unions and environmentalists. On the Mexican side of the border, the manufacturing jobs created have not necessarily translated into prosperity for the Mexican people. In Tijuana, gleaming maquiladora *assembly plants stand in sharp contrast to the homes of their workers. The long-term effects of NAFTA for the United States and Mexico are almost impossible to calculate.*

border to take advantage of the much lower wage scales found in Mexico. These plant relocations would translate into higher rates of unemployment for U.S. blue-collar workers. Second, there is a real potential for severe environmental damage both in Mexico and along the U.S.-Mexican border as a result of Mexico's less stringent pollution laws. Many environmentalists see NAFTA as an invitation for U.S. companies to pollute at will. Finally, U.S. agricultural and other labor-intensive jobs currently rely on illegal immigrants for cheap labor. If employers would suddenly find themselves without an adequate supply of undocumented workers willing (or compelled) to work for lower wages, they would be forced to raise wages significantly in order to attract U.S. workers. The resulting higher production costs undoubtedly would be passed along to consumers in the form of much higher prices for supermarket produce; landscaping, house-cleaning, and child-care services; and even new houses and home remodeling. Thus, living standards would be lowered for a significant segment of the U.S. population.

Given these considerations, what conclusion can be drawn about the net impact of the North American Free Trade Agreement on the United States? Is NAFTA functional or dysfunctional for the United States? How does one calculate a final score for the various positive and negative economic consequences of this arrangement for the diverse interests and groups that make up the population of this society? Functionalist theorists (as well as the U.S. Congress) might find this an almost impossible task. Conflict theorists, however, would be spared such mental gymnastics. They simply would assume that NAFTA served the interests of some particular groups over all other groups in U.S. society.

CONFLICT PERSPECTIVES

Conflict sociologists (e.g., Collins, 1975; Dahrendorf, 1959; Eitzen & Baca Zinn, 1991; Mills, 1956; Wright, 1985) view social problems very differently than functionalist theorists. Conflict sociologists see these problems as the inevitable byproducts of power differences among the various groups that make up societal populations.

From the conflict perspective, human societies are not orderly systems designed to promote the collective well-being of populations united by shared values, beliefs, and interests. Rather, societies form the arenas within which population subgroups distinguished by opposing world views and conflicting interests attempt to promote their individual well-being by exercising power and coercion over one another. Societal settings provide specific resources and impose specific limitations that have tremendous impacts on the outcomes of intergroup conflicts. Thus, different groups will attempt to seize control of the machinery of society in order to promote their own objectives. Once in control, ruling groups create and carry out political, economic, and social policies that invariably create adverse—perhaps fatal—consequences for other groups.

MARXIST THEORY

The most widely known and influential statement of the conflict perspective is that of Karl Marx (Marx, 1967, original 1867; Marx & Engels, 1955, original 1848). According to Marx, human social history has been a continuing story of class conflicts pitting the "haves" of the world against the "have-nots." The size and membership of these two groups are determined by individuals' relationships to the economic systems in their respective societies.

Marx claimed that the economic system of any human society (what he called the *mode of production*) is the single most important fact of life for that society. The arrangement by which wealth is produced and distributed forms the foundation, or **societal sub-**

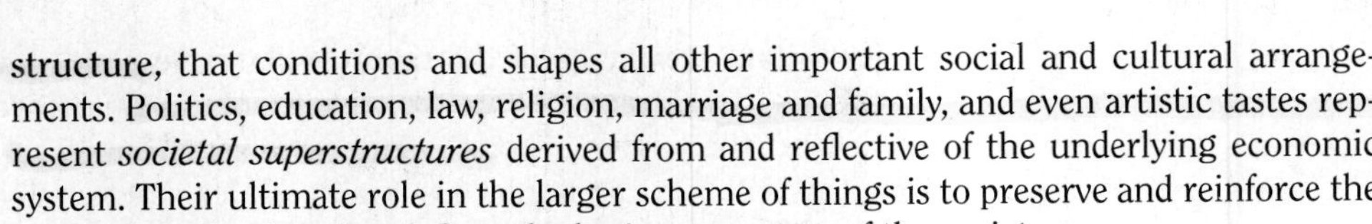

structure, that conditions and shapes all other important social and cultural arrangements. Politics, education, law, religion, marriage and family, and even artistic tastes represent *societal superstructures* derived from and reflective of the underlying economic system. Their ultimate role in the larger scheme of things is to preserve and reinforce the mode of production that defines the basic parameters of the society.

Within a given society, all important social positions and social interactions are defined by the **relations of production**—that is, by individuals' standings with regard to the mode of production. For Marx, the essential distinction was that between those whose ownership of private property gave them control over the mode of production (and, thus, over political, legal, and other superstructures) and those whose lack of property ownership forced them to sell their own labor to make a living. Each group formed what Marx called a "class in itself," defined in terms of its objective condition of property ownership or nonownership and independent of individuals' perceptions of their own respective situations. However, such perceptions played a critical role in the development of true social classes. An accurate awareness of one's own objective class position and of the consequences of that position led to class consciousness and deliberate attempts to organize with others in the same situation to promote collective class interests. At this point, the objective class becomes transformed into a subjectively aware "class for itself," prepared to engage in the historic struggle for its own survival.

Marx argued that the goals and interests of the two great classes in modern societies—the powerful and propertied **bourgeoisie** and the nonpropertied and powerless **proletariat**—are inherently incompatible. The bourgeoisie owners want to maximize the profits from their economic investments; the proletarian workers want to maximize the wages earned by their labor. Because the economic rewards available from the existing mode of production exist in limited supply, relations between owners and workers unfold within the context of a **zero-sum game**, in which one group's success comes at the expense of the other group's failure.

For example, suppose the net monthly revenue of a certain local restaurant is currently $30,000, and it is divided equally between the restaurant owners' profits and the restaurant workers' wages. At the end of each month, $15,000 goes to the owners and $15,000 to the workers. However, imagine that each side wishes to increase its share of the revenue by $5,000. If the owners' monthly profit were to increase to $20,000, the additional $5,000 would have to come from the workers' wage pool, which would decrease to $10,000. If the workers' monthly wages were to increase to $20,000, that additional money would have to come from the owners' $15,000 profit pool, which would shrink to $10,000. Barring any increase in the restaurant's net monthly revenue, any financial win by either owners or workers requires a corresponding financial loss by the other side. And even in the event of such revenue gains, it remains almost a certainty that the workers will be deprived of anything resembling a fair share of the increase.

Marx claimed that the enormous economic, political, and legal resources of the bourgeoisie owners give this group an insurmountable power advantage over the much larger group of proletarian workers who make up the masses in modern societies. Coupled with the incessant bourgeois greed for greater profits, this power differential translates into lives of untold and increasing misery for the millions of individuals who toil as wage slaves in capitalist societies. These workers' rightful share of the wealth their labor has helped produce is routinely confiscated by the property-owning ruling class. Poverty, war, disease, and other wretched living conditions that might broadly be termed "social problems" thus are endemic to private property–based economic systems. For Marx, the only effective solution to the host of social problems facing modern societies was the dismantling and rebuilding of the economic substructure responsible for the creation of these problems.

Human societies could and would become problem free only after private property held for individual gain had been replaced by communal property used for the common public good, only after capitalism had been replaced by socialism and then by communism.

NON-MARXIST APPROACHES

Marx's claim that social problems would be eliminated by the overthrow of capitalist economic systems has not been supported by events since his time. The socialist and communist societies that attempted to embody Marx's ideas have faced economic, health, crime, and other problems similar to those that plague capitalist societies. Indeed, some of these societies (most notably, the Soviet Union) ultimately collapsed as a result of their inability to solve those problems.

Contrary to the central assertion of Marxist theory, then, many major societal problems are not inevitably linked to capitalism in a simple cause-and-effect relationship. However, this fact alone does not necessarily invalidate the fundamental premises of the conflict approach itself. Other theorists in this tradition have developed explanations whose applications are not limited to social problems in capitalist societies.

RALF DAHRENDORF

German sociologist Ralf Dahrendorf (1959) revised and extended Marx's theory of class and class conflict to include all modern industrial societies, whether capitalist, socialist, or something in between. According to Dahrendorf's reformulation, the basic principle that divides the populations of these societies into distinct and conflicting classes is not position within the societal property system (the relations of production) but, rather, position within the societal authority system. In modern industrial societies, economic, political, educational, and all other important institutionalized activities now are carried out by what Dahrendorf (1959, p. 138) termed "imperatively coordinated associations." These are large-scale structures—corporations, governments, and schools, for instance—characterized by socially accepted authority relations in which some positions (and the people who occupy them) are granted the legal and moral right to direct and control the activities of other positions (and the people who occupy them).

For example, in schools, students are subject to the authority of classroom teachers. Teachers are allowed to give orders and otherwise control activities within their classrooms, and students are supposed to follow orders and otherwise do what teachers tell them. In turn, teachers are subject to the authority of principals and other administrators who have been given charge of particular schools. Individual school principals are themselves ultimately subject to the authority of local school boards, which have final jurisdiction over all individual schools (and administrators and teachers) within a given geographic territory.

These authority relations, which are recognized and accepted by the various involved parties, establish important power differences within and among particular organizations. Since the interests of the different authority positions (and of the organizations in which they are embedded) normally do not coincide, established societal authority relations create the bases for conflicts among the groups occupying different levels within the overall hierarchy. They also create the bases for a variety of social problems, as policies enacted to further the interests of some authoritative positions create effects that work against the interests of others. And since imperatively coordinated associations exist in all societal types (not just capitalist) and in all societal sectors (not just the economy), the elimination of capitalist economic structures in favor of some other arrangement will not bring an end to social conflicts or social problems. In this sense, conflicts and problems are endemic to modern social organization itself.

GERHARD LENSKI

In a similar vein, sociologist Gerhard Lenski (1966) argued that any attribute or trait that differentiates population members into socially recognized subgroups has the potential for becoming the basis for the kinds of class conflicts described by Marx and by Dahrendorf. Both sex and age, for example, cut across property and authority lines, dividing populations into groups that typically are defined, evaluated, and treated as social unequals. Regardless of economic position, women in many parts of the contemporary world receive a lesser share of their societies' rewards than their male peers. (Sex and gender inequalities are examined in Chapter Eight.) In sociocultural systems in which youth is highly valued, older members of the population may be devalued and treated as lesser beings than their younger counterparts. Lenski claimed that, in particular, tensions between what he termed "age classes" have grown tremendously in modern societies and that struggles between different age groups not only will become more frequent but "are likely to take violent and even revolutionary forms" (1966, pp. 426–427).

The basic point, according to Lenski's argument, is that any status-related factor—race, religion, ethnicity, or sexual orientation, to name only a few possibilities—can become the flashpoint for social problems and societal upheavals if the various groups so defined do not see their best interests being served by existing social arrangements. So long as the supply of societal resources remains smaller than the collective needs and wants of the different groups that make up the societal population at large, problems and conflicts will be integral, inevitable parts of human social life.

SYMBOLIC-INTERACTIONIST PERSPECTIVES

Despite the obvious and profound differences that separate them, both functionalist and conflict perspectives take what amounts to an **objectivistic** view of society and of human social relations. That is, both theories focus on factual or objective conditions—the structure of a particular society's economic system, or a particular group's position within that economic structure, for example—as crucial causal variables in their attempt to explain human social patterns. Society X's free-market economic structure is more successful in providing needed goods and services to its population than society Y's state-controlled market structure. Because of its lack of property ownership, group A's share of economic rewards is not as large as group B's share.

In contrast, sociologists in the symbolic-interactionist tradition assume a **subjectivistic** approach in their attempts to understand human social phenomena. From this perspective, it is not so much the objective, factual conditions of life that shape people's social beliefs and behaviors as it is their subjective perceptions and interpretations of those conditions. Two people facing exactly the same objective situation—the sudden onset of blindness, for example—might well respond to it in very different ways, depending upon how they come to define the experience. The individual who views the loss of sight as a disability or handicap might become less active and more withdrawn from social life. The person who interprets blindness as a challenge or an opportunity might become more active and more socially involved than ever before.

Symbolic interactionists acknowledge that the objective circumstances of people's lives are an important consideration in explaining human social phenomena. However, these theorists claim that, in the final analysis, it is the subjective "spin" that people give these phenomena—how they perceive and interpret events in their world—that is of critical importance in structuring their subsequent actions. As W. I. Thomas, a founding figure of the symbolic-interactionist perspective, once phrased the argument: "If men define situations as real, they are real in their consequences" (Thomas & Thomas, 1928, p. 572).

SOCIAL CONSTRUCTIONISM

As applied to the study of social problems, the central premises of symbolic interactionism translate into what has been called the *social constructionist* perspective (Berger & Luckmann, 1966; Holstein & Miller, 1993). According to social constructionist theorists, like all other aspects of organized human life, social problems are human constructs or creations. They represent the outcome of a given population's attempt to make sense out of its surrounding physical world by assigning meaning and value to objects and events as they are encountered. Social problems do not and cannot exist in an absolute sense, independent of some particular group's perception and definition of particular situations as being morally objectionable. That is to say, there are no social conditions that, in and of themselves, are inherently wrong or evil. They become wrong or evil only after someone interprets them and responds to them as such. (Recall our earlier discussion on the objective and subjective components of social problem definitions.) For social constructionist theorists, then, the fundamental goal of the sociological analysis of social problems is to identify and chart the processes by which some events or conditions—but not others—become defined and treated as problems (Spector & Kitsuse, 1987).

LABELING THEORY

One illustration of the social constructionist approach is that of the so-called **labeling theory of deviance**. According to this interpretation (and unlike other scientific interpretations of crime and deviance), social deviance is not the result of some detectable biological or psychological flaw in certain individuals. Nor is it the result of some observable flaw in the structure or operations of a given group or society. Rather, what a particular group or society comes to regard as a *deviant* behavior, belief, or attribute represents the result of a social process that defines certain phenomena and people as deviant and also establishes an official response to such deviance. Howard Becker, one of the pioneers of labeling theory, argued (1963, p. 9) that "social groups create deviance by making the rules whose infraction constitutes deviance, and by applying those rules to particular people and labeling them deviant."

According to labeling theorists, all members of a given group or society at some time or other engage in behaviors that violate established rules. However, these occasional, random acts of **primary deviance** become socially significant only if and when the individuals performing them are observed and apprehended by what Becker called "moral entrepreneurs." At that point, these unlucky individuals are subjected to "status degradation ceremonies" (Garfinkel, 1956), in which they are stripped of their previous social identity as law-abiding citizens and given a new identity or label: that of deviant. Once so labeled, these individuals find themselves increasingly shut out of social opportunities and social relations with "normal" members of their group or society. Deprived of the chance to conduct their lives in a socially acceptable manner with socially accepted people, they must turn increasingly to other stigmatized people like themselves and to other disapproved behaviors (in the words of labeling theory, to acts of **secondary deviance**) simply to stay alive. In turn, this secondary deviance becomes proof of the individuals' fundamentally deviant nature. It legitimizes their further exclusion from polite society and acts of punishment from the guardians of the moral and legal order.

Labeling theory is a very controversial interpretation of social rule breaking. In at least some of its versions, the labeling approach seems to take all the burden of responsibility for what sometimes are violent, dangerous, and bizarre actions from those committing them and to place it, instead, on the group or society that has come to regard those behaviors as violent, dangerous, and bizarre in the first place. If only society didn't insist on having rules, we wouldn't be bothered by people breaking those rules. Be that as it may, the labeling approach nonetheless adds an important dimension to our understanding of problems of crime and deviance. It directs our attention to the processes through which deviance and deviants are "discovered" in a given society, as well as to the various consequences—both to society at large and to those who have been so labeled—of those discovery processes.

TOWARD AN UNDERSTANDING OF CONTEMPORARY PROBLEMS

In the best of all possible analytical worlds, the different theoretical approaches we have overviewed would all arrive at identical conclusions regarding the causes, the patterns, and the consequences of social problems, as well as their solutions. In the next-best possible world, these different theories could at least be synthesized and integrated into one coherent whole to yield a comprehensive paradigm for the sociological analysis of contemporary social problems. However, as we noted earlier, the real social world seldom behaves as nicely or in as orderly a way as we might wish. In this instance, the functionalist, the conflict, and the symbolic-interactionist perspectives simply do not lend themselves readily or easily to attempts to blend them into some seamless single product. Because they start from very different premises and proceed in very different ways, each approach tends toward very different conclusions than the others. Consequently, any attempt to force these three perspectives into a unitary mold would be both premature and fruitless.

In the chapters that follow, we will examine a number of specific social problems confronting this and other societies, utilizing several or all of these different theoretical models. As we proceed, we will highlight the major points of similarity and of departure among the three major paradigms, comparing and contrasting their effectiveness in furthering our understanding of environmental destruction, overpopulation and underpopulation, war and conflict, inequality, and other problematic aspects of life in the modern world. Our approach, then, might best be described as *eclectic,* in that it draws upon the varying individual strengths of the different interpretive frameworks without attempting to amalgamate them into one, all-encompassing model. You should be aware of several important points as you read through these discussions.

CONNECTIONS

In each following chapter, we have isolated one social problem (or one set of problems) for detailed analysis. Chapter Two, for example, examines conflict and war; inequality and poverty form the focus of Chapter Six; drugs, alcohol, and gambling are treated in Chapter Eleven. Please keep in mind, however, that although these problems are being presented serially, one topic at a time, this format represents an artificial simplification of these phenomena as they occur in the real world. It is a device used strictly for analytic purposes—that is, as a tool to allow us to examine more closely the large and small

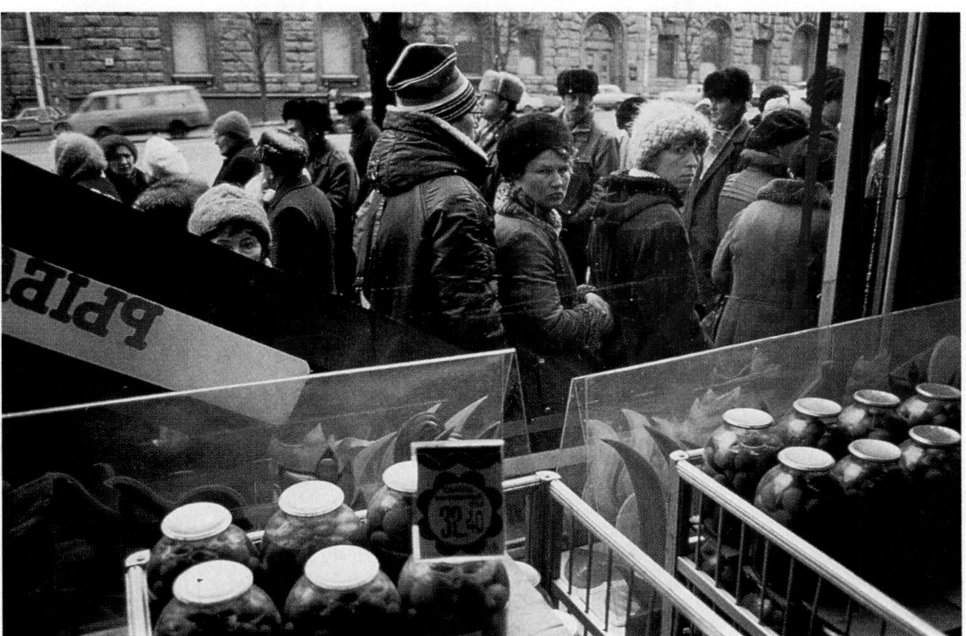

The demise of the Soviet Union in 1991 was viewed by most Western observers as a triumph for democracy. However, these former Soviet citizens, who must now wait in long lines to buy scarce and expensive food supplies, most likely are more concerned about the economic rather than the ideological consequences of the collapse of communism in Eastern Europe. Very often, solutions to particular social problems generate serious and unexpected problems in other sectors of society.

details of each problem area in turn. In the empirical social world, the individual problems we describe are never found in such isolation. Rather, they are interconnected and interwoven in very intricate patterns, most often displaying what classical functionalist theorists called **interdependence.** Events that take place in any one of these problem areas both affect and are affected by events in other areas.

For example, the breakup of the Soviet Union, an event generally hailed by Western observers as positive and long overdue, has turned out to be something less than positive for many of its constituent populations. With the lifting of what often were ruthless and repressive tactics by the communist government, old ethnic conflicts that, in some cases, had been simmering for decades suddenly exploded. New nationalist conflicts were created as now-free peoples in the former Soviet states and throughout Eastern Europe pushed for recognition of their traditional homelands as independent republics. (These conflicts are examined in Chapter Seven.) The hundreds of thousands of deaths and the paralysis of normal social affairs brought about by these conflicts have had a devastating effect upon societal economies that, in many cases, were already in very precarious positions. As economies throughout the former Soviet Union have collapsed in the chaos, millions of people have been thrown into dire poverty—politically free, perhaps, but economically chained.

This widespread poverty, in turn, has generated a series of survival responses from people that often have had serious negative consequences for them, for their societies, and for the world at large. Deprived of other occupational opportunities, women throughout the former Soviet Union have turned to prostitution in dramatically increasing numbers (Hornblower, 1993), and child prostitution is also on the rise (Serrill, 1993). Strapped for other sources of revenue, some now-independent governments have planned "fire sales" of nuclear weapons from the ex-USSR arsenal, raising the specter of future nuclear wars throughout that and other regions of the world (Nelan, 1993). Finally, the territory has become a major conduit for drugs from Asia to Western Europe, as out-of-work people do what they feel they must in order to survive, and local or regional governmental attention has been directed elsewhere (Dahlburg, 1993).

Just as individual social problems are tied to one another in complex cause-and-effect relationships, so also are problems and their attempted solutions. Efforts to eliminate or lessen the negative effects of one particular problem often generate unintended and unforeseen effects that may increase, rather than decrease, the scope of the problem. (Recall our earlier summary of Merton's discussion of manifest and latent functions and dysfunctions.) For example, some years ago, the United States began a program in which fields of marijuana being grown in Mexico for the U.S. drug market were sprayed with a chemical that caused violent nausea to the user when the drug was smoked. The aerial spraying, which was carried out by the Drug Enforcement Administration, an agency of the U.S. government, raised serious questions about Mexican political sovereignty and put a severe strain on U.S.-Mexican relations.

Political issues aside, however, the ultimate objective of curbing drug use in the United States was not fulfilled by this tactic. If anything, spraying the Mexican pot fields had just the opposite overall effect. In the absence of imported marijuana and the subsequent price increase for the drug, growers in some parts of the United States (most notably, in northern California) stepped up their production of domestic pot, thus filling the void. Further, with their supply of marijuana cut off, some normal users of the drug turned to cocaine, a drug that, especially in the form of "crack" cocaine, apparently is much more powerful and more addictive than the Mexican-grown marijuana it replaced. The net effect of the spraying of Mexican marijuana fields, then, was to increase the seriousness of the U.S. drug problem.

Similarly, efforts to curb one social problem may generate consequences that have an impact, for better or worse, on other problems (or create new problems), as well. For example, in an attempt to comply with local, regional, and federal laws concerning air quality, many plants and factories in the United States turned to much taller than usual smokestacks to keep soot and other pollutants from dropping on surrounding towns and cities. As a result, however, these emissions were carried into the upper atmosphere, where they mingled with those from other plants and factories, becoming more concentrated. They ultimately descended as acid rain, hundreds or even thousands of miles from their points of origin. Among the other results of this situation has been the destruction of thousands of acres of forests and of hundreds of lakes in the eastern United States and Canada. Canadians, in particular, have taken great offense not only at the decimation of their lands and lakes by U.S. private industry but also at the refusal of the U.S. government to concede that a problem in fact exists, much less to accept at least partial responsibility for its creation.

In no single chapter in this book will we be able to capture entirely the many linkages that exist between the specific problem being discussed and other social problems; however, we will attempt to make you aware of these complexities. In each chapter, we have included a section called "Connections," in which we examine the webs of relationships—some direct and obvious, some indirect and not so obvious—existing between and among different social problems. In this regard, we will draw heavily upon Robert K. Merton's ideas of multiple functions and dysfunctions. The basic point to remember here is that, in the real world of human social relations, things seldom are as simple as they seem.

SCOPE AND LEVEL

We have further simplified reality by dividing our examination of social problems into three broad segments, based upon the general scope or level of the particular problem being considered. In Part One, "Global-Level Problems," we discuss various aspects of conflict and war, population dynamics, and environmental destruction that seem worldwide in nature. That is, they entail conditions that affect humanity at large, rather than any one society or region alone. In Part Two, "Societal-Level Problems," we examine problems such as urbanization; socioeconomic inequality; racial, ethnic, and gender inequalities; and crime, whose shape and severity vary from one society to another. These phenomena reflect the specific structuring of groups and group relations in a given society and have significant consequences for the continued viability of the society in question. Finally, in Part Three, "Individual- and Family-Level Problems," we consider a series of phenomena—family disorganization, sexuality, addiction, and illness and health care—whose most immediate and primary impacts appear at the individual or small-group level. However, once again, the treatment of these particular problems in separate clusters or sections represents an analytic consideration more than an accurate reflection of real-world events.

For example, although we treat environmental destruction as a global-level problem, we could and will just as easily discuss the relationships that exist between certain social and cultural elements—a corporate economy and a widespread ethos of material comfort, for instance—and the nature and dimensions of environmental problems in a given society. Environmentally speaking, the world in general may be in serious long-term trouble, but both the timing and the content of those troubles may be experienced in very different ways by the populations of different societies. Similarly, although we discuss illness and health care as individual-level problems, both phenomena possess societal-level and even global-level dimensions. In the United States and in many other societies, for example, the incidence of different physical and mental illnesses varies consistently and significantly by race, class, and gender. Individuals' access to quality health care is very much a function of their location within the larger societal stratification system, and the quality of their society's health care system itself is a function of that society's position within the international stratification hierarchy. The moral here is that specific social problems do not affect people at only one level, whether global, societal, or individual. The consequences of these conditions range up and down the entire spectrum of humanity, impacting us at the personal, the national, and the international levels. To repeat an earlier point: Things never are as simple as they seem.

GLOOM AND DOOM

In all fairness, we should offer one final note of caution before proceeding to our inventory and discussion of the world's social problems. If past experience serves as any guide, there seems to be a genuine tendency for first-time students of social problems to become infected with a certain amount of pessimism and despair as they consider the various woes of their society and their world. Faced with an imposing and apparently unending chronicle of destruction, decay, misery, and misguided or failed cures, some people may be tempted to throw in the towel and call it quits. "Has anyone in your social problems classes ever committed suicide?" one of us once was asked by a freshman student after viewing a particularly depressing film on toxic waste disposal in which the basic message was that we are all going to die or mutate as a result of the contamination of our drinking water. The answer, then and now, was "No, nobody ever has, nor is there any reason to. Things might not be as bad as they seem."

As you will discover soon enough, serious social problems have been an ongoing part of human social organization for centuries, perhaps since the beginning of human societal life. The factors that continue to generate these conditions sometimes appear to be rooted in the basic structure of a given society. Consequently, successful solutions—if any are possible—likely must entail major sociocultural surgery, and this type of surgery can be very painful. If serious and scientific studies, or serious financial expenditures, were all that were needed to eradicate social ills, we would now be living in a problem-free world. However, as gloomy as all of this might sound, do not lose sight of the fact that progress in dealing with many social problems can be made and has been made. Solutions to social problems typically do not come easily or cheaply, but with a combination of pushing and persistence, they can come eventually.

SUMMARY

1. Since its beginning as an academic field, sociology has been concerned with the study of social problems. Pioneer thinkers such as Comte, Marx, and Durkheim engaged in sociological analyses to help comprehend the major problems of their times. In the United States, this tradition has continued since the late 1800s, with many American sociologists assuming very activist orientations to the study of problems in their society.
2. *Social problems* are conditions arising from the operation of the social order that are perceived as unacceptable by an influential segment of a society's population and that become the target of attempted corrective social action. By itself, no objective condition constitutes a problem. It becomes a problem only if and when it is subjectively defined as such by powerful members of the given society.
3. Scientific analyses of social problems are hindered by ethical constraints in dealing with human subjects, as well as the fact that social problem definitions and solutions often are surrounded and confounded by political considerations.
4. Early structural-functionalist theorists viewed social problems either as pathologies resulting from the actions of misguided or evil persons or as indicative of some type of social disorganization. According to the culture lag hypothesis, social problems were the consequence of changes in technologies outstripping changes in cultural norms and values. Robert K. Merton modified these early explanations by introducing the concepts of manifest and latent functions and dysfunctions.
5. From the conflict theory perspective, social problems are the results of differences in power and interest among members of societal populations. Karl Marx viewed these differences as embedded in private property–based capitalist economies. Non-Marxists, such as Dahrendorf and Lenski, see such differences arising from authority, age, gender, and other status-relevant structures found in all modern societies.
6. From the symbolic-interactionist perspective, social problems are social constructions resulting from attempts by humans to give meaning and value to their surrounding world. In this sense, all problems are essentially subjective in

nature, dependent upon people's perceptions that some situation or event is morally offensive and in need of correction.

7 Operating within the symbolic-interactionist framework, labeling theorists claim that the fundamental cause of norm- or law-breaking behaviors by individuals is the creation and enforcement of social rules by "normal" society. From this perspective, deviants are individuals whose initial acts of primary deviance have been observed and negatively responded to by moral entrepreneurs, leading to the deviants' exclusion from society. Deviants then are forced to engage in later acts of secondary deviance for survival, thus ensuring their total separation from normal social affairs.

8 Although most social problems texts treat these phenomena as discrete topics, in the empirical social world, social problems are tied together in very complex cause-and-effect relationships. Given social problems typically impact people at the personal, the societal, and even the global levels, and attempted solutions to one set of problems may generate unforeseen and unfortunate effects upon other problems. Social problems are very difficult to eradicate, but with understanding and persistence, they can be overcome.

CHAPTER TWO

THE WORLD AT WAR
Apocalypse Now

Civil War General William Tecumseh Sherman is credited with uttering the now-famous phrase "War is hell." Like so many millions of men, women, and children, both soldiers and civilians, who have witnessed or experienced warfare, Sherman had firsthand knowledge of the absolute evil of armed conflict. Unfortunately, Sherman's apt observation no longer conveys the emotional impact of the horrors and madness of war—if, in fact, it ever did. This three-word phrase that rolls off the tongue as effortlessly as a long-playing television advertising slogan has become just another trite, meaningless cliché. Because of the way war has been carefully packaged and delivered to the American public, neatly wrapped in a veneer of glory and patriotism, this is hardly surprising. In the 20 years or so following World War II, our image of that monumental struggle was viewed largely in terms of John Wayne–type movies that sang the praises of young, confident soldiers, going off to fight the good fight. The following generation of Americans was treated to the heroics of Sylvester "Rambo" Stallone, a one-man wrecking crew who took on whole battalions of enemy soldiers at one time and won.

While Hollywood gave us heroes, the Pentagon and news media all too often presented a view of the conflict that best served the war effort. Anything that accurately portrayed the brutal realities of combat was likely to be eliminated by censors. This was especially true in the recent Persian Gulf War, when the Pentagon imposed some of the most severe restrictions on press coverage in U.S. history (Neier, 1992). In addition, some elements of the news-reporting industry appear to have engaged in self-imposed censorship.

Video footage taken by reporters from two of the major television news networks captured the devastated Iraqi countryside and grieving families— an image that sharply contradicted the government's claim that so-called precision bombing had resulted in only a limited number of civilian casualties. In both cases, these photojournalistic pieces were killed by network executives, in one instance, the night before it was to be broadcast. Instead of seeing some of the destruction wrought by American bombs, the American public was fed a nonstop television diet of military officers with pointers standing in front of maps, as well as a parade of experts on various aspects of the war being interviewed one after another.

Just as images of the Persian Gulf War were carefully controlled, our view of World War II 50 years ago was "sanitized and romanticized almost beyond recognition by the sentimental, the loony patriotic, the ignorant, and the bloodthirsty" (Fussell, 1992). In his work *Wartime,* World War II combat veteran Paul Fussell offers some vivid examples of what one soldier noted was the "real war" that "will never get in the books" (p. 267):

- Ten percent of the soldiers in one division admitted they had been so frightened during combat that they urinated in their pants. Twenty-five percent said that at the most terrifying moments, they had vomited and/or had a bowel movement. As Fussell notes, one can only speculate on how many other men had lost control of bodily functions but were too ashamed to admit it.
- In Berlin, during the final days of the war, after the city had been bombed for years, some 50,000 children were found living in destroyed buildings and holes in the ground like animals. Some of them were "one-eyed or one-legged veterans of seven or eight or so"; many were "so deranged by the bombing and the Russian attack that they screamed at the sight of any uniform, even a Salvation Army one" (Botting in Fussell, 1992, p. 273).
- Forced by the conditions of battle to stay in rain-soaked foxholes for a week, U.S. Marines on Okinawa endured the stench of decomposing bodies all around them and had to use their dug-out quarters as toilets, shoveling out excrement whenever they could.

  If a Marine slipped and slid down the back slope of a muddy ridge he was apt to reach the bottom vomiting. I saw more than one man lose his footing and slip and slide all the way to the bottom only to stand horror-stricken as he watched in disbelief while fat maggots tumbled out of his muddy dungaree pockets, cartridge belt, legging lacing, and the like. (Sledge in Fussell, 1992, p. 294)

- Starvation and thirst were so grave among prisoners of the Japanese and among downed American pilots adrift on boats in the ocean that many went insane. Some resorted to drinking their own urine; others tried to bite the necks of their comrades and suck blood from the jugular vein.

These grotesque, terrifying images of war are hardly the stuff of enlistment commercials ("Be all that you can be in the army"), news coverage, or Hollywood films, even the supposedly more realistic ones like *Apocalypse Now* or *Platoon.*

"War is hell."

QUESTIONS TO CONSIDER

- 1. How many people have been killed in wars fought around the world since 1900? Why have conflicts in this period of history been especially deadly?
- 2. What are the major symptoms of *posttraumatic stress disorder?*
- 3. In the 1980s, how much did the nations of the world spend each year for military purposes?

- 4. What are the major explanations for why nations go to war with one another?
- 5. What are the major explanations of war crimes?
- 6. What are the most significant problems associated with dismantling and controlling nuclear weapons?
- 7. Which countries are involved in the new arms race? What can be done to halt the arms buildup in these countries?
- 8. What problems are associated with the economic conversion of a country heavily dependent on arms production? What is the so-called peace dividend?
- 9. How will future wars differ from conventional wars?
- 10. What is terrorism? Is there a "terrorist personality"? Do any strategies successfully combat terrorist activities? If so, what are they?
- 11. Can a lasting peace be achieved in the modern world? Why or why not? What steps can the world community take to bring about the end of international conflict?

UNDERSTANDING CONFLICT AND WAR

CAUSES OF WAR

The sociological enterprise can be thought of as having two fundamental objectives. The first is to describe recurring events in the social world (like wars) as accurately as possible; the second is to explain why these events happened—that is, to uncover their causes. This latter task is much more difficult than the former because, contrary to conventional wisdom, facts do not speak for themselves. To discover, for example, that agrarian-based revolutions have been fought in a number of developing nations is not the same as knowing *why* these events took place.

At least four categories of explanation attempt to determine why nations go to war with one another. The *nature-of-human-nature* perspective focuses on humankind's tendency to engage in aggressive, violent behavior. Numerous social scientists and other observers of human behavior have looked inward and discovered the roots of our war-producing tendencies. The Viennese psychiatrist Sigmund Freud (1961, original 1930) wrote that we are "not gentle creatures who want to be loved" but creatures whose "instinctual endowment" leads to aggression. For Freud, the atrocities of conquering Huns and Mongols as well as the horrors of World War I could lead to no other conclusion, forcing us to "bow humbly before the truth of this view." Another psychiatrist, Anthony Storr (1968), argued similarly that humans had a "physiological mechanism" that, when stimulated, led to anger and violence.

Anthropologists, on the other hand, examine war from a cultural perspective. Louis Leakey (1983) is convinced that human beings are not inherently "killer apes," nor are we innately peaceful creatures. Rather, we are cultural animals whose actions (including violent behavior) are products of our particular cultural environments and learning experiences. Ashley Montagu (1976) adds that no human being has ever engaged in any form of violence without learning to do so. Nor is aggressiveness on the part of humans or animals spontaneous; rather, this behavior is a reaction to some external stimulus.

The *population-and-technology* perspective of Stanislav Andreski (1964) suggests that rapid population growth (especially in the developing world) has resulted in poverty and misery for tens of millions of people, which in turn has led to hostility and war. The natural tendency for populations to grow beyond the available supply of food needed to prevent starvation assures the permanence of internation conflict. However, even a reduction in the standard of living in prosperous nations (resulting from a depression, for example) can cause heightened aggression that may culminate in warfare.

Sophisticated long-range killing machines (automatic rifles, missiles, and bombers), readily available to all but the poorest of the nations of the world, have made it possible to kill people "without exertion, without passion, and without guilt" (Barnet, 1983, p. 52). The person who pulls the trigger or pushes the button of one of these weapons does not have to witness the devastating impact of his or her actions. In a very real sense, modern instruments of war do the dirty work of killing for us, work that many people, perhaps most, could not stomach. "Very few air crews who are willing, indeed eager, to drop their bombs 'on target' would be willing to strangle, stab, or burn children (or, for that matter, adults) with their own hand" (Tinbergen, 1968). Richard Barnet (1972) argues that we have become victims of a "technological imperative" of our own making. Organizations in the modern world have pushed technological development to the limit and then have used what they have created. Barnet argues that after investing $2 billion and four years of hard work developing the atomic bomb during World War II, the government was determined to use it even though there was evidence that Japan was considering surrender.

Societal structure theories are concerned with the form and workings of society's economic and political institutions. Often referred to as an "economic determinist," Karl Marx argued that all aspects of human social life are contingent on the material or economic conditions that exist in society. In capitalist states, the bourgeoisie own and control the "modes of production" (factories, machinery, land) and make enormous profits by exploiting the proletariat (working class), who survive by trading their labor for meager wages. While the bourgeoisie, or capitalist class, grows wealthy as a result of this relationship, it eventually leads to the problem of underconsumption—that is, the proletariat do not have enough money to purchase what they have produced.

Vladimir Lenin believed that at this point in the evolution of capitalist states, the owning/ruling class begins to develop new markets for their products through colonization. In the latter years of the nineteenth century, the British, the French, and the Germans each claimed a significant part of what we now call the Third World in Asia and Africa to act as suppliers for raw materials as well as markets for their overproduction. When there were no more weak nations left to exploit, these European powers fought each other for control of the capitalist "world-system" (Chirot, 1977). It follows from this perspective that the recent transformation of numerous societies from socialism to capitalism will eventually result in heightened tension and possibly war as these nations seek to expand their economies.

Critics of the Marxist world view contend that Marx and his followers put too much emphasis on economic relationships, noting that political policy and decisions (including the decision to go to war) are not made solely in line with the concerns and interests of big business. In addition, the type of government a country has will go a long way in determining if it goes to war. In democratic nations, where citizens end up paying for a war with their money and their lives, people rarely support the initiation of war (as opposed to when they are attacked). Conversely, in totalitarian states, powerful leaders have a significant amount of control over the people and can force them to pay the cost of warfare (Kiser, 1992). The logical extension of this position would be that democratization of numerous countries (especially in Europe) in the 1980s will lead to a more peaceful world.

People can be casualties of war long after the fighting has stopped. These individuals in Vietnam had their legs blown off after stepping on so-called antipersonnel mines that were planted over 25 years ago.

The *relations-among-states* explanations focus on the military strengths of nations vis-à-vis each other in the geopolitical world. According to the balance-of-power position, an equitable distribution of military might (such as that between the United States and the USSR during the Cold War) produces a state of mutual deterrence—and peace—as neither country has the wherewithal to defeat its adversary. Hegemonic-stability theory suggests, to the contrary, that peace follows when one state has the military power to dominate other nations. The strongest country has no need to engage in warfare because its objectives can be realized without the use of force, and the militarily weaker countries are not inclined to start a losing war against a more powerful opponent (Kiser, 1992).

Because these four explanations for war are very different, comparing and contrasting these divergent positions is difficult, if not impossible. What is needed at this point, as Kiser (1992) notes, is an overarching, general theory of the causes of war that takes one or more aspects of all of these perspectives into consideration.

THE COST OF WAR

FATALITIES

To be sure, we will never know how many human beings have lost their lives as a result of war. One obvious problem is that during and after the chaos of battles, it would be impossible to find and count all the casualties, even if someone were interested in performing such a task.

Another problem is that of definition. Ruth Leger Sivard (1991), author of the annual *World Military and Social Expenditures,* defines war as "any conflict involving one or more governments and causing the death of 1,000 or more people per year" (p. 25).

Another researcher accepts this basic definition but adds "including deaths from war-related famine and disease" (Eckhardt in Copeland, 1991, p. H53). The utilization of these definitions will yield very different fatality counts.

However, experts in this field agree that both the intensity and the frequency of wars have increased steadily from the time of the Roman Empire to the present. Approximately 75 percent of all wartime deaths since the era of Julius Caesar have occurred in the twentieth century (Renner, 1993).

In her survey of 142 countries since the year 1500, Ruth Sivard (1991) concluded that these nations collectively fought 589 wars at the cost of almost 142 million lives. Starting with the seventeenth century, every successive century was characterized by an increase in both the number of wars and the number of fatalities associated with these conflicts. The period from 1900 to the present has been especially deadly, with estimates ranging from approximately 115 million (Sivard, 1991) to 175 million (Brzezinski, 1993) war-related deaths to date.

An examination of the geography of warfare reveals an interesting and informative trend: As the battleground for two world wars in this century, Europe has been the locale for two-thirds of all war-related deaths since the year 1500 (Sivard, 1991). However, in the post–World War II era, the killing ground has shifted almost exclusively to the developing countries, where 40 million people have been killed in more than 125 wars since 1945 ("Let Them Eat Guns," 1991).

A major distinction between twentieth-century wars and all those preceding conflicts is that civilians are now the principal victims of the hostilities. Whereas in previous times, wars were often limited to battles fought between armies of professional soldiers, the strategy of modern warfare is to destroy the enemy's ability to fight. This means attacking weapons production and general supply centers located in major cities. Contemporary strategists also believe that striking the enemy deep in his homeland (with bombs and long-range missiles, for example) will have a demoralizing effect and reduce the will to fight. This overall strategy, coupled with the mass-destruction capabilities of modern weapons, is a major reason why 74 percent of all wartime casualties in the 1980s were civilians. In 1990, almost 90 percent were civilians (Sivard, 1991, p. 20).

Even when commanders are not specifically targeting the civilian population, the realities of modern warfare make it impossible not to kill (often in very large numbers) innocent people. For example, in the recent Gulf War, we heard continuously of "precision bombing" and "surgical strikes" conducted by long-range bombers and fighter pilots of the U.S.-led coalition forces. These carefully chosen phrases and labels are meant to convey the message that enemy soldiers and weapons can be targeted and destroyed with pinpoint accuracy, incurring little, if any, "collateral damage" (the killing and maiming of civilians). While this military *doublespeak* (from George Orwell's *1984*) may permit us to get behind the war effort with a clear conscience, "precision bombing" and "surgical strikes" are usually anything but that.

Estimates of the number of Iraqis killed in the Gulf War range from 150,000 to 200,000 people. According to the calculations of demographer Beth Osborne Daponte (in Colhoun, 1992) of the U.S. Census Bureau, 40,000 Iraqi soldiers were killed during the war (the official Defense Intelligence Agency number was 100,000). Another 83,000 Iraqis (mostly women and children) died as a result of air strikes. Approximately 13,000 people were killed during precision bombing, and another 70,000 perished as a result of the collapse of the public health system that was destroyed in surgical strikes. The destruction of water purification and sewage systems created conditions for the outbreak and spread of water-transported diseases that are especially deadly to children and the elderly

(Daponte in Colhoun, 1992). (The Bush administration attempted—unsuccessfully—both to prevent Daponte's work from being published and to fire her.)

Although it would have been almost impossible for anyone living in the United States in the latter half of 1990 and the first few months of 1991 not to have any knowledge of the Gulf War, most armed conflicts that take place in the world today (that is, in the developing world) are all but ignored by the international community. How many people know that over 100,000 people have died in Angola's 18-year civil war? In Somalia, 14,000 people were killed in one 5-month period in 1991 and 1992 (Hiltzik, 1992). Had the United States not become involved in that country, the story of these wars would be relegated to the back pages of local newspapers. If these little noticed but highly deadly wars, which kill so many people and alter the lives of millions of others, are ever to end, the world community must become as aware of them.

PHYSICAL AND PSYCHOLOGICAL INJURIES

The number of people physically maimed and psychologically scarred as a result of war usually exceeds the total number of fatalities. In fact, one component of wartime strategy is to wound rather than kill one's opponents because more resources are expended in caring for 100 seriously wounded people than in burying a like number of bodies.

Land mines have rendered the maiming of people easier and more vicious than ever before, and they victimize more civilians than soldiers. Over the past 15 years, tens of millions of antipersonnel mines have been laid in regions of at least 10 developing nations, most notably Cambodia and Afghanistan. In Cambodia, a nation of fewer than 9 million people, over 30,000 individuals have had limbs (typically legs) amputated as a result of stepping on mines. With the highest percentage of amputees in the world, Cambodia has been called "the land of one-legged men." These hidden weapons take a heavy toll on people returning to their homeland after the hostilities have ended. Men, women, and children in rural areas herding livestock, tilling fields, and looking for firewood are especially at risk (Stover & McGrath, 1992). The United Nations estimates that 800 people are killed and another 450 are wounded every month by land mines (Carvel, 1994). In Afghanistan, Soviet troops planted mines in abandoned homes, mosques, on roads, and on farmland—that is, just about any place they could. One Afghan man in a Pakistani refugee camp noted that "the ground will be fighting us for years after the Soviets have left" (Carvel, 1994, p. 6). Utilizing present technology, these antipersonnel weapons, which cost about $3 each to plant, require $975 each in workers' time and technology to remove (Carvel, 1994).

A United States Senate report released in May 1994 listed over a dozen incidents in which U.S. combat forces appear to have been exposed to various chemical weapons during the Gulf War (Baumann, 1994). Six hundred witnesses testified before the Senate committee that they continue to suffer as a result of chemical attacks in 1991; their symptoms include chronic fatigue, headaches, diarrhea, and aching joints. A number of veterans reported that their spouses and children have some of the symptoms, causing fear that exposure to debilitating chemical and/or biological agents can be passed on (Ritter, 1994).

Those individuals fortunate enough to emerge from wars physically intact may well suffer psychological trauma that can hamper their ability to function in society long after the last shots of combat have been fired. The disorientation, fatigue, and trauma referred to as "shell shock" in World War I and "combat fatigue" in World War II were often attributed to cowardice by military commanders. However, in the post–Vietnam War era, these symptoms have been assigned a diagnostic category (Scott, 1990). **Posttraumatic stress**

disorder (PTSD) is the product of one or more experiences of overwhelming terror, a threat to a person's well-being and safety over which he or she has no control.

Symptoms of PTSD (Davidson & Neale, 1994) include reexperiencing the traumatic event, often through vivid dreams and disturbing nightmares. Cars backfiring, firecrackers exploding, and thunderclaps can remind veterans of combat situations and trigger flashbacks of events. Attempting to avoid stimuli associated with disturbing experiences, individuals try to refrain from thinking about traumatic events. PTSD is associated with a long list of problems, including difficulty sleeping and concentrating, anxiety, depression, anger, guilt, suicidal thoughts, violent behavior, marital problems, and drug abuse (as a form of self-medication). A 1988 congressional study estimated that 479,000 of the 3.5 million Vietnam veterans suffer significantly from PTSD, and another 350,000 individuals exhibit more moderate symptoms (Witteman, 1991).

THE MONETARY COST OF WAR

We will never know how much money and resources someone like Alexander the Great spent on his conquests; however, relatively accurate figures exist on the monetary cost of warfare in the modern world. By the end of the 1980s, the nations of the world were collectively spending almost $1 *trillion* a year for military purposes—or approximately $2 million a *minute* (see Figure 2.1). During the Reagan and Bush presidencies, which spanned the largest and most expensive military buildup in our history, the United States allocated almost $3 trillion for national defense, or $45,000 for each family in the country (Sivard, 1991). The final bill for the recent Gulf War came in at $61.5 billion, which included expenditures of one-half billion dollars a day just for ammunition.

FIGURE 2.1 World Military Expenditures: 1950–1990

By the time they peaked in 1988, world military expenditures were approximately $1 trillion a year. Between the end of World War II and 1990, roughly $30 trillion was spent on all aspects of the military.

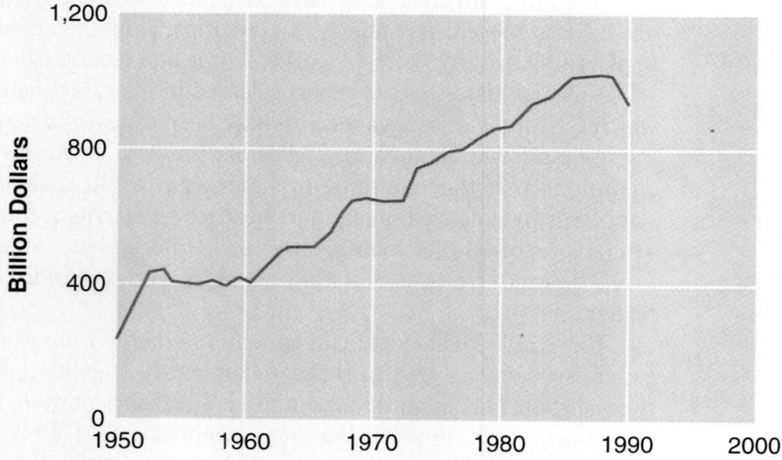

SOURCE: Reprinted from *Vital Signs 1992—The Trends That Are Shaping Our Future,* edited by Lester R. Brown, Christopher Flavin, and Hal Kane, with the permission of W. W. Norton & Company, Inc. Copyright © 1992 by Worldwatch Institute.

There are at least two reasons for the incredibly high costs associated with war. The first is the amount of money spent on the research and development (R&D) of increasingly sophisticated weapons. Since 1955, the United States has spent more than $1 trillion on the R&D of nuclear and conventional weapons. This figure represents 62 percent of all federal government research expenditures (Broad, 1992). On a global basis, the military accounts for between 25 and 33 percent of all money spent for R&D (Renner, 1990).

The second reason for these spectacular prices has to do with the high cost of space-age materials and a significant amount of waste and fraud. As a consequence of these collective factors, the price index of weapons has increased about 200 times since the end of World War II, while the U.S. price index for all other goods and services has gone up but 7 times since that date. In other words, an item that cost $1 in 1945 now costs $7. However, a tank today costs 88 times what it did during World War II, and a bomber is 130 times more expensive. Stealth fighter planes are priced at almost 2,000 as much as World War II–era fighters. If prices in the civilian world had increased as much as the cost of a fighter airplane has, an average family car today would cost about $20 million (Sivard, 1991).

Even though the United States has decreased military spending between 10 and 15 percent over the past few years, defense expenditures are still very high. The 1993 defense budget of $272.2 billion represented 17.8 percent of all money spent by the federal government. Expenditures at the federal level in that same year for education, health, and Medicare combined totaled $299.5 billion.

ENVIRONMENTAL DESTRUCTION

The words *national defense* are the two most ecologically destructive words in English; so are their equivalents in many other languages. In the name of maintaining a strong national defense for their respective nations, the world's military organizations have become the largest polluters of the earth. In the United States, the armed forces produce more toxic substances each year than the top five chemical companies combined (Sivard, 1991). Rather than allocate any significant portion of their budgets for environmentally sound practices, the military superpowers often dispose of the poisonous byproducts of their war machines whenever and wherever it suits them.

Since the 1960s, the Soviet military has used its bordering oceans as a dumping ground for nuclear waste. Between 1965 and 1988, the Soviets disposed of 18 nuclear reactors—6 of which still contained radioactive fuel—into shallow waters of the Arctic Ocean. In what one commentator referred to as a "nuclear atrocity," a weapons factory poured radioactive waste into a river that was the source of water for 28,000 people. The practice continued unabated for over four years (Murkowski, 1993).

In 1991, residents of a small Hungarian town began hauling up buckets full of a black, slippery substance from their wells. The townspeople thought they had discovered oil that would make them rich. What they really found was a significant amount of approximately 900 tons of jet fuel that was dumped at a nearby abandoned airbase by the homeward-bound Soviet military. Near another former Soviet air base, Hungarian officials "discovered that the water of a small lake was covered with a layer of jet fuel three feet thick" (Nagorski, 1993, p. 185).

In the process of cutting back up to two-thirds of its European forces in the aftermath of the Cold War, the United States military initially located 358 contaminated sites (fields, underground storage areas) near its bases. Experts expect to locate more such sites, no doubt escalating the cleanup cost originally estimated at $162 million (Charles, 1990). In Savannah, Georgia, a major center for the production of plutonium used in nuclear weapons, there are 51 storage tanks—each the size of the Capitol dome in

Washington, D.C.—filled with high-level radioactive waste. The estimated cost of properly disposing of this material runs into the tens of billions of dollars (Budansky, 1992b).

Perhaps even more startling examples of ecological destruction are evident both during and after open conflict. In the final days of the Gulf War, retreating Iraqi troops set fire to 732 of Kuwait's approximately 900 oil wells, producing one of the worst environmental disasters in history. Thick, black smoke from the raging fires that burned for almost 9 months formed a 600-mile-long blanket over the region that blocked out the sun and produced record-low temperatures ("Last of Kuwait's 762 Oil Wells," 1991). Pollution from the burning oil fields was expected to reduce crop yields in countries as far away as India (Sivard, 1991).

Not only are farmlands and animals destroyed during the intense bombing that is an integral part of modern warfare, but in some parts of the world, the tens of thousands of craters formed from these blasts produce a major health hazard. In Vietnam, Laos, and Cambodia, these craters fill with water during the rainy season and serve as breeding grounds for malaria-carrying mosquitoes.

WAR CRIMES

Although the capacity to torture and kill has been greatly expanded with advanced technology, what are today considered *war crimes* can be traced back hundreds if not thousands of years. Victorious, rampaging armies routinely annihilated enemy soldiers and civilians as punishment for resistance, a normal aspect of conquest, or a way of spreading terror (Kuper, 1992).

Only since the Age of Enlightenment (beginning in the eighteenth century) created a newfound regard for the rights of humanity has genocide been considered a crime. According to the United Nations' definition, **genocide** is "the deliberate destruction of a racial, ethnic, national, or religious group, in whole or appreciable part, by killing members of that group or imposing conditions inimical to survival" (Kuper, 1992, p. 758).

The most infamous and barbaric episode of genocide in human history was Nazi Germany's attempt to exterminate European Jews and Gypsies. Slavic groups (Poles, Russians, Slovaks) as well as other so-called inferior people were targeted for forced labor, torture, and/or death. In the largest World War II concentration/extermination camp at Auschwitz (located in southern Poland, near the city of Krakow), approximately 800,000 to 1,000,000 people were murdered. During the course of World War II, the Nazis slaughtered some 6,000,000 men, women, and children—tens of thousands of them in gas chambers.

Pery Broad (1991), a soldier in the German Army, kept a journal during his three-month tour of duty at Auschwitz. He described how prisoners accused of crimes (stealing a piece of bread or being a member of the Polish resistance movement, for example) were tortured:

> Two tables had been placed side by side with a gap of one meter between them. The victim had to sit down on the floor and cross his hands in front of his drawn up knees. His wrists were then bound. A thick bar was put between his elbows and his knees. The ends of the bar lay on both tables. He was helplessly swinging between the tables, his head downwards. Then his posterior and naked feet soles were flogged with a bull-hide whip. The blows were so violent that the tortured man rotated wheelwise. Every time his posterior came into a convenient position—a powerful blow was dealt, with all of the strength the torturer could muster. When

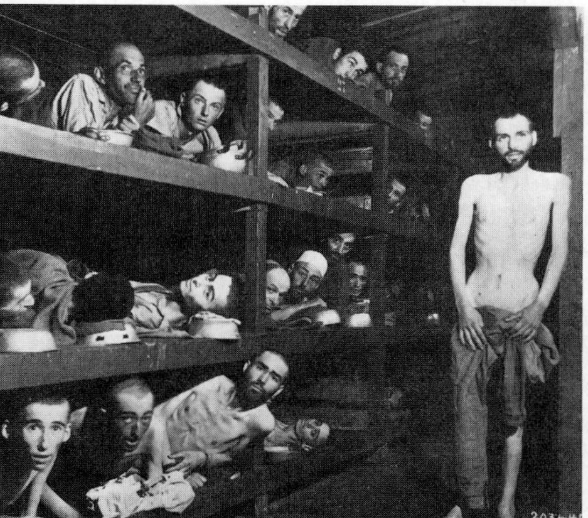

The photo on the left, which was taken by an American soldier during the closing days of World War II, shows emaciated prisoners in a Nazi concentration camp. The seriously malnourished prisoners in the photo on the right are victims of the fighting in the former Yugoslavia, which has been torn apart by a nationalistic war that began in 1991. War crimes of the twentieth century are among the worst in the history of humankind.

the cries grew too piercing, the fiendish Gestapo man smothered them by putting a gas mask on the victim's head. (Broad, 1991, p. 114)

After the victim passed out, the torturers poured scalding water up his nose. Broad reported that at this point, the inquisitor got the confession he wanted. Once they confessed their supposed crimes, prisoners were taken to a mortuary and executed (shot in the head) in groups of 10.

It didn't take the death-camp administrators long to figure out that shooting prisoners and dumping their bodies in mass graves was a slow and cumbersome method of killing people. If whole groups were to be removed from the face of the earth, a much more expedient process of murdering undesirables would have to be implemented. Engineers, technicians, and designers who worked for private German firms helped solve the technical problems (Pressac, 1993): Gas chambers were built to kill as many as 4,000 people at one time. After the chambers had been opened and ventilated of the deadly Cyclon B gas, prisoners were forced to drag out the bodies of their slaughtered comrades. Using a tool designed specifically for the task, gold fillings were extracted from the jaws of the dead.

Anything of value the prisoners brought to the camps was used in some way to pay for or enhance the German war effort. Useable clothes, luggage, shoes, crutches, and artificial limbs were sent back to Germany. Human hair was used to make jacket linings for soldiers' cold-weather uniforms. The bodies of gas-chamber victims were burned in one of four crematoria at Auschwitz. Broad (1991, p. 138) reported that the stench of burning flesh could be smelled for miles. Because of overuse, the ovens were constantly in need of repair; on at least one occasion, a chimney burst because of the intense heat. In

a final act of indignity, the ashes of the deceased were often shipped back to Germany to be used as fertilizer.

In a letter to General George Marshall in April 1944, Supreme Allied Commander and future president Dwight D. Eisenhower recounted his visit to a German internment camp:

> The things I saw defy description. . . . In one room, where there were piled up twenty or thirty naked men, killed by starvation, George Patton would not even enter. He said he would get sick if he did so. I made the visit deliberately, in order to be in a position to give *first hand* evidence of these things if ever, in the future, there develops a tendency to charge these allegations merely to be "propaganda." (emphasis in the original) (in Chandler, 1970, p. 2616)

Sadly, some 50 years after the war, it seems that many Americans need to be reminded of the atrocities that Eisenhower witnessed. A 1993 poll conducted by the American Jewish Committee found that 38 percent of adults and 53 percent of high school students did not know what the term *holocaust* (the deliberate and systematic killing of 6 million Jews before and during World War II by the Nazis) referred to or used this word incorrectly ("Testing Awareness of the Holocaust," 1993).

Because they are more likely to be victimized sexually in addition to being tortured by other means, women are subject to additional horrors of war upon captivity. During World War II, as many as 250,000 Korean (up to 80 percent of the total), Chinese, Manchurian, and Filipino girls and women (from age 13 to the mid-20s) were forcibly abducted and raped for extended periods of time by Japanese soldiers (Lee, 1992). Called *jung-shindae,* "comfort girls," these females were used to satisfy the sexual demands and appetites of the troops. Given weekly injections of antibiotics to control sexually transmitted diseases, each of the captives was forced to have sex with an average of 30 men a day. Listed as "ammunition" on military supply records, these women and girls were abandoned when they were too sick or too beat up to work and perform sexually (Lee, 1992).

When women on the opposing side of the conflict are sexually brutalized by soldiers, these attacks are usually crimes of opportunity—that is, soldiers will rape young girls or women if and when they find their victims accidentally during the course of their duties or free time. However, at other times, the rape and impregnation of enemy women is part of a deliberate and systematic military strategy.

In Bosnia-Herzegovina, Serbian troops have been engaging in a campaign of so-called ethnic cleansing—a euphemism for genocide (MacKinnon, 1993). This campaign includes the rape, impregnation, torture, and murder of Muslim and Croatian women toward the end of eliminating these ethnic groups. Savage sexual assaults were often filmed by Serbian soldiers making pornographic movies to be shared with their comrades. A woman who survived one of these rape/execution camps (MacKinnon, 1993) recounted her experience: "In front of the camera, one beats you and the other—excuse me—fucks you, he puts his truncheon in you, and he films all that. . . . We even had to sing Serbian songs in front of the camera" (in MacKinnon, 1993, p. 27). To keep them alive until the next attack, the victims were given one thin slice of bread a day.

Any serious discussion of war crimes invariably leads to the question of how individuals can possibly commit such unspeakably cruel, heinous acts. There are at least three—not necessarily mutually exclusive—answers to this query. One stimulus for excessive brutality may be the very training that is necessary to transform civilians to soldiers—people whose job it is to kill other people (Dyer, 1985). In a speech to U.S. forces preparing for combat duty in 1942, Lieutenant General Lesley J. McNair (1983) exhorted his men to become killing machines: "We must lust for battle; our object in life must be to kill, we must scheme and plan night and day to kill. . . . It is the avowed purpose of the army to make killers of all of you" (pp. 110, 111). More recently, a U.S. Marine Corps drill instructor (in Dyer, 1985) noted that during his boot camp training, recruits yelled "Kill!" every time their left foot hit the ground while running. One can only imagine how many thousands of times these young men uttered this word during the course of their training.

Historian Arnold Toynbee (1983, original 1971) correctly observed that it is very difficult to turn young men and women who have been socialized for the first 18 to 25 years of their lives into an ethos of "thou shall not kill" into soldiers who will take the life of another human being on command. However, "once this taboo has been broken it is difficult to set limits to the breach of it by confining the killing to 'enemy' soldiers" (p. 126). The killing can more easily spill over to the civilian population if the soldiers come to believe directly (from an order, for example) or indirectly (subtle encouragement of their superior officers) that the brutalization of nonmilitary people is acceptable.

Another aspect of training that is used to prepare civilians as well as soldiers for war is the dehumanization of the enemy. This dehumanization of one's opponent accomplishes in whole or part at least two objectives:

1. It serves as a justification to the larger society why this particular enemy must be defeated and/or exterminated.
2. Stripping the enemy of his humanity—that is, reducing him to some subhuman level—makes it that much easier for soldiers to kill their opponents. If "thou shalt not kill" (or its equivalent in other religions) only applies to human beings, then nonhumans no longer have the protection of this moral imperative.

To the extent that the administrators and guards of Nazi death camps internalized the idea that Gypsies "had to be removed from the face of Europe as an inferior race" (Broad, 1991, p. 139), these men could murder and burn the bodies of their victims and still feel good about themselves. A loving father or brother of a 13-year-old girl who would do anything to protect that child can sadistically and repeatedly rape the 13-year-old daughter or sister of another man whom he considers less than human and feel perfectly justified in his actions.

While the military training and dehumanization interpretations go a long way in helping us understand why soldiers commit war crimes, they are in and of themselves incomplete explanations. Virtually all soldiers receive similar training and are exposed to the same propaganda concerning their enemies, but not all soldiers commit war crimes. This leads to the final explanation for these atrocities—the circumstances of the existing, immediate situation.

Research by social scientists has demonstrated that when people believe they are following the orders of a legitimate authority, they will administer powerful electric shocks to other individuals who have done nothing illegal or morally wrong (Milgram, 1963, 1965). Also, people will conform to the decision of a group even when they know that decision is wrong (Asch, 1951). The very strong desire of soldiers to be accepted by their comrades, coupled with the belief that their superiors are legitimate authority figures, make these individuals particularly susceptible to committing war crimes.

In March 1968, a company of U.S. soldiers killed most of the inhabitants (innocent civilians) in the village of My Lai, Vietnam. Rather than condemning the members of Charlie Company as a group of cold-blooded killers, at least one observer viewed these young soldiers as a "frightened group of poorly trained, poorly led, psychologically scarred young draftees" (Gershen, 1983). Three weeks prior to the My Lai massacre, the company was trapped in a mine field; 4 soldiers were killed and 24 were injured. One member of the company stated, "The psychological effect of the mine field was more devastating than the physical effect" (in Gershen, 1983, p. 134). The company was told that it was going to My Lai to get the guerrillas responsible for the death of their comrades. To what extent did the mind-set of these soldiers and the situation they found themselves in contribute to the events that followed? Can their actions be understood as the tragic, yet inevitable conclusion to the "wild confusion of combat" (Elliot in Gershen, 1983, p. 133)?

THE COLD WAR AND ITS AFTERMATH

October 4, 1957, is one of the most important dates of the twentieth century: The Soviet Union announced to the world that it had successfully launched a satellite—*Sputnik*—that was orbiting the globe. In retrospect, the technological significance of that event was probably minimal. However, the symbolic impact of the Soviet achievement triggered a series of events that dramatically changed the geopolitical situation—probably forever. Up until that fateful autumn day in 1957, Americans had pretty much thought of the Soviet Union as a vast country populated by boorish communists who lived in acres of drab, mostly concrete-slab apartments. Although they had a formidable military force that could not be underestimated, the "Ruskies" were basically techno-peasants (that is, technologically primitive) whose ability to do anything of importance in the world of engineering and science was completely stifled by the Marxist/Leninist system under which they lived.

The launching of *Sputnik* ("fellow traveler" in Russian) took Americans by surprise. Senate majority leader Lyndon Johnson spoke of the "decline and fall of the Roman Empire" (the United States was the new Rome), and another senator proposed a "National Day of Shame and Danger" (in Moore, 1992, p. 2). Determined not to be eclipsed by a nation of "godless communists," the United States resolved to match and then surpass the Soviets' aeronautical feat. The space race and the Cold War arms race had begun.

By the time the arms race reached its peak some 30 years later, in 1988, the global stockpile of strategic long-range warheads (those that travel 3,000 miles or more) had reached almost 25,000, with another 30,000 tactical weapons (those that travel less than 3,000 miles) also ready for deployment. The United States and the former Soviet Union accounted for more than 95 percent of this total (Renner, 1992) (see Figure 2.2). The explosive power of 3 decades of nuclear weapons building was approximately 3,000 times that of all munitions used in World War II (see Figure 2.3). In addition, by 1967, when the government stopped producing chemical weapons, the United States had stockpiled 30,000 tons of various toxic substances. According to the American Chemical Society, that was enough to kill everyone in the world 5,000 times over. The new Commonwealth of Independent States may have 10 times that amount—some 300,000 tons of chemical weapons ("Turning Off the Gas," 1989). In 1992, the United States and Russia (principal recipient of the former Soviet arsenal) agreed to reduce their combined stockpile of nuclear weapons to approximately 3,000 to 3,500 warheads by the year 2003 (Renner, 1992).

This proposed (and to some degree, already implemented) and long overdue reduction of nuclear weapons is the "good news." The "bad news" is just about everything else. To begin with, even when the proposed arms reductions have been completed, the United States and Russia will have enough firepower to annihilate life on Earth. And while the

FIGURE 2.2 Shrinking Nuclear Arsenal

The world's combined nuclear arsenal hit 25,000 strategic (long-range) weapons in the late 1980s; 95 percent of these bombs belonged to the United States and the Soviet Union. The United States and Russia (which has the bulk of the nuclear weapons from the former Soviet Union) have agreed to reduce their nuclear arsenals to 3,000–3,500 warheads by the year 2003. Despite this formidable reduction, enough firepower will remain intact to kill everyone on the planet many times over.

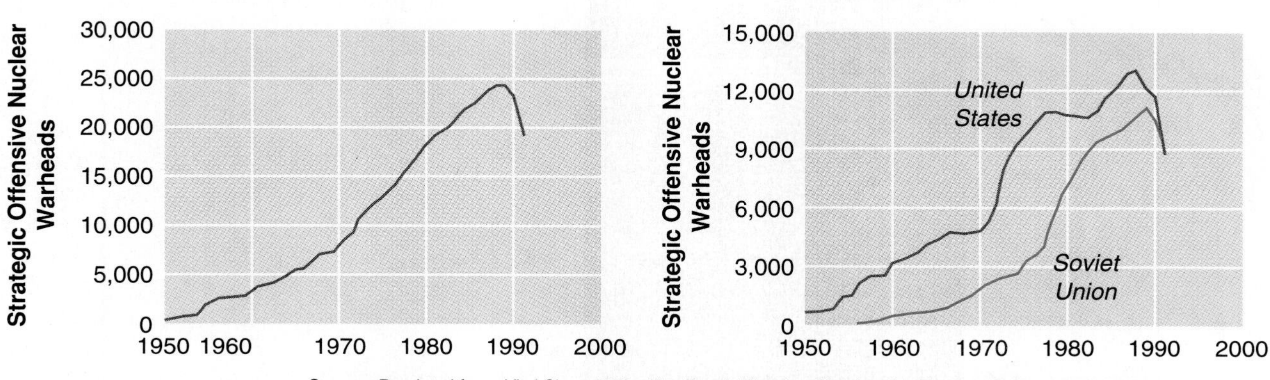

SOURCE: Reprinted from *Vital Signs 1992—The Trends That Are Shaping Our Future,* edited by Lester R. Brown, Christopher Flavin, and Hal Kane, with the permission of W. W. Norton & Company, Inc. Copyright © 1992 by Worldwatch Institute.

two superpower rivals are scaling back their arsenals, France, Britain, and China (the other nations with the largest numbers of nuclear weapons) are planning a combined increase of some 500 nuclear warheads.

DISMANTLING THE ARSENAL AND CONTROLLING THE WEAPONS

When the "evil empire" collapsed, the world immediately inherited 3 more nuclear powers. In addition to Russia, which had 19,000 nuclear weapons, the Ukraine (4,000), Kazakhstan (1,800), and Byelorussia (1,200) each became a formidable military power. With the exception of Russia, the new republics have almost no accounting systems for their tons of highly enriched uranium and plutonium. These key ingredients for construction of nuclear weapons could be siphoned off, given away, or sold without local officials being any the wiser.

Because the new republics have such enormous financial problems, Western leaders are fearful that sizeable portions of their military hardware will be sold to the highest bidder, no matter who those individuals are and what cause they represent. There have already been reports of "shopping expeditions" to Russia and Kazakhstan by delegations from Iraq, Libya, and Iran (Robbins, 1992).

If military hardware is not sold outright by government officials, weapons may change hands by way of former officers who have seen their military careers come to an end or have been forced to take drastic cuts in pay. According to a U.S. national intelli-

FIGURE 2.3 Destructive Power Compared: Nuclear Weapons Stockpile of 1993 versus All Munitions Used in World War II

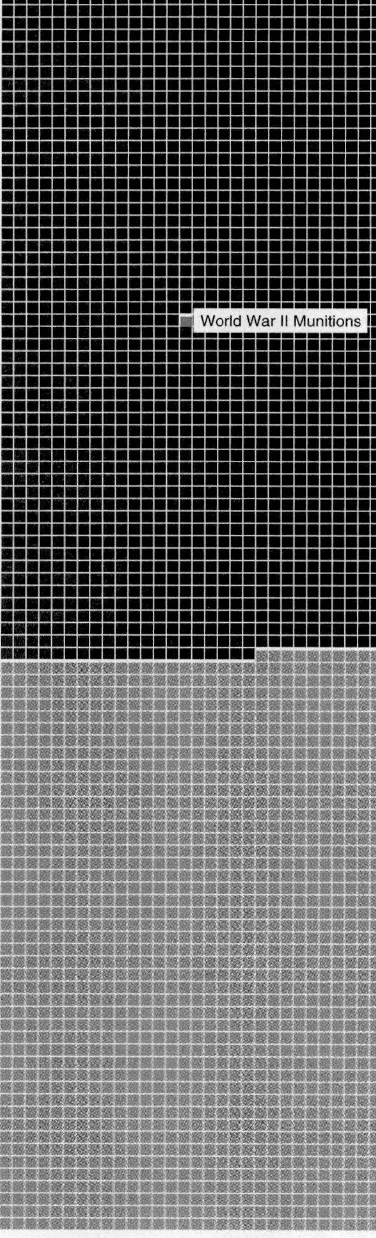

A single red square above represents the TNT equivalent of all munitions used in World War II. An estimated 6 million tons were used in that war and 40–50 million people died.

The entire block of squares represents the TNT equivalent of world nuclear stocks at their peak.

Black squares are the operational stockpiles of 1993 after planned reductions take place, and lavender squares the stocks now being removed.

SOURCE: Reproduced, with permission, from *World Military and Social Expenditures 1991* by Ruth Leger Sivard. Copyright © 1991 by World Priorities, Box 25140, Washington, DC, 20007 USA.

gence estimate, there is at least a 10 percent chance that some ex-Soviet military officer will try to sell a relatively portable tactical nuclear warhead to foreigners (Watson, 1992). The U.S. Department of Energy disagreed with this assessment and added a footnote to the report; it estimated the danger at 30 percent.

Organized crime groups in Russia may prove to be a more serious threat to international security than disgruntled ex-Soviet military officers. In May 1994, Federal Bureau of Investigation (FBI) Director Louis J. Freeh told a Senate Permanent Investigating Committee, "Russian organized-crime members may have already attained or will attain the capacity to steal nuclear weapons or weapons grade material" (in Goldstein, 1994, p. A5). Commenting on the implications of such an occurrence (including the possibility that these weapons could be sold to terrorists who would use them against the United States), Senator Sam Nunn of Georgia noted that organized crime in the former Soviet Union is "a potential national security nightmare" (in Goldstein, 1994, p. A5). Reacting to the threat of nuclear thefts in this region of the world, the FBI opened a field office in Moscow.

Even though governments have the ability to control military hardware to a greater or lesser extent, it is much more difficult for these new democratic states to curtail the movement of their citizens. At the height of its military power in the late 1980s, the Soviet Union had a workforce of approximately 100,000 technicians, engineers, and scientists in atomic research, of whom some 2,000 to 3,000 individuals had intimate knowledge of nuclear weapons design (Barnaby, 1992; Watson, 1992). Their careers were changed significantly or came to an end with the events of 1991. A combination of high inflation and a near-worthless ruble reduced the value of their salaries to about $15 a month in 1992. Although there is no evidence to date of a nuclear "brain drain," there have been reports of recruiters from developing nations attempting to entice these world-class scientists to work for their weapons programs. In an effort to prevent the buying of these individuals, the United States pledged (in February 1992) $25 million toward the creation of an international science and technology center that will employ former Soviet nuclear scientists and put them to work on more peaceful projects (Robbins, 1992).

The unpredictability of political events and nuclear weapons philosophy in Ukraine, Kazakhstan, and Byelorussia is a major concern to many people. For example, although Ukraine has continually stated that it wants to become a nuclear-weapons-free nation, government officials continue to drag their feet concerning when and under what conditions those weapons will be removed and/or dismantled (Katz, 1993). Another possibility is a nuclear confrontation between feuding republics, with nuclear warheads ultimately being deployed (B. Schneider, 1991). The political instability in that part of the world, coupled with the lack of accountability and control over nuclear weapons, makes for a dangerous situation.

THE RISE OF NATIONALISM AND ETHNIC CONFLICT

One advantage of the Cold War period, according to political scientist John Mearsheimer (in Talbott, 1992), is that the United States and the Soviet Union were able to keep their allies and subordinates (in the case of the Soviet Union) in check. However, now that the USSR no longer exists and the chances of an East-versus-West nuclear confrontation have been drastically reduced, Mearsheimer sees the emergence of a multipolar Europe awash with tension and shifting alliances. While he does not predict a war involving the major European states—France, Britain, Germany, and Italy—Mearsheimer suggests that they may experience tension as they jockey for position and supremacy in the post–Cold War era. With progress toward an integrated European Community stalled, these concerns are even more relevant.

On the other side of the continent, Hungary, Poland, Romania, the Czech Republic, and Slovakia might resurrect long-standing border disputes that could erupt into armed conflict. This is especially problematic considering the political geography of the region. For example, of the 5.3 million inhabitants of Slovakia, approximately 600,000 are ethnic Hungarians. These individuals are pushing the new Slovak government for increased cultural autonomy (e.g., education for children in the Hungarian language). Many Slovaks, including prominent government leaders, believe that Slovakia was victimized by approximately 1,000 years of Hungarian domination, and they are not about to make that concession. Equally adamant in their position, Hungarian officials have made it known that they will not permit members of their ethnic group to be oppressed. A latent consequence of the democratization of numerous societies that began in the 1980s is an increase in political identification and action on the basis of in-group characteristics (ethnicity, religion, and common culture).

An equally savage episode of ethnic violence occurred in the central African nation of Rwanda beginning in April 1994; as many as 200,000 to 500,000 Hutu and Tutsi tribe members were killed in a seven-week period. Thousands of men, women, and children were murdered in the streets. Hospital patients were slain in their beds; others were pulled out of a church and slaughtered, many hacked to death by machetes (Gerstenzang & Marshall, 1994).

Some of the world's most populous and more heterogeneous nations may become involved in protracted internal warfare that would be significantly more destructive than any such conflict in Eastern Europe. Violent clashes between many of the more than 700 million Hindus and 130 million Muslims in India over the past few years have resulted in the deaths of thousands of people as well as the destruction of homes, temples, and mosques. Because any economic and/or political gains made by Hindus are viewed by Muslims as coming at their expense and vice versa (a *zero-sum game*), there is little chance that the intense rivalry that exists between millions of people in these two groups is likely to be resolved in the near future. This extremely volatile situation is exacerbated by the pressures of a rapidly growing population and a scarcity of resources in a poor country. Pakistan and South Africa are also vulnerable to this kind of internal disorder. Iraq has already demonstrated its willingness to use chemical weapons on the Kurdish minority. If the right-wing Hindu fundamentalist Bharitya Janata Party were to come to power, perhaps something equally as gruesome could happen in India.

State-versus-state confrontations are typically more dangerous than internal conflicts because the former can draw in other nations and quickly escalate to large-scale wars involving millions of combatants. In the post–Cold War period, the likelihood of nation-versus-nation conflict does not appear to have been reduced as much as altered. Although a United States-versus-Russia confrontation seems unlikely, the proliferation of nuclear weapons and nuclear weapons–making technology has increased the chances of devastating wars both between and among nations. For example, would nuclear-armed Israel, which sees itself as a vulnerable island in a hostile sea of Arab states, use those weapons if it believed the nation's survival were threatened? Conversely, will not some (if not all) of the surrounding Arab states, knowing that Israel has the bomb, work diligently to obtain or produce nuclear weapons of their own? Would Iran and Iraq hesitate to use nuclear weapons against each other in a future confrontation if those weapons were available? While the global stockpile of weapons of mass destruction may be shrinking, the number of people with access to them is increasing, and that does not bode well for humankind as we approach the twenty-first century.

DEVELOPING NATIONS AND THE NEW ARMS RACE

Whereas the contest for military superiority among the global superpowers received a great deal of attention, few people noticed that many developing nations were arming themselves as fast as their much less endowed military budgets would permit. By early 1994, North Korea had produced as many as five nuclear weapons, a development that could destabilize, militarily and politically, its entire region. Not only are South Korea and Japan troubled by this situation, but a financially desperate North Korea (a country where eggs cost $9 *each*) could sell nuclear technology to Iran, which could in turn pass it on to terrorist groups (Pritchard, 1994; Thompson, 1994).

This arming of the poorer nations of the world was, in large part, the result of both Soviet and U.S. foreign policy. Always looking to increase the number of people in the capitalist or communist camps, the world's two most powerful countries attempted to entice developing nations to join their side by supplying them with, among other things, weapons and military advisers. Between 1983 and 1987, the Soviet Union provided arms to 42 countries; during the same period, the United States helped arm 59 Third World nations. Just over $200 billion worth of weapons was transferred from the superpowers to developing nations between 1981 and 1988 (Klare, 1990) (see Figure 2.4). In the 10-year period ending in 1988, the poorer countries of the world accounted for three-quarters of the total trade in arms ("Let Them Eat Guns," 1991). Purchasing these arms put a tremendous strain on Third World economies.

Inasmuch as the United States and the former Soviet Union were by far the two largest arms exporters during the Cold War, they basically decided which developing nations received military aid and weapons as well as the quantity and quality of these commodities. However, by the end of the 1980s, this situation changed considerably. As a result of losing their monopoly on arms technology, the superpowers lost control of what had shaped up to be a full-fledged arms race in the developing world. With the proliferation of all forms of technology, including military technology, in the post–World War II era, it was only a matter of time before some of the nations that were at the forefront of the modernization process gained access to that technology.

This recently acquired military know-how led to a modest although hardly insignificant arms industry in some of the Third World's more economically successful nations. Brazil now produces its own line of armored vehicle tanks, tank destroyers, and personnel carriers. India manufacturers a wide range of fighter aircraft, armored vehicles, missiles, and naval vessels. South Korea is one of the world's largest ship builders and constructs a wide range of combat vessels (Ross, 1990). To further maximize their technological capabilities, some developing nations have formed arms-development partnerships. Israel has allegedly helped Taiwan and South Africa develop ballistic missiles, and China and Brazil have formed a joint venture to develop space launch vehicles with military uses (Nolan, 1991). It remains to be seen if these cooperative arms-developing ventures will have diplomatic implications, such as the formation of military alliances.

In the latter years of the Cold War, the more prosperous developing countries found that they could circumvent the United States and former Soviet Union entirely and buy the weapons they wanted on the world market. Not to be left out of an ever-growing, increasingly more lucrative arms industry, France, the former West Germany, Italy, and Switzerland also sold billions of dollars' worth of armaments to Third World countries.

While many of the more than 140 developing nations increased their military prowess over the past 30 years, the majority of weapons transferred to Third World countries were sent to only 14 countries. These nations, plus Argentina, Brazil, China, and South Africa, comprise the developing world's "18 militarized states." Michael Klare

FIGURE 2.4 Major Arms Exporters: 1969–1988

Between 1969 and 1988, international trafficking in arms was a lucrative business for both capitalist and communist countries. The 10 nations shown in this chart exported 89 percent of the $558 billion worth of weapons sold to other countries during this nine-year period. The United States and the former Soviet Union alone accounted for 65 percent of the total.

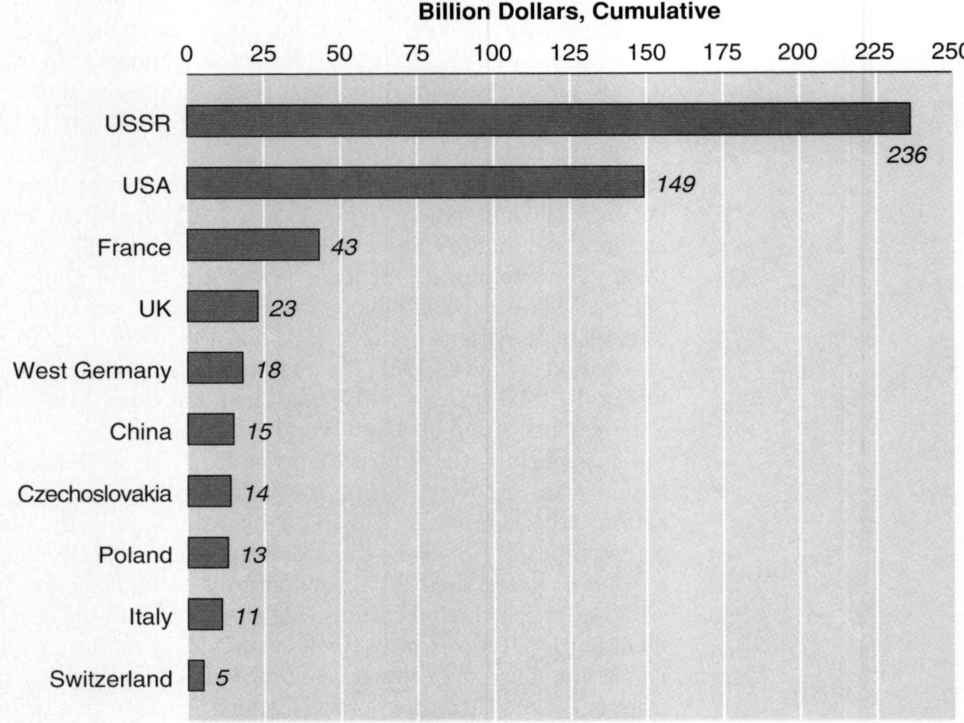

SOURCE: Reproduced, with permission, from *World Military and Social Expenditures 1991* by Ruth Leger Sivard. Copyright © 1991 by World Priorities, Box 25140, Washington, DC, 20007 USA.

(1990) argues that this lopsided arms buildup has produced an especially dangerous situation because most of these new regional military powers have been or are likely to be competitors. In this group of 18 nations, Klare identifies at least 12 antagonistic pairs (Klare, 1990, p. 11): Argentina and Brazil, China and India, China and Taiwan, Egypt and Israel, Egypt and Libya, India and Pakistan, Iran and Iraq, Iran and Saudi Arabia, Iraq and Syria, Iraq and Turkey, Israel and Syria, and North Korea and South Korea. Some of these pairs have already had armed skirmishes or full-scale wars. For example, Iran and Iraq have engaged in the deadliest conflict in the post–World War II era; India and Pakistan have fought three wars since the Indian subcontinent was partitioned in 1947. To make matters even worse, an estimated 40 nations, including many if not all of the above-mentioned countries, will have the technical ability to manufacture their own nuclear weapons by the year 2000 (U.S. Commission on Long Term Strategy in Klare, 1990).

Unlike nuclear arms, chemical weapons are inexpensive to produce, and the technology to do so is easily acquired. As of 1991, at least 12 developing countries were believed to have such weapons, and another 19 were trying to obtain them. Because of the relatively easy accessibility of these weapons, they have been referred to as the "poor nations' atomic bomb" (Adams, 1991).

One would be hard pressed to find a better example of the law of supply and demand in the international marketplace than the buying and selling of weapons. Even the former Second World countries of Poland and (then) Czechoslovakia that, ideologically at any rate, abhorred capitalism, joined China and the former Soviet Union as four of the ten largest arms-exporting nations between 1969 and 1988 (Sivard, 1991). It hardly mattered who was buying these weapons and to what end they would be used, as long as a profit could be made.

In the mid-1980s, the Japan Steel Works was heavily involved in the construction of a facility in Rabta, Libya, that would permit Libya to produce from 22,000 to 84,000 pounds of chemical weapons *every day*. When confronted with this fact, the Japanese said the giant complex was a desalination plant—that is, an operation for transforming salt water to fresh water. The plant was located 50 miles from the sea (Adams, 1991, p. 47).

A few days after the end of the Gulf War, President Bush told Congress, "It would be tragic if the nations of the Middle East and the Persian Gulf were now, in the wake of the war, to embark on a new arms race" (in "F-15 Sale: Wrong New World Order," 1992). Within the next 12 months, his administration had approved $8.6 billion in arms sales to that region, the highest 1-year total in history. During the Iraq-Iran War of the 1980s, 45 nations sold arms to the combatants, and 28 of those countries supplied both sides with weapons.

A major confrontation (like the Gulf War, for example) between two or more well-armed nations is one of the best things that can happen to weapons merchants. Not only do they get to replenish the stock of arms and ammunition used (to say nothing of selling weapons to worried neighbors of the combatants); they can tell potential buyers that their products are battle tested. The approximately 70 "weapons bazaars" that take place around the world each year in cities such as Las Vegas, Kuala Lumpur, and Paris are always well attended. Booths and displays (much like those in an auto show) with brochures and videos inform customers of the killing and maiming potential of everything from pistols and rifles to state-of-the-art antitank weapons and missiles. South Africa even markets access to a missile test and launch site to countries with poor weather conditions and/or dense populations that have difficulty perfecting their own weapons. The price, $500,000 a week, is much cheaper than comparable facilities offered in the United States and France (Millman, 1992). And for those weapons testers who are concerned with the ecological impact of their work, the South Africans offer a comforting message: "Before every test, we do an environmental impact statement. For example, when the whales are breeding, we shoot further out to sea, to not upset the mothers and their babies" (Millman, 1992, p. 21).

The developed countries continue to account for the great bulk of world military expenditure. Their spending amounts to 85 percent of the world total (see Figure 2.5). But when these expenditures are measured in terms of income equivalents, the Third World, with per capita gross national product (GNP) averaging only 5 percent of that of the developed countries, carries the heavier burden by far (Sivard, 1991). Despite some retrenchment in military spending recently, Third World annual outlays still take the equivalent of 180 million human years of income versus 56 million human years for the developed countries. In other words, the burden of the arms race in relation to income is more than three times as great in developing than in developed countries (Sivard, 1991).

FIGURE 2.5 Military Expenditures and the Burden of These Expenditures in Equivalent Human-Years of Income

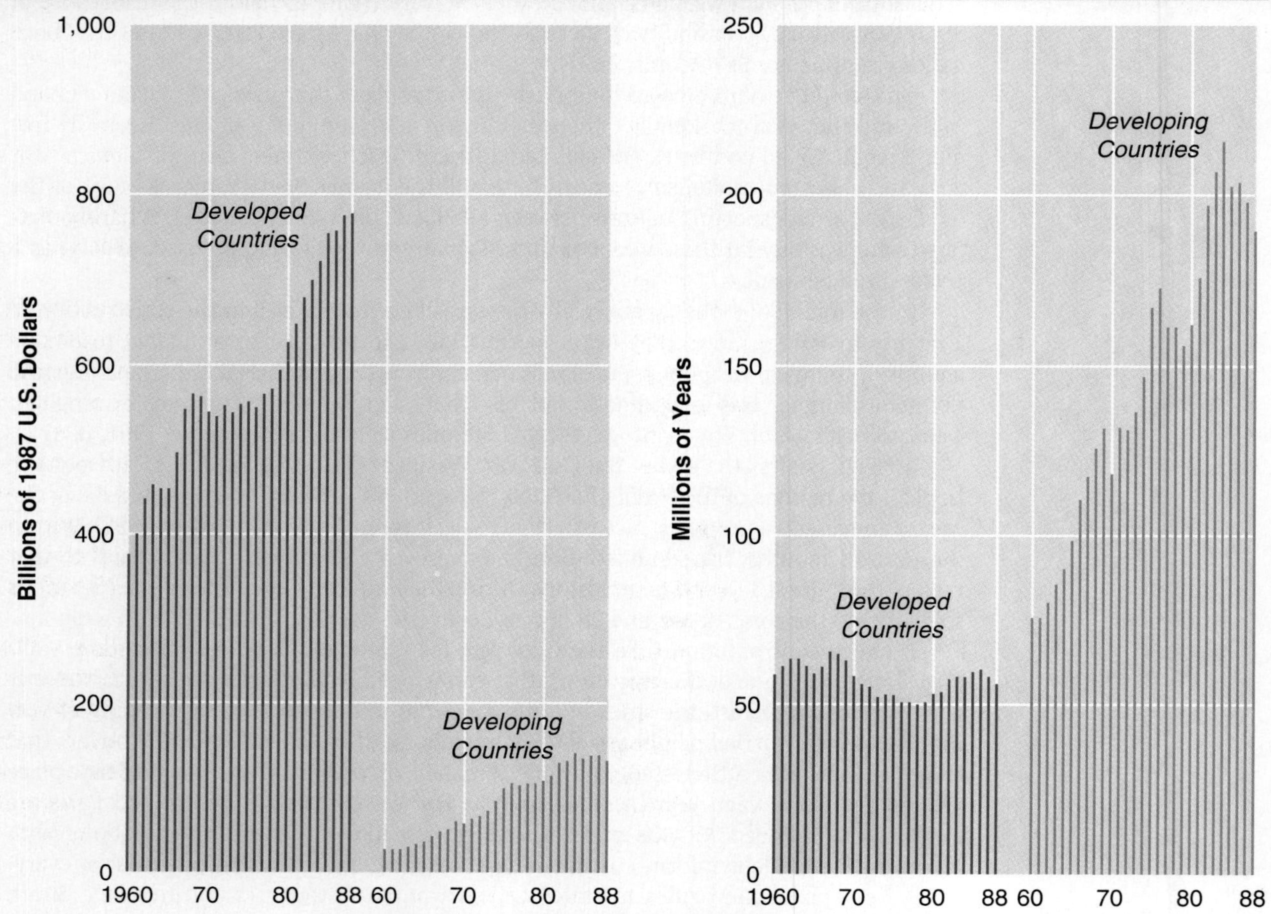

SOURCE: Reproduced, with permission, from *World Military and Social Expenditures 1991* by Ruth Leger Sivard. Copyright © 1991 by World Priorities, Box 25140, Washington, DC, 20007 USA.

FUTURE WARS

In a February 1994 interview ("Apocalypse Right Now?"), futurist Alvin Toffler offered his conviction that tactical (small-scale) nuclear weapons will be used in the next Bosnia-style conflict sometime during the next five years. Israeli historian and military expert Martin van Creveld (1991) has offered a very different scenario of what we can expect regarding armed confrontations. He believes that **low-intensity conflicts (LICs)**, which have occurred on a regular basis in the post–World War II era (approximately 120 between 1945 and 1990), will be even more numerous as we move into the twenty-first century.

LICs usually occur in less-developed countries and typically involve an army fighting guerrillas, terrorists, or civilians (including women and children). Rather than involving major battles fought with aircraft, tanks, and heavy artillery, LICs are characterized by small-arms fighting, skirmishes, bombings, ambushes, and massacres. Because LICs are often revolutionary wars, the armies cannot use heavy bombing and long-range weapons, lest they destroy much of their own countries, kill countless civilians, and alienate the ones who survive. (Ongoing hostilities between guerilla forces and the central government in El Salvador and Guatemala during the 1970s and 1980s are recent examples of LICs.)

Conventional wars—like the Persian Gulf War—that involve hundreds of thousands of professional soldiers and an enormous amount of military hardware, will diminish, as will the importance and usefulness of large armies and standard military strategy, which "have been caught in a vise between nuclear wars on the one hand and low-intensity conflict on the other" (van Creveld, 1991, p. 207). In the future, government forces may have more in common with police than with soldiers as we now know them, especially in urban areas.

U.S. Army Major Ralph Peters (in Levins, 1994, p. A18), who also writes about the changing nature of warfare, argues that a new "warrior class," which is "habituated to violence, with no stake in civil order," is springing up in poor nations around the world. This new breed of warriors—"who have acquired a taste for killing, who do not behave rationally according to our definition of rationality, who are capable of atrocities that challenge the descriptive powers of language" ("Mushrooming Ragtag Armies Worry Pentagon," 1994, p. F7)—would be formidable opponents for U.S. soldiers (should they ever engage each other in combat), because U.S. soldiers are not trained to mutilate and kill people indiscriminately and savagely. This predominantly underclass of robbers, terrorists, and guerrillas will be led by more or less charismatic leaders who command the fanatical devotion of their followers.

In the course of these often long-running conflicts, large numbers of civilians will be captured and held for ransom by forces hostile to the government. To protect themselves, more affluent people will hire security personnel and use sophisticated security devices. If van Creveld is correct, millions of people in some of the world's poorest nations will have to contend with LICs in addition to the many problems they now face. These "dirty little wars" will be clashes of car bombs and "men killing each other at close quarters, and of women using their purses to carry explosives. . . . It will be protracted, bloody and horrible" (1991, p. 212).

ECONOMIC CONVERSION AND THE PEACE DIVIDEND

In his presidential farewell address to the American people before leaving office in January 1961, former general Dwight D. Eisenhower warned the nation of the danger of a growing military-industrial complex that threatened to eventually control the federal government and undermine the democratic process. This alliance had the potential to propel the nation into war and make economic giants out of those industrialists who controlled the production of weapons.

The politically conservative Eisenhower echoed the writings of radical sociologist C. Wright Mills (1956), who presented his view of the American political-economic system in a book entitled *The Power Elite.* According to Mills, the power elite was a coalition of the highest-ranking officials from the nation's largest corporations ("corporate chieftains"), the military services ("warlords"), and the executive branch of the federal government ("political directorate"). The production of weapons, coupled with the country's wartime posture, when not actually fighting a war, was at least one point of "convergence" for members of the "higher circle of power." Corporate leaders made enormous profits, military leaders enhanced their careers, and the executive branch orchestrated the operations of a country always ready for war.

It is interesting how two men from opposite sides of the political spectrum could arrive at the same conclusion regarding the romance—some would say "illicit affair"—between the military establishment and corporate America. One would not have to subscribe to either of these perspectives to realize that in a nation that spent trillions of dollars on defense in the post–World War II era, a lot of people made a great deal of money producing and selling weapons.

However, of greater national significance than the fortunes made from armaments is the direction the military-industrial alliance steered the country. Every dollar the federal government spent developing and purchasing arms was a dollar not available for the development and support of other aspects of the economy. This point was humorously as well as sadly depicted in a political cartoon at the conclusion of the Cold War. Resplendent in his red, white, and blue suit, Uncle Sam is asking a brutish-looking Soviet general, "The Cold War is over—so who won?" Standing in the background, with a grin that stretches from ear to ear, is a man waving a Japanese flag.

Figure 2.6 shows the relationship between military spending and the growth of manufacturing productivity in 10 developed countries. Nations like the United States and the former Soviet Union, which pumped significant portions of their GNPs into the military, had the lowest rates of economic growth. Conversely, Japan, whose rate of economic growth between 1960 and 1988 was nothing short of spectacular, devoted less than 1 percent of its GNP for defense. Regarding the relationship between military expenditures and economic growth, Kevin Phillips, author and political theorist for the Republican Party, lamented, "We won the battle with the Soviet Union but we lost the battle for control of the 21st century economy" (in Joseph, 1990, p. 146).

If Phillips and the many other people who share his pessimistic view are to be proved wrong, the United States will have to undergo a rapid and successful economic conversion. That is, the many industries that are geared largely (if not exclusively) toward developing and producing military hardware will have to be transformed to produce nonmilitary goods that will be competitive in the international marketplace. As Michael Renner (1990) of the World Watch Institute, who has closely examined the conversion issue, noted, there will be strong opposition to altering the economic organization of the country. This opposition will come in three forms:

1. Weapons manufacturers who have long been accustomed to serving a single customer (the federal government) that had precise demands and bottomless pockets are not interested in now trying to meet the whims and fickle buying habits of an increasingly cost- and quality-conscious public (Corcoran, 1992). For arms producers, economic conversion is akin to killing the goose that laid the golden egg.
2. A report by the Office of Technology Assessment (OTA) stated that some 2.5 million jobs will be lost in the defense industry over a 9-year period ("Side Effects of the U.S. Peace Dividend," 1992). Approximately 37 percent of the 342,000 engineering jobs in the military-industrial complex will disappear in a 4-year period. People affected by these cuts can be expected to dig in their heels and wage a vigorous campaign to protect their livelihood.
3. A significant portion of the American public firmly believes that economic prosperity is spearheaded by defense spending. This view goes back to the 1940s, when massive military expenditures during World War II helped pull the United States out of the Great Depression.

FIGURE 2.6 Military Expenditures and Productivity: 1960–1988

During the height of the Cold War, the major industrial countries of the world with high rates of military expenditure had low rates of productivity growth. The former Soviet Union, which devoted an average 10 percent of its GNP (gross national product) to the military, had the lowest rate of productivity growth, averaging just 2.4 percent annually. Conversely, Japan, which spent only 0.9 percent of its GNP on the military, had a very healthy 7.8 percent annual rise in productivity.

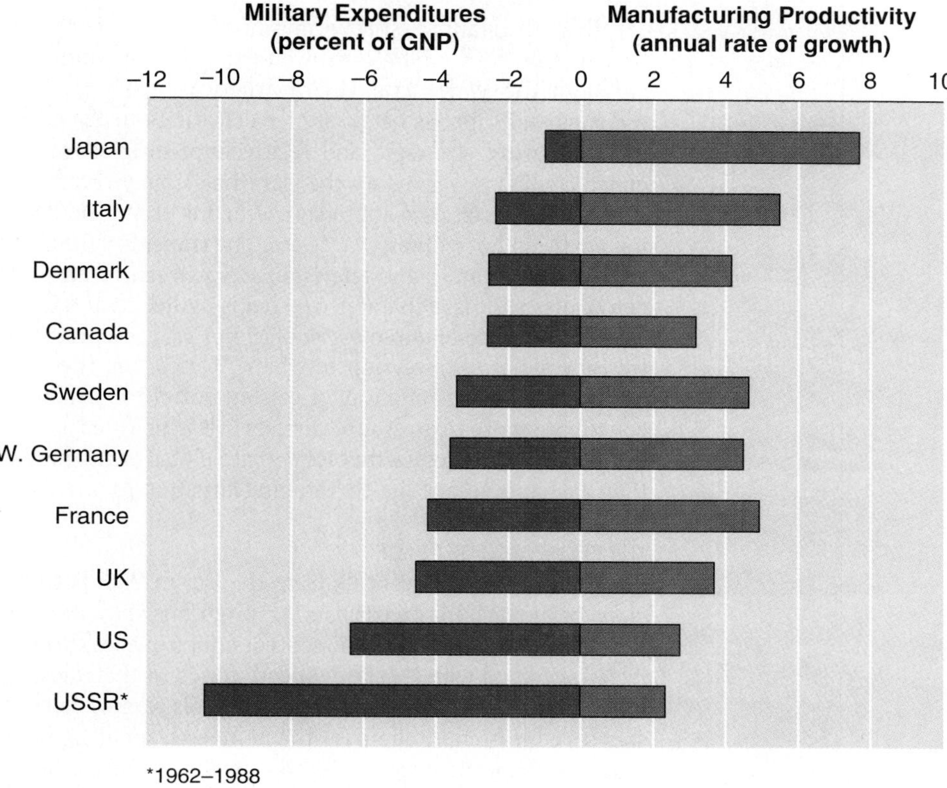

*1962–1988

SOURCE: Reproduced, with permission, from *World Military and Social Expenditures 1991* by Ruth Leger Sivard. Copyright © 1991 by World Priorities, Box 25140, Washington, DC, 20007 USA.

Inasmuch as defense contractors have low-risk operations that yield large profits, they may never be persuaded that economic conversion is in the country's (or their own) long-term financial interest. However, supporters of economic transformation hope to convert both defense workers and the general public with the following arguments. Although the transition period will be painful, eventual gains in the civilian employment sector generated by a restructured economy will more than offset losses in weapons production industries. To help ease the difficulties during this period, the federal government can establish a special conversion fund for job retraining programs and provide more generous unemployment compensation.

Renner (1990) makes a strong case against the myth of military-led prosperity. One recent study showed that 321 of the 435 congressional districts in the United States paid a "net Pentagon tax"; that is, more money left their districts in the form of defense taxes than was returned via military salaries and defense contracts. Another study concluded that while $1 billion (in 1981 dollars) created approximately 7,000 missile production jobs or 14,000 positions in manufacturing military aircraft, that same amount of money spent on local transit (buses and subways) would have produced 21,500 jobs; on educational services, approximately 63,000 jobs; and on the control of air, water, and solid waste pollution, 16,500 jobs. Research in the former West Germany and India reached similar conclusions.

Even the staunchest advocates of economic conversion realize that this transformation so vital to the long-term well-being of the country will be difficult. For example, although the World War II–era American economy was centered on producing the weapons and supplies necessary for defeating our enemies, the conversion to peacetime manufacturing was rapid and relatively painless. Because most of these factories produced civilian goods before the war, they simply reverted back to this practice after the conflict. However, many of today's weapons producers have little, if any, experience making anything but military hardware. The transition from producing missile guidance systems to video games and television sets will not be easy or perhaps even possible. These companies will have to enter new fields of business, retool, and start all over again.

This leads to an often overlooked but very important question concerning economic transformation: Conversion to what? Abandoning the production of tanks to manufacture automobiles is one way of getting out of the defense industry, but that would only contribute more toxins to the already overly polluted air. The creation of new factories or innovative technologies that exacerbate global environmental problems is nothing more than exchanging one life-threatening situation for another (Renner, 1990).

THE ECONOMICS OF PEACE

No sooner had the last brick from the Berlin Wall been torn down in 1989 than politicians began making "wish lists" of programs they were going to fund with the money saved from future defense budget reductions in a less threatening world. Much of the projected spending with "peace dividend" funds, as this unexpected windfall was being called, broke down along ideological lines. Liberals wanted to spend money for social programs such as education, shelters for the homeless, and drug rehabilitation centers—programs that were shortchanged during the massive military buildup during the Reagan presidency. Conservatives favored giving the money back to the public in the form of tax cuts. There was more bipartisan support for using these funds to help repair the nation's crumbling infrastructure—roads, bridges, and mass transit systems. And just about everybody agreed that a healthy chunk of these savings should be used to pay off some of the government's more than $3 trillion debt.

What nobody seemed to be sure of was how large the peace dividend was going to be over a period of 10 to 15 years. Some observers predicted a 4 percent reduction of the $300 billion-a-year defense budget, which would yield some $12 billion in extra funds annually. Others, like former President Carter (1990), expected that the U.S. military budget could be cut in half by the year 2000, yielding a peace dividend in the neighborhood of $150 billion annually.

While politicians had all but spent the eagerly anticipated funds, some observers (Hackett & Barry, 1989) believed that the peace dividend was nothing more than a myth that would simply never materialize. In a country like the United States, with a $3 trillion debt, not spending money on the military means that less money will have to be borrowed from banks in the future.

THE IRAN/IRAQ WAR
God, Guns, and Poison Gas

In Baghdad, on September 19, 1981, Saddam Hussein addressed a meeting of senior Gulf States officials. After apologizing for arriving three hours late, the president of Iraq informed his audience that he intended to declare war on Ayatollah Khomeini and the state of Iran (Lamb, 1987). Three days later, 45,000 Iraqi troops (the better part of 4 divisions) swept across the border and invaded their eastern neighbor. The war Hussein expected to last no more than a few weeks would last for 8 years and become the "bloodiest and most destructive military conflict since World War II" (Swearingen, 1988, p. 405).

Between 1983 and 1988, the conflict degenerated into the brutal trench warfare of World War I, characterized by long, bloody battles that yielded insignificant territorial gains. Less-than-accurate missiles falling short of their military targets rained on Iraqi and Iranian cities and killed hundreds of civilians. Because of military blunders on both sides, the war dragged on as the casualties mounted. One Pentagon official quipped that the Iran/Iraq war was "a case of the incompetent fighting the inept" (Swearingen, 1988). Thousands of soldiers became prisoners of war, and 1 million people were forced to flee their homes to escape the fighting and destruction. The prolonged conflict cost each country $1 billion a month, for a total of approximately $300 billion (Swearingen, 1988). By the end of the war, 1 million people had been killed and hundreds of thousands more wounded.

One of the most gruesome incidents of the war occurred in mid-March of 1988, after Iranian Revolutionary Guards pushed enemy soldiers out of the Iraqi city of Halabja. The Iraqi high command decided to bomb with chemical weapons this city populated by Kurds who had been fighting a guerilla war against Hussein (and now Iranian soldiers) for over 20 years. Planes dropped mustard gas, cyanide, and possibly sarin, one of the deadliest chemicals ever made, on the inhabitants of Halabja ("New Horrors," 1988). *Time* magazine correspondent Jill Smolowe (1988, p. 46) describes the hideous effects of chemical warfare:

> First, one detects an odd odor, something like the scent of garlic. Then the burning sets in, blurring the vision as the eyes begin to smart and itch. Uncontrollable bouts of sneezing and coughing follow, often attended by nausea and vomiting. As the hours crawl by the inflammation slowly spreads. When it reaches the respiratory tract, swelling the internal lining, the breath shortens, the chest tightens. The skin darkens to a sickly purplish color, the armpits and other cavities turning almost black. Excruciating blisters appear on the neck, chest,

The bodies of infants and young children lay strewn in a field, like so many broken dolls, young victims of a deadly poison gas attack during the Iran/Iraq War. In modern warfare, which is characterized by the use of weapons of mass destruction aimed at densely populated areas, there are often more civilian casualties than deaths of military personnel.

thighs, causing patches of skin to fall off. Large lesions discolor the genital area. For some, the blisters and the terror eventually fade, although they may be plagued by side effects like bone-marrow or gastronomical problems for years to come. Others perish quickly, the silenced victims of a silent killer.

Within minutes of the attack, between four and five thousand people died and thousands more were badly injured. Entire families perished in their homes, in the streets, and in their cars. Bloated corpses, many with the waxy appearance indicative of cyanide poisoning, were scattered throughout the city. As often happens, civilian casualties were mainly women, children, and the elderly. Survivors with severe burns caused by mustard gas were taken to available hospitals, where they lay in agony. Earlier in the war, Iraq used gas to repel Iranian attacks on Basara, the nation's second largest city ("If You Can Think," 1988).

Whereas Iraqis gassed their enemies, the government of Iran did not hesitate to sacrifice schoolchildren for military purposes. Armed with wooden sticks to detonate explosives, boys as young as 12 and 13 years old walked across enemy minefields. Thousands were ripped apart by explosions and Iraqi machine-gun fire ("New Horrors," 1988). In one incident, 5,000 young martyrs died clearing a minefield. Immediately following the carnage, Iranian tanks made their way over the blood-soaked terrain (Lamb, 1987).

Populations of 16 million (Iraq) and 42 million (Iran) meant that almost every family in these Middle East nations was affected by the war. Journalist David Lamb (1987), who covered the conflict for the *Los Angeles Times,* reported that the Iraqi people knew *who* they were fighting against but were not quite sure *what* they were fighting for. They were certain, however, that the war was a battle of wills between Saddam Hussein and Ayatollah Khomeini and would last as long as both men remained in power.

To some extent, the people of any nation are captives of their government during wartime. They must fight and support the war effort or be prepared to face unpleasant consequences. Consider the number of young men who went to prison or fled the United States rather than serve in the armed forces and possibly fight and die in Vietnam. The less democratic governments are, the more power they have to compel people to do their bidding. This is exactly what happened in the one-party (some would say totalitarian) regimes of Hussein and Khomeini.

Exiled in 1963 by the Shah of Iran, Ayatollah Khomeini returned triumphantly to his native country in 1979 and ascended to near-absolute power on a wave of Islamic fundamentalism. Khomeini legitimated his position, and his domestic and foreign policy (including the war with Iraq), on religious principles. Extolling his countrymen to battle the forces of Hussein, Iran's new leader stated, "The purest joy in Islam is to kill and be killed for God" (in Lamb, 1987). For Khomeini, the war was an "Islamic duty," implying that it was not an option but a necessity (Chubin & Tripp, 1988). Koran (Islam's holiest text) in hand, hundreds of thousands rushed to join the battle, some taking their own coffins to the front lines. Teenagers who were used to clear minefields were presented plastic keys to heaven that they proudly wore around their necks. Illiterate peasant youths were given fake maps that showed holy Shiite Muslim cities located approximately a hundred yards across the Iraqi border. In reality, these cities were 200 miles away (Lamb, 1987). Iran's leaders presented themselves as defenders of the Islamic revolution while mobilizing support for a war of an undetermined duration (Chubin & Tripp, 1988).

Iranians who resisted the war effort often received harsh punishment. In 1986, the government moved to take direct control of the nation's medical establishment, demanding compulsory service of physicians on the front lines. When the medical association balked at this directive, 450 doctors were arrested and many were tortured. Those Iranians opposed to the war remained "marginal figures, or hidden, or unseen, critics within the ranks of the regime" (Chubin & Tripp, 1988).

In Iraq, the war was supported by Hussein's generals, who were handpicked for their political loyalty as opposed to professional competency (Pearson, 1988). No doubt this was a factor in the bad advice Hussein received from senior media officials, including the counsel to go to war in the first place. To keep soldiers fighting a seemingly never-ending war, troops were given one week of leave for every three weeks spent at the front. For each two or three years of wartime service, officers received Volkswagens, many of which were sold on the black market for cash (Kirk, 1988).

Lest they forget their enemy, Iraqi schoolchildren learned that when Babylon was at its zenith in 500 B.C., the ancient land was overrun by Persia (now Iran). Donald Kirk (1988) argues that after a lifetime of brainwashing, young Iraqis were "spontaneously supportive" of Hussein. They sang, "Oh, father, take us to the front" in classrooms and meetings of the Young Pioneers—the Iraqi equivalent of the Boy Scouts (Kirk, 1988, p. 10).

Not taken in by its own propaganda, and ever careful to present the war as favorably as possible, the government took steps to insure that people did not learn how many soldiers were being killed and wounded. Trucks bringing casualties to the cities only did so after dark, and grieving families were ordered to keep funeral ceremonies brief. Public displays of mourning were forbidden (Kirk, 1988) and people who opposed the war were subjected to "draconian penalties." Serious critics of government policy simply disappeared; entire families have vanished.

The consequences of a war of this magnitude and duration will be felt in both Iraq and Iran for many years.

With 1 million deaths and hundreds of thousands of wounded soldiers in countries with a combined population of approximately 60 million people, the war affected most extended families in one way or another. Apart from the staggering loss of life, thousands of people had to flee their homeland with few possessions to face an uncertain and probably dismal future. After the gas attack on Halabja, some 50,000 Kurdish people escaped to Iran; another 75,000 took refuge in Turkey.

While so many people suffered horribly as a result of the eight-year conflict, arms manufacturers in countries all over the world reaped enormous profits. The two oil-rich combatants had the money to buy sophisticated weapons in the international marketplace, and there was no shortage of companies willing to sell them anything they could pay for. David Lamb (1987) notes that arms-producing nations supplied military hardware to both sides openly, which not only boosted sales but intensified research and development programs for new weapons. The Iraq/Iran War also allowed them to learn how these armaments would perform under actual battle conditions. Salesmen could now inform potential customers that these weapons were "combat proven."

Although the Soviet Union was Iraq's major arms supplier, French and German manufacturers made important sales to Saddam Hussein. The Iraqis also purchased weapons from South Africa, Brazil, Chile, and Holland. The Austrians sold tens of millions of dollars' worth of weapons to Jordan's King Hussein, who turned around and shipped them off to Iraq, making a handsome profit for himself in the deal (*60 Minutes,* 1991). During the Reagan years, the United States sold Hussein satellite imagery to help him target his growing arsenal of sophisticated weapons (Timmerman, 1992). The United States also capitalized on Arab fears of Khomeini with huge sales of arms to Arab states (Lamb, 1987). Iran bought weapons from France and received "essential items and services" from the Soviet Union, Syria, and Libya (O'Ballance, 1988).

David Lamb (1987) argues that the superpowers viewed the Iraq/Iran conflict as a useful war as long as it didn't spill over to neighboring countries. Two "unsavory" and unpredictable leaders (Saddam Hussein and Ayatollah Khomeini) were locked in a long-term struggle that could only weaken both nations. The Soviet Union was pleased to see the strength and influence of its oil-producing, troublemaking neighbors decline. The sentiment of the United States was cogently summarized by Henry Kissinger: "The ultimate American interest in the war [is] that both sides should lose" (in Lamb, 1987, p. 288). As long as the flow of oil to Europe, Japan, and North America was not impeded, and other nations were not sucked into the conflict, the war could be viewed as a positive factor for the United States and the rest of the world.

The use of chemical weapons by Iraq and Iran and the response or lack thereof to these incidents by the international community does not bode well for future conflicts. Despite strong verbal condemnation by the United States and other nations, there was no attempt to bring Iraq before the International Court of Justice. In the final days of the war, a United Nations staffer noted, "In the interest of peace I doubt that we will hear much more about the issue" (in Smolowe, 1988, p. 47). This lack of forceful action sends a message to Third World countries that they can engage in chemical warfare without having to pay a high political price for their actions (Smolowe, 1988). At a time of arms proliferation in a developing world rife with heightened racial, ethnic, and various cultural tensions, the passive acceptance of chemical warfare sets a very dangerous precedent.

The Iran/Iraq conflict contained all the horrors of modern warfare in a rapidly changing world: tremendous loss of life, agonizing death resulting from chemical weapons, and the destruction of billions of dollars' worth of property. But the real tragedy is that so much of the suffering could have been prevented. Although world leaders were not responsible for starting or continuing the hostilities, many were culpable for supplying the combatants (directly or indirectly) with the instruments of war. In an era of economic uncertainty and change, when the production of weapons is a major source of profit, there can be little hope for global tranquility if the profit motive continues to supersede values of peace and justice.

TERRORISM

The emotional-laden "slippery subject" of terrorism, as sociologist Brian Jenkins (1992) notes, is a difficult one to define, yet this is precisely what must be done if we are to discuss and understand this important issue. For Jenkins (1992, p. 2168), *terrorism* is "the use or threat of violence, calculated to create an atmosphere of fear and alarm and thereby bring some political result." While this definition of terrorism provides a framework to work within, it also leaves us with some difficult ethical issues. For example, were the reputed 24 attempts on Cuban leader Fidel Castro's life (including the planting of poison cigars) by the Central Intelligence Agency (CIA) acts of terrorism? Were the U.S. Army Air Corps pilots who dropped thousands of bombs on Tokyo in 1944 that burned to death 180,000 people terrorists? Certainly, these acts were designed to bring about "some political result" through "the use or threat of violence." Why is blowing up innocent people in a crowded restaurant a terrorist act, while burning to death men, women, and children with incendiary bombs dropped from airplanes an "unavoidable act of war" tolerated by the international community?

The above-mentioned problems aside, there is a good deal we can say about terrorism as it is usually defined. To begin with, there are at least three prevalent forms of terrorism recognized by most experts. **Political terrorism** is a form of unconventional warfare without any humanitarian restraints or rules that is waged against governments (Wilkinson, 1986). The goal of political terrorists is to bring about a significant change in or overthrow the existing government. The Palestine Liberation Organization (PLO), the Irish Republican Army (IRA), the Red Brigades in Italy, and Basque separatists in Spain fighting for an independent homeland are all considered political terrorist groups.

State terrorism is the use of violence by the government against its own citizens with the goal of terrifying them into submission. As with other forms of terrorism, the *actual victims* of psychological and physical brutalization serve as an example to the larger *target audience,* creating a pervasive atmosphere of helplessness and fear (Jenkins, 1992; Wilkinson, 1986). In Rangoon, Burma, in 1988, thousands demonstrated against one of the world's most oppressive regimes. A news reporter describes what happened when soldiers opened fire on the marchers and indiscriminately killed hundreds, perhaps thousands of people (Neumanin, 1991, p. G7): "I saw machine guns trained and firing on unarmed, peaceful civilians; soldiers moving methodically through the streets, pausing only to kill. Students were summarily executed on street corners as an example to others. . . . I am not exaggerating when I say that the evil I witnessed was unspeakable." There were no more antigovernment demonstrations in Burma for quite a while.

Typically, revolutionary groups use **enforcement terrorism** to gain the support of local people as well as to insure that they do not collaborate with the government. In Peru, the *Sendero Luminoso* ("Shining Path") captured eight civil defense workers in a small village. After a mock trial, the men were tortured and beheaded. This technique of gaining people's allegiance through fear, intimidation, and murder has been especially prevalent in the Middle East (Bremmer, 1988).

Questions regarding the psychological profile of political terrorists and what their primary motivation for joining these organizations may have been have prompted research yielding inconclusive and often contradictory results. About the only thing the experts in this field agree on is that almost all terrorists are young; the vast majority are in their twenties. Paul Bremmer (1988) studied members of the Red Army Faction and the Red Brigades in Italy and Germany and found that a "high frequency" of these individuals were educational and occupational failures. Rather than being committed to the "cause," they joined terrorist organizations because these groups offered a tightly knit, familylike atmosphere. The cause served as a rationale for their actual motivation: to become members—perhaps for the first time in their lives—of a "family." Bremmer also found that terrorists are not as eager to be imprisoned or to give up their lives for the cause as is commonly believed.

Paul Wilkinson (1986) gives us a very different interpretation of the terrorist personality. He sees most "hard-core" terrorists as well-educated individuals with above-average intelligence, people who are fully prepared to sacrifice their lives for some noble purpose. Perhaps these diverse findings can be explained in part by the terrorist organizations the researchers examined. One Italian study discovered that left-wing terrorists exhibited fairly normal personality patterns, whereas members of extreme right-wing groups were more likely to be psychopathological. There may be a self-selection factor at work here, as individuals with different personalities, family backgrounds, and life experiences (educational and occupational successes and failures, for example) are drawn to different types of terrorist organizations.

Although terrorism is overwhelmingly a male occupation, at least some organizations that have recruited or permitted women to join have been pleased with their capabilities and performance. In fact, 10 of the 14 most wanted terrorists in Germany in 1981 were women. Female members of several terrorist organizations "have proved to be tougher, more fanatical, more loyal" as well as demonstrating a "greater capacity for suffering" than their male counterparts (Laquer, 1987, p. 80).

Inasmuch as only a small number of terrorists are ever apprehended, and few of them are willing to undergo a full range of personality tests and evaluations, we will never have an accurate "terrorist psychology." However, the political geography of terrorism is much more straightforward and easily understood. Whereas some degree of state terrorism is a hallmark of totalitarian governments, revolutionary terrorism is virtually unheard of in these countries, where any opposition to the state is rapidly and often ruthlessly crushed. On the other end of the political spectrum, there appear to be what Jenkins (1992) calls "terrorist prone societies." It is not hard to see why "economically and politically advanced states" like the Western European democracies and the United States are especially vulnerable to this type of violence. In democratic countries like the United States, people enjoy almost complete freedom of movement. There is no internal passport system of the type that existed in the former Soviet Union. This gives terrorists the freedom to move about when and where they choose. One senior intelligence official stated, "Give me $1 million and 20 people and I'll shut America down. . . . I'll shut down the computers that drive our production lines, our communications systems, etc." (in "Apocalypse Right Now?" 1994). In addition to citizens' unrestricted movement in societies like the United States, all democratic governments have to work within procedural rules of law. This means that police cannot conduct random searches and seizures, nor can they arrest and detain people for an indefinite period of time without formally charging them. Finally, if captured in a democratic society, terrorists are all but guaranteed a lengthy and well-publicized trial, giving them the media coverage they desire.

The vast majority of revolutionary terrorist activity is confined to the following (Laquer, 1987; Wilkinson, 1986):

1. *Assassinations*—The killing of prominent government and business leaders serves as a mechanism for attacking the hated status quo and generating instantaneous publicity for their organization. Unlike street criminals, terrorists very often claim responsibility for their actions.

2. *Indiscriminate killing*—Detonating bombs in public places and taking the lives of people who are "guilty by association" (that is, citizens of the government they oppose) has been one of the most effective terrorist weapons. On February 26, 1993, high explosives jammed into a van parked in a garage underneath New York City's World Trade Center were detonated, resulting in what authorities described as the single most destructive terrorist act ever committed on U.S. soil. The powerful explosion that created a seven-story-deep crater killed five people and injured more than 1,000 others (Church, 1993a). Continued over a prolonged period, bombings of restaurants, stores, railway stations, airports, and important commercial establishments like the World Trade Center

can severely curtail the everyday operations of a society. This can lead to hostility toward a government that is perceived as ineffective in stopping these attacks.

3. *Robbery*—Terrorists need money to finance their operations. While cars can be stolen, places to live ("safe houses") cannot. In addition, money is needed for daily expenses. Robbing banks and armored cars is one solution to this problem. Some terrorist organizations have come to be involved in the international drug trade to support their activities. Others counterfeit some of the world's major currencies. Copies of U.S. $100 notes have been described as "excellent."

4. *Kidnapping*—Taking prominent people hostage and holding them for ransom has the dual benefit of raising money and getting news coverage.

5. *Liberation of colleagues*—Terrorists often place a high priority on freeing members of their group who have been apprehended and imprisoned. One strategy for achieving this goal is to step up the indiscriminate bombing of public places until imprisoned terrorists are set free.

6. *Hijacking*—The skyjacking of airplanes was a favorite terrorist activity in the 1960s and 1970s until the introduction of armed sky marshals and agreements with countries like Cuba (which would no longer give these individuals a safe haven) brought about a significant reduction in this behavior. Terrorists had hijacked airplanes to escape from one country to another or for hostage-taking and ransom.

Strategies for successfully combating terrorist activities are as controversial as other aspects of this phenomenon. The *soft-line* approach advocates negotiating with terrorists in order to secure the release of hostages and/or to end a terrorist attack as quickly and bloodlessly as possible. Although governments hope that once they resolve a terrorist incident through negotiation and appeasement, their tormentors will go away and never return, typically just the opposite happens. Terrorists are likely to pounce on this evidence of government weakness and increase both the frequency of their attacks and the boldness of their demands (Wilkinson, 1986). Another liability of this course of action is that it invites the attacks of other extremist groups who are attracted and reinforced by the success of the organization that previously negotiated with authorities. As Paul Wilkinson (p. 15) notes, "In terrorism nothing succeeds like success."

For *hard-liners,* any negotiation with or concessions to terrorists is simply out of the question. In addition, adherents to this position advocate the death penalty for convicted terrorists. While this get-tough, no-nonsense approach (especially executing terrorists) has a gut-level appeal for many people, there are some formidable arguments against it. Hardcore, fanatical terrorists will hardly be deterred by the death penalty. In fact, they may relish the thought of becoming martyrs (after a highly publicized trial) and securing their niche, as Wilkinson notes, in "revolutionary history." Martyrdom can also be a powerful force in gaining converts to the terrorist cause and, quite possibly, attracting new members to the organization. Finally, terrorists may engage in an escalated wave of attacks (assassinations, bombs in crowded places, taking hostages) to secure the release of condemned colleagues, or they may extract a high measure of revenge if their comrades are executed.

Hard-liners like Paul Bremmer (1988) argue that after the United States bombed the headquarters of Libya's Colonel Qaddafi in 1986, incidents of terrorism declined dramatically—as many as 35 attacks planned for the coming weeks were aborted. Opponents of this position counter by stating that no nation has been more forceful in lashing out against terrorists than Israel. Yet terrorist attacks against this country continue on a regular basis.

KEEPING THE PEACE

George Orwell, whose literary masterpiece *1984* vividly portrayed the structure and workings of human society at its worst, stated: "If you want a picture of the future, imagine a boot stomping a human face—forever" (in Winokur, 1987, p. 105). Many people would think that Orwell's vision of humankind's destiny is overly pessimistic. However, some 40 years after the British author's death, wars continue to snuff out the lives of people in countries all over the world. If the pattern of collective violence and war that has been escalating since the sixteenth century is to be broken, some major changes regarding how nations resolve their differences will have to be implemented. In addition, the way we think about war and the prospects for a lasting peace will also have to be transformed. Michael Klare (1992), Wendell Berry (1991), and Michael Renner (1993) offer a number of constructive steps for beginning this process. To their list, we have added some ideas of our own:

1. We must reject the idea that war is an inevitable, inescapable part of the human condition. This perspective is increasingly found in newspaper editorials and general social commentary. The perpetuation and dissemination of this way of thinking has the danger of turning into a self-fulfilling prophecy. If we convince ourselves that war is normal activity for our species, we are likely to behave in ways that increase if not guarantee that wide-scale armed conflict will continue (Berry, 1991).
2. We must overcome the legacies of almost a half-century of the Cold War. Campaigns for nuclear and chemical disarmament, which have been somewhat successful, should be continued. In 1992, 39 nations signed a chemical weapons disarmament treaty that had been negotiated for 10 years. By way of incentive, signatories of the treaty are guaranteed that if attacked they will receive immediate help in the form of protective, detection, and decontamination equipment from the other nations party to the agreement. This serves to reduce the value of chemical weapons to potential aggressors as well as further isolate them from the international community ("Curbing Chemical Warfare," 1992; Klare, 1992).
3. Funding the conversion process from a largely military-oriented to a peacetime economy should be a top priority of the military superpowers as well as the developing nations.
4. Increased economic and technical assistance to developing countries should be contingent on those nations' reducing their military spending. Some portion of the peace dividend could be used to fund this assistance program. While this policy would help developing nations, it would also insure our own safety and security, inasmuch as Third World conflicts always run the risk of involving one or more of the military superpowers (for example, U.S. involvement in the Vietnam War, the Persian Gulf War, and in Somalia) (Klare, 1992).
5. Although it is a difficult task, governments—especially in the developing countries where the problem is most serious—must do everything possible to diffuse fundamentalist movements within their borders. Whether they be Islamic fundamentalists in the Middle East, Hindu fundamentalists in India, or skinheads in Germany, these groups are very divisive and extremely dangerous. In religiously, ethnically, and linguistically heterogeneous nations, they keep burning bright the fires of intolerance and hatred that can explode in orgies of arson, looting, and killing, as in India, for example.
6. International institutions will have to be revamped to give real authority to Third World nations, where most of humanity lives. The Security Council of the United Nations

CONNECTIONS

Although the end of the Cold War was cause for celebration in the United States, it has had some latent consequences:

- Developing nations that received financial help and technological assistance from the United States (in part with the expectation that they would not turn communist) and from the former Soviet Union (to keep them away from capitalism) have been some of the biggest losers to date in the post–Cold War era. Recently, the attention—and money—of the developed nations have shifted to the new Commonwealth of Independent States and to Eastern European countries like Poland and Hungary that are transforming their economic institutions from socialism to capitalism. Partially as a result of these events, Africa's share of all the money invested in the world fell from over 4 percent in 1960 to less than 2 percent in 1990. Now that a sizeable portion of the funds heading from the rich to the poor countries of the world has dried up, the already enormous income gap between the "haves" and "have nots" will increase even faster (Kempton, 1991).
- The end of the Cold War has left us, for the first time in over 40 years, with no clearly defined enemy. Two generations of Americans (including the baby boomers) grew up learning to fear and hate Russian communism. If the "evil empire" out to "destroy our way of life" has collapsed, who or what will take its place? Columnist Charles Krauthammer (1992, p. 76) believes that we have already set our sights on

could be expanded from five members (currently the United States, Russia, China, France, and England) to eight members, including one representative from each of the major regions of the developing world, Asia (other than China), Africa, and South America. If the rich countries expect their poorer brethren to abide by the directives of international organizations, they will have to give those nations the opportunity to help formulate those directives (Renner, 1993).

7. If a lasting peace is ever to be attained, the nations of the world will have to forego the long-held notion of retribution or *lex talionis* ("an eye for an eye, a tooth for a tooth"). Wendell Berry (1991, p. 28) makes the following argument:

> If somebody raped or murdered a member of my family, would I not want to kill him? Of course I would, and I dare say I would enjoy killing him. If asked, however, if I think that would do any good, I must reply that I do not. The logic of retribution implies no end and no hope. If I kill my enemy and his brother kills me and my brother kills his brother, and so on and so on, we may all have strong motives and good reasons.

Berry notes that although retribution has been outlawed in our private lives, it remains an established and honor-bound principle in our international lives.

8. Striving for and attaining peace should be given the same rewards and prestige as preparing for and fighting wars. Toward this end, the United States and other countries should establish "peace academies" that have the same standing and prestige as today's military academies (Berry, 1991).

9. The United States must relinquish its role as the world's police officer. Although the United States was part of the 36-nation coalition that defeated Iraq in the Persian Gulf

a new adversary. This time, however, the nation to be feared is not a military threat but a ruthless economic opponent. "The emerging consensus is that Moscow's successor in infamy is Tokyo, which stands accused of mercilessly shelling the United States with reliable cars." If Krauthammer is correct in his assessment of Japan as the new target of our collective scorn, what does this say about us as a nation? Have we grown so accustomed to an external threat (real or imaginary) as part of our world view that we now find it hard to live without one? Psychiatrist Robert Coles (1983, p. 60) argues that "we crave scapegoats, targets to absorb our self-doubts, our feelings of worthlessness and helplessness."

If Coles' assessment is accurate, the Japanese make perfect scapegoats for us at this moment in history and, in time, could become even more loathsome foes than the Russians. For all their military prowess and diabolical activity, the Soviets were burdened (in the eyes of many) with an inferior economic system that eventually collapsed around or on top of them. However, the Japanese do not have this shortcoming. In the postwar era, they have proved to be the world's most successful capitalists. And herein lies the reason why they make such a perfect target for many people. Nobody likes to get beat at their own game, as the saying goes, and a growing consensus is that we are getting trounced at ours. Whereas the Cold War was primarily an ideological clash between capitalism and communism, twenty-first-century conflicts between any two or more of the world's rich nations may be fought primarily for economic reasons.

War, there can be little doubt that the United States was the major player in that action. Even though Iraq had the world's fourth-largest army at the time of the war, that army was controlled by incompetent, unimaginative leaders. The next time we may not escape with so few casualties. A long, costly, nationally divisive war like Vietnam is always a possibility (Klare, 1992).

10. It follows, therefore, that a truly international military force should respond to hot spots around the globe with the intent of preventing nations (or opposing factions in a civil war) from destroying one another. This intervention should take place when tempers reach a boiling point, not when war is well under way and hundreds of thousands of people have been killed, as was the case in Rwanda. The United Nations needs a mandate to intercede in a country's internal affairs if the situation warrants such action. Although political leaders of all stripes are loath to permit any interference in their nations' internal problems, only a policy like this can prevent wide-scale death and destruction from occurring.

Although the world community has been more apt to allow the United Nations to perform its peace-keeping mission as of late, it has been less than forthcoming in paying for these ventures. In 1992, member nations owed that world body almost $450 million, with the United States and Russia (which acquired the debt of the former Soviet Union) the chief debtors. If there were anything even approaching annual equivalency on the amount of money spent gearing up for war as keeping the peace, the world would be a much safer and saner place. The international community currently spends "three times as much in a *day* preparing for war as it does in a *year* keeping the peace" (Sommer, 1992, p. 18).

Michael Sommer (1992), of the Peace and Conflict Studies Program at the University of California, Berkeley, has posed an innovative and practical way for the United Nations and other international organizations to raise the funds they need. Just as governments levy "sin taxes" on items such as cigarettes and alcohol—with the funds going in part to rehabilitate people harmed by these products—arms manufacturers, dealers, and buyers should have to pay a "war tax" on every transaction they engage in. A tax of only 1 percent levied on the $300 billion a year spent on the purchase of arms by the world community would generate $3 billion for the United Nations' general operating budget. A 2 percent tax could go a long way toward helping countries make the transformation from military-oriented to nonmilitary-geared economies. The $9 billion generated each year from a 3 percent tax could be used to establish an Earth Corps to, among other things, begin cleaning up and repairing the environmental destruction caused from conflict and stockpiling weapons around the world (Sommer, 1992). Funds might also be used to begin repairing the lives of those individuals physically and/or psychologically injured by war.

No doubt military leaders and defense contractors around the world would do everything in their power to derail such a plan. However, if the international community is going to get down to the business of building a peaceful future, some method of generating funds must be found and implemented. Nobody likes paying taxes, yet opposition to such revenue-enhancing schemes has rarely stopped any government from demanding money from its citizens when the need arises.

The success or failure of these ideas is contingent, to a large extent, on whose view of human nature and the inherent structure and working of society is correct. If human beings are biologically programmed to be aggressive and, as the conflict theorists argue, society is continuously beset by dissension, strife, and periodic open conflict, the twenty-first century will bring us 100 years of horror that will make the destruction and killing of the period since 1900 seem tame by comparison. If, on the other hand, we are the products of our own making, destined to be combative by neither our genetic inheritance nor by our social institutions, the long historical record of humankind's murderous, self-destructive behavior can be broken. Created by humans, wars can be abolished by them as well—"given sufficient will and perseverance" (Renner, 1993, p. 157).

SUMMARY

1 According to one estimate, approximately 142 million people were killed in almost 600 wars between the years 1500 and 1990. The period from 1900 to the present has been especially deadly. In this latter time frame, civilians have been the principal victims of hostilities. Most armed conflicts today occur in the developing world.

2 There may be as many as 100 million land mines buried in countries around the world, especially in the developing nations. Approximately 800 people a day are killed by these mines, and another 450 are wounded. Posttraumatic stress disorder (PTSD) is the consequence of one or more experiences of overwhelming terror. Almost 850,000 Vietnam veterans suffer moderate or severe symptoms resulting from this disorder.

3 During the Reagan and Bush presidencies, the United States spent almost $3 trillion on national defense, about $45,000 for each family in the country. About $1 trillion has been spent on research and development of nuclear and conventional weapons since 1955. The world's military organizations are the single largest polluters of the planet. Pollution from burning oil wells in the Persian Gulf War was one of the greatest humanmade disasters in history.

4 There are four basic explanations for why nations go to war with one another. The *nature-of-human-nature* perspective focuses on humankind's innate propensity to engage in aggressive and violent behavior. The *population and*

technology argument is that rapid population growth has led to poverty and misery for tens of millions of people, which in turn has led to hostility and war. *Societal structure theories* see international conflict resulting from society's economic and political institutions. According to the *relations-among-states* perspective, wars are the outcome of military strengths of nations vis-à-vis each other in the geopolitical world.

5 *Genocide* is the deliberate, systematic killing of a group of people. During World War II, the Nazis slaughtered some 6 million men, women, and children, tens of thousands of them in gas chambers. Heinous war crimes have occurred during the fighting in the former Yugoslavia.

6 One explanation for wartime atrocities focuses on the training people receive as they are transformed from civilians to soldiers. A second explanation looks at how military organizations dehumanize the enemy, making it easier for soldiers to torture and kill their opponents. Finally, war crimes are viewed as the result of brutal circumstances that exist during wartime. In other words, the fear, hatred, panic, and pressure of battlefield conditions produce wartime atrocities.

7 The end of the Cold War is producing strains in the world's military superpowers. Their economies near collapse, Russia and other republics of the former USSR may end up selling some of their weapons (nuclear and otherwise) to the highest bidders for badly needed capital. The United States will face many problems changing from a military-oriented to a peacetime economy.

8 Just over $200 billion worth of weapons were transferred from the developed countries to the developing nations between 1981 and 1988. These sales resulted in the loss of badly needed funds for modernization on the part of Third World countries. According to van Creveld (1991), future wars will take the form of *low-intensity conflicts,* primarily in the developing world.

9 *Terrorism* is the use of violence calculated to create an atmosphere of fear and alarm to result in some political objective. Terrorist organizations engage in assassinations, indiscriminate killings, robbery, kidnapping, hijacking, and the liberation of colleagues.

10 A number of strategies have been put forth for limiting or eliminating future wars. Implicit in these approaches is the assumption that humans are not inherently violent beings.

CHAPTER THREE

POPULATION DYNAMICS
Too Many and Too Few People

As a result of a national census taken approximately every 10 years in most countries of the world, the enumeration of the population receives a good deal of attention. However, this "head count," as a census is sometimes called, yields much more information than simply the number of people who reside in a particular country. Data gathered from such an extensive project can give us a fairly accurate picture of many population-related problems and may even suggest what courses of action will have to be followed if these situations are to be rectified.

For example, environmental destruction is directly related to the absolute size of a population as well as its rate of growth, level of technology, and affluence. While slower-growing populations like the United States' are major polluters because of the vast quantities of energy and products they consume, poor countries (with significantly lower consumption of resources) can still be hard on the environment because of high birth and growth rates. Conversely, the industrialized nations of the world, with very slow or even negative growth rates resulting from low birth and death rates, are increasingly susceptible to a whole set of difficulties related to aging populations.

The often large-scale movement of people within a particular society as well as between nations can also result in a number of significant problems for all concerned. For example, a wealthy nation like the United States attracts people from all over the world who are seeking a higher standard of living. Many of these individuals enter the country legally. Others arrive illegally, like thousands of people from China, often after spending as long as 114 days at sea on overcrowded ships in miserable conditions. These Chinese "illegals," whose immigration is sometimes referred to as the "modern slave trade," pay $2,500 up front to gang members called "snakeheads" and agree to pay as much as $30,000 from their meager wages once they arrive in the United States (Frankel, 1993). Failure to make good on their debts can result in severe, sometimes fatal, beatings at the hands of gang members. In poor, heterogeneous societies like India, migration within the country (especially rural-to-urban migration) can lead to conflict—often of an extremely violent nature—as people of different races, ethnic backgrounds, religions, castes, and languages compete for wealth, status, and power in a rapidly growing society with limited resources.

The three principal measures of population dynamics—birth or fertility, death or mortality, and migration—are intimately related to some of the most significant problems facing the human race. However, because these problems do not contain what demographer Joseph McFalls (1991) calls the "dramatic event—the startling calamity or outrageous incident," they do not get the attention that humanmade and natural disasters such as wars, assassinations, typhoons, and earthquakes routinely receive. Until recently, population problems were most often "out of sight, out of mind" as far as the majority of people and most world leaders were concerned. This is especially unfortunate when one considers the scope of these problems and the enormity of their consequences.

QUESTIONS TO CONSIDER

1. What are the three stages of the *demographic transition?*
2. Which two groups of people are primarily responsible for much of the environmental damage taking place in the world today? What types of behavior do these individuals engage in that is so destructive?
3. In what region of the world is the problem of hunger most severe? Why?
4. Why is the economist and clergyman Thomas Malthus sometimes referred to as the "Parson of Doom"?
5. What is the *Green Revolution?* Where has it been most successful? What are some of the undesirable latent consequences of this revolution?
6. What is the *Biotechnology Revolution?* Can this revolution solve the problem of world hunger?
7. What strategies have been most successful in reducing fertility in Third World nations?
8. What is the *population implosion?* In what region of the world is this phenomenon occurring? What are the short- and long-term consequences of this event?
9. What are "push" and "pull" factors, and how are they related to migration?
10. What are the major arguments of both the anti-immigration and the pro-immigration movements?

OVERPOPULATION

UNPRECEDENTED GROWTH

Anyone who has ever traveled in the developing nations or visited a major city in these countries may find it hard to imagine that only 2,000 years ago (a short period of time in the history of our species), the population of the world was no more than 250 million people—slightly less than today's U.S. population. However, beginning in the modern age

FIGURE 3.1 World Population Growth through History

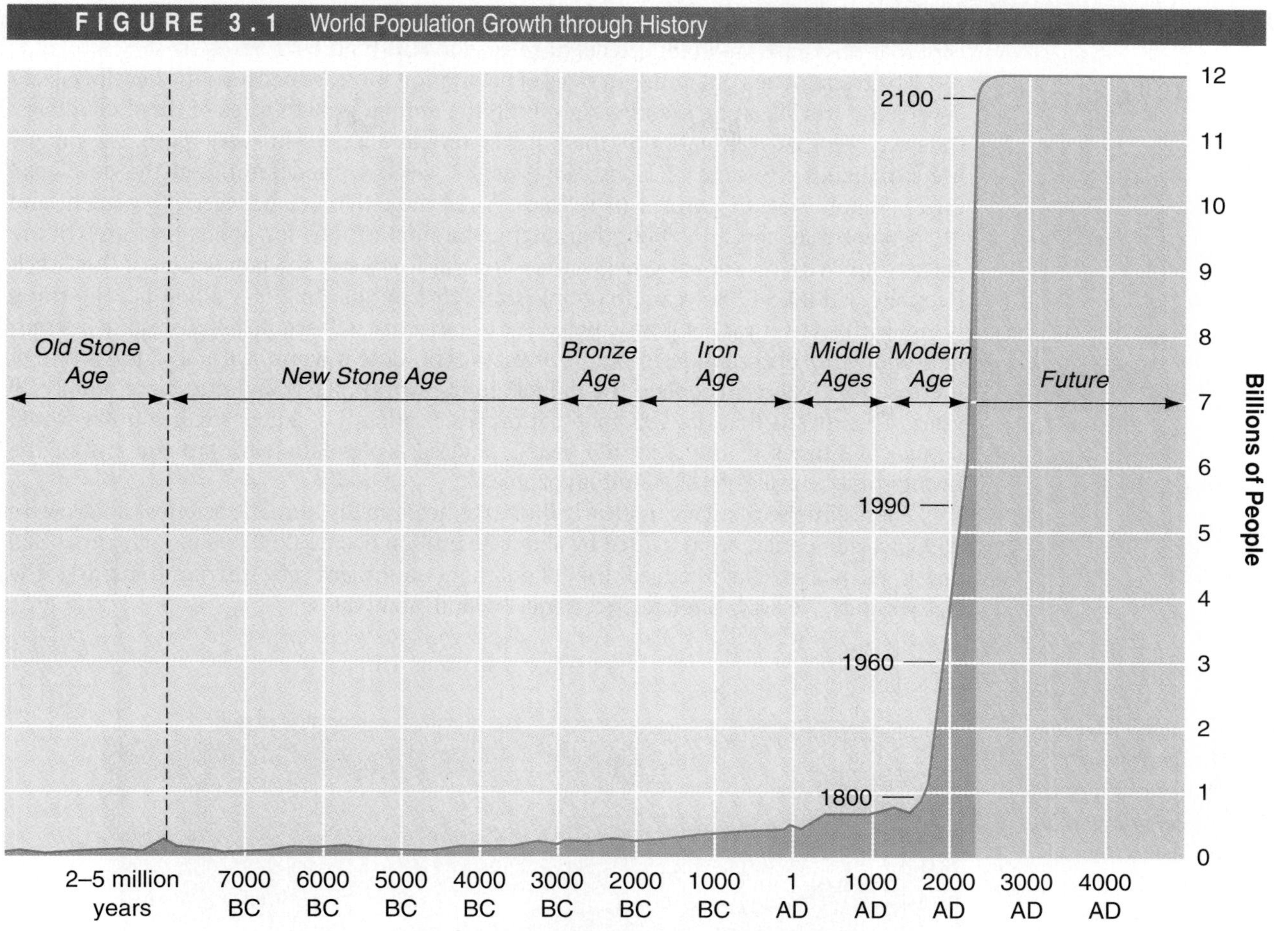

SOURCE: Reprinted by permission of the Population Reference Bureau.

(for reasons to be discussed in the following section), societal growth accelerated at an unprecedented rate (see Figure 3.1). The world population grew at a rate of 2 percent every *thousand years* for most of human history. Today, in the developing nations, growth is occurring at the rate of 2 percent *per year.* While it took from the time of Christ to 1927 for world population to increase from approximately 250 million to 2 billion people, it will take only 71 years (until 1998) for the population to triple to 6 billion individuals. With a doubling time of 42 years (at the current rate of growth), the population of planet Earth will reach 12 billion during your lifetime.

Every 24 hours, another 250,000 individuals—enough people to populate the cities of Akron, Ohio, or Anaheim, California—are added to the world's population: 237,000 to the population of developing countries and 13,000 to the remaining nations (i.e., North America, Europe, the former Soviet Union, and Oceania) ("Today on the Planet," 1992). Over the past 45 years, approximately 85 percent of population growth has occurred in the developing world (see Figure 3.2). This proportion will increase to 96 percent by the year 2001 as a result of the control of numerous communicable diseases, improved health care that has drastically reduced death rates, and still-high birth rates.

The tremendous difference in rates of population increase between the developed and developing world can be seen by examining the annual growth rates of three countries: the developing African nation of the Cote d'Ivoire at 3.5 percent (very high), the rapidly industrializing city-state of Hong Kong at 0.7 percent (moderate), and the developed Czech Republic at 0.1 percent (very low). While the difference between 3.5 percent and 0.1 percent may appear to be rather slight, the implications for population growth are staggering. With an annual growth rate of only 0.1 percent, the population of the Czech Republic will take 1,386 years to double from 10.3 million to 20.6 million people. Hong Kong, with a faster rate of yearly increase (0.7 percent), will see its population of 5.8 million double to 11.6 million in only 100 years. The Cote d'Ivoire, with an annual rate of increase of 3.5 percent (one of the highest in the world), has a doubling time of only 20 years. This means that the 1993 population (13.4 million) of a now small country would double five times in the next 100 years, yielding a population toward the end of the twenty-first century of 428.8 million people!

These simple calculations clearly illustrate how rapidly human societies can grow. In 1993, world population increased by about 91 million people (250,000 per day times 365 days), as planet Earth added the population equivalent of Austria, Denmark, the Netherlands, Norway, England, Scotland, Ireland, and Wales.

Babies born in developing nations typically weigh less than those born in the developed world. Because these children are smaller and weaker than their counterparts in rich countries, they are more likely to die sometime during the first year of life from a variety of diseases. This high infant mortality rate is a primary reason why fertility rates in the developing world are so high: People compensate for the deaths of so many children by having large families.

FIGURE 3.2 Population Trends in Developed and Developing Countries: 1750–2100

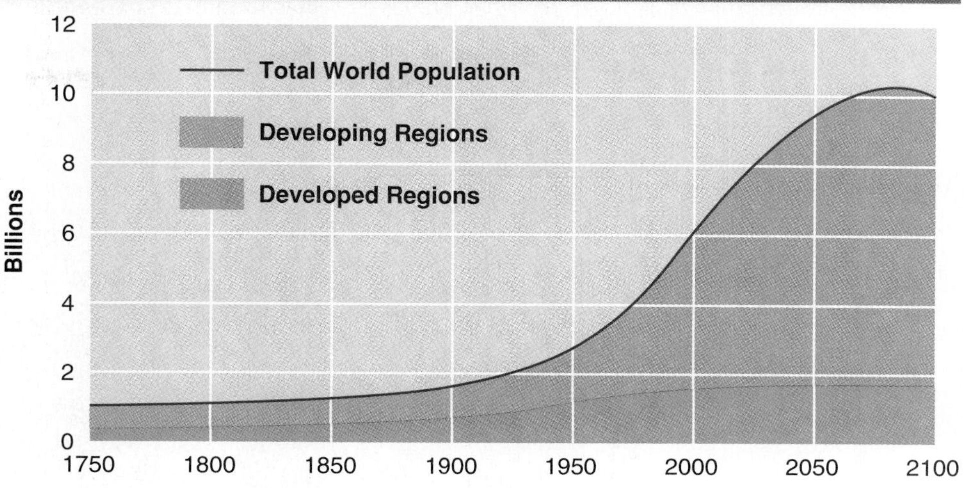

SOURCE: Reprinted by permission of the Population Reference Bureau.

THE DEMOGRAPHIC TRANSITION

The unprecedented growth in human populations that began in the modern age is best explained by the **demographic transition**, a perspective originally developed by Warren Thompson in 1929 and further developed by Frank Notestien in 1945. According to this theory, the birth and death rates of a society will change, which will determine its rate of growth as it passes through four stages (see Figure 3.3), neatly summarized by McFalls (1991) and Haupt and Kane (1991).

The first stage, which lasted for almost all of human history, was characterized by high birth rates and equally high death rates that essentially canceled out each other. This resulted in a very slow and intermittent rate of population growth. Death rates were high because of poor health and sanitation, limited medical knowledge, and harsh living conditions. Many children died before their fifth birthday. On the other hand, religious teachings and social pressures kept birth rates high. McFalls (1991, p. 33) notes that "if birth rates had not also been high, societies would simply have died out—and many did!" Hunting-and-gathering and later agricultural societies were particularly labor intensive and required steady population growth just to survive. These labor requirements were reinforced by religious teachings that were the equivalent of the Christian prescription to "Go forth and multiply." Large families also increased the economic, political, and military power of a society and helped insure survival following unexpected disasters such as droughts or contagious diseases. Because of high birth rates, this stage is sometimes referred to as one of *high growth potential.*

Signaling a dramatic break in our demographic history, stage two began when death rates fell at the beginning of the Industrial Revolution because of advances in medicine, better nutrition, and a slightly more equitable distribution of income. This stage marked the inception of the population explosion. At this point, it is important to understand that population increase is not simply the result of high birth rates. Rather, population

FIGURE 3.3 Stages of Demographic Transition

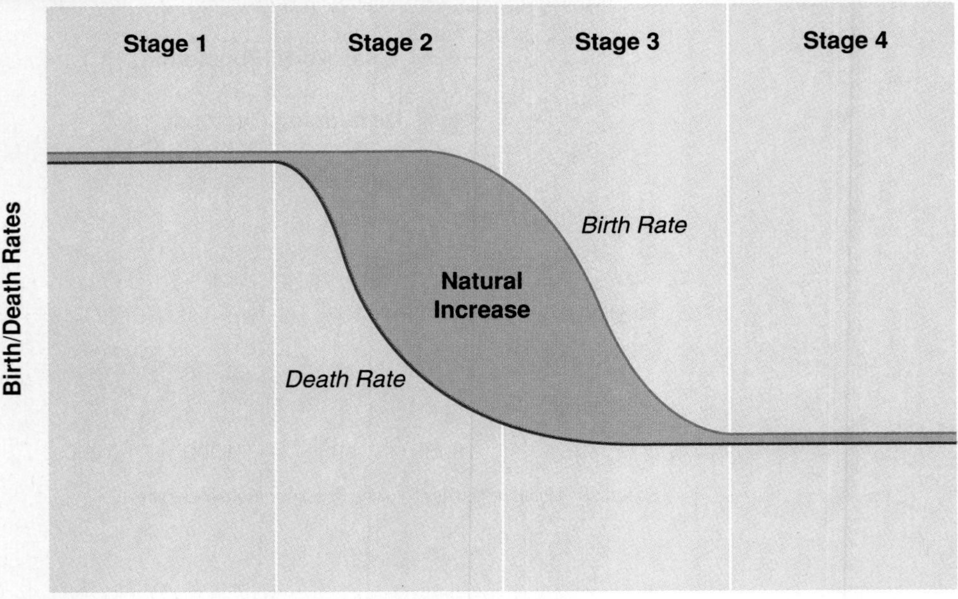

SOURCE: Reprinted by permission of the Population Reference Bureau.

growth (either positive or negative) is the difference between a society's birth rate *and* its death rate. In stage one of the demographic transition, a high birth rate was nullified by an equally high death rate. However, when the same (not increasing) birth rate is coupled with a sharply declining death rate, as it is in stage two, population growth is rapid and significant. Birth rates did not fall in accord with death rates at this time because of a phenomenon that sociologist William Ogburn (1950) refers to as *cultural lag*—the process whereby one component of a society changes faster than another related aspect of society.

While virtually every society embraced the medical and technological advances that could forestall "the universal enemy: death" (McFalls, 1991, p. 34), those social, cultural, and religious forces and beliefs that had supported large families for hundreds of years were much harder to change. In other words, a society's system of beliefs and patterns of behavior do not quickly and automatically change in line with every technological innovation. Regarding population dynamics, for example, it may take generations for people to accept the fact that a family with six or eight children is dysfunctional in a larger, more technologically advanced society.

In the third stage of the transition, birth rates "catch down" with death rates as people gain both the desire and the ability to control fertility. For most of human history, children began working at 6 or 8 years of age, and their labor was an economic asset to the family. However, as societies modernized, children became economic liabilities, consuming food, clothing, shelter, tuition, and recreational goods and services that were paid for by their parents until they reached the age of 21. The desire to reduce family size is more easily realized in this stage with the introduction and widespread availability of contraceptive devices. Although population growth remains quite high during the beginning of this stage, it falls to near zero by its conclusion.

Whereas the first stage of the demographic transition has high birth and death rates, the fourth stage is characterized by low birth and death rates. As Figure 3.3 illustrates, both stages have low rates of population growth. At stage four, contraceptive use is extensive and widely accepted. Partially as a result of increases in economic power and political rights, women marry later and have fewer children. Couples may view children not only as economic liabilities but also as detriments in a consumer-oriented society where people often have strong desires for material possessions and recreation and travel.

Some population experts have attracted attention by speculating about a fifth stage of the demographic transition, when death rates fall below birth rates and heretofore slow rates of population increase (as in stage four) turn into negative growth, or a decline in the size of the population. The dynamics and consequences of this fifth stage will be discussed in the section on underpopulation later in this chapter.

Societies differ in the length of time it takes to complete the transition, but once the process begins, it cannot be reversed. To date, there is no record of a society moving, for example, from stage three back to stage two. Developing nations are in stages two and three as their populations are increasing rapidly. One of the shortcomings of this theory is its failure to predict how long countries will remain in each stage. Although the developed countries of the world completed the transition (the first four stages) somewhat in unison in roughly 200 years, "it is clear that as a result of contemporary political and economic forces, developing nations are following very different timetables" (McFalls, 1991, p. 34). This will have tremendous implications for world population growth. If a country like India (with about 17 percent of the world's people) gets demographically stuck in stages two and three for any length of time, the planet's population will grow much faster than it will if India moves quickly to stage four.

All the industrial societies have progressed to stage four, but only a handful have moved to the fifth stage. As of this moment, it is unclear whether all the developed nations will follow suit and/or if those countries in stage five (negative growth) will eventually experience increases in their birth and growth rates and move back to stage four.

POPULATION, THE ENVIRONMENT, AND DEVELOPMENT

Much of the environmental destruction taking place in the world today is due to the ways of life of two groups of people: the richest billion individuals who reside in the developed nations and those 1 billion destitute people (sometimes called "the poorest of the poor") who live in developing countries. The former destroy the environment indirectly through their consumption of tremendous amounts of resources and, as a consequence of this pattern of consumption, generate enormous quantities of waste. The poorest billion individuals destroy their environment out of sheer necessity to survive (Sadik, 1991, p. 4).

IMPACT OF POPULATION ON ENVIRONMENT

The impact any one group of people has on the environment can be determined through the application of a formula developed by population biologists Paul and Ann Erlich (in *Population and the Environment: The Challenges Ahead,* 1991):

$$I = P \times A \times T$$

In this formula, I stands for environmental impact, P stands for population (its size, rate of growth, distribution, etc.), A stands for affluence (determined by level of income and lifestyle), and T stands for the environmentally harmful technology that supplies A.

The $I = PAT$ equation demonstrates why both the richest and the poorest billion people in the world are so environmentally destructive. Consider a country like the United States, with a 1993 population of 258 million: a relatively small nation when compared to India with over 900 million and China with 1.178 billion people. Although the *P*, or population, of the United States is less than one-third of India's and one-fourth of China's, the level of income and lifestyle (*A*) in the United States and also the amount of environmentally harmful technology (*T*) are all much greater than they are in the other two countries. As a result of U.S. affluence and technological sophistication, Americans probably have a destructive impact on the environment greater than that of the populations of India and China combined.

If this final statement seems somewhat hard to believe, consider the lifetime environmental impact (*I*) of a typical middle-class individual in the United States ("Today on the Planet," 1992). During the course of his or her life, this person will:

- Go through 12,000 grocery bags
- Drive 700,000 miles and use 28,000 gallons of gasoline
- Use and throw away 27,500 newspapers, 3,900 weekly newsmagazines, and 225 pounds of phone books
- Throw away 55 tons of garbage
- Consume enough electricity to burn over 8 tons of coal
- Account for the use of 35 tons of steel and 23 tons of cement
- Eat 8,486 pounds of meat
- Eat over 17,000 eggs, the lifetime supply of 35 chickens

Looking at this only partial list of lifetime consumption, it is easy to understand how the United States, with approximately 5 percent of the world's population, uses roughly 25 percent of the planet's resources. Per capita use of energy in the United States, which would fall under *T* in our formula, is 10 times as great as that of Brazil and 35 times that of India (Valentine, 1992). Not just the United States but all the developed countries, with only 15 to 20 percent of the world's population, use the majority of the earth's resources and produce most of the pollution.

While developing nations currently produce about 33 percent of the carbon dioxide that is pumped into the earth's atmosphere, their populations (*P*) are growing so rapidly that by the year 2025, that figure could exceed 66 percent. And if some of these countries (especially the most populous ones) begin to make significant strides economically, increasing the overall affluence, *A*, and technology, *T*, in the equation, their levels of carbon dioxide pollution will rise accordingly.

As previously noted, the poorest billion people also contribute to environmental destruction. For example, these individuals often clear-cut forests and woodlands in their search for firewood and building material. And because almost all these nations are in debt (collectively, they owe world banks over $1.3 trillion), they are also selling off the nonrenewable natural resources that are in many cases their only sources of foreign currency. "Like a consumer forced to hock the family heirlooms to pay credit card bills, developing countries are plundering forests, decimating fisheries, and depleting water supplies regardless of their long-term consequences" (Kane, 1992a, p. 68).

The poorest region of the developing world, which also has the highest rate of population growth, sub–Saharan Africa's external debt was over four times as great as its annual earnings from exports in 1989. With a population doubling time of only 23 years, what other alternative is open to these countries than to sell anything and everything they have of value, with little regard for the long-term consequences of their actions?

Even water, which we normally think of as a renewable resource, has a finite dimension and as such is affected by population growth. Although the supply of water necessary for drinking, cooking, and irrigation is continually being replenished by rainfall, a nation with a population doubling time of 20 years cannot expect that its water supply will also double. The United Nations predicts a 25 percent increase in water demand worldwide during the 1990s alone ("Running Dry," 1993). To meet this demand, underground aquifers are being overpumped and water tables are diminishing. Water shortages will inevitably lead to diminished food production, slower growth in local economies, and further destruction of the local environment ("Running Dry," 1993).

Even some so-called natural disasters that result in heavy loss of life are linked to the pressures of overpopulation. The 114 million people of Bangladesh reside in every possible area of that small country, including the continually shifting low-lying islands called *chars.* In 1991, a powerful cyclone ripped across this area, killing 139,000 people and hundreds of thousands of animals and damaging more than one million homes. If Bangladesh were not so densely populated, these low-lying areas would probably be uninhabited. The saddest aspect of this entire tragedy is that it will certainly happen again to one degree or another as people in one of the poorest countries in the world struggle to survive wherever they can. As one survivor said to a reporter, "Where shall we go?" (in Drogin, 1991).

Paleoanthropologist Louis Leakey argues that just as the earth has experienced five extinctions over the hundreds of millions of years of its existence, human beings may soon be responsible for a sixth extinction: that is, the environmental destruction in the coming three decades of 50 percent of the planet's species. Not only would this be a tragedy in and of itself, but plants unknown and uncatalogued by botanists and biologists could have been key ingredients in cures for some of our deadliest diseases (in Germani, 1992b). This is hardly farfetched considering that nearly one-half of all medical prescriptions dispensed in the world today have their origins in wild organisms (*Population and the Environment: The Challenges Ahead,* 1991). In a worst-case scenario, Leakey speculates that the sixth extinction could take humankind with it.

IMPACT OF POPULATION ON QUALITY OF LIFE

The International Human Suffering Index (HSI) (1992), compiled by the former Population Crisis Committee (now Population Action International), indicates that just as the environment is affected by the size and rate of growth of a population, so is a nation's overall quality of life. An index consisting of the following 10 measures of human welfare was translated into a final summary HSI score for 141 countries: life expectancy, daily intake of calories, clean drinking water, infant immunization against disease, secondary school enrollment, per capita gross national product (GNP), rate of inflation, communications technology, political freedom, and civil rights.

Results showed that countries with the highest suffering scores also had very high rates of population growth. For example, of the 27 countries in the "extreme human suffering" category, 20 were in Africa, the fastest-growing region in the world. Conversely, of the 24 nations in the "minimal human suffering" group, only Barbados could be considered a developing country ("Human Suffering Index," 1992). The HSI clearly illustrates the tremendous gap in living conditions between the most prosperous billion people in the world and the most poor billion inhabitants. Population Action International argues that slower rates of population growth would go a long way toward reducing the suffering of this latter group of people.

One of the HSI items, per capita gross national product, is an important indicator of economic development. The debate about the relationship between population growth and economic development has raged "loud and long" (P. Harrison, 1992). One group argues that population growth stimulates the demand for products and services, which in turn creates both jobs and capital. From this perspective, population growth fuels the motor of economic advancement. Critics contend that if this argument is valid, countries like India and Bangladesh, as well as the entire sub–Saharan Africa region, should have some of the fastest-growing and healthiest economies in the world. Instead, these nations are struggling to survive and, in many instances, do so only with massive amounts of aid from wealthier nations. Critics argue further that an annual increase in a country's gross national product of 3.5 percent (a healthy rate of growth) is negated by a yearly population increase of 3.5 percent. And if the rate of economic growth should falter while yearly increases in population remain the same, the nation will lose ground. A country that is continually putting its capital into schools and hospitals to care for society's newest members will have less to invest in economic development.

Prior to the mid-1970s, it did not appear that population growth adversely affected economic development. However, a 1992 United Nations Population Fund (UNFPA) (P. Harrison, 1992) report indicates that since the 1980s, the situation has changed dramatically. A slowdown in the world economy during that period, coupled with the massive debt incurred by developing nations, effectively halted growth in these countries. Of the 82 developing countries examined by the UNFPA, the 41 nations with slower rates of population growth saw incomes increase an average of 1.25 percent per year, while the 41 countries with faster rates of population growth saw incomes decrease by 1.25 percent per year.

Even though the health of the world economy is certainly a key factor in the population growth/economic development relationship, it does not appear that the global economic situation is going to improve significantly in the near future. That being the case, the developing nations, and especially those where the poorest billion people reside, may have to find a way to reduce population growth or face the consequences of a continued erosion of their quality of life.

WORLD HUNGER

Today, there are more people in the world without enough to eat than ever before. As of 1991, more than one-half billion people (approximately twice the population of the United States) experienced continuous hunger, and even more people are vulnerable to hunger. Over 20 percent of the world's population live in households that are too poor to provide the foodstuffs their bodies need for an active work life. One-third of the children under age 5 in Third World nations (177 million) have so little to eat that their physical and mental development is permanently impaired (Reeves & Cohen, 1991a). An estimated 40 to 60 million people (mostly children) die annually from hunger and hunger-related diseases.

By the end of the 1980s, 40 low-income countries with approximately 40 percent of the world's population failed to produce enough food to feed their inhabitants. Five of these countries were in Latin America and the Caribbean, seven were in Asia, and 29 were in sub–Saharan Africa. By far the fastest-growing region on Earth today, the 46 nations that comprise sub–Saharan Africa have a population doubling time of 23 years as well as the world's least productive output of food (Power, 1991). As of 1991, half of Africa's population had less food to eat than they did in 1970 (see Figure 3.4).

The consequences of these observations are both staggering and frightening. With a population doubling time of 24 years (that is, for the entire continent), Africa's food pro-

FIGURE 3.4 Food Deficit in Africa

The food deficit is measured technically in terms of million tonnes of food grain equivalent (FGE): the deficit being the difference between the estimated FGE produced and the quantity of FGE needed to support a given population. The World Bank's 30-year forecast for Africa proposes three scenarios:

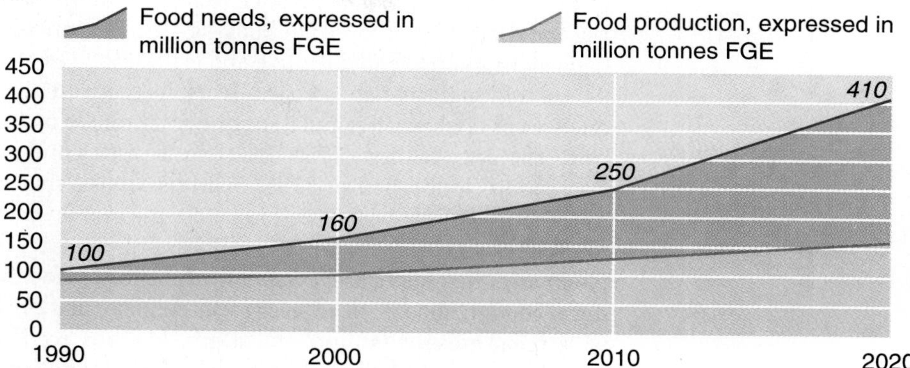

1. In this first scenario, the population continues increasing at its current rate, while the production of FGE improves by 2 percent annually. This would mean an increase in food deficit from 10 million tonnes FGE in 1990 to 245 million tonnes in 2020.

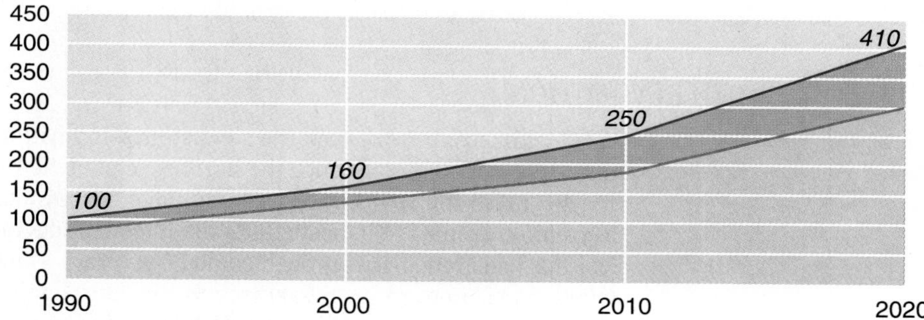

2. A second possible scenario would mean that, while there was no change in the population growth rate, the rate of food production would double to 4 percent. The 2020 deficit would drop to 110 million tonnes FGE.

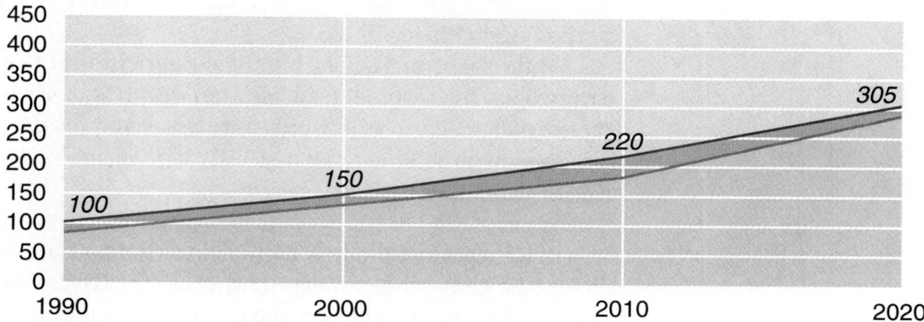

3. The third scenario presumes the same improvement in food production as the second, but postulates a drop in population rate to 3.3 percent. The 2020 deficit would then drop to 5 million tonnes FGE (i.e., half the 1990 deficit).

In the World Bank's estimation, this most optimistic scenario is also the least likely.

duction would also have to double during that same period just to keep the same levels of hunger, starvation, and starvation-related diseases and deaths that currently exist. Anything less than a 100 percent increase in agricultural production and/or the import of vast amounts of food aid from developed nations would mean that the terrible suffering and death that occurred in Somalia, Ethiopia, and the Sudan in 1992 and 1993 would happen on a continentwide scale and claim the lives of tens of millions of people.

If this nightmarish scenario were to occur, it would seem to validate the consequences of unchecked population growth outlined by the English clergyman and economist Thomas Malthus (1766–1834) in a work entitled "An Essay on the Principle of Population," published in 1798. Malthus argued that while food production increased arithmetically (one-two-three-four, etc.), the human population grew geometrically (two-four-eight-sixteen, etc.). Therefore, it was only a matter of time before the number of people in any one region, and eventually the entire planet, would outstrip the ability to produce enough food to feed ever-escalating populations. At this point, there would be widespread misery, famine, and death. Malthus realized that before people starved to death many would be killed off by disease, war, and vice. He referred to these gruesome limits of growth as "positive checks." This tragedy could be avoided if people used "preventive checks" (delayed marriage or moral restraint, i.e., celibacy). As a conservative clergyman, Malthus strongly disapproved of any form of contraception, abortion, or infanticide (the killing of infants).

THE GREEN REVOLUTION

Was Malthus right? Are even the slowest-growing nations and regions of the world destined to eventually experience the horrors he predicted?

Begun in the 1940s, with the first major success occurring in the 1960s, the **Green Revolution** seemed to indicate that even if food production did increase arithmetically as Malthus had argued, that growth could be very fast. The Green Revolution, as Critchfield (1990, p. 44) notes, is a "breakthrough in plant genetics that allows man to breed and grow artificially short, stiff-stemmed wheat, rice and other grains," often in two-thirds the time it takes to produce other species. India's wheat production jumped from 11 million metric tons in the early 1960s to 56 million tons in 1990. Using Green Revolution technology and chemical science, China was able to increase its grain harvests at a very fast pace, to a point where it now leads the world in wheat, rice, and overall grain production (Critchfield, 1992).

While these incredibly high-yield agricultural breakthroughs appeared to be the cornucopia that would feed all the world and stave off (perhaps indefinitely) the Malthusian scenario of misery, starvation, and death, there were, and continue to be, some major problems (Baron, 1992; Critchfield, 1990; Mellor, 1991; Reeves & Cohen, 1991b; Wolf, 1986):

1. If they adopt the new high-yield wheat and rice, farmers have to purchase the fertilizer, pesticides, and new equipment that the Green Revolution agriculture demands. In addition, these new hybrid plants require a steady supply of water that can only be met by irrigation. These costly requirements are beyond the range of all but the most prosperous farmers who own the largest tracts of land. As a consequence of this rather capital-intensive method of farming, the already tremendous inequality that existed between prosperous and poor farmers has increased significantly in some parts of the world. Rather than spend their increasing earnings at home, a practice that would have helped

This African farmer is spraying his crops with pesticides in order to maximize the yield per acre of his harvest. However, due to the fast rate at which the population is growing in sub–Saharan Africa, the number of people on that continent already exceeds the ability of the people to feed themselves.

small merchants and bolstered the local economy, in some regions farmers have used most of this money to purchase foreign-produced goods.

Also, increasing agricultural output has resulted in a decline in the price of rice and wheat, which benefited poor people (and helped maintain peace and stability in overcrowded Third World cities) but has been detrimental to small farmers who cannot successfully compete with their wealthier counterparts. Poor farmers who eventually lost their land have not been able to work for wealthier neighbors because labor once done by people and animals has been turned over to machines. The mechanized Green Revolution has added to unemployment problems in poor countries that already have millions of people with little if any means of earning a living.

2. Large-scale farming operations that have adopted Green Revolution agriculture tend to raise wheat, corn, or rice year after year. Known as *monocropping,* this failure to rotate crops weakens the genetic structure of plants, making them more susceptible to disease and requiring increasing amounts of fertilizers and pesticides. The careless, indiscriminate use of fertilizer pollutes both surface and ground water, creating a health hazard for human beings and killing the fish that provide a valuable source of protein. In some regions (India, for example), this environmental degradation, as well as overworking croplands and rapidly depleting the underground watershed, have been so severe that "future food production has been jeopardized" (Baron, 1992; R. D. Kaplan, 1994). The irony is that a promising scientific breakthrough that produced so much food in the short run may contribute to the problem of hunger in the not too distant future.

3. Food production has gone up significantly in Latin America and increased to a level in Asia that few would have thought possible, but the African continent has benefited the least from these innovations. One of the major problems is Africa's soil, leached of valuable nutrients by thousands of years of heavy rains and high temperatures. Plant biologist Norman Borlaug (in Critchfield, 1990, p. 45), who helped launch the Green Revolution,

states that much of the soil on the world's fastest-growing continent is infertile and "incapable of sustaining a very dense population." Africa's poor soil can be replenished by applying the necessary nutrients (as South Africa and Zimbabwe have done), but this procedure takes skill and requires a great deal of money. In addition, soil erosion, which is of serious concern worldwide, is especially problematic in Africa. A study by the United Nations Environmental Program estimated that because of this erosion, Africa's agricultural output could be reduced by 25 percent between 1975 and the end of the century.

4. Finally, because few of Africa's 50 million farm families grow wheat or rice (the principal crops of the Green Revolution), they have gained little from Green Revolution technologies. Only in the past 15 years have researchers turned their attention to millet, sorghum, yams, and a number of other traditional foodstuffs of Africa.

Many of the examples noted indicate the latent (unintended or unanticipated) consequences of the Green Revolution. Like any other piece of scientific knowledge or technology, it is neither inherently good nor inherently bad. Rather, the Green Revolution can have a varying impact on poverty and hunger, depending on governmental policies, the existing structure of income and power in a region or country, and how farmers spend their added income (Mellor, 1991). While the Green Revolution has not solved the problem of world hunger, it was never meant to be the ultimate solution. Norman Borlaug and others who pioneered these techniques wanted this revolution to buy time and stave off Malthusian consequences until fertility could be lowered and population growth halted.

THE BIOTECHNOLOGY REVOLUTION

Global food production that rose significantly between 1950 and 1984—partially as a result of the Green Revolution—slowed considerably in the mid-1980s because of drought, the overuse of fertilizer, new plant-attacking diseases, and soil deterioration. However, some individuals believe that a new *Biotechnology Revolution* will help alleviate the gap between worldwide food production and rapid population growth in the twenty-first century. Whereas the Green Revolution focused on developing stronger and more nutritious strains of wheat and rice, biotechnology encompasses more and refers to any technique that uses living organisms to modify or improve plants *and* animals or develops microorganisms for specific uses (Kennedy, 1993). Through oftentimes extensive genetic manipulation, biologists hope to accomplish in a matter of months or years what would normally take decades using conventional methods of breeding plants and animals.

Researchers have already produced genetically engineered growth hormones that increase the milk output of cattle (currently used in the United States by some dairy farmers) and are developing plants that will be insect and disease resistent. Unfortunately, a number of physiological and socioeconomic obstacles will have to be overcome before the biotech revolution can deliver the desired results. For example, hogs injected with growth hormones are subject to ulcers, arthritis, and other diseases that can render them unfit for human consumption.

Whereas previous agricultural breakthroughs that resulted in record harvests (the Green Revolution) were made in the government-subsidized public sector, most of the current biotech experimentation is being conducted in the profit-oriented private sector by corporations that have little concern about the economic and social consequences of their products (Kennedy, 1993). Poor developing nations may find that high-priced agricultural innovations are well beyond their meager budgets, making them increasingly food dependent on more prosperous biotech-oriented countries. In addition, because things like cattle growth hormones are relatively expensive and require monitoring by skilled technicians, the biotech revolution could increase the income gap between prosperous farmers (who can afford this technology) and poorer agriculturalists in some regions of the developing world in much the same manner as did the Green Revolution.

IMPACT OF BEEF CONSUMPTION

At least one more perspective is worth mentioning in any discussion of world hunger: the tremendous consumption of beef in the industrialized world, the United States in particular. Jeremy Rifkin (1992) argues that the 1.28 billion cattle on Earth, which have a combined weight greater than that of all humanity, are a major cause of pollution, deforestation, desertification, and world hunger. Cattle and other livestock consume one-third of the grain produced on this planet and more than 70 percent of the grain grown in the United States. If this land were used to grow food rather than feed, we could provide nourishment to an additional 1 billion people.

People in the industrialized countries are not only devoting a significant portion of their farmland to the growing of cattle feed; they are also using the land of poor countries to feed the livestock that they (the developed nations) will consume. Rifkin estimates that since 1960, more than 25 percent of Central America's forests have been cleared to create pasture for cattle grazing. If these oxygen-producing forests and wetlands were used to produce food for local people, it would be one thing. However, two-thirds of all agricultural land in Central America is used by livestock destined for the United States. Each hamburger derived from imported beef requires the clearing of six square yards of forest for pasture and saves the American consumer approximately five cents. This land could have been used to grow traditional crops for the local populace instead of subsidizing the meat-eating habit of the world's richest nation.

CONTROLLING FERTILITY

Approximately 3 billion young people are entering their reproductive years this generation—a figure equal to the total world population in 1960. The decisions these individuals make regarding how many children they will bring into the world will go a long way in determining if the current world population of 5.6 billion people will double and then stabilize sometime during the next 100 years or will increase some fivefold to 27 billion by the end of the twenty-first century (see Figure 3.5) (Fornos, 1991a; *Report on Progress Towards Population Stabilization,* 1990).

Even with rapid growth rates in most of the developing world, people continue to have large families for a number of social, political, and religious reasons. Relatively early marriage and the almost immediate pregnancies that follow are intertwined with the roles of women. A World Fertility Survey found that approximately 30 percent of women in Latin America, 40 percent of women in Asia, and 50 percent of women in Africa are married by age 18. In some cultures, a woman's value is directly related to how many children she produces. For example, women are likely to be physically abused and/or abandoned if they do not deliver the expected number of offspring, especially sons (Stutsman, 1992). Important rituals in some religions can only be performed by sons, which means that a woman with two or more daughters will be under pressure to become pregnant as many times as necessary to produce a male child. For young and old women, having many children within a short time period is unhealthy and greatly increases their likelihood of

FIGURE 3.5 Alternative Futures: Population Projections to 2150

Ahead lie four decades of the fastest growth in human numbers in all history. The three outlooks shown here only diverge significantly after 2050, when the world's population will be about double today's.

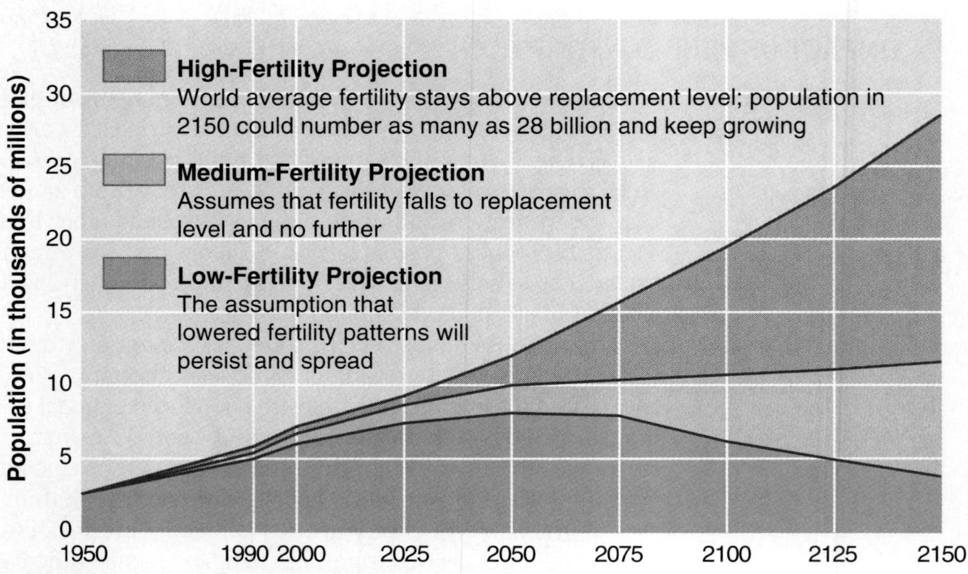
Population (in thousands of millions)
35
30
25
20
15
10
5
0
High-Fertility Projection
World average fertility stays above replacement level; population in 2150 could number as many as 28 billion and keep growing
Medium-Fertility Projection
Assumes that fertility falls to replacement level and no further
Low-Fertility Projection
The assumption that lowered fertility patterns will persist and spread
1950
1990 2000
2025
2050
2075
2100
2125
2150

Source: VanPelt in *The Christian Science Monitor* © 1992 TCSPS.

Note: Data from United Nations Population Fund.

untimely death (Stutsman, 1992). With little if any political power in most poor countries, women do not have much of an opportunity to change a centuries-old way of existence that keeps them pregnant and bound to child care for most of their lives.

Echoing the frightening demographic conclusions of Malthus, population biologist Paul Erlich argues that high rates of fertility and the growth of human societies cannot continue indefinitely. "We should not delude ourselves: The population explosion will come to an end before very long. The only question remaining is whether it will be halted through the humane method of birth control, or by the wiping out of the surplus population" (in Nixon, 1992, p. 44).

CHANGING ATTITUDES AND BEHAVIOR

If fertility in the developing world is to be reduced, governments of developing nations must vigorously support and become heavily involved in the drive to reduce family size. Only national governments have the funds, organization, and in some cases the necessary legitimacy to get the message out and continue to keep it a high-profile item: Family size must be reduced.

This includes attacking (both socially and legally) *machismo* (a component of which is that manliness is measured by how many children an individual has fathered) or its cultural equivalent that exists to one extent or another in virtually every society. In

Nigeria as well as other developing nations, fathers are now required by law (previously it had just been mothers) to support their children financially. A member of the Population Council notes that "until men bear parallel costs, what incentive do they have to cut fertility?" (in D. C. Scott, 1992b, p. 11).

In Mexico, radio and television commercials as well as subplots in soap operas promote the advantages of small families. The Mexican government's top priority in the area of family planning is to reach the rural population (where fertility is highest), adolescents, and men (D. C. Scott, 1992b). In Nigeria (see "Focus" box in this chapter), the government has enlisted the support of some of the nation's top entertainers to get the family-planning message out. Hairdressers in Haiti have been recruited to distribute contraceptives and family-planning information, and the Philippine government has even been successful in getting the local Catholic hierarchy to support its reduced fertility campaign.

With approximately 37 percent of the world's population between them, India and China hold the key to lower global fertility. India's population of more than 900 million has a doubling time of 34 years, whereas China's population of almost 1.2 billion will double in 60 years. Although the controversial one-child policy has been successfully implemented in urban areas for the most part, the norm in much of rural China is still two children per family, with authorities trying to prevent the birth of a third child.

The poster in the background proclaims the Chinese government's policy of one child per family. As a nation of almost 1.2 billion people and with a population doubling time of 60 years, China will face massive food shortages in the next century if population growth is not controlled.

People must be convinced that having smaller families is not only good for the larger society but is in their best interest, as well. This can be very difficult to accomplish in countries—almost all of the developing world—where programs like Social Security and other forms of old-age and retirement benefits do not exist. People's children are their old-age insurance in these nations, and it makes perfect sense from a young couple's point of view that the more children they have, the more secure and comfortable they will be in their declining years. Expanding economies can begin to provide some of these old-age benefits. However, as previously mentioned, economic growth may be slowed considerably (if not halted) by rapid population growth.

Concerned over the continuing growth of the world's most populous nation, the Chinese government in 1979 instituted a system of formal and informal mechanisms of social control as well as a comprehensive propaganda campaign aimed toward the goal of limiting families to only one child. This policy was intended to last for 100 years and cap the population at 1.5 billion. As of 1993, China had 1.178 billion people and an annual growth rate of 1.2 percent per year, one of the lowest in the developing world. However, China is paying a high price for controlling population growth. One of the latent (unintended) consequences of the one-child program has been a sharp increase in female infanticide. Wanting a son to carry on the family name, among other reasons, some people, especially in the rural areas, kill a firstborn baby girl in the hope that the next pregnancy will result in a male child.

INCREASING CONTRACEPTIVE USE

Population control is not only a matter of changing people's attitudes regarding the number of children they should have: The means of controlling fertility must be readily available and affordable. The birth control devices on the market today are useless if poor people cannot afford to purchase them. Governments (including those of industrial nations) can make contraceptives available either at no charge or at a price even the most destitute family can afford. Two of the world's most widely used methods of reducing fertility—intrauterine devices and female sterilization—are currently too costly for millions of women. Also, family planning is available only in the urban areas of many African countries. This is one reason why only 2 percent of these women are using contraceptives, as opposed to 75 percent of females in the industrialized world (Moffett, 1992b). The Secretary General of the International Planned Parenthood Federation stated that "at least 500 million women around the world are left at the mercy of repeated pregnancies because they are out of reach of any services, or because the services are simply not good enough" (Mahler in "IPPF," 1992).

Contraceptives are not likely to be used (even if available) if health care workers and women are not properly educated about the implementation and effects of these devices. For example, studies of Indian villages revealed that 92 percent of the women had gynecological diseases. Because they were not examined by health care workers prior to the distribution and use of contraceptives, the women's gynecological problems were often aggravated by the devices. Thus, women come to believe that "contraception leads to suffering," and they often discontinue their use (Stutsman, 1992). Two-thirds of Mexican women surveyed in one study believed that oral contraceptives caused birth defects. One-third of women polled in Chile thought the pill accumulated in the stomach and eventually caused stomach cancer. Almost half of the women surveyed in the Philippines were convinced that the use of oral contraceptives resulted in sterility.

OCUS ON NIGERIA

POPULATION GROWTH IN NIGERIA

Politics, Pop Music, and the Changing Role of Women

The phrase *population explosion* is commonly used to describe the incredible rate of growth in the world's developing nations. While this expression may be overused (and is inaccurate in some cases), it is appropriate when speaking of Nigeria.

The population of this former British colony (independence came in 1960) increased from 19 million in 1931 to approximately 52 million in 1952. By 1990, Nigeria's population was estimated at between 100 and 130 million; projections of 301 million have been made for the year 2025. The 301 million figure would represent an almost sixteenfold increase in less than 100 years. Werner Fornos (1987) of the Population Institute notes that, at current rates of growth, Nigeria would have 1 billion inhabitants in the year 2065. However, Nigeria cannot continue growing at the same rate due to ecological, economic, and social factors.

That Nigeria is the most populous nation in Africa and one of the world's fastest-growing countries is an incontrovertible demographic fact, although there is considerable uncertainty and debate regarding this West African nation's actual size and rate of growth. The first complete census, in 1952–1953, was undercounted by more than 10 percent (Nelson, 1982) because many individuals believed the government's nationwide enumeration was a trick to increase their taxes or spy on people and their property (Diamond, 1988). Every census since the initial British head count has been surrounded by controversy, with regional population figures either grossly exaggerated or undercounted by millions. The appearance of phantom people occurs because an enumeration of the populace is a highly political act. The final count of the country's 21 states and 4 major regions determines who gets how much money from the federal government. In a poor, rapidly growing, heterogeneous nation like Nigeria, the larger the population of a given region and/or ethnic group, the more seats it has in Parliament, which translates into increased state contracts, jobs, loans, and other resources (Diamond, 1988).

Viewed against a backdrop of cultural values, rapid social change, and the economic realities of a developing country, the relationship between mothers and their children provides an insight into Nigeria's population growth and may shed light on the prospects for slowing this rate of increase. To begin, most Nigerians believe a female's primary responsibilities in life are to bear and raise children. For females, status is attained through marriage and a growing family. Toward this end, girls often marry as young as 11 or 12 years of age and spend up to 60 percent of their adult lives either pregnant or breast-feeding children (Entwisle & Coles, 1990). Although years of pregnancy, nursing, and looking after children can be a drain on a mother's health and productivity, children contribute to a woman's psychological and economic well-being. Older children help with the housework and look after younger siblings; as adults, they support their mother in her old age, especially if she has been widowed (Entwisle & Coles, 1990).

Introduced in 1976, universal primary education has resulted in more girls and young women attending school. This may be a factor in the increase of age at first marriage and could also contribute to reduced childhood mortality (Entwisle & Coles, 1990). More women are gaining the knowledge to better care for their children, as well as the skills needed to find a job. Employed women are more likely to improve their socioeconomic status, which often translates into a higher standard of living for the entire family. As infant mortality declines, women may be under less pressure to have more babies. The education of women, therefore, could be a crucial component in slowing Nigeria's rate of population growth, as it has in other countries.

However, women's education and exposure to nontraditional values and patterns of conduct can also bring about changes in behavior that may also *increase* fertility rates. Educated women tend to reduce the period of postpartum sexual abstinence as well as the time spent breastfeeding. This means that if the woman is not practicing birth control, she can become pregnant sooner than she could if she followed traditional practices.

In 1989, King Sunny Ade, one of Nigeria's most popular entertainers, released an album (*Wait for Me*) with song lyrics that urged people to have fewer children (Sobo, 1990). Two things were particularly interesting about this recording. First of all, Ade, the father of 12 children, had previously cut records supporting high fertility and large families. (Presumably, listeners would take this latest message to heart while ignoring the behavior of the messenger.) Second, the cost of producing and distributing the recording ($350,000) was financed by the U.S. Agency for International Development (AID). The Nigerian recording was but one part of a five-year anti–large family campaign sponsored by AID in cooperation with the Population Communication Services Center at Johns Hopkins University. The university was to develop "culturally appropriate communications" to influence family-planning acceptance and use (in Sobo, 1990). Records with similar messages were released in Mexico and the Philippines.

Nigeria is Africa's most populous nation. In order to reduce the rate of population growth, the Nigerian government enlisted the help of a popular entertainer to sing the praises of having smaller families. It remains to be seen how much influence King Sunny Ade will have on young adults in his country.

AID involvement in Nigeria was to remain a secret for fear that revealing the source of the record would have been "counterproductive" (Sobo, 1990).

News of the U.S. government's attempt to influence fertility in Africa reached the United States in February 1990. While it was unnoticed by most Americans, there was some predictable outrage in the Black community. One commentator on an African American radio station in Washington, D.C., stated, "African countries have seen their economic resources depleted first by colonialism and now by huge debts to international lending institutions and enormous interest payments. The human resources of Africa are the latest thing they want to take away from us" (in Sobo, 1990).

Nigeria's high rate of population growth has put that country on a collision course with the most serious population-related problems discussed in this chapter. (Only China, India, Indonesia, and Brazil in the developing world have to cope with more people.) The demands of this growing population can only exacerbate ethnic and tribal tensions that could erupt in wide-scale violence (and possibly civil war) with a staggering number of casualties. Unpredictable oil prices in the international marketplace will make the Nigerian government's job that much more difficult as it attempts to reduce foreign debts and generate funds needed to produce jobs and upgrade the country's infrastructure. Even the most optimistic scenarios for economic development will be negated by rapid population growth if fertility is not controlled.

Although family-planning recordings may be construed as pressure in the right area, it will take much more than songs by pop stars to convince Nigerians that having significantly smaller families is in their interest as well as that of the entire nation. The changing role of women and the extent to which these changes are accepted by men will go a long way in determining if Nigeria's future will be something other than a demographic catastrophe.

INCREASING FEMALE LITERACY

Research indicates that educating women leads to lower rates of fertility (see Figure 3.6). The key component in this process, as numerous studies have documented, is education. For example, the World Health Organization reported that in the African country of Sudan, women with seven or more years of education averaged 2.7 children, while females without any formal schooling averaged 6.5 children ("Fertility Choices Vital in Raising Status of Women," 1992). Female literacy is also closely related to rates of infant mortality (the number of infants per 1,000 live births who die before their first birthday); that is, as female literacy increases, infant mortality decreases (Kane, 1992b). Literate mothers tend to have higher status and better health and are more likely to be earning some money than women without any education.

FIGURE 3.6 Women's Literacy and Population Growth

There is a close connection between education and fertility: the more education women have, the more likely they are to have small families.

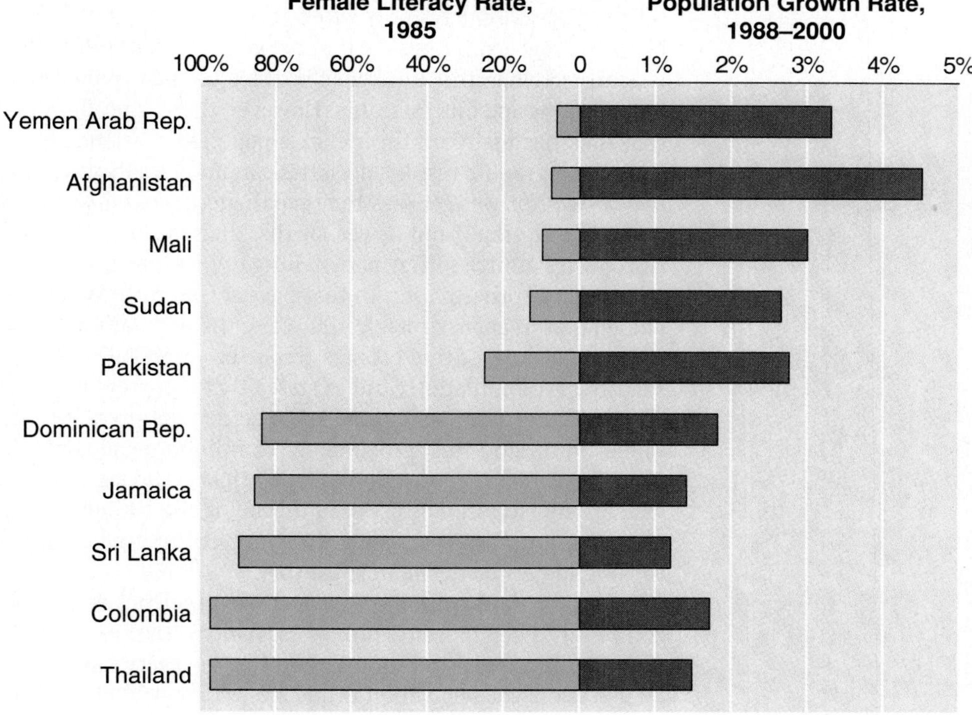

SOURCE: VanPelt in *The Christian Science Monitor* © 1992 TCSPS.

NOTE: Data from United Nations Population Fund.

These factors contribute to a woman's ability to provide food, fuel, and water for her children as well as to cook nutritious meals for the entire family. Healthy children translate into lower rates of infant mortality. This is vitally important for reducing fertility rates because women who have some assurance that their children will survive beyond infancy are more likely to find family planning and the use of contraceptives acceptable.

The efforts of governments and family-planning agencies have paid off in dramatic results over the past 30 years: The number of couples using contraceptives increased from 8 percent to 50 percent from 1960 to 1990 (Moffett, 1992). However, if world population is to stabilize at less than 11 billion people in the next century, the proportion of people using modern birth control methods will have to reach 75 percent (the percentage of people in developed nations using contraceptives) by the year 2000 ("World Access to Birth Control," 1992). Although population experts note that in a short period of time, we have come more than halfway toward reaching this goal, the latter part of the journey will be more difficult than the initial stage.

UNDERPOPULATION AND SOCIETAL AGING

SLOW GROWTH AND NEGATIVE GROWTH

By the time a society moves into the fourth stage of the demographic transition (low birth and low death rates), it is at or near *zero population growth* (ZPG), a condition that is achieved when the number of births plus the number of in-migrants equals the number of deaths and out-migrants. However, there is no "homeostatic mechanism" to insure that societies maintain this delicate population balance (McFalls, 1991). At this point in their demographic history, societies can quite easily pass through ZPG into NPG—*negative population growth*—as they experience a *population implosion:* that is, a population decline resulting from fewer births than deaths. This has already occurred in six European countries (Germany, Hungary, Bulgaria, Latvia, Estonia, and Ukraine), and almost every other nation in that part of the world is approaching ZPG. One study concluded that in approximately 100 years, the population of Europe could be reduced by 50 percent because of this process (reported in McFalls, 1991). The director of the Italian Institute for Population Studies stated that if current birth and death rates continue into the next century, by the year 2100, the population of his country will decline from just under 58 million to approximately 15 million people, and half those individuals will be over 60 years of age (in Montalbano, 1994). The significantly higher number of people who are moving into as opposed to leaving the United States (to be discussed in the section on migration) is the only thing preventing this country from passing through ZPG to NPG sometime in the next century.

The age composition of industrialized societies at or near ZPG or those with NPG is completely different from Third World nations that are presently in the second or third stage of the demographic transition and growing at a very rapid pace. On the European continent, 20 percent of the population is under age 15 and 14 percent is 65 years of age or older. The corresponding numbers for Africa are 45 percent under age 14 and only 3 percent in the older age bracket. Both slow and negative population growth resulting from low fertility *and* low mortality inevitably produce an older and continually aging population.

Over the next 40 years, the aging of populations that is well underway in the industrial world will also occur in developing nations (Grigsby, 1991), as fertility rates in these latter countries fall and reduced mortality rates lead to increased life expectancy. Whereas developing countries are much more concerned with lowering their fertility rates today than with worrying about tomorrow's old-age associated problems, many European nations are currently dealing with the consequences of an increasingly elderly society.

FRANCE: STIMULATING POPULATION GROWTH

Over 20 percent of France's 58 million people are 60 years of age or older (the age used by the United Nations to determine the percentage of people who are elderly). As a result of younger people moving to cities in search of work, 23 percent of people in the countryside are in that age bracket. These numbers will increase as fertility remains low and mortality continues to decline (Hershey, 1993). This aging of the population, coupled with a move toward ZPG (and quite possibly NPG) and an influx of immigrants from other nations, has some people worried that the nation is losing its "Frenchness" (Root, 1988). In an effort to increase the birth rate, stimulate population growth, and slow down the societal aging process, the government started a pronatalist incentive policy that pays couples approximately $125 a month for two years in addition to other monetary incentives upon the birth of a third child. Billboards with a smiling infant that state *"La France a besoin des'enfants"* ("France needs children") can be seen across the country. To date, these efforts have been only minimally successful.

JAPAN: MOVING TOWARD NPG

With a growth rate of less than one-third of 1 percent in 1993, Japan's population of 125 million people will reach NPG by the year 2011. The Japanese government released a long-range report to the year 2090, projecting the country's population based on the average number of births a woman has during her lifetime. The high, middle, and low series call for a population of 131 million, 96 million, and 62 million, respectively (Yanagashita, 1993). The last figure represents less than half of Japan's current population. The 1990 census revealed that Japan's **total fertility rate (TFR)**—the average number of births per woman—was 1.57.

A smaller population makes sense from a land-use point of view. Japan is approximately the same size as California, with four times as many people. Garbage processing plants in large cities are fast approaching their limits. Electricity and water supply systems are also producing near capacity, and sewage treatment plants are "over utilized and under maintained" (do Rosario, 1992).

From an economic standpoint, the problem of NPG is clear: How can a nation that already imports guest workers to rectify a labor shortage (especially in low-paying jobs) maintain its position as one of the world's leading economies if its workforce continues to shrink? To cope with the problems of an older and smaller population, the Japanese government is considering a program that would keep people working additional years before retirement. This would also provide needed funds to care for the aged through increased social security taxes (Yanagashita, 1993). The proposed plan, which would also encourage females to participate in the marketplace to a much greater extent than they do now, could have the unanticipated consequence of strengthening the financial position of women in Japan. This would probably translate into more political power and social equality for females in the future.

To capitalize on the increasing geriatric population at home as well as in other nations, the Japanese government and manufacturers have already begun working to produce high-tech electronic medical devices. Whereas companies in the United States have an edge in the production of therapeutic instruments, the Japanese are concentrating on biomedical engineering (Crawford, 1991). In addition to producing artificial hearts and pancreases and synthetic bones, companies are attempting to develop tunneling microrobots that, after being installed in arteries, will eat away at cholesterol deposits. There can be little doubt that the consumer health care market in aging societies all over the world will change dramatically, and the Japanese are poised to take advantage of this market.

THE GRAYING OF THE UNITED STATES

The aging of U.S. society has been rightfully described as "the most important demographic event occurring in the United States today" (Ahmed & Smith, 1992). In 1950, some 12 million people were 65 years or older, a number that increased to 33 million by 1993 (see Figure 3.7). Demographers estimate that by the year 2030, almost 65 million people in the United States (approximately 20 percent of the population) will be 65 or older. Within this group, the fastest-growing segment of the population is the more than 8.6 million persons age 85 and above (Ahmed & Smith, 1992; *America in the 21st Century,* 1989).

FIGURE 3.7 Americans Age 65 or Older for Selected Years (number and percentage)

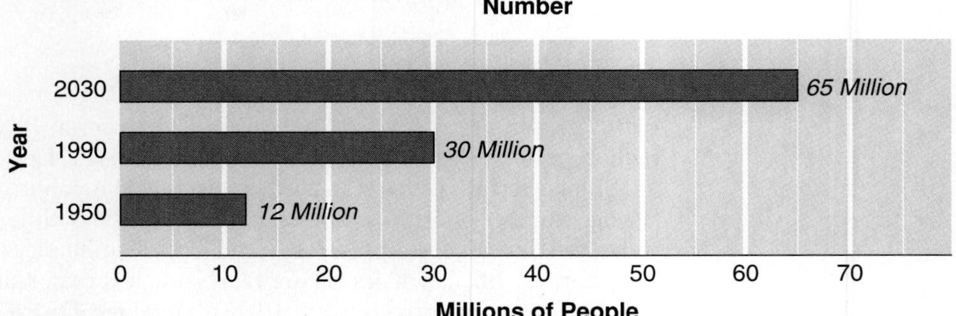

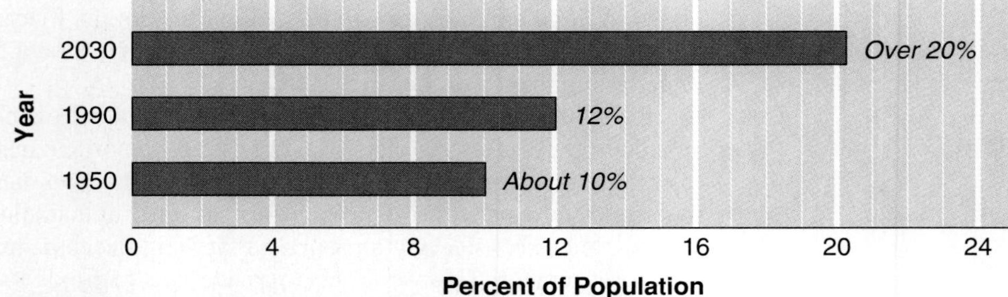

SOURCE: Reprinted by permission of the Population Reference Bureau.

The large number of people born between 1895 and 1925 are responsible for the rapid growth in the elderly population between 1960 and 1990. Even though growth in this segment of society will slow for the next 20 years because of the relatively low birth rates during the Great Depression and World War II era (1929 to 1945), it will escalate rapidly in the year 2010, when the baby boomers—those millions of people born between 1946 and 1964—begin reaching retirement age (Frey, 1993). Senior boomers will have a profound effect on this country, just as this generation always has.

IMPACT ON THE ECONOMY AND THE WORKFORCE

Due to the "birth dearth" that followed the baby boom, there may be a shortage of workers to take the place of retiring boomers starting in the second decade of the twenty-first century. This would result in a less productive, smaller, older, and increasingly illness-prone workforce. This labor scarcity may call for a relaxation of immigration laws, with people migrating to the United States in significant numbers to fill tens of thousands of vacant positions. Even if the nation's gross national product were to go down as a result of fewer workers, real incomes could rise because of a smaller population (Kaye, 1988).

Productivity will also be affected by shortened work weeks as people in their middle years spend increasing amounts of time and energy looking after aging mothers and fathers. Already, an estimated 25 percent of all employees take some time off from work each year to care for their parents. Some companies provide flexible working hours and arrangements for their employees who chauffeur parents to medical appointments, hospitals, and rehabilitation programs (Crowell, 1991). This work-related flexibility will have to be greatly enhanced in the future if elderly Americans are to be adequately cared for.

SUPPORTING THE COST OF AGING

While senior citizens may not be drawing salaries, they will have retirement incomes that will be funneled back into the economy, creating demands for more products oriented toward the needs, desires, and consumption patterns of aging Americans. This transition will no doubt cause problems for many industries (children's toys) and companies and create opportunities for others (pharmaceutical companies).

The elderly population consumes a disproportionate share of society's medical resources, approximately three-and-one-half times as much per capita as a working adult and seven times as much as a child (Hurd, 1992). Also, as the proportion of the population that is elderly increases, the elderly population itself ages (Grigsby, 1991). This means that the number of people in the old-old category—85 and older—will triple between now and the year 2030. The near round-the-clock care required by many of the 8.6 million people in this category at that time will cost hundreds of billions of dollars a year.

A significant amount of the money needed to pay for medical costs comes from taxes. In 1992, 3.4 workers supported each recipient of Social Security, Medicaid, and Medicare. However, by the year 2020, each recipient will be supported by only 2.4 workers (Hurd, 1992). Will the government have enough funds to support a large and growing elderly population, or must members of the birth-dearth generation pay more taxes?

Already, there is debate regarding the continued viability of Social Security. While government officials are quick to point out that the system is solvent and will meet the needs of an aging population well into the next century, other people believe that it is only a matter of time before the system runs out of money. Some individuals advocate raising the retirement age (which will go up to age 67 in the year 2027) to age 70 to help insure that Social Security funds never dry up (Ignelzi, 1992).

REGIONAL GROWTH IN AGING POPULATIONS

The geographical concentration of the elderly means that some cities and states will be more involved in dealing with an aging population than others. Many cities in the Sunbelt states of the South and Southwest have attracted a substantial number of retirees to add to their own aging populations and will no doubt continue to do so. As a result of this movement, Florida's age structure is the oldest in the nation. The 10 metropolitan areas in the country with the highest concentration of elderly people are all in Florida (Frey, 1993; Grigsby, 1991). Metropolitan areas in the Northeast and Midwest (Rustbelt) that experienced the out-migration of a substantial number of young people in search of better jobs and a different life in the Sunbelt also have a relatively high percentage of elderly residents.

Local governments in these cities (many with severe economic problems) will be hard pressed to increase their support systems to meet the needs of aging residents. In addition, the tremendous amount of money needed to rebuild heavily damaged urban infrastructures (schools and hospitals, for example) in the aftermath of natural disasters (such as the Los Angeles earthquake, hurricanes in south Florida and the Carolinas) and humanmade calamities (urban riots) can reduce funds originally earmarked for social services, including programs for the elderly.

The graying of America should also result in some positive changes. Inasmuch as older people are more likely to vote and become politically involved than younger individuals, the United States may well become a more democratic society. However, to the extent that aging is associated with political and social moderation, we will also become a more conservative nation. In addition, street crimes (burglary, robbery, rape, etc.) usually committed by younger offenders (age 15 to 29) will in all likelihood decrease, resulting in a less dangerous society and a less costly criminal justice system (police, courts, and correctional institutions).

Although not an exhaustive list, the consequences of an aging population described earlier clearly demonstrate the tremendous impact this demographic phenomenon will have on the United States. No doubt other unanticipated ramifications of this societal aging will also be felt.

MIGRATION

Since the days of our hunter-gatherer ancestors thousands of years ago, human beings have migrated, sometimes over vast distances, in search of animals, land, resources—anything that would provide them with a better life. Demographers define *migration* as the movement of people across some specified boundary for the purpose of establishing a new and permanent residence. *Internal migration* is movement within a country; *international migration* is the relocation of people between countries. The process of leaving one nation for the purpose of taking up residence in another nation is called **emigration,** while the process of entering one country from another to take up permanent residence is referred to as **immigration** (Haupt & Kane, 1991).

INTERNAL MIGRATION

Next to the population explosion, the movement of people from the countryside to cities has been the most significant global demographic trend of the twentieth century. Unfortunately, movements of this magnitude are likely to be fraught with problems.

People on the receiving end of these migrations often resent newcomers who may intensify the competition for jobs, education, housing, and recreational activities. The sudden influx of migrants may drive down wages, increase the cost of housing, and disrupt local communities that have been relatively stable for years. Resentment can turn to hostility and violence when the migrants are of a different racial, ethnic, religious, or social class than local residents. For example, some of the ugliest incidents in U.S. social history have resulted from the clash between new African American arrivals and the more established local White city residents. To the extent that in-migration to a city is often associated with increased rates of crime, drug abuse, alcoholism, pollution, and overall congestion, those people who have fueled urban growth (especially identifiable minorities) are rightly or wrongly blamed for these and other problems.

The United States has experienced three major movements of people over the past 200 years. The first was the rural-to-urban migration of millions of people that contributed to the growth of giant metropolitan areas such as New York and Chicago and helped produce a country where 75 percent of the population live in cities. The second was the movement of African Americans from the South to cities in the Northeast and Midwest in the first half of this century and to the far West in the post–World War II era. Finally, beginning in the late 1960s, there was another exodus of large numbers of people from the Frostbelt (the Northeast and the Midwest) south to the Sunbelt and west to the Pacific Coast.

A worldwide phenomenon to a greater or lesser extent, the exodus of people from the countryside to the cities has resulted in a tripling of the global urban population since 1950. In China, 60 million rural peasants (a figure slightly larger than the 1993 population of Italy) have recently made their way to that nation's cities, where they perform the difficult, dangerous, and dirty jobs shunned by local inhabitants (Tyson & Tyson, 1992). These *mangliu* ("blind drifters") represent one of the largest peacetime population relocations in human history. The people who have flooded into urban areas are motivated by a combination of **"push"** and **"pull" factors:** pulled by the hope of a more prosperous life and pushed by rural corruption, tight government control, and a low standard of living. The influx of so many individuals in a relatively short period of time has put a tremendous strain on the infrastructures of cities and has created tension between the mostly young migrants and their more conservative elders in the countryside. The latter are more likely to tolerate political abuse and a lower standard of living (Tyson & Tyson, 1992).

INTERNATIONAL MIGRATION

While an internal population shift in the form of rural-to-urban migration has transformed or is currently transforming the distribution of people and their way of life in almost every country in the world, international migration—the permanent movement of people from one nation to another—has altered the destiny of entire countries (see Figure 3.8). The push and pull factors responsible for international migration often occur in "great waves in response to world events" and fall into four categories (McFalls, 1991, p. 14):

1. Persecution on the basis of race or ethnicity and/or political and religious beliefs
2. Communal violence and war

FIGURE 3.8 World Population

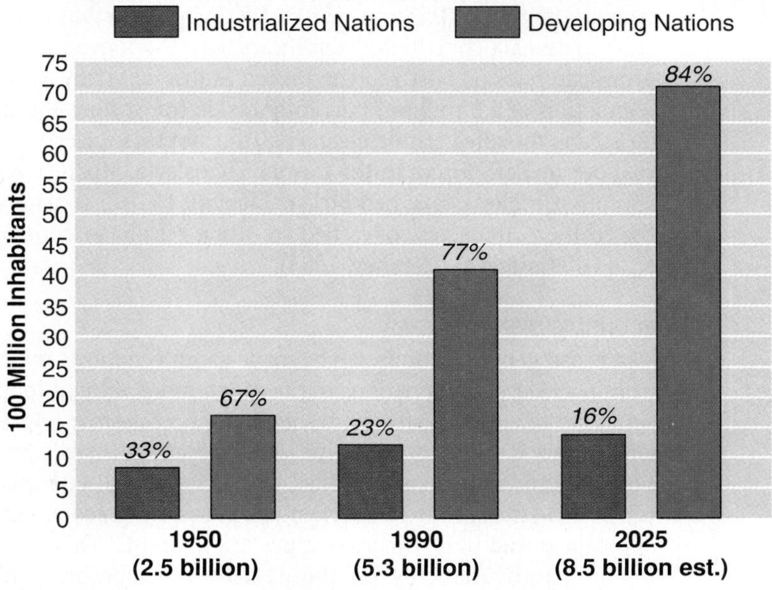

SOURCE: Copyright, 1994, U.S. News & World Report.

3. Perceived economic opportunities
4. Environmental destruction

These migration-precipitating conditions are not mutually exclusive; that is, people can move as a result of factors associated with two or more of these categories. A number of major migrations can be used to illustrate these push/pull factors.

RACIAL/ETHNIC, POLITICAL, AND RELIGIOUS PERSECUTION

As a result of the Russian Revolution of 1917, tens of thousands of people fled their native land, as did large numbers of Jews, Gypsies, and Slavic people who left Germany when the Nazis came to power in the 1930s. With the independence of India in 1947 and the partition of the subcontinent, millions of Hindus found themselves residents of the new nation of Pakistan, while an almost equal number of Muslims became citizens of the Hindu-dominated India. Fearful about their status as members of a religious minority group, streams of Hindus moving to India and Muslims heading for Pakistan often attacked each other. Thousands of people of both religions were brutally killed, often hacked to death with machetes, axes, and knives—simple but gruesomely effective weapons of the poor.

COMMUNAL VIOLENCE AND WAR

As a result of the civil war in Afghanistan during the late 1970s and early 1980s that matched Soviet troops against U.S.-sponsored Afghan troops, more than 2 million people left that country for neighboring Pakistan, a very poor nation with over 122 million people and enormous problems of its own. Many of these wartime refugees (most of whom are women and children), along with another 1 million immigrants from other countries, continue to reside in refugee camps under poor conditions with little hope of a more prosperous future (Barbour, 1991).

Approximately one-third of Liberia's 2.5 million people have fled to neighboring countries to escape the civil war in their homeland. Over 1 million people in Mozambique have left because of civil unrest and resettled in Malawi, one of the poorest countries in the world (Barbour, 1991). Civil war and revolutions in Nicaragua, El Salvador, and Guatemala contributed significantly to the movement of people from these Central American nations north to the United States. As many as 300,000 El Salvadorans (1993 population of 5.2 million) currently reside (most illegally) in Los Angeles County alone. To escape so-called ethnic cleansing (the systematic destruction of an ethnic group) carried out by Serb forces in the former Yugoslavia, Muslims from Bosnia and Herzegovina and other regions have had little choice but to flee. To date, almost 500,000 people from the former Yugoslavia have fled to other European countries, most notably Germany (220,000 refugees) (Hershey, 1993).

ECONOMIC OPPORTUNITIES

Two broad generalizations can be made about economic migrants: First, most are moving from poor developing nations to the much more affluent industrial nations. This is a continuation of a long historical trend wherein economic migrants have gravitated to more affluent areas. Second, these individuals come primarily from the extremes of the economic hierarchy—poor, unskilled workers and well-educated, highly skilled individuals. When this latter group of people move in search of economic advancement, their country of origin is said to be experiencing a "brain drain." This is especially harmful to developing nations that not only lose those relatively few people with much-needed skills in medicine and industry but that also have nothing to show for the money and time expended training these individuals. However, the brain drain is not just a problem for poor nations. Many scientists, engineers, and college professors have left Great Britain and other developed countries and migrated to the United States (McFalls, 1991).

Prior to the 1991 Gulf War, some 6 million people from poor countries such as Egypt, Jordan, and Syria were working in oil-rich nations such as Kuwait and Saudi Arabia. Japan has some 300,000 legal and illegal migrants (mostly from Bangladesh, Thailand, and the Philippines), and that number will certainly grow inasmuch as Japan may have as many as 2.7 million more jobs than workers by the end of the century. A significant number of economic migrants are also expected to search for employment in the rapidly developing Asian countries of Hong Kong, Malaysia, Taiwan, Singapore, and South Korea.

With the demise of communism in the former Soviet Union and Eastern Europe, thousands of people unwilling or unable to wait for robust capitalist economies to evolve in their homelands have migrated to Western and, to a lesser extent, Northern Europe. The departure of these people, which is already being felt, will become especially problematic when the fighting is over and the newly independent states created from this turmoil are rebuilding their devastated economies and infrastructures.

The influx of migrants may be tolerated or even encouraged during periods of economic expansion; however, immigrants in many countries have been made to feel less than welcome during the sluggish world economy of the late 1980s and 1990s. Many people would like to see the 1 million plus Turks who came to Germany as guest workers during a period of rapid postwar growth sent home as soon as possible. Resentment against the Turks turned violent in 1993. In one of a number of attacks, three Turkish girls and two women were killed after their home was firebombed. In a nation with a liberal policy toward both economic migrants and political refugees, the question of immigration has become a hotly debated and extremely divisive topic. Initially an issue confined to right-wing political parties, ridding the country of foreigners is a sentiment increasingly heard across the political spectrum. In the absence of a tremendous surge in the economies of these countries that would employ most of the legal and illegal immigrants, the so-called immigration problem will only intensify and become more violent.

Even in the absence of major international political and economic events, international migration will be stimulated for decades to come by tremendous population growth in the developing world. For example, Latin America's 1993 population of 460 million people is expected to double in 36 years. No doubt millions of these people from overcrowded cities and impoverished rural areas will gravitate to the nearest developed countries—the United States and Canada—in their search for employment.

ENVIRONMENTAL REFUGEES

Of the estimated 30 million people who have left their countries of origin to take up permanent residence in other nations, *environmental refugees* may already be the largest single category of displaced individuals (Barbour, 1991; "Environmental Refugees: A Growing Problem," 1993). By the middle of the twenty-first century, the number of people forced to leave their homelands because of toxic pollution, desertification, global warming, flooding, hurricanes, and other environmental disruptions may be several times greater than the number of people displaced by all other means combined (Fornos in "Environmental Refugees: A Growing Problem," 1993). Millions of people in overpopulated developing nations will be forced to find homes in other nations because the ecosystems they inhabit can no longer support so many individuals. In other words, the *carrying capacity* of the land has been surpassed because of deforestation, the gradual poisoning of land and water by toxic wastes, soil erosion, overgrazing, and the depletion of underground aquifers.

In some areas of Africa, desertification has become so widespread that sand dunes have covered entire villages and agricultural fields. People have no choice but to completely abandon the entire area (Jacobson, 1988). A United Nations report noted that "throughout the Third World, land degradation has been the main factor in the migration of subsistence farmers . . . producing desperate populations vulnerable to disease and natural disasters and prone to participate in crime and civil strife" (in Jacobson, 1988, p. 10).

While millions of Third World people will become refugees directly as a result of overpopulation and the accompanying environmental degradation, millions more will be forced to seek new lives in other countries because of the tremendous use of fossil fuels and global warming brought about in large measure by residents of the rich nations of the world. A one-meter (approximately 39 inches) rise in ocean levels induced by this warming could result in the creation of 50 million environmental refugees around the world. People living in the delta regions of the Nile and Ganges Rivers of Egypt and India as well as along the coast in Bangladesh will see their life-sustaining farmlands under water (Jacobson, 1988). In Bangladesh (with a population doubling time of 29 years), approximately 120 million people (four times the population of California) live in an area approximately the size of Wisconsin. The loss of farmland and living space will become a powerful push factor, forcing people to migrate to poor neighboring countries like India that have serious population-related problems of their own.

In 1986, the explosion of a nuclear reactor in Ukraine spread a cloud of radiation that stretched from Kiev to Krakow, Poland. In addition, the land around the accident site (Chernobyl) is permanently contaminated and uninhabitable. A similar disaster in a bigger nuclear facility near a large concentration of people or the detonation of one or more nuclear weapons could produce a tide of environmental refugees of historic proportions. One can only imagine the political, economic, health, and social problems such a sudden mass exodus of people would create.

THE UNITED STATES AND IMMIGRATION

Between 1820 and 1987, some 54 million people left their homes in countries around the world and emigrated to the United States. Given this historical reality, it is somewhat puzzling but nevertheless accurate to note that although we are a nation of immigrants, "Americans have never really liked immigration" (Lane in Dudley, 1990, p. 13). Since people began coming to this country en masse 175 years ago, immigration has been a highly controversial issue. In recent years, both defenders and critics of the government's immigration policy have been especially vocal.

THE ANTI-IMMIGRATION ARGUMENT

Opponents note that the 880,000 people who come to this country legally and the 400,000 or more who enter illegally every year are, for the most part, an unacceptable burden on the citizens (taxpayers) and major institutions (health, education, welfare) of the United States. There are three major components to the anti-immigration argument (Hardin, 1990).

The first and most notable objection is that immigrants take jobs from U.S. citizens or become unemployed themselves. Whereas business and agriculture employed virtually everyone who wanted to work in a rapidly expanding labor-intensive economy for much of U.S. history, the last thing we need in a modern, slow-growth, capital-intensive economy are tens of millions of unskilled and semiskilled workers. With between 4 and 10 million workers (from unskilled to highly trained professionals) out of a job at any one time, today's immigrants only swell the list of the unemployed or take jobs from people born in this country.

The second argument against immigration holds that employers take advantage of the newcomers' willingness to work, paying them lower wages and offering few if any benefits. This drives down the wage scale in low-skill, low-paying occupations and undermines the hard-won benefits earned over many years by established workers.

Finally, legal and illegal immigrants who are unemployed or working for low wages overuse the welfare system as well as public health and education services and cost taxpayers billions of dollars annually. A significant number of these individuals represent a double loss to the United States; that is, they contribute little if anything in the way of taxes while they consume much more than their share in benefits.

THE PRO-IMMIGRATION ARGUMENT

A staunch defender of the current immigration policy, economist John Simon (1990, 1991) argues that newcomers contribute so much to the betterment of this nation that, if anything, we should admit even greater numbers of people. First, Simon points out that the United States has benefited enormously from the addition of top scientific talent trained in some of the world's leading universities. We need the intellectual resources of these talented people to help us successfully compete with Japan, Europe, and the rapidly industrializing countries of the world. Even those opposed to immigration would probably agree that the nation has benefited from the influx of highly educated immigrants. Simon also claims that relatively unskilled newcomers should be welcomed.

Numerous studies indicate that immigrants do not take jobs from U.S. citizens and are not especially dependent on government services and money. In fact, after they begin earning money, immigrants also create jobs with their purchasing power and the new businesses they open. Simon concludes that immigrants create at least as many jobs as they fill.

Also, because immigrants are typically young and healthy when they arrive in this country, they are less likely to use welfare services than the average native family. Nor do these individuals receive expensive Social Security benefits and other aid to the elderly. Immigration is really the best way to lighten the Social Security burden of an aging population. The taxes paid by young immigrants will help finance the hundreds of billions of dollars it will cost to care for baby boomers when they begin retiring early in the next century. In addition, because schools and hospitals are financed by bond issues on a pay-as-you-go basis, immigrants pay much of their share in taxes for the use of these facilities. Compared to people born and raised in the United States, immigrants save a greater proportion of their earnings, typically apply more effort during working hours, are twice as likely to be self-employed, and are unusually self-reliant and creative. These are all highly desirable traits that contribute to the nation's economic growth and industrial expansion.

Like the very controversial issues of abortion, gun control, and capital punishment, the subject of immigration is likely to trigger intense feelings and lead to passionate debate. This topic often goes to the core of people's beliefs regarding the direction in which this country should be moving. While the nation's immigration policy may become more stringent and drastically reduce the number of people who legally enter this country at some future date, push factors associated with ever-increasing Third World populations virtually guarantee that millions of individuals will illegally cross over into the United States for many years to come. The full impact of the benefits or problems (or some combination of the two) of continued immigration on the country are yet to come.

CONNECTIONS

As we have seen in this chapter, the pressures of overpopulation are responsible for a wide range of problems. In addition to the tremendous strain placed on a rapidly deteriorating ecosystem and the economic difficulties already discussed, consider these additional problems associated with rapid population growth in developing nations:

- The labor force in the developing world will increase from 1.7 billion in 1992 to 3.1 billion people by the year 2025. Some 38 million jobs will have to be created every year if unemployment is not to exceed the already high rate of 40 percent that exists in many developing countries ("Population and the Environment: The Challenges Ahead," 1991). Millions of mostly young, unemployed individuals residing in urban areas may prove to be a very receptive audience for radical political parties that will not hesitate to engage in violence to overthrow a government and economic system they consider to be hopelessly ineffective. While in some, perhaps even most, of these situations this behavior is justified, there is always the danger that the revolutionary fervor in one nation may spill over into neighboring countries and result in regional instability that could eventually involve major military powers.
- Economist Robert Heilbroner (1980) speculates that increasingly poor and overpopulated countries that have ravaged their environments and have few resources left to trade or sell could engage in "wars of distribution" against the developing world. This would involve international blackmail as a group of terrorists from these nations, armed with small, yet incredibly powerful nuclear weapons, present an ultimatum to leaders of the world's richest countries: "Give us the food and resources we need to survive, or we will start destroying your cities." The partial destruction in 1993 of the World Trade Center in New York City by what appears to be polit-

SUMMARY

1. The doubling time of the world's population is 42 years; approximately 85 percent of this growth occurs in the developing nations. World population increases by 91 million people (about the size of Mexico) every year.
2. According to the demographic transition perspective, the birth and death rates of a society will change as it passes through four stages. Stage one is characterized by both high birth and death rates and very slow population growth. Stages two and three have high birth rates and low death rates and rapid population growth. With low birth rates and low death rates, modern industrial states are in the slow-growth, final stage of this transition.
3. The world's richest 1 billion individuals, who reside in the developed world, and the poorest 1 billion people, who live in the developing nations, are responsible for the greatest amount of environmental destruction.
4. There are more people in the world today without enough to eat than ever before; the problems of malnutrition and starvation are most severe in sub–Saharan Africa. The Green Revolution resulted in a tremendous increase in the production of wheat and rice in some parts of the world but will not stave off a nightmarish Malthusian scenario if population growth continues at the present pace.

ical terrorists indicates that the wars-of-distribution scenario is not just the stuff of adventure movies.

- With more countries than ever (including the former Soviet Union and Eastern European nations) asking for aid from the developed world, a phenomenon called *donor fatigue* by international relief agencies has been reported over the past few years. This refers to a reduction of monetary and material aid on the part of individuals and governments that increasingly define the poverty and starvation in these countries as overwhelming and hopeless. Rather than give more as the situation in, for example, sub–Saharan Africa, deteriorates, people will give less. As a result of scaling back (or not increasing) aid, the suffering in these countries will be much worse.
- A major problem in countries like the United States is coming up with the funds to support an aging population. Does it make sense for a society to pay almost $50 billion a year (by the year 2025 this figure could be a trillion dollars or more) to keep millions of people (mostly 85 years of age and older) alive who must be fed, taken to the toilet, and put to bed by caretakers? In other words, should this staggering sum of money be spent on people who require attention 24 hours a day and who will live this way in many instances for a number of years before they die? If the answer is no, what is the alternative? Just as China has a one-child policy, will some developed nations eventually consider a policy that, in effect, functions to limit the upper boundaries of life? Louis Shattuck Baer (1978) suggests that elderly patients communicate to their doctors their choice not to be admitted to a coronary unit, to stay more than a brief time in an intensive care unit, or to receive intravenous feeding or antibiotics for pneumonia or urinary tract infections. People would be given medication to reduce pain but not to extend their lives beyond their seventy-fifth birthday. Could this suggestion someday be mandated by law? Although this notion of withholding treatment and medicine to the aged seems draconian today, it may be discussed as a viable alternative sometime in the next 30 years.

5 A growing body of research indicates that educating women leads to lower rates of fertility as well as a reduced rate of infant mortality.

6 The rich nations of the world are characterized by slow, and in some cases negative, population growth. The population of Europe could be reduced by as much as 50 percent in the next 100 years. Whereas in developing nations, half the people are under 19 years of age, in countries in the developed world, the population is increasingly elderly, causing unique social problems.

7 By the year 2030, approximately 20 percent of the U.S. population, some 65 million people, will be age 65 or older. The medical costs of caring for senior citizens who consume a disproportionate amount of the nation's health resources will be very high.

8 Next to the population explosion, the migration of people throughout the world from rural areas to the cities has been the most notable demographic trend of the twentieth century.

9 People who want to restrict immigration to the United States argue that newcomers to this country take jobs away from U.S. citizens or become unemployed. The pro-immigration position is that people moving to the United States contribute both socially and economically to this country.

CHAPTER FOUR

ENVIRONMENTAL PROBLEMS Trashing the Planet

A little over 10 years after becoming the first and only country to experience atomic bomb attacks, Japan was targeted for another round of nuclear assaults. In 1956, Godzilla, a 40-story-tall, radiation-breathing dinosaur, roared out of Japanese film studios and cut a swath of destruction across the countryside. Awakened from ages-long slumber by atomic weapons testing, the angry beast trampled Tokyo and other large cities under him until finally being subdued by a partnership of Japanese military forces and American scientific know-how. However, the humans' triumph was short lived: Down but not out, the fierce monster soon returned to take on the hapless Japanese a second time. In later cinematic encounters, Godzilla was joined by an assortment of other nuclear creatures, including a giant caterpillar (Mothra) and a giant flying turtle (Gamera), each of which took its best shot at the country in retaliation for having its rest disturbed by human meddling into the secrets of the atom.

Students of Japanese popular culture are well aware that the original Godzilla film and the raftload of imitative "creature features" that followed are symbolic of the Japanese people's very real and horrible experiences with the destructive power of nuclear energy. In these enormously popular movies, the monster (be it Godzilla himself or one of his atomic pals) is a metaphor for the terrible force that obliterated Hiroshima and Nagasaki in August of 1945, killing tens of thousands of people and dooming thousands more to lives that were both physically and emotionally scarred. Seen in this light, the Godzilla films represent the Japanese people's attempt to come to grips with what they had endured during the war as well as a warning to the rest of the world about the all-too-real potential for an atomic Armageddon unless humans changed their violent ways.

This covert symbolic theme becomes clearer if we examine the evolution of these fearsome and deadly creatures over the course of the film series. Just as Japan itself was able to overcome its fear and loathing of the atom and begin developing nuclear energy for peaceful uses, in later movies, Godzilla, Mothra, and Gamera emerged as "good guy" monsters. Having apparently worked out their differences with humankind, the three former horrors teamed up with the Japanese to take on a lineup of newer and even more dangerous creatures—including Hedorah, the 200-foot-tall, sulphuric-acid-belching Smog Monster—accidentally created by humans as a byproduct of our own ravaging of planet Earth.

Not coincidentally, this cinematic metamorphosis occurred precisely at the same time that real-world Japan was beginning to recognize the extent and depth of its own environmental pollution problems. As personified by a now kinder, gentler Godzilla, nuclear power had become humans' companion and helpmate. Environmental decay and pollution were our new worst threats and enemies. Using the potential nuclear energy had to offer, humans might yet be able to overcome the terrible mess they had managed to get themselves into by contaminating their natural habitat. But ultimate success would require a truly monstrous effort.

The business-oriented Japanese government has been reluctant to legislate environmental policies that might impede economic expansion, and the country's environmental movement is "generally fractionalized and weak" (Suzuki, 1992). Nonetheless, Japan now is engaged in the kind of monstrous effort needed to deal with its escalating environmental problems. As an island nation whose own energy resources have been depleted, Japan relies entirely on imported petroleum, coal, and uranium to power its economy. In turn, it bears the brunt of air and water pollution created by its export-oriented production system and must also deal with the increasing physical debris generated by its modern economy and its population's modern lifestyle. As the Japanese people have become increasingly aware of the fragility of their world, they have begun to embrace a new environmental ethos that is growing in other societies, as well (Sawa, 1992).

In this chapter, we examine the nature and scope of the mounting destruction of the physical environment and the growing impact of that process on all our lives. Paralleling the call of many environmentalists to "reduce, reuse, and recycle," we investigate a series of problems related to the depletion, the destruction, and the disposal of natural environmental resources and human artifacts. Much as depicted in the later Japanese monster movies, these problems represent the often-unintended consequences of widespread and accepted human actions. And like the portrayals in these films, in the real world, countless numbers of people have been killed or maimed as a result of these conditions. However, unlike the fantasy world of film, real-life solutions to these problems cannot and will not be reached in the space of one or two hours. Yet unless humans are able to devise some effective way of dealing with the continued destruction of our environment, there may be no one left for the making of a sequel to this particular horror story.

QUESTIONS TO CONSIDER

- 1. With so much of the earth's surface covered by water, why has water depletion become such a problem in the modern world?
- 2. What are the major sources or causes of land and soil depletion in the contemporary world?
- 3. Why are fossil fuels such as oil and coal being depleted so rapidly?
- 4. What factors have led to the decline of nuclear power as a replacement for conventional fossil fuels?

5. What have been the main barriers to the widespread commercial use of wind, geothermal, solar, and other alternative energy sources?
6. What have been the major causes of acid rain and ozone depletion?
7. What is the *greenhouse effect,* and why is this phenomenon a matter of great controversy?
8. What factors have been responsible for the creation of so much solid waste in the contemporary world?
9. Why has toxic waste become such an enormous problem in most developed societies?
10. What specific characteristics of radioactive or nuclear waste make these materials perhaps the most serious waste problem facing the contemporary world?

PROBLEMS OF ENVIRONMENTAL DEPLETION

Each year—indeed, each day—the roughly 5.6 billion people who make up the world's population consume a staggering amount and variety of the earth's natural resources in their attempt to stay alive. Some of these materials (for example, water, solar energy, and thermal energy) in theory are **perpetual resources.** As long as the rain keeps falling, the sun keeps shining, and the wind keeps blowing somewhere in the world, these materials will constantly renew themselves, despite the level of human usage. Other natural materials are considered to be **renewable resources,** in that they can be recreated or replaced within a relatively short period of time through human intervention. Foods such as corn, rice, wheat, and oats fall into this category, as do forest products such as lumber, bark, and a variety of resins. Finally, some materials, such as coal, oil, natural gas, and other fossil fuels, are **nonrenewable resources.** They exist in fixed supplies, and, once used up, they cannot be replaced, as the particular physical climatic conditions that originally created fossil fuels have long since changed. Even if these conditions somehow could be replicated, millions of years would be required to turn decaying organic materials into usable coal or oil.

Although humans have been drawing on the supply of natural resources since our first appearance as a species, the rate at which these materials are being consumed has skyrocketed within the past three centuries. As we discussed briefly in the last chapter, two factors are particularly significant in explaining this quantum leap in resource depletion: the enormous growth in the world's population size and the technology-based shift to modern industrial economies.

In contemporary times, billions rather than millions or hundreds of thousands of individuals around the planet are trying to sustain their own physical existence. The sheer number of people competing for water, land, energy, and other resources has severely taxed the ability of renewable resources to replenish themselves and has greatly accelerated the speed at which various nonrenewable resources are vanishing altogether. If nothing else about human social life had changed, this dramatic surge in global population by itself would have created a tremendous strain on the physical environment. However, other aspects of human social life *have* changed.

The effects of increasing world population size have been magnified by the increasing number of contemporary societies grounded in industrial or postindustrial economic organization. In these societies, machine power has replaced human or animal power as the primary source of economic energy, and machines of all sorts must draw heavily on physical resources to create their own power. Additionally, the economic well-being of these modern industrial systems depends on the mass production and mass consumption of goods and services, all of which entail the utilization (and, hence, depletion) of natural resources. The larger and more advanced the societal economy, the greater the drain on local environmental resources. And as local resources are exhausted, distant sources of needed materials will be located and exploited. According to some estimates, the 25 percent of the world's population who constitute the Western industrial nations currently consume over 85 percent of all natural resources used worldwide each year. At about 6 percent of the world's total population, the United States consumes over 50 percent of all nonrenewable resources used and over one-third of all raw materials produced in the world each year (Bharadwaj, 1992).

As we will discuss in more detail in Chapter Six, many social scientists argue that the current global socioeconomic inequality system of wealthy developed nations and struggling developing countries is based squarely on this pattern. Developed industrial societies are the voracious consumers of enormous supplies of raw materials, and developing nations are the suppliers. In the process, both parties exact a heavy toll on local and global physical environments. The vast array of global environmental problems facing humankind today thus is one consequence of the complex international economic and political arrangements that have come to distinguish and dominate the post–World War II era.

PERPETUAL RESOURCE DEPLETION

WATER SHORTAGES

At first glance, it might seem a little odd to speak of water as a depleted environmental resource. After all, approximately 70 percent of the entire earth's surface is covered by water, and, in many parts of the world, rain falls abundantly and frequently. Be that as it may, a growing number of observers have begun to recognize, and a growing number of populations have begun to encounter, serious water shortages in the Middle East, in Africa, and in many other regions of the developing world. This growing water scarcity has been described as a crisis that "in some parts of the world . . . may be to the 1990s what the oil price shocks were to the 1970s—a major source of economic and political instability" (Postel, 1993b).

WATER, WATER, EVERYWHERE . . .

The world's supply of water is quite large: about 335 million cubic miles' worth, or enough to cover the entire United States under 93 miles of water. However, only about 2.5 percent of that total represents potable (drinkable) or otherwise usable freshwater, and most of that supply is out of easy human reach ("Speaking of: Water," 1993). Consequently, people must rely on rainfall, lakes, rivers, streams, and accessible groundwater (aquifer) supplies for their agricultural, industrial, and residential needs. These needs have been rising at such a rapid pace that water usage has far outstripped natural water renewal mechanisms, leading to long-term depletion. Global water use has more than tripled since 1950, currently standing at about 2,713 cubic miles a year.

Of this aggregated amount, on average, 69 percent of the world's water is used for agriculture, 23 percent for industry, and 8 percent for domestic or household purposes. However, in some especially dry areas of the developing world, such as Sudan and

Afghanistan, crop irrigation accounts for up to 99 percent of all freshwater usage. Conversely, in modern Belgium, about 85 percent of all water is used by industry. In countries such as Zambia and Kuwait, which have very little agriculture or industry, 65 percent of all water goes to domestic household use ("Speaking of: Water," 1993). To the extent that both industrial and agricultural economies have grown in scope during the past half-century, global and regional water use rates have increased much faster than population growth rates and promise to continue to do so in the foreseeable future.

BUT NOT A DROP TO DRINK

By 1993, the available per capita supply of water worldwide had shrunk to two-thirds of its 1970 level (Postel, 1993a). One result of the increasing imbalance between growing water consumption and stable or shrinking water supplies is the increasing number of societies around the world whose populations' health and societal economies are being harmed by a lack of adequate water. As of 1992, 26 countries with a combined population of 230 million people were experiencing *water scarcity,* the condition of having annual water supplies of less than 1,000 cubic meters per person. An additional 8 countries currently defined as *water stressed* (annual water supplies of 1,000 to 2,000 cubic meters per person) could join this group by the year 2010 if current trends continue ("Running Dry," 1993). Some studies estimate that between 2.8 billion and 3.3 billion people could be living in water-troubled countries by the year 2025 (Feldmann, 1993d).

WATER AND WAR

A second consequence of the water consumption/water supply disjuncture is the growing potential for inter- and intranational conflicts over this basic resource. In his apocalyptic preview of the twenty-first century, "The Coming Anarchy," Robert Kaplan (1994) calls the environment "*the* national-security issue of the early twenty-first century," with questions of water resources and water rights a likely catalyst for future wars in Africa, in the Middle East, in Eastern Europe, and on the Indian subcontinent. Kaplan argues that, in particular, countries bordering the earth's major waterways (in many cases, already mutually antagonistic by virtue of long-standing ethnic, religious, and other differences) could well go to war over the contents of those rivers, "a classic case of how environmental disputes fuse with ethnic and historical ones" (Kaplan, 1994, p. 58). Nearly 40 percent of the current world's population depends on river systems shared by two or more countries, so the potential for water-based strife is enormous (Postel, 1993b).

But we will not have to wait until the twenty-first century to see if water could generate international conflicts. In many water-scarce regions of the world, it already has. Following the 1947 partitioning of the Indian subcontinent, the Indian state of East Punjab tried to stop the flow of water from within its borders into neighboring Pakistan—an action that nearly led to all-out war between the two countries. In the Middle East, where Israel, Jordan, the West Bank, and Syria depend on water from the Jordan River basin, the question of who controls that supply has brought the area dangerously close to war. Part of Israel's spoils from the 1967 Arab-Israeli War include important water sources that the Israeli government now is reluctant to return to Jordan. Insisting on their return, Jordan's King Hussein has stated that water is the one single issue that could take his country to war again against Israel (Postel, 1993b).

Control over water resources has also led to significant conflicts within societies, as well. For example, in the southwestern region of the United States, questions of water rights have pitted one state against another (Colorado, New Mexico, and Arizona against California and against one another), one part of a given state against another (northern California against southern California), and one sector within a specific part of a given state against another (rural agricultural interests against urban industrial and domestic interests in central California) (Wood, 1992). These disputes most often have been waged in the federal courts but at times have taken the form of violent acts among the various contending parties (Knickerbocker, 1993a).

In Mexico, 85 percent of the country's water is located in areas under 500 meters in altitude (primarily in the southern part of the country), whereas 70 percent of the population and 80 percent of industry are located above that altitude (primarily in the northern part of the country, as well as in Mexico City, the nation's capital). Ironically, people in the water-rich but otherwise impoverished Mexican states are far less likely than their counterparts in water-poor but otherwise more affluent states to have access to municipal drinking water and sewage discharge systems ("While Mexico's People," 1992). This imbalance, as well as the projected high costs of moving water to and from population and industrial centers, has exacerbated what already is a significant north-south split along socioeconomic and racial lines in Mexico.

SOLVING WATER SHORTAGES

Strategies for dealing with the world's growing water shortage have taken several major forms. At the global and regional levels, international agencies, such as the United Nations, and hemispheric or regional agencies, such as the European Community and the North American Free Trade Agreement nations, have attempted to develop a body of laws or working agreements to establish both rights and obligations over control and usage of transnational water resources. The 1960 Indus Waters Treaty between India and Pakistan is one example of these attempts (Postel, 1993b). For the most part, however, these efforts have been directed at the peaceful resolution of disputes concerning the distribution of existing water supplies. Issues surrounding the depletion of these supplies typically have been addressed by other mechanisms.

SUPPLY-SIDE MEASURES

One strategy for arresting the growing depletion of water resources involves increasing the supply of usable freshwater. In the past, this most often took the form of constructing large dams and other structures to capture, store, and manage water resources. For the most part, these water management projects seem to have worsened rather than ameliorated environmental problems (Sattaur, 1989; Tyson, 1992). A second and equally unsuccessful strategy involves the mining of "fossil" aquifers (that is, groundwater reservoirs hundreds or thousands of years old that receive little replenishment from current rainfalls). Saudi Arabia presently uses this source for 75 percent of its total current water needs but faces the distinct likelihood of completely depleting its water reserves within 50 years. In Texas, overuse of the regional Ogallala aquifer already has resulted in the exhaustion of about one-fourth of that massive groundwater reservoir's supply (Postel, 1993a). Though perhaps effective for meeting immediate water needs, these policies are not suitable for dealing with long-term problems.

More recently, **desalination**, the removal of salt and other substances from seawater or mineral-rich water, has been instituted in a number of different regions of the world, most notably, in the Middle East. As of 1992, about 7,500 desalination units around the world were treating 13 million cubic meters of water a day, with half this total concentrated in Persian Gulf states (Bior, 1992). The main drawback to desalination is the requirement of cheap and plentiful energy sources, an obstacle that has rendered desalinated seawater too expensive for widespread agricultural use. Some experts predict that, within the next 20 years, inexpensive power sources will allow the cost of desalinated seawater to be cut by two-thirds, making bargain-priced water available to water-parched populations in unlimited amounts. However, in the Middle East, a region in which water scarcity has already led to near-war, 20 years may be too long a wait. "If one wishes to make peace and bring prosperity to these countries, one must make sure that in the next decade 500 million to 600 million cubic meters of water will be desalinated. The investment needed for such a project is about $2.5 billion, less than the cost of a small war" (Zaslavsky, in Bior, 1992).

DEMAND-SIDE STRATEGIES

Perhaps a more effective, longer-lasting solution to the world's water shortage problem lies in the conservation and more careful use of existing resources—that is, in decreasing water demand rather than increasing water supplies. As Postel (1993a, p. 23) notes:

> Modern society has come to view water only as a resource that is there for the taking, rather than a life-support system that underpins the natural world we depend on. Instead of continuously reaching out for more, we must begin to look within—within our regions, our communities, our homes, and ourselves—for ways to meet our needs while respecting water's life-sustaining functions.

A growing number of societies around the world already have taken significant steps in reducing water consumption. Israel, for example, has pioneered the widespread use of drip-irrigation systems for agricultural production in the Negev Desert. Drip irrigation is a technique that reduces water usage by about 60 percent compared to conventional irrigation methods and also permits the use of brackish water that would otherwise be wasted (Kahana, 1992). In California, state- and locally imposed water conservation measures during the recent 6-year drought reduced overall water consumption by about 20 percent, partially through the implementation of drip irrigation for home gardening ("Speaking of: Water," 1993). The trick seems to be getting people to recognize and accept the fact that water conservation is a long-term fact of life, rather than a temporary inconvenience.

In the long run, the ultimate success or failure of water conservation measures will hinge on the large-scale adoption of water-efficient policies and processes in agriculture and in industry. It will also depend on the recognition by individual countries that water shortage is a global and regional problem that requires cooperation, rather than antagonism, among the nations of the world (P. M. Johnson, 1992). Reaching that level of awareness may prove to be one of the most difficult barriers to slaking the thirst of both people and the environment itself in the years to come.

SOIL AND LAND DEPLETION

In addition to a growing shortage of usable freshwater, people and societies throughout the modern world face a growing shortage of usable land. According to some estimates, since 1945, about 10.5 percent of the earth's most fertile soil, representing an area about the size of India and China combined, has been seriously depleted by human activity (Stammer, 1992a). Since 1972, some 480 billion tons of topsoil, roughly equivalent to the combined farmlands of France and India, have been lost to agricultural use ("Threats to Earth," 1992), raising the specter of massive crop shortfalls and a food crisis within the next 25 to 30 years. Each year, the world loses an area of productive land almost the size of Ireland (Grier, 1993). About two-thirds of the most seriously depleted land lies in Africa and Asia, two of the poorest regions of the world. Sub–Saharan Africa already suffers from populationwide malnutrition and starvation, and the situation will only get worse as remaining agricultural land continues to be depleted (Stammer, 1992a).

DESERTIFICATION

Although most of the moderate to severe soil and land loss is concentrated in developing countries, no region of the world has escaped. For example, although North America constitutes only about 4.5 percent of the world's total damaged lands, 40 percent of the hemisphere's range and cropland has undergone **desertification**, the process of having literally been turned into desert. The U.S. Soil Conservation Service estimates that about one-fourth of the remaining cropland in the United States is eroding at a rate faster than can be corrected (Stammer, 1992a). Similarly, almost one-fourth of all range and cropland in Australia has been turned into largely unusable desert areas (Rohr, 1992). According to the UN Environmental Program, about 73 percent of the world's 8.25 billion acres of dry rangeland has become at least moderately desertified, having lost more than 25 percent of its carrying capacity—that is, its ability to support plant and animal life ("Threats to Earth," 1993).

Scientists at the World Resources Institute, who conducted an extensive study of the soil depletion problem in conjunction with the UN Environment Program, cite three factors as being most significant in bringing about this growing problem: overgrazing of cattle and other livestock, deforestation, and unsuitable agricultural practices. Of the three, overgrazing by livestock is perhaps the most serious contributing factor.

OVERGRAZING

Since the mid-1940s, overgrazing has destroyed some 1.7 billion acres of pasture and rangelands worldwide, nearly 35 percent of all depleted lands (Postel, 1994). In addition to stripping the land of virtually all vegetation, cattle, sheep, and other hooved livestock

A combination of overgrazing, deforestation, and unsuitable agricultural practices has led to the desertification of much of the planet's croplands and rangelands, especially in sub–Saharan Africa. As once fertile topsoil dries up and blows away, poverty and starvation follow. According to one UN estimate, approximately 22 million acres of land around the world have been so destroyed by desertification that they are beyond any hope of restoration.

compact the denuded soil, making it impervious to water absorption and thus easily washed away by heavy rains. According to one observer, "The impact of countless hooves and mouths over the years has done more to alter the type of vegetation and land forms of the West than all the water projects, strip mines, power plants, freeways, and subdivision developments combined" (Fradkin in "Damage Done by Cattle-Raising," 1993, p. 2).

DEFORESTATION

A second major cause of worldwide land depletion is the deforestation of many areas across the planet, a process taking place at the rate of an estimated 40 million acres a year (Brown, 1991). Of the estimated 4.9 billion acres of formerly productive land lost worldwide since 1945, deforestation accounts for about 1.45 billion acres, or about 30 percent of the total (Postel, 1994). This stripping of the world's forests is most widespread in Central and South America. It is estimated that, by the year 2000, Honduras and Nicaragua each will lose half their remaining forest lands, and Colombia will lose a third of its remaining forests. More than 95 percent of Brazil's Atlantic forest areas already have been lost, and the country's remaining forests are currently being removed at the rate of 5,335 square miles per year (Rohr, 1992).

UNSUITABLE AGRICULTURAL PRACTICES

The third significant factor contributing to the depletion of the earth's soil and land is composed of a variety of agricultural practices that cause or accelerate the depletion process. These practices include the overuse of fertilizers that acidify the soil, poor plowing practices that expose the land to the eroding effects of wind and rain, poor drainage that increases soil salinity, and cultivation of steep hillsides that results in soil erosion after a short period of time (Grier, 1993; Stammer, 1992a). Since 1945, these and other "agricultural mismanagement" practices have accounted for approximately 1.38 billion acres, or about 28 percent, of the total world's land depletion (Postel, 1994).

SOLVING LAND DEPLETION PROBLEMS

As is also the case with water depletion problems, any real solution to the growing problem of soil and land depletion will necessitate both a rethinking of humans' relationship to the land and international cooperation at the regional and global levels. Such a solution also will require large expenditures of money, effort, and time. For example, in India, the cost of reclaiming damaged soil has averaged from $2,000 to $3,000 per hectare (a hectare is equal to 2.5 acres) (Stammer, 1992a). Regardless of the cost, in some instances, it is already too late to do much to correct the damage already done. According to the UN Environmental Program report, approximately 22 million acres of land around the world have been so depleted and ruined that they are beyond hope of restoration (Stammer, 1992a). The critical issue, then, involves taking steps to halt or slow down the depletion process before it reaches the point of no return.

ONE SMALL STEP

One approach to soil depletion is to attempt new agricultural methods that retard the process. For example, a growing number of farmers throughout the United States now have begun practicing what has been called *residue management* ("Revolution on the Farm," 1992). **Residue management** consists of a series of techniques including planting new crops in the decomposing residue of the previous year's harvest, crop rotation, and the use of rapidly degradable and environmentally friendly herbicides. According to the chief of the U.S. Soil Conservation Service, residue management currently is used on about 25 percent of all U.S. croplands, a figure that likely will double within the next two or three years. In the Dominican Republic, a small group of graduates of the country's Regional Center for the Study of Rural Alternatives are instructing rural farmers in many of these same techniques (Elkin, 1993). These are steps in the right direction, but only very small steps.

ONE GIANT LEAP

To make any real dent in the world's soil depletion problem, the deforestation and desertification of lands in the developing world must be addressed. This is not simply a matter of educating "backward" or "ignorant" people about the theory and practice of environmentalism. Rather, it is more a question of insuring adequate food, water, and other resources for impoverished populations while addressing the needs of the physical environment. As we discussed briefly in Chapter Three on population, poor people engage in environmentally harmful practices not so much out of ignorance as out of a need to survive.

In the final analysis, what must be accomplished is a breaking of what Alan B. Durning (1989, p. 40) calls "a self-feeding downward spiral of economic deprivation and ecological degradation" that "forces landless families to put rain forest plots to the torch and mountain slopes to the plow." The successful ending of this vicious circle of economic poverty and environmental depletion in turn will require a reordering of the international socioeconomic stratification system that has left most people in the developing nations trailing far behind their counterparts in the affluent developed world. In essence, the solution to environmental depletion in less developed countries lies largely in the hands of developed industrialized societies.

NONRENEWABLE RESOURCE DEPLETION

During the winter of 1973–1974, U.S. consumers first learned the hard way that the fate of modern societies hinges on a large and steady flow of energy resources. Thanks to production cutbacks and price hikes by the members of the OPEC (Oil Producing and Exporting Countries) cartel, many people in the United States suddenly found themselves facing severe shortages of heating fuels, as well as long lines and rationed supplies at gas stations. Not quite 20 years later, again facing the distinct possibility of disrupted oil supplies from the Persian Gulf states, the United States and other Western industrial nations sent military forces into the Middle East to turn back Iraq's invasion of Kuwait and maintain the flow of petroleum to the West. The allies' involvement in the Persian Gulf War proved costly in both financial and human terms. However, the likely consequences of another round of oil shortages seemed to justify the action. Oil has become the lifeblood of most developed societies, and without that sustaining force, the world's leading economies would soon wither and die.

As we discussed earlier, oil and other fossil fuels are nonrenewable resources. They exist in finite (albeit large) amounts, and once those supplies have been used up, the resources are gone for good. Since the coming of the Industrial Revolution and the modernization of many of the world's societies, the rate at which these energy resources have been consumed has risen dramatically and continues to do so. In the past three decades alone, world energy consumption has nearly tripled, and most of that energy still is provided by fossil fuels (see Table 4.1). These resources are being depleted so rapidly that many observers predict the complete exhaustion of specific fuels within the foreseeable future. For example, some esti-

TABLE 4.1 World Energy Consumption, by Region and Energy Source (in metric tons of coal equivalent)

Region and Energy Source	Consumption (and Percent Distribution) (millions of metric tons)							
	1960		1970		1980		1990	
World Total	3,924	(100.0)	6,440	(100.0)	8,544	(100.0)	10,412	(100.0)
North America	1,599	(40.7)	2,502	(38.9)	2,796	(32.7)	3,061	(29.4)
United States	1,454	(37.1)	2,217	(34.4)	2,594	(27.7)	2,572	(24.7)
South America	79	(2.0)	143	(2.2)	251	(2.9)	307	(2.9)
Europe	1,039	(26.5)	1,720	(26.7)	2,145	(25.1)	2,153	(20.7)
Asia	514	(13.1)	903	(14.0	1,579	(18.5)	2,552	(24.5)
Japan	96	(2.4)	333	(5.2)	435	(5.1)	519	(5.0)
Soviet Union (former)	595	(15.2)	999	(15.5)	1,473	(17.2)	1,931	(18.5)
Oceania	41	(1.0)	71	(1.1)	105	(1.2)	147	(1.4)
Energy Source								
Solid fuels	1,940	(49.4)	2,159	(33.5)	2,632	(30.8)	3,324	(31.9)
Liquid fuels	1,306	(33.3)	2,835	(44.0)	3,778	(44.2)	4,038	(38.8)
Natural gas	593	(15.1)	1,292	(20.1)	1,834	(21.5)	2,532	(24.3)
Electricity	84	(2.1)	154	(2.4)	301	(3.5)	518	(5.0)

SOURCE: Adapted from *Statistical Abstract of the United States: 1993,* Table 943.

mates claim that half of all the recoverable oil in the world will have been used up by as early as 1997 and no later than the year 2017 (Courtney, 1993).

OIL DEPLETION

"Black gold" remains the primary energy source for many of the world's contemporary societies. Collectively, the nations of the world consumed a total of nearly 66 million barrels (about 2.77 billion gallons) of petroleum per day in 1990, a 40 percent increase from 1970 rates (see Table 4.2). Petroleum represents about one-third of the total current industrial energy consumption in the United States, although, since 1970, all energy-use sectors except transportation have moved away from petroleum and other fossil fuels toward increased use of electricity. However, according to U.S. Department of Energy projections, petroleum consumption will grow steadily through the year 2010, with an increasing amount of that oil coming from foreign sources. Thus, the United States, much like Japan and other industrialized societies, will remain heavily dependent on petroleum imports and vulnerable to price fluctuations on the world market (Energy Information Administration, 1993). As oil reserves are depleted, these prices are likely to

During their withdrawal from Kuwait in the Persian Gulf War, Iraqi military forces set fire to nearly 800 oil wells. In addition to accelerating the depletion of this important energy resource, these fires caused a tremendous amount of pollution in surrounding air, land, and sea environments.

rise significantly, placing additional burdens on the economies of societies dependent on imported petroleum.

In many developing countries, where energy consumption has quadrupled since 1960, energy-import costs already constitute a major foreign exchange expenditure, drawing away capital that otherwise could be utilized for domestic economic and social development. Seventy-five percent of all developing countries are oil importers, and 29 of the world's 38 poorest countries import more than 70 percent of their commercial

TABLE 4.2 Petroleum Consumption, World and Major Consuming Nations: 1970, 1980, 1990 (millions of barrels per day)

Country	Petroleum Consumption		
	1970	1980	1990
World Total	46.81	63.07	65.92
United States	14.70	17.06	16.99
USSR (former)	5.31	9.00	8.40
Japan	3.82	4.96	5.14
West Germany	2.61	2.71	2.38
United Kingdom	2.10	1.73	1.75
France	1.94	2.26	1.81
Italy	1.71	1.93	1.87
Canada	1.52	1.87	1.69
China (PRC)	0.62	1.77	2.28

SOURCE: Adapted from *Statistical Abstract of the United States: 1993,* Table 950.

energy, primarily in the form of oil (Lenssen, 1993). As these countries' energy needs continue to rise and those of developed nations also increase or remain steady, the international competition for remaining oil supplies likely will intensify, conceivably to the point of overt conflict (Kaplan, 1994).

COAL DEPLETION

Next to petroleum, coal is one of the most widely used energy sources in the modern world. For example, in 1991, 23 percent of the total energy consumption in the United States came from coal (U.S. Bureau of the Census, 1993a). In that same year, coal produced nearly 40 percent of the world's electricity (Flavin & Lenssen, 1994). As of 1993, coal still provided 28 percent of the world's commercial energy (Flavin & Kane, 1993).

According to most estimates, the world's remaining coal reserves are much larger than those of petroleum. However, much of this coal is of poor quality, more difficult and expensive (in terms of both economic and environmental costs) to mine, or both. Additionally, coal is a significant source of both greenhouse gas (carbon dioxide) and acid rain–producing gas (sulfur dioxide); consequently, coal burning is a major contributor to contemporary air pollution and global warming problems.

For the most part, heavy use of coal now is confined to developing countries that cannot afford the widespread use of oil. For example, China still gets about 75 percent of its total energy from coal and consumes one-fourth of all the coal used in the world each year. Planners in that country estimate that coal use in China will increase by 40 percent within a decade (Flavin & Kane, 1993).

NUCLEAR ENERGY

As of 1992, 364 commercial nuclear-powered reactors were in operation around the world, producing a total of nearly 1,900 billion kilowatt hours of electricity (see Table 4.3). These

TABLE 4.3 Commercial Nuclear Power Generation, World and Selected Countries: 1992 (in billions of kilowatt hours)

Country	Reactors	Electricity Generated
World Total	364	1,868.3
United States	112	650.1
France	57	337.6
Japan	42	215.8
Great Britain	37	78.5
Germany	22	158.8
Canada	20	81.3
Sweden	12	63.5
South Korea	9	56.4
Spain	9	55.8
India	8	6.3

SOURCE: Adapted from *Statistical Abstract of the United States: 1993,* Table 961.

numbers represented a sixfold increase in the number of reactors but less than a tripling in the amount of electricity generated since 1970. Nuclear energy was once hailed as the most viable solution to the world's energy needs, but construction and operation of nuclear energy plants have slowed considerably since the inception of commercially produced nuclear energy in the 1950s. In the past two decades, many once-planned nuclear reactors have not been constructed at all, and many others under construction have been abandoned before completion. Rapidly rising construction and operating costs of nuclear plants, as well as mounting questions about the health and safety hazards of nuclear energy, have led to significant reversals in this once-booming area. In large measure, this turnaround was intensified as a result of several dramatic accidents that caught the attention and magnified the fears of people throughout the world.

On March 28, 1979, a partial meltdown of a nuclear reactor at Three Mile Island, Pennsylvania, released radioactive steam into the atmosphere, threatening local communities and both shocking and angering many people around the country. Seven years later, on April 26, 1986, an explosion at the Chernobyl nuclear power plant in Ukraine (part of what was then the Soviet Union) resulted in the release of over 100 tons of contaminated debris, the world's worst nuclear power accident (Dahlburg, 1992). Official Soviet government figures placed the death toll from the accident at 31; however, other estimates claim that thousands of people had died from radiation effects by 1991 (in Holloway, 1993).

ADDRESSING THE ENERGY CRISIS

The combination of diminishing fossil fuel supplies and growing concerns about the cost and safety of nuclear power has led many nations to explore novel approaches to solving their energy problems. These solutions include efforts to restructure current energy consumption rates and patterns as well as attempts to identify and develop as yet untapped energy sources.

DEMAND-SIDE MANAGEMENT

In recent years, many developed and developing countries have made increased efforts to slow down the depletion of local and global energy resource supplies through a series of techniques known collectively as **demand-side management**, or **DSM** (Roodman, 1993). Designed to reduce energy (in particular, electric energy) consumption, the DSM approach has begun to generate what some observers have called a "negawatt revolution" around the world (Flavin & Lenssen, 1994, p. 69). Governments in dozens of nations throughout various regions, including North and South America, Western Europe, and East and Southeast Asia, have already initiated programs to curtail both industrial and residential electric consumption.

Some specific DSM measures, such as designing and constructing more energy-efficient buildings or retrofitting older buildings to make them more energy efficient, are costly. However, these costs are far lower than those required to build and operate additional power plants. By taking steps to reduce the demand for electric energy rather than building new generating facilities to meet increasing demands, over time, both governments and consumers will realize substantial economic savings. According to some estimates (in Roodman, 1993), over the next 30 years, DSM programs could cut energy investments in developing countries by 40 percent and in developed nations by 50 percent, resulting in total savings of approximately $2.2 trillion. Additionally, reduced energy consumption translates into a reduced drain on existing energy resource supplies.

In the United States, DSM spending rose from $900 million in 1989 to $2.3 billion in 1992. By 1990, DSM programs had reduced overall electric energy consumption by 1 percent and by nearly 4 percent during peak electricity demand periods. Some estimates claim that, in the next 15 years, these programs could cut overall electricity consumption in the United States by 7 percent and by 10 percent during peak demand periods (Roodman, 1993). Demand-side management has proved so effective that it has led the U.S. electricity industry to begin moving toward a more comprehensive planning view that takes into account the cost effectiveness of various alternative energy sources and policies. *Integrated resource planning,* as this new model is called, now is required by law in 30 states (Mitchell in Roodman, 1993). Some experts project that comprehensive, integrated energy planning could cut between 75 and 80 percent of energy use in commercial and residential buildings, resulting in annual energy savings of more than $130 billion (Scholand, 1993).

RENEWABLE ENERGY TECHNOLOGIES

In spite of the potentially large global and societal energy savings that can be realized through DSM conservation and efficiency strategies, many informed observers agree that "no matter how much waste is squeezed out of the way energy is used . . . over the long term energy supplies must be increased" (Lenssen, 1993, p. 111). Growing problems with fossil and nuclear fuels have led to increasing explorations of alternative power sources, especially renewable energy.

According to some estimates, solar, thermal, and geothermal power resources are "sufficiently abundant to supply all the world's electricity scores of times over" (Flavin & Lenssen, 1994, p. 68). However, until recently, widespread commercial use of renewable energy technologies has been stymied by high research and development costs, as well as by the unwillingness of many governments to underwrite these costs. For example, in the United States, only 2 percent of all federal subsidies to the energy sector are used to promote renewable energy development. By way of contrast, a total of nearly 90 percent of these monies have been allocated to fossil fuels (58 percent) and to nuclear power development (30 percent) (Courtney, 1993). Nonetheless, more and more countries are starting to develop these potentially unlimited power supplies.

In the United States, renewable energy–based technologies produced 87.4 gigawatts of electricity (roughly the equivalent of the combined productive capacity of 88 state-of-the-art electric power plants) in 1990, a figure that is expected to increase significantly over the next few decades (see Table 4.4). Of this total amount, about 86 percent was derived from conventional hydroelectric power; however, increasing opposition to the large dams required for hydroelectric power generation makes it likely that other renewable energy sources will steadily increase in importance over the next two decades. U.S. Department of Energy projections indicate that, in particular, the roles of municipal solid waste, biomass (wood, vegetation, and other organic materials), geothermal, and wind power sources will expand greatly.

To date, concerns about the reliability of many of these otherwise promising alternative energy sources have led their actual usage levels to remain far below their potential applications. Because natural phenomena such as wind velocity, cloud patterns, and rainfall are variable over time, power generation from these energy sources can also vary significantly over time. For this reason, "renewable energy must be considered a supplemental, rather than baseload, source of power" (Energy Information Administration, 1993, p. 54). However, in spite of this perceived serious limitation, a large number of public- and private-sector-sponsored power generation projects utilizing wind, geothermal, or solar energy already are in place, and many more are being planned.

TABLE 4.4 U.S. Renewable Electric Generating Capacity (1990) and Projected Capacity (2010) (in gigawatts)

Technology	Generating Capacity (1990)	Projected Capacity (2010)
Conventional hydropower	75.1	76.9
Biomass/other waste	6.0	8.1
Geothermal	2.6	8.5
Municipal solid waste	2.0	11.4
Wind	1.4	6.3
Solar thermal	0.4	1.9
Total Renewable	87.4	113.1

SOURCE: Adapted from *Annual Energy Outlook 1993,* Table 13.

1. *Wind power*—European countries, in particular, have stepped up their development of wind-powered electrical generation. By the year 2000, the combined wind-generated electrical power capacity of Britain, Denmark, Germany, Greece, Italy, and the Netherlands will exceed 2,600 megawatts (MacLeod, 1992a). In the United States, wind farms in California already produce 1,350 megawatts of power, and other states are expected to follow suit as wind-generating technologies improve and wind-power costs continue to fall. In 1982, the average kilowatt-hour cost of wind-generated electricity was 50 cents, compared to 6 cents for coal and 15 cents for natural gas. By 1990, that cost had dropped to 7.5 cents compared to 6 cents for coal and 7 cents for gas, making wind power an increasingly attractive alternative energy source (Thompson, 1992).

2. *Solar power*—Once hailed and then dismissed as the single most promising prospect for alternative renewable energy, solar power also has been making a significant comeback in recent years. This rebirth has been especially prominent in developing countries, whose economies do not permit the commitment of huge sums of capital for conventional or nuclear power plants (Reddy & Goldemberg, 1991). These nations currently buy about 65 percent of all solar panels produced in the United States. Mexico, in particular, is using inexpensive and portable solar panels to help bring electricity to the roughly 28 million people in that country who currently lack electric power. Mexico's efforts have been described as "the most ambitious solar electrification program in the world" (Sklar in Greenwald, 1993a). As is the case with wind-generated power, a critical factor in the future of solar power is the cost of the involved technologies. If the price of solar power drops significantly in comparison to the costs of other power sources, solar power could well become a major player in meeting future energy needs in both the developing and the developed worlds.

3. *Geothermal power*—Unlike the wind or the sun, geothermal power, which is drawn from natural heat and steam from within the earth, is a much more stable (and, thus, more reliable) source of energy for commercial use. Japan and a number of European societies have substantial government-funded geothermal energy development programs, although the United States still leads the world in hot dry rock (HDR) geothermal technology. In the HDR process, water injected into a well is warmed by the earth's heat from below and then extracted from a second well and converted into elec-

trical power (Glasser & Pardue, 1993). However, according to some reports, geothermal energy development in this country has received a number of significant setbacks, including the potential withdrawal of HDR research funding by the Department of Energy. If this abundant and promising source of energy is to play a significant role in lessening U.S. and world dependency on fossil or nuclear fuels, a much more aggressive research and development program will have to be undertaken in the very near future.

PROBLEMS OF ENVIRONMENTAL DESTRUCTION

The global and societal consequences of environmental resource depletion have been compounded by a series of problems involving the increasing worldwide destruction of air, water, and other critical ecosystem components. In many cases, these two phenomena are directly linked. For example, as older, deep-shaft sources of higher-grade coal have run out, many countries have turned to the mining of lower-grade coal closer to the surface of the land. In the United States, such strip mining has literally laid bare huge tracts of land in the Appalachian and Rocky Mountains, leaving them unfit for other use. The subsequent processing and burning of lower-grade coal have contributed significantly to local water and air pollution levels as well as to global warming problems. Similarly, as other cultivatable lands have been depleted, rural peasants in many developing countries have resorted to clearing and burning rain forests to create new farmlands. The wholesale deforestation of large areas in South America, Africa, and Asia has resulted not only in the destruction and loss of forest plant and animal species but, ultimately, in the depletion of the land itself through accelerated erosion (Durning, 1989).

WATER POLLUTION

In 1991, the Natural Resources Defense Council reported more than 2,000 beach closures across the United States, primarily as a result of untreated human sewage polluting coastal waters. Of these closings, 588 involved the stretch of California coastline between Los Angeles and San Diego. Another 715 closures took place along the New Jersey, New York, and Connecticut shorelines, an area that had been affected by other pollution problems only three years earlier (Germani, 1992a). Throughout the summer of 1988, people up and down the northeastern United States found the waters and sands of their favorite beaches littered with a vast and unwholesome array of medical and solid waste debris that made safe recreational use of the Atlantic coastline impossible (Toufexis, 1988). Similar coastal pollution problems turned up in many other parts of the world, including some once-fabled beaches of the Mediterranean Sea that had been made useless and dangerous by sewage and chemical pollutants (Morello, 1992).

At the same time that pollution is cutting sharply into the recreational possibilities of beaches throughout the United States and the world, other and more sinister water pollution problems also are manifesting themselves. Largely as a result of contamination from nonpoint-source pollution—that is, aggregated agricultural, industrial, and residential waste runoffs (Spaid, 1993c)—water supplies and waterways across the world are showing increasingly higher levels of harmful pollutants. Water that once was safe to drink no longer is. Fish and other aquatic creatures that once were safe to eat no longer are. Communities and industries that depended on water for their livelihood have been figuratively, if not literally, hung out to dry (Toufexis, 1988).

U.S. WATER PROBLEMS

In the United States, the 1972 Clean Water Act and the 1974 Safe Drinking Water Act were enacted to insure reasonable and continuing supplies of potable or otherwise usable water. However, in the more than 20 years since the passage of these bills, national water quality has declined. According to some reports, 250,000 violations of the Safe Drinking Water Act, affecting 120 million people, occurred in 1991 and 1992 alone, especially in the 83 percent of the nation's smaller water systems that collectively serve about 20 million people across the country. Because of their size, these systems are exempted from expensive purity testing and other rules designed to protect consumers from contaminated drinking water. As a result of these exemptions and the overburdening of many larger municipal water systems, "Americans are ingesting such noxious pollutants as bacteria, viruses, lead, gasoline, radioactive gases and carcinogenic industrial compounds" (Lemonick, 1993, p. 85). For example, in the spring of 1993, nearly 300,000 Milwaukee-area residents became ill and 6 died from drinking Great Lakes water contaminated with a common parasite that somehow had slipped through the municipal water filtration system (Rumbaitis-del Rio, 1994).

Many of the United States' earlier water pollution problems were the result of point-source pollution—pollution that can be traced to a particular origin, such as a waste discharge pipe from a factory or a chemical processing plant. As a result of the heavy penalties imposed by the 1972 Clean Water Act, much of this point-source pollution has been eliminated. Most contemporary water pollution in the United States results from the continued flow of waste runoff from farms, city streets, and industry (that is, from nonpoint-source pollution), rather than from any one specific source (Spaid, 1993c).

Dealing with contemporary water pollution problems is a much more difficult challenge because the fundamental cause of these problems is a technology-based economic and social system that encourages or requires massive use of water-contaminating substances in nearly all aspects of daily life. For example, according to U.S. Geological Survey estimates, U.S. farmers use a total of 200 to 300 million pounds of agricultural chemicals each year (Holmstrom, 1993b). Overall, some 740 million pounds of toxic chemicals pour into streams, rivers, and municipal sewers each year (Knickerbocker, 1994a). Many of these chemicals eventually find their way into the ocean, turning many once-thriving waters into "nothing more than cocktails of highly toxic substances" (Houck in Toufexis, 1988, p. 46).

Any significant attempt to lessen or eliminate water pollution permanently would necessitate a radical restructuring of the chemical infrastructure that makes possible the lifestyles currently enjoyed and taken for granted by people in developed societies. Given a choice between cleaner water and a less affluent standard of living, many individuals might opt for the accustomed material lifestyle, in effect, conceding water pollution as an acceptable "price of progress" (Ogose, 1993).

WATER POLLUTION IN THE DEVELOPING WORLD

In contrast to the United States and other industrialized nations, the main causes of the enormous water pollution problems found in many industrializing countries are their disadvantaged position within the global economy and their all-out efforts to achieve higher levels of economic and social development. As we discussed earlier, developing countries occupy positions on the periphery of the international economic system. In this capacity, they largely serve as suppliers of many raw materials required by industrialized nations. For example, we have already seen that much of the petroleum imported by the United States comes from Persian Gulf states. Mexico, Venezuela, and other LDCs (less developed countries) also are significant exporters of oil to the industrialized world. Similarly, a large amount of the aluminum used for commercial and residential purposes in the United States is derived from bauxite that is mined and processed in Jamaica. Both the oil and bauxite industries are environmentally unfriendly, resulting in (among other things) significant water contamination from spills, discharges, and runoffs of pollutants. It is the suppliers' environments and populations, rather than the purchasers', that normally bear the brunt of this damage.

Many developing countries have made modernization their top priority and are prepared to do whatever is necessary to upgrade their economies as quickly as possible. What often has resulted is the destruction of both local and international waterways by industries given virtual "blank checks" to operate in the most economically productive way, even if that entails significant environmental costs. In comparing the environmental situations of the rich, industrialized nations of the north and the poor, developing countries of the south, United Nations environmental planners (Grenon & Hoballah in Morello, 1992) were led to conclude:

> In the south, the word "environment" is written in miniscule letters. Their major preoccupation is development. . . . The north has an environmental problem. People can afford to look at the environment to preserve a way of life. In the south, people worry about what they will eat.

In the developing world, then, water pollution represents one price of economic development. And if the experiences of the industrialized nations are any guide, once those societies have developed, continued water pollution may well become a price of continued affluence.

AIR POLLUTION

Since the advent of the Modern Age and the industrialization of the world's societies, the earth's natural ability to cleanse itself of atmospheric pollutants has been strained to the point of collapse. Each year, the United States and other developed countries pour millions of tons of toxic pollutants into the air in the course of heating, cooling, and powering the economies that sustain the social well-being of their populations (see Table 4.5). And each year, the developing nations of the world disgorge rapidly growing amounts of the same fossil fuel and chlorofluorocarbon (CFC) emissions into the atmosphere as they industrialize and modernize in an effort to improve their own populations' levels of well-being. Ironically, one of the net results of this attempted global upgrading of human societal life has been the global downgrading of the physical environment and, ultimately, of human societal life, as well. The atmosphere that is meant to sustain us is now dirtier, unhealthier, warmer, and thinner than at any previous point in recorded history.

In 1993, the residents of Mexico City, arguably the smog capital of the world, enjoyed exactly 37 days of "satisfactory" air quality, as measured by the Metropolitan Air Quality Index. During the remaining 328 days of that year, they were confronted by air that was either "unsatisfactory" or "very bad" (Walker, 1994). In Japan, tourists hoping to photograph Mount Fuji, a site long treasured for its tranquil beauty, must wait until nearby factories are closed or a strong north wind is blowing. Otherwise the summit remains obscured by industrial smoke ("Mount Fuji," 1992). San Diego, which boasts of being "America's Finest City," has now attained the dubious distinction of possessing one of the

TABLE 4.5 Air Pollutant Emissions in the United States: 1991 (by pollutant and source)

Pollutant	Source					
	Total Emissions	Transportation	Fuel Combustion[1]	Industrial Process	Sold Waste Disposal	Miscellaneous
Carbon monoxide[2]	62.1	43.5	4.7	4.7	2.1	7.2
Sulfur oxides[2]	20.7	1.0	16.6	3.2	0.2	0.1
Volatile organic compounds[2]	16.9	5.1	0.7	7.9	0.7	2.6
Particulates[2]	7.4	1.6	1.9	2.6	0.3	1.0
Nitrogen oxides[2]	18.8	7.3	10.6	0.6	0.1	0.2
Lead[3]	5.0	1.6	0.5	2.2	0.7	0.0

SOURCE: Adapted from *Statistical Abstract of the United States: 1993,* Table 369.

[1] Stationary sources
[2] Millions of metric tons per year
[3] Thousands of metric tons per year

worst regional air quality levels in the entire country. And across Western Europe, the Colosseum in Rome, the Cathedral of Notre Dame in Paris, the Roman Aqueduct in Segovia, and many other historical monuments are disintegrating under the impact of air pollution (Pollack, 1992). While the "free world" may be breathing a lot easier since the collapse of the Soviet Union and the end of the Cold War, they are by no means breathing cleaner or healthier. Their counterparts in Eastern Europe and the former USSR are hardly better off, having inherited a legacy of environmental pollution that at times staggers the imagination. Throughout much of the world, humans are literally, as well as metaphorically, choking on the consequences of modern life.

FOSSIL FUEL POLLUTION

Environmental Protection Agency estimates claim that half the population of the United States breathe air that is heavily polluted (Cylke, 1993). According to the American Lung Association, almost 23 million people in the United States face a "deadly public health threat" because their communities are polluted by soot and other excess particulates that turn the air thick and hazy ("Thick, Hazy Air," 1994). In China, three cities (Xi'an, Shenyang, and Beijing) currently rank among the 10 worst sites in the world for concentration of sulfur dioxide, and in each city, large numbers of people suffer from serious respiratory problems (Lide, 1990). In Mexico City, drugstores do a thriving business selling bottled oxygen to the rich, and even street-corner oxygen kiosks sell brief shots of clean air to the less affluent masses who must deal with that city's unparalleled air pollution (Cleeland, 1991). Much of this pollution emanates from the burning of fossil fuels for transportation and power purposes—that is, from the exhaust pipes of private and public vehicles as well as the smokestacks of factories and power plants. The basic cause of global air pollution is the world's continued dependency on the fossil fuels that power societal economies.

ENVIRONMENTAL DISASTER
Communism versus the Smog Monster

Beginning in 1989, the world was stunned by a series of rapid-fire events culminating in the collapse of the Soviet Union in December 1991. As the Berlin Wall fell and the Iron Curtain lifted, secrets long hidden from Western eyes finally started coming to light. Among the secrets that many people perhaps wish had remained in the dark was an almost unbelievable litany of environmental horrors dating back to the early years of the USSR.

Scientists certainly had been aware of some of the region's environmental problems long before the Soviet government decided to call it quits. But as details of the full extent of these ecological nightmares unfolded, it became clear that the regime that had prided itself on being the friend of the worker had been no friend of the environment. "We cannot expect charity from nature," former Soviet leader Josef Stalin once said. "We must tear it from her" (quoted in Holloway, 1993). His subsequent attempts to transform nature on behalf of economic development through a series of giant civil engineering projects wreaked havoc on the air, the water, the land, and, eventually, on the people themselves (Waters, 1990). More than 40 years after Stalin's reign of environmental terror, observers both inside and outside the former Soviet Union are wondering if that tear can ever be mended. According to one recent analysis of the Soviet environmental track record, "When historians finally conduct an autopsy on Soviet communism, they may reach the verdict of death by ecocide" (Feshbach & Friendly quoted in Stanglin, 1992, p. 42).

The assertion that the Soviet Union itself was killed by its environmental policies is open to debate. But it is becoming very apparent that many of its inhabitants are being killed and maimed as a result of those policies. For example, less than five years after the world's worst nuclear disaster at Chernobyl sent tons of radioactive clouds across Ukraine and Belarus, children living in those regions began to develop thyroid cancer more quickly and in larger numbers than health officials had expected ("More Thyroid Cancer," 1992). Stomach and kidney illnesses likewise have increased 450 percent since the 1986 explosion (Dahlburg, 1992). However, these post-Chernobyl cases are only the most recent tragic manifestations of the continuing consequences of living on what has been described as "the world's biggest pile of nuclear waste" (Bogert, 1992).

From the late 1940s through the late 1980s, hundreds of atom bombs were detonated above ground across the Soviet Union. Many of these explosions, like those taking place in the United States during the same period, were tests conducted in pursuit of nuclear superiority in the Cold War arms race. But more than 100 others were so-called peaceful detonations—that is, atomic explosions used as part of the Stalin-era effort to remold the physical landscape to serve the needs of the industrial economy.

One result of both the production and the detonation of so many nuclear devices has been the radioactive contamination of vast expanses of territory that are now unfit for human habitation. A second result has been the health and genetic damage suffered by humans living in areas they did not know (and had not been told) were contaminated. Residents of Chelyabinsk, a site that may well be the most radioactive region on Earth, face a contamination level estimated to be 20 times that of Chernobyl (Sommer, 1993). Throughout these irradiated regions, physical and psychological health problems including deformities and mental retardation plague residents at record rates; and in a few especially contaminated areas such as Semipalatinsk (site of 122 above-ground blasts), significantly impaired children described by some Russian scientists as "nuclear mutants" are being born in unprecedented numbers. Researchers have begun to voice fears that sustained exposure to such high doses of radioactivity, coupled with exposure to other widespread forms of pollution, may have altered the genetic code carried by human chromosomes (Dahlburg, 1992).

This nuclear waste threat extends well beyond the territory and the population of the former USSR. During their regime's heyday, Soviet government leaders authorized the dumping of spent nuclear fuel and spent nuclear reactors in the Kara Sea, posing a very real danger of leakage and contamination of international waters (Bogert, 1992). Even after the collapse of the Soviet government, Russian ships continued to dump additional tons of radioactive waste into the Sea of Japan (Knickerbocker, 1993b). Many former Soviet republics that now face enormous radioactive waste disposal problems just do not have the tremendous financial resources needed to solve these problems safely. They have simply resorted to doing nothing at all or to disposing of these wastes as cheaply as possible, regardless of the consequences. In the absence of the hundreds of billions of dollars needed to deal with such massive contamination, the former USSR's nuclear debris could well remain the most enduring legacy of communism for decades to come.

Radioactive wastes may be the most serious environmental problem facing post-Soviet Russia and Eastern

Located in the "black triangle" that encompasses portions of Poland, Slovakia, and Germany, the city of Copsa Mica is almost constantly covered in soot from nearby smelters and factories. As bad as it is, such air pollution may not be the most serious environmental legacy of the now defunct communist regime in Eastern Europe.

Europe, but they are not the only serious threat to those societies' populations. Conventional air and water pollution levels in these countries are among the highest in the world. Some of the region's most important waterways, including the Volga River, the Black Sea, and the Baltic Sea, have become little more than "toxic soup" as a result of heavy sewage and chemical contamination from cities and industries as yet largely unequipped with purification and filtration systems (Green & Bartal, 1992; Pope, 1992). In Poland, water pollution is so severe that 95 percent of all rivers are unsuitable for municipal use, and 42 percent cannot be used even for industrial purposes (Kabala, 1991). One-third of all forests throughout Eastern Europe have been damaged by air pollution, and nearly 80 percent of the forests in the "black triangle," a 700-square-mile region of southern Poland, northern Slovakia, and southeastern Germany, have been destroyed entirely ("Acid Rain from 3 Nations," 1991). Continuously burning oil well flare-offs in Siberia have created acid rains that have ruined more than 1,500 square miles of forest over the past 20 years and may be contributing significantly to global warming and global ozone destruction (Goldberg, 1993). Russia's Kola peninsula, site of two of the world's largest and most antiquated nickel smelters, is so polluted by sulfur dioxide and heavy metals that its neighbor, Norway, has a sightseeing post on the border inviting tourists to "Come see the dirtiest place on the globe" ("Russia's Kola Peninsula," 1994).

Most analysts agree that this hellish ecological situation represents the outcome of decades of deliberate Soviet policy decisions to pursue economic development by investing primarily in resource-intensive, environmentally destructive industries such as coal mining, steelmaking, and chemical manufacturing (Kabala, 1991). The problem was compounded by the Soviet government's mania for secrecy, as well as its feelings of invincibility. The net result was that "natural resources were squandered; investments in efficient, modern technology were lacking, and free discussion on the consequences was not allowed" (Havel in Nagorski, 1993). This combination of short-sightedness and arrogance has created a contemporary situation in which post-Soviet governments of the ravaged lands are stuck with outmoded industrial systems that are economically inefficient and environmentally harmful. Struggling to meet their respective populations' economic needs and demands, and lacking the enormous funds required either for restructuring their economies or for restoring their environments, these newly free nations may find themselves shackled to the practices of their former overlord for the foreseeable future.

When nitrogen and sulfur exhaust gases from fossil fuel combustion are further oxidized in the atmosphere, they convert into nitric acid and sulfuric acid. The result is heavily acidic moisture known as **acid rain** (Cylke, 1993). And when acid rain falls on lakes, forests, and other sensitive ecosystem elements, the long-term result is their ultimate destruction. Acid rain effects have already been noted across the northeastern United States and eastern Canada. In these areas, thousands of acres of forests and hundreds of lakes and ponds have been ravaged by pollutants originating, in many cases, as factory exhausts in the western or midwestern United States. Even larger-scale destruction has been charted across Europe. According to one British study, acid rain is responsible for $500 billion to $1.5 trillion in damages to lakes, forests, crops, buildings, and human health throughout Europe each year ("Acid Rain's High Cost," 1991). Japanese scientists also have calculated that 10 percent of that country's forests will suffer significant damage from acid rain by the end of the decade, in spite of Japan's highly alkaline soil and rapid rain runoff (Huggett, 1991). As fossil fuel use for transportation, industry, and power has steadily increased around the world, the incidence and magnitude of acid rain damage have increased, as well.

CURBING FOSSIL FUEL POLLUTION

To the extent that the automobile is a major source of contemporary air pollution, eliminating air pollution problems will be a formidable challenge. An estimated 600 million automobiles currently travel the roads of the world, most of them in developed countries. The United States alone had 125 million registered automobiles in 1993, a ratio of one car for every two people living in the country (Nauss, 1994a). Each year, U.S. drivers log about 2 trillion miles, traveling back and forth between home, work, school, malls, and the other centers of daily life (Dean, 1994). The geographic separation of many of these facilities, as well as the general absence of efficient and comprehensive public transit systems, have made many members of this society particularly dependent on cars as personal means of transportation (Snell, 1994).

In spite of the demonstrated linkage between automobiles and serious air pollution, car sales are booming across the world, especially in developing countries. Cities such as Mexico City and São Paulo, Brazil, are already suffocating in smog produced by automobile exhaust emissions (Long, 1994), and even the People's Republic of China is being targeted as the next frontier for the world's car manufacturers (Tempest, 1994). If significant strides are to be made in lessening air pollution, the world's passion for the automobile will have to be dampened.

Although the inhabitants of the world are a long way from giving up their cars, some real progress in curbing automobile-exhaust pollution has been made. In the United States, all new vehicles are equipped with catalytic converters and other antipollution devices, and the use of leaded gasoline has been phased out. California, which has the most stringent antipollution laws in the country, has also mandated that 2 percent of all new cars available for sale in the state in 1998 must be electric powered. The net result of these changes has been that, between 1970 and 1991, pollutants from vehicle emissions were reduced over 500 percent nationwide, from 263.3 million metric tons to 48.6 metric tons per year (U.S. Bureau of the Census, 1993a, Table 369). Some other societies that have begun to encounter serious auto smog problems, such as Brazil, are also requiring antipollution devices on personal vehicles, but leaded gas–burning automobiles remain a significant source of air quality problems in developing countries. As much as 80 percent of Mexico City's air pollution has been attributed to the more than 5 million cars that jam that city's roads (Long, 1994; Romero, 1992). In countries such as Japan, where public transportation accounts for about half of all vehicular travel, mass transit systems have helped reduce smog problems substantially. However, public resistance to mass transit, as well as the enormous costs incurred in retrofitting communities with these systems, so far have limited the widespread adoption of this cleaner alternative to the personal automobile (Bleviss & Walzer, 1991).

Significant progress has also been made in reducing air pollution from fossil fuels burned for power generation and industrial purposes. Scrubbers, filters, and other devices required on manufacturing and electric utility plants in the United States reduced air pollution emissions from these sources 30 percent between 1970 and 1991, from 49.9 million metric tons to 35 million metric tons per year (U.S. Bureau of the Census, 1993a, Table 369). Of course, 35 million metric tons is still an immense amount, so a great deal more needs to be done before the nation can begin to breathe easier. The problem is that the pollution controls needed to reduce these emissions further are very expensive. In some cases, these devices account for as much as 45 percent of the costs of new plants (Flavin & Lenssen, 1994). Barring any quantum breakthrough in alternative fuel development, additional air pollution emission reductions will have to await significant cost reductions in antipollution technologies.

OZONE DEPLETION: THE CFC EFFECT

The **ozone layer** is the portion of the stratosphere that protects the planet's surface against excessive ultraviolet (UV) radiation from the sun. Without the shielding effect of ozone molecules, human, animal, and plant life would be seriously—perhaps fatally—injured from UV burning. According to mounting data gathered from around the world by research scientists, the planet's ozone layer has been dangerously weakened as a result of chlorofluorocarbon (CFC) emissions (Lemonick, 1992). Found primarily as coolants in air conditioners and refrigerators and as propellants in aerosol sprayers, CFCs are byproducts of industrialization and modernization that are simultaneously making life more comfortable for some but less possible for many others (Larmer, 1991).

Recognizing the global danger inherent in the deteriorating ozone layer, in 1987, the major nations of the world signed the Montreal Protocol, an international treaty designed to reduce CFCs and other ozone-destroying chemicals 50 percent by the end of 1999. In 1990, stung by news of further ozone losses over Antarctica and other regions, members of the international community signed an agreement to phase out CFCs entirely by the end of the century (Begley, 1991; Stammer, 1992b).

However, some scientists claim that this still may be too long a period to wait, since the destructive effects of these chemicals accumulate and persist over an extended period of time. Evidence of a growing number of animal and plant anomalies, as well as skin cancer cases in humans living in areas located under "ozone holes" (such as the southern tip of Chile), suggests that the health and economic tolls of widespread ozone destruction could be catastrophic (Larmer, 1991; "Naked Planet," 1992). These observers claim that, if such tolls are to be avoided, all production and use of CFCs and similar harmful substances must cease at once. Their concerns were given greater weight by the discovery of significant ozone losses over a wide band of the northern hemisphere, raising the specter of ozone holes opening over many heavily populated urban areas of the developed world (Lemonick, 1992).

But the economic costs of immediately abandoning worldwide CFC use also are enormous, well beyond the financial capacity of developing societies and the newly independent Eastern European countries. For such a plan to work, the United States, Japan, and other affluent nations would have to at least partially subsidize their poorer neighbors' efforts (Elmer-Dewitt, 1992). Barring such economic assistance, it is unlikely that these countries can or will do much in the very near future to eliminate the flow of destructive elements into the world's ozone layer. And according to at least some reports, it may well be the case that successful efforts to halt the erosion of the ozone layer could exacerbate another air pollution–generated environmental problem: global warming brought about by the so-called greenhouse effect (Begley, 1991).

GLOBAL WARMING

According to some scientists, of all the negative consequences of increasing air pollution, the most serious threat to humankind may be that posed by accumulations of CFCs, carbon dioxide, nitrous oxide, and methane gases. These greenhouse gases trap heat reflected from the planet's surface in the atmosphere, resulting in temperature increases and, conceivably, long-term changes in global climate (Cylke, 1993). Even modest increases of 4 to 8 degrees in global temperatures would generate a series of catastrophic effects, including polar ice cap melting, rising sea levels and the consequent destruction of many densely populated areas across the world, frequent droughts, and the extinction of many plant and animal species. Some reports claim that these temperature changes already have begun as a result of the doubling of carbon dioxide levels in the atmosphere since the beginning of the Industrial Revolution. And if, as currently projected, these accumulated gases double again in the next 100 years, the worst-case scenario will become a reality.

Alarmed by these grim predictions, many developed nations in attendance at the 1992 Earth Summit in Rio de Janeiro sought an international treaty that would severely limit future greenhouse emissions, beginning with a reduction to 1990 emission levels by the year 2000. However, the terms of this agreement were modified to meet the objections of the United States, whose representatives argued that existing scientific data concerning global warming do not justify the gargantuan economic costs that would be incurred in meeting these imposed emission levels (Stevens, 1992). A large number of developing countries, including China, refused to sign even this much weaker version of the agreement, claiming that economic development had to remain their number-one priority ("China Won't Put a Curb," 1992).

In point of fact, a growing number of studies have begun to question the validity of the earlier global warming forecasts and their computer-based "doomsday" projections (Balling, 1992). New satellite data show both much smaller temperature increases over the past several decades and much faster dissipation of carbon dioxide gases from the atmosphere than commonly believed, raising important questions about the need for immediate drastic social and economic changes that would affect the lives of millions of individuals worldwide ("New Study Casts Doubt," 1994). Using these new data, more recent greenhouse and global warming models project a more modest world temperature increase and, therefore, less catastrophic environmental and human damage. These forecasts do not entirely dismiss the threat of global warming, inasmuch as the cooler than anticipated observed temperatures may be a result of ozone depletion and the accumulation of sulfate aerosols from coal burning. Both of these phenomena, which are consequences of other forms of air pollution, have the effect of counteracting increased temperature buildups in the atmosphere. But if both ozone-destroying gases and acid rain–producing emissions are eliminated or reduced significantly in the future, the dramatic global warming trends predicted by earlier greenhouse theorists could very well begin (Begley, 1991; Dolan, 1992).

Given the incompleteness of current scientific understanding of climatic forces, the final word on the controversial global warming issue has yet to be written. As one participant in this debate has observed, "We may be overstating the problem. We may be understating the problem. That's what makes it a very difficult situation for government and industry" (Watson in Dolan, 1992). At this point, the best possible conclusion may be that global warming is a problem of some unknown magnitude that people should be aware of and concerned about, a problem that will require some responses of unknown scope and costs.

PROBLEMS OF WASTE DISPOSAL

The same set of factors that have led to problems of increased environmental resource depletion and increased environmental destruction over the past two centuries have created a third set of environmental problems, as well: how to dispose of the various waste materials that are threatening to engulf the world. To the extent that both developed and developing societies extract and process numerous resource materials for later economic or social uses, these actions create waste products that somehow must be disposed of safely. To the extent that the conversion of these raw resources into finished consumer products also creates waste byproducts, these materials likewise must be disposed of. And finally, to the extent that the eventual use of finished products results in additional waste materials, these, too, become part of a disposal problem.

For example, consider the textbook you are now holding in your hands. Although this particular book happens to be printed on recycled paper, at one point in its dim past, it began life as a tree that was felled to make paper. The felling process created waste materials (in the form of leaves, needles, cones, and the like) that had to be disposed of by the paper mill because they were of no use in making pulp. The processing of the wood into pulp and then of the pulp into paper entailed the use of acids and other chemicals that had to be disposed of once they had served their purpose. As the paper was being cut to the final size specified by the publisher, scraps and other trimmings were created, and as the various colored dyes and inks were applied to the paper's surfaces, yet more waste products were generated. If you happened to purchase a shrink-wrapped package of the text and its accompanying study guide, the plastic wrapping had to be disposed of once it had been removed from the brand-new books. Finally, at some point in the future, when your grandchildren reluctantly part with a classic text that gave the family so much enlightenment over the years, the now-faded and worn-out paper will need to find a final resting place.

Multiply this one little example by the number of products made, bought, and used around the world in any given 24-hour period, and you begin to get some idea of the mind-boggling amount of trash confronting the world each day. Modern economies depend on mass production and mass consumption, and those mass production and consumption processes create massive amounts of wastes, as well. Determining how to rid ourselves of these waste materials without doing significant harm to the environment or to ourselves has become a problem of epic and growing proportions.

SOLID WASTES

Solid wastes is a catch-all term that refers to items such as paper, cardboard, glass, metals, plastics, textiles, wood, food, lawn and shrub clippings, and other leftover materials created through residential or business activities. Essentially, solid wastes represent the kinds of "stuff" that end up in the nation's and the world's landfills. As the sheer volume of solid wastes generated in contemporary societies has exploded in recent years, finding a good home for it all has become a much more expensive, difficult, and frustrating experience than ever before. The number of landfill sites deemed suitable enough or safe enough to handle solid waste disposal has failed to keep pace with the increasing millions of tons of solid waste materials produced each year. For example, between 1960 and 1990, municipal solid waste generation in the United States increased from 87.8 million tons to 195.7 million tons per year. In more personal terms, this represented an increase in the amount of waste generated by each member of the population (and there were many more people in the population in 1990 than there were in 1960) from 2.66 pounds to 4.3 pounds each day of the year, not counting scrapped cars (U.S. Bureau of the Census, 1993a, p. 227). Worldwide, about 30 million automobiles are scrapped each year, about 9 million in the United States alone. And even though recycling can salvage about 75 percent of the materials in scrapped autos, each abandoned car results in about 600 pounds of nonrecoverable materials that end up in landfills (Nauss, 1994b).

As dramatic as these figures may be, they constitute only a minor component of the solid waste disposal problem. According to some studies, municipal solid wastes at most make up under 10 percent of total solid waste materials currently generated in the United States and other industrialized societies. A much larger percentage of societal solid wastes consists of concrete, metal, wood, and other building construction and demolition debris (in particular, from industrial sources), and these wastes are growing at startling rates ("Waste and the Environment," 1993). For example, in Japan, industrial solid wastes increased 700 percent between 1985 and 1989, literally filling up many legal disposal sites and creating a serious illegal dumping problem in many parts of the country ("Japan Battles," 1992). In addition, municipal solid wastes figures do not include sewage sludge, a waste product that is also growing at a significant rate and generating its own particular set of disposal problems (K. Schneider, 1991). As we saw in our earlier discussion of water pollution problems, much of this sewage finds its way untreated into the rivers, oceans, and other waterways of the world.

DOWN IN THE DUMPS

In Tokyo, municipal solid wastes find a final resting place in a 100-foot-high, 490-acre island of trash in Tokyo Bay, a burial spot that is expected to close by 1996 (Chung, 1993). Japanese Health and Welfare Ministry estimates claim that the country's industrial and household waste disposal sites will all be completely filled before the end of the century (Sugio, 1991). In the United States, a barge loaded with solid wastes from one Long Island, New York, community cruised the nation's waterways for months, looking for a place to dispose of its cargo, before heading home in defeat. Some of that trash was ultimately shredded, bagged, and sold or given away as souvenirs of the highly publicized event. The United States and many other countries in the developed world appear to be running out of places to store solid waste refuse. But appearances often can be deceiving.

According to an international review and survey of the solid waste disposal problem conducted by *The Economist* in 1993, "the availability of landfill space is more a matter of politics than geology" (p. 5). That is, on a country-by-country basis, there is more than enough suitable and otherwise unused land to handle the present and projected solid waste disposal needs of most modern societies. The problem lies not so much in finding a physically appropriate site for waste disposal but, rather, in gaining public support and government approval to use the site for landfill purposes. The permitting process is both

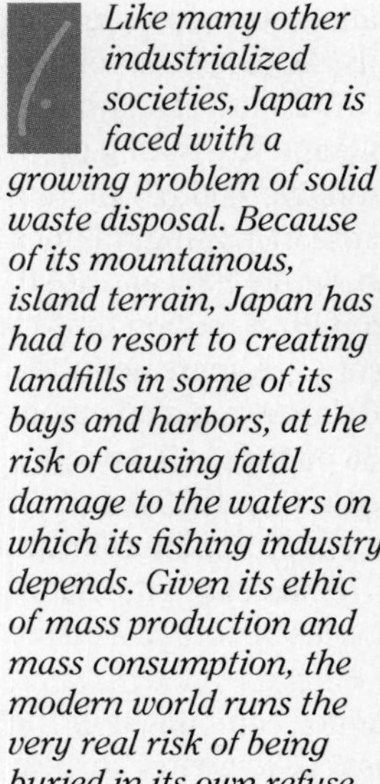

Like many other industrialized societies, Japan is faced with a growing problem of solid waste disposal. Because of its mountainous, island terrain, Japan has had to resort to creating landfills in some of its bays and harbors, at the risk of causing fatal damage to the waters on which its fishing industry depends. Given its ethic of mass production and mass consumption, the modern world runs the very real risk of being buried in its own refuse.

expensive and time consuming, even for waste disposal companies that employ state-of-the-art landfill technologies.

Ironically, a good deal of the current solid waste disposal problem in many developed nations may be a consequence of those societies' active and strong environmental movements. Responding, in many cases, to past situations of improper and unsafe solid wastes disposal, environmental groups have often vigorously opposed any new landfill proposals. Some observers claim that this opposition makes it increasingly unlikely that communities will be able to keep up with their growing waste disposal needs. Consequently, well-intentioned environmentalists may inadvertently be creating a climate that encourages an increase in illegal and unsafe dumping, thus exacerbating what already is a serious problem ("Waste and the Environment," 1993, p. 3).

TOXIC WASTES

According to required toxic release reports filed with the Environmental Protection Agency, in 1990, over 400 million pounds of cancer-producing chemicals and 1.2 billion pounds of chemicals believed to cause birth defects were legally disposed of in the United States (Knickerbocker, 1992b). It is not clear just how much more may have been disposed of otherwise. As of 1992, 1,224 hazardous waste sites across the country had been included on the national priority list for the Superfund cleanup program (U.S. Bureau of the Census, 1993a, p. 228), but that number represents only those toxic waste sites identified as presenting the most immediate and serious dangers among all such problem areas known as of that year. There very well could be many more hazardous waste sites that remain undiscovered. For example, by the end of 1992, officials of the U.S. military, now regarded by some as the country's top toxic polluter, had publicly acknowledged the existence of nearly 11,000 hazardous waste areas at 1,877 military installations around the country (Van Voorst, 1992).

No one seems to know exactly how much hazardous waste must be disposed of in the world each year, but it is undoubtedly a staggering amount. According to one estimate, the two dozen most industrialized nations of the world produce 98 percent of all hazardous wastes and collectively generate about 300 to 400 million tons of hazardous waste materials each year (Fogel, 1993). The United States and other developed societies depend on a sea of toxic chemicals to help fuel their economies, and at times, that sea threatens to wash their populations away. Toxins buried in the earth often work their way into groundwater systems or to the surface, posing serious health risks. Chemicals buried in the oceans eventually escape as their containers corrode, imperiling human and aquatic life along coasts and beaches (Ferrell, 1992). Incinerated hazardous wastes typically release equally hazardous exhausts into the air, endangering local populations (Gascoyne, 1993; Rotella, 1992).

Escalating costs brought about by expensive hazardous waste disposal procedures imposed by environmentally conscious nations have led to the increased exportation of these toxic materials to less costly (and safely distant) disposal sites in the developing world. For example, according to Greenpeace, between 1990 and 1993, five developed countries—the United States, Canada, Germany, Britain, and Australia—shipped 5.4 million tons of toxic waste to Asia alone (Wallace, 1994a). Here, they have added to an already long list of serious environmental and health problems plaguing the members of these poorer societies.

This wholesale use of less developed countries as a convenient dumping ground for the industrialized world's dirty laundry has further widened the growing rift between the more affluent northern nations and the less affluent southern countries, which have begun to take measures to protect themselves from further exploitation. In 1987, only three developing countries banned hazardous waste imports; as of 1994, that number had risen to 103 (Satchell, 1994). With the urging of the Clinton administration, the United States has agreed to end its exportation of some toxic wastes. But Germany, Finland, Japan, Australia, Canada, and Britain so far have resisted all attempts by the international community to impose a complete export ban on these hazardous waste materials (Knickerbocker, 1994b). The world is rapidly running out of places to dump its toxic wastes, but the production of these wastes continues to grow each year, as more and more societies start or continue on the road to industrial development.

RADIOACTIVE WASTE

Of all the different forms of waste that are piling up around the world, the most serious dangers to human life and health are those posed by radioactive waste materials, ranging from spent nuclear power plant fuel to contaminated clothing worn by X-ray technicians or other medical personnel. Given the fact that many of these wastes require thousands of years for radioactivity to decay to the point of being harmless, they constitute what has been described as a "deadly residue of the nuclear age . . . [that] may be our civilization's longest-lasting legacy" (Lenssen, 1991, p. 5).

By 1990, the world's 433 commercial nuclear reactors, source of 95 percent of all global waste radioactivity, had produced an accumulated total of 84,000 tons of used fuel

CONNECTIONS

The individual, societal, and global effects of environmental depletion, destruction, and disposal problems cut across a very wide spectrum. Some of these issues have already been discussed in previous chapters; others will be examined more closely in the chapters that follow.

- In the international societal stratification hierarchy, the poorer countries that make up the developing world often have been forced to bear the brunt of the environmentally harmful practices of developed nations. Now, these countries are being asked to bear the brunt of the costs of environmental conservation (Sugio, 1992). However, as the 1992 Rio de Janeiro Earth Summit made clear, China, India, and other members of the developing world are no longer willing to put the developed world's environmental concerns ahead of their own economic development goals (Stevens, 1992). This growing split between the northern/developed and southern/developing nations could become the basis for future international or global class conflict (Kaplan, 1994).
- In addition to dumping unwanted hazardous wastes on the poorer nations of the world, affluent nations such as the United States also have been accused of dumping these dangerous wastes on their own poorer and less powerful citizens, as well. Critics charge that U.S. racial and ethnic minorities, in particular, have been the victims of "environmental racism" practices that locate hazardous waste pro-

(Lenssen, 1991). Largely stored on site at individual power plants, these wastes had been generated in the absence of any established method of safe disposal. However, many of these plants have reached their on-site storage capacities and now are threatened with early closure if a more permanent disposal arrangement cannot be found. The U.S. federal government, which was supposed to have begun accepting these wastes by 1998, no longer appears able to meet that deadline, leaving the future of many U.S. nuclear power plants up in the air ("Time Running Out," 1994). To further complicate the problem, as nuclear weapons facilities and nuclear weapons themselves have been phased out following the end of the Cold War era, thousands more tons of dangerous radioactive wastes now must be reckoned with, as well (Knickerbocker, 1992a).

According to U.S. Department of Energy estimates, the cost of cleaning up the nation's known radioactive waste sites likely will exceed $200 billion dollars (Levy, 1993). Coming up with these funds, especially at a time when the U.S. economy remains in a prolonged slump, will be a tremendous challenge. Finding an effective and lasting method of safe disposal may well prove to be even more of a challenge.

Increasing concerns about the environmental and human health consequences of past radioactive waste disposal techniques have significantly decreased the range of viable disposal options available at present. International treaties now ban the dumping of nuclear wastes at sea (Knickerbocker, 1993b), and problems of leakage have effectively ruled out underground burial. Attempts to license nuclear waste recycling facilities in Britain and

cessing and landfill facilities in their communities (Boulard, 1993; Morgan, 1993). However, other observers claim that the siting of these potentially dangerous facilities has more to do with lower economic class status than it does with lower racial or ethnic group status (Satchell, 1992).

- Air and water pollution exact a heavy societal and global toll on human lives and human health, thus placing an additional burden on health care systems that in many cases already may be strained to the point of collapse. For example, some researchers claim that toxic air pollution may be responsible for the deaths of more than 30,000 U.S. citizens each year (Cylke, 1993). In Mexico City, as many as 30,000 children may have died in 1990 as a result of that city's incredible air pollution (Romero, 1992).
- Environmental destruction has resulted in the permanent loss of many formerly thriving plant and animal species. The U.S. Fish and Wildlife Service named over 1,000 different flora and fauna throughout the world on its endangered species list and another 207 on its threatened species list in 1992 (U.S. Bureau of the Census, 1993a).
- The economic costs of cleaning up and restoring environments damaged through human actions consume enormous sums of money that otherwise might be directed toward other vital or important goals. For example, the estimated $200 billion that will be required to dispose of hazardous radioactive wastes in the United States could go a long way in alleviating the poverty currently experienced by nearly 37 million members of this society's population, or in providing adequate health care coverage for those 38 million Americans who currently lack any form of health insurance.

elsewhere have met with strong opposition from environmentalists and other concerned groups (MacLeod, 1993). Vitrification, the process of heating radioactive waste materials to create glass, is costly and creates pollution from escaping gases. One new and promising technique involves bioremediation, the use of plants such as alfalfa to extract low-level radioactive materials from large areas of contaminated soil (Levy, 1993). However, this relatively inexpensive and environmentally friendly process is not well suited for dealing with the highly radioactive reactor fuels that constitute the bulk of the nuclear waste problem. Radioactive wastes remain very much a problem in dire need of a solution.

SUMMARY

1. Depletion of water, land, and energy resources; destruction of water and air quality through pollution; and disposal of solid, toxic, and radioactive wastes are three significant environmental problems confronting the contemporary world. These problems have been accelerated by the sheer number of people alive today and the industrialization of many societal economies.
2. Only a very small percentage of the world's water supply is drinkable or otherwise usable freshwater, and that supply has been shrinking rapidly as a result of agricultural, industrial, and residential overuse. A growing number of societies in

Africa and the Middle East are either water scarce or water stressed. Competition for dwindling water supplies could well become a source of future societal and regional conflicts. The most effective strategy for dealing with water shortages would appear to be scaling back water use and making better use of existing supplies.

3 Billions of tons of topsoil are lost around the world each year as a result of desertification. Overgrazing of livestock, deforestation, and unsuitable agricultural practices are three major causes of this massive land and soil depletion problem. Many land-depleting practices in developing countries are a result of the widespread poverty found among the populations of these societies, who harm the land in their quest for survival.

4 Although found in vast quantities, nonrenewable fossil fuels such as oil and coal nonetheless are being rapidly depleted by industrialized and industrializing nations whose economies run on these energy resources. Safety and cost problems have made nuclear energy a much less promising source of power than it appeared to be in past years. Alternative energy sources such as geothermal, wind, and solar power are being developed, but problems with reliability so far have limited their application for commercial use.

5 In much of the developed world, water and air quality have become increasingly fouled by an assortment of nonpoint-source chemical and waste substances from agricultural, industrial, and residential activities. In the developing world, societal goals of economic advancement often have taken priority over concerns about the environment. Environmental destruction and pollution are viewed as a necessary price of economic and social development.

6 Acid rain and the destruction of the earth's protective ozone layer are two documented consequences of the massive burning of fossil fuels and the exhausting of industrial and agricultural chemicals throughout the industrialized world. The so-called greenhouse effect, in which pollutants that trap the sun's reflected heat result in a global warming process, is still a matter of great continuing controversy. As more developing countries complete the industrialization of their economies, it seems likely that these atmospheric problems will grow even faster.

7 The same factors that have spawned problems of environmental depletion and destruction are also largely responsible for growing problems of waste disposal. Municipal and industrial solid wastes are rapidly filling available landfill spaces, and new landfills are not being developed quickly enough to meet many societies' and communities' needs. In some cases, delays in siting new landfills have been the result of concerns about their impacts on local environments.

8 Toxic wastes pose a large and growing problem in most industrialized societies, whose economies depend on widespread use of chemicals and fossil fuels. In many cases, these toxic wastes have been disposed of unsafely and improperly, creating serious health problems. In other cases, developed societies have begun exporting toxic wastes to poorer developing nations. These countries have begun to pass laws banning these hazardous waste materials. This toxic dumping has become another issue polarizing developed northern societies and developing southern societies.

9 Spent nuclear fuels and other radioactive wastes constitute the most serious danger to human life. Some of these materials will take thousands of years to disintegrate to the point of harmlessness, and their safe disposal in the meantime is very problematic and very costly. In particular, the former Soviet Union is a potentially lethal source of radioactive debris not only for its own populations, but for the world at large.

CHAPTER FIVE

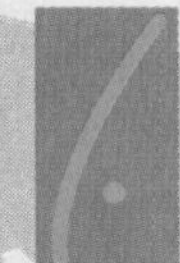

URBAN PROBLEMS
Cities under Siege

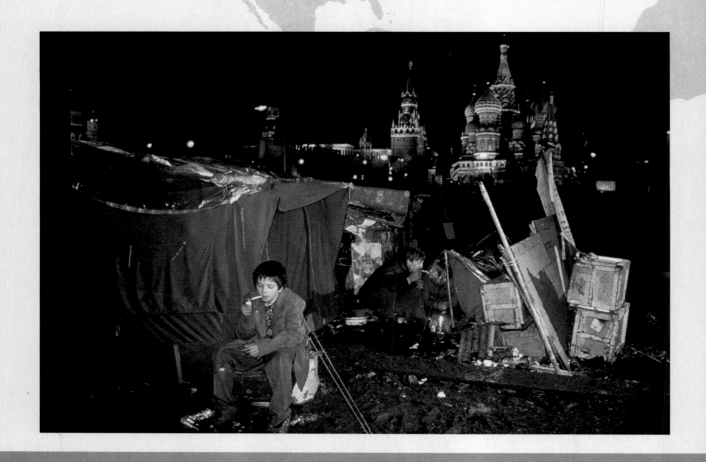

The Taj Mahal Hotel in Bombay is reputed to be one of the 10 best such establishments in the world. A magnificent Victorian structure built at the turn of the century, when India was part of the British empire, it has beautifully decorated, spacious rooms and outstanding food. The staff of immaculately dressed men and women are ever present to take care of any desire a guest might have. During India's long, hot, humid summers, the Taj Mahal's well-to-do clientele relax on the veranda, where they sip exotic drinks and watch the world go by.

Just outside the hotel, a stone's throw from where people are eating gourmet food, is a completely different world. Inhabited by a fragment of the city's homeless population, or "pavement dwellers" as they are called in India, the individuals who live on this end of the socioeconomic spectrum exist on a meager diet. Their annual income is less than the cost of a one- or two-night stay at the Taj.

While the gap between India's "haves" and "have-nots" is startling, even painful to behold, one need not travel halfway around the world to a developing country to see the contrast between the urban rich and poor. A drive of less than 20 or 30 minutes from decaying inner cities to prosperous suburbs in almost any major urban center will reveal the tremendous economic gap that exists in U.S. metropolitan areas.

Cities have always been a microcosm of a society's distribution of wealth. Cities also showcase the achievements of a civilization—the arts, education, medical and technological sophistication, and sports—as well as the moral conscience of its people, revealed through social programs.

Cities in all nations have to contend with issues of crime, drugs, unemployment, poverty, homelessness, and pollution, to name only the most egregious contemporary problems. But particularly in wealthy countries, urban centers are often afflicted with vicious street gangs and the strife (occasionally erupting in riots) that typically comes from cultural and economic conflict between two or more groups in an ethnically and racially diverse nation. These problems also exist in catastrophic proportions in many Third World cities. However, unlike societies in the developed world, the main problem in most developing societies is rapid urban growth (see Figure 5.1). Fueled by unprecedented rural-to-urban migration, the total collapse of one or more of these rapidly growing urban giants might occur in the near future.

While Tokyo in wealthy Japan continues to grow as a result of that nation's prosperity, rapid population increases in Mexico City have occurred by way of grinding poverty. Driven by deteriorating conditions in the countryside both during and after World War II, 6.2 million people streamed into Mexico's capital between 1940 and 1970. Beginning in the late 1970s, Mexicans moving to their country's capital city have been joined by a relatively small but ever-increasing stream of individuals coming from Nicaragua, El Salvador, Guatemala, and Honduras. Most of these Central American immigrants are fleeing war and repression in their homelands. While many end up staying in Mexico City permanently, others live and work there for an undetermined amount of time before embarking on their final destination—the United States (O'Dougherty, 1989).

At current rates of growth, Mexico City's population of approximately 25 to 27 million people will be well over 50 million by the year 2025. Mind-boggling problems associated with pollution, sanitation, sewage disposal, and providing fresh water for so many people prompted one of Mexico's former presidents to state, "If we become careless, Mexico City can become uninhabitable. Catastrophe is not out of the range of possibilities" (in Vasquez, 1983). With limited resources to expend, governments in Mexico and other developing countries have little chance of reducing the size and scope of their

FIGURE 5.1 Urban and Rural Growth Projections to 2025

Between 1950 and 1990, the world's urban population more than tripled to 2,390 million. In the 1990s, the world's urban population will grow at the rate of 10 Paris-sized cities a year. (This chart is based on medium-fertility projection.)

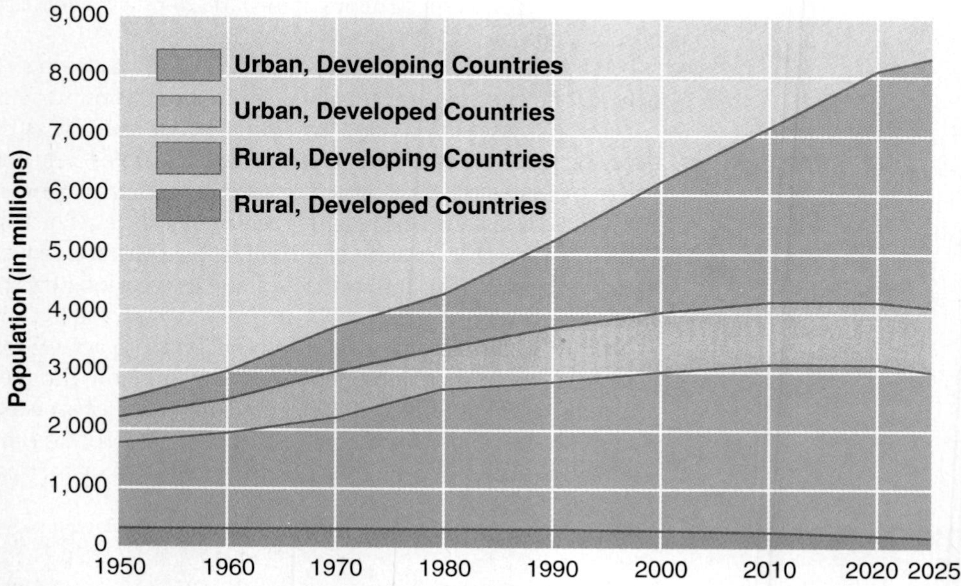

SOURCE: VanPelt in *The Christian Science Monitor* © 1992 TCSPS.

urban problems. The day-to-day suffering of millions of people and the chaos that will inevitably follow in some of these giant cities will be of major proportions.

Centuries ago, a Roman sage noted that "cities are immortal." No doubt he was correct, and cities will endure as long as we as a species survive. The question is, Will they be worth living in?

QUESTIONS TO CONSIDER

1. What is the most severe problem facing the urban United States today?
2. What is the culture-of-poverty position regarding the problem of chronic urban poverty? What is the concentration-effects explanation of William Julius Wilson?
3. How have the suburbs contributed to the nation's urban problems?
4. Why has gang violence increased in so many U.S. cities over the past few years?
5. What are the major explanations for urban riots?
6. What group makes up the fastest-growing segment of the urban homeless population? What are the major causes of homelessness in the United States? Is homelessness a problem in any other developed nations?
7. What are the major characteristics of the *global city?*
8. What are *enterprise zones?* Can these zones help bring about economic recovery in the poorest neighborhoods of the nation's most financially troubled cities?
9. Who are the new immigrants to the United States? Where do they come from? Why did they decide to come to this country?
10. What are the major problems facing cities in the developing world?

THE U.S. URBAN PROBLEM: DYING CITIES, THRIVING SUBURBS

The 1990 census revealed that for the first time in U.S. history, the majority of Americans (approximately 125 million people) lived in metropolitan areas of 1 million or more residents. However, most of these people did not reside in large cities themselves but rather in the surrounding suburbs (Bencivenga, 1992).

In fact, many of these suburban enclaves have grown so large that they are not "sub" anything, having turned into *edge cities* (Garreau in "America's Cities," 1992). The last census showed a continuation of a trend that demographers have noticed in the post–World War II era: While Americans choose to live in large metropolitan areas, they do not want to reside in big cities. People have fled to the suburbs to escape a variety of urban problems, including violent crime, widespread poverty, pollution, dilapidated housing, and the racial and ethnic minorities who inhabit inner-city areas.

STRUCTURAL CHANGE AND THE URBAN UNDERCLASS

In 1991 and again in 1992, more than half of 620 cities in the United States polled by the National League of Cities were spending more money than they were accruing in revenues. Technically, these municipalities were bankrupt. Many of these cities continue to have financial problems in part because a sizeable percentage of their residents are desperately poor. In the past 20 years, the number of inner-city neighborhoods that can be classified as areas of extreme poverty (comprised of 40 percent or more poor people) has significantly increased. Two-thirds of the increase in ghetto poverty during the 1970s occurred in five cities: New York, Chicago, Philadelphia, Detroit, and Newark. New York City alone accounted for 33 percent of the rise in ghetto poverty during this decade (Wilson, 1991–1992).

Big-city poverty has also deepened in recent years. The poorest urban dwellers were further below the poverty line in the 1980s than were their counterparts in the 1960s (Commission on Cities, 1988). Although members of every race and almost any ethnic group can be counted as members of the urban poor, the most destitute inner-city neighborhoods in the Northeast and Midwest are primarily comprised of Blacks and Latinos.

While virtually everyone agrees that poverty is the most debilitating urban problem and that it is related to other big-city maladies, such as violent crime (especially urban gangs), the distribution of drugs, and the rise in single-parent families, no one agrees on the root cause or causes of urban poverty. Of the numerous perspectives offered to account for the origin and rapid escalation in urban poverty over the past 20 to 25 years, the two most frequently cited explanations are the restructuring of the urban economy and the culture of poverty.

First used by anthropologist Oscar Lewis (1961), the **culture of poverty** refers to a self-perpetuating and self-defeating world view among the poor that helps insure that they will remain in economic deprivation from generation to generation. Children are socialized into a set of values and attitudes that makes it difficult for them to plan for the future, sacrifice immediate gratifications in favor of future ones (Banfield, 1970), and accept the discipline necessary to acquire and spend money. This world view is linked to low motivation in school and, therefore, inadequate preparation for employment (Leacock, 1971).

Living in a world where the prospects of employment are often scant and entry-level jobs are low paying and dull, many teenagers opt for the more exhilarating life of the ghetto streets. Here they hang out, brag about their real and imaginary experiences, and plan and attend parties. These young people often choose to join groups or more structured gangs that provide support, protection, friendship, and excitement (Peterson, 1991–1992). One observer referred to this emphasis on male toughness, sexual activity, and liquor consumption as a "ghetto specific complex" (Hannerz in Greenstone, 1991). An often neglected consequence of urban gangs is that these groups weaken the bond between individuals and society and, in so doing, perpetuate the culture of poverty.

Although William Julius Wilson rejects the politically conservative culture-of-poverty explanation, he does not completely rule out cultural forces in his interpretation of chronic urban poverty. He notes that "a jobless family in such a neighborhood is influenced by the behavior, beliefs, orientations, and social perceptions of other disadvantaged families, disproportionately concentrated in the neighborhood" (1991–1992, p. 651). He refers to this process as **concentration effects**—"the effects of living in an overwhelmingly impoverished neighborhood." In other words, these individuals are doubly disadvantaged: They have "weak labor force attachments" (limited job opportunities), and they are socially isolated in communities with other extremely poor, very often thoroughly disadvantaged people (p. 651).

Despite the cultural component of poverty, Wilson (1987, 1991–1992, 1992) believes that a stronger explanatory factor has been the post–World War II restructuring of the urban economy that significantly reduced the number of manufacturing jobs. For example, in the 1940s, two out of every three workers in Cleveland had a job in manufacturing, while only one of three is similarly employed today. In Pittsburgh, a city once noted for its steel industry, no more than one of five workers makes a living in factories and mills (Frieden, 1989).

In the past 30 to 40 years, manufacturing has given way to a more service-oriented economy. While many factories closed, others made cost-cutting moves out of the cities to suburbs and/or Third World countries that offered cheap labor. Not only did cities suffer from the loss of jobs, but the factories also took with them a large percentage of the tax base that had always supported city services and social programs. Not surprisingly, northeastern and midwestern urban areas were hit hardest by this economic transformation. The 1980s were particularly tough on cities. For example, New York City lost half its production jobs between 1969 and 1987, and during that same approximate time period, the number of *Fortune* 500 firms (many of them associated with the manufacturing sector) headquartered in that city declined from 128 to 53 (Sassen, 1991).

While New York was losing hundreds of thousands of high-paying manufacturing positions, a new class of highly educated, highly paid professionals was being created—the "brains." At the same time, a growing labor force comprised of delivery people, cleaning crews, file clerks, and others who provide routine, everyday services for these professionals was working in low-paying, often temporary dead-end jobs. In addition, there was a proliferation of stores and services that catered to the tastes and wealth of the new urban elite. Businesses such as luxury hotels, gourmet shops, boutiques, and special cleaners, as well as exotic services like French hand cleaners, employed thousands of people at low wages (Sassen, 1991).

What remains of the manufacturing sector has been significantly downsized as a result of the disappearance of many unionized factories and the growth of sweatshops in the textile and electronics industries. Newly arrived immigrants (both legal and illegal) work under poor conditions (excessive heat and noise, unsafe equipment) for miniscule salaries and few if any benefits. The loss of so many middle-class production jobs has contributed to the economic woes of the poorest half of the labor force in another way. Urban manufacturing was important not only for the number of jobs created directly by companies but for the number of jobs created indirectly, as well—the so-called *multiplier effect.* People who earn more money than just enough to get by from week to week strengthen the housing market and, with the higher taxes they pay, the building of roads, schools, and other local and state projects that employ thousands of people. It was precisely these working- and middle-class individuals who comprised, in large part, the suburbanization process that was such a vital component of life in the post–World War II United States (Sassen, 1991).

During the period when plant closings and relocations were an everyday occurrence, the Reagan and Bush administrations cut federal funds to the cities by 70 percent (Kaslow, 1992). At a time when social services, job retraining programs, and education in general were needed most, less and less money was available. Innovations in technology as well as job cutbacks during years of recession have also taken their toll on workers who managed to keep their jobs in the manufacturing sector. Wages were reduced in remaining jobs, and a less organized and unionized labor movement has been almost totally powerless to slow down, much less halt, the erosion of production workers' salaries and benefits. Whereas cities have been centers of upward of mobility for tens of millions of poor Americans over the years, rags-to-riches success stories are now fewer and farther in between. Economist John Kenneth Galbraith (1991) remarks that the urban poor are now "frozen" in their underclass status.

Bernard Frieden (1989) offers three reasons why the urban underclass has not taken advantage of opportunities in the service sector:

1. Living among unemployed family members and friends, they lack a network of informal contacts in the workplace who can notify them about job openings. This explanation fits with Wilson's notion of social isolation and concentration effects.

2. Many companies have discovered that a large number of inner-city residents do not have reading and math skills. In 1987, the New York Telephone Company found that only 16 percent of applicants could pass entry-level job examinations. This lack of marketable skills could also be related to the concentration effects of poor schools in poverty-stricken neighborhoods.

3. An undetermined number of inner-city residents are not looking for work at all. A study by Wilson and his colleagues (in Whitman, 1991) discovered that Black respondents frequently told interviewers that some of their friends were lazy and didn't want to work hard. However, another study in Chicago found that so-called shiftless individuals (people who did not want to work and preferred other forms of support, even if that support was inadequate) were far from the majority; to the contrary, willingness to work was the norm among inner-city residents (Tienda & Steir, 1991).

THE SUBURBS' CONTRIBUTION TO URBAN WOES

The year 1980 was a demographic milestone of sorts in the United States, as the number of people living in suburbs topped the 100 million mark, making it the world's first suburban nation (Henderson, 1987). In that year, approximately 42 percent of the population lived in suburbs, whereas only 25 percent resided in the cities (Fava, 1991). Unfortunately, much of this growth has come at the expense of big cities. As we have seen, the corporate sector has contributed to this growth by moving its factories and headquarters to the suburbs. However, the federal government has also fueled this growth by abandoning the cities financially.

Transportation has always been a key component in the suburbanization process. Its importance was seen as early as the nineteenth century, when ferry boats first carried workers back and forth from their places of employment on Manhattan Island to the then-fashionable suburban community of Brooklyn (Jackson, 1985). Since factories, offices, and shops were located in cities (especially the central downtown areas), suburbs could not exist without regular, reliable commuter systems linking them to the cities. In the 1850s, ferries left Manhattan for Jersey City every 15 minutes. Commuter trains and the expansion of railroads in general gave a tremendous boost to the suburbanization process, with Chicago boasting almost 100 suburbs by the 1870s (Jackson, 1985).

If public transportation allowed people to trickle out of cities, the mass production of affordable automobiles in the years following World War I opened the flood gates. In 1915, there were less than two-and-one-half million cars registered in the United States. By 1945, that number had increased to almost 26 million, and in 1989, there were just under 144 million cars in this country, more than one for every two people. The concomitant proliferation of trucks meant that factories no longer had to be located near waterways and railroads, freeing industries to relocate, expand, or commence operation in the suburbs. However, cars and trucks needed roads, and roads were and still are built by state and federal tax dollars. This means that urban taxpayers have helped finance locally constructed roads as well as the post–World War II interstate highway system that has encouraged the middle class to abandon the cities and the factories and corporate headquarters to relocate to the suburbs. And while it can be argued that everybody benefits from increasing the network of roads, it is also true that some people (suburban residents) benefit more than others.

Suburbs also benefited directly and indirectly by a variety of government subsidies. The Home Owners Loan Corporation (HOLC), signed into law by President Roosevelt in 1933, provided millions of dollars for new home buyers. The Federal Housing Administration of 1933, supplemented by the GI bill of 1944, helped make the dream of home ownership possible for civilians and 16 million veterans in the post–World War II era (Jackson, 1985). In addition to providing money for homes (often at reduced interest rates), the federal government still permits interest payments on these loans to be deducted from declared income for tax purposes. This $50 *billion* annual subsidy flows overwhelmingly to suburban residents and comes at the expense of urban dwellers, who saw federal aid to cities decline from $47.2 billion in 1980 to $21.7 billion in 1990.

Finally, once suburbs incorporate and become politically and economically independent of an adjacent big city, they can, as the saying goes, "have their cake and eat it, too." Suburbanites who work and play in a city use that city's resources (roads, parks, baseball and football stadiums, fire and police protection, etc.) without paying any income taxes to support these services. These same suburbanites also have the luxury of good schools and recreational facilities in their towns, strong tax bases, and few social/economic programs to support (homeless population, AIDS patients, the unemployed).

However, signs that the isolation of suburbs is backfiring are already evident. Increased air and water pollution means that even the most prosperous suburbanites have witnessed their quality of life reduced by environmental problems in metropolitan areas. Violent crime, drug use, and gang activity are increasing in many suburban neighborhoods. A social service worker on the outskirts of Minneapolis stated, "The first-ring suburbs are starting to reflect what we saw in inner cities 10 to 20 years ago" (in Bonfante & Painton, 1992, p. 33).

Individuals in the wealthiest suburban communities may be able to keep one step ahead of encroaching urban problems, but the vast majority of people who live adjacent to big cities do not have the finances to pick up and leave. If racial and ethnic prejudices on the part of many Whites have not eroded in the years since they left the cities, there will be tension and inevitably some degree of violence in the suburbs. Many heretofore racially homogeneous suburban neighborhoods (a product of "White flight" and oftentimes housing discrimination) are being integrated, as college-educated Blacks, Latinos, and Asians leave the cities.

Additionally, an increasing number of suburbs are facing problems rooted in the age structure of their inhabitants. The optimistic newlyweds who came to the suburbs 40 years ago are now senior citizens who need health care, home maintenance, Meals on Wheels, and other programs. These individuals may demand that they be taken care of, and some will vote against bond measures that would finance local schools and recreational services.

URBAN GANGS AND COLLECTIVE VIOLENCE

Street crimes such as burglary, robbery, and aggravated assault constitute a major problem in the urban United States. The economic, physical, and psychological costs of these crimes to individuals who reside in cities, and even more for people living in inner cities, are very high. Especially debilitating to the social fabric and economic well-being of an urban community is ongoing gang activity that creates a constant climate of fear for the inner-city residents, in particular. In a matter of two or three days, urban riots can all but wipe out the economic resources of a poor neighborhood, making a difficult situation significantly worse. Local businessowners who have seen their shops and restaurants go up

in flames may not have the funds to rebuild, while outside investors will be even more reluctant to put money in neighborhoods that now resemble war zones.

STREET GANGS

Youth gangs have been part of the urban landscape of the United States for most of the twentieth century (Vigil & Long, 1990). As cities on the East Coast swelled with European immigrants between 1900 and 1930, teenagers who shared a common cultural heritage socialized with each other, some engaging in criminal activity. The combination of greater economic opportunity and more young people along the eastern seaboard explains why the growth of gangs has been more rapid in this region than in the Midwest and South (Taylor, 1990).

The other area of the nation with a long history of gang activity is California, especially the cities of Los Angeles and San Francisco. Chicano (barrio) neighborhood gangs in southern California are among the "longest-lived gangs in America," with some maintaining a continuous presence in Los Angeles barrios for more than 50 years (Vigil & Long, 1990). An especially heterogeneous city with a growing immigrant population (both legal and illegal), Los Angeles is home to gangs comprised of White, Black, Mexican, Vietnamese, Chinese, Filipino, Korean, Samoan, Jamaican, and Guatemalan youths, among others (Vigil, 1988).

During the latter half of the 1980s, gang violence increased dramatically in numerous American cities. In Los Angeles, for example, gang-related homicides increased from 271 in 1985 to over 700 in 1991 (Katz, 1991). Many of the victims were innocent bystanders, gunned down by stray bullets in drive-by shootings. Some gangs, like the Jamaican posses, have a reputation for being even more violent than the Mafia (Morganthal, 1988). Speaking of the blood being spilled in urban America, Louis Sullivan, Secretary of the Department of Health and Human Services, stated, "During every 100 hours on our city streets we lose more young men than were killed in 100 hours of ground war in the Persian Gulf" (in Witkin, 1991, p. 27).

Gang violence has also become a serious problem in Canada. Officials in Toronto report that roaming bands of young males engage in "swarmings"—mass attacks on teenage or adult victims and rapid-fire strikes on stores. Some businesses have lost up to $80,000 worth of merchandise in two minutes (Kiahla, 1989).

The increase in gang violence over the past few years can be attributed to at least five factors:

1. Many cities have recorded dramatic increases in gang populations and activities. For example, the Los Angeles County gang population is estimated to have increased from approximately 50,000 to 100,000 in a six-year period ending in 1991 (Katz, 1991).

2. Whereas some gangs fight over territory ("turf") for bragging rights, others fight ruthlessly to increase the size of their sales territory (Morganthal, 1988). Carl S. Taylor (1990), who has done extensive research on gangs, argues that just as organized crime flourished by quenching the nation's thirst for illegal alcohol during Prohibition (1919 to 1933), some street gangs have grown rich and powerful by partially satisfying the demand for illicit drugs in the United States. Through intimidation and violence, the most powerful gangs have greatly expanded their area of operations. Some Los Angeles drug-dealing gangs are reported to be active in 32 states and over 100 cities. Miami-based gangs have established cocaine-selling operations in Atlanta and Savannah; Chicago gangs in the drug business have moved into a number of other midwestern cities.

These young Cambodian American gang members use hand signs to express their group identity (name and location). Gang-related violence is especially problematic in large U.S. cities, where gangs are typically comprised of individuals of the same race or ethnicity.

3. Established Chicano gangs in Los Angeles are fighting rival groups made up of newly arrived immigrants from Central America (Katz, 1991).
4. Territorial disputes between rival gangs are likely to produce fatalities because of the availability of semiautomatic and automatic weapons. Gangs, it has been noted, are oftentimes better armed than local police.
5. From a psychological perspective, "gangbanging" (fighting) may be a form of suicide on the part of individuals raised in poverty, surrounded by various forms of crime and deviance and with little if any hope for the future. A pastor who has buried 15 youths killed in gang violence stated, "I have never heard so much despondent talk as I do now . . . , kids saying they want to die" (in Katz, 1991).

There are at least two explanations for why someone would enter the dangerous, often deadly world of gangs. M. Sanchez-Jankowski (in Horowitz, 1990) argues that joining a gang is the end result of a rational decision-making process. Gangs offer delinquents more parties, more sex, and the opportunity for greater income (sometimes as high as six figures) than any other available alternative. Gangs that promise sufficient incentives and deliver on those promises will survive (sometimes for generations); others will simply collapse. James Diego Vigil (in Horowitz, 1990) thinks that individuals are pushed into gangs as a result of poverty and their minority status. Although most ghetto residents are subject to one or more stressors (economic, social, cultural, and psychological), some people have difficulty in all these areas. These individuals are prime candidates for gang membership (Horowitz, 1990).

Even relatively peaceful, nonviolent Japan is having trouble with gangs. Members of *bosozoku* ("violent running tribes") are made up of young men and women from age 16 to the mid-20s who refuse to live in accord with the rules of a conforming, disciplined society. With names like "Black Emperor," "Killer Alliance," and "Death Lover," these gangs have been increasing over the past few years. Gang members who drink, fight, and roar around the city streets on big, unmuffled motorcycles travel in packs of up to 150 people, annoying, intimidating, and beating up passersby. Capable of explosive fits of violence, *bosozuku* beat a prominent journalist to death in front of his wife and dozens of witnesses after the man chastised them for making too much noise (Yates, 1990).

In 1989, Japanese police received approximately 115,000 calls for assistance from people who were threatened or attacked by *bosozuku,* a 34 percent increase over the previous year. A report by the National Research Institute of Police Science (*Mainichi Daily News* in Adler et al., 1991) concludes that this gang activity is rooted in a number of societal problems, including education, family relations, living space, and dissatisfaction with school and employment. A Tokyo psychologist views the proliferation of *bosozuku* as a manifestation of his country's strict rules of conduct. "I think *bosozuku* are a direct result of Japan's failure to allow young people to express themselves openly and honestly" (in Yates, 1990).

During the 12-year civil war in the Central American nation of El Salvador (in the 1970s and 1980s), approximately 20 percent of the population (about 1 million people) left that country and settled in the United States, particularly in Washington, D.C., and southern California. When the war ended, many Salvadorans returned to their homeland by choice, whereas others were deported as a result of criminal convictions in this country (Wilkinson, 1994b). Among those returning to El Salvador were young gang members from Los Angeles, many of whom had spent most of their lives in the United States and spoke little Spanish. These Americanized youths brought their gang affiliations and violent behavior with them. Authorities in the capital city of San Salvador report that more than 230 gangs, comprised in part of thousands of former L.A. gang members, are responsible for a significant upsurge in crime in that city (Wilkinson, 1994b).

Widespread poverty in a war-torn nation such as El Salvador, coupled with an inadequate criminal justice system, make it likely that gang-related crime will be a problem in the city of San Salvador for years to come. These streams and counterstreams of migrants turned gang members are a telling example of how civil war can have significant long-range consequences, both nationally and internationally.

URBAN RIOTS

Riots are relatively large-scale, spontaneous outbreaks of violence and destruction engaged in by a fairly sizeable group of people (Goode, 1992). While riots are infrequent, they are hardly unknown in U.S. history. From pre–Revolutionary War times to the present, colonists and later American citizens have occasionally taken to the streets in angry bouts of looting, arson, assault, and murder. Prior to independence and the birth of the republic in 1776, indignant colonists engaged in demonstrations that turned into riots over harsh and unfair tax laws. With the first American urban explosion between 1820 and 1860, newly arrived Roman Catholic immigrants who settled in eastern cities were often attacked by gangs determined to keep the country free of foreign influence.

With the passage of the Union Enrollment Act (1863) during the Civil War, White males between 20 and 45 were liable for military service in the Union Army unless they could find an able-bodied substitute or pay the government the sizeable sum of $300. Rioting erupted in New York City as working-class Whites vented their frustration and anger on the area's Black residents. By the time federal troops restored order three days later, 70 people were dead and another 1,700 wounded.

Conflicts between labor and management have a long, violent history in the United States, as workers have demanded the right to unionize and bargain collectively and management has steadfastly refused to take these demands into consideration. During the so-called Great Strike of 1877, violent labor disputes broke out in cities across the country, with a considerable loss of life and property. Rioters in Pittsburgh destroyed 39 buildings, 104 locomotives, and 500 freight cars (Lewis, 1991; Wade, 1972).

In terms of the number of casualties, loss of life, and destruction of property, race riots have been the costliest and most painful incidents of collective violence in the United States. As far back as the eighteenth century, mobs of Whites invaded Black neighborhoods in northern cities, beating up and sometimes killing people while plundering and robbing their homes. During the "Red Summer" of 1919, race riots broke out in Chicago and other northern cities because working-class Italians, Poles, and Irish, among others, resented the influx and economic inroads of Blacks from the South (Howard, 1974, p. 22).

Riots erupted in Black neighborhoods in numerous cities during the summer of 1964, and over 160 disturbances were reported in 1967. After the assassination of Martin Luther King, Jr., in 1968, there was collective violence in over 100 United States communities (Caplan & Paige, 1968). In 1992, after four police officers were acquitted of beating Rodney King in Simi Valley, California, three days of rioting in Los Angeles left 58 people dead and 226 critically wounded. Approximately 3,700 fires were started, and property damage was just under $800 million ("Death and Destruction Spread," 1992; Methvin, 1992).

The pattern of collective violence that occurred during the 1960s and afterward was significantly different from almost every riot in which a significant number of Blacks were involved in previous years on at least two counts. First, whereas Blacks had previously been attacked by Whites (occasionally Blacks fought back) (Howard, 1974), of late Blacks sometimes have taken a very aggressive posture at an early stage of the hostilities. Second, race riots occurred when Whites invaded Black neighborhoods, attacked residents, destroyed property, and then left. In more recent years, most people in the area of the disturbance (rioters, spectators, and victims) have been residents of the community where the riot took place.

CAUSES OF URBAN RIOTS

Documenting the number and scope of urban riots is a rather straightforward task; however, explaining why these episodes of collective violence transpire is a much more difficult assignment. There are three primary explanations for these events (Caplan & Paige, 1968). According to the **riffraff theory**, rioters are the "dregs of society," "the criminal element" (Goode, 1992, p. 111), a group of irresponsible, emotionally disturbed individuals who go crazy, attack people, destroy property, and steal anything they can get their hands on.

The **frustration-aggression theory** holds that frustrations caused by low social, economic, and political status in society (Berkowitz, 1968) lead poor, inner-city residents to explode periodically in a deadly, destructive rampage of collective violence. A variant of the frustration-aggression perspective is the *relative deprivation theory*. Relative deprivation is a state of mind that exists when there is a gap between what people believe they deserve (for example, to live in safe neighborhoods, with good schools and jobs) and what they think their chances are of attaining these things (Gurr, 1968). If people are poor but do not expect much, they are likely to be content. However, if individuals are poor but believe they deserve an opportunity to be as successful as other members of society, they will eventually grow resentful and may turn to violence.

In a third, somewhat related explanation, race riots are the result of the build-up of anger resulting from **blocked opportunity**. Living in a White-dominated society, Blacks

have had limited economic success because of policies of systematic discrimination leveled against them. Last to be hired, first to be fired, even well-educated Blacks may find that many doors are closed to them because of the color of their skin.

Interviewing 773 residents of Detroit and Newark in the aftermath of the 1967 riots in those cities, Caplan and Paine (1968) attempted to test the aforementioned explanations of urban riots. The riffraff theory had no empirical support. "The rioters are not the poorest of the poor. They are not the hard-core unemployed. There is no evidence that they have serious personality disturbances or are deviant in their social behavior" (p. 19). The major difference between rioters and nonrioters was that rioters were better educated. While the relative deprivation perspective also failed to explain why some inner-city people engaged in collective violence, the data supported the blocked opportunity theory. As long as race and not ability (or lack of ability) is perceived as a fundamental determinant of economic success, young people who are especially angered by discriminatory hiring and firing practices will be a powderkeg of potential violence.

The blocked opportunity perspective as well as the relative deprivation thesis have serious shortcomings. If the opportunity for upward mobility is limited for Blacks (especially young Blacks) in urban areas across the United States, why doesn't rioting occur in all these cities? And why are riots in Black neighborhoods such rare events? Why don't they occur much more often? It appears that while relative deprivation and lack of opportunity may be *necessary* conditions for these types of disturbances, in and of themselves, they are not *sufficient* conditions. That is, some factor or factors in addition to lack of opportunity and feeling of deprivation must also be present for riots of this type to occur.

One researcher found that rather than living conditions or the economic well-being of inner-city Blacks, the variable that best predicted whether an urban area in the late 1960s would experience a riot was the size of its Black community (Spilerman, 1976). If an urban Black population reached a large enough proportion of the total population, a

The frequency of riots in U.S. cities may escalate because urban dwellers have become exceedingly polarized. One class is comprised of relatively affluent residents, while the other is made up of a growing number of poor people who have little chance of achieving economic prosperity.

riot was likely to occur. With a growing number and percentage of Black residents, many American cities have reached, or will reach, that point where they are at greater risk of having a riot triggered by an incident (such as the Rodney King verdict) that enrages the minority community.

In his research on race riots of the 1960s, Spilerman (p. 790) concluded that television conveyed "the intensity and emotion" of the disturbance and was an "essential mechanism for riot contagion." Black television viewers could see and identify with how Black rioters in another city were dealing with the same discriminatory practices and poor living conditions that they experience. In short, by continuous coverage of the disturbances, television provided rioters role models and helped fuel the rage that turned into riots in a significant number of U.S. cities.

Finally, sociologist Erich Goode (1992) reminds us that not all participants in a riot are similarly motivated. A "most common motive" (p. 112), such as political protest, may exist among rioters in a particular disturbance, but for other rioters, the incentive could be personal gain (looting), settling old scores (burning a house), or enhancing the tough-guy image of gang members (beatings). Some individuals may be simultaneously motivated by a number of factors, or a person's reasons for engaging in collective violence may change in riots that last for several days.

RIOTS IN DEVELOPING NATIONS

In poor, desperately overcrowded Third World cities, where too many people compete for too few jobs and affordable places to live, urban riots are relatively common and typically deadly events. This is especially true in heterogeneous nations, where poverty-stricken urban residents are also divided by race or ethnicity, language, religion, and, in the case of India, caste. Over the past 10 to 15 years, there have been hundreds of riots—many of them large-scale confrontations—between Indian Hindus and Muslims. During the summer of 1980, in the northern city of Mordabad, a rumor rapidly spread through the Muslim community that local (Hindu) police had permitted a defiling pig to enter a mosque. Enraged Muslims began shooting at police, who did not hesitate to return the fire. Hindus then joined in the battle, which eventually spread to 18 other cities. A few days later, when pieces of pork were found in a mosque in Allahabad, the army had to be called in to prevent the ensuing fracas from turning into a minor war. By the time the fighting was over, 150 people were dead and thousands more injured (Bryjak, 1984). In the spring of 1984, fighting between Hindus and Muslims claimed 230 lives. Twenty-seven people trapped in their homes during the fighting burned to death. With a core of fanatics in both the Hindu and Muslims camps only too willing to engage in violence at the slightest provocation from the other side, the numbers of urban riots and ensuing casualties are sure to increase in the coming years.

URBAN HOMELESSNESS

With the exception of suffering some long-term debilitating injury or illness, probably the worst thing that can happen to someone in U.S. society is to find himself or herself with little if any money and no place to live. The often devastating psychological trauma of trying to survive in the streets can destroy people's spirit and ability to function to the point that they never fully recover. *Homelessness* has become a much-discussed social problem over the past 15 years, a highly visible problem that exists to some extent in virtually every American city with a population of more than 100,000 people.

WHO ARE THE HOMELESS?

While homeless individuals share a common status of living without benefit of private shelter, they are a diverse group of people (see Figure 5.2). A brief overview of the homeless population in the United States will give us some insight to the causes and possible solutions to this problem (Marin, 1988).

- Veterans, mostly from the Vietnam War, account for as many as 50 percent of the homeless in some cities. An undetermined number of these individuals are afflicted with posttraumatic stress disorder (see Chapter Two).

FIGURE 5.2 Profile of U.S. Homeless

The majority of people who are homeless in the United States are men. A disproportionate number of individuals who live on the streets are from minority groups, especially African Americans.

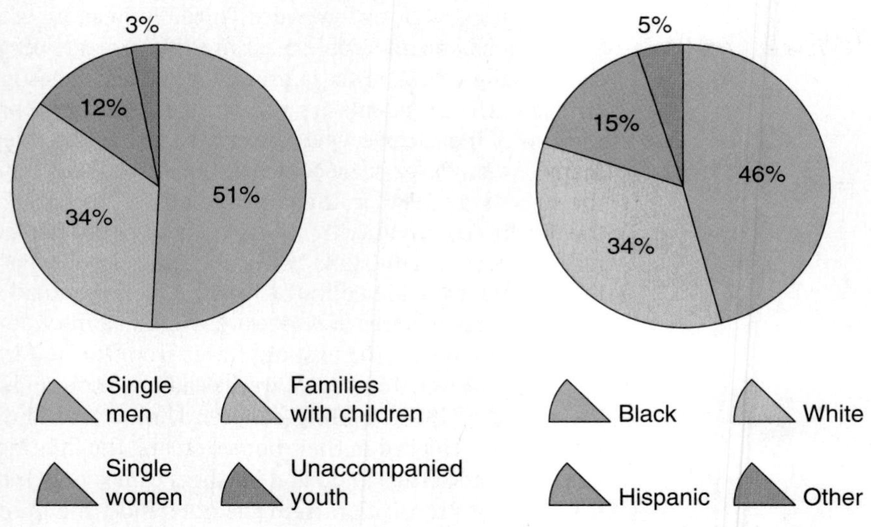

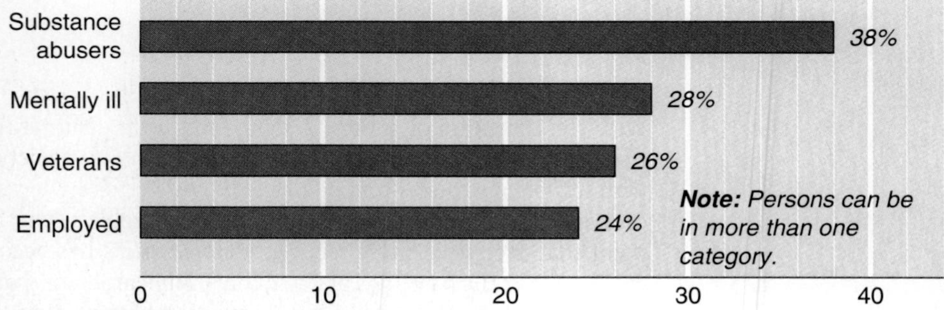

SOURCE: Reprinted by permission: Tribune Media Services.

- Individuals who are physically disabled, chronically ill, and mentally ill make up a large portion of the homeless population. As a result of deinstitutionalization policies in the 1960s and 1970s, thousands of people who are mentally ill ended up in the streets. Up to 30 percent of the homeless population suffers severe mental problems, especially schizophrenia and manic depression (Toufexis, 1990).
- Both ends of the age spectrum are represented among the homeless. The elderly poor on fixed incomes lack money for even a minimal level of subsistence—food, clothing, and shelter. Runaway children, many escaping abusive families, often take up lives of prostitution and hustling on the streets.
- A survey of 13 major cities discovered that the HIV virus had infected the homeless at rates up to 40 times the national average. In the skid row section of Los Angeles, 10 percent of the homeless population had AIDS and another 20 percent were HIV positive (Stoner, 1991).
- The fastest-growing segment of the homeless population, single-parent (mothers) families, comprise approximately 34 percent of those without permanent shelter. Many homeless women have been abused by their husbands and are not capable of supporting themselves and their children. One study found that 89 percent of homeless mothers had been victims of sexual and physical abuse at some point in their lives, most when they were children (Bassuk, 1991). Street life can be especially difficult for women, who not only have to worry about surviving from day to day but also must protect themselves from violent crimes, especially rape.
- An estimated 10 to 30 percent of homeless mothers abuse alcohol or drugs such as cocaine and "crack" cocaine. While drug abuse led to homelessness for some of these women, for others, the habitual use of alcohol and drugs may be the result of having no permanent place to live, or it may be the outcome of other problems, such as being abused by husbands and boyfriends.
- Legal and illegal immigrants are often not counted as part of the homeless population because of their immigrant status; nonetheless, they are on the streets with other homeless people.

The number of homeless people in the United States is unknown, with rough estimates ranging from 250,000 (Rossi, in Ellickson, 1990) to 3 *million* (National Coalition for the Homeless, in "Homeless Women," 1992). Although there is considerable disagreement among scholars and government officials regarding the scope of this phenomenon, virtually everyone believes the number of people living on the streets is increasing.

CAUSES OF HOMELESSNESS

As with so many other social issues and problems, explanations for the root causes of homelessness in the United States fall along a liberal-conservative continuum. Conservatives have taken two approaches in this controversy. They either deny a problem exists or argue that homelessness is the result of individual shortcomings and personal pathologies (Tucker, 1991). As one observer put it, street people are viewed as either "lazy" or "crazy" (Raskin, 1992). This explanation ignores children, elderly people, people with disabilities, abused women, and others who certainly are not without shelter because they are lazy or incompetent.

From the liberal point of view, the majority of homeless people are working- and middle-class individuals who have fallen off "the ladder of opportunity" (Raskin, 1992) or were knocked down by economic policies of the Reagan/Bush era that favored the wealthy at the expense of the poor. From this perspective, conservatives only add insult to injury when they state, as President Reagan did, "Some of those people are there, you might say, by their own choice" (in Bassuk, 1991).

William Tucker (1991) argues that neither the conservative nor the liberal position stands up very well to close inspection. Not surprisingly, he notes, rates of homelessness that often vary considerably from city to city are primarily a function of local housing policies. Toward their real goal of slowing population growth and hindering or stopping development, many cities adopted strict rent control laws in the name of keeping monthly payments low for their poorer citizens. However, these ordinances worked to the detriment of low-income people by discouraging profit-minded developers from constructing new apartment buildings. Vacancy rates declined, apartments became much harder to find, and some people ended up on the streets.

In addition, **gentrification**—the return of middle- and upper-class people to deteriorating inner-city neighborhoods—means that old, dilapidated buildings that once provided shelter for many of the poorest residents of the city have been torn down. These structures have been leveled to make way for high-priced condominiums as well as shops and boutiques that cater to upscale clients. Inexpensive, single-room-occupancy (SRO) hotels that were found in the downtown areas of large cities have also fallen victim to urban renewal and "clean up downtown" movements (p. 36). Of the 10,000 cheap hotel rooms (sometimes as low as $2 a night) in Chicago in 1963, only 2,000 remain (Tucker, 1991).

According to Tucker, homelessness is primarily the result of housing regulations at local levels. This problem, therefore, can only be rectified by city governments. While most residents will tolerate higher-priced housing (the value of their homes also increases), they are not very anxious to see an expansion of low-income housing, nor do they particularly welcome the poor people who inhabit those dwellings.

While housing policies have certainly contributed to homelessness in the United States, the parent cause of this problem (as well as many others) is extreme poverty (Bassuk, 1991). Even if low-income housing were more readily available, how would people living on the streets possibly save enough money to pay the first and last months' rent as well as the security deposit on an apartment that costs even as little as $400 a month? In a society with a realistic unemployment rate upward of 10 percent and millions of people making little more than minimum wage, it is difficult, and in some cases impossible (for people who are elderly or disabled, for example), to pull oneself up by one's proverbial bootstraps. To make the situation even more difficult, city governments may be able to do little to prevent the growth of poverty and homelessness. We may be entering an era when localities are powerless to control (to any great extent) the global economic forces that are shaping their destinies (Sassen, 1991).

More than 100 years ago, sociologist William Graham Sumner wrote a book entitled *What Social Classes Owe to Each Other* (1883). His answer was a resounding "nothing." Regarding the homelessness crisis, Robert Marin (1988, p. 44) asks similar questions: "What does a society owe to its members in trouble, and *how* is that debt to be paid?" In large measure, we have not yet responded to the second question because the current answer to the first query echoes the response of Sumner: "nothing."

HOMELESSNESS—THE INTERNATIONAL SITUATION

If a summary statistic regarding the number of homeless people in the United States is only a rough estimate, a comparable figure concerning the number of people worldwide without permanent shelter is little more than a guess. To begin, most developing nations do not even keep such statistics. Nevertheless, the Worldwatch Institute (in Boyden, 1993) estimates that globally, some 100 million people have no choice but to live on the streets.

In Brazil, a nation with the world's third most inequitable income distribution, approximately 200,000 children live on the streets of Rio de Janeiro (Harris, 1994). These individuals often victimize each other in their struggle to survive and/or are gunned down by death squads (the police have been implicated in many of these murders) under the hire of local businessowners who argue that young street criminals are stealing from them and scaring away customers.

Abandoned by parents who do not have the money to care for them, homeless children in African cities support themselves by doing makeshift work, like watching parked cars (so they will not be vandalized) and carrying luggage for tourists (Makombe, 1992). Young girls in this situation often turn to prostitution; many of them will become carriers and ultimately die from AIDS.

As many as 3 million people in the relatively prosperous European Community nations have no permanent place to live. The situation is especially severe in France and Germany, the latter nation having 150,000 so-called registered homeless. The most often heard explanations for this problem are familiar to Americans: runaway children from troubled and abusive families, people with AIDS, drug addicts, women who have been abused and their children, and the long-term unemployed ("Homelessness Grows," 1992).

The situation is much worse in some republics of the former Soviet Union. In the old Soviet Union, homelessness did not officially exist, and people without shelter were kept off the streets by local police. As a consequence of this policy, people lived in cemeteries, railway stations, subway tunnels, and construction sites as well as ventilation pipes and heating ducts in high-rise apartment buildings (Remnick, 1992). The political and economic turmoil in Russia following the downfall of communism has brought this problem

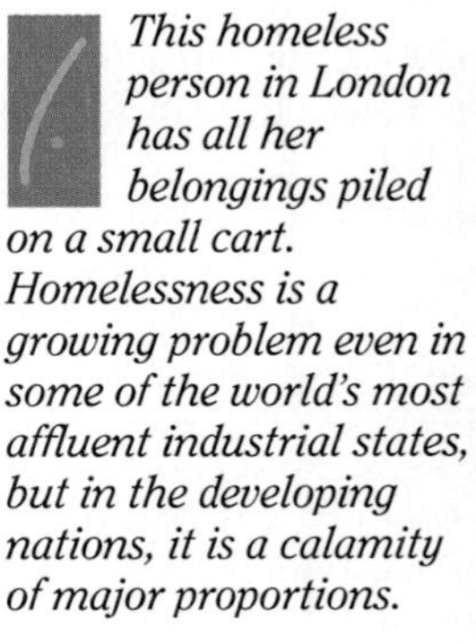

This homeless person in London has all her belongings piled on a small cart. Homelessness is a growing problem even in some of the world's most affluent industrial states, but in the developing nations, it is a calamity of major proportions.

THE URBANIZATION OF INDIA
Giant Cities, Giant Problems

For most of its 4,000-year history, India has been a rural nation. By 1901, only 26 million people residing in present-day Indian territory, or 11 percent of the population, lived in cities (Nagpaul, 1988). In 1993, 26 percent of the population, or 233 million Indians, made their homes in urban areas. This represents almost a tenfold increase in less than a century.

However, as incredible as India's urban evolution has been to date, growth projections for the first quarter of the next century are nothing short of mind boggling. By the year 2025, approximately one-half of the country's projected 1,380,000,000 people will be urban residents (Dogan & Kasarda, 1988). This translates to 687 million city dwellers, a figure larger than the combined 1990 populations of the United States, Brazil, Japan, Mexico, and France. If this scenario comes to pass, Indian cities will have added 465 million people in a mere 35 years. Mattei Dogan and John D. Kasarda (1988) speculate that the Indian subcontinent could have as many as 30 to 40 metropolises, each with between 4 and 10 million people. Fifty million people will likely live in India's biggest cities—Bombay, Calcutta, Delhi, and Madras—by the year 2000.

Whereas India's population has been growing at a rate of 2.1 percent per year, the cities are increasing by an average of 3.8 percent per year, with many urban centers increasing between 4 and 7 percent annually (Chengappa, 1988). A significant portion of this growth is a product of rural-to-urban migration, especially in the four big cities. Delhi attracts 300,000 new residents a *year,* Bombay 25,000 a *month,* and Calcutta approximately 2,000 people a *day.* One Indian sociologist described the influx of 5 million rural peasants into the cities each year as "several thousand lifeboats heading for a few islands" (in Chengappa, 1988, p. 57). A Calcutta newspaper publisher noted, "Survival is why all these people came. Whatever little they earn is more than they could in the villages where they were born" (in Kaylor, 1984, p. 46). As is the case in other developing nations, the movement of so many people from impoverished rural areas to Indian cities is primarily a function of an uneven policy of development that has favored urban industrialization at the expense of the agricultural sector.

HOUSING SHORTAGE AND UNEMPLOYMENT

The number and severity of problems directly and indirectly caused by rapid urban growth has resulted in hardships and misery for tens of millions of people. The most serious of these problems are squalid living conditions and a drastic shortage of housing units. Surveys of the big four Indian cities indicate that between one-third and one-fourth of their residents live in substandard dwellings "considered unfit for human habitation even by applying a criterion of subsistence living" (Dogan & Kasarda, 1988). A Delhi health official claims that 4.8 million people in his city live in "subhuman conditions" (in Bhatia, 1989). Storage rooms, garages, even outdoor toilets have been converted into living space (Chengappa, 1988). Nagpaul (1988) reports that even in the much less crowded 1950s, half the households in Bombay had living space of less than 40 square feet per person (less than 50 percent of a parking space), with two households often sharing a one-room tenement. A "considerable portion of the population" lived on porches or underneath stairs. To make matters worse, most people currently living in crowded conditions and/or substandard structures could not afford the cost of the most modest single family accommodations were they available.

Even for wealthy Indians, the housing shortage in Bombay, Calcutta, Delhi, and Madras is serious. Sitting atop a long peninsula on land reclaimed from the sea, Bombay can only expand vertically. An apartment with 1,000 square feet of floor space in India's most cosmopolitan city costs approximately $200,000 (Nagpaul, 1988), this in a country with a 1993 per capita income of $330. The acquisition of an apartment may require a so-called deposit of up to 50 percent of the selling price that does not count toward the eventual purchase of the dwelling. Both parties realize this initial payment is little more than a bribe (Bryjak, 1982–1983).

Unable to find or afford housing in the city, Bombay's middle-class residents have been forced to live in distant suburbs and surrounding towns. They spend up to four hours a day commuting to and from work (Chengappa, 1988). In Calcutta, housing is simply not available; in Delhi, the price of suburban homes has skyrocketed in the past few years. Housing costs in the southern city of Madras have also increased steadily (Nagpaul, 1988).

As a result of high rates of natural population increase (births over deaths) and substantial in-migration, unemployment is high in most Indian cities. In 1973, the Calcutta Municipal Development Authority (CMDA) conducted 10,000 interviews with "pavement dwellers"—the poorest of the city's poor (Mukherjee & Singh, 1981). The CMDA study found that 98 percent of these people who live, work, and oftentimes die on the streets were migrants to Calcutta, with the overwhelming majority of these desperate individuals coming to the city for economic reasons. Inasmuch as they have few if any job skills, low incomes, and less than secure employment, their chances of finding adequate housing are almost nonexistent. Slightly less than half those surveyed were engaged in some form of manual labor, including pulling rickshaws and carts and selling cheap goods and services as well as picking rags and paper. Twenty-two percent were beggars. Living in such deplorable conditions was not a transitory, short-term affair for many of these people. Approximately one in five reported they had lived on the streets for 15 years or more (Mukherjee & Singh, 1981).

HEALTH AND ENVIRONMENT

Like the inhabitants of other poor countries, residents of India have a life expectancy (59 years) significantly shorter than that of individuals living in developed nations (74 years). Health problems are especially severe for slum residents and pavement dwellers. Undernourished if not chronically malnourished, many of these individuals are more susceptible to a long list of illnesses, including "respiratory diseases, gastrointestinal disorders, skin diseases, fever worms; ear, nose and throat problems and tuberculosis." (Nagpaul, 1988, p. 269).

Further complicating matters, the deadly specter of AIDS is spreading across India. Although the number of HIV-infected people in urban areas was relatively small as of 1990 (250,000 cases), the director general of the Indian Council of Medical Research stated that India is entering a "disaster phase" regarding AIDS ("Disaster Looms," 1990, p. 499). In India, AIDS is transmitted primarily by heterosexual intercourse, and in some red-light districts of Bombay and Madras, 30 percent of prostitutes examined were HIV positive. Sometime early in the next century, India could surpass sub–Saharan Africa as the region of the world hardest hit by the AIDS epidemic.

While impoverished residents of Indian cities are especially vulnerable to a wide variety of physical maladies, rich and poor people alike are victimized by rapidly increasing environmental pollution. In 1982, Indian environmentalists estimated that just breathing the air in Calcutta was the equivalent of smoking one pack of cigarettes a day. A 1991 study reported that Delhi had the fourth-worst quality of air in the world. India's air pollution problems are a direct result of motor vehicle emissions, power plants, and the engines that fuel heavy industry. A growing number of vehicles (10,000 more each month in Delhi) burning low-grade fuel spew out voluminous quantities of foul-smelling, noxious fumes, while factories and coal-burning power stations fill the skies with dangerous toxins (Bhatia, 1989; Bryjak, 1984). Like other developing nations, India is fouling the physical environment in its effort to modernize as quickly as possible.

Contaminated water is a major health problem in cities and a source of numerous water-borne diseases, such as hepatitis and cholera. While India's urban population more than quadrupled between 1951 and 1991, the infrastructures of these cities, including water purification and sewage treatment plants, hardly kept pace. For example, in Calcutta, there was no major construction of water and sewage lines between 1906 and the mid-1970s (Kaylor, 1984). The lack of such basic facilities, combined with the fact that as many as one-third of the residents in some cities use the streets as a toilet, means that cities are breeding grounds for a host of disease-carrying parasites. The situation is especially problematic during the monsoon season, when torrential rains quickly back up antiquated sewer systems and many streets (as well as entire neighborhoods) are flooded and awash in raw sewage. A six-week-long cholera and gastroenteritis epidemic affected 28,000 Delhi residents in 1988, claiming almost 300 lives (Bhatia, 1989).

The custom of leaning on the horn almost nonstop while driving in traffic has created a serious noise pollution problem in urban India. Noise levels in Bombay, for example, range between 57 and 91 decibels—significantly higher than the 55-decibel safety limit recommended by the World Health Organization (Chengappa, 1988).

WHAT CAN BE DONE?

Over the years, planning commissions in a number of Indian cities have embarked on master plans to partially alleviate some of these monumental problems (Nagpaul, 1988). Slums have been torn down and squatters moved from one section of the city to another. Programs have been initiated to provide urban residents with minimal levels of water, sewage treatment, paving, and street lighting in the slums of the nation's 20 largest cities. Unfortunately, in a country with few resources (monetary and otherwise) and rapidly expanding cities, partial solutions to these monumental afflictions are quickly negated by population growth.

The scenario for India's urban future is anything but encouraging. What nation (no matter how wealthy) could possibly provide even the most minimal standard of living for the projected 400 million plus people who could inhabit urban India in the year 2025? Commenting on the difficulty of managing an Indian city, Raj Chengappa (1988, p. 57) stated, "Whatever can go wrong, will go wrong." There is little if any reason to believe that the quality of life will improve in what will soon be the world's most populous urban environment.

out into the open. As is the case in Africa, thousands of Russian children have been abandoned by their desperately poor parents, with as many as 10,000 youngsters and adolescents living on the streets of St. Petersburg alone (Dammann, 1993).

THE FUTURE OF CITIES IN THE UNITED STATES

The city of the future as presented in science fiction movies and novels is a wonder to behold. Gleaming skyscrapers are interconnected by a maze of tunnels and tubes as silent, fast-moving trains transport people in a world free of congestion, pollution, and crime. However, the realization of this urban dream is contingent on the allocation of generous amounts of time, money, energy, resources, and desire (Spates & Macionis, 1987).

No doubt, the most important of these commodities are money and desire. As we approach the twenty-first century, our major cities are at a crossroads, and anything short of making the revitalization of American urban centers a top priority is likely to end in disaster. Numerous metropolitan areas (especially inner cities) are just as likely to turn into the nightmare scenarios presented in films such as *Bladerunner* and *Escape from New York* as they are to become space-age habitats where everyone lives the good life. Some observers note that the turmoil in Los Angeles in 1992 may be a sign of the times to come for cities in many nations (in Merrill, 1992).

We can take a significant step toward the metropolis of the future or find ourselves in a situation where the revitalization of some segments of urban America is all but lost. Many urban neighborhoods in the United States are already beginning to resemble depressed areas of Third World cities.

THE GLOBAL CITY

In a skillful sociological analysis entitled *The Global City: New York, London, Tokyo,* Saskia Sassen (1991) examines the linkages between a changing international economy and the structure and workings of some of the world's largest metropolitan areas. She argues that the large-scale dismantling of industrial productivity in postwar England, the United States, and Japan, in combination with the industrialization of some Third World nations, has dramatically altered the international financial industry and the cities in which it is located. With the production of goods ranging from inexpensive clothing to high-priced automobiles now taking place in developing societies (known as *spatial dispersal*), and a concentration of financial planning and other services in a small number of urban centers (primarily New York, London, and Tokyo), these municipalities are now functioning in ways quite unlike other cities.

These three cities on a global scale—as well as Amsterdam, Hong Kong, Sao Paulo, Sydney, Toronto, and a few others on a regional basis—are the knowledge centers, or "brains," of the world economy (Sassen in Coughlin, 1994, p. A8). They are the key locations for specialized accounting, legal, advertising, banking, and investment firms that give direction to and handle much of the growth that fuels the international economy.

Sassen notes that although the globalization of manufacturing altered the economic and social structures of New York City, this transformation came at the expense of production in the midwestern and northeastern regions of the country. This "new growth rests on the decline of what were once significant sectors of the national economy, notably key branches of manufacturing" (p. 328). In other words, even though New York City lost tens of thousands of manufacturing jobs in the post–World War II era, it was able to make up for this exodus of positions by expanding its already formidable base of internationally oriented financial institutions. On the down side, in contrast to the high-paying positions of the urban financial elite, thousands of low-skill, low-paying jobs have been created in the service sector—jobs that have contributed to the "social and economic polarization" of New York's workforce.

Inasmuch as the new international economic order only needs a limited number of financial centers ("brains"), cities such as Cleveland, Buffalo, Pittsburgh, and many more will never be in a position to make this transition. If Sassen is correct, the transformation of the world economy has produced a handful of winners in the developed world, cities like New York and Toronto that will remain vibrant financial centers, and many more losers that have experienced the loss of thousands of never-to-return manufacturing jobs.

SAVING CITIES: ACTION AT THE INDIVIDUAL LEVEL

If cities are to prosper in coming years, action will have to be taken at both individual and institutional levels. Individually, we will have to adopt the practice of what Schumacher (in Spates & Macionis, 1987, p. 467) calls "Buddhist Economics." This means a more austere lifestyle of wanting, using, and wasting far less than we do today. Curbing our collective material appetites and recycling would result in less strain on highly polluted urban environments in terms of both reduced demand for natural resources and significantly less pollution. Even the once seemingly trivial problem of trash disposal is becoming a difficult problem, as cities like New York and Philadelphia, among others, have already learned. Many of the country's largest cities are increasingly hard pressed to get rid of their trash as nearby landfills have reached capacity.

If impoverishment is the root cause of many of the problems currently plaguing urban America, then interrupting the cycle of poverty should be a high priority for saving our cities. Toward this end, Robert Conot (1992) advocates paying teenage girls 14 to 19 years old in low-income urban families $50 for every month they avoid pregnancy. This money would accrue and be paid to young women when they graduate from high school. For those who go on to college, the stipend would continue four additional years. These women would also be given free birth control information and devices. Conot argues that his plan would not only reduce urban poverty but would also pay for itself in a relatively short period of time. The funds for this new policy would come from the Aid to Families with Dependent Children Program, which would no longer need such a sizeable budget.

REVITALIZING CITIES WITH ENTERPRISE ZONES

The most serious problem facing U.S. cities is the erosion of the tax base that is leaving many of them teetering on the edge of bankruptcy. One heretofore untapped source of funds for urban maintenance and development in many cities is user fees (Durr, 1971). If commuters from the suburbs (in some cases, from neighboring states) are going to demand and use police, fire, emergency, street maintenance, and traffic control services provided by cities, they must be willing to pay for those services. Likewise, churches and civic groups with tax-free status would also have to pay their fair share of support. Cities can no longer foot the bill for nonresidents who utilize their labor and services on a regular basis and then go home to the suburbs or the country. There is no practical (or moral) reason why increasingly poor cities should subsidize activities of the entire (usually more affluent) geographical area.

If the largest U.S. metropolitan areas (especially the inner cities) are to prosper, business leaders must be encouraged not only to keep their companies in the United States but to relocate and/or expand facilities in center cities where rates of unemployment and poverty are especially high. However, businesspeople have been reluctant to move into areas where the pool of skilled labor is low and rates of both property crime and violent crime are high.

To encourage investment in the poorest sections of the city, the federal government has designated many of these neighborhoods *enterprise zones* and offered businesses healthy tax breaks and discounted utilities if they will set up shop in these locations. Not only will enterprise zones create jobs, but they will simultaneously restore the tax base (more employed people) of near-bankrupt cities and cut the number of people collecting welfare benefits. The enterprise zone strategy is sometimes referred to as "the conservative answer to liberal welfare programs."

Critics of this program contend the 2,200 enterprise zones existing in 38 states as of 1992 have made no more than a small dent in a very large problem. The 258,000 jobs created by this program is a minuscule figure in relation to the numbers of inner-city people who remain unemployed. If enterprise zones are to be successful, poor neighborhoods must also receive government subsidies in the form of free drug treatment centers, low-cost housing, and increased police protection ("Morning News," 1992). Even if the infrastructure of the poorest neighborhoods is revitalized and generous tax breaks are extended to businesses, many companies will conclude that it is in their financial interest to relocate to Mexico or some other developing nation, where wages are typically less than a dollar an hour.

However, staunch defenders of this program ask that critics give enterprise zones a chance. At the very least, it is one of the few urban programs that both liberals and conservatives can agree on.

THE NEW IMMIGRANTS

Between 1820 and 1940, over 38 million people immigrated to the United States. Approximately 26 million of these individuals arrived during the 50 peak years of immigration—1871–1920. Settling primarily in cities, the newcomers of this latter period helped turn the United States into a nation of city dwellers, as the urban population passed the 50 percent mark in 1913 (Spates & Macionis, 1987). The overwhelming majority of these early immigrants came from Europe and settled in the Northeast, near their ports of entry (Abu-Lughod, 1991).

Also heavily concentrated in urban areas, today's immigrants come predominantly from Central and South America, the Caribbean, and Asia (see Figure 5.3). Of the 7,338,062 people who arrived in the United States between 1981 and 1990, fewer than 10 percent were of European ancestry. While New York and Pennsylvania are still popular destinations for these newcomers, California, Texas, Florida, and Louisiana (the new ports of entry) also receive significant numbers of immigrants (McLemore, 1994).

Today's immigrants also have more diverse educational and occupational backgrounds than did those individuals who came predominantly from Europe in the nineteenth and early twentieth centuries. Of those newcomers who arrived in the 1990 fiscal year, 12.7 percent were **professional immigrants** (doctors, for example), managers, or executives or had technical skills. These types of people come to urban America not to escape grinding poverty but because they want to enhance their economic position, to further their careers (McLemore, 1994; Portes & Rumbaut, 1990).

FIGURE 5.3 Immigrants to the United States by Region of Origin: 1820–1985

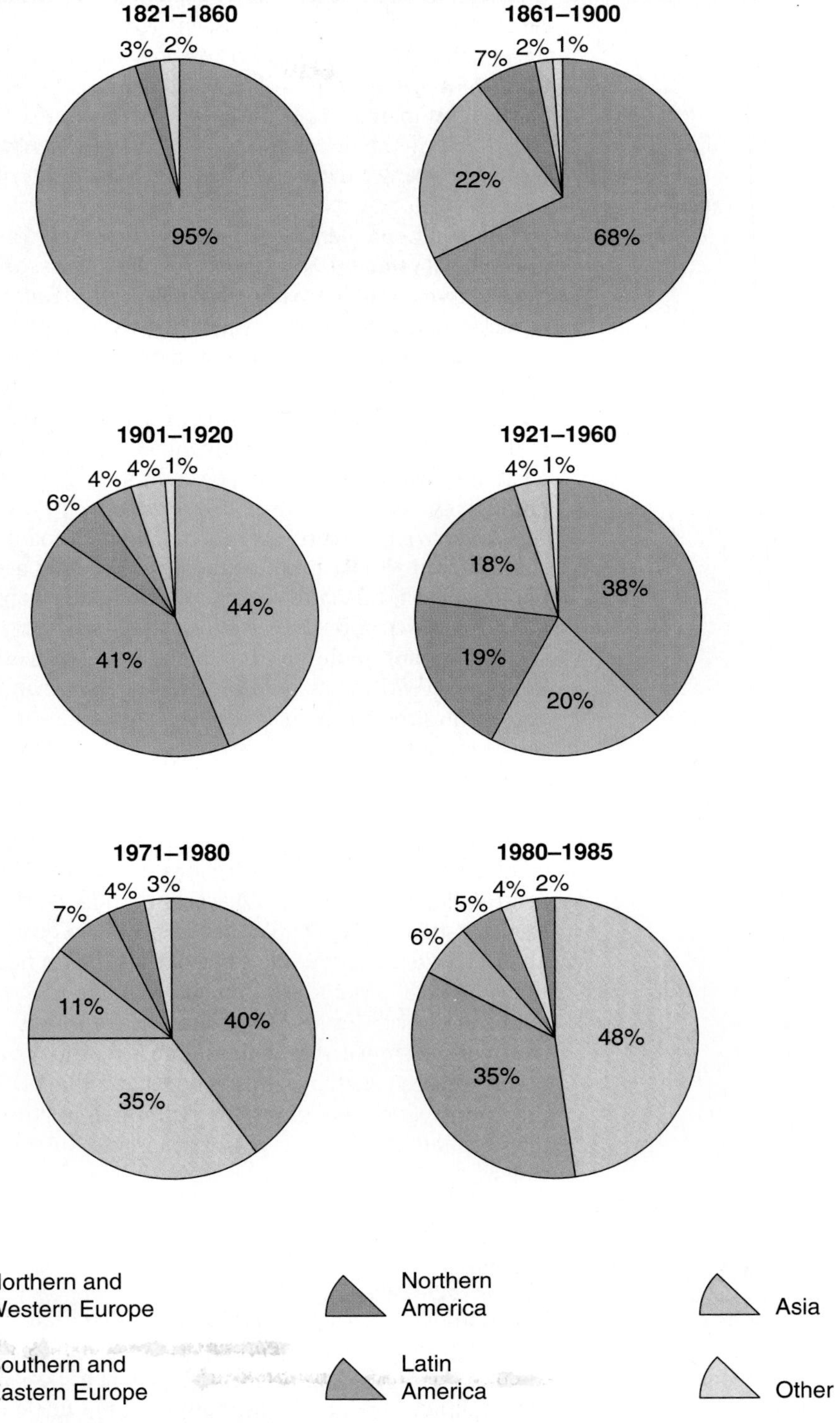

SOURCE: Reprinted by permission of the Population Reference Bureau.

Entrepreneurial immigrants come to this country and start their own businesses. Immigrants from Korea, for example, have opened thousands of grocery stores, restaurants, gas stations, liquor stores, and real estate offices in Los Angeles and New York City. Residents of Koreatown in Los Angeles are three times more likely to be self-employed than the population as a whole. The number of Cuban-owned firms in Miami's Little Havana has increased from 919 in 1967 to approximately 28,000 in 1990, with the average business employing 8.1 workers. Urban neighborhoods with a high concentration of immigrant-owned and -operated businesses are called *ethnic enclaves* (Portes & Rumbaut, 1990).

An additional defining characteristic of this latest wave of immigrants is that many are **political refugees**. Some of these individuals—an "elite of former notables"—have left their native countries because of ideological and political differences with the existing power structure. A second, much larger group of people have come to the United States to escape the economic hardships imposed by that same government (Portes & Rumbaut, 1990). Offering a different interpretation (especially as it relates to this latter group), S. Dale McLemore (1994) argues that the primary reason political refugees cite for leaving their homeland is much more compelling (and urgent) than merely ideological differences they have with those in power. Rather, they are fleeing to avoid persecution, imprisonment, and execution for political reasons.

Aside from the controversy revolving around the issue of whether the United States should admit almost a million mostly city-bound people annually in a period of slow economic growth, this latest period of immigration appears to have triggered a resurgence in *nativism*—a movement to eliminate foreign persons, customs, and ideas. Groups with anti-immigrant philosophies, like the Ku Klux Klan (KKK) and the White Aryan Resistance (WAR), increased their memberships and activities during the 1980s. The latter organization has advocated shooting people attempting to enter the United States illegally from Mexico.

There is also conflict among some groups of recent immigrants as well as friction between new arrivals to this country and other minority groups. In California, Vietnamese gangs battle Laotian gangs for dominance, and newly arrived El Salvadoran youths fight long-established gangs of Mexican Americans and African Americans for control of neighborhoods and access to the lucrative drug trade. In New York City, there has been an ongoing conflict between Korean businessowners and many of their African American customers. While some of these differences are cultural (to what extent should shoppers be allowed to pick up and examine the produce, for example), others are economically based. Some African Americans resent what they believe is the preferential treatment accorded recent immigrants by the government in terms of social and economic welfare benefits, pointing out that millions of Blacks, whose families have been in this country for generations, are still mired in poverty. The very different perceptions of the situation held by African Americans and Korean Americans have, on occasion, turned violent.

WHY SAVE THE CITIES?

Regarding the future of cities in the United States, one observer commented, "Babylon fell; what's so special about Detroit?" (Gerreau, in "America's Cities," 1992). When put in those terms, the answer (though people in Detroit would certainly disagree) is "nothing." Taking this line of reasoning one step further, a similar question could be asked: The Roman Empire fell; what's so special about the United States? No doubt far fewer Americans would be willing to state that nothing is special about this country.

If Detroit is to fall, we can be absolutely sure of one thing—it won't die by itself. The demise of the Motor City would be but one loss, since many urban centers would perish. Inasmuch as we are a nation of urban dwellers with most of our financial, educational, health, communication, transportation, and cultural resources concentrated in metropolitan areas, what kind of a future would the United States have—a nation of bankrupt, dilapidated cities—in an increasingly complex and competitive world?

Former Boston Mayor Raymond J. Flynn stated, "We're the only country that ignores its cities; Japan would not think of ignoring Tokyo, Germany would not think of ignoring Bonn" ("If Nation's Economy," 1992). While this statement may be somewhat of an exaggeration on the mayor's part, there can be little doubt that other industrial nations are far more concerned about the welfare of their cities than we are. During the 1980s and early 1990s, when the United States was cutting back federal funds to the cities, Japan embarked on a 15-year, $8 *trillion* program to bolster that nation's metropolitan areas. Japanese leaders, like their counterparts in numerous other nations, have discovered that a country's prosperity is firmly grounded in the well-being of its cities.

CITIES IN THE DEVELOPING WORLD

The two major demographic trends of the latter half of the twentieth century are the tremendous increase in world population (the population explosion) and the heretofore unprecedented rapid growth of cities (Brown & Jacobson, 1987). In 1900, only 1 of every 10 people was an urban resident. By the year 2000, 1 out of 2 people will live in cities (see Figure 5.4). Most of this urban growth has occurred in developing countries, where cities are doubling in population every 10 to 15 years (Lowe, 1992a). In the next 20 years, many Third World metropolitan areas will equal if not surpass the population of Mexico City, currently the largest city in the world. It is estimated that by the year 2025, Africa will have 36 metropolises of over 4 million (as compared to 2 in 1985), and Latin America will have

As a result of significantly more births than deaths and high levels of rural-to-urban migration, cities in the already overcrowded developing world are growing at unprecedented rates. These cities are potential centers of collective violence, as increasing numbers of people compete for scarce resources such as jobs and places to live.

21 cities of this size or more (as compared to 8 in 1985) (Dogan & Kasarda, 1988). One observer notes that these giant cities will be "twice as big, three times as big, four times as big" (Naciri, 1989).

These projections may seem farfetched until one realizes that a city like Cairo adds on average 2,050 residents *each day,* or almost three-quarter million people each year (Murphy, 1992). By the year 2020, the 10 largest urban areas in the world will all be located in developing nations. The great cities of the first countries to become industrialized (New York, Paris, London, Berlin, and Tokyo, to name a few) will be relatively small in comparison to these urban behemoths. Already over half of the world's largest 100 cities are in the developing world (see Figure 5.4).

The continuing growth of these cities is being fueled by the natural increase in population (more births than deaths) and by rural-to-urban migration. On average, natural increase accounts for 60 percent of the growth of these cities, and in-migration con-

FIGURE 5.4 Distribution of the World's 100 Largest Metropolitan Areas (by population)

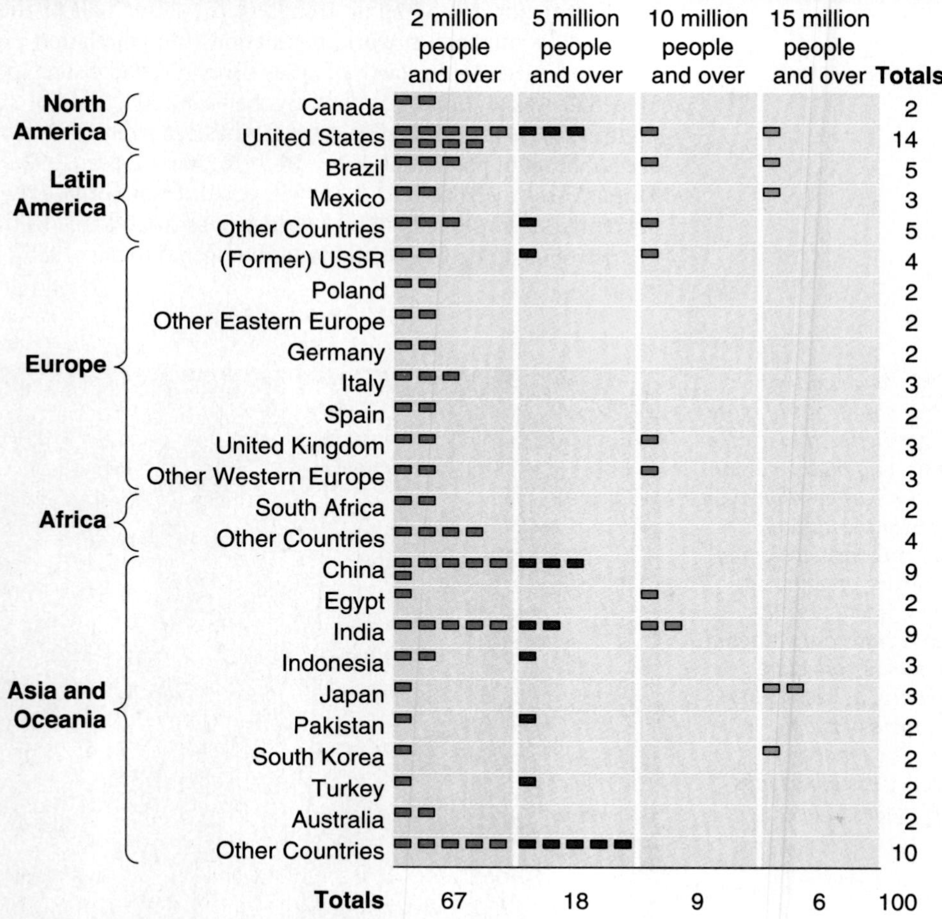

Source: Reprinted by permission of Population Action International (formerly Population Crisis Committee).

tributes to the remaining 40 percent (Gugler, 1988a). However, in Africa, most of this growth is a result of rural-to-urban migration, and in some countries, people moving into cities comprise 70 percent of annual urban population growth. Not only do rural-to-urban migrants contribute to urban growth, but because they are disproportionately adolescents and young adults between the ages of 15 and 25, they have higher rates of fertility than those of the general population. A newly married 20-year-old couple arriving in a Third World city from the countryside may have 5 or 6 children in a 10-year period.

It does not take an advanced degree in the social sciences to understand that rapid urban growth is accompanied by a host of problems such as unemployment and underemployment; air, water, and noise pollution; power shortages and blackouts; and severely overtaxed institutions: education, health care, transportation, communication, and sewage treatment and disposal. These staggering problems may become so severe that some cities will become giant warehouses of humanity, where people do not live but barely survive in a marginal environment. Consider Robert Kaplan's (1994, p. 54) description of Conkary, the capital of Guinea in West Africa:

> The forty-five minute journey in heavy traffic was through one never-ending shanty-town. . . . The corrugated metal shacks and scabrous walls were coated with black slime. Stores were built out of rusted shipping containers, junked cars, and jumbles of wire mesh. The streets were one long puddle of floating garbage. Mosquitoes and flies were everywhere. Children, many of whom had protruding bellies, seemed as numerous as ants. When the tide went out, dead rats and skeletons of cars were exposed on the murky beach.

Today, all over the developing world, the water supplies in cities like Conkary carry diseases such as hepatitis, typhoid, jaundice, and diarrhea. During heavy monsoon rains, overburdened drainage systems often back up, depositing untreated sewage in the cities' water supplies. The water is so polluted in the Indian city of Agra (site of the Taj Mahal) that one has to boil it before washing in order to avoid skin infections (Awasthi, 1992).

Egypt's capital city of Cairo, with some 16 million people, is one of the noisiest places in the world. Nonstop traffic, streets full of people trying to talk over one another, and thousands of mosques with loudspeakers calling the faithful to prayer five times a day combine to produce an almost never-ending barrage of noise that has become a major health hazard. A 1990 study by the Egyptian Academy of Scientific Studies found that more than half of Cairo's residents use sleeping pills and sedatives to escape from and cope with the noise (Murphy, 1992). Almost one-third of the population suffers from high blood pressure.

Polluted air from automobiles and trucks burning low-quality leaded gasolines and the fumes from thousands of factories turn the air a sickening orange-brown color. During the hot and humid summer months, toxic clouds comprised of a wide array of chemicals hang over Third World cities and poison their inhabitants. Just breathing the air in Mexico City is the equivalent of smoking two packs of cigarettes a day. Fifty percent of newborn infants tested in the Mexican capital had toxic levels of lead in their blood; the figure was 70 percent for unborn children (Gardels & Snell, 1990). The presence of lead at these high levels can reduce a person's IQ as much as 10 percent.

Swelled by natural population increases and rural-to-urban migration, cities in the developing world have a tremendous surplus of workers with limited skills, resulting in high rates of unemployment, underemployment, and misemployment (Gugler, 1988a). Urban unemployment rates range from 6.5 percent in Latin American cities to 10.8 percent in African urban areas. **Underemployment** is the underutilization of labor and takes

Living in cities (especially large urban areas) can be detrimental to one's physical and mental well-being. Although few people suffer the equivalent of smoking two packs of cigarettes a day just by breathing the surrounding air, as do the inhabitants of Mexico City, most urban residents are subject to the ill effects of a wide variety of humanmade pollutants to one extent or another.

- People who moved to Sunbelt cities for health reasons have found that rapid growth in some of these urban areas has polluted the air to the extent that the Arizona Lung Association has warned people with respiratory problems to stay away from Phoenix. Children from inner cities subject to high amounts of toxic automobile emissions have more lead in their systems than do children from smaller cities and rural areas. Lead levels in the air of the fastest-growing Third World cities, which typically do not use more expensive unleaded gasoline, will undoubtedly approach that of Mexico City, where on particularly bad days, the air smells like gasoline.
- In Russia, in the first nationwide survey of the water supply, the Environment Ministry found that outdated purification facilities, dirty pipes, and widespread pollution left about half the country with substandard water. As a result, one-third of Russia's 148 million people suffer each year from intestinal disorders caused by ingesting poor water. The survey found that drinking water was especially bad in the

a number of forms. Seasonal work, like construction and tourism, plus fluctuations in a nation's economy mean that some workers will be sporadically employed. So-called solidarity groups, which employ members of an extended family or specific caste, may choose to keep everybody working at reduced wages during economic slowdowns rather than terminate some employees. Finally, the ever-present surplus of labor means that millions of people in overcrowded cities engage in makeshift work, such as picking through garbage and selling or trading any usable items they salvage. Individuals whose labor does not supposedly contribute to the social welfare or undermines that welfare are underemployed. Begging, prostitution, as well as a myriad of other forms of illegal activity would be considered **misemployment**.

Next to acquiring enough food to stay alive, the most serious problem facing the urban poor in developing countries is housing. Demographer Nathan Keyfitz (1992) estimates that of the almost 2 billion people living in metropolitan areas in poor countries, 1.3 billion are living in poverty. These people are forced to reside in squatter settlements, live in the streets, or inhabit any makeshift form of shelter they can improvise. Known by a variety of names (Mexico: *los villas miserias,* "cities of the miserable"; Turkey: *gacekondu,* "built overnight"; and Brazil: *favelas,* "slum" or "shantytown"), these settlements are home to the most destitute people on Earth.

More than half the urban residents in India live in households with one room and an occupancy rate of 4.4 persons per room (Gilbert, 1988). In Calcutta, over 1,000 people live in small cubicles beneath a railway station only 4 or 5 feet from the tracks (Banerjee,

Moscow, Kurgan, and Kalmykia regions ("Much of Russia's Water," 1994).

- A review of ten studies that compared mental disorders in urban and rural settings showed that eight found higher rates of mental problems in cities, although these differences were not very large (reported in Link & Dohrenwend, 1989). Whereas physical health hazards like air pollution and contaminated water typically affect city dwellers regardless of where they reside in the metropolitan area (or of their political, economic, and social standing in the community), mental health problems are often linked to social class.
- A number of studies have found that living in a chronically poor, inner-city neighborhood is detrimental to one's psychological well-being (Link & Dohrenwend, 1987). Impoverished African Americans experience a particularly low level of mental health in urban ghettos characterized by high crime rates, substandard housing, inferior schools, poor services, and inadequate transportation. These problems may be even more severe for males, who face chronic unemployment and are often under the jurisdiction of the criminal justice system (Amato & Zuo, 1992). However, poor women (especially single mothers) have more than their share of psychological stress as they struggle to provide for their children financially in dangerous, crime-ridden neighborhoods with inferior schools. This overall lower level of psychological well-being makes it that much more difficult for poor urban residents to perform at the highest level of their ability. As a consequence, these individuals have less of a chance of being hired in the first place and, if hired, to be promoted on the basis of merit and/or productivity.

1992). In Cairo's notorious City of the Dead, as many as 500,000 people live among the tombs in cemeteries. Other residents of the city live in condemned buildings that often collapse, killing scores of people (Murphy, 1992). Brazilian authorities estimate that as many as 7 million children live in the streets. Because governments in many developing countries cannot afford to build shelters for their rapidly increasing urban populations and because poor people do not have the money to pay for apartments even if they were available, the plight of these individuals will only become worse.

Not only do the urban poor in developing nations suffer many physical hardships; they also experience chronic anxiety resulting from their limited resources and lack of political power. These people must deal with irregular employment; illness and accidents, with a minimum (if any) health care; the theft of their precious few items at the hands of other desperate people; finding places to live; and the possibility that police will destroy their illegal squatter settlements (Lloyd, 1982).

If the quality of life of poor urban dwellers is so low, why do tens of millions of people move from the countryside to cities every year? The answer is that conditions in rural areas are even worse, and there is little if any chance of improvement. The rural labor force has been destabilized as a result of overpopulation, technological innovations in agriculture, the displacement of small farmers as large-scale farming has expanded, and the cycle of rural catastrophes (floods, droughts, pestilence, and the fall in cash crop prices) (Bromley & Gerry, 1979). These factors push people from the countryside to the cities, where they have a chance (no matter how slim) to escape the grinding poverty of the countryside. In a complete rejection of the culture-of-poverty thesis, Perlman (in Gilbert, 1988, p. 85) notes that these people have "the aspirations of the bourgeoisie, the perseverance of pioneers, and the values of patriots."

SUMMARY

1 In the post–World War II era, millions of city residents fled to the suburbs to escape increasingly serious urban problems and distance themselves from racial and ethnic minorities. By the early 1990s, virtually every major U.S. city had financial problems, and many were technically bankrupt.

2 According to the culture-of-poverty explanation, the urban poor have a set of values and a lifestyle that make it difficult for them to prepare for employment and hold down jobs. Others have argued that values of inner-city residents (if in fact they are significantly different from those of others) are not as important in explaining urban poverty as is the tremendous loss of manufacturing jobs that has occurred over the past 40 years.

3 Low-interest home loans helped fuel the exodus of mostly White Americans to the suburbs. Not only did the urban tax base erode with the departure of these people, but suburbanites who work and play in the cities use the resources of these municipalities (roads, parks, police) without paying taxes to support them.

4 Violence has increased dramatically in many American cities over the past 20 years, with a sizeable percentage of these assaults and murders attributed to gangs. Many urban gangs have grown rich and powerful by satisfying the demand for illegal drugs. In some cities, long-established gangs are fighting newly arrived groups of Central Americans and Asians who are challenging the established gangs' dominance and control of the drug trade.

5 Urban riots have taken place in the United States intermittently for well over 200 years. Confrontations between labor and management (most notably in the nineteenth and early twentieth centuries) as well as race riots between Blacks and Whites have been especially numerous. There are three primary explanations for these occurrences. According to the *riffraff theory,* rioters are the dregs of society, comprised of criminals to a large extent. The *frustration-aggression* view holds that the low social, economic, and political status of inner-city residents results in collective violence. Anger emanating from a *blocked opportunity* structure in a racist society leads to many urban race riots.

6 Homelessness is a problem in the United States as well as many other nations in the world. Some individuals believe that a significant percentage of the homeless are mentally ill and lazy people who choose not to work. Others see the homeless problem as rooted in high unemployment and the loss of affordable housing.

7 American cities can be significantly helped at the individual level by a less wasteful, polluting lifestyle and at the structural level by creating enterprise zones that attract new and expanding businesses.

8 Immigrants to U.S. cities today come predominantly from Central and South America, the Caribbean, and Africa. Many of these people are poor, but others are

professionals; still others arrive with some capital and start their own businesses. Political refugees are fleeing persecution in their home countries.

9 As a result of a high rate of natural growth (more births than deaths) and unprecedented rural-to-urban migration, cities in the developing world are dealing with serious problems of unemployment/underemployment, pollution, a lack of clean water, and a monumental housing shortage.

CHAPTER SIX

INEQUALITY AND POVERTY
Chasing the Dream

With former *Saturday Night Live* stars Eddie Murphy and Dan Aykroyd playing the lead roles, the 1983 film *Trading Places* offered a somewhat lighthearted look at the very top and the very bottom of the American social class ladder. In this popular comedy, a wager between the Duke brothers, two patrician but ruthless multimillionaires, turned the lives of Murphy's and Aykroyd's characters completely upside down. Billy Ray Valentine, the streetwise scam artist from the inner-city ghetto, suddenly found himself trading places with Louis Winthorpe III, the cultured and pampered uptown financier. For the brothers who had engineered the transformation, the object of this experiment was to determine which factor—heredity or social environment—was responsible for individuals' economic and social successes or failures in life. The Dukes were willing and able to destroy two innocent people to settle their bet and, as the story line unfolded, they proceeded to do just that.

After having their lives nearly demolished by the Dukes' plotting, Billy Ray and Louis at last caught on to what had been happening to them. Outraged by the brothers' shallowness and callousness (at stake for the Dukes was a wager of one dollar), they joined forces with a prostitute and a disgruntled butler to craft their revenge. Learning of the Dukes' scheme to corner the nation's orange juice market, Billy Ray and Louis torpedoed the plan. Financially and legally ruined, the Duke brothers were led away in disgrace by the police. As the film closed, audiences saw Billy Ray and Louis basking in the Caribbean sun, enjoying their victory. Justice, in the form of an unlikely alliance between the uncouth African American hustler and the well-bred White Anglo-Saxon Protestant entrepreneur, had triumphed over elegant but heartless wealth.

As entertaining as it may be, *Trading Places* is hardly reflective of the realities of inequality in this or any other society. (After all, as the closing credits point out, the film is purely a work of fiction.) In most human societies, population members display what often are enormous differences in economic and other resources, as well as grim dispari-

ties in the quality of their respective lives. Throughout the world, more than 1 billion people are literally unable to sustain their minimal survival needs on a long-term basis, while a much smaller number of their fellow humans live in almost unimaginable luxury. For example, a designer handbag in Paris costs $1,500, a sum larger than the annual per capita income in more than 40 countries (Wright, 1994).

On the societal level, the situation is much the same. A small group of affluent, developed nations consume a disproportionately large amount of the world's resources, while a much larger group of poor, developing countries must struggle just to maintain their existence. Although they may share the same physical space, the members of these "have" and "have-not" countries exist worlds apart economically, socially, and politically. The likelihood that either group will be able (or will be forced) to trade places with the other is almost zero. Though such stories may be the stuff of which film comedies can be made, they more often fall into the realm of fantasy. Conditions of extreme poverty for many and extreme wealth for a few are historical and continuing facts of social life.

The development of a true global society as a consequence of growing international economic, political, and communications linkages has generated an increasing awareness of these stark contrasts. As we saw in Chapter Three on population problems, it has also led to a rising world tide of economic refugees. People are leaving their homelands in unprecedented numbers in search of the better lives they have heard about or seen. However, their mass movement into countries that may be unprepared and unequipped to deal with their needs has often translated into additional problems of enormous proportions for these host societies. It remains to be seen if this growing recognition of societal and global inequalities will also translate into an insistence that something be done to alter one of the oldest facts of human social existence.

QUESTIONS TO CONSIDER

1. Why is social inequality most often measured in terms of economic differences among people or societies?
2. What is the difference between *income* and *wealth* as measures of economic standing?
3. How has the corporation affected economic inequalities in industrial and postindustrial societies?
4. What is meant by the concept *political economy?*
5. What factors have contributed to the loss of so many traditional blue-collar jobs in contemporary societies?
6. How have corporate mergers affected white-collar occupations in developed societies?
7. How has formal education contributed to increasing inequality in many contemporary societies?
8. What is *world system theory?*
9. What is the difference between *absolute* poverty and *relative* poverty?
10. What are the three main perspectives concerning the causes of poverty in contemporary societies?
11. What is the connection between race and poverty in the United States?
12. Why are current workfare programs not likely to reduce poverty in the United States to any great extent?

ASSESSING CONTEMPORARY INEQUALITY

Confirming the presence of widespread social inequalities in the contemporary world is not a very difficult undertaking, even for the sociologically impaired. Newspapers, news magazines, films, and television have given millions of people at least secondhand experience with the lifestyles of both the rich and famous and the poor and obscure. And thanks to increasing personal and job-related travel, millions of other individuals have had firsthand exposure to these social disparities. In a very real sense, it would require much more effort to deny than to verify the reality of inequality.

However, accurately charting the depth and breadth of these individual and societal inequalities is a task that challenges the abilities of even the most sophisticated social scientists. As commonly understood, inequality is a multifaceted phenomenon that includes intangible as well as material dimensions. Some aspects of inequality, such as income and education, lend themselves readily to quantification and measurement. But others, such as prestige, power, and a sense of personal well-being, are much less tangible (though no less real) and, thus, much more difficult to measure with confidence. For this reason, existing data concerning social inequality at the societal and global levels typically reflect only those components that can be quantified and compared empirically. As such, they are more approximate than precise measures that in all likelihood underreport the true scope of modern social inequality.

ECONOMIC DIMENSIONS OF INEQUALITY

To a large extent, national and cross-national studies of social inequality have focused on the distribution of economic factors such as income and wealth within and among societies. These economic resources are by no means the only important dimensions of inequality, but they obviously play a critical role in shaping an individual's (or a society's) chances for obtaining other resources necessary for maintaining a high-quality level of existence. Additionally, various economic factors can easily be translated into a common denominator (U.S. dollars, for example) that makes meaningful cross-societal comparisons possible. In analyzing the amount of inequality within a specific society, then, sociological research typically examines income and wealth-distribution patterns among the members of the given population. In examining international or global-level systems of inequality (as we do in more detail later in this chapter), sociological research typically compares the given countries in terms of their average per capita gross national product (GNP), gross domestic product (GDP), or some similar indicator of their overall level of economic development. Both levels of analysis indicate that significant social inequalities are pervasive throughout virtually every contemporary society.

INTERNATIONAL ECONOMIC INEQUALITY

Both the World Bank and the United Nations Development Program (UNDP) collect economic and other quality-of-life data from a large number of contemporary societies. These data are then analyzed and interpreted in the World Bank's annual *World Development Report* and the UNDP's annual *Human Development Report*. Table 6.1 and Figure 6.1, which are based on information from these two sources, show the extreme variations in per capita economic resources that existed across the world as of 1990, the most recent year for which comparable cross-cultural information is available.

TABLE 6.1 Variations in Annual per Capita Gross National Product: 1990

Average per Capita GNP (in U.S. dollars)	Number of Countries
Less than $1,000	66
$1,000–$3,999	36
$4,000–$7,999	11
$8,000–$11,999	9
$12,000 and over	19

SOURCE: Compiled from data in Population Action International (formerly Population Crisis Committee), 1992, *International Human Suffering Index.*

In that year, according to World Bank data analyzed by the former Population Crisis Committee, nearly half (66) of the 141 countries examined had per capita GNPs under $1,000. In contrast, only about 14 percent of those societies (19) had per capita GNPs of $12,000 or more. For the world at large in 1990, according to data presented in *Human Development Report 1993,* per capita GNP averaged slightly over $4,000. For industrial-

FIGURE 6.1 Average per Capita Gross National Product for Industrialized and Developing Countries: 1990

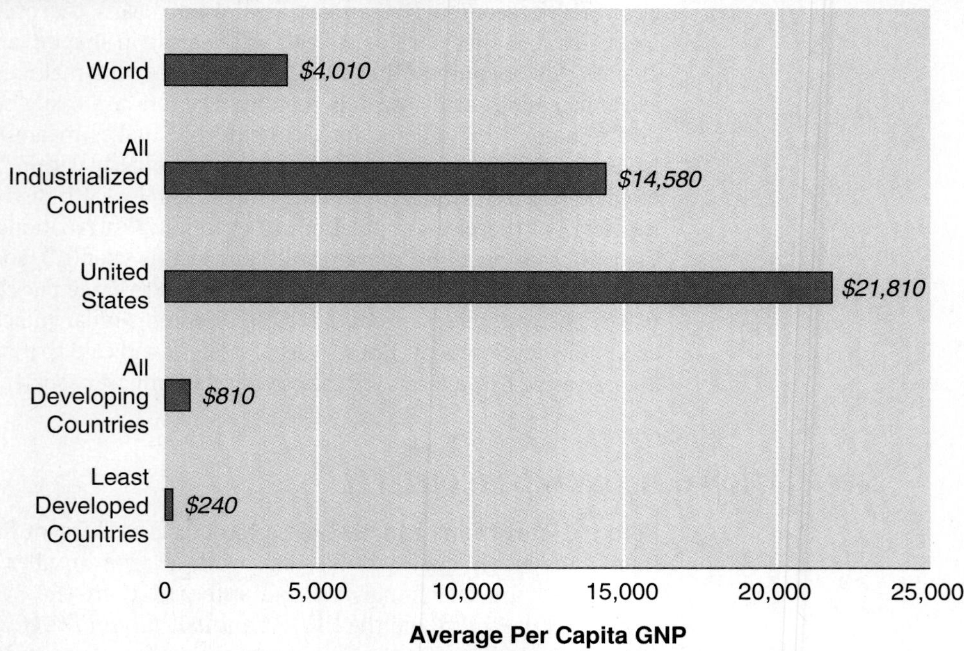

SOURCE: Adapted from United Nations Development Program, *Human Development Report 1993,* Tables 18 and 40.

ized nations as a whole, that figure soared to over $14,500, whereas for developing countries, it plunged to a little over $800. On average, then, the populations of the industrialized nations enjoyed about 14 times the level of economic resources received by their counterparts in developing societies. And some developing nations were far worse off than others: Per capita GNP in the least developed countries averaged a mere $240 in 1990, or one-sixtieth that of people living in industrialized societies.

ECONOMIC INEQUALITY IN THE UNITED STATES

To a large extent, the economic disparities that exist between developed and developing countries are reflected within developed societies such as the United States, as well. The United States as a whole is one of the world's more affluent societies, but this general affluence is not shared equally by its population segments. U.S. Census Bureau (1993b) data indicate that, in 1992, the mean yearly income of all households in the country was slightly over $39,000. However, for those households that made up the lowest one-fifth of the income-receiving population that year, the average was only $7,328. By way of contrast, the mean income ($91,494) for households in the highest quintile was almost 13 times greater. And for those households within the top 5 percent of all income-receiving units, the average was $145,244—over 20 times as high as the lowest quintile. Table 6.2 shows not only the very unequal shares of total U.S. yearly income distributed to the various household quintiles but also that this pattern has been growing more unequal over the past 25 years. And with regard to the distribution of wealth, these inequalities are even more pronounced.

Whereas *income* is a measure of all monies obtained from different sources, *wealth* is a measure of the economic value of all one's assets, including stocks, bonds, checking and savings accounts, and real estate holdings. Reliable data relating to wealth are much harder to obtain than reliable income data; consequently, estimates of how wealth is apportioned in this society at times amount to little more than educated guesses based on information provided by individuals and families to government agencies.

TABLE 6.2 Share of Aggregate Income Received by Each Fifth and Top 5 Percent of U.S. Households: 1967–1992

	Distribution of Aggregate Income (percent)					
Year	Lowest Fifth	Second Fifth	Third Fifth	Fourth Fifth	Highest Fifth	Top 5 Percent
1967	4.0	10.8	17.3	24.2	43.8	17.5
1972	4.1	10.5	17.1	24.5	43.9	17.0
1977	4.2	10.2	16.9	24.7	44.0	16.8
1982	4.0	10.0	16.5	24.5	45.0	17.0
1987	3.8	9.6	16.1	24.3	46.3	18.3
1992	3.8	9.4	15.8	24.2	46.9	18.6

SOURCE: U.S. Bureau of the Census, *Current Population Reports,* Series P60-184, adapted from Table B–3.

According to Federal Reserve and Internal Revenue Service data, by the end of 1989, the 834,000 households that constituted the top 1 percent of the American population had amassed more wealth than the 84 million households that made up the bottom 90 percent. The top group's net worth of $5.7 trillion (compared to the $4.8 trillion net worth of the bottom 90 percent) was founded on its holding of 49 percent of all publicly held stocks, 62 percent of all business assets, 78 percent of all bonds and trusts, and 45 percent of nonresidential real estate in the United States. Government figures show that the top 1 percent group's share of the country's net wealth had increased from 31 percent to 37 percent during the period 1983–1989, the first significant rise in the concentration of wealth since the 1920s. As the United States moved into the 1990s, the richest 10 percent of the population possessed an estimated 68 percent of all the nation's wealth (Nasar, 1992).

To a large extent, this growing concentration of immense wealth in the hands of a miniscule portion of the U.S. population has been fostered by a system of "wealthfare" that allows the rich to escape substantially the federal and state income taxes that were designed to promote the greater equalization of wealth in this society. For example, Internal Revenue Service data show that 779 couples and individuals with reported earnings of $200,000 or more each and an aggregated income of $340 million paid no federal income taxes at all in 1990. An additional 1,817 couples and individuals with reported incomes between $100,000 and $200,000 also escaped any federal taxation that year ("Life on EZ Street," 1993). These government-sponsored welfare benefits for the rich have not changed appreciably under the Clinton administration, nor are they likely to (Goodgame, 1993). Like all other contemporary societies, the United States continues to be marked by substantial wealth inequalities.

Like income and other economic resources, wealth is distributed very unequally among as well as within societies. It is unlikely that these New Delhi street children could even imagine the wealth of this couple from Sarasota, Florida, much less ever experience it. The old cliché that "An ordinary dog in America eats better than a child in the developing world" is quite possibly true in this instance.

INDUSTRIALISM, POSTINDUSTRIALISM, AND INEQUALITY

In a wide-ranging attempt to understand contemporary patterns and predict future trends in human inequality, sociologist Gerhard Lenski (1966; Lenski & Lenski, 1991) argued that, as societies developed from agriculture-based to industrialized economies, long-standing social inequalities began to give way to newer, more egalitarian arrangements. This "revolutionary movement," as he called it, was grounded largely in the domination of the economy by jobs that required increasing amounts of technical expertise and in the development of mass educational systems that provided this expertise to more and more population members. In turn, these higher-paying, more prestigious occupations served to end the monopoly of wealth and power previously enjoyed by small privileged groups of elites, distributing these two important resources more evenly among various population segments. The net result of these dramatic changes, according to Lenski, is the modern, middle-class society.

Both Lenski and fellow sociologist Daniel Bell (1973, 1976) argued that, as industrial economies began to give way to postindustrial systems, remaining socioeconomic inequalities would lessen even more. Populations would continue to become more formally educated, automation would free workers from routinized blue-collar manufacturing tasks, and information-based service and administrative occupations would dominate the economy. What already was a broad middle class would expand further, leaving only small population segments at the top and bottom extremes of the social hierarchy.

Lenski's and Bell's arguments notwithstanding, events have proved these predictions wildly and unrealistically optimistic. If anything, economic inequalities in the United States and other postindustrializing societies have grown, rather than decreased, in recent years. A number of significant changes in the nature of modern economies and the nature of modern education have combined to give these inequalities the appearance of permanency.

CORPORATE POWER

One factor contributing to the perpetuation of many existing inequalities and the creation of significant new inequalities is the domination of national and international economies by large, powerful corporations. Corporations' ability to amass enormous pools of financial, administrative, labor, and other productive resources has allowed them to assume control over most important markets and fields in capitalist economies. Given their clout, these modern institutions have made the idea of a free market system shaped by the collective economic decisions and activities of numerous individual producers and consumers just that—an idea, rather than a reality. The reality is economic systems in which most important policies reflect the interests and goals of a relatively small handful of corporate participants whose power extends well beyond the purely economic sphere (Dye, 1990; Marger, 1987). Corporations' "prime directive" is to make money for their owners, and within broad limits, they are free to pursue any policies that maximize their profit making.

Controlling ownership of these powerful organizations rests in the hands of the top 1 percent of the population in the United States, and within equally small population segments in other capitalist societies, as well. In practice, then, the economies of many developed countries are operated in the best interests of a select group of their members, and not according to "the public interest" or some supposed common good.

POLITICAL ECONOMY

Corporations' ability to dominate and control many important economic activities in developed societies has been assisted by the close, symbiotic relationship between political institutions and economic institutions in these social systems—that is, by the **political economy.** To a large extent, political stability in modern industrial and postindustrial societies is dependent on the support of those elite groups who control the corporations that, in turn, dominate the economy. And to an increasing extent, economic success is dependent on the support of political elites, who help maintain an atmosphere conducive to corporate profits. "The business of America is business," a statement made decades ago by then-president Calvin Coolidge and resurrected not that long ago by then-president Ronald Reagan, summarizes the essence of this close intertwining of government and corporate sectors.

In the interest of establishing or enhancing a favorable climate for economic development, governments often have been led into policies that have the effect (at least in the short run) of maintaining or exacerbating existing inequalities. For example, for decades, the Liberal Democratic Party that controlled Japan's postwar government aggressively pursued actions designed to transform the country's devastated economy into a superpower (Jones, 1993b). Among other things, this emphasis on building a world-class economy imposed a work ethic for white-collar "salarymen" that literally has Japanese workers dropping dead on the job. Some estimates claim that *karoshi* (or "death from overwork," as this phenomenon is called) was responsible for as many as 10,000 fatalities in 1992 (Watanabe, 1992a). Until pressed by mounting public pressure to do so, the Japanese government was reluctant to investigate the problem seriously, apparently in fear of disrupting a relationship with business that has been described by its critics as "Japan, Inc." (Silk & Kono, 1994). At the same time, government import and export policies created through the Ministry of International Trade and Industry (MITI) have led to extraordinarily high prices for many goods and services needed or desired by Japanese consumers. The result has been what many Japanese call "rich Japan, poor Japanese": a level of general affluence for the country as a whole that masks the inability of many of its citizens to maintain even a moderately comfortable level of personal daily existence (Shear, 1990).

In Mexico, the administration of President Carlos Salinas de Gortari was marked by a similar emphasis on economic development, with social and political reforms relegated to a much lower priority. Many significant economic advances were accomplished for the country as a whole, but this strategy came back to haunt both Salinas and the Institutional Revolutionary Party (PRI), which has controlled Mexican politics for more than 65 years. On New Year's Day, 1994, Indian peasants in the southern state of Chiapas began the most serious uprising against the Mexican federal government since the famous Revolution of 1910–1920 that created the modern Mexican state (Golden, 1994; Paz, 1994). According to the Zapatista Liberation Army, which spearheaded this action, the rebellion was a response to continued federal government indifference to the desperate plight of the local people: "For [the government] it doesn't matter that we possess nothing, absolutely nothing, not a home, not land, not work, not education" (quoted in "Indian Peasants in Southern Mexico," 1994).

The Mexican government's initial brutal response to the uprising drew heated criticism from the U.S. government and a number of international human rights organizations at a time that President Salinas and the PRI could least afford it. The North American Free Trade Agreement (NAFTA), which had barely survived intense opposition in the U.S. Congress, had just taken effect, and the national election that would decide

Mexico's next president was just around the corner (Scott, 1994). That election was thrown into disarray when, on March 23, 1994, Luis Donaldo Colosio, the PRI presidential candidate (and, therefore, the likely next Mexican president), was assassinated after completing a speech in Tijuana, the first assassination of a Mexican presidential candidate since 1928 (Gross, 1994). Although many different theories about the shooting surfaced in the aftermath of the assassination, some observers cited widespread uncertainty and concern about the country's dramatic economic changes (including NAFTA) as a significant contributing factor.

Even in avowed Marxist societies such as the People's Republic of China (PRC), governments now are encouraging their citizens to succeed economically and get rich. Communist party leaders in the PRC apparently have come to the conclusion that the creation of a wealthy socioeconomic class—and, thus, the development of a significant inequality hierarchy—is a necessary consequence of that country's recent attempts to reform and strengthen its economy (Tempest, 1993). Regardless of ideological or economic developmental differences, it would seem that political bodies in many, if not most, contemporary societies are encouraging or tolerating substantial economic and social inequalities within their populations.

STRUCTURAL CHANGES AND RISING UNEMPLOYMENT

A third factor that has contributed to continuing or growing inequality in modern societies is the changing profile of the occupational structure. With the onset of postindustrial economic organization, the skilled and semiskilled blue-collar occupations that had been the hallmark of industrialism began to give way to professional, managerial, and administrative white-collar occupations, as well as service jobs. As industries have become more fully automated, computers and robots have replaced human workers on factory assembly lines. The result, in the United States and in other developed societies, has been the loss of millions of traditional working-class jobs. According to one International Labor Organization report, 120 million workers around the world are now unemployed and another 700 million are underemployed, earning less than required to maintain a minimum standard of living. The report calls the situation "the worst global employment crisis since the Great Depression of the 1930s" ("Global Unemployment," 1994).

For example, the relatively low unemployment rates enjoyed by Finland and Sweden through the 1980s have more than quadrupled in the past few years, placing a crushing burden on what had been smooth-running social welfare systems. Facing unprecedented numbers of people out of work (in Finland, the unemployment rate rose to nearly 20 percent in 1993), these countries have been forced to begin cutting back on social welfare benefits and services that had been the most generous in the industrialized world. Old-age pensions now begin at age 67 rather than 65, sickness benefits have been reduced from 100 percent of lost salary to 80 percent, fees for medicines are being increased, and unemployment benefits that once paid 90 percent of previous earnings are being trimmed ("Farewell, Welfare," 1993).

PERMANENT JOB LOSSES

In a large and growing number of cases, this displacement of blue-collar workers represents permanent job losses, as positions have been eliminated along with the workers (Church, 1993b; Greenwald, 1991). For example, throughout Western Europe and the United States, many manufacturing jobs have disappeared entirely as the result of plant closings or industry relocations to areas with less expensive operating costs (Dillin,

1993b; Havemann & Kempster, 1993). This situation has added to unemployment rates that at times are extraordinarily high. Among the 12 member-nations that make up the European Community, for example, nearly 18 million people, or 11 percent of the total labor force, were out of work at the end of 1993, making the unemployment problem the top priority of economic and political leaders across Europe (LaFranchi, 1993b). At a meeting of the Group of Seven industrial democracies (Britain, Canada, France, Germany, Italy, Japan, and the United States) in March 1994, the situation was termed a "structural crisis" in which "even strong growth . . . will not create enough new jobs to replace those lost" (Biedenkopf in Friedman, 1994a).

Because they most often represent work in the service sector of the economy, many of the new jobs that are being created do not offer the same wages as those being lost. For example, though more than 35 million new jobs were created in the United States over the past two decades, the number of full-time workers earning poverty-level wages—the "working poor"—increased by 50 percent since 1979. As of 1992, according to U.S. Census Bureau reports, 18 percent of Americans with year-round, full-time jobs earned less than $13,091, the poverty threshold figure for that year (Rosenblatt, 1994).

All indicators point to the fact that things are not likely to improve for displaced blue-collar workers in the near future. Overall, according to U.S. Bureau of Labor Statistics reports, the number of workers now employed in "contingent" jobs—that is, who are working only part time—has increased to 25 percent of the labor force and could rise to 50 percent by the year 2000 (Dillin, 1993a). The part-time wages associated with these jobs have contributed to the continued deterioration of blue-collar workers' wages, a decline that began in the late 1970s and accelerated through the 1980s (Francis, 1993a). Similar increases in the number of contingent workers have taken place in many other industrialized nations, as well. According to one study by the International Labor Organization (reported in Belsie, 1993), part-time workers now constitute one-third of the labor force in the Netherlands, one-fourth in Norway, and one-fifth in Britain and New Zealand.

WHITE-COLLAR BLUES

The members of the blue-collar working classes have not been the only segments of modern societies negatively affected by occupational structural changes. A combination of factors in many postindustrial economies has led to a shrinking, rather than growing, number of the white-collar positions that created and sustained the broad middle classes in these societies. According to some observers (Newman, 1988; Phillips, 1993; Strobel, 1993), these forces have been at work in the United States since at least the late 1960s or early 1970s and are largely responsible for the increasing "pauperization" and disappearance of the middle class in this society.

One factor contributing heavily to the loss of millions of white-collar positions is the restructuring that has taken place in many national and multinational corporations. In their efforts to cut costs and increase efficiency, companies have "downsized" their operations by eliminating many full-time administrative and service positions. Ironically, many staff workers who lost their jobs to downsizing have been hired back by those same companies to perform the same duties, but now as lower-paid, part-time temporary workers without medical or retirement benefits (Dillin, 1993a). Overall, the wages of U.S. white-collar workers have been slipping since 1987 (Francis, 1993a).

A significant amount of corporate downsizing represents one effect of the large number of mergers and takeovers throughout the corporate world during the past two decades. These alliances often are hailed as a stimulus to economic growth and development for the organizations involved (Halverson, 1994), but the impact on their constituent staffs often has been far less benign. For many midlevel managers and service personnel, these mergers signify impending unemployment. As Newman (1988, p. 34) has observed: "When two corporate bureaucracies fold together, only one emerges in the end." For example, when Bank of America merged with Security Pacific Bank in 1992, over 10,000 southern California workers found, to their horror, that they were part of what Bank of America executives had blandly termed a "release of resources" that would accompany the closing of many branch offices and the consolidation or transferring of their operations to the bank's corporate headquarters ("Gee, Thanks, Boss," 1992). Vice-presidents and managers who had been with Security Pacific for many years suddenly had to scramble for comparable positions elsewhere, as they were let go in favor of their Bank of America counterparts. For these individuals, the merger was anything but the "win-win" situation it may have been for stockholders.

Governmental downsizing has also played a major part in the disappearance of many white-collar positions. In the United States, the Clinton administration has already begun laying off federal employees as part of its plan to cut the federal workforce by over one-quarter million by the end of 1999 (Ingwerson, 1994). In Argentina, a relatively advanced and affluent developing nation, the federal government also has embarked on a campaign to slice expenses by effecting major cuts in its huge bureaucracy (Long, 1992). As a result of these cost-cutting measures, hundreds of thousands of government staff workers have lost their jobs—and their middle-class lifestyles—over the past few years. Some local observers have described the destruction of what had been a healthy and growing middle class as "one of the country's big social problems" (Pessah in Green, 1993).

EDUCATION

Economic and occupational structural changes have by no means been the only obstacles to greater equality in industrial and postindustrial societies. Formal education has played as much of a role in preserving and creating social inequalities in these societies as it has in eliminating them. In particular, as the 1994 Group of Seven meeting emphasized, educational systems in most industrialized nations have been unable to keep up with the changing technological skill requirements of their rapidly changing economies. Schools continue to teach occupational skills that have become obsolete or no job-related skills at all to their students who are not college bound. The result has been both a growing number of students completing their high school education without ever acquiring the technological skills necessary for finding initial employment and a growing number of displaced employees throughout the developed world who lack access to the technological retraining necessary for finding replacement jobs. To a large extent, the current unemployment crises facing many industrialized countries across North America and Western Europe are based on what amount to educational crises (Friedman, 1994b).

Modern economies depend on an adequate supply of trained, knowledgeable personnel who can understand and utilize (and create) the technological, informational, and other sophisticated tools that support the productive system. As far as we presently can tell, talent in any society is not confined to any single social group. All races, nationalities, classes, sexes, and other identifiable groups are capable of producing people of genuine ability. It clearly is in the best collective interests of all modern societies, then, to do whatever they can to promote the search for and development of individual talent, regardless of its origin. Formal education can play exactly such a role, if at least two important conditions are met.

First, all members of society must be provided equal access to formal education. There can be no barriers that categorically restrict or exclude certain kinds of people from participating in the formal educational process simply on ascriptive grounds (that is, because they come from the "wrong" race, ethnic group, class, or gender). Second, once enrolled in the educational system, all individuals must be provided the same opportunities for success. The system itself must not operate in such a way that certain categories of people are much more likely than others to do poorly or to fail. Academic success or failure must be a function of individual talent and effort, rather than membership in some particular favored or unfavored group. In short, like the larger economic and occupational systems whose needs it was designed to serve, formal education must follow pure achievement principles in recruiting, training, and evaluating its students.

To the extent that formal education meets these criteria, society as a whole benefits from the increased talent available for service in economic, government, and other critical social institutions. Individuals likewise benefit from the educational credentials that allow them to improve their own social status and life situations. However, in many modern societies, as we will discuss in more detail in the next chapter, one or both of these necessary conditions are missing. The result is systems of formal education that more often reflect and reinforce, rather than reshape, prevailing socioeconomic inequalities (Collins, 1979; Kozol, 1992; Weis, 1988).

COLLEGE AND UNIVERSITY ACCESS

Although most individuals in modern societies complete primary education and many also finish a secondary education, a much smaller number typically complete college or university studies. For example, among people aged 25 to 64 in various OECD (Organization for Economic Cooperation and Development) industrialized countries in Western Europe, 65 percent of British respondents had completed high school as of 1989, whereas only 9 percent had completed college. In Germany, 78 percent had completed high school, but only 10 percent college. In Denmark, 57 percent had completed high school, and 10 percent college. And in France, 50 percent were high school graduates, but only 7 percent had completed college (reported in Havemann, 1993).

Students who do continue their formal education beyond the secondary level are drawn largely from those economic, racial, and ethnic groups that constitute the middle and upper rungs of their societies' socioeconomic ladders. Students from less advantaged backgrounds are far less likely to undertake undergraduate and graduate education (Farkas et al., 1990; Navarrette, 1992; Steele, 1992). Ironically, those who, in a sense, have less need for the social mobility that university degrees make possible (since their social class standing is already at or above the middle of the ladder) are much more likely to attain those degrees than individuals from the lower classes, for whom the need is far greater and the gains from being educated would be more significant.

It is very unlikely that this pattern is the result of any policies deliberately instituted to exclude members of the lower social echelons from the rewards of higher education. Where such legalized practices once existed (as, for example, in the "Jim Crow" system of racial segregation in the U.S. South or in the apartheid system of South Africa), they have been overturned. Rather, a series of factors have combined to create what amounts to a de facto (in practice) college "Head Start" program for members of the more affluent social strata. Some of these contributing elements are functions of the ability of higher-strata families to send their children to more exclusive and better-equipped private schools rather than to the public school system. In these schools, children will receive whatever benefits can be obtained from what literally may be the best—or at least the most expensive—education that money can buy. Armed with experiences and information not ordinarily available to their lower-class counterparts, they may possess enough of an edge to perform at consistently higher academic levels in their classes and on college entrance exams (Katsillas & Rubinson, 1990; Levine, 1980).

EDUCATIONAL TRACKING

Other contributing factors, however, may be related to lingering beliefs about the presumed lesser abilities of specific racial, ethnic, or class groups. Many critics (for example, Kozol, 1992; Navarrette, 1992; Oakes, 1985; Pasternak, 1993) claim that such beliefs underlie the educational *tracking* systems found at the secondary-school level in many modern societies. These differentiated curricular tracks are intended to channel students of different abilities into career lines best suited for their own individual talents. Their overall effect often has been to categorically steer minority and lower-class students into vocational training and other noncollege tracks and upper-middle- and upper-class students into college-prep studies. The consequences of such tracking upon future economic prospects can be enormous.

Some industrial societies, such as Austria, Denmark, France, Germany, and Switzerland, have begun to establish apprenticeship training programs in conjunction with private enterprise to insure that non-college-bound high school students will be well prepared for employment in high-paying, skilled trades positions after they graduate (Havemann, 1993). But other modern societies, including the United States, have no such programs. The needs of students not enrolled in college-prep tracks often are virtually ignored, so that these students face what has been described as an "occupational void" after graduation, destined for long-term unemployment or employment in low-paying, marginal jobs (Fiske, 1992). The reality of the U.S. situation has been described by one close observer, an educational adviser to President Clinton and himself president of the National Center on Education and the Economy:

> Ours is one of the most elitist educational systems of all the advanced industrial world. We concentrate all resources on college-bound kids, [while the others] leave high school having achieved only a seventh- or eighth-grade level of literacy. The result is that we are forced to compete not with Japan and Germany on quality, but with Thailand and Mexico on wages and hours. (Tucker quoted in Levine, 1993)

Whether intended or not, one crucial effect of contemporary tracking systems and practices has been the shunting of many lower-socioeconomic-background students onto what amount to dead-end educational sidings while the college-bound express roars by on the fast track. In an era in which as many as 30 percent of college graduates find themselves unemployed or underemployed each year (Greenwald, 1993b), viable job prospects for these nondegreed individuals remain extremely grim. College diplomas have become "the great divider" in shaping occupational careers and economic attainment among the members of modern industrialized societies (Jones, 1994). As Table 6.3 illustrates, the likelihood of poverty is 12 times lower for college degree holders than for high school dropouts and 5 times lower than that for high school graduates. Many minority and lower-class students are finding themselves on the wrong side of that educational divide and may never be able to cross to the other side.

RISING COSTS

In past years, state-supported, four-year colleges and two-year junior or community colleges made undergraduate and (in some cases) graduate degree programs accessible to a broad spectrum of the population, at costs well below those of the private schools. The

TABLE 6.3 Educational Level and Poverty Rates for Householders 25 Years and Over: 1992

Educational Level of Householder	Below Poverty Level (percent)
No high school diploma	24.1
High school diploma, no college	11.0
Some college, less than bachelor's degree	7.2
Bachelor's degree or more	2.2

SOURCE: U.S. Bureau of the Census, *Current Population Reports,* Series P60-185.

academic currency value of their degrees often was below that of degrees from many private colleges and universities (Useem & Karabel, 1986), but these public colleges did offer higher educational credentials to individuals at a time of overall economic growth when positions requiring college degrees were expanding rapidly. However, that time now appears to be over.

The economic changes that have dramatically slowed or stopped growth in many modern societies (as discussed earlier in this chapter) have also placed tremendous strains on their ability to maintain quality higher educational systems at what amount to below-market costs to students. Falling revenues and other pressing economic needs have led governments to slash their budgets supporting higher public education. The results of these cuts have included rising tuition and related academic fees, cutbacks in faculties and in classes, and lower enrollment caps (Feldmann, 1993a). As a consequence, growing numbers of students from lower-socioeconomic backgrounds have been priced out of what had been a free or nearly free college education, thus closing off what had been an important channel for occupational and social advancement. If recessions continue throughout the industrialized world and public college and university systems continue to downsize, members of the lower-socioeconomic ranks may find themselves increasingly locked into place. Now a vehicle for individual achievement, formal education in these societies could once again become a badge of ascription.

GLOBAL INEQUALITY

Just as contemporary societies are stratified into unequal segments whose constituent members are individual people, the contemporary world is likewise stratified into unequal segments. However, in the case of this global inequality system, the constituent members are individual societies. *Developed,* or *northern,* and *developing,* or *southern,* are terms often used to describe a particular society's general position on this global stratification ladder with respect to economic, educational, nutritional, health care, and other resources vital to human existence.

Developed, or northern, countries are composed of the more economically developed and politically democratic nations. These societies feature free-market economies dominated by advanced-technology industrial and administrative occupations, and display generally high levels of collective and per capita income. Many population members occupy what could be called middle-class socioeconomic positions and enjoy relatively comfortable lives. Japan, Canada, and the United States are representative examples of developed societies.

Developing, or southern, countries currently are undergoing societal modernization. Their economies represent a mixture of a large percentage of traditional agrarian activities and a growing proportion of industry-oriented, factory-based manufacturing and processing occupations. In contrast to their counterparts in the developed world, these developing societies generally are characterized by much lower levels of overall and per capita incomes. Many, perhaps most, population members occupy very low positions in the socioeconomic hierarchy. They often lead lives at or near the basic survival level and experience great economic and physical hardships. Often, though not always, developing societies are characterized by political systems that are nondemocratic and "less free."

Although all developing societies share this modernizing status, they differ significantly from one another in many other ways. Both Mozambique and South Korea are developing countries, but they are located at very opposite ends of the modernization continuum with regard to economic and political development and the quality-of-life levels of their respective populations. Mozambique may well be the least developed society in the world, whereas South Korea is poised on the edge of "developed nation" status in many ways. Truly representative societal examples are difficult to provide, since the term *developing* includes such a wide array of individual nations at different levels of social and economic development.

According to World Bank data (World Development Report, 1992, p. 25), more than 1 billion people throughout the world continue to live in "abject poverty," and most of these poor people live in developing societies. This number represents an increase of over 100 million individuals since the mid-1980s and is related significantly to rapid population growth in these less developed countries. (Recall our discussion of population dynamics in Chapter Three.) Population Action International (formerly The Population Crisis Committee) (1992) has attempted to operationalize the concept of abject poverty by translating it into more tangible form. Their International Human Suffering Index (HSI) represents a composite measure of living conditions in 141 nations in the developed and developing worlds. The index includes information on life expectancy, daily calorie supply, clean drinking water, infant immunization, per capita GNP, enrollment in secondary schools, inflation rate, civil rights and political freedom, and communications technology. Based on their standings on these dimensions, individual countries are rated as "extreme," "high," "moderate," or "minimum" with respect to human suffering.

According to the most recent HSI figures, "extreme" and "high" human suffering countries are concentrated squarely in the developing world. The 83 countries that fall into these two categories have a collective population of nearly 4 billion people, or 73 percent of the present world population. At the other end of the spectrum, the 24 countries that comprise the "minimum" human suffering category are, almost without exception, industrial or postindustrial societies of the developed world. Collectively, these nations hold 14.8 percent of the world's population, or 797 million people. These figures parallel those of the United Nations Development Program's *Human Development Report 1993,* which indicates that the most affluent 20 percent of the world's population received 150 times the earnings of the poorest 20 percent that year (see Figure 6.2).

South Asia and sub–Saharan Africa are two regions that are particularly poor: In 1990, nearly half of all people living in these two geographic areas fell below the poverty level (World Development Report, 1992). Since 1990, poverty numbers and rates have improved in South Asia and other developing nations, but the individual societies of sub–Saharan Africa continue to fall even farther behind the rest of the developing and

FIGURE 6.2 Disparity of Global Wealth

The wealthiest fifth of the world's population control about 85 percent of total economic activity as measured by four key indicators. The bottom fifth control about 1 percent.

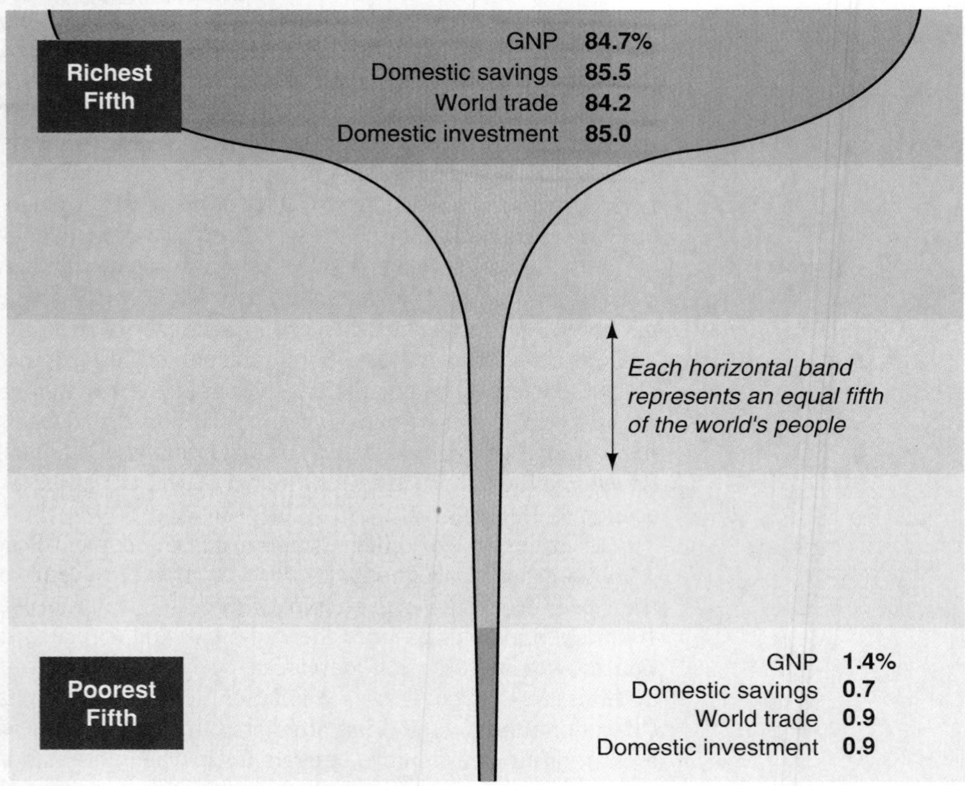

Source: Herring in *The Christian Science Monitor.* © 1994 TCSPS.
Note: Original data from United Nations Development Program, 1991.

developed world (Scherer, 1993). At current rates, 9 million more people will be added to the ranks of the poor in this region each year. In these countries, economic poverty translates into misery, disease, hunger, malnourishment, and starvation for countless individuals each day.

It is extremely doubtful that simply pumping large sums of money in humanitarian aid into these impoverished countries would do much to change their situation. Their problems, and those of other developing nations, stem from their unfavorable positions within the global economic system. The historical forces that created such widespread poverty and misery in the developing world are the same as those responsible for the relative affluence of developed societies that have been more favorably positioned within that system.

WORLD SYSTEM THEORY

Immanuel Wallerstein (1974, 1979, 1984) has largely been responsible for the development of a theoretical model of the global political economy known as *world system theory*

(*WST*). According to this interpretation, the origins of and relations between the developed and the developing worlds can only be understood in the same framework as relations between the lower and upper classes within given societies.

Throughout much of the past millenium, superior technology allowed England, Spain, Germany, France, and other European countries to colonize large portions of the Asian, African, and American continents. These colonies were established as sources of wealth for the mother country, whether through the direct shipment of precious commodities (for example, gold and silver from the New World or ivory from Africa) or from the goods and services provided for economic trade markets (tea and spices from the Far East and slaves from Africa, for instance). As centuries passed and the destruction and exploitation of indigenous peoples evolved into political control and then to economic domination (Bergesen, 1980), the old colonial (and now industrialized) powers came to form the core countries or what amounted to the upper class of an evolving world stratification system. Most of the former colonies (especially in Africa and Asia) fell to periphery or lower-class international status, and the lesser powers of the industrialized world (the Scandinavian countries, for example) assumed a middle-class position as semiperiphery nations.

Just as the relations between the upper and lower classes within individual societies inevitably entail conflict as both groups struggle for limited and scarce resources in a zero-sum societal environment, relations between core and peripheral societies in the context of a zero-sum international environment likewise involve inevitable conflict. And in both instances, the results are the same. Societal upper classes dominate and exploit lower classes, and world system core nations dominate and exploit peripheral countries. It is the self-serving economic and political policies of the industrialized core, and not any local cultural, political, or social deficiencies within the periphery, that keep the developing countries in such crushing poverty.

Under the logic of the WST model, peripheral countries will experience significant and sustained improvement only if and when they acquire enough economic, political, or other power to force a change in the international stratification system. Since they are the beneficiaries of the existing order, societal and international ruling groups are not likely to permit dramatic structural changes to systems that work so well to their advantage. Much as it would take a proletarian revolution to excise entrenched societal inequality (according to Marxist theory), it will take a peripheral revolution to effect similar results in the entrenched world inequality system. However, the immense firepower advantages industrialized nations historically have had over developing countries make large-scale military assault by the periphery against the core extremely remote.

One promising approach for improving the status of developing societies has been that of concerted economic action. Inspired, perhaps, by the amazing success of the so-called little dragons of East Asia—South Korea, Hong Kong, Taiwan, and Singapore—developing countries around the globe have forged alliances that promote their collective economic interests and magnify their individual economic resources. For example, Pakistan, Turkey, Iran, and five Islamic Asian republics of the former USSR have formed an Economic Cooperation Organization embracing one-quarter billion people; the five nations that border the Caspian Sea, the world's largest land-locked body of water, have joined to form the Caspian Sea Pact (R. Wright, 1992). These and other alliances have helped make Asia one of the fastest-growing economic regions (with Latin America) in the world.

According to World Bank projections, if current development trends in the modernizing societies were to continue, the developing world's share of world income would rise to almost half (from less than one-quarter) by the year 2050 and to three-quarters by the end of the twenty-first century (World Development Report, 1992, p. 33). Not all developing countries would share equally in this gain, of course, but their socioeconomic inequality profiles would begin to more closely resemble those of developed societies. Though far from perfect, this would be a distinct improvement for the hundreds of millions of people in developing countries who now have virtually nothing at all.

UNDERSTANDING POVERTY

When we picture socioeconomic inequality, the first image that typically comes to mind is that of poverty. Whether it is the massive and profound impoverishment of a developing country's population (epitomized, for example, by photographs and horror stories of starving African children) or the more selective but no less profound poverty of developed nations (portrayed, for example, in newspaper articles about the local city's plans for its homeless people), conditions of poverty and groups of poor people may be the most obvious manifestation of societal inequality systems in action.

It may or may not ultimately turn out to be the case, as the Bible claims, that "the poor we shall always have with us." What has been true is that, for the past several thousand years, all but the smallest and simplest of human societies have had their shares of poverty and of the poor. Tales of the economically distressed abound in ancient and recent historical accounts of the human condition. People fleeing poverty in Old World Europe found it (or brought it with them) in New World America. Many people and nations now emerging from long-standing political repression remain as economically repressed as they were under the old regimes (Drew, 1993). But although poverty might be thought of as a more or less constant human phenomenon, humans' perceptions of what poverty is and who the poor are have varied tremendously from one time and place to another.

DEFINING AND MEASURING POVERTY

On the surface, it might seem that conceptualizing and studying poverty would not present any real difficulties. *Poverty* is the lack of money. *The poor* are those people who do not possess and cannot afford the basic necessities of life that other people possess.

By now, however, you should be aware that *the* fundamental principle of sociology—"things never are as simple as they seem"—applies here as in all other aspects of human social life. Is poverty really just a matter of lacking money? What exactly are "the basic necessities of life" that one must possess in order not to be poor? Who exactly are "the other people" to whom the poor are compared and contrasted?

ABSOLUTE DEFINITIONS

According to what are sometimes referred to as *subsistence definitions* (George, 1988), poverty is an objective phenomenon, a state of absolute deprivation. From this perspective, poverty is that condition experienced by individuals and families (and societies) who lack the economic resources to maintain a minimally adequate level of existence. In terms of sheer physical survival, poverty represents the inability to "make it" on a long-term basis—and, throughout the contemporary world, quite a few people just aren't making it.

According to estimates by the United Nations Development Program (as reported in "One-Fourth of Humanity," 1993), about one-fourth of the population of the entire world (some 1.4 billion people) were living in absolute poverty in 1993, primarily in countries of the developing world. But absolute poverty is hardly unknown in the developed nations. The members of these industrialized societies generally enjoy much higher absolute income levels, as measured by some common denominator (U.S. dollars, for example), but this fact alone does not mean there is no real poverty, since these people face much higher living costs, as well. Simply knowing per capita income figures for various societies, therefore, may tell us very little about the extent of absolute poverty that exists within each society.

Poverty may be an absolute phenomenon in the sense that some specific and measurable amount of income is needed to maintain basic physical survival. It is nonetheless a relative phenomenon in the sense that the number of dollars so required varies with cost-of-living expenses, rates of inflation, and other factors specific to individual societies. For example, the per capita yearly income level in Japan, an economic superpower considered second only to the United States, was $27,132 in 1992, compared to $22,204 in the United States (Greenhouse, 1993). However, the cost of basic consumer goods in Japan, especially housing, was about 40 percent higher than that in the United States, so that the extra $5,000 was not enough to keep the average Japanese on a par with the average American. Looking at the two countries just on the basis of their populations' gross per capita incomes would therefore be misleading.

To avoid problems in making valid comparisons between two or more countries, poverty rates for individual societies ordinarily are calculated on the basis of the number of dollars needed to purchase survival-level resources in those particular societies. For example, in the United States, 36.9 million people were defined as living in "official" poverty in 1992. This figure was based on government estimates that, in that particular year, incomes of $14,335 and $7,143 formed the poverty thresholds for four-person families and for individuals, respectively (Eaton, 1993). Over the past decades that poverty rates have been tracked, these threshold dollar amounts have risen steadily from year to year, with the cost of living. However, some critics contend that they have yet to rise to realistic levels, so that official poverty estimates greatly understate the true extent of subsistence-level existence in this country (Ruggles, 1990, 1992). In this capacity, poverty rates serve an important political role, as it is clearly to the advantage of an incumbent government to present a best-case scenario when assessing its own performance in economic and other realms. Too much economic bad news can mean political bad news, and so poverty data are as much subject to political manipulation as they are to mathematical analysis (Ingwerson, 1992). For this reason, so-called objective poverty figures should be treated with caution (George, 1988).

An additional problem that seems to be built into absolutist conceptions of poverty is determining which resources are truly necessary for survival. For example, food, clothing, and shelter obviously are required to maintain life over time. But what about transportation? In a society in which one's job is located outside the home, some means of getting to and from work (whether by public transit or personal automobile) is essential. No transportation means no work, and no work means no income for food, clothing, and shelter. Similarly, it could be argued that, in an information-based modern society, some way of accessing mass communications channels may be necessary for survival. Does that then mean that a television should be added to the list of items essential for long-term physical survival? As George (1988) has observed, the extent of absolute deprivation in a given society and across different societies can vary significantly depending on how generous government or other officials are in compiling lists of "essential" survival resources.

RELATIVE DEFINITIONS

One way or another, the various absolute definitions of poverty attempt to draw a line that demarcates the poor from the rest of society by calculating the dollar cost of those objective resources deemed necessary to sustain human life over time. In contrast, relative poverty approaches argue that poverty is the condition of being deprived in comparison to some other person or group. For example, most blue-collar workers in industrial societies may live comfortably above the subsistence level. They earn wages, own or rent homes, and drive personal automobiles. However, their lesser incomes, more modest houses, and older cars would make them relatively poor when compared to attorneys, physicians, and other professionals whose greater incomes make possible much more affluent lifestyles. And even these professionals could be regarded as experiencing relative deprivation when their lifestyles are compared to those of their society's rich and famous.

Though such arguments seldom if ever have been made seriously, it could be claimed that anyone not at the very top of the societal socioeconomic hierarchy is, by definition, relatively poor. However, a serious claim could be made that such conceptualizations of poverty as a relative condition are not very helpful in examining poverty as a social problem. Given the logic of this approach, so long as income and wealth are distributed at all unequally among different population segments (regardless of just how more or less unequal those distributions may be), poverty will persist, even if the lowest economic group is well above the subsistence level. Anything short of a perfectly equal distribution of economic resources amounts to relative poverty. In contrast, treating poverty as a condition of absolute or extreme deprivation implies that, at least in theory, such conditions could be eliminated by raising all societal members above the poverty threshold. Disputes about how his objective might best be accomplished generally begin with questions about the origins of poverty.

THE CAUSES OF POVERTY

Just as perceptions and definitions of poverty have fluctuated across social space and time, so also have beliefs about those factors responsible for such economic deprivation. Although there have been a fairly large number of individual variations, three general themes have dominated social thinking and public policy concerning the fundamental causes of poverty. They have centered on economic development, on the psychological and cultural attributes of the poor, and on structural conditions as having the most significant impact on creating and preserving poverty.

ECONOMIC DEVELOPMENT

According to one interpretation, the level of poverty within a given society is a direct function of that society's level of economic development. From this perspective, widespread and persistent deprivation is one consequence of a societal economy that fails to meet its population's needs for basic resources. This is especially likely if the society is experiencing rapid population growth, as is the case for a large number of developing countries. Many or most people in these less developed countries are poor for the simple reason that there just isn't enough food, clothing, shelter, and other necessities of life to go around. These societies have begun to modernize but are unable to complete the process. The pressures of trying to meet the present needs of a growing population mean that the enormous amount of monetary and other resources required for the economic expansion that could lift the country out of poverty normally aren't available. Governments that attempt to ignore current demands and to channel resources instead into economic development for future population needs do so at the risk of a political and social upheaval sparked by what James Davies (1962) termed a "revolution of rising expectations." Population members who have had a glimpse or a small taste of the better life made possible through modernization may experience an intolerable level of relative deprivation should that hope be blocked. For example, the 1994 Chiapas revolt against the Mexican federal government was deliberately timed to coincide with the start of the North American Free Trade Agreement. Peasant farmers in this southern state were convinced that the Salinas government that for years had ignored their needs had now sacrificed them in the name of international trade. They were convinced that NAFTA would undercut the price of locally grown corn and thus destroy the only source of their livelihood (Golden, 1994).

Since developing nations ordinarily are unable to finish modernizing their economies on their own, they must rely either on foreign investment capital or on loans from international banks. Should they then encounter a recession or other slowdown in their economic progress, as happened throughout Latin America in the 1980s, payments on these loans then would become an additional barrier to development (see "Focus on Brazil"). After collectively paying $296 billion in interest to world banks on their modernization loans, Latin American countries still owed another $430 billion as of 1992 (Cockburn, 1992). In any event, evidence from the developed nations suggests that even if less developed countries could complete their modernization, that fact alone would not eradicate poverty. Significant poverty remains in most societies long after advanced stages of economic development and economic productivity have been attained (George, 1988).

PSYCHOLOGICAL AND CULTURAL TRAITS

A second interpretation of poverty assigns causal priority to psychological or cultural traits exhibited by poor people. In essence, people become poor and remain poor because of some defect in their individual personalities or their group culture—an argument sometimes described by its critics as "blaming the victim" (Ryan, 1976).

In the early 1900s, at a time when many U.S. cities were being crowded by large numbers of foreign-born immigrants, both urban poverty and urban crime levels rose rapidly.

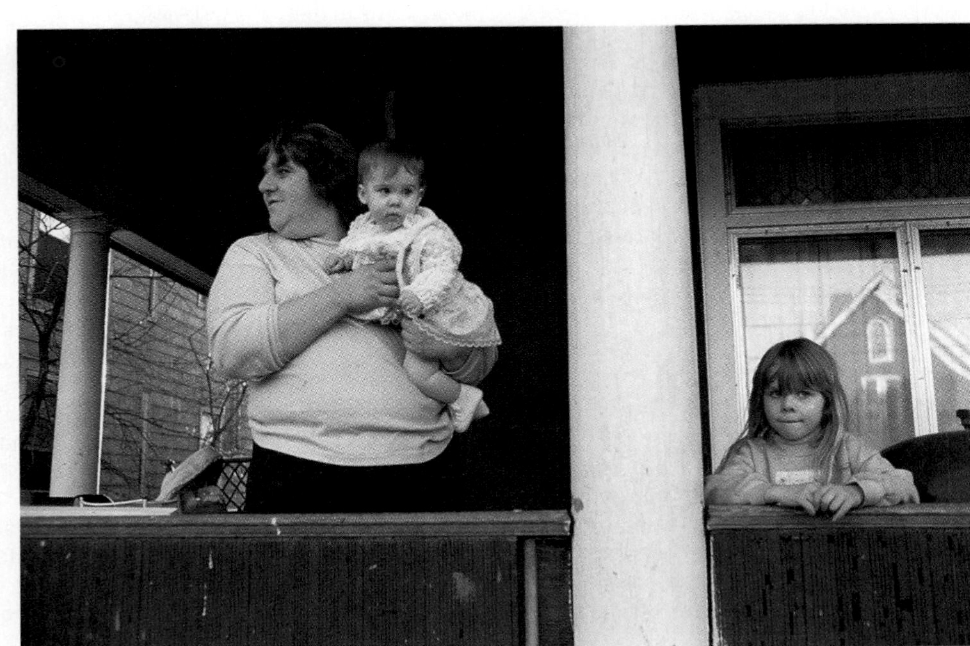

Contrary to portrayals in the popular media, poverty in the United States is an overwhelmingly White phenomenon. Although many minority groups have higher rates *of poverty, in terms of the total number of people living in poverty, most are White. Single-parent families headed by women have been among the fastest-growing poverty group in this country, especially families with young children.*

OCUS ON BRAZIL

THE BOYS FROM BRAZIL
Poverty, Life, and Death in Latin America

With a total land area of over 3.275 million square miles and a total population of close to 160 million people, Brazil is geographically and demographically the dominant country in all of Latin America. Brazil's $450 billion economy is approximately the same size as China's and Russia's, and ranks the country tenth among the world's 200 economies in terms of real gross domestic product (Maddison & Associates, 1992). A growth rate of 4.5 percent in 1993 put Brazil squarely in the forefront of economic development among all Latin American societies that year, while a per capita yearly income of approximately $3,000 gives its population one of the highest average incomes in the region. On the surface, it might seem that Brazil could be a model of what a modernizing society might hope to become in the best of all possible scenarios. Brazil appears to be a nation that, like Japan, has pulled itself out of economic darkness in the relatively short space of less than 50 years. But these impressive figures tell only half the story.

A major portion of Brazil's startling economic growth during the late 1960s and early 1970s—the period of the so-called *milagre brasilerio* ("Brazilian miracle")—was made possible by a series of loans arranged through the world bank members of the International Monetary Fund and a heavy infusion of foreign investment capital. However, during the decade-long economic slump of the 1980s that hit the entire Latin American region, Brazil's economic expansion came to a sudden halt. The country was left saddled with a foreign debt of $115 billion, the largest of any country in the developing world (Bruner, 1993a). It was also left with mind-boggling yearly inflation rates that in 1993 reached 2,244 percent and pushed the inflation rate for the Latin American region as a whole to 797 percent (Long, 1993b). Brazil's current monthly inflation rate of 35 percent is higher than annual inflation rates in Argentina, Chile, and Mexico (Bruner, 1993a) and has a near-fatal impact on the lives of the nearly 50 percent of the Brazilian population living below poverty level. For the estimated 20 percent of the population living in abject poverty, the impact often *is* fatal.

HOW THE LOWER HALF LIVES (AND DIES)

Brazil's per capita income figures mask the reality of a highly skewed income distribution that varies significantly, among other things, by geographic region. The more urbanized and industrialized southern and southeastern states are relatively better off compared to the more impoverished northern and northwestern hinterland states. Overall, the top 20 percent of Brazil's population receives 32 times the income of the bottom 20 percent—a quintile income ratio that is widely regarded as the most unequal in the Western world (Wright, 1994). Approximately 32 million people earn just about enough money (the equivalent of $150 per month) to provide for the most basic survival resources, whereas another 15 million earn only half that amount. The 5 million individuals who constitute the lowest of the low receive no income at all for their labor (Margolis, 1993). For them, "Will work for food" is a daily fact of life, rather than a ploy for charity. Very often, there is no work—and no food.

Hunger and malnourishment are very serious problems among the Brazilian poor, especially among children. The country's rate of infant mortality—the number of infants who die before age 1 per 1,000 live births—is 55, or two and a half times that of China. To date, the Brazilian government has been unable (or, according to some critics, unwilling) to take systematic steps to address the infant mortality problem and the widespread hunger that feeds it. Local citizens in a number of particularly hard-hit states have taken matters into their own hands, forming programs that at times have achieved a high level of success at very little cost (Brooke, 1993). But for many children who have survived infancy and fled to Brazil's cities, these programs are too little and too late. Seeking a better life in Brazil's urban centers, they instead more often encounter a miserable death.

MENINOS DE RUA

On July 23, 1993, seven street children (*meninos de rua*) were brutally massacred as they slept on the streets of Rio de Janeiro. An eighth died of his wounds a few days later. Although these particular killings shocked both local residents and members of the international community, they were hardly unique, nor were they the last such events. In 1992, an official investigation conducted by the Brazilian congress had reported that more than 4,600 street children had been killed during the previous three years (Muello, 1993). Since that time, an estimated average of four more have been killed each day, some of them by other street children or by the various criminal gangs for whom they often perform services. Many others, however, have apparently been the victims of death squads allegedly hired by middle-class merchants to drive the children away from their stores and their customers. Further allegations claim that these execution squads are composed of moonlighting members of the military police,

As is so often the case in the world, children have been among the groups hit hardest by Brazil's struggling economy. According to some estimates, as many as 7 million meninos de rua *("street children") may be living in Rio de Janeiro and other large Brazilian cities. Often turning to criminal and gang activity in order to survive, these children have been increasingly targeted by death squads allegedly hired by middle-class merchants and shopkeepers.*

an organization widely believed by Brazilians to be both completely corrupt and completely without mercy toward the poor who live in the *favelas* ("slums") that spread out through Rio, São Paulo, and other large cities (Long, 1993a). Most military police officers themselves have been recruited from the lower classes and have become accustomed to doing whatever they feel they must in order to survive.

According to those who work in shelters set up for them, the street children who have been the targets of these death squads are most often boys (although the number of girls has been growing) who have fled abusive family situations in suburban slums. Most frequently, they are Black or mulatto—that is, of mixed racial heritage (Michaels, 1993). Once on the streets, they turn to theft and other crimes—sometimes violent crimes—in their efforts to scratch out an existence. It is the combination of this growing urban crime problem and what many people see as government laxity in punishing street children criminals that, in the words of one observer, "has pushed the middle class into a fascist attitude. It wants criminals to be killed" (Saboia in Long, 1993a).

GOVERNMENT GRIDLOCK

The Brazilian government's inability to deal effectively with the country's growing poverty problem and with growing urban crime stems from its own criminal difficulties. After 20 years of military rule, Brazil's first popularly elected president, Fernando Collor de Mello, was impeached and forced to resign over his apparent involvement in widespread political corruption. Since his departure, other charges of influence-peddling, bribery, fraud, and other acts of corruption have been leveled against members of the Brazilian congress popularly referred to as "the Budget Mafia" (Long, 1993c). Public support and confidence are at an all-time low as government leaders spend more time on resolving their own and their colleagues' potential legal difficulties and less time on resolving the country's worsening economic and social difficulties.

This same lack of confidence on the part of foreign investors is lessening their willingness to commit the massive funds vital to Brazil's economic and social improvement (Bruner, 1993b). Should that source of financing be closed off, the results could be truly disastrous. As we saw earlier, in the political economies of the contemporary world, bad news in either the political or the economic sector is bad news for the other. In Mexico, the 1994 Zapatista-led rebellion against the federal government of President Salinas reflected the growing disenchantment and anger of poor people tired of being passed over in the country's push for economic development. The subsequent assassination of the ruling PRI party's candidate to succeed Salinas may also have been tied to increasing frustration against a government that had been unable (or unwilling) to address the continuing poverty of much of its people. If Brazil's leaders cannot make immediate and significant gains against that country's worsening poverty problems, a similar grass-roots uprising could be in the offing.

Some social scientists of the day claimed that these problems were the result of the inferior intellectual, emotional, or moral attributes of these immigrant groups, which doomed their members to lives of poverty and crime. These people failed in the game of life because they lacked the intelligence and ambition needed to succeed in the competitive social world. For example, in a book intended as a text in "civic sociology" for high school students, Edward Alsworth Ross, one of the most influential sociologists of his time, addressed the poverty that was then quite pervasive throughout the United States. He claimed that, among those cases of poverty that were not "acts of God," the leading causes of such economic misery were the laziness, stupidity, and vice of the poor (Ross, 1931). In some instances, these inferior traits were biologically inherited and therefore beyond social solution. In other cases, they could be eradicated and replaced with more wholesome and productive traits through a rigorous resocialization program.

"Natural superiority theories," as these arguments are called, have been scientifically discredited by later research, which has failed to verify either the natural superiority or the natural inferiority of any particular racial or ethnic group relative to any other specific group. But the belief that the poor are more lazy or sinful or stupid than other people still persists. An editorial cartoon that appeared in the daily newspaper of the sixth-largest city in the United States in February 1994 showed a welfare recipient talking with his tax accountant. In response to the accountant's news that, under the Clinton proposal to tax welfare benefits, he could deduct the cost of equipment used to produce his income, the client replied, "That would be my TV and my sofa" (Kelley, 1994). The rich may be just like ordinary folks, but the poor apparently are not.

As we saw in the last chapter, some contemporary social scientists explain the continuing poverty of the urban underclass in terms of this group's possession of a set of unique beliefs and values. This so-called culture of poverty fosters a fatalistic, present-oriented world view that traps the poor into permanent poverty status. Like the earlier natural superiority approach, this perspective places the ultimate blame for poverty squarely on the shoulders of the poor.

STRUCTURAL EXPLANATIONS

In contrast to explanations of poverty that center on the psychological or cultural characteristics of the impoverished, structural interpretations of poverty focus on characteristics of the larger society that permit or encourage poverty. Functionalist theorists and conflict theorists have offered two very different structural explanations for the same phenomenon.

According to the functionalist model of inequality and poverty proposed by sociologists Kingsley Davis and Wilbert E. Moore (1945), all societies face the problem of attracting talented individuals to perform difficult and demanding, but necessary, social roles. To encourage the most capable people to seek out the most important roles, these positions will be rewarded with high levels of income, prestige, and other desired resources. For example, because physicians are needed to help maintain the physical well-being of population members and the job itself demands great intellectual and physical skills, medicine is one of the highest-paid, most prestigious professions in modern societies. By the same token, social roles that are not of such importance to societal survival and that do not require specific talents that may be in short supply will offer lesser economic rewards. Restaurant dishwashers, for example, do not ordinarily command high salaries, given the nature of the job and the large number of population members who could easily do the work. From this perspective, then, the unequal amounts of income rewards attached to different social positions lead those people who occupy the lowest-rewarded positions to experience economic deprivation and those individuals who occupy the highest-rewarded positions to experience economic affluence. Poverty thus is an unintended consequence of a structural arrangement that otherwise operates to promote societal survival by guaranteeing a steady supply of talented people to perform critical tasks.

For conflict theorists, poverty and inequality in any society are both consequences of the same structure of power that is responsible for many other social problems. (Recall our discussion of social problems perspectives in Chapter One.) In all societies, population groups or segments that have controlling power will use that resource to structure economic, political, and all other important activities to suit their own best interests, regardless of the consequences for other groups. Poverty in modern societies results from the operations of a corporate economy designed to make money for its owners, not to offer a decent living for its workers. For example, as we saw in Chapter Five, much of the growing problem of urban poverty and homelessness in the United States has stemmed from the restructuring of the U.S. economy from a manufacturing-based system that offered many high-paying, skilled blue-collar jobs to a system now dominated by low-paying, service-sector jobs. From this perspective, solutions to poverty lie in altering the larger societal structure, not the personal or cultural characteristics of the poor.

POVERTY IN THE UNITED STATES

A large plaque on the base of the Statue of Liberty, in New York Harbor, invites the nations of the world to give the United States "their poor, their tired, their huddled masses." Over the years, many countries have taken us up on that generous offer, but the United States doesn't really need to solicit poor people from other lands. For some time, this country has had, hidden away in out-of-sight pockets of rural poverty and in out-of-mind inner-city ghettos, a significant supply of homegrown poor who were periodically "discovered" by social scientists and politicians. However, as the number of U.S. poor has grown steadily over recent decades, their presence and their plight have been working their way increasingly into the daily vision and consciousness of mainstream America. Poverty in the United States is a problem that has refused to hide or go away.

WHO ARE THE POOR?

The 36.9 million people who constituted the U.S. poor in 1992 represented a wide array of population segments. Nearly all recognized societal groups contributed to the 14.5 percent of the total population who fell below the official poverty line that year, but they did not contribute in equal proportions. As has been the case in preceding years, specific racial, ethnic, sex, and age categories were overrepresented within the ranks of the poor. These patterns are summarized in Table 6.4.

RACE AND ETHNICITY

Contrary to what may be widespread popular beliefs, the majority of all poor people in the United States—66.5 percent in 1992 (U.S. Bureau of the Census, 1993c)—are White. This may come as a surprise to some people, since, for better or worse, the mass media appear to have seized on the idea that poverty is a state inhabited primarily by people of color and have passed that idea to the general public as an established fact. Whenever television programs or newspapers or magazines feature stories about poverty in America, it seems, the settings invariably are the inner-city ghetto, the migrant labor camp, or the reservation, and the faces are always of a darker hue. But this image of poverty does not

TABLE 6.4 Poverty Status of Persons by Family Composition, Sex, Age, and Race: 1992

	Below Poverty Level (percent)			
Characteristic	White	Black	Latino	All Races
All Ages	11.6	33.3	29.3	14.5
Male	10.1	29.3	27.0	12.7
Female	13.0	36.8	31.6	16.3
Under 18 Years	16.9	46.6	39.9	21.9
Male	16.6	45.9	39.2	21.5
Female	17.2	47.3	40.7	22.3
Family Composition				
Married couple	6.7	14.3	21.4	7.5
Female head, no spouse present	30.2	53.7	51.2	38.5
Female head, no spouse present, children under 18	40.3	60.4	58.5	48.3

SOURCE: U.S. Bureau of the Census, *Current Population Reports,* Series P60-185.

mirror reality. Most poor people in the United States are not members of racial or ethnic minority groups.

What is true, however, is that membership in a minority group appears to magnify one's likelihood of falling below the poverty line. Whereas most poor people are White, most Whites aren't poor—fewer than 12 percent of all White persons were living below poverty level in 1992. However, persons of African American descent, who constituted 12.6 percent of the total U.S. population that year, had a poverty rate of 33.3 percent; and people of Latino origin, who made up a little under 9 percent of the entire population in 1992, had a poverty rate of over 29 percent. This pattern of significantly higher rates of poverty among African Americans and Latinos holds across different age, sex, and family composition categories.

SEX AND AGE

The probability that one will fall below the poverty level is significantly associated with sex and age status, as well. For women, poverty rates in 1992 were higher than those for men in all age and racial or ethnic categories. This was particularly true for women who were heads of single-parent households with children under the age of 18. For this group as a whole, the poverty rate in 1992 was over 48 percent, and the rates were even higher for minority women—slightly over 60 percent for African Americans and slightly under 60 percent for Latinos. These figures may be indicative of a trend termed "the feminization of poverty" (Pearce, 1978, 1990), which we will examine in more detail in Chapter Eight.

Age also plays a significant role in U.S. poverty. Children constituted 40 percent of the poor in 1992, even though they represented only about 25 percent of the societal population. In particular, according to the U.S. Bureau of the Census (1993c), children under age 6 are especially prone to poverty and its effects. One in every four children in the country under age 6 was living in poverty in 1992, and once again, these figures were elevated for minority children. These children, and many others, have become part of a widespread hunger problem that has been described as an epidemic (Grossfeld, 1993) and currently affects an estimated 12 million children (Yenkin, 1993). Overall, the number of poor children has been rising steadily over the past decade, and if present trends continue, half of all African American and Latino children and one-fourth of all Anglo children will be living in poverty by the year 2010 (Mehren, 1993).

FAMILY COMPOSITION

Vulnerability to poverty in 1992 was very much a function of family structure. Across the different races, 7.5 percent of persons living in intact married families—that is, in families with both spouses present—experienced poverty. This rate quintupled to 38.5 percent for persons in female-headed families and rose even higher (to 48.3 percent) for persons in female-headed families with children under age 18. The number of people living in single-parent family structures has increased steadily since the 1960s, and the majority of these single-parent situations involve females as family head. And once again, these rates increased substantially for African Americans and Latinos.

URBAN POVERTY

Although nonmetropolitan poverty rates were higher than metropolitan rates in the United States in 1992 (16.8 percent versus 13.9 percent), central cities were the sites of large numbers of the poor. Over 42 percent of all poor people lived in central city areas that year; the concentration of such large numbers in such confined areas may help explain the tendency to associate poverty with minority-group and inner-city status. It may also give some clues about the basic causes of poverty in American society.

As we discussed in great detail in Chapter Five, many of the largest cities in the United States have become financially destitute as a result of a series of postwar economic changes that included the shutting down of many once-thriving urban-based manufacturing industries. The loss of millions of jobs from plant closings and factory relocations has stranded increasingly large numbers of urban residents—especially members of ethnic and racial minority groups—in inner-city neighborhoods in which no work of any kind is to be found. Once in poverty and "out of the loop" with respect to job retraining and access to the now distant few blue-collar jobs that remain, many of these individuals sink into the ranks of the underclass, the hard-core poor. In those same urban centers, a growing number of people have been pushed into the ranks of the homeless, contributing even further to the cities' collapsing financial base. Given these realities, it is evident that any attempt to eliminate poverty in the United States will have to address these structural conditions.

ADDRESSING THE POVERTY PROBLEM

Although many different attempts have been made to deal with the poverty problem in the United States, none has been very effective to date. For the most part, public policies have focused on meeting the immediate needs of the poor and on correcting their presumed personal or cultural defects. Attending to the immediate needs of impoverished people for food, shelter, and other basic resources is a necessary and praiseworthy response. However, concentrating efforts on people alone while substantially ignoring the

Inequality and poverty are such pervasive phenomena that they intersect virtually all other national and international social institutions in the contemporary world. Socioeconomic inequality has impact not only on humans from the individual to societal levels but also on the physical environments within which all humans conduct their daily lives.

- Our earlier discussion of environmental problems in Chapter Four noted that the depletion and destruction of many natural resources are especially pronounced in developing societies. In these poverty-stricken nations, the economic development that government leaders hope will improve people's quality of life (and their own political futures) often takes priority over most other competing concerns, including environmental quality of life. The destruction of rain forests in Latin America and Asia (Bokhari, 1994) and the toxic contamination of numerous rivers throughout Eastern Europe (Hunt, 1993) are two examples of this shortsighted approach to economic development.
- Developing countries are not the only settings for economically driven, environmentally destructive practices. As we observed earlier in this chapter, some areas in the United States have been hit especially hard by the loss of factories and industries and the threatened loss of yet more. In an effort to keep what may be the few remaining sources of employment in a particular area from shutting down, local and state governments have sometimes granted them exemptions from otherwise costly environmental regulations. The argument is that, for a time at least, safeguarding local jobs must take precedence over safeguarding local environments (Armstrong, 1993b).
- Poverty and inequality translate into growing military conflicts and political instability at the societal level. Hundreds of thousands of people in Angola, Nigeria, and Somalia have lost their lives as warring factions have struggled for political control, plunging these societies' populations even deeper into

larger structural setting that shapes the possibilities and the limits of those people's lives is not likely to result in anything but, at best, a short-term and temporary solution. A case in point is the U.S. welfare system.

WELFARE AND WELFARE REFORM

By nearly everyone's estimate, the program presumably designed to provide short-term economic relief to people until they could get back on their feet has just not worked (Shogren, 1993). Nationally, welfare rolls have grown each year, as have the costs of running the various welfare programs. Estimates of exactly how many tens of billions of dollars the federal government spends each year on welfare vary, but it is clear that more and more of the cost increases represent monies spent on administration rather than on payments to recipients. According to a report issued by the inspector general at the Department of Health and Human Services, federal administrative costs rose by 43 percent between 1987 and 1991, whereas the number of welfare recipients rose by only 18 percent during that same time period ("Federal Cost," 1994). Should the nearly 27 percent of the poor who received no benefits of any sort in 1992 (U.S. Bureau of the Census, 1993c) enter the welfare program, the costs to federal and state governments would skyrocket.

poverty and misery (Esipisu, 1994). Sometimes, these national and regional conflicts have drawn in armed forces from the developed nations in an attempt to safeguard the lives of local population members and to maintain or restore basic principles of human rights. However, these incursions into the internal affairs of other countries have raised many serious questions about the sovereign rights of nations, as well as controversies concerning possible hidden political or military agendas on the part of developed nations toward less developed (and less powerful) countries (Mouat, 1994).

- Over the space of the past few years, the United States has been shocked by a series of homicides committed by recently fired or chronically unemployed workers against those they apparently perceived as responsible for their plight. In one southern California incident, for example, several people in a state unemployment office in the city of Oxnard were shot to death by a gunman frustrated and angered by his lack of success in obtaining work. Following the shootings, he was pursued by local police, who finally shot him to death outside a second state unemployment office in a neighboring city. Psychiatrists and job counselors described this case not as an aberration or fluke but, rather, as indicative of a trend in which thousands of long-term unemployed people are showing signs of growing anger, depression, and mental illness as their situation persists over time (Reed, 1993).
- Finally, although the phenomenon may or may not be causally linked to mental or physical health issues, U.S. Bureau of the Census data indicate a large and growing number of young adults—currently, over 52 percent of those between the ages of 18 and 24 and nearly 12 percent of those between ages 25 and 34—now living with their parents in the parents' homes. This is the largest number observed over the past 24 years and has been attributed to the declining job prospects and wages, increasing job layoffs, and increasing financial debts of young adults (Reese, 1992). The potential for clashes between parents and their adult children who find themselves in a living arrangement that perhaps none of them would have chosen voluntarily is great, and may be connected to increasing family violence (to be examined in Chapter Ten).

With a collective state government welfare tab estimated at $15.3 billion in 1993 (Lacayo, 1994), many individual states have begun to cut back on welfare payment levels, to limit the length of time individuals can remain on welfare, and to require welfare recipients to find employment within some specified period of time—the so-called workfare program (Ross, 1993). President Clinton has made similar provisions a central part of his package of federal welfare reforms but has offered increases in child-care and job-training benefits to recipients to make their successful exit from welfare a realistic possibility (Kaslow, 1994). The Clinton plan faces serious opposition in Congress, since, in the short run, at least, these changes would cost more than they would save (Lacayo, 1994).

The most serious flaw in various plans to trim the welfare rolls is the absence of jobs to accommodate individuals once they leave the welfare program (Trumbull, 1994). Lacayo (1994) cites estimates that claim welfare reforms could put an additional 1.5 million people into the job market at a time when 8.3 million individuals already are unemployed. In addition, many people currently receiving welfare benefits already are working full time but in minimum wage jobs that do not provide incomes above the poverty threshold (Rosenblatt, 1994). Attempts by the Clinton administration to increase the minimum wage level to $4.50 per hour and to index the wage level to cost-of-living increases have met with strong opposition from the private business sector. The likelihood that a minimum wage increase bill will succeed at a time when the White House is trying to pass a comprehensive health program package seems remote (Risen, 1993a).

LONG-TERM PROSPECTS

Inequality and poverty in the United States and throughout the modern world have been maintained and inflamed by the combined effects of a number of significant structural factors. The loss of so many manufacturing jobs and the rise of so many lesser-paying service jobs, the merging and downsizing of companies and industries that have dumped so many managerial and other white-collar workers into the ranks of the unemployed, educational systems that provide only minimal training for large segments of the population, and recession-driven cutbacks in government budgets have all contributed heavily to the declining living situations faced by millions of people in contemporary societies. Given this reality, it is not likely that anything short of major economic structural changes will succeed in finally eradicating the poverty problem. Given the equally low likelihood that such changes will take place quickly or easily, it may indeed be the case that the poor we shall have with us, at least for the foreseeable future.

SUMMARY

1. Data from a wide variety of sources indicate that significant economic inequalities in income and wealth exist within almost all contemporary societies, as well as between societies at the international level. Developed industrial societies show much higher levels of per capita economic resources than developing countries.
2. The contemporary United States shows income and wealth distribution patterns that are both highly unequal and growing more so over time. The wealthiest 1 percent of all U.S. households possess more total assets than the bottom 90 percent.
3. Two factors that have contributed to growing inequalities in developed societies are the increasing power and control of large corporations over the economy and the mutually supportive close relationship between governments and corporations.
4. Structural changes associated with the shift to service-based postindustrial economies, as well as the merging and downsizing of many corporations, have created unprecedented unemployment problems across Europe and North America.
5. The failure of formal education to keep up with changing technological requirements of societal economies, as well as the tendency of educational systems to "track" students into different career lines, has relegated many lower-class and minority students to the likelihood of long-term unemployment or underemployment as adults.
6. Poverty and economic deprivation are especially acute problems in developing countries. Population pressures in these countries have created widespread misery and suffering for their members and have seriously handicapped their chances to complete economic development.
7. According to world system theory, the widespread poverty of developing countries is a result of their peripheral positions in a global economic system controlled by powerful developed core societies.

8 *Absolute poverty* refers to the inability to sustain one's existence on a long-term basis. *Relative poverty* refers to the feeling of being poor in comparison to some other person or group. Absolute poverty is a growing problem in both developing and developed societies.

9 Some explanations of poverty have focused on the level of economic development within a given society as the prime cause of poverty. Others have focused on the presumed inferior personal or cultural traits of the poor. Still others have interpreted poverty as the result of societal structural conditions that permit or encourage economic deprivation for some societal members.

10 In the United States, some 37 million people were living in poverty in 1992. Although most of these individuals were White, racial and ethnic minority groups were overrepresented among the poverty population. Poverty rates also were high for women and children who formed single-parent households. A significant number of poor people are clustered in inner-city neighborhoods, where occupational structural changes have eliminated most or all jobs and created rising numbers of people who are homeless.

11 To date, welfare programs in the United States have focused on people rather than on structural conditions. Since many poor people are already working full time, various workfare proposals are not likely to reduce poverty significantly. In all likelihood, poverty will be reduced only when the structural sources that continue to create the poor are altered.

CHAPTER SEVEN

7 PROBLEMS OF RACE AND ETHNICITY
The Melting Pot Boils Over

In May 1992, following four days of rioting that left 58 people dead, hundreds more injured, and over $1 billion in property destroyed, Rodney King addressed the stunned citizens of Los Angeles. King, an African American, had been beaten by four White police officers in an incident that had been captured on video and replayed on local, national, and international TV news. It was the acquittal of those officers by an all-White jury that had triggered the worst U.S. civil disturbance of the twentieth century. "Can we just get along?" a shaken King now wanted to know.

Judging by events not just in Los Angeles but in the world at large, the answer to King's plaintive question would have to be "Apparently not." In what used to be Yugoslavia, Serbs, Croats, and Bosnians continue their attempts to wipe one another out. Throughout the former Soviet Union, other ethnic peoples have rekindled old conflicts or begun new ones as they attempt to establish nation-states. In the East-Central African country of Rwanda, an estimated 200,000 to 500,000 people were slaughtered in one month alone as long-standing tribal hatreds exploded after the apparent murder of the country's president. In Long Beach, California, members of a Cambodian gang calmly opened fire on a group of Chicanos at a street festival, killing three and wounding three others—just the latest incident in the growing warfare between one of southern California's newest immigrant groups and one of its oldest. All in all, the prospects for the world's diverse racial, ethnic, and national groups just getting along seem pretty bleak.

In this chapter, we examine the explosive dynamics of racial and ethnic group relations in the developing and the developed worlds. These relations, as we will see, continue to be shaped and colored by what are often profound misperceptions and misunderstandings of exactly what being a member of some particular racial or ethnic group is all about. As may be the case with beauty, race and ethnicity often are in the eyes of the beholder, and those eyes frequently seem myopic. But such distorted vision has not made the hostility and misery that so often flow from racial and ethnic clashes any less real. If anything, it may have added to their intensity.

QUESTIONS TO CONSIDER

- 1. What is the difference between a *racial group* and an *ethnic group?*
- 2. In what sense is it true that *race* is a social creation?
- 3. What are the differences between *majority groups* and *minority groups?*
- 4. How does *de jure discrimination* differ from *de facto discrimination?*
- 5. In what way is *discrimination* different from *prejudice?*
- 6. What is the distinction between *assimilation* and *multiculturalism?*
- 7. In what ways has the collapse of political empires such as the Soviet Union affected racial and ethnic group relations in the modern world?
- 8. What is so-called *ethnic cleansing?*
- 9. What are *indigenous peoples?*
- 10. What was the "melting pot"?
- 11. How has the historical experience of slavery affected relations between African Americans and Whites in the modern United States?
- 12. Why is Latino immigration regarded as a serious problem by many Anglos in the United States today?
- 13. How do recent immigrants from Southeast Asia differ from earlier Asian immigrants from China and Japan?

UNDERSTANDING THE PROBLEMS OF RACE AND ETHNICITY

RACE

In the 1860 census of the U.S. population, three categories—"White," "Black," and "Mulatto" (mixed)—were used to identify the racial composition of the society. By 1890, this number had increased to eight as a result of an elaboration of various Black/White mixtures ("Mulatto," "Quadroon," and "Octoroon") and the addition of "Chinese," "Japanese," and "Indian" categories. By the time of the 1990 census, the number of racial categories had more than doubled again. "Mulatto," "Quadroon," and "Octoroon" were gone, replaced by "Vietnamese," "Aleut," "Samoan," and other exotic-sounding groupings (O'Hare, 1992). If these categories had at all captured the spirit of the scientific meaning of the term *race,* some pretty remarkable changes had taken place within the space of an evolutionary wink of the eye.

From a purely scientific standpoint, the term race denotes a classification of human beings based on genetic differences, or the relative frequency of some gene or genes.

Races are groups defined on the basis of specific genetic characteristics (what are termed *genotypical* differences). These characteristics develop over time, are hereditary, and often—but not always—manifest themselves as *phenotypical* differences in skin color, hair texture, body shape, and other observable physical features (Schaefer, 1990).

This definition seems fairly straightforward and clear, but so far, it has not translated very easily into empirical terms. For example, do all possible combinations of gene frequencies establish different racial groups (in which case there may be an infinitely large number of races in the modern world), or do only certain combinations matter? If the latter is the case, which particular combinations are most significant?

Ethnologists (scholars who study races and their origins) often speak of three major races or racial groups: *Caucasoid,* or "White," *Negroid,* or "Black," and *Mongoloid,* or "Yellow." At best, this classification scheme is imprecise. Variations in physical traits (including skin color) among individual members of the same racial group often are greater than variations found between individuals in different racial groups (Gould, 1981). For this reason, some societies have developed racial classification systems that are much more complex and fluid than the Caucasoid/Negroid/Mongoloid trichotomy.

For example, in Brazil, membership in a particular racial category is defined in terms of such phenotypical features as skin color and hair color. The result is a classification system that includes as many as 400 different categories and movement of individuals from one category to another as their skin and hair color lighten or darken over time from exposure to the sun or as a result of other climatological factors. To complicate matters even further, socioeconomic class position also helps determine the socially defined lightness or darkness of an individual's skin. For Brazilians, race is anything but the fixed category it is for Americans (Kottak, 1994).

In practice, *race* is a social construct that reflects the experience of a particular society at a given time (Tamayo Lott, 1993). For example, in the nineteenth-century United States, considerations of "Blackness" were much more important in establishing legal rights and a variety of social relations than they may be now. Hence, racial distinctions were made on the basis of what percentage or proportion of an individual's ancestry was Black—three-eighths to five-eighths for Mulattos, one-quarter for Quadroons, and one-eighth for Octoroons. In the late twentieth century, many people of Asian and Pacific Island origin form significant subgroups within our population. The designations "Filipino," "Vietnamese," "Guamanian," "Korean," and "Asian Indian" in the 1990 U.S. census reflect the contemporary presence of groups not found to any appreciable extent in this country a century ago.

In and of itself, there may not be anything particularly negative or harmful about the fact that a given society's racial categories do not coincide with natural biological divisions. However, these artificial distinctions can become very harmful if they are utilized to explain real or imagined intellectual, psychological, or behavioral traits in certain groups and then to justify discriminatory policies toward these groups. For example, in Nazi Germany during the 1930s and 1940s, members of the Jewish "race" were believed to be inherently sneaky, conniving, and driven by a lust for money. According to prevailing beliefs, it was their greed that was responsible for the economic ruin of Germany following the end of World War I. Since in the Germans' view, these behaviors were an inborn racial trait, there was little that could be done to change them short of wiping out the race itself. The fact that Jews are not a race at all and do not exhibit the attributes ascribed to them proved to be irrelevant. In the ensuing program of genocide carried out against the Jews by Hitler, more than 6 million individuals were put to death. The widespread tendency to attribute particular characteristics to all members of a supposed race and then erroneously conclude that these traits somehow are natural to that race represents a sinister example of symbolic interactionists' argument that situations defined as real can have consequences that are all too real.

ETHNICITY

Like race, *ethnicity* is a concept that has been subject to a variety of interpretations. Whereas racial groups are defined, in some manner, on the basis of biological or physiological differences among people, ethnic groups are defined on the basis of cultural differences. An **ethnic group** consists of people who possess a distinctive, shared culture (such as ancestry, language, folklore, foods, traditions, music, and residential patterns) and a sense of common identity or "peoplehood." Ethnic groups are seen by others as being culturally distinctive (Alba, 1992; Bahr et al., 1979).

Although ethnicity per se does not necessarily have anything to do with race, common physical characteristics do constitute an important shared attribute for many ethnic groups (Weber, 1978, originally 1921). For example, many Chicanos or Mexican Americans possess a number of "racial" features, including skin tone and hair color, that distinguish them as much physically from their Anglo neighbors as their ethnic heritage does culturally. On many occasions, their physical resemblance to undocumented Mexican nationals attempting to enter the United States illegally has led to embarrassing confrontations with U.S. Border Patrol agents in the Southwest.

In contrast, the members of a given ethnic group may be drawn from any number of different racial groups. For example, the U.S. Bureau of the Census uses the umbrella term *Hispanic origin* to describe individuals of Spanish culture or origin, regardless of

These Vietnamese women (left) and this Korean woman (right) would have no trouble distinguishing members of their own groups, but many non-Asians might, especially in the United States. Although there is no necessary link between ethnicity and physical appearance, cultural groupings often overlap with racial groupings. In recent years, "Japan bashing" has resulted in deaths or injuries to members of other Asian groups mistakenly believed to be Japanese.

race. In the 1990 census, a total of 57 percent of Hispanic respondents identified themselves as being members of one of the four "minimum race categories" ("White"; "Black"; "American Indian or Alaskan Native"; "Asian or Pacific Islander") employed by the Bureau of the Census that year, but 43 percent identified themselves in the residual "Other Race" category. Most people in the "Other Race" category—96 percent—were of Hispanic origin (O'Hare, 1992).

Finally, in still other cases, people who appear (at least to outsiders) physically indistinguishable from one another may be members of very different ethnic groups. The Vietnamese, Thai, Cambodian, and Laotian people who settled in some areas of the United States following the war in Southeast Asia represent distinctive cultural groups but are most often referred to under the blanket term *Indochinese* by local Anglos, Latinos, and Blacks.

And in Japan, a population segment estimated at between 2 and 3 million who are Japanese in terms of race, ancestry, language, and other cultural traits nonetheless are defined as a distinctive and inferior ethnic group. The *burakumin,* as these people are called, occupy a place in Japanese society roughly similar to that once held by African Americans in the U.S. South or that of the so-called unscheduled castes in modern India. Once legally barred from a host of occupational, educational, residential, and other social opportunities, the *burakumin* still face a great deal of de facto discrimination that effectively keeps them out of the Japanese mainstream and frozen in place at the bottom of their society's socioeconomic hierarchy (Magagnini, 1992; Schoenberger, 1990; Yoshino & Murakoshi, 1983).

As the case of U.S. Hispanics shows, common ancestry or an ancestral homeland forms an important component of ethnic group identity (Alba, 1992). But *nationality* and *ethnicity* are not always the same thing. *Nationality* refers to individuals' geographic and political backgrounds—that is, their nation of origin. For example, *Lithuanian American* describes a U.S. population group based on common national origin. However, not all individuals who happen to have come from (or who still live in) Lithuania are members of the same ethnic group. In that country of 3.8 million, about 80 percent of the population are ethnically Lithuanian, 9 percent are Russian, 8 percent are Polish, and the remaining 3 percent are composed of Belarussians, Ukrainians, Tartars, Latvians, Germans, and Lithuanian Jews (Barberis, 1993).

Switzerland is a recognized political unit whose citizens claim Swiss nationality, but there is no "Swiss" ethnic group to speak of. The country's population is divided into French, German, and Italian subgroups that occupy different geographic regions and maintain their own languages and sense of peoplehood. The Germans make up about two-thirds of the population and live primarily in the northern and eastern parts of the country. At 18 percent of the total population, the French Swiss live primarily in the western cantons, and forming 10 percent of the population, the Italian Swiss reside principally in the south ("Switzerland," 1992).

The distinction between race and ethnicity is one that has not always been consistently maintained by sociologists, much less by the general public. Some observers prefer to use *ethnic group* as the more inclusive term and to treat *race* as a special case of ethnicity. In this view, a race is "an ethnic group whose members are believed, by others if not also by themselves, to be physiologically distinctive" (Alba, 1992, p. 576). To a large extent, these classification problems may reflect the reality of a world in which social definitions of race and ethnicity are imprecise and subject to constant change. The important consideration is the consequences that flow from people's tendency to categorize one another on the basis of assumed physical or cultural differences and to act on the basis of those categorizations.

INEQUALITIES BETWEEN MAJORITY GROUPS AND MINORITY GROUPS

In many societies, interactions among the different racial and ethnic groups that define the population have taken the form of majority group/minority group relations. Based largely on their possession of certain valued physical or cultural traits—and, more importantly, on their possession of effective power—some recognized groups come to constitute **majority groups.** They dominate economic, political, and educational institutions and can structure most important societal activities to their own best advantage. In contrast, those other groups whose nonvalued physical or cultural traits—and, more importantly, whose lack of effective power—block them from control over important societal institutions come to constitute **minority groups.** Denied access to essential opportunity structures, they are relegated to the bottom rungs of their societies' socioeconomic hierarchies. Once in those subordinate positions, they experience a variety of dysfunctional consequences that affect virtually all aspects of their lives. As we saw in our discussions of inequality and poverty in Chapter Five and Chapter Six, these disadvantages include limited access to the education and training required for most white-collar and professional occupations, so that many minority group members are likely to remain unemployed or underemployed on a long-term basis. Additionally, as we will discuss in more detail in Chapter Twelve, minorities have higher likelihoods of illness and lower likelihoods of having medical insurance to help pay the high cost of treatment. When they do get sick, they often must remain sick until they get better on their own or they die.

DISCRIMINATION, PREJUDICE, AND STEREOTYPING

To understand the dynamics of majority/minority group relations, first, it is necessary to understand the underlying conceptual, attitudinal, and behavioral factors that structure them. At the most obvious and immediate level, these factors begin with **discrimination,** or unfair and unequal treatment of members of some specific group (usually members of minority groups by members of majority groups). In some instances, significant restrictions in housing, employment, and educational opportunities may be supported or required by law (**de jure discrimination**), as was the case in the South African system of apartheid. In other instances, these restrictions may be the result of common and accepted practice (**de facto discrimination**), even though these practices may be prohibited by law. For example, even though the *burakumin* now are guaranteed equal protection under Japanese law, they continue to experience a great deal of discrimination in housing and employment (Magagnini, 1992; Schoenberger, 1990).

Unfair practices directed toward members of certain minority groups are often—though not always—the result of prejudices held against those particular groups. Unlike *discrimination,* which refers to the way members of certain groups behave toward one another, **prejudice** denotes the way that certain people or groups think about one another in terms of fixed and rigid mental images. These images most often are based on information (whether factually correct or not) and beliefs that are irrational or negative and that consequently may predispose people to act negatively toward the objects of their prejudices.

In many cases, prejudice entails stereotyped portrayals of the groups in question. **Stereotypes** are oversimplified and categorical beliefs in which all members of some particular group are assumed to possess specific traits that distinguish them from all members of other groups. In stereotyping, what may be very significant differences among individual members of a group are ignored in favor of an "all Xs are Y" conclusion. For example, all the members of one particular racial group may be perceived as being deficient in some particular mental or physical ability, whereas all members of a second group may be seen as excelling in that same ability. Once formed and in place, these beliefs tend to accentuate the importance of observations that confirm the stereotype and to discount or ignore altogether the importance of observations that challenge the stereotype.

INSTITUTIONAL AND INSTITUTIONALIZED DISCRIMINATION

In many societies, the continued subjugation of minority racial and ethnic groups is maintained through a variety of formal and informal structural mechanisms that operate to preserve these groups' subordinate positions in the socioeconomic hierarchy. The institutional repression of South African Blacks through the imposed system of **apartheid** is the most blatant recent example of the formal subjugation process. In South Africa, established laws required strict racial segregation for many years, resulting in severe political, economic, and social restrictions on the lives of millions of people. Among the many other negative consequences of apartheid is the now emerging realization that millions of Black citizens who ultimately will participate in the governing of their country have been denied any sort of formal education. Described as one of the worst legacies of apartheid, the collapse of Black education is likely to become the "hidden crisis and challenge" as South Africa moves toward democratic rule (Drogin, 1993).

In other instances, what once had been a system of formal subjugation of minorities has evolved into an informal system. To a large extent, these informal systems are maintained by established practices that continue to discriminate covertly and perhaps unintentionally against minorities—a phenomenon known as **institutionalized discrimination.** The current system of formal education in the United States provides an example of institutionalized discrimination.

DISCRIMINATION IN U.S. EDUCATION

Given the nearly universal enrollment in primary and secondary schools in the United States, it might at first appear that equal educational opportunity has been accomplished in this society. Regardless of social, racial, or ethnic background, all members of society can acquire the same initial sets of educational tools that will permit later entry into lucrative blue-collar, white-collar, and professional occupations as adults. But such appearances are deceiving.

More than 40 years after the historic 1954 U.S. Supreme Court *Brown v. Board of Education* decision that declared segregation in public education unconstitutional, neighborhood schools around the country continue to be racially and ethnically segregated (Brownstein, 1994; Kozol, 1992). Overt housing discrimination against minorities in the past created racially segregated neighborhoods that in many communities remain largely segregated in the present. Local schools designed to serve children in the area then became segregated by default, as a result of the racial and ethnic composition of the surrounding neighborhood. Jonathan Kozol (1992, p. 3) describes this pattern in his scathing analysis of the "savage inequalities" evident in inner-city public schools throughout the country: "Most of the urban schools I visited were 95 to 99 percent nonwhite. In no school that I saw anywhere in the United States were nonwhite children in large numbers truly intermingled with white children."

Because many minority urban neighborhoods have high rates of unemployment and poverty (and consequently low tax revenues), inner-city schools tend to be greatly underfunded and have far fewer resources to offer local students. Equal opportunities in primary and secondary education are more an illusion than a fact (Pasternak, 1993; Toch, 1993; Tyson, 1994). In addition to defective and antiquated facilities that place their minds at risk, minority students in many of these schools also find their bodies and their lives at risk, as well. A study of 729 school districts conducted in 1993 by the National School Boards Association called violence in public schools an "epidemic," with 39 percent of all schools reporting a shooting or knifing that year (reported in Holmstrom, 1994a). In a 1992 study of public school tenth-graders, only half the students surveyed said they always felt safe at school, and 10 percent admitted to having brought a weapon to school the previous month (reported in Walters, 1993). In Maryland, one school district installed surveillance cameras on its buses in an attempt to curb violence by students traveling to and from district schools in nearby Washington, D.C. (Sweeney, 1992b). Under these conditions, it is difficult to maintain the argument that the quality of primary and secondary education experienced by different racial and ethnic minorities in the United States constitutes equal opportunity.

LEGAL PROTECTION OF MINORITIES

In some societies, the civil rights of various racial and ethnic groups that otherwise might be jeopardized by local prejudices and discriminatory practices are safeguarded by political and judicial actions. This legal protection of minorities may be accomplished through laws, constitutional amendments, court directives, or other mechanisms. For example, in the United States, the Thirteenth, Fourteenth, and Fifteenth Amendments to the Constitution; various civil rights laws passed during the past three decades; and a number of affirmative action directives have helped establish and maintain the legal rights of African Americans, women, and other minority groups. In Australia, some two hundred years after European settlement drove aboriginal groups from their ancestral lands, the senate in 1993 passed the Native Title Bill, which guaranteed a number of territorial rights to the continent's indigenous peoples. The passage of the bill had been resisted fiercely by Australian farmers and miners, who were concerned that they might have to surrender vast tracts of profitable lands to the aboriginal groups (Foster, 1993a). These lands originally had been claimed by Europeans under the doctrine of *terra nullius* ("the land was unoccupied"), despite the fact that aboriginal groups had occupied the area long before the arrival of the first Europeans. Government leaders saw the bill as a necessary step in their attempted reconciliation with Aborigines and hailed its final passage as "a turning point for all Australians" (Keating in Foster, 1993b). Indigenous peoples in Brazil and Ecuador also have been granted a growing number of territorial and other legal rights by those nations' governments, although their status as equal citizens remains more a dream than a reality (Michaels, 1992b; Yarbro, 1992).

PATTERNS OF RACIAL AND ETHNIC GROUP RELATIONS

With a few notable exceptions, virtually all modern societies display what demographers call *population heterogeneity*. Unlike most traditional societies, whose populations shared physical and cultural identity, contemporary societies are composed of groups of people who are unlike one another in many important respects. For example, modern India has a population that is more racially, ethnically, linguistically, and religiously diverse than the combined populations of all the independent nations of Europe. Physical and cultural diversity is a fact of life in most modern social systems, though one that has been greeted in different ways from one place and time to another. Population heterogeneity has elicited an array of responses ranging from enthusiastic attempts to weave a rich tapestry of racial and ethnic subgroups to enthusiastic attempts to eliminate these groups by any means necessary.

ASSIMILATION

Assimilation refers to the process by which minority ethnic and racial groups are absorbed into the mainstream sociocultural system, eventually losing their distinctive cultural and physical identities. At times, assimilation has been the avowed goal of many developed societies throughout the modern world. Milton Gordon (1964) identified several different types or stages of minority group assimilation. The process began with **cultural assimilation**, or the adoption of majority group cultural and behavioral patterns by different minority groups, followed by **structural assimilation**, or successful entrance of minority group members into primary and secondary group relations with the majority. Finally, **physical assimilation**—that is, biological reproduction across majority/minority group lines—completed the process. Gordon's description was based on the U.S. historical experience but is applicable to other societies, as well.

For example, in Japan, the Koreans who constitute that country's largest foreign population subgroup are expected to learn the Japanese language and to adopt Japanese customs, and many have. However, the estimated 1 million members of the Korean population have not achieved structural assimilation. Defined by prevailing prejudices as profoundly inferior to the Japanese, Koreans remain excluded from economic, political, and social opportunities otherwise available to members of Japanese society (Hirao, 1993; Kang, 1993). According to some observers, their continued exclusion is a reflection of the fact that "most Japanese do not think that 'Japaneseness' can be acquired. People can speak perfect Japanese and have grown up within the Japanese school system, as have many Koreans, and still be regarded as aliens" (Oka, 1993).

Even foreign-born Japanese remain on the outside of Japanese society, looking in. Many Latin Japanese workers have recently returned to their ancestral homeland from Brazil, Peru, and other South American countries to which their grandparents or parents migrated as contract laborers. Even though their Japanese racial heritage has given them immigration priority over all other groups seeking entry into Japan, these *dekasegi* have found themselves treated as second-class citizens. They are subject to the same kinds of prejudice and discrimination as Koreans and other foreigners (Jones, 1992; Michaels, 1992a). The fact that racial or ethnic minorities have adopted their host society's cultural patterns does not automatically guarantee their acceptance into mainstream group life.

Physical assimilation is also not an automatic process. It depends on the willingness of the majority group to accept the minorities as marital and reproductive partners, as well as on the desire of the minorities to marry and have children with members of the majority group. Regardless of their inclinations in this matter, Koreans in contemporary Japan are restrained by powerful traditions (and previously by law) from marrying native Japanese. Consequently, they have yet to achieve physical assimilation to any measurable extent.

PLURALISM AND MULTICULTURALISM

Pluralism and multiculturalism both refer to the retention, rather than the blending, of racial and ethnic group identities within a given society. Both patterns entail an appreciation of each group's symbolic world view by all other groups, as well as an acceptance of the attitudinal and behavioral differences these divergent world views generate. In addition, true pluralism also entails a sharing of political power by the different groups within the larger system. These groups must constantly work to accommodate themselves to one another's interests, rights, and needs. Success therefore requires sustained effort by all participating groups.

Modern Switzerland is perhaps the best-known contemporary example of a successful pluralist society. As discussed earlier, there is no real Swiss ethnic group that forms the country's population. Rather, German, French, and Italian subpopulations maintain their respective languages and cultural traditions while still cooperating with one another on political matters of mutual importance, such as decisions concerning alliances with other nations. For example, as a nation, the Swiss have voted not to join either the European Community or the United Nations.

According to evidence summarized by anthropologist Conrad Kottak (1994), multicultural societies have the highest chance of success when their constituent ethnic and racial groups interact in what amounts to a non-zero-sum game setting. (Recall the discussion of the zero-sum game in Chapter One.) In these societies, ecological interdependence resulting from the different activities of each ethnic and racial group within the same region, or from the occupation of different regions within the same nation-state by individual groups, allows noncompetitive group relations. If and when those intergroup relations become competitive, as the different groups pursue the same resources or the same goals, multicultural or pluralist societies can easily be transformed into systems marked by ethnic and racial group conflict. As we will discuss in greater detail later in this chapter, it is just these sorts of real or imagined zero-sum game situations that have given rise to significant racial and ethnic violence around the world and within U.S. society.

POPULATION TRANSFER

One way racial or ethnic groups who find themselves in competition and conflict with other such groups have attempted to resolve the situation is by voluntary or involuntary population transfer, or movement of minority group members from one geographic region to another to avoid contact with majority group members. For example, in the United States, Native American tribes were forcibly removed from the eastern states to lands west of the Mississippi River in the nineteenth century. Similarly, Japanese American citizens were relocated to internment camps by order of the federal government during World War II.

In Southeast Asia, tens of thousands of ethnic Vietnamese people have "voluntarily" left Cambodia for the southern provinces of Vietnam in response to an escalating series of assaults and killings carried out against them by the Khmer Rouge (Jones, 1993a). Similarly, over 100,000 Lhotshampas, or ethnic Nepalese, have "voluntarily" left Bhutan after the Drukpa ethnic group in the world's oldest Buddhist monarchy began a systematic campaign of repression against them. Their return to Nepal has placed a tremendous burden on what already is a poverty-stricken country and has generated growing tension between local populations and the refugees (Chatterjee, 1993).

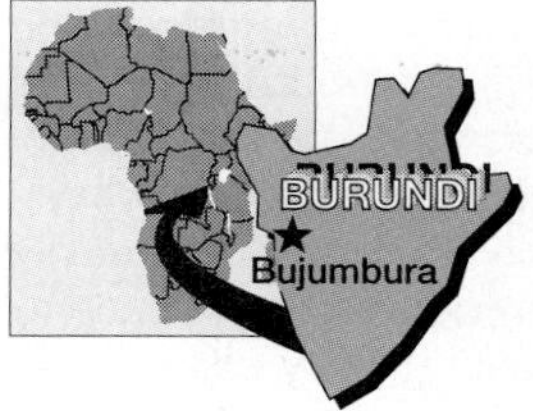

BATTLE IN BURUNDI
Old Tribalism and New Politics

When most people think of race or ethnic relations in Africa and the subjugation of large minority populations by smaller ruling majority groups, what comes to mind is South Africa. For many years, the South African White minority was able to dominate and virtually enslave millions of Blacks through the institutional system of apartheid. Won only after years of struggle and bloodshed, the dismantling of that system has been a cause of celebration and a source of inspiration for people of color and people of goodwill around the world.

But South Africa is not the only African nation in which a numerically small but politically powerful population group has been able to structure and control the lives of numerically superior but politically weaker groups defined as different and inferior. In many of the new nations that emerged following the breakup of the European colonial empires after the First World War, old ethnic antagonisms that had been suppressed and remained dormant under colonial rule resurfaced in the same way they did following the much later collapse of the Soviet Union in the early 1990s. The East-Central African nation of Burundi is one of the more violent examples of this widespread pattern of "Black-on-Black" tribal subjugation in the modern era. Although one of Africa's smallest countries, Burundi has had one of the largest ethnic conflict death tolls in the world (Press, 1993b).

Once described by early German explorers as "the Switzerland of Africa" because of its size and alpinelike topography and climate, what was then called *Urundi* was part of German East Africa from 1885 to 1916 (Melady, 1974). From 1919 to 1962, the country formed half of a League of Nations/United Nations Trust Territory (Ruanda-Urundi) under the administration of the Belgian government. On July 1, 1962, after a trial year of limited self-government, Urundi attained complete independence from Belgium and was established as the Kingdom of Burundi. From 1966 to 1992, what was now the Republic of Burundi moved in and out of extended periods of military control, interspersed by brief interludes of constitutional democracy (Banks, 1993).

Although Burundi's geographic climate may resemble that of Switzerland, its social and economic climate is anything but Swisslike. With a 1991 per capita GNP (gross national product) of only $210, Burundi is one of the least-developed countries in the world—about 90 percent of the population is engaged in subsistence-level farming. Most land suitable for agriculture is devoted to the growing of coffee, which accounts for about 80 percent of the country's export revenue. And unlike Switzerland, in which German, French, and Italian ethnic populations have managed to coexist peacefully in democratic pluralism, for over 400 years, Burundi existed as a feudal monarchy based on the complete domination of one ethnic/tribal group over others.

Prior to Burundi's colonial period, the country was governed by a *mwami* (king or paramount chief) and a group of *ganwa* (royal princes) drawn from among the Tutsi tribe, who have historically constituted about 14 percent of Burundi's total population. The much more numerous Hutu people, who make up about 85 percent of the overall population, and the much smaller group of Twa (about 1 percent of the population) were reduced to the status of serfs. They depended on the Tutsi for military protection and were required to surrender their labor and the bulk of their material goods to the Tutsi rulers as tribute (Weinstein, 1976).

Under German and then Belgian colonial administration, the country's loose system of government was centralized. Virtually all important offices in the expanding, European-style government bureaucracy were allocated to the Tutsi who, in turn, found it increasingly necessary to work the Hutu peasants harder in order to meet various production quotas imposed by the Europeans. Some degree of ethnic resentment had existed in the past, but these new conditions generated an accelerating awareness of ethnic distinctions that began to overshadow older clan and regional identities. The net effect of the colonial period, according to Weinstein (1976, p. x), was to make the ethnic cleavage "the primary social division" in Burundi and to create a growing feeling of hostility on the part of the Hutus towards the Tutsi puppet government officials. These feelings exploded soon after the move to independence in 1962.

In 1965, a Hutu uprising attempted to seize control of the government. It was a dismal failure, leading not only to the death of over 5,000 Hutu people, including most intellectuals, but also to a military takeover of the monarchical government by Tutsi forces under the leadership of Michael Micombero. In 1972, a second failed overthrow attempt led to a bloodbath and "the tragic years" (Melady, 1974), during which an estimated 100,000 Hutus were killed and additional tens of thousands fled Burundi in fear of their lives. The Tutsi remained in control of both the government and the military, and they made life even worse for the Hutu people who stayed behind.

Following a series of renewed Hutu/Tutsi conflicts, in 1992, the then-current military government of President Pierre Buyoya adopted the results of a popular referendum calling for an end to military rule and the establishment of a multiparty democratic political system. On June 28, 1993, a true democratic election was held in Burundi, and for the first time, a Hutu—Melchior Ndadaye—was elected president in a landslide victory (Banks, 1993). It appeared that, after more than four centuries, the numerical majority group in Burundi was about to become the political majority group, as well. However, this turned out to be more an illusion than a reality.

In the best tradition of political patronage, once President Ndadaye assumed power, he began a systematic program of replacing most officials at all levels of government with members of his own Hutu group. Fearing an end to their centuries-long rule and possible reprisals from the Hutu, Tutsi military leaders staged an unsuccessful coup just one week after the national election. President Ndadaye responded by appointing a Tutsi, Sylvie Kinigi, prime minister. However, this gesture angered some of the more militant Hutu factions, who wanted a complete purge of all Tutsis from government, and it failed to satisfy the Tutsi-controlled army (Press, 1993b). On October 21, 1993, the military attacked the capital (Bujumbura), capturing and then killing President Ndadaye and dissolving the new government (Press, 1993c). A second bloodbath began against the Hutu, who fled by the tens of thousands into neighboring Rwanda, Tanzania, and Zaire. By November 1993, an estimated 700,000 refugees had left Burundi, most ending up in Rwanda, a country with the same ethnic population mix as Burundi but a Hutu government (Peterson, 1993b; Press, 1993g).

The sudden influx of so many Hutus threatened to destabilize Rwanda, which had just come out of its own ethnic civil war and the violent overthrow of a long-standing Tutsi government. Both the ousted Burundi government and the Rwandan government appealed for military intervention from the outside world to help restore order, leading to the arrival of first an OAU (Organization of African Unity) advisory group and then a larger United Nations peacekeeping force (Press, 1993e). At the same time, foreign governments responded to the military takeover and consequent ethnic massacres by withdrawing the financial aid on which Burundi so heavily depended for its economic well-being. As world condemnation of the coup grew, some senior military officers also began to condemn the takeover and call for a return of the elected Hutu government. As one observer analyzed the situation, "They made a coup without taking into account the change in the world. . . . This is the first time there has been a [world] consensus on Burundi" (Mulami quoted in Press, 1993f).

Unwilling to run the risk of an all-out ethnic war that would shatter the fragile situation throughout the region, concerned foreign parties took steps to stop the Burundi conflict before it spread (Press, 1993d). However, their efforts were too late. On April 6, 1994, a plane carrying Cyprian Ntayamira and Juvenal Habyarimana, the presidents of Burundi and Rwanda, was shot down as it approached the airport in Kigali, Rwanda's capital, killing both men ("Burundi, Rwanda Presidents Die," 1994). The Rwandan Hutu responded to the killing of their president with retaliatory killings against local Tutsi civilians. In turn, the Tutsi rebel army countered by launching attacks against the Hutu government and against Hutu civilians, and the situation quickly escalated to a nationwide bloodbath (Lorch, 1994). According to some estimates, by the end of 5 weeks of fighting, as many as 500,000 Rwandans from both tribes had been killed and over 2 million more had been displaced from their homes in the intertribal war ("Enemies Negotiate U.N. Control," 1994). So long as old ethnic and tribal hatreds prevail in Rwanda and in Burundi, successful new democratic politics will remain an impossibility.

EXTERMINATION

Extermination, or *genocide,* is the process by which majority groups attempt to resolve their minority group "problems" by physically annihilating or destroying the members of particular groups. As we saw in Chapter Two, this practice has had a long history in racial and ethnic group relations.

In the 1940s, Adolf Hitler exterminated over 6 million Jews as part of his "final solution" to the Jewish problem. Over 1.5 million Cambodians were put to death by the Khmer Rouge government in the early 1970s, and hundreds of thousands of people have been exterminated so far in Bosnia-Herzegovina as part of the so-called ethnic cleansing instituted by Serbian forces against Muslims and Croats (Watson et al., 1992). In Africa, similar extermination campaigns directed by ethnic tribes against other tribal groups have swept across Angola, Burundi, Kenya, Rwanda, and Somalia as these factions have fought for political control of their nations. The result has been the deaths of millions of people (Peterson, 1993a, 1993b; Press, 1993a).

RACE AND ETHNIC RELATIONS IN THE GLOBAL VILLAGE

THE EMPIRES STRIKE OUT

Since the end of World War II and especially since the mid-1980s, many European, Asian, and African countries that had been under the control of powerful First World and Second World nations gained their independence. For the first time in many years, hundreds of millions of people around the world came out of the shadows of repression and into the light of political and economic self-determination. It was a time of joyous celebration and great optimism for the free world. However, it now appears that both the celebrations and the optimism were premature. In a great many cases, the passing of the old political order has been followed by the coming of new racial and ethnic disorders. Group civilities that may have been imposed by force under totalitarian rule have been replaced (in the absence of such rule) by waves of racial and ethnic brutality that often rival atrocities committed under the old regimes.

For example, since the breakup of the Soviet Union in late 1991, the various members of what is now called the Commonwealth of Independent States, particularly those in Central Asia, have been wracked by ethnic violence. Many of these conflicts have been generated by the nationalistic spirit sweeping across the region. Attempts by these newly freed peoples to establish nation-states in what they regard as their ancestral homelands have resulted in campaigns to remove foreign ethnic groups whom they perceive as occupying "their" territory. This is especially true if those others are members of groups who once politically dominated the territory.

In Moldova and Georgia, for example, government-led forces launched campaigns described as "genocide" by Russian Vice-President Alexander Rutskoi against ethnic Russian and Ossetian minorities, prompting a threat of Russian military intervention to protect the rights of ethnic Russians in those areas (Sneider, 1992b). Similar violence erupted between Armenia and Azerbaijan to decide the fate of Nagorno-Karabakh, an enclave of Christian Armenians who wanted to break away from Islamic Azerbaijan and establish their own independent state (Sneider, 1992a). In this particular case, ethnic differences between the Armenians and the Azerbaijanis were compounded by questions of religion. Beyond these conflicts, a growing wave of anti-Semitism is spreading throughout the former Soviet republics, largely in the mostly Moslem Central Asia (Simon, 1992).

A FOURTH REICH?

The dismantling of the Berlin Wall and the later reunification of East and West Germany in 1990 likewise have been accompanied by rises in anti-Semitism, racism, and escalating violence against all foreign immigrants in the former East Germany. The situation was brought to a head by the large flow of refugees from the war-torn former Soviet republics and from North Africa and the Middle East, all of whom were attracted by Germany's liberal political asylum policies (MacLeod, 1992b). Problems were further fueled by incendiary actions from members of a growing right-wing nationalist movement sparked by high rates of unemployment and poverty in the eastern German states ("Racism Shadows," 1992).

This neo-Nazi movement has been especially successful in recruiting a "new lost generation" of young Germans, who view foreigners as the main source of their country's and their own problems. As expressed by one woman, "I think the foreigners here should die. They take our jobs and apartments, and the government doesn't care. I have no optimism. There is nothing" (quoted in M. Fritz, 1992). This sense of nihilistic despair was the same sort of sentiment that helped bring Hitler to power in 1933. The painful memory of the first Nazi movement and its world-shattering consequences has led tens of thousands of other Germans to repudiate the neo-Nazis and try to defuse growing internal tensions that now threaten to blow the new Germany wide apart.

INTERNATIONAL MIGRATION

As we saw in the population chapter (Chapter Three), racial and ethnic persecution has been a powerful force in generating the waves of mass migrations that have moved entire populations across the world's landscape in the past and in the present. The biblical story of the Jewish exodus out of Egypt was completed in 1948 with the creation of the Jewish state of Israel following the United Nations–directed partitioning of Palestine. The result has been nearly 50 years of hostility between Jews and Arabs that at times has threatened to plunge not just the Middle East but the entire world into open warfare. In the contemporary era, the estimated 17 million refugee immigrants who have fled across national borders in Asia, Africa, and Latin America are a significant part of what a 1993 UN report called "the human crisis of our age" (Meisler, 1993). Regardless of the compelling reasons that led them to flee their homelands, these immigrants often are regarded as invaders whose sheer numbers threaten the economic and cultural survival of their reluctant host countries. The result has been increased intergroup friction in many of these societies.

In Western Europe, the influx of large numbers of racially and ethnically distinct refugees has led to growing right-wing nationalism in Italy and in Germany, increasing racism in Great Britain, and heightened attempts in France to preserve French culture from foreign contamination through "zero immigration" laws (LaFranchi, 1993a; Leeman, 1992). A growing number of nations have tightened or rescinded formerly liberal political asylum laws in an attempt to halt the steady flow of minorities from Eastern Europe, the former Soviet Union, and Africa (Games, 1993).

In the United States, some legislators have called for the use of National Guard troops to control the 2,000 mile border with Mexico and help stem the "brown tide" of illegal immigrants they fear is threatening to engulf the American way of life. This and other aggressive attempts to block off the U.S.-Mexican border have drawn heated responses from Mexico, adding to existing tensions between the two countries (McDonnell, 1993).

NATIONAL FRAGMENTATION?

At the same time the flow of ethnic peoples across societal borders is generating international problems, a growing sense of ethnic identity among peoples within societal boundaries is creating problems in maintaining national cohesion. In the United States, some observers have raised concerns that increasing multiculturalism and "the cult of ethnicity" (Gray, 1991; Schlesinger, 1991) are threatening to destroy the cultural ideals that have historically bound Americans together. Others see the growing emphasis on defining and preserving the rights of racial and ethnic groups as leading eventually to the erosion of the individual rights that have been a hallmark of U.S. society (Perlmutter, 1992).

In Europe, what has been described as a "burst of micronationalism" ("Europe's New Flags," 1992), set in motion by the collapse of old political empires and the rise of new democracies, has threatened to split established Western nations such as Belgium and Scotland into dozens of small states defined by ethnic ties and divided by divergent ethnic interests (Hottelet, 1992). Such a partitioning and "balkanization" of the developed world during a time of growing global economies and politics could well prove catastrophic for the populations of these countries.

INDIGENOUS PEOPLES

When Spanish explorers led by Christopher Columbus "discovered" the New World in 1492 and Spanish armies led by Hernando Cortés began the conquest of that New World in 1519, the continent had already been occupied for thousands of years by a variety of native peoples. Mistakenly called *Indians* by the Europeans who thought they had discovered a new route to India, some of these groups had developed sophisticated social and cultural systems that matched or surpassed those of the Old World. What the natives lacked, however, was the military technology and firepower of the Europeans. No match for Spanish weaponry, the native peoples in what is now Mexico and Central and South America were quickly reduced to the status of conquered peoples. In many cases, what followed was mass impoverishment, slavery, and death.

What also ensued was a new European racist ideology that defined these physically and culturally different peoples as inherently inferior to White Europeans, thus setting the pattern for social, political, and economic relations between the two groups for the next 500 years (Bonacich, 1992; Russell, 1994). That pattern has been one of increasing affluence and dominance for the descendants of the European conquerors and increasing poverty and misery for the descendants of the conquered natives. Five hundred years after the armies of the Old World powers "steamrolled" the inhabitants of the New World (Espada, 1992), the survivors of that onslaught are still confronting the ghost of Cortés (Miller, 1992). And now, so is the rest of the world.

To focus the attention of the developed world on the plight of native peoples not just in the Americas but throughout the globe, the United Nations declared 1993 "The International Year of the World's Indigenous People." According to estimates, there are more than 300 million **indigenous peoples**, groups whose ancestors were the original inhabitants of lands that were later colonized, settled, or invaded by others (Mouat, 1993). These peoples represent thousands of separate cultures and over 6,000 different languages.

The 1993 UN declaration followed an escalating series of actions by indigenous groups around the world to push for social and political rights. For example, in Canada, Inuit people (so-called Eskimos) finally won approval for a new self-governing homeland, Nunavut ("our land"), to be implemented in 1999 ("Canada's North," 1992), and members of the Cree Nation successfully blocked construction of a new hydroelectric dam that would have destroyed much of their ancestral lands in northern Quebec (Clayton, 1992). In Ecuador, several confederations of indigenous peoples led nationwide uprisings demanding human rights and title to ancestral lands in the Andes highlands and in the interior rain forests (Holmstrom, 1993a). Bolivia, Brazil, Colombia, and Venezuela have also returned some lands to local indigenous peoples, although "the majority of indigenous people in Latin America remain in a very difficult economic, social, and political situation" (Berger in Mouat, 1993). In Australia, as noted earlier, aboriginal people have been granted legal claims to vast areas of land that had been seized and developed by European settlers under the *terra nullius* doctrine (Foster, 1993b).

Despite these modest gains, the situation of indigenous peoples worldwide remains precarious. In Brazil, for example, members of the Yanomami tribe apparently have been massacred by miners stripping the forests in the Amazon basin in their pursuit of gold

(Bruner, 1993c). Both the massacre and the mining occurred within the boundaries of the Yanomami reservation, an area as big as Portugal. Local political and business interests had opposed the creation of the preserve, which they saw as depriving the local economy of valuable sources of revenue, and the Brazilian government has resisted creating additional reservations for much the same reason (Long, 1993d). In the meantime, indigenous forest people like the Yanomami remain in jeopardy of losing not only their culture but their lives, as well.

Tens of thousands of highland Indians have been killed in Guatemala since the 1980s by government security forces, leading many to seek refuge in Mexico (Nelan, 1992). However, depressed conditions in that country have led Mexico's government to close many of the refugee camps and send their inhabitants back to Guatemala—and possible death (D. C. Scott, 1992a). As we saw in the last chapter, Mexico's own indigenous Mayan groups in the southern state of Chiapas rose in revolt against the federal government in early 1994 to focus attention on their desperate situation after years of neglect and abandonment by Mexico City. With its own indigenous groups in insurrection, Mexican officials are not overly anxious to harbor another country's native problems.

In northern Canada, alcoholism affects over 95 percent of all adults in some Labrador Inuit villages, and as many as one-half of the villages' populations have attempted suicide (Scott, 1993). In Japan, members of the aboriginal Ainu population are still fighting for official recognition and guaranteed rights in what Japanese government leaders insist on describing as a "monoethnic" society (Wetherall, 1993). Whether actively attacked or quietly forgotten by more powerful societal groups, many of the world's indigenous peoples remain in serious peril, their continued survival threatened by larger forces beyond their control.

RACE AND ETHNIC GROUP RELATIONS IN THE UNITED STATES

THE MYTH OF THE MELTING POT

For well over a century, one of the most powerful and persistent images of racial and ethnic group relations in the United States has been the "melting pot." This metaphorical portrayal of the immigrant experience envisioned the inpouring of European, African, Asian, and other groups to the developing American nation (see Table 7.1) as being akin to the smelting of individual metals to form a new and superior alloy. This American alloy possessed new characteristics and abilities created by the smelting process itself, as well as the best traits of each of its individual racial and ethnic components (Parrillo, 1994).

THE REALITY OF DIVERSITY

As a description of the reality of the U.S. immigrant experience, the melting pot is as short on historical accuracy as it is long on charm. That reality was one of forced conformity to a cultural model that was based largely on a British standard and regarded as an essentially finished product. And *Anglo conformity,* as this pattern is called, never really was intended to apply to the people of color who were so obviously physically different from the host (and dominant) Anglo cultural group. To the extent that beliefs in the natural superiority of Caucasians over darker-skinned people permeated (and continue to permeate) U.S. society, African, Asian, indigenous, and other Americans of color

TABLE 7.1 U.S. Population by Selected Ancestry Group: 1990

Ancestry Group	Number of People (in millions)
German	57.9
Irish	38.7
English	32.7
African American	23.8
Italian	14.7
Mexican	11.6
French	10.3
Polish	9.4
Native American	8.7
Dutch	6.2
Scotch-Irish	5.6
Scottish	5.4
Swedish	4.7
Spanish	2.0
Puerto Rican	2.0
Chinese	1.5
Filipino	1.5
Hispanic	1.1

SOURCE: U.S. Bureau of the Census, *1990 Census of the Population, Supplementary Report.*

found themselves "out of the loop" as far as assimilation and complete acceptance were concerned. These groups might adopt the cultural patterns demanded and expected by the majority group, but their physical traits would keep them from structural and physical assimilation so long as these attributes were defined as marks of natural inferiority.

THE NEW IMMIGRANTS

As we saw in our discussion of urban problems in Chapter Five, the composition of immigrants to the United States has changed dramatically since 1960. For the most part, these new immigrants come from Central and South America, the Caribbean, and Asia, rather than from Europe. For example, Mexicans alone accounted for 22 percent of all immigrants arriving in the United States in 1992 ("Numbers Game," 1993). To a large extent, these new arrivals are characterized by increasing rather than decreasing physical, cultural, and religious differences from the dominant WASP (White Anglo-Saxon Protestant) group. These differences, coupled with a growing refusal on the part of many immigrants to surrender their ethnic identities to the assimilation process, have created a volatile situation across the country.

As they seek their share of economic success, political power, and other goals, these new immigrants have found themselves competing against older, more established minorities, as well as against the majority group. This competition for what, in many cases, are scarce resources (the declining number of lucrative white-collar and skilled blue-collar jobs, for example) has translated into growing hostility between African American, Latino, and Asian subpopulations across the United States (Holmes, 1994). It has likewise translated into growing conflicts within particular racial minority groups—for example, confrontations between Haitian Black immigrants and longer-settled "American" Blacks in cities such as Miami (Portes & Stepick, 1993) and battles between Laotian gangs and Vietnamese gangs in Los Angeles and other California cities. More significantly, perhaps, this growing cultural and racial diversity has generated growing xenophobia (the fear and hatred of anyone or anything foreign) by segments of the White majority against "un-American" groups.

As far back as the beginning of the twentieth century, prominent sociologist Edward Alsworth Ross had warned the American public about the menace posed by the millions of so-called **new-wave immigrants** then entering the country from Central, Southern, and Eastern Europe, as well as from Asia and other non-European sources. Depicting these very different-looking and -acting people (in comparison to the earlier and more assimilated **old-wave immigrants** from Northern and Western Europe) as barnacles that had been scraped off the rocks of their native shores and then allowed to drift to the United States, Ross claimed that their sheer numbers eventually would overwhelm the superior Anglo host population (Ross, 1922). If these inferior people were permitted to enter the United States unchecked, the result would be "race suicide" and the passing of American civilization.

As we saw in our discussion of migration in Chapter Three, many of these same beliefs (although generally couched in less obvious terms than Ross's) continue to shape contemporary arguments about immigration in the United States and in the world at large. They are also significant factors in the shaping of the lives of those racial and ethnic minority groups already settled within this society.

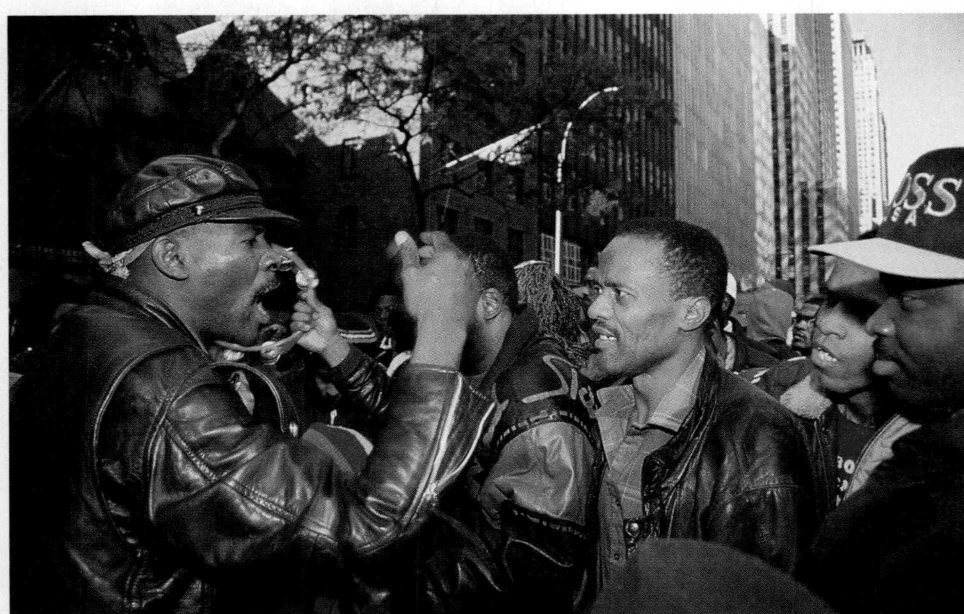

The arrival of new and impoverished immigrants (such as the Haitians pictured here, demonstrating in New York City) has intensified intergroup strains in the United States. In many cases, these new groups compete and conflict with other members of the same racial (but different ethnic) groups, as well as with members of different racial groups. Reports indicate that minorities harbor as many hostile feelings against other minorities as they do against majority group members.

AFRICAN AMERICANS

In 1968, after a year-long investigation, the National Advisory Commission on Civil Disorders—popularly known as the Kerner Commission—issued its final report to the American public. The Commission had been assembled by President Lyndon B. Johnson in the aftermath of a wave of destructive riots that had hit Newark, Los Angeles, Philadelphia, Detroit, and many other large cities earlier that decade. Its report on the causes of these widespread outbursts perhaps surprised some members of the Anglo majority group but came as no real surprise to the members of the African American community who were forced to live the experiences described by the commission.

According to the Kerner Commission (National Advisory Commission on Civil Disorders, 1968, p. 1), the United States was well on its way to becoming "two societies, one black, one white—separate and unequal." The combined effects of discrimination in employment and education and segregation in housing and schools had kept most African Americans from any real social equality with Whites. The resulting frustration and bitterness of African Americans at being denied a chance to attain the benefits taken for granted by their White counterparts had finally exploded, plunging the ghettos of America's largest cities into what surely seemed like anarchy. And, the commission concluded, unless basic social and economic conditions for African Americans improved dramatically, there was every reason to expect future urban disorders that would equal or surpass anything seen to date.

By the beginning of the 1990s, over two decades after the Kerner Commission report, there had been no appreciable change in the living conditions of millions of members of the United States' largest racial minority. (African Americans constitute approximately 13 percent of the total population.) As Table 7.2 demonstrates, on average, Blacks have continued to trail significantly behind Whites across a wide range of fundamental quality-of-life indicators. For example, the rate of infant mortality (the number of infants per 1,000 who die before reaching the age of one year) was over twice as high for African Americans in 1990 as it was for Whites—17.0 versus 7.7 (Stief, 1993). In that same year, mortality rates for some inner-city African American men were more than twice as high as those

TABLE 7.2 Selected Quality-of-Life Indicators for Whites and African Americans

Indicator	Whites	African Americans
Life expectancy at birth (years)	75.2	69.2
Infant mortality rate (deaths per 1,000 infants under age 1)	7.7	17.0
Below poverty level (percent)	11.6	33.3
Children below poverty level (percent)	16.0	46.3
Female-headed households (percent)	13.6	46.6
Over age 25 without high school diploma (percent)	11.2	29.6
1992 median family yearly income	$37,783	$21,548

SOURCE: U.S. Bureau of the Census, *Current Population Reports,* Series P-60, No. 180; Series P-60, No. 185; Stief, 1993.

for White men, 50 percent higher than those for Blacks as a whole, and actually higher than the mortality rates for men living in Bangladesh, one of the poorest developing countries in the world (McCord & Freeman, 1990). In 1991, African Americans had, on average, a life expectancy 6 years shorter than that of Whites—69.2 years compared to 75.2 years (Johnston, 1991). In 1992, poverty rates for African Americans as a whole (33.3 percent) and for African American children in particular (46.3 percent) were nearly three times as high as those for Whites (11.6 percent) and for White children (16.0 percent) (U.S. Bureau of the Census, 1993c).

Given this continuing litany of Black/White differentials, it is hardly surprising that, in late April and early May 1992, Los Angeles erupted in violence following yet another seemingly glaring demonstration of African American social inferiority. The wonder may be that more people in more cities around the country did not follow suit.

THE LEGACY OF SLAVERY

To understand the historic and continuing "separate and unequal" status of African Americans in the United States, it is necessary to remember their previous status as slaves for a period of approximately 250 years. From the early 1600s, when Africans first were brought to Jamestown, to the early 1860s, when the Emancipation Proclamation and the Civil War formally ended the practice, African Americans were held in legal bondage as unwilling workers in the labor-intensive agricultural economy of the South. As slaves, they were defined as property and denied basic human rights otherwise accorded members of this society. Subject to conditions of absolute social and economic poverty, African Americans came to be defined by popular beliefs as naturally inferior to Whites by virtue of their race—an ideology that, according to many observers, was necessary to reconcile the glaring contradiction between the human liberties guaranteed by the Constitution and the inhuman conditions imposed on the slaves (Bonacich, 1992).

Long after the legal system of slavery had been abolished, this notion of the basic natural inferiority of Blacks compared to Whites continued to structure the dominant (White) group's occupational, educational, political, and other social policies toward African Americans. The resulting high rates of poverty, illiteracy, and other indicators of social inferiority within this population group then served to confirm the supposed correctness of the original belief—a classic example of what sociologists term a "self-fulfilling prophecy" (Merton, 1968). Even at a time in which many individual African Americans have been able to achieve occupational and educational success, in spite of a system largely stacked against them, these stereotypes and prejudices continue to haunt their lives. Recent studies of African American business leaders, professionals, and other elites have documented the daily humiliations they face at the hands of the larger White society—and the growing feelings of rage that so far have not been vented in a way similar to those of lower-class Blacks in the ghettos (Benjamin, 1991; Cose, 1993).

For the far larger number of African Americans struggling to stay afloat economically, the situation has continued to worsen. As we saw in Chapter Five, significant changes in the occupational structure and employment picture have left large numbers of African Americans stranded in the inner cities and without significant work. For many African American blue-collar and lower-middle-class workers who have become casualties of the recession, entrenched prejudices and discrimination have made it more difficult to find new jobs. In 1992, Black unemployment rates were over twice as high as those for Whites (14.5 percent versus 6.5 percent), especially in the industrial areas of the midwestern states. As one observer close to the problem has put it, "Corporate America doesn't believe in the black male. The black male is left out of the middle class, then we point the finger at him, and say, 'Why doesn't he do something with himself?' It's the old 'blaming the victim' " (Lacey in S. Cohen, 1992).

AN AMERICAN MARSHALL PLAN

The National Urban League's 1992 *State of Black America* report described "a community under siege, fighting for its economic survival while victimized by the rise of a resurgent racism and abandoned by fiscally pressed state and federal governments" (Jacob, 1992, p. C-1). Calling poverty-stricken inner-city populations "a threat to the survival of our urban centers" and continued racial inequality "a threat to the well-being of a democratic society," the report called for the creation of a Marshall Plan for America, similar to the original economic plan formulated to rebuild West Germany after World War II. Under the proposed plan, an additional $50 billion per year over current funding would be made available by the federal government. These monies would be used for rebuilding crumbling urban infrastructures and for establishing educational and occupational training centers to develop human capital resources and prepare all members of the population to compete successfully in the new global economy. Although intended specifically for the Black and other minority communities "that have paid the price for America's past economic failures," this American Marshall Plan ultimately would "serve America's overriding national interest" and "help the nation lay the foundation for sustained, long-term economic growth and rising living standards for all Americans" (Jacob, 1992, p. C-7).

Given the structural roots of many (if not most) problems currently affecting African Americans, it is clear that something like the Marshall Plan for America is necessary for making significant and lasting changes in their lives and in the life of the country itself. However, given current economic climates and political realities, it remains to be seen whether such a plan is remotely possible. Past experience would seem to indicate that, given a choice between "major surgery" and "band-aid" policy alternatives, the tendency has been to cover things over and hope they'll heal themselves. Convincing members of the majority group that a more radical procedure now is called for undoubtedly would be a formidable task, though one that must be undertaken if any real progress is to occur. Unless the effort is made, the Los Angeles civil disorder of 1992 could mark the beginning, not the end, of urban racial unrest in the late twentieth century.

NATIVE AMERICANS

Like most other indigenous peoples in the Americas, "Indians" in what is now the United States have fared poorly during the 500 years since the beginning of contact with Europeans. The early period of that contact was characterized by cultural and physical conflicts, a pattern that was repeated throughout much of the history of the United States following the country's break from Britain. Viewed as foreign nations by the U.S. government, Native American tribes became the opponents of that government in a series of "foreign wars" that almost invariably resulted in defeat for Native Americans. By the mid-1800s, all tribes living in the eastern half of the nation had been forcibly relocated west of the Mississippi River. Estimated to have once been as large as 8 million, their numbers had been reduced by this time to about 250,000 as a result of dwindling food resources and the effects of previously unknown diseases transmitted by European settlers (Parrillo, 1994).

The opening of the western frontier following the Civil War led to further conflicts with White settlers who, in their search for land, gold, and other fortune, simply swept native tribes aside. Because they were unable to assimilate to Anglo culture and posed a physical threat to settlers, Native Americans once again were forcibly relocated, this time to lands that typically were so resource poor as to be of no interest to Whites. Tribal members languished in "benign neglect" on these reservations as wards of the federal government for many years, their lives controlled and structured by the Bureau of Indian Affairs (BIA).

For the most part, BIA policies seemed to be directed to forcing the assimilation of Native Americans to White cultural patterns and to breaking up traditional tribal groupings. For example, children often were taken from the tribes to be educated in distant "Indian schools" that utilized Anglo curricula and taught traditional Anglo subjects rather than the knowledge and customs of their particular tribe. The result was large groups of people who were unable to cling to old ways of life that had been virtually destroyed and who were unable to adapt to a new way of life that was both culturally foreign and unwilling to accept them.

Tired of their steady decline under the BIA, in the 1960s and 1970s, Native American groups undertook a series of dramatic acts of protest to focus public attention on their plight. These actions included the seizure of Wounded Knee, South Dakota, the site of the massacre of 300 Sioux by U.S. Army troops in 1890, and the occupation of Alcatraz Island, California. Native Americans also organized a pan-Indian movement, a coalition of various tribal groups united in common cause to pursue common interests against a common enemy: the federal government. This was an extraordinarily difficult undertaking, inasmuch as it required groups whose world views in some respects were poles apart to bridge that cultural chasm.

TABLE 7.3 Selected Quality-of-Life Indicators for Native Americans

Indicator	Native Americans	U.S. National Average
Family income level	$21,750	$35,525
Poverty rate	31.7%	13.1%
Married couple	17.0	5.5
Male, no wife	33.4	13.8
Female, no husband	50.4	31.1
Unemployment rate		
Males	16.2%	6.4%
Females	13.5	6.2
Leading Causes of Death (per 100,000 population)		
Accidents	93.1	35.0
Liver disease/cirrhosis	30.0	9.0
Diabetes	29.1	10.1
Suicide	17.5	11.4
Homicide	15.4	9.0

SOURCE: "A Look at Native Americans across the USA," *USA Today,* 28 April 1994, p. 7A. Copyright 1994, *USA Today.* Reprinted with permission.

NOTE: Data from U.S. Bureau of the Census and Indian Health Service.

Although the pan-Indian movement achieved some positive results in securing tribal land rights and in pursuing several court cases against the government and private corporations, its overall success has been mixed (Parrillo, 1994). Whether measured in terms of economic, educational, or physical health, most of the estimated 1.96 million Native Americans today remain near the bottom of the U.S. socioeconomic hierarchy (see Table 7.3). For example, Native Americans in the 15- to 24-year-old age bracket have the nation's highest death rate, largely as a consequence of their extremely high incidence of alcoholism. For Native Americans, rates of cirrhosis of the liver and diabetes are three times higher than the national average, and their accident rate is two-and-a-half times higher than the national average. As a group, Native Americans also have the highest suicide rate of any group in U.S. society (Johnston, 1991).

Unemployment and poverty rates among some individual tribal groups are extraordinarily high. For example, in 1988–1989, according to data presented before a U.S. congressional committee in 1990, 87 percent of the 10,300 Lakota Sioux who inhabit the Standing Rock Reservation in North and South Dakota were unemployed, and 90 percent were living in poverty (Kennedy, 1991). It is both ironic and tragic that the people who first lived in this land have been relegated to the bottom of the social heap.

LATINOS

Sociologist James W. Russell (1994, pp. 8–9) notes that "the naming of Latin American-origin people is a problem in the United States and Canada. A wide number of terms are in use, some of which are considered objectionable, but by different people." For example, the term used by the U.S. Bureau of the Census—*Hispanic*—is most widely used in the eastern part of the United States but does not exist among people in Mexico, Central America, or South America. Some groups oppose the use of *Hispanic* because it implies a complete Spanish background as well as a single cultural identity among Spanish-speaking peoples that does not mirror reality. In like manner, the term *Latino,* which is widely used in the western and southwestern parts of the United States, also implies the same sort of monolithic cultural identity that is at odds with the realities of racial, ethnic, and national differences among Spanish speakers. However, following Russell (and recognizing the possible distorting effects of the term), *Latino* will be used here as an umbrella term to designate the various people of Latin American origin currently residing in the United States. These people include Mexican Americans, Puerto Ricans, Cubans, Argentines, and a variety of other specific nationality groups.

Collectively, Latinos make up a sizeable (21.5 million in 1990) and rapidly growing (34 percent growth rate during the 1980s) segment of the U.S. population (Savage, 1990). According to the most recent census figures (1990), Latinos now constitute over 42 percent of the roughly 20 million foreign-born people living in the United States; Mexicans alone represent nearly 22 percent of all U.S. foreign born (Winsberg, 1993). In some portions of the country, especially in South Florida and Southern California, Latinos already constitute a numerical majority, and their numbers continue to grow. At least one commentator has predicted that, by the year 2010, the Los Angeles area will have become "a Latino subcontinent—demographically, culturally and economically distinct from the rest of America"—as a result of the *reconquista* ("reconquest") brought about by the large numbers of Mexican Americans streaming across the border each year and by the high birth rates exhibited by Latinos already living in the United States (Meyer, 1992, p. 32). It is this possibility that has many Anglos (non-Latino Whites) concerned.

NEW IMMIGRANTS FROM MEXICO AND CENTRAL AMERICA

Latinos are perceived as a genuine threat to the economic well-being of both the Southwest and society as a whole because of their willingness to accept lower wages than "American" workers, thus displacing deserving citizens from the labor force (Graham & Beck, 1992). One controversial study conducted by economist Donald L. Huddle (reported in Wood, 1993) claimed that immigration was responsible for the loss of 914,000 Californians' jobs in 1992—a figure that has been hotly contested by critics of the study. Latinos also are seen as a tremendous drain on educational, health care, legal, and other social services ultimately supported by tax funds (Johnson, 1993). The Huddle study found that, in 1992, the 7.4 million legal and illegal immigrants who have settled in California since 1970 cost the state $18 billion more than they paid in taxes (Wood, 1993). Less controversial studies have placed the taxpayer cost of immigration closer to $3 billion annually, a figure cited by California governor Pete Wilson in his "get tough on immigration" reelection campaign theme in 1994. Other local California politicians have also made the immigrant issue part of their election or reelection campaigns, and at least 20 bills have been introduced in the state legislature to curb illegal immigration (Armstrong, 1993a). Federal officials have also moved to introduce legislation that would seal off the southern U.S. border to illegals from Mexico and Central America, citing the tremendous burdens these immigrants have imposed on federal as well as state budgets (Dillin, 1994a). Immigration is an extremely volatile issue, and Latino immigrants are widely seen as being the crux of the problem.

Latino immigrants are also seen as a threat to the cultural well-being of U.S. society because of their continued refusal to assimilate, retaining their native Spanish language and cultural traditions. In response, the dominant Anglo group is forcing the issue. For example, in 1986, Californians voted to make English the official language of the state, becoming one of 19 states that now have such laws. Nationally, the USA English movement represents a similar attempt to legislate the use of English as the official language of the United States. According to supporters, this movement is an effort to preserve a critical and fundamental aspect of U.S. culture—its grounding in a common language.

QUALITY-OF-LIFE FACTORS

Much like those of African Americans and Native Americans, the life circumstances of many Latinos in this country are characterized by significantly lower economic, educa-

TABLE 7.4 Selected Quality-of-Life Indicators for Anglos and Latinos

Indicator	Anglos	Latinos
Infant mortality rate (deaths per 1,000 infants under age 1)	7.7	7.8
Below poverty level (percent)	11.6	29.3
Children below poverty level (percent)	16.0	38.8
Female-headed households (percent)	13.6	23.2
Over age 25 without high school diploma (percent)	11.2	43.6
1992 median family yearly income	$37,783	$23,895

SOURCE: U.S. Bureau of the Census, *Current Population Reports,* Series P-60, No. 180; Series P-60, No. 185; Stief, 1993.

tional, occupational, and other quality-of-life standards (see Table 7.4). For example, in 1992, nearly 30 percent of all Latinos and nearly 40 percent of all Latino children lived in poverty, a reflection of the fact that nearly one-quarter of all Latino households were headed by women. In that same year, nearly 44 percent of all Latinos over age 25 lacked high school diplomas, the minimum credential needed for a relatively decent job. The widespread lack of higher-educational degrees may be an important factor in the significantly lower than average income levels of Latinos compared to Anglos. Relegated to lower-paying and less-secure jobs, Latino workers are also likely to get hurt on the job more often and more seriously than either Anglo or Black workers ("Hispanics More Often Hurt," 1992).

Some of these disparities between Anglos and Latinos can be explained by the fact that many members of the Latino population are recent immigrants from Mexico and Central America. They have fled economic or political repression in their home countries and arrived in the United States with little or nothing in the way of personal resources. Trapped in minimum wage or subminimum wage jobs that do not carry medical or other benefits, they quickly sink into poverty and must struggle just to survive. Generally uneducated and unrepresented politically, they often become the targets of local racial and ethnic antagonisms.

In a few instances, elected Latino representatives have begun to exercise some political clout at the local and state levels, primarily as a result of demographic shifts (Gillam, 1993). However, for the most part, Latinos have yet to translate their large population numbers into effective political power. Individually, a growing number of upwardly mobile young Latinos have taken on an educational system they see as unresponsive to their cultural needs and have often won (Frammolino, 1993). However, on the whole, Latinos have been unable thus far to get past the many diversities and disagreements that subdivide their various constituent nationality groups and form anything like a "pan-Latino" coalition to challenge Anglo dominance ("Despite Political Gains," 1991; Natividad, 1992).

ASIAN AMERICANS

Like *Latino, Asian American* is an umbrella term that embraces a large number of distinct ethnic and nationality groups, including Japanese American, Chinese American, Korean American, Vietnamese American, and several other Indochinese groups. Asian Americans currently number about 6.5 million people and represent slightly over 25 percent of the U.S. foreign-born population (Winsberg, 1993). With Latinos, Asian Americans constitute over two-thirds of all U.S. foreign-born people; like Latinos, Asian Americans are a very visible group in the current immigration controversy. As a result of recent increases in "Asian bashing" on the part of a growing number of Anglos, Asian Americans once again are being singled out for special negative treatment from members of the dominant group.

Historically, Asians were the first group to be marked for restricted access to this country through the Chinese Exclusion Act of 1882. This legislation against Chinese immigrants, like the World War II executive order that led to the forced relocation of thousands of Japanese American citizens to special internment camps, seems to have been the result of racist-inspired fears of a possible Oriental takeover of the White world (Hoppenstand, 1992). This "Yellow peril" stereotype appears to have been reborn in the aftermath of the U.S. military loss in Southeast Asia in the 1970s and the current economic trade war being waged with Japan in the 1990s. Renewed antagonisms against

CONNECTIONS

The prejudices, discriminatory actions, and outright conflicts that so often characterize racial and ethnic group relations in the contemporary world have restricted and reduced the lives of countless millions of people. Aside from their obvious and often fatal impacts on the physical well-being of victimized groups, these hostilities create a host of other problems with enormous consequences for all members of the affected societies:

- In addition to having higher rates of illness than Whites, Blacks in the United States also receive medical care significantly inferior to that of Whites in every type of hospital in America, according to a major study that found that "the quality of care varies tremendously with a patient's race, and not . . . based on whether a person has health insurance" ("Hospital Care Found Worst," 1994).
- As a result of their continued treatment as second-class citizens, many African Americans have grown increasingly pessimistic about their social and economic futures and increasingly radical in their political views. A University of Chicago study reported that about 50 percent of African Americans now favor the formation of a separate Black political party to further their interests (Tyson, 1994). The polarization of such a large segment of the U.S. population represents a potential threat to political stability and perhaps to democracy, as witnessed by the cases of ethnic and racial conflicts now taking place in many other countries.
- In their attempt to deal with the crushing poverty that traps so many of their people, a number of

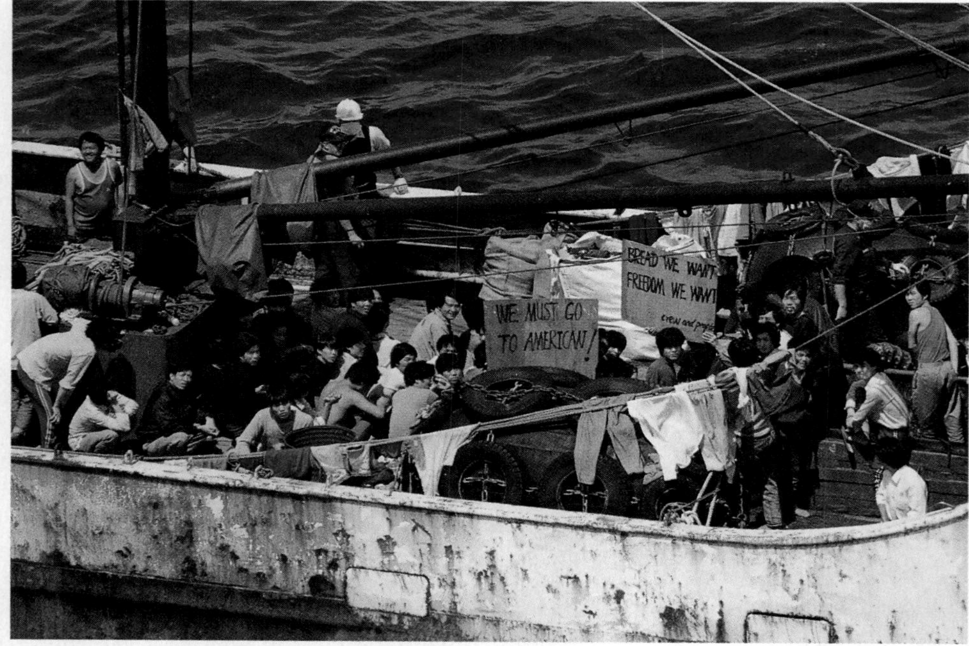

The "superminority" stereotype of Asian Americans obscures the reality of widespread poverty among recent immigrants. These illegal Chinese are part of a wave of economic and political refugees fleeing their homelands for a better life in the United States. This particular group was apprehended off Baja California by the Immigration and Naturalization Service and returned to China; many others have managed to slip past the INS, only to find poverty and despair in their new home.

Native American tribes around the country have embarked on controversial policies aimed at improving their economic conditions. In California, the once-bleak Sycuan Indian Reservation now sports an upper-middle-class air as a result of that tribe's entry into the casino gambling business. However, concerns about issues of morality and crime have led many local Anglos to oppose further gaming enterprises by other California tribal groups (Barfield, 1994). In what well may be a much more serious situation, some tribes have offered their lands as sites for solid waste and toxic waste landfills that have been blocked from other areas. Fears of the potential health hazards posed both to tribal members and to other local residents have led to attempts to block these "Dances with Garbage" plans that critics have viewed as a manifestation of environmental racism (Hager et al., 1991).

- At the same time that it has blinded Americans to the very real economic plight of many Asian immigrants, the spectacular success of some Asian Americans has been cited as one of the contributing factors to the growing wave of "Asian bashing" across the United States. This increasing anti-Asian sentiment is not confined to Anglos but has been exhibited by some Latinos and African Americans through acts of violence against Koreans and other Asian groups (J. Walsh, 1993).
- Increasing cultural awareness and multiculturalism around the world promise to keep that world in almost constant turmoil and conflict for years to come. Since many of the claims of ancestral homeland made by various ethnic groups overlap with those of other groups, territorial border disputes between established and would-be nation-states likely will increase in number and in magnitude (Grier, 1994).

Asian Americans have begun to mar what in many other ways has been an amazing success story of the type envisioned in the "melting pot" myth.

Asian Americans have sometimes been called a "superminority" (Schwartz, 1987) or a "model minority" (McLeod, 1986). They have the highest median annual family income of any ethnic group in the United States ($35,900), as well as the highest average level of formal education of any group in the country, including Anglos. Nearly twice as many Asian Americans as Anglos have completed college—33 percent compared to 17.5 percent of the two respective groups. However, Schaefer (1990) observes that these profile figures are very deceiving.

NEW ASIAN IMMIGRANTS

Whereas many Asian Americans are employed in high-paying, high-status professional and managerial positions, an equally large number are employed in low-paying, low-status service jobs. Many established Asian Americans have been able to fulfill the American dream of upward mobility and success. But many of the recently arrived immigrants, who have contributed to the rapid growth of the Asian American population since 1970, have sunk to the bottom of the income and occupation ladders.

A major government-sponsored study found that Southeast Asian immigrants currently have the highest rate of welfare dependency of any racial or ethnic group in the United States. More than 30 percent of all Southeast Asian households depend on welfare (almost 4 times the 8 percent national average), and welfare rates are as high as 77 percent among Cambodians and Laotians in California (Dunn, 1994). With the assistance of the federal government, a growing number of these new Asian immigrants are leaving the West and moving into the heartland of Kansas and other states. There, they can find steady though difficult work in meat-packing and other industries and receive at least civil treatment from local residents. However, as Asians' and other immigrants' numbers have grown in these rural areas, so have the rates of crime. The result, in some cases, has been increasing antagonism toward the newcomers. One Dodge City, Kansas, official was reported to have compared some immigrants to cockroaches: "If you spray for them there, they only end up here" (quoted in Sontag, 1993).

Unfortunately, the persistence of the "superminority" image has blinded federal and state governments and many members of the general public to the plight of these refugee people, leaving them, in many cases, with no place to turn for assistance (Shaw, 1990). Like many Native Americans, who live in profound poverty on reservations around the country, these new Asian immigrants remain a hidden minority group.

SUMMARY

1 From a scientific standpoint, *races* are groups of people who differ from other groups genetically. Gene differences may manifest themselves as overt differences in skin color and other physical features. *Ethnic groups* are composed of people who share common cultural traits and have a sense of peoplehood. Members of specific ethnic groups often share common physical features, but this is not always the case.

2 In practice, *race* is a social construct that depends on people's perceptions and often incorrectly attributes cultural patterns to genetic or biological characteristics. This confusion between *race* and *ethnicity* has been and remains the source of many intergroup problems and conflicts.

3 *Majority groups* are those groups who dominate and control the most important institutions within a given society. *Minority groups* are those groups whose lack of effective power consigns them to subordinate positions within the socioeconomic hierarchy. Minorities often are stereotyped as being categorically different and inferior to other groups. These prejudicial feelings often lead to *discrimination,* the unequal and unfair treatment of minority groups.

4 *De jure discrimination* is required or supported by law in some societies. However, *de facto,* or *informal, discrimination,* is more often the case. Such informal discrimination often is institutionalized in common practices that may operate to the disadvantage of specific groups without intentionally intending to do so. Neighborhood schools in the United States are an example of *institutionalized discrimination.*

5 Whereas assimilation models envisioned the eventual blending of racial and ethnic minorities with majority groups, the reality more often is multicultural or pluralistic societies in which individual groups retain their cultural identities. True pluralism also entails a sharing of political power by the different groups, as is the case in Switzerland. Given the competition for scarce resources that often marks relations between ethnic and racial groups, successful multiculturalism is very difficult to accomplish. Conflict between ethnic and racial groups more often appears to be the case.

6 Conflict between different ethnic or racial groups sometimes has taken the form of extermination, or *genocide,* in which an attempt is made to physically destroy some particular group. Genocidal wars are being fought in several countries in Eastern Europe and the former Soviet Union as well as a number of African and Asian countries. In many cases, indigenous peoples, whose ancestors originally occupied the given area, have been targeted for extermination by more powerful, later arrivals.

7 Contrary to the myth of the "melting pot," cultural and racial diversity has been characteristic of U.S. society. Prevailing beliefs in the innate inferiority of certain groups have relegated them to severely disadvantaged positions in most important spheres of life. As a legacy of slavery, African Americans continue to be treated as second-class citizens. Native Americans also constitute an especially poverty-prone group, though one more hidden from public consciousness as a result of their effective segregation on reservations. Some of these reservations are characterized by near-universal unemployment and poverty.

8 One of the fastest-growing minorities in the United States, Latinos from a number of Central and South American countries are viewed by many Anglos as an economic and cultural threat to the traditional American way of life. Because of their very large numbers in California, Texas, and Florida, Latinos have been targeted for a variety of immigration law reforms, ranging from restriction to exclusion.

9 Although Asian Americans often are stereotyped as a "model" or "superminority" group because of their educational and economic successes, many newer immigrants from Southeast Asia live in abject poverty. Some Vietnamese, Cambodian, and Laotian groups are being assisted by government programs to find steady employment in the rural areas of the Midwest, but the plight of many others remains unnoticed by local governments and the general public.

CHAPTER EIGHT

INEQUALITIES OF SEX AND GENDER
The Longest War

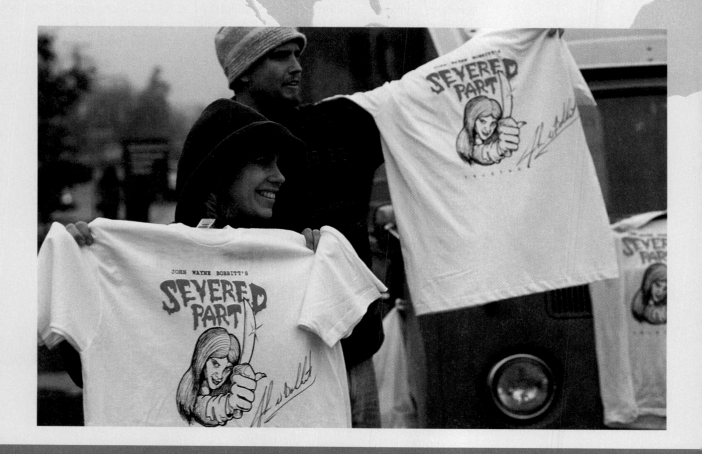

On June 23, 1993, the long-simmering battle between the sexes in the United States took a dramatic and lurid turn. Lorena Bobbitt, a suburban Virginia housewife, carved a small niche for herself in contemporary American history when she took a 12-inch fillet knife, amputated her sleeping husband's penis, and then tossed it into an empty field. The severed organ later was retrieved and surgically reattached, but the long-term prognosis for a complete recovery remained cloudy. As the distraught Ms. Bobbitt later told police, hers was an act of utter desperation, triggered by what she described as a long series of physical and sexual abuses by her husband, John Wayne Bobbitt. Feeling trapped and unable to endure the thought of any further humiliations, she claimed that she had snapped, striking out unthinkingly with the nearest weapon at hand. Unimpressed by her story, the district attorney's office charged Lorena Bobbitt with the malicious wounding of her husband and bound her over for trial. In turn, John Wayne Bobbitt was charged with raping his wife and likewise held for trial. It was a case destined for media greatness: every man's worst nightmare (and, according to at least some radical feminists, every woman's secret revenge fantasy) come true.

The subsequent trials of the star-crossed couple riveted the attention of the American public and seemed to widen the rift between women and men, as well as that between militant feminists and their more moderate counterparts (Ehrenreich, 1994; D. A. Kaplan, 1994). In his trial, John Wayne Bobbitt was acquitted of the rape charge, thus apparently undercutting the basis for much of Lorena's planned defense. In her later trial, played out in intimate and painful detail on prime-time national television, Lorena Bobbitt was found not guilty of the malicious wounding of her husband by reason of temporary insanity. She was remanded to a psychiatric facility for evaluation; 45 days later, she was declared sane and released back into the community. In the meantime, her husband, seemingly well on the road to recovery, made several lucrative guest appearances on television to promote his version of the bizarre story. He spent additional time signing some of the many graphic

T-shirts ("Revenge Is Sweet," "Love Hurts") that had been rushed into production to commemorate this singular event.

At the same time the genital mutilation of John Wayne Bobbit was etching itself into the national (and international) consciousness, millions of other cases of genital mutilation were going largely unnoticed. Their victims were not invited on the TV and radio talk-show circuit to discuss their traumas, nor did they autograph any commemorative wearing apparel. According to the World Health Organization, more than 84 million young girls throughout Africa and the Middle East have undergone a forced "female circumcision" in which part or all of their clitoris was cut away. Described as "ritual mutilation" by its critics, this procedure typically is done without anesthetics or sterilization (Boxall, 1993; Greenhouse, 1994). Despite the many deaths that result, the practice persists in some societies because cultural beliefs define uncircumcised girls as not desirable or proper marriage partners (Spaid, 1993b). Concerned that a large number of Ethiopians, Eritreans, Somalis, and other African immigrants were bringing this particular tradition with them to North America, in 1993, Congresswoman Pat Schroeder introduced a bill to outlaw the practice in the United States (Brinkley, 1993). To date, however, the genital mutilation of millions of girls in the developing world has attracted nothing like the attention given to the mutilation of one U.S. man.

In this chapter, we examine the separate and unequal lives of women and men throughout the developing and developed worlds. Based on cultural beliefs that define them as naturally inferior and institutionalized practices that make them socially inferior, nearly half the world's population faces daily political, economic, educational, and other experiences that are psychologically and spiritually, if not physically, mutilating. Women's attempts to confront and change the forced circumstances of their lives constitute one of the great civil rights movements of the age. These efforts mark the latest battle in what has been described as "the longest war" (Tavris & Offir, 1977).

QUESTIONS TO CONSIDER

- 1. What is the difference between *sex* and *gender?*
- 2. How do gender stereotypes shape the lives of women and men in societies such as the United States?
- 3. What is the difference between *gender assignment* and *gender socialization?*
- 4. How does formal education affect the occupational careers of women and men in contemporary societies?
- 5. What are *human capital factors?*
- 6. With respect to sex and gender, what are *dual labor markets?*
- 7. What is the difference between *quid pro quo sexual harassment* and so-called *hostile environment harassment?*
- 8. In what sense do contemporary rape laws treat women as second-class citizens?
- 9. Why is abortion regarded by many feminists as the single most important gender equality issue of the late twentieth century?
- 10. What are the main sources of factionalism within the women's movement in the United States?

DECONSTRUCTING SEX AND GENDER

Much like *race* and *ethnicity, sex* and *gender* are terms often used interchangeably (and, consequently, incorrectly) by many people. Inasmuch as they both represent ways of categorizing individuals on biological and physiological grounds, the two concepts are related; however, they are by no means identical phenomena.

From a strictly scientific standpoint, **sex** is a method of classifying individuals based entirely on consideration of anatomical, chromosomal, and gonadal factors. Although these three sex-related dimensions do not coincide perfectly in all cases, individuals are defined as being male if they possess a penis, testicles, an XY chromosome pattern, and predominantly androgen hormones. They are defined as being female if they possess a vagina, ovaries, an XX chromosome pattern, and predominantly estrogen hormones.

The concept of gender is likewise grounded in physiological differences between females and males, but it adds psychological and sociocultural dimensions, as well. A given individual's **gender** is a result of that person's self-definition as female or male, as well as an acceptance of the psychological and behavioral characteristics defined as appropriate for one's particular sex. In most cases, people's gender identity coincides with their biological sex category—that is, females think of themselves and act like girls or women, and males think of themselves and act like boys or men. It is precisely in the construction and communication of the particular psychological, emotional, and behavioral traits deemed natural and proper for each sex that gender classification systems move well beyond the realm of the purely biological (Lorber & Farrell, 1991).

GENDER STEREOTYPES AND GENDER ROLES

In most human societies, popular cultural beliefs have generated **gender stereotypes**, or images of women and men as fundamentally and categorically different from one another. Because of their natural and intimate connection with biological reproduction, women have been thought to be inherently gentle and nurturing. By virtue of their hormonal cycles, they are likewise believed to be very emotional and more subject to mood swings than men. Because of their presumed higher intellectual powers and less intimate connection to hormonal cycles, men are thought to be more logical and more emotionally stable than women. By virtue of their larger size and assumed greater natural aggressiveness, men are also defined as inherently better suited for protecting women and children.

These are the widespread beliefs about the psyches of women and men, but what are the realities? What difference does it make that women and men display different ratios of estrogen and androgen hormones? Does the testosterone level in the human male have the same impact on aggressiveness that it seems to have in males of other species? Are women more slaves to their hormones than are men?

Whereas the existence of hormonal changes associated with menstruation, childbirth, and menopause is a matter of verified fact, the precise impacts of these changes on female psychology and temperament are matters of continuing debate. So, also, are questions concerning the relationship between sex-linked hormones and intellectual, emotional, and behavioral patterns in both men and women. A number of reviews of the relevant research literature (Deaux, 1992; Jacklin, 1989; Shapiro, 1990) conclude that the actual range of consistent female/male differences in these patterns may be much smaller than is commonly believed. Males and females do differ from one another in various respects, but it's not entirely clear just what these differences mean.

This research indicates that females show somewhat higher levels of verbal ability than males and that males demonstrate somewhat higher mathematical and visual-spatial abilities as well as higher levels of physical aggression than females. However, these differences are not always large or statistically significant (Jacklin, 1989). Collectively, research findings presently do not support the conclusion that women and men are significantly different in temperament or in intellectual abilities (Deaux, 1992; Shapiro, 1990). Nevertheless, many people remain convinced that women and men are fundamentally different from one another in many, if not most, important respects.

In all societies where they have existed, these stereotyped beliefs and assumptions about the respective basic natures of men and women have led to the creation of specialized social statuses and roles for the two sexes. These **gender roles** categorically assign people to different positions and activities specifically because of their sex and its presumed associated attributes. In most cases, these gendered statuses and roles generate unequal income, power, and other desired rewards for women and men, leading to inequality hierarchies based on sex. As a result, **gender stratification** has been a basic and persistent feature of most human societies (Crompton & Mann, 1986; Lorber, 1992). In these societies, a simple accident of birth—being born female rather than male or male rather than female—generates life-and-death consequences for hundreds of millions of people around the world each day.

PRESERVING GENDER STEREOTYPES

Once in place, gender stereotypes and their resulting systems of gender inequalities are maintained in much the same way as other social constructs. They are deeply embedded within a matrix of cultural beliefs and social patterns, supported by individual and institutional practices that have the effect of confirming and perpetuating them over time. These conceptions of gender form an intrinsic part of the "world taken for granted" into which members of a given society are born. Through the lifelong process of **gender socialization,** societies imprint their particular images of men and women on their populations. As they move through the age cycle, individuals learn and internalize cultural beliefs and values about the differing natures of males and females, as well as each sex's proper place in the larger scheme of things.

INFANCY AND EARLY CHILDHOOD

The long teaching and learning process that ultimately will lead individuals to define themselves and their linkage to the world in gendered terms begins at (or, in an increasing number of cases in which amniocentesis or sonogram tests have established the sex of the fetus, before) the moment of birth. **Gender assignment,** the announcement that "It's a girl!" or "It's a boy!" presents the newly born (or not-yet-born) child to its parents and to the rest of the world as a member of a predefined category with predefined attributes and limitations. This sex categorization is crucially important in structuring the infant's initial social experiences and relationships both inside and outside the family (Fagot et al., 1985; Rossi, 1984).

By the time children are three to four years old, they already have formed an image of themselves as "girl" or "boy." They also have gained knowledge of what being a girl or a boy means in terms of their own behaviors (La Freniere et al., 1984). Even though children have had relatively little outside social experience at this point in their lives, through their interactions with parents and other family members, they already have been exposed to (and have absorbed) their society's definition of what they should be like

In many societies, the gender socialization process is characterized by gender-specific coming-of-age rites that mark individuals' passing from childhood to adulthood and reinforce traditional gender roles. These children in Zaire are preparing for a menstrual ceremony. Are there any comparable gendered rites-of-passage ceremonies in the United States?

as individuals because of their sex. Notions of "she" and "he" are becoming important ingredients in the development of "I" and "me."

ADOLESCENCE AND EARLY ADULTHOOD

For most individuals in modern societies, the years of transition between childhood and adulthood form a critical period for gender socialization. It is during this time that gender identities and roles are reinforced and integrated (Eccles, 1987), and the joint actions of parents, teachers, counselors, and the educational curriculum seem to operate (or conspire) to achieve an overall acceptance of the gender patterns to which individuals were exposed during earlier childhood. Training for future adult occupational and social roles most often focuses on learning activities appropriate for members of one's own sex. Learning to be an adult means learning to be a proper adult man or adult woman. At the point that most individuals finally cross the threshold into adulthood, they have internalized the gender information provided for them by the appropriate agents of socialization in their particular society.

MIDDLE AND LATE ADULTHOOD

For most adults, the middle years are defined by increasing participation in familial and occupational roles. Entering and maintaining a marriage, having and raising children, and crafting a successful career are activities that occupy the bulk of the time and energy of adults in contemporary societies. In most societies, many of these roles are defined by prevailing values and beliefs as being the proper domain of one sex rather than the other: Men are most often seen as providers and women as nurturers (Boyden, 1993; United Nations, 1991). Fulfilling these role expectations cements individuals into a set of structured behaviors and relationships that reinforce and confirm their sense of masculinity or femininity.

For many people, movement into the "golden" years of late adulthood brings anything but gold. Women who have defined themselves primarily in familial and domestic terms may face a crisis of self-identity and self-worth with the deaths of their husbands and the passage of their offspring from childhood into adulthood (Williamson et al., 1980). Many of these women in the United States also face the very real prospect of impending poverty as they grow older. Given their own past employment histories and a Social Security system that drastically limits their share of their husbands' retirement benefits, women aged 65 and over are three times as likely to be poor as men the same age (Barringer, 1992b). These women now constitute nearly 75 percent of the elderly poor in the United States, and their situation is likely to get worse unless Social Security laws are changed. Nearly half of all women over age 65 live alone, and only about 25 percent of all retirement-age women receive some sort of pension. In 1960, women's basic Social Security benefit was 75 percent of the average benefit for men; by 1990, that average had dropped to 59 percent (Gardner, 1992).

For many other women and for most men, retirement from an occupational career serves as the catalyst for significant gender role changes. In many developed societies, cultural values and beliefs define the adult role as one involving active mastery of some occupational task and productive contribution to society. Employment provides people positive social and self identities and also serves as an important indicator of their position in the socioeconomic hierarchy. (Recall our discussion of occupation and inequality in Chapter Six.) Retirement thus may symbolically tell the retirees—and the world—that their days of productive contribution to societal well-being have ended. This realization, coupled with the economic decline that often follows retirement, may generate a severe identity crisis (Chown, 1977).

The decline of physical abilities and physical health that ultimately accompanies advancing chronological age forms an additional source of personal identity crisis for many people, especially in cultures in which adult status is defined in part by physical vigor. In cultures that define and judge females largely in terms of physical attractiveness, physical aging can be particularly damaging for those women who have accepted the stereotypes and have defined themselves in terms of physical criteria. For these women, the assurance that they're getting better, not older, often rings hollow.

As they age, both women and men face the likelihood of being forced to redefine their image of who and what they are. This process of unlearning an old social identity and learning a new one mandates a reassessment of one's femininity or masculinity. This reevaluation may consist of the realization that one no longer can measure up to existing ideals of gender appearance and activities. In cultures in which youth is valued and old people are subject to negative stereotyping, the new self-identity of many older people may be that of someone who is a lesser person than before.

PATTERNS OF GENDER INEQUALITY

Demographic data strongly suggest that females have a biological advantage over males when comparisons are made in terms of infant mortality rates, overall longevity rates, and other measures of birth and death (Baker et al., 1980; United Nations, 1991). However, other sociological data suggest just as strongly that, in virtually all societies, the period between birth and death is characterized by overwhelming male social advantages in such fundamental realms as educational and occupational opportunities, health care, and legal and political representation.

For example, throughout the world, a disproportionately large and growing number of women live in poverty—a phenomenon known as the *feminization of poverty* (Pearce, 1978, 1990; Peterson, 1987). According to some estimates, over 550 million women in the rural areas of developing countries now languish in abject poverty as "the forgotten oppressed of our planet" (Power, 1992). In the United States, according to U.S. Bureau of the Census data (1993c), women now constitute 63 percent of all poor persons over the age of 18. Whether the specific setting is developing countries or developed nations, the pattern remains essentially the same. Men dominate major social institutions, and women are subordinated to those structures.

GENDER AND EDUCATION

As we saw in Chapter Six, formal education has become perhaps the single most important vehicle for the attainment of socioeconomic status and social mobility in modern industrialized societies. Access to the educational system and to a successful passage through that system has become a critical factor in shaping a whole range of social, economic, and political consequences for people in the contemporary world. Restricted or blocked formal educational opportunities typically result in constricted or impoverished life conditions for those so denied. In a large number of societies, women are greatly overrepresented among that denied group.

In spite of tremendous advances in women's education during the past two decades, women as a whole remain far behind men in terms of educational attainment, especially in developing countries. The United Nations survey of the world's women (1991, p. 45) estimated that, as of 1985, there were 597 million illiterate adult women compared to 352 million illiterate adult men throughout the world and that this gap likely would continue "well into the next century in all the developing regions." This same report indicated that younger girls now are approaching universal primary education in most Asian, Latin American, and Caribbean countries but not in southern Asia or sub–Saharan Africa. With regard to secondary (high school) and tertiary (college and university) education, men still dominate in all but 33 countries. As Figure 8.1 illustrates, in developing countries, women's enrollment in university-level education on average was slightly more than half (51 percent) of men's by the end of the 1980s. By way of contrast, in the developed nations, women's tertiary-level enrollment as a percentage of men's during that same time period ranged from a low of 48 percent in Switzerland to a high of 130 percent in Sweden. For the most part, women's proportional enrollments were equal to or somewhat higher than those of men across Europe and North America. In a few instances, they were considerably higher: For example, in the Scandinavian countries as a whole, female college and university enrollment averaged 123 percent of that for males.

When women do achieve college or university education in significant numbers, they tend to be concentrated in traditional liberal arts or humanities majors rather than the potentially more employable and more lucrative engineering and science-related fields. In the developing countries as a whole, women constitute only 20 percent of all students enrolled in these areas of study; for developed industrial societies as a whole, women's enrollment in these fields averages only about one-third that of males. In only one industrialized country—Italy—does women's enrollment in engineering and science-related fields exceed one-half—51 percent—that of men's (United Nations Development Program, 1993, p. 196).

This tendency for women to major in the humanities and social sciences may reflect the combined effects of cultural beliefs and social practices concerning the presumed

FIGURE 8.1 University Education Gender Gaps in Developing and Developed Countries

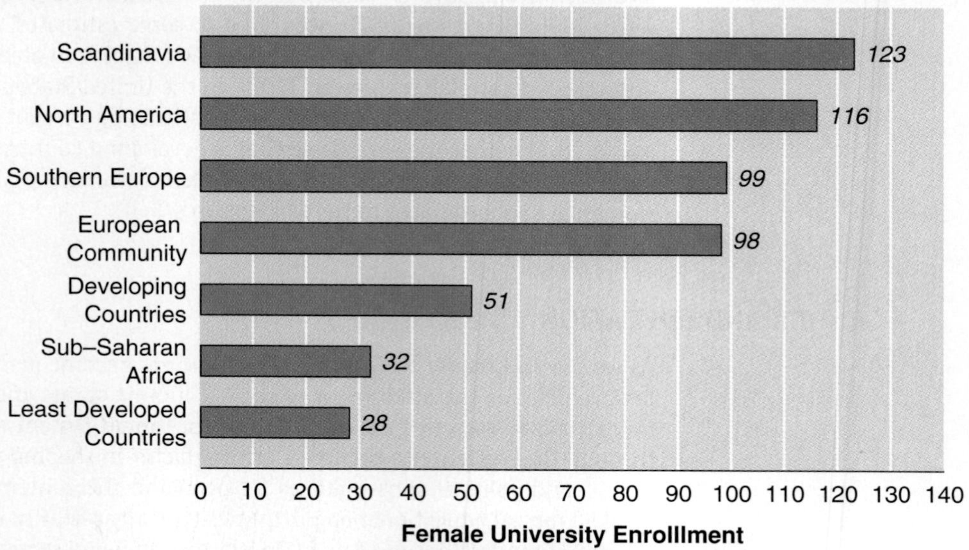

SOURCE: Compiled from data in United Nations Development Program, *Human Development Report 1993*, Tables 9 and 34.

lesser abilities and interests of females in science, engineering, and mathematics. Whatever the causal mechanisms involved, the net result is that college and university women throughout the contemporary world are concentrated in fields likely to be rewarded with lesser-paying jobs after graduation. For example, in 1992, women constituted less than 9 percent of all engineers, less than 28 percent of all natural scientists, one-third of all mathematical and computer scientists, one-fifth of all physicians, and less than 9 percent of all dentists in the United States (U.S. Bureau of the Census, 1993a, p. 405).

GENDER AND THE WORKPLACE

A United Nations report issued during that international agency's Decade for Women (1976–1985) observed, "Women comprise about half the world's population, perform about two-thirds of its work, receive only one-tenth of its income, and own less than one-hundredth of world assets" (quoted in Boyden, 1993). Nearly a decade later, a United Nations Development Program (UNDP) human development report concluded that it still is the case "no country treats its women as well as it treats its men" (United Nations Development Program, 1993, p. 16).

For example, in the developing world, women on average work up to 25 percent more hours per week than men, dividing their time between family responsibilities and unpaid work in the agricultural or other nonindustrial activities that form the majority of economic roles in these societies. In Africa, women account for as much as 80 percent of total food production, especially in the rural areas of countries such as Lesotho

(Boyden, 1993). In the developed world, a large number of women—over 60 percent in Japan, Great Britain, and the United States and 80 percent in Sweden (cited in "Mirror on the U.S.," 1992)—have joined the workforce as full-time employees in the years since the end of World War II, primarily to help their families survive economically. Like their counterparts in the less-developed countries, these women also are expected to assume primary responsibility for families and households.

Despite the amount of time and effort involved, women's domestic labor for the most part remains unnoticed and excluded from worldwide calculations of societal economic productivity. As the United Nations 1990 survey of the world's women noted, "If their unpaid housework and family care were counted as productive outputs in national accounts, measures of global output would increase 25 to 30 percent" (United Nations, 1991, p. 2).

GENDERED INCOME DIFFERENCES

Because so much of women's work in developing countries takes the form of unpaid labor in the agricultural sector or paid domestic work outside the regular labor force, reliable information about gender-based income disparities in the developing world is spotty and often nonexistent. For the most part, what we possess in the way of hard data on this issue comes from developed nations. These numbers tell us that, in every industrialized country in the contemporary world, women trail behind men in wages derived from their employment in the paid labor force.

In all contemporary societies for which comparable income and employment figures exist, the available data indicate "a remarkable pattern of discrimination" against women (United Nations Development Program, 1993, p. 101). By combining measures of the relative wages of women and men and their relative rates of participation in the labor force, the UNDP created an "adjusted real GDP" (gross domestic product) figure that shows female per capita income as a percentage of male per capita income in these nations. According to the UNDP, this index in all likelihood still understates the actual extent of gender-based income inequality, inasmuch as it is based on a number of conservative assumptions about male and female nonwage incomes that are known to be flawed. However, in spite of the limitations of the index, the results are nonetheless striking (see Figure 8.2).

For the 22 developed and 11 developing nations included in the report, adjusted female incomes as a percentage of male incomes ranged from a high of 82 percent in Sweden to a low of 26 percent in Costa Rica. The female-to-male income ratio was 60 percent or greater in only 9 cases (the Scandinavian nations, Australia, New Zealand, Paraguay, and the former Czechoslovakia), whereas it was below 40 percent in 10 cases—including Japan, a country that otherwise ranked first in the world in terms of overall human development. For the United States, the figure was 48.7 percent—that is, taking into account both the percentage of women in the labor force relative to men and the average gap between female and male wages, women in this society on average earn only 49 cents for every dollar earned by men. In 1993, according to one study, women holding chief executive officer or similar rank within *Fortune* 500 corporations averaged only two-thirds the salary of their male peers ($187,000 versus $289,000) (Brooks, 1993).

HUMAN CAPITAL FACTORS

These female/male income discrepancies have been interpreted in a number of different ways by economists and sociologists. Economists have focused on what are termed **human capital factors**, the resources that people bring with them to the labor market that make them more or less successful in finding good jobs. These resources include formal

FIGURE 8.2 Gender Income Disparities in Selected Developing and Developed Countries

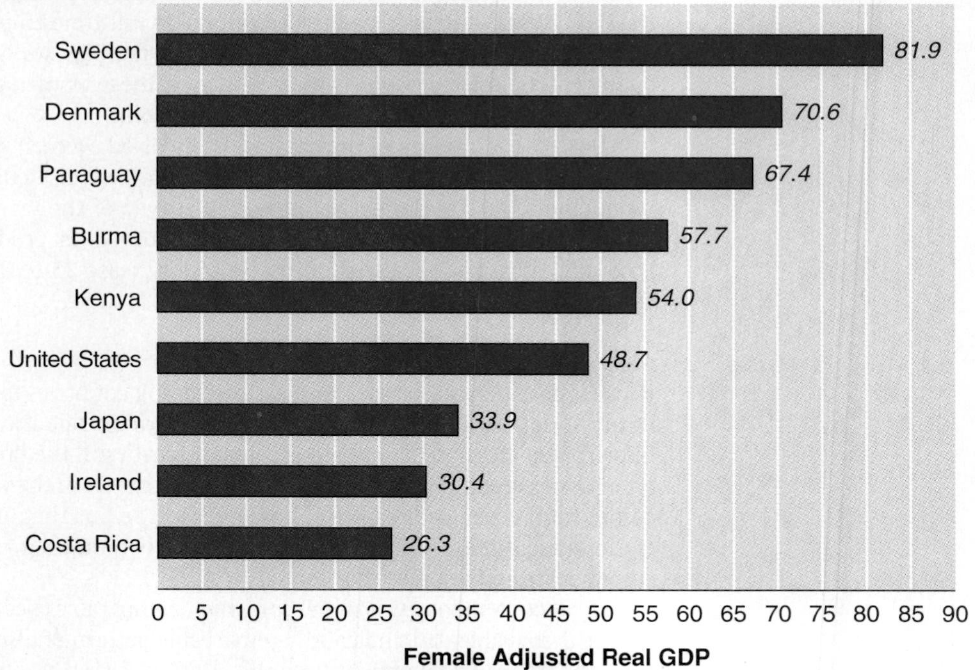

SOURCE: Compiled from data in United Nations Development Program, *Human Development Report 1993*, Technical Note Table 1.1.

NOTE: Figures are expressed in terms of adjusted real GDP: the gap between male and female wages multiplied by the gap between male and female labor force participation.

education, aptitudes, occupational training, and various other "investments" that make some individuals more attractive to employers, thus increasing their employment prospects. Higher incomes represent the "return" on the human capital investments made by these successful job candidates.

According to this argument, female/male income differentials are indicative of the fact that men generally possess more human capital resources than women. On average, men have more interest, formal training, and previous work experience in law, medicine, science, engineering, business, and other professions that command the highest salaries in modern societies. Because they have more human capital to offer, men are able to negotiate good positions and high salaries for their employment services. In contrast, women are at a comparative disadvantage when it comes to human capital factors. Some women choose to invest their time and energy in having children rather than in having occupational careers. Their childrearing activities often keep them out of the full-time labor force for a lengthy period of time, thus causing them to fall behind their male counterparts in seniority and in job experience. These family responsibilities also lead many women to accept jobs closer to home or that offer flexible hours so they can be with their children more often. Because the obligations attached to their domestic roles put them at a human capital disadvantage, these women are not in a good position to bargain with potential employers. They must settle for whatever jobs and wages they are offered.

This human capital argument has received some support from a number of studies of gender-based wage differentials in the United States and other modern societies (England & Farkas, 1986; Roos, 1985). But these same studies concluded that human capital resources are not the only or even the most influential contributing elements in the gender-based income gap. The dual labor markets of many contemporary societies, as well as continuing discrimination against women, play roles that are equally or more significant.

DUAL LABOR MARKET

Throughout the world, women entering the paid labor force find their employment prospects limited in ways that those of men are not. Depending on their formal educational credentials, both women and men might have access to a variety of blue-collar, white-collar, or managerial and professional jobs. However, within these major occupational categories, women are steered into a much narrower range of choices, relegated to jobs defined as "women's work" and to status and incomes substantially lower than those of men (Seager & Olson, 1986). Thus, women come to occupy what have been called "pink-collar" jobs (Bernard, 1981).

Some observers (Bielby & Baron, 1984; Roos, 1985; Trieman & Roos, 1983) claim that these sex-segregated occupational structures and their resulting pink-collar ghettos are indicative of what are called **dual labor markets.** Dual labor market systems contain two distinct segments or tiers of jobs, each of which demands different types or levels of skills and training and offers different levels of rewards. The top tier is composed of professional, administrative, and technical occupations that require high-level skills and training but deliver high status and income rewards in return. The bottom tier is made up of service, domestic, and other unskilled jobs that do not require much training but do not offer many prestige or income rewards. Because far greater wage and prestige rewards are associated with the top-tier occupations, this segment of the labor market will be filled disproportionately by members of powerful majority groups in a given society. (Recall our discussion of majority groups and minority groups in Chapter Seven.) With less opportunity to gain high-level skills and training, most minority group members will be consigned to less desirable, less rewarding, lower-tier positions. In this respect, women in male-dominated societies may be considered a minority group that must compete against other minorities for low-echelon jobs in the dual labor market (Hacker, 1951, 1974).

In large measure, the sex-segregated occupations that form the bulk of women's employment alternatives are extensions of the traditional female nurturing role: dental and medical assistants, licensed and practical nurses, prekindergarten and kindergarten teachers, child-care workers, and tellers, receptionists, and secretaries, for example. Even when they're employed outside their own homes, many women end up performing traditional female domestic roles. Over 95 percent of all U.S. workers employed in private households as child-care providers or as servants are women (U.S. Bureau of the Census, 1993a, p. 407). In Latin America and the Caribbean, up to 80 percent of all wage-earning women work as servants (Seager & Olson, 1986).

In a cross-cultural study of work and gender across a dozen modern industrial and postindustrial societies, Roos (1985) found very similar clusters of sex-segregated occupations in all 12 countries. Women were concentrated primarily in lower-prestige clerical, sales, and service jobs, whereas men greatly outnumbered women in managerial and administrative positions, as well as in high- and medium-status production jobs.

According to Roos, these patterns could be interpreted as being indicative of continuing gender stereotypes that transcend individual societies and cultures, pressuring women and men to seek work compatible with their presumed basic natures. Although the specific details of these gender-differentiated job markets vary from region to region or country to country, it is universally true that jobs defined as "women's work" carry low pay, low status, and little job security (Seager & Olson, 1986).

GENDER DISCRIMINATION

The final element that has to be taken into account in explaining female/male income differences is gender discrimination. Simply stated, the fact remains that women continue to be treated unequally and unfairly in the labor markets of most contemporary societies (England et al., 1988; United Nations, 1991). Besides being categorically excluded from many occupations, women are subject to very different promotion experiences once on the job.

In particular, women executives at middle-management levels in some of the industrial world's largest national and international corporations have experienced what has come to be called the "glass ceiling." Entrenched male prejudices and practices create a set of invisible and informal barriers that effectively keep women out of their companies' highest-level positions. Throughout the modern industrialized world, women filled less than one-quarter (24 percent) of all administrative and managerial staff positions at the end of 1989 (United Nations Development Program, 1993, p. 151), and very few of these were of chief executive officer or similar rank. In the United States, a 1991 study by the Feminist Majority Foundation indicated that, of 6,502 officers at the level of vice president or higher among *Fortune* 500 corporations that year, only 175 were women (reported in Aburdene & Naisbitt, 1992). And those few women who do make it to the top still have a rougher time than their male peers. Most reported having experienced sexism and sexual harassment during their ascent to the top (Brooks, 1993). Recent evidence also points to the development of "glass walls" that keep corporate women from moving laterally from support staff positions (public relations and human resources managers,

TABLE 8.1 Median Annual Earnings by Education Attainment and Sex: 1992

Education Attainment	Male	Female
Fewer than 9 years	$16,980	$12,176
9–12 years (no diploma)	21,179	13,760
12 years (high school diploma)	26,766	18,648
Some college, no degree	31,413	21,987
Associate's degree	32,349	24,849
Bachelor's degree	40,381	29,264
Master's degree	47,260	35,018
Doctoral degree	56,590	43,699
Professional degree	73,942	44,405

SOURCE: U.S. Bureau of the Census, *Current Population Reports,* Series P-60, No. 184, Table 29.

NOTE: Figures are for year-round, full-time workers, 25 years of age and older.

TABLE 8.2 Median Weekly Earnings by Type of Occupation and Sex: 1992

Type of Occupation	Male	Female
All workers	$505	$381
Managerial and professional	777	562
Technical, sales, and administrative support	519	365
Service	330	248
Precision production	503	336
Operators, fabricators, and laborers	393	279
Farming, forestry, and fishing	269	223

SOURCE: U.S. Bureau of the Census, *Statistical Abstract of the United States, 1993.*

for example) into line positions (for example, sales, production, and marketing managers). Blocked from the horizontal moves within a given rank needed to acquire the practical hands-on experience required for top executive positions, many women are excluded from achieving higher rank before they ever encounter a "glass ceiling" effect (Lewis, 1992).

Finally, gender discrimination is evidenced in the fact that, even in those cases in which their formal educational credentials and occupational titles match or exceed those of men, women continue to receive lower wages than men. Table 8.1 clearly shows these education/wage disparities as they existed in the United States in 1992. In this table, the figures are for year-round, full-time workers, age 25 and older.

Table 8.2 shows the across-the-board disparities between women's and men's 1992 median weekly earnings in identical occupational categories. In every instance, women's wages trailed those of men employed in the same types of jobs, often by significant amounts. Evidence suggests that, in part, these widespread wage differentials are the lingering results of deliberate policies instituted in the past to create lower pay scales for women (Kim, 1989).

COMPARABLE WORTH ISSUES

In the continuing presence of large wage disparities between women and men, some feminists have begun to press the issue of comparable worth. Comparable worth arguments in the United States are based on principles set forth in the Equal Pay Act of 1963 and provisions of Title VI of the Civil Rights Act of 1964. These acts established that the nature of the job, rather than the nature of the job holder, should determine the level of compensation for paid labor. People who perform the same work (two welders or two administrative assistants, for example) are entitled to the same compensation, regardless of their sex, race, age, or other personal characteristics. "Equal pay for equal work" is the mandated principle at work here.

Comparable worth proponents take this principle one step farther. Recognizing that structural and cultural barriers have created sex-segregated labor markets, **comparable worth** calls for equal pay for jobs that, while different, are of substantially equal difficulty and importance (Renzetti & Curran, 1992). For example, if kindergarten teachers (most of whom are women) perform activities that require a level of skills and provide a level of benefits comparable to those of high school football coaches (most of whom are men),

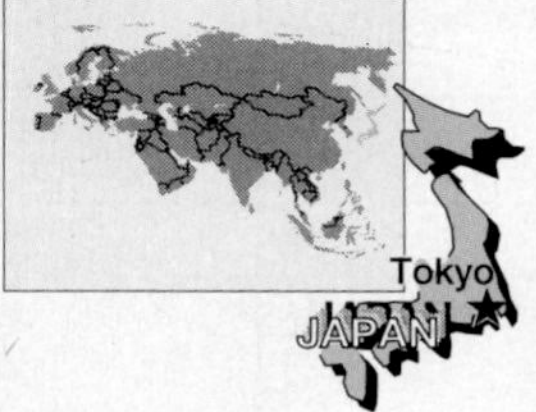

ISSUES OF GENDER EQUITY
Sinking Daughters in the Land of the Rising Sun

Japan often has been described as a modern economic "miracle." Beginning in 1945, within the remarkably short space of less than 50 years, the country literally rose from the ashes of its crushing World War II defeat to become one of the foremost powers in the world. For the past several years, Japan consistently has ranked at or near the top of all the nations of the world in per capita income and gross domestic product levels. The United Nations Development Program (UNDP) 1993 annual report also ranked Japan first in the world in terms of its human development index (HDI), a composite measure of average levels of life expectancy, income, and education within societal populations. By way of comparison, the United States' HDI rank was sixth in the world that same year (United Nations Development Program, 1993, p. 11). Considering the state of the Japanese economy and the Japanese people just half a century ago, "miracle" is an apt description of this amazing comeback.

As is the case in so many other societies, however, the fruits of this rebuilding effort have not been shared equally by Japanese women and men. When the country's HDI score is adjusted to reflect average income, education, and longevity disparities by gender, Japan slips to the seventeenth-ranked position in the world. On average, Japanese women earn only 51 percent of the wages of Japanese men, the lowest female/male wage ratio among all modern industrial societies (United Nations Development Program, 1993, p. 196). Only two-thirds as many Japanese women as men are enrolled in college- or university-level studies, and most of these women attend junior colleges rather than four-year universities, as do most men. In these two-year colleges, women learn traditional feminine skills and prepare for eventual employment as *o-eru* ("office ladies," the equivalent of clerks or secretaries in the United States), while men prepare for careers as managers and *sararimen* ("salarymen," or white-collar employees) (Brinton, 1988, 1989). In the dual-track Japanese business system, most men enter the high-prestige managerial track, and most women still are relegated to the dead-end, low-prestige "office lady" track. According to one Japanese Labor Ministry study, in 1990, over 97 percent of career-track workers were men, whereas 99 percent of all clerical-track workers were women (in Watanabe, 1992b).

Once on the job, many Japanese women experience sexual harassment and other widespread forms of sexism. Until recently, women in Japan have had little choice but to put up with the situation; however, within the past few years, Japanese courts have begun to grant substantial damage awards to women who were subject to sexual harassment or discrimination (Graven, 1990; Murakami, 1992a). The fact

Many of the societal changes symbolized by the "bullet train" pictured here, waiting at the station, have forced Japan to rethink its traditional beliefs about women. Will Japanese women be able to join Japanese men on the ride to economic, social, and political prosperity in the wake of the country's recent problems?

that women finally began to file civil and criminal suits against their male tormentors may indicate a growing sense of political awareness and political empowerment.

According to some scholars (Bingham & Gross, 1987; Warshaw, 1988), in ancient times Japanese society was a matriarchal system in which women exercised a great deal of social and political influence. The Japanese believe their land originally had been settled by the descendants of *Amaterasu Omikami* ("Great Heaven-Shining Mother"), the sun goddess. The heirs of the goddess became the first Japanese emperors, and to this day, emperors trace their lineage to this supreme deity in the Shinto religion (Cherry, 1987). However, this matriarchal structure did not last long. In the sixth century A.D., Japanese emperors began to accept the teachings of Buddhism and Confucianism that had been introduced into the country from Korea and China. In particular, the rise of Confucianism marked the beginning of a patriarchal system that was to last in Japan for over 1,000 years.

For more than a millennium, Confucian principles that prevailed in Japan held to the belief that women are inferior to men in the hierarchical ordering of the natural world because of their "five weaknesses—disobedience, anger, slanderousness, jealousy, and the lack of intelligence" (Warshaw, 1988, p. 195). Subject to "the three obediences"—obedience to their fathers before marriage, obedience to their husbands after marriage, and obedience to their sons (especially their eldest son) after their husbands' death (Fewster & Gorton, 1987)—Japanese women were barred from any educational or political opportunities under a rigid patriarchal social arrangement that lasted until the end of World War II and the resulting postwar Allied occupation of the country. As part of the social reforms mandated by the occupation forces, women were granted full access to formal education, as well as the legal right to vote and to hold political office (Bando, 1986). However, for years, women's political involvement remained low. A 1991 United Nations analysis of the gender composition of legislative bodies in 130 contemporary nations ranked Japan 110th among the total—only 12 women sat in the 500-member Lower House of the Japanese Diet (Murakami, 1992b).

Following a dramatic loss of power by the Liberal Democratic Party that had controlled Japanese government for over 35 years and the formation of a new coalition government, in 1993, Takako Doi, former head of the Social Democratic Party of Japan, became the first woman speaker of the country's House of Representatives (Daimon, 1993). She is one of a small but growing number of women gaining a foothold in positions of political power throughout Japan. Collectively, however, Japanese women still have a long way to go. The bursting of the Japanese "bubble" economy in the early 1990s has moved the country into a serious recession and washed away many economic and social advances scratched out by women in recent years. Much as in other recessions in other times and places, in Japan, it is women who so far have borne the brunt of rising unemployment and falling income trends. The country as a whole may come out of the current economic downturn stronger than ever, as some observers have predicted (Powell, 1992), but it is not clear that women's overall position will in any way be improved. When and if Japan rises again, its women may find themselves sinking even farther behind its men.

then kindergarten teachers and high school football coaches should receive equal pay. In this instance, the proposed principle is "Equal pay for comparable work."

Nationwide, a few state- and local-level governments have instituted comparable worth policies, with mixed results (Evans & Nelson, 1989). However, the movement as a whole has met with a good deal of resistance on the basis of its potential costs to employers and the intrinsic difficulties of attempting to measure the comparable worth of occupations and occupational categories that, at least on the surface, may appear to be very different (Christensen, 1988). To the extent that governments and the courts have not been overly energetic in their support of comparable worth proposals, the widespread implementation of this program may have to await the infusion of greater numbers of feminists into the political and legal systems.

WOMEN IN POLITICS AND LAW

The persistence of significant gender-based inequalities and the dramatic growth of female poverty in the contemporary world are testimonies to the fact that, to a large extent, women remain excluded from political power in most societies. Election or appointment to political office brings with it some measure of influence or control over the state (that is, the political structure). The state constitutes the primary mechanism for allocating the different rewards society has to offer its members, and those who control the state can shape this allocation system to meet their own specific interests and needs. Throughout the world, control of the offices of state rests squarely in the hands of men.

As of the early 1990s, women held just under 11 percent of all parliamentary representative seats in the world's political systems—12 percent in developing nations and 9 percent in the developed or industrial world. Perhaps not surprisingly, the Scandinavian countries displayed the highest levels of female representation, averaging 36 percent (United Nations Development Program, 1993, p. 195). Norway, "the most feminized democracy in the world" (Aburdene & Naisbitt, 1992, p. 306), has a female prime minister as well as about 50 percent female representation in the country's cabinet; in addition, the leaders of all three of Norway's major political parties are women. In Finland, 40 percent of parliamentary positions now are held by women, as are 38 percent of similar positions in Sweden. Vigdis Finnbogadottir, president of Iceland since 1980, is the world's first popularly elected female head of state (Aburdene & Naisbitt, 1992, p. 303). Hers was one of only 6 United Nations member-states (out of 159) headed by a woman at the end of 1990. Women hold cabinet-level positions in less than 5 percent of all countries of the world, and they hold no ministerial offices at all in 93 countries. They are excluded entirely from decision-making positions at the four highest levels of government in 21 African countries, 16 Asian and Pacific nations, 8 countries in the Caribbean and Latin America, and 4 nations in Europe and North America (United Nations, 1991).

In the United States, women's political office profile is not appreciably better. As of 1993, only 54 women served in the 103rd Congress—48 representatives out of a total of 435 and 6 senators out of a total of 100 (Baum, 1992). Although small in absolute terms, these figures represent the largest number of women in the U.S. Congress in the history of that body. They also reflect the outcome of elections held in what was widely portrayed as "the year of the woman" in U.S. politics (Goodman, 1992; Randall, 1992). In 1992, U.S. women were radicalized and mobilized in unprecedented numbers as a result of the highly publicized and televised Anita Hill–Clarence Thomas sexual harassment hearings, as well as a perceived growing attack on women's reproductive rights. Twenty-one women ran for Senate seats, and more than 140 women ran for seats in the House (Bayer, 1992), but with only moderate success. Although the number of female senators tripled and the number of female representatives nearly doubled, their absolute and proportional numbers in Congress remain low. So, too, do their numbers at the state government level. In 1992, only three states had female governors, and women constituted only about 20 percent of all state legislators in the country (Belsie, 1992).

The presence of some particular number or percentage of women in political office in and of itself does not guarantee that "the women's view" will automatically be considered and promoted. Indeed, the idea that there is a single and unified women's view is an exaggeration and a stereotype. There are many different kinds of women (as there are many different kinds of men), and the racial, ethnic, class, religious, and other differences that distinguish and divide women throughout the world create many women's views. Be that as it may, however, it would be a mistake to assume that the presence of female office holders makes no significant difference. An absence of women from important political decision-making positions increases the likelihood that female perspectives and interests will not be taken into account at all in the creation and implementation of political and social policies. Increasing women's participation in politics remains a primary objective in the promotion of true human development throughout the modern world (United Nations Development Program, 1993).

Like politics, law is a social institution that has critical ramifications for the distribution of socioeconomic opportunities and rewards in contemporary societies. And like politics, law is a social institution that historically has been dominated by men, who overwhelmingly make up legislative, judicial, and police agencies in most societies. Consequently, women around the world continue to be treated quite differently than men in their daily interactions with their societies' legal structures.

Some conflict theorists have interpreted this widespread pattern of gender-based legal differences as the result of the deliberate actions of men, who have seized control of legal mechanisms and created, interpreted, and enforced laws that help maintain their own socioeconomic advantages in a patriarchal hierarchy (Jaggar, 1983). Other less conspiratorial interpretations view these patterns as the result of a unified male world view that inadvertently develops from the gender composition of these legal bodies. From this perspective, law reflects men's beliefs in the natural intellectual and physical inferiorities of women. These stereotyped beliefs define women as logically impaired and therefore helpless, in need of protection by and from men. The result is legal systems that operate to preserve existing gender inequalities and to create new ones (Kirp et al., 1986). Laws regarding rape and abortion typify what Laurel Richardson (1988, p. 104) calls a "double standard of morality based on biological deterministic thought" built into the legal processes of most societies. With the growing question of sexual harassment in the workplace, rape and abortion issues have become major battlegrounds in the war between the sexes.

SEXUAL ISSUES AS A BATTLEFRONT

Among the various fault lines that mark contemporary gender relations in the United States and around the world, some of the most heated issues have revolved around sex and sexuality in and out of the workplace.

SEXUAL HARASSMENT

In 1991, television viewers in the United States witnessed a series of hearings conducted by the Senate Judiciary Committee that pitted Clarence Thomas, President Bush's nominee to the U.S. Supreme Court, against Anita Hill, a University of Oklahoma law professor. At issue was Professor Hill's charge that she had been repeatedly sexually harassed by Judge Thomas while working as his aide at the Equal Employment Opportunity Commission in the early 1980s. Following days of intense questioning, the all-male committee voted to support Thomas's nomination. He was later confirmed by a vote of the full Senate, despite Hill's graphic testimony and despite cries of outrage from women around the country angered at committee members' grilling of Hill and their reluctance to take her charges seriously.

At about the same time, a San Diego, California, newspaper broke a story about widespread sexual assaults that had taken place in September of that year at the annual Tailhook Association Convention, a meeting of active and retired U.S. Navy pilots. In that episode, dozens of women, including several officers, were fondled and sexually abused by a gauntlet of male officers. After a long period of what seemed to be foot-dragging, the military began an investigation that resulted in the firing, forced retirement, or disciplining of a number of senior navy officials, including H. Lawrence Garrett III, Secretary of the Navy (Vistica, 1992b). After a Pentagon study reported that 64 percent of all women in the military had experienced some form of sexual abuse or harassment in a single year, the navy instituted a get-tough policy that would automatically discharge first-time offenders (Vistica, 1992a).

Sexual harassment refers to "any unwelcome tactile, visual, or verbal communication of a sexual nature" (Cohen, 1991). The term originated in the United States, where, in 1975, federal courts recognized sexual harassment as a form of sexual discrimination prohibited under the provisions of the 1964 Civil Rights Act ("Sexual Harrassment a Problem," 1992). Work-related sexual harassment cases brought before the courts have been of two different types:

1. Quid pro quo charges that submission to unwelcome sexual communication was made an express or implied condition of employment
2. So-called hostile environment charges that unwelcome sexual communication created an environment that made work impossible for female employees (Lauter & Silverstein, 1991)

According to polls taken in the United States in 1982 and 1991, 40 percent of female workers have experienced sexual harassment in one or both of these two forms ("Forty Percent of Women," 1991). However, many victims have been reluctant to come forth with charges since, in many cases, filing a sexual harassment complaint is tantamount to "career suicide" (Braun, 1991).

Although sexual harassment was first given a name and a legal status in the United States, the problem is hardly confined to this society. Cross-cultural studies conducted by the UN-based International Labor Organization indicated that sexual harassment plagues women in most developed societies throughout the world, with as many as 58 percent of Dutch women and 74 percent of British women claiming experience with some form of harassment ("Sexual Harrassment a Problem," 1992). About 50 percent of female workers in European Community member-nations have been the targets of minor sexual harassment, 25 percent have encountered strong physical or verbal harassment, and 3 percent have been the victims of violent sexual attacks, according to other studies that have characterized the situation as an "international sickness" (Bustelo, 1992).

According to some observers, an unknown portion of sexual harassment incidents reported by women may be the result of differences in the respective world views of women and men. Men generally see sexual jokes, remarks, and gestures as acts that are qualitatively different from violence or sexual assault. They also view these behaviors in terms of sexuality. In contrast, women see sexual harassment as abuse of power and tend to view its various manifestations as points on a continuum, rather than as qualitatively different categories. Consequently, women often feel threatened by acts that men perceive as innocent (Klein in Lauter & Silverstein, 1991). These observers claim that attempts to legislate and regulate individuals' personal behaviors in the workplace could have unintended but nonetheless very significant negative effects on what is now a widespread pattern of marriages forming from social relationships begun at work (Dichter in Lauter & Silverstein, 1991). As a result of changing attitudes and laws concerning sexual communication, "men and women aren't sure how to act around each other anymore" (Wilkens, 1992). As Cohen (1991, p. 13) argues:

> For an increasing number of people the workplace represents by far the best avenue for finding and pursuing romantic interests. . . . At work they can flirt and in other

> ways get the ball rolling in a controlled, largely non-threatening environment. . . . Should this marketplace be substantially damaged by regulations, the lives of those affected will be diminished. They will have more difficulty finding partners and will have to search in less attractive places.

Feminists counter this argument by pointing out the possible millions of women whose professional and personal lives have been substantially damaged and diminished as a result of unwanted sexual advances from supervisors or co-workers. Additionally, sexual harassment imposes financial burdens on the companies in which the incidents occur. According to one study (cited in Wilkens & Hearn, 1992), even when workers don't sue their employers for damages, sexual harassment costs the typical *Fortune* 500 company close to $7 million per year in employee turnover, absenteeism, and reduced worker productivity.

Finally, sexual harassment has been moving out of the workplace and down the age ladder. According to one national study conducted by the American Association of University Women (AAUW) Educational Foundation in 1993, 85 percent of girls and 76 percent of boys in public school grades 8 through 11 claimed to have been targets of some form of sexual harassment (Spaid, 1993a). Increasingly, girls in their early teens or even preteens have been singled out for violent sexual assaults (Pederson, 1993). Responding to such incidents, California now has a law permitting school districts to suspend students as young as fourth-graders who sexually harass their fellow students (Wilkens, 1992).

RAPE

Although rape has been called "the all-American crime" (Griffin, 1973), it is hardly confined to the United States. Virtually all other contemporary societies evidence this crime, and many conceptualize and deal with rape in similar ways (Seager & Olson, 1986; United Nations, 1991). Historically, rape has been regarded legally as a crime that could be committed only against women. Rape laws were created specifically to protect the chastity of women, especially girls (Richardson, 1988). Girls below a specified legal age are defined as being incapable of consenting to sexual intercourse, whereas women over the defined legal age often are implicitly seen as inciting or tempting men to commit rape. They are regarded as somehow being responsible for their own rapes in ways that victims of other crimes are not. Rape victims' past sexual histories can be used as evidence in court, whereas the past sexual histories of their alleged attackers, including past accusations and convictions for rape, cannot. Consequently, a high percentage of rapes are never reported to authorities, even though the number of rapes continues to skyrocket (Salholz et al., 1990).

According to one study conducted by the National Victims Center, in 1990, a total of 683,000 women were raped in the United States, a number five times higher than that reported in official estimates by the U.S. Department of Justice. Only 16 percent of the women reported their rapes to police, even though nearly 80 percent of these victims knew their attackers. This same study estimated that as many as 12.1 million U.S. women—1 out of every 8 adult women in the country—have been raped at some point in their lives ("Rape Rate in America," 1992). More recently, a U.S. Department of Justice study revealed that girls younger than 18 were the victims of more than half of all reported rapes in 1992 ("Fifty-One Percent of Rape Victims," 1994).

Feminists claim that rape is an act of power and violence, not sex (Brownmiller, 1975; Richardson, 1988). In this view, rape is a terrorist tactic, a tangible and symbolic method for men to keep women in their presumed proper place. There is ample historical and contemporary evidence to support this argument. In the 1937–1938 Japanese conquest of Nanking, an estimated 20,000 Chinese women were raped by Japanese troops. In both World War I and World War II, tens of thousands of women were raped by German armies sweeping their way across Europe. More recently, as many as 50,000 Muslim women may have been raped by Serbian soldiers during the "ethnic cleansing" program in Bosnia-Herzegovina ("Action Alert," 1993; Post, 1993). Carried out in "rape camps," these repeated mass assaults appeared to be part of a deliberate plan both to impregnate Muslim women and to have them ostracized from their own communities (Brownmiller, 1993; Post, 1993).

Because of their low status and lack of power, women in many developing nations are subject to assault and rape at the hands of both street criminals and the criminal justice system. One study (reported in "Women in Double Jeopardy," 1992) found that 70 percent of Pakistani women in police custody were sexually tortured and physically abused by police agents; in India, women offenders and victims alike often are molested and subjected to "custodial rape" by government officials (Shrivastava, 1992). In Guatemala and some other Latin American countries, women who are part of dissident political or social movement groups have been subjected to gang rape as a way of punishing their activism (Nelan, 1992). Where cultural values and beliefs place a high premium on female chastity, the deliberate violation of this purity can be a powerful political weapon.

ABORTION

Many observers regard abortion as *the* single most important gender issue of the recent past and the near future. Abortion is a complex and volatile question that has divided societal populations as few other issues have in the past few decades. For many people, abortion rights have become a measure of the continued possibility of the whole gender equality movement. From this perspective, the outcome of the abortion struggles unfolding in many societies across the world will determine not only women's social and economic viability but their physical viability, as well.

As we saw earlier, female embryos have a higher probability of surviving to birth than male embryos, and once born, females in general have higher longevity rates than males. However, in some regions and nations of the developing world, girls and women who otherwise might be expected to outlive men have mortality rates greatly exceeding those of males. Based on comparisons of expected population sex compositions with observations of actual female/male population ratios, some observers have concluded that about 100 million women are "missing" from the developing world (United Nations Development Program, 1993, p. 17).

A number of different factors contribute to these unexpectedly high female mortality rates, but one major component is the very large number of women in the developing world who die during pregnancy and childbirth. These countries have been described as "a recognized danger zone for childbearing women and their children" (Seager & Olson, 1986, Map 10). The United Nation's survey of women in the world (1991, p. 57) found that "rates of maternal mortality show a greater disparity between the developed and developing regions than any other health indicator." At the end of 1988, the average maternal mortality rate per 100,000 live births for all the world's industrial countries was 26; for all developing countries the figure was 420. In the least developed countries, for every 100,000 live births, 740 women died—a maternal mortality rate nearly 30 times higher than that in the developed world (United Nations Development Program, 1993, p. 151).

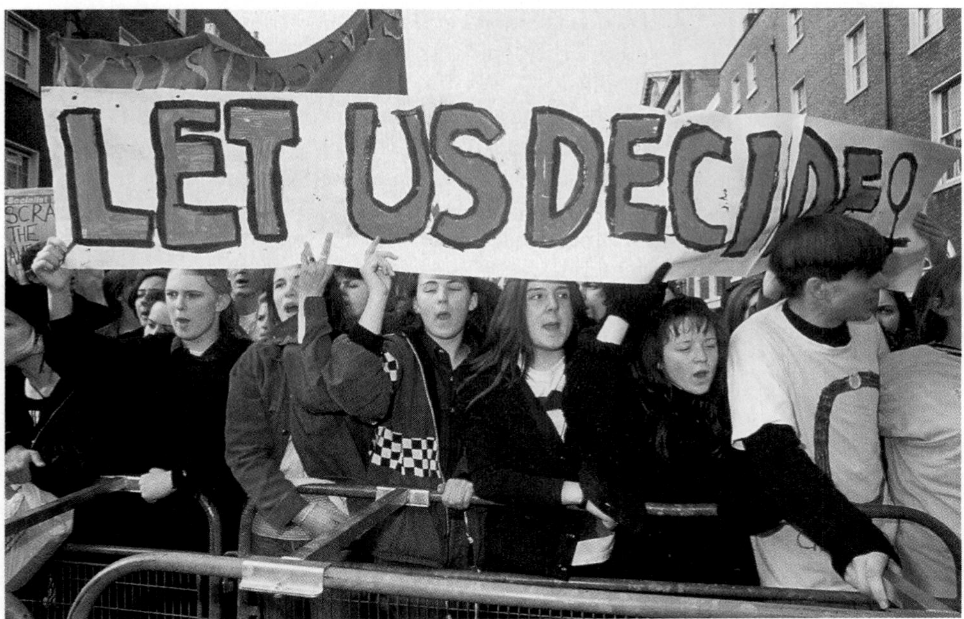

Many feminists regard abortion as the single most important gender rights issue of the contemporary era. "Pro-choice" advocates, such as the Dublin group pictured here, demonstrating against Ireland's restrictive abortion laws, claim that women must retain final control over their own reproductive destinies. "Pro-life" advocates claim that any terminated pregnancy is tantamount to murder and that the state must safeguard the rights of the unborn.

As of 1990, 53 countries, making up 25 percent of the world's total population, prohibited abortions except to save the life of the pregnant woman. Twenty-one of these nations were located in Africa and constituted some of the world's least developed countries. Another 42 nations (nearly half of them African), whose combined populations make up an additional 12 percent of the world's population, restricted abortions to specific medical grounds (Henshaw, 1990). For many women in the Third World, then, the inability to have their pregnancies terminated under safe conditions leads to their own termination. In these countries, prevailing social and economic conditions make the lack of access to safe abortions not so much a matter of personal inconvenience as a matter of life or death.

By way of contrast, 37 other countries, constituting about 63 percent of the world's total population, as of 1990 had more liberal laws that permit abortions under a wide range of social and sociomedical situations. To a large extent, these societies represent the industrialized nations of Europe, North America, and East Asia (Henshaw, 1990). For women in these countries, the most serious abortion issue is accessibility. Even in countries with the most liberal abortion policies, legislation establishing abortion rights most often is not matched by laws guaranteeing adequate service to all women. These discrepancies create (Sachdev, 1988, p. 12)

> inequality of access to legal abortion, especially for poor or socially disadvantaged women as in Australia, Canada, the FRG [Germany], India, Italy, New Zealand, and the United States. Consequently, many women who want an abortion are forced to travel a considerable distance to other regions or to another country. Others are compelled to resort to illegal abortions available through paramedics or untrained personnel (e.g., countries of Latin America and the Caribbean).

World Health Organization studies estimate that from 115,000 to 204,000 women throughout the world die each year as the result of illegal abortions. Many of these illegal

abortions take place in those countries in which abortion itself is illegal; others occur in countries in which legal abortions are too difficult or too expensive for poor women to obtain (Costa, 1991, p. 94). For women in the first group of countries, the basic abortion fight is for the establishment of legal abortion rights; for women in the latter group of societies, the basic struggle is to preserve previously established abortion rights. The United States has become one such battleground.

The U.S. Supreme Court's 1973 *Roe v. Wade* ruling affirmed the constitutional right of women to decide for themselves whether or not to terminate a pregnancy during the first trimester. This historic decision, based on an interpretation of constitutional guarantees to individual privacy (Dworkin, 1993), was hailed by many feminists as a major step in granting women control over their own bodies and freedom from male domination of women's reproductive activities. It was attacked by many conservative and antifeminist groups as legalized murder of unborn human beings.

These two very different interpretations of abortion—homicide versus reproductive rights—continue to define the boundaries of the debate and to make any sort of real compromise on the issue virtually impossible. During the more than two decades since the *Roe* decision, antiabortion, "pro-life" groups have succeeded in promoting a number of state laws that significantly restrict abortion by imposing several legal requirements on women seeking to terminate their pregnancies. In some instances, these laws have redefined and narrowed the conditions under which abortions may be performed legally (Costa, 1991). Other state laws have imposed counseling sessions, required warnings of the potential physical and psychological risks of abortion and mandatory information about alternatives to abortion, and set a variety of other stipulations whose net effects are to make abortions more difficult to obtain, especially for socially disadvantaged women ("In the State Courts," 1994).

After a great deal of speculation that a Supreme Court made increasingly conservative by Reagan and Bush appointees would overturn *Roe v. Wade,* in June 1992, that Court narrowly upheld the essential provisions of the 1973 *Roe* decision. However, at the same time, the Court also affirmed the rights of the individual states to impose broad restrictions on women's access to abortions (Hearn, 1992). The 1992 ruling technically was a victory for "pro-choice" (pro-abortion) advocates but left *Roe* "hanging by a thread" (Clinton in S. Fritz, 1992).

Since 1992, pro-life forces have attempted to cut that thread by a combination of additional antiabortion legislation and increasing activism against abortion providers. At times, this activism has assumed what some see as terrorist proportions. For example, in March 1993, an abortion physician, Dr. David Gunn, was shot and killed by an antiabortion demonstrator outside a clinic in Florida. Rejecting the claim that Michael Griffin had been made temporarily insane by antiabortion rhetoric, in March 1994, a jury found Griffin guilty of first-degree murder ("Anti-Choice Protestor Found Guilty," 1994). If this incident and the growing number of arson attacks against abortion facilities are any indication of things to come, abortion rights in the United States are likely to become a bloodshed, as well as a watershed, issue for feminists and for the gender equality movement at large.

FEMINISM AND THE WOMEN'S MOVEMENT

Much of the material presented thus far paints an overall picture of monolithic male domination over females in virtually all important aspects of human social existence. Although this image is true to a large extent in many countries, the pattern is not as entirely one sided or irrevocable as it first might seem. The dramatic gaps that remain between women and men throughout some areas of the contemporary world obscure the fact that progress toward gender equality has been made in other regions. A great deal of this progress has been brought about through the actions of feminists—those persons of either sex who believe in social justice and equality for members of both sexes—as well as by major changes in contemporary political and economic landscapes.

For example, the disintegration of the Soviet Union and the subsequent economic chaos in many of the former Soviet republics have propelled women into a growing political activism throughout Eastern Europe (Nadle, 1992), especially in Russia, the largest of those republics (Barry, 1992; Goldberg, 1994; Sloane, 1993). Much of this new activism was born of necessity, as women in the new democratic nations found that economic, political, and social freedom had not been extended to include them. In Somalia, South Africa, Eritrea, and other war-torn countries in one of the world's least developed areas, women first drawn into leadership roles by default (that is, by the absence of the men who normally dominate economic and political activities) have attempted to expand those roles into a springboard for greater social equality (Battersby, 1993a; Press, 1993h; Williams, 1993). In Pakistan and Turkey, two modernizing, male-oriented Islamic societies, women have also begun carving out many very nontraditional economic and political gains (Bokhari, 1993; Montalbano, 1993). Indeed, the new (as of mid-1993) female prime minister of Turkey, Tansu Ciller, is a former economics professor. Although such advances generally have met with stiff resistance from entrenched male interests, they appear to be the wave of the future. In the new global economic and political alliances that are coming to define the last segment of the twentieth century, there may be little room left for old gendered social arrangements.

But these changes will not come automatically. If women in other parts of the world are to realize gains on the order of those made by women in the United States, they will

In the midst of sweeping political and economic changes, women have made significant and surprising gains in many societies. Pictured here is Tansu Ciller, a former economics professor who became Prime Minister of Turkey in 1993. Ciller's rise to government office is indicative of the gender role changes taking place even in very traditional Islamic cultures, such as that of Turkey. In many cases, these changes have come as a result of the feminist activities of women's movements.

CONNECTIONS

Gender inequality is pervasive throughout the world, and the consequences of gender stratification cut across a wide range of female experiences and opportunities. In some ways, it might be easier to talk about those few (if any) situations in which sex and gender considerations *don't* seem to have a significant impact or make a real difference in people's lives, as the spillover from gendered arrangements into other social dimensions is enormous. We examine some of the vast multitude of gender-related social problems in later chapters dealing with crime and criminal justice, family disorganization, addictions, and health issues. In this section, we simply offer a brief sampling of a few of the many ways in which established gender-based inequality systems have worked to the detriment of women and men alike.

- Despite a lack of evidence to support the claim that women are systematically or consistently inferior to men in science, mathematical, or engineering abilities, they nonetheless are grossly underrepresented in these fields in most contemporary societies. Available evidence indicates that women's exclusion from these critically important disciplines is largely the result of prevailing cultural and social forces that either steer females away from advanced formal education altogether or track them into traditional liberal arts studies. One major result of this pattern has been the restricted occupational and income alternatives available to women, leading to categorical socioeconomic differences between the two groups. At the same time that women are deprived because of this arrangement, society as a whole may be deprived of talents of both women and men lost or misapplied through traditional gendered divisions of labor. Women who have the potential to become world-class engineers may never get a real opportunity to demonstrate and develop their potential, and men whose nurturing skills could make them world-class kindergarten teachers may never get an opportunity to develop these talents. In this respect, gender stratification, like any other sort of stratification system, ultimately strangles, rather than encourages, the search for societal talent (Tumin, 1953). This wholesale loss of female talent may be especially acute in the developing world, where economic development could benefit signifi-

have to form women's movements that duplicate the successes of that movement in this society.

THE WOMEN'S MOVEMENT IN THE UNITED STATES

The contemporary U.S. women's movement had its roots in the abolitionist movement of the early nineteenth century. Recognizing their own subordinated social position as they worked with free men to eliminate the enslavement of African Americans in the South, women met in Seneca Falls, New York, in 1848. There they drafted a Declaration of Sentiments calling for social equality with men (Banner, 1984). Following the Civil War and the granting of voting rights to former slaves, women turned to their own political emancipation—that is, to the extension of voting rights to women. This suffragist orientation, which dominated the women's movement for the next 50 years, finally led to the passage of the Nineteenth Amendment in 1920, guaranteeing women's constitutional right to the vote.

cantly from the greater participation of women who so often are cut off entirely from access to formal education and technological training (United Nations, 1991, p. 47).

- As long as employment and wage discrimination, as well as existing divorce and child-support laws, continue to consign large numbers of women to poverty, gender inequality will exact a high cost from state and federal government social service budgets in the form of welfare benefits to women and dependent children. At a time when many industrialized societies are experiencing economic recessions, these large and increasing welfare expenditures constitute a severe drain on these political bodies. In the absence of organized, supervised, and reasonably priced public day care for their children, single mothers often are unable to find the full-time employment that could get them off welfare and into the labor force as contributing participants (Gardner, 1994).
- To the extent that women in large numbers continue to be the victims of rape, spouse battering, and other forms of physical violence, sexism places additional strains on emergency health care facilities that in many cases are in imminent danger of collapse (Duerksen & Cleeland, 1994). Besides tying up medical personnel and equipment, such gender-based violence imposes significant financial costs on city and county health care budgets already strapped for operating funds.
- Since these acts of violence against women are pursued as criminal matters, sexism contributes to the increasing frustration and fragmentation of criminal justice systems swamped by an abundance of cases and a shortage of time and personnel. Moreover, there is evidence to suggest that physical violence against women may contribute to the growing rate of crimes committed by women. Between 1980 and 1993, the number of women in federal and state prisons in the United States rose by 275 percent, and more than half of all female prisoners nationwide had been physically abused at some point in their lives. In conjunction with women's restricted educational and employment opportunities and income possibilities associated with the widespread drug trade, such physical violence has taken many women out of their homes and away from their children. About 80 percent of female prisoners are mothers, and their incarceration strains both their families and the social service agencies that often must tend to the needs of children left motherless by their parents' crimes (Tyson, 1993).

The Civil Rights movement to establish social equality for African Americans in the still-segregated South, as well as their own increasing participation in the U.S. labor force and their increasing encounters with pay and other forms of discrimination, led women to again become active in establishing their own civil rights during the 1960s (Ferree & Hess, 1991). The growing movement was crystallized, to a large extent, by the publication of Betty Friedan's *The Feminine Mystique* in 1963 and the founding of the National Organization for Women (NOW) in 1966 (Kramer, 1986). The primary agenda of the movement during this period was the establishment of social equalities for women. Among other things, feminist efforts assisted in the passage of the Civil Rights Act of 1964, which became the legal foundation for a host of significant changes in education, the workplace, and other major societal institutions during the 1970s, 1980s, and 1990s.

However, as the women's movement grew in numbers and organizational structure, it began to encounter a series of problems that sociologist Robert Michels (1966, original 1915) claims are endemic to any social movement over time: increasing conservatism and a distancing of the organizational structure from the needs and interests of rank-and-file members. The moderate, liberal orientation of the mainstream women's movement, with its emphasis on reformist measures to insure women's civil rights, has become increasingly alienating for socialist and radical feminists, who view the source of gender inequality as residing in the basic structure of capitalism (in the case of socialist feminism) or in the basic structure of male/female relations (in the case of radical feminism) (Ferree & Hess, 1991).

From a conflict perspective, the critical issue facing the gender equality movement in the 1990s is whether feminists can successfully overcome the often intense opposition of established male groups that continue to hold the balance of power in U.S. society. To do so, feminists first must overcome the divisions within the ranks of the women's movement that currently block the development of an effective, unified power base. These divisions are based on racial, ethnic, religious, and other group affiliations that often lead to very different experiences for members of these subgroups.

For example, African American women may find that, to the extent that they must deal with racism in their daily lives, they have less in common with White women than they do with African American men. According to the reports of many African American corporate women, the promotion-blocking "glass ceilings" encountered by their White counterparts more often translate into "concrete walls" where their own careers are concerned. Compared to White women, these African Americans more often speak of being "ghettoized" in positions of little or no power, of receiving little or no organized support in career counseling and training, and of having no access to corporate mentors (MacLachlan, 1993).

In the political realm, the Congressional Caucus for Women's Issues has found its work hampered by the fact that its 45 members, in the words of its co-chair, "are not a homogeneous group" (Snowe in Feldmann, 1993b). In many instances, the plurality of social class, political party, and other constituencies represented by its members seems to override the commonality of their sex. Women speak with many different voices rather than a single voice, and sometimes these voices cancel out each other. Issues such as the right of sexual assault victims to sue producers and distributors of pornography if these materials contributed to their attackers' behavior have split many liberal feminist groups, pitting free speech questions against those of the civil rights of abused women (Elson, 1992). At the same time, a growing number of "separate sisters" have evidenced increasing dissatisfaction with what they perceive as the elitism of the feminist movement (MacFarquhar et al., 1994). From their perspective, groups such as NOW have focused largely or exclusively on issues of interest to "successful, upper-middle-class, professional white women" at the expense of "most blue-collar, working-class women of color" (Simon quoted in "To Some, Elitism," 1992). If the women's movement is to have any real chance of success in bringing about true gender equality, its leaders somehow must resolve the issues that continue to keep real power out of reach.

SUMMARY

1. *Sex* is a classification of individuals on the basis of anatomical, gonadal, and chromosomal characteristics. *Gender* is based on sex but includes an acceptance of the psychological, emotional, and behavioral traits deemed appropriate for one's sex, as well.
2. In most societies, stereotyped beliefs about the presumed different natures of females and males have created specialized and differentiated gender roles for women and men. Gender stratification in these societies reflects the fact that women's roles most frequently receive lesser income, prestige, and power rewards than those of men.

3 Gender stereotypes, roles, and stratification are maintained through a lifelong process of socialization that begins with the assignment of individuals to an appropriate sex category. Throughout this gender socialization process, individuals learn and internalize attitudes and behaviors defined as suitable for their sex by prevailing cultural standards and social practices.

4 In most societies, women's lower levels of formal education (compared to those of men) and their "tracking" into traditional liberal arts studies in college result in their underrepresentation in higher-paying mathematics, science, and engineering occupations. Some economists claim that these human capital factors are responsible for most observed income inequalities between the sexes. Sociologists claim that sex-segregated, dual labor market structures, as well as overt and covert discrimination against women, are of greater importance in understanding these gendered pay differences.

5 The failure of legislative and judicial bodies to pursue comparable worth and other gender equality issues vigorously is a reflection of women's underrepresentation in politics and law. Around the world and in the United States, relatively few women hold positions of real power in the political or legal spheres. As a result, women's issues often receive little or no support.

6 Sexual harassment, involving any unwelcome tactile, visual, or verbal sexual communication, is reportedly a serious and widespread problem in workplaces across the world. As many as half of all female employees in the United States and even larger percentages of women in some European countries claim to have been the targets of either quid pro quo or hostile environment sexual harassment.

7 Rape is also a serious and growing problem in many developed and developing countries. Feminists view rape as an act of power rather than passion and see rape as a terrorist tactic used by men to keep women in their proper place. In many societies, existing rape laws subject the victim to humiliating treatment in court; as a result, many rapes go unreported to authorities.

8 Many feminists regard abortion as the single most important gender rights issue of the past several decades. In many developing countries, lack of access to safe abortions results in the deaths of thousands of women during childbirth each year. In many developed countries where abortion is legal, lack of access to safe abortions places many poor and minority women at risk.

9 In the United States, the Supreme Court *Roe v. Wade* decision that established women's right to abortion has come under a great deal of challenge from pro-life groups. In 1992, the Court narrowly reaffirmed the basic principles of the *Roe* decision but gave individual states much more latitude in establishing abortion regulations.

10 With the many great changes brought about by the collapse of the Soviet Union and other world political and economic events, women in many parts of the world have been making significant strides toward greater equality. However, their ultimate success will depend on their ability to establish and maintain powerful women's movements. In the United States, the continued viability of the women's movement has been challenged by ideological differences among liberal, socialist, and radical feminists, as well as by concerns of many minority and lower-class women that the movement does not meet their needs. If true gender equality is to be attained, these differences will have to be resolved.

CHAPTER NINE

CRIME, VIOLENCE, AND CRIMINAL JUSTICE
Getting Busted

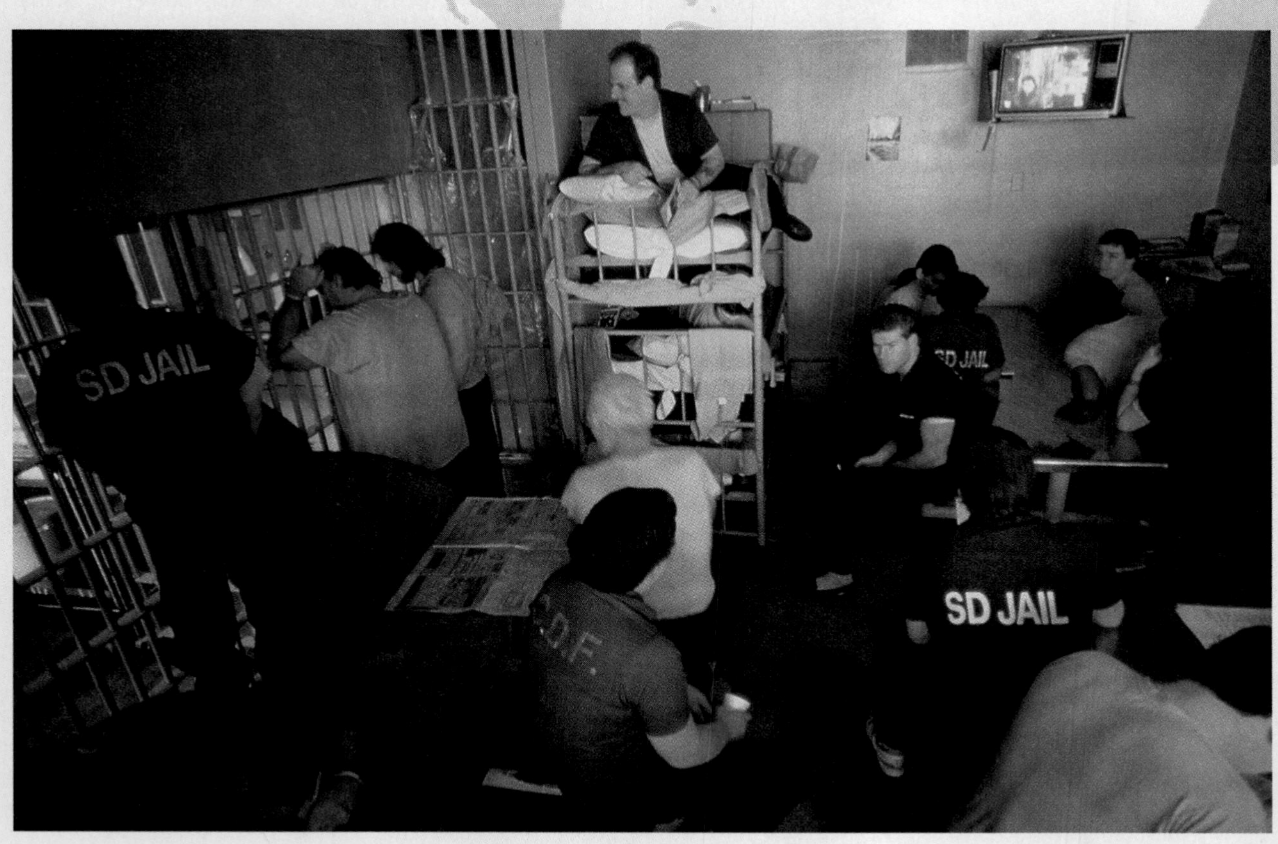

Crime patterns observed in many nations over the past 200 years exhibit a consistent pattern of evolution—that is, as societies modernize, rates of criminal behavior increase (Shelley, 1981). The association between modernization and crime found in the relatively poor nations of the world also occurred in the rich countries beginning in the late eighteenth century with the Industrial Revolution. Sweeping economic changes at this time were accompanied by one of the greatest demographic transformations in history, as millions of Europeans, Americans, and Canadians left their rural farms and moved to the cities in search of employment. This phenomenon was most pronounced in North America, where rural-to-urban migrants were joined by a steady stream of newcomers from Europe.

The rapid growth of cities was accompanied by a sharp increase in crime—especially property crime. Prior to the Industrial Revolution, rural peasants lived a poor to modest existence, often in the shadow of wealthy nobles. Inasmuch as the rigid class distinction between the "haves" and "have-nots" had persisted in feudal societies for centuries, peasants had virtually no hope of acquiring the status or wealth of the privileged few. Consequently, few property crimes were committed by the poor at the expense of the rich. And because peasants lived in close-knit communities with a high degree of informal social control—that is, they were under the control of family, friends, and church—they rarely stole from each other.

Crime rates began their steady rise when people moved to the cities en masse. The acquisition of material possessions took on greater importance as societies became increasingly oriented to the production and consumption of goods. Of no small importance was the fact that now there were many more things of value to steal. In addition, the traditional informal mechanisms of social control, so important for keeping deviance at relatively low levels among the rural poor, began to crumble.

The tremendous increase in crimes committed by youths (what would later be called *juvenile delinquency*) was also a product of this period. Less supervision from adults as a result of parents working away from home coupled with an emerging school-centered youth subculture were major contributors to adolescent criminal activity (Shelley, 1981). Prior to the Industrial Revolution, there were no "teenagers" and no concomitant high rates of criminality associated with this phase of life. In traditional societies, individuals between 13 and 18 years of age were simply considered smaller, younger adults with most, if not all, of the responsibilities and obligations of older individuals.

The comparative work of criminologist Louise Shelley (1981) suggests that not only is the overall process of development "conducive to criminality," but the achievement of development, as experienced by the United States and other rich nations, also contributes to high rates of crime. At this stage of modernization, property crimes (as well as some profit-driven violent crimes, such as robbery) are committed not so much out of survival needs but as a result of the "relative deprivation" experienced by people (even economically successful individuals) who are determined to succeed at all costs in a society obsessed with material wealth.

Shelley's analysis makes for a rather bleak scenario as we move toward the twenty-first century. On the one hand, there is no compelling reason to believe that crime rates—including increasingly more violent acts—will substantially decline in rich societies like the United States. On the other hand, rapidly growing Third World nations will see their crime rates keep pace with overall development, a condition, as we have noted, that will not diminish once a high degree of modernization has been achieved. With 85 percent of the world's total population and a doubling time of only 35 years, developing nations are collectively poised to undergo the greatest expansion in criminal behavior in human history. And if these countries begin experiencing anything even close to the level of urban violence taking place in the United States today, hundreds of thousands of people will be raped, beaten, and murdered each year.

QUESTIONS TO CONSIDER

1. How does the crime rate in the United States compare to rates of criminal behavior in other nations?
2. What are the three major sources of criminal statistics used in the United States?
3. What are the relationships among variables such as age, race/ethnicity, gender, social class, and crime?
4. Why do crime victims fail to report millions of offenses to the police each year?
5. Does unemployment cause crime?
6. What major sociological theories explain crime?
7. What is the relationship between watching violence on television and engaging in violent behavior?
8. Is there a subculture of violence in the United States?
9. What are some of the major characteristics regarding murder in the United States?
10. What is the relationship between guns and violent crime in the United States?

- 11. What are the four major types of occupational crime?
- 12. What are the principal explanations for the origin and growth of organized crime in the United States?
- 13. Why is the job of policing much more difficult in democratic nations than it is in totalitarian countries?
- 14. What is *plea bargaining?* Why is it such an integral part of the criminal justice system in the United States?
- 15. What are the major solutions to the problems of prison overcrowding?

COUNTING CRIME AROUND THE WORLD

The success or failure of any crime-prevention program depends in part on the accurate assessment of the amount and distribution of criminal activity. In addition, our theories of crime causation will be all but useless if criminal statistics significantly underestimate or overestimate the actual amount of crime in a given time and place. While all crime data are subject to error, statistics from developed nations (like the United States) are probably more accurate than figures from developing nations if for no other reason than that these former states have more resources to carefully collect this information than do the latter nations. Also, many authoritarian, nondemocratic countries in the developing world are apt to publish misleading or blatantly false crime statistics for political reasons.

THE UNITED STATES

Published every August by the Federal Bureau of Investigation (FBI), the *Uniform Crime Report* (UCR) is the most widely used source of criminal statistics. The UCR gives detailed information on seven *index* crimes—four crimes of violence (murder, robbery, rape, aggravated assault) and three property crimes (burglary, larceny, and auto theft) as well as limited statistics on arson. These offenses are expressed in terms of the total number of crimes committed in an area and a *crime rate*—that is, the number of crimes committed per 100,000 population. This latter statistic permits the comparison of criminal activity across cities of differing sizes as well as across time. The UCR has been criticized (especially by conflict theorists) because it is primarily a count of street crimes (burglary and robbery) committed by poor people and portrays criminality as a lower-class, minority problem. Another shortcoming is that the UCR is only a measure of those crimes reported to police. The crime index (see Table 9.1) indicates how both the absolute number of crimes and the crime rate (the number of crimes per 100,000 population) have increased between 1983 and 1992.

In an effort to learn more about crime victims (who they are and why they do not always contact the police), the National Crime Survey was begun in 1972. This annual *victimization survey* questions approximately 135,000 people representing 60,000 households nationwide. Household members over 12 years of age are interviewed twice a year and asked how many times in the past 6 months they have been victims of particular crimes. These surveys have found a substantial "dark figure"—the number of crimes that occur but are not recorded by police and, therefore, do not show up in the UCR (Conklin,

TABLE 9.1 Index of Crime, United States: 1983–1992

Population	Crime Index Total	Violent Crime	Property Crime
Total Number of Crimes Reported: 1983–1992			
Population (by year)			
1983—233,981,000	12,108,600	1,258,090	10,850,500
1984—236,158,000	11,881,800	1,273,280	10,608,500
1985—238,740,000	12,431,400	1,328,800	11,102,600
1986—241,077,000	13,211,900	1,489,170	11,722,700
1987—243,400,000	13,508,700	1,484,000	12,024,700
1988—245,807,000	13,923,100	1,566,220	12,356,900
1989—248,239,000	14,251,400	1,646,040	12,605,400
1990—248,709,873	14,475,600	1,820,130	12,655,500
1991—252,177,000	14,872,900	1,911,770	12,961,100
1992—255,082,000	14,438,200	1,932,270	12,505,900
Percent Change: Number of Offenses			
1992/1991	–2.9	+1.1	–3.5
1992/1988	+3.7	+23.4	+1.2
1992/1983	+19.2	+53.6	+15.3
Number of Crimes per 100,000 Inhabitants: 1983–1992			
Year			
1983	5,175.0	537.7	4,637.4
1984	5,031.3	539.2	4,492.1
1985	5,207.1	556.6	4,650.5
1986	5,480.4	617.7	4,862.6
1987	5,550.0	609.7	4,940.3
1988	5,664.2	637.2	5,027.1
1989	5,741.0	663.1	5,077.9
1990	5,820.3	731.8	5,088.5
1991	5,897.8	758.1	5,139.7
1992	5,660.2	757.5	4,902.7
Percent Change: Rate per 100,000 Inhabitants			
1992/1991	–4.0	–.1	–4.6
1992/1988	–.1	+18.9	–2.5
1992/1983	+9.4	+40.9	+5.7

SOURCE: Federal Bureau of Investigation, U.S. Department of Justice, *Uniform Crime Reports: Crime in the United States 1992* (Washington, DC: U.S. Government Printing Office, 1993).

1972). Victimization surveys indicate that approximately one out of two violent crimes are not reported to authorities.

A final mechanism for gaining information on the incidence and distribution of crime in society is the *self-report study*. Guaranteeing anonymity, researchers ask individuals about their involvement in various types of criminal behavior such as illegal drug use and cheating on tax returns. As a result of these studies, we know that:

1. There is significantly more crime in society (the "dark figure") than is being reported to police.
2. Almost everyone has broken the law at one time or another, although most of these infractions are minor.
3. Some populations of law violators are involved in a staggering number of offenses (narcotics users or opportunistic burglars, for example).

DEVELOPED COUNTRIES

The Dutch Ministry of Justice recently conducted a victimization study involving 55,000 respondents in 20 industrialized countries (in Tuohy, 1993). With the exception of Japan and Switzerland, all the nations surveyed had appreciable levels of property and violent crimes. The English-speaking countries of the United States, England, and Australia had the highest rates of criminal behavior in the 11 crimes surveyed, registering approximately twice as many per capita offenses as France or Germany.

In 1990, Toronto had approximately 90 murders, while Washington, D.C. (a city one-quarter of Toronto's size) reported 473 homicides. In the same year, Canada, with a population of approximately 27 million people, had 656 murders, while Los Angeles had 983 murders and New York City 2,245.

Comparisons of other violent crimes (robbery, rape, and aggravated assault) also yielded wide disparities between the United States and just about every industrialized country in the world. An individual is approximately 200 times more likely to be robbed in New York City than in more tranquil Tokyo. The United States, Canada, England, Germany, and Poland topped the list of sex offenses. National levels of crime are linked to the level of urbanization, with Japan being the lone exception to this finding. Investigators also found a positive relation between a country's level of affluence and its rate of property crime—that is, as national income and wealth increased, so did the theft of material goods.

DEVELOPING NATIONS

Rates of criminal activity have been rising in modernizing nations for all offenses, especially drug-related crimes, property crimes, and prostitution. The highest rates of crime in the developing world are found in the Caribbean nations and the lowest rates in the Middle East. Modernizing countries in Africa, Asia, and Latin America are between these two extremes (Shelley, 1981).

As noted in the introduction, this upsurge in crime is taking place predominantly in metropolitan areas. Tens of millions of high-crime-risk young men have migrated from the countryside to the city. Fast-growing urban areas offer the greatest opportunity for committing a wide range of offenses. "Consequently, such huge cities as Bombay, Calcutta,

Colombia is one of the most violent societies in the world, in part because it is a center of warring drug cartels and in part because of the emergence of terrorist and paramilitary groups on the political right and left. In this photo, police officers arrive at the scene of a murder in the capital city of Bogota.

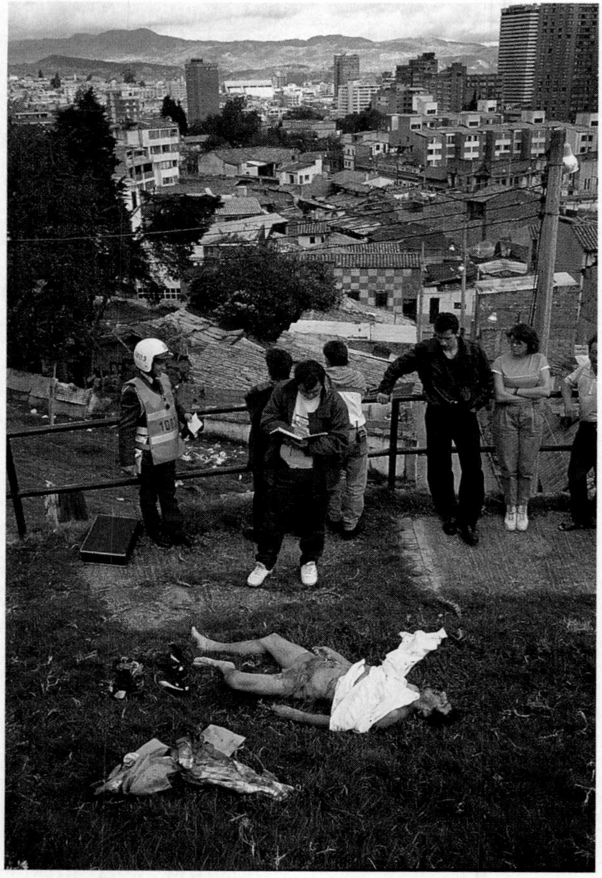

Bangkok, Seoul, Manila, Caracas, Bogota, Mexico City, Cairo, Lagos, Abijan, and Nairobi experience far higher—and more sharply rising—crime rates than their respective country averages" (Clinard, 1983). The scarcity of material possessions on the part of so many people means that even the simplest object—a used shirt, an iron pipe, or a lightbulb—is of value to someone and therefore subject to theft (Clinard, 1983).

Many women with few job skills have resorted to prostitution as the only way to survive in overcrowded cities with high rates of unemployment. Brazil has more than 500,000 child prostitutes, with 8-year-old girls the norm in one state (Associated Press, 1993). Rapid population growth in Third World cities means the rate of prostitution—and the number of people who contract the HIV virus and AIDS—will only increase.

OFFENDERS AND VICTIMS

Few attitudes or behaviors are randomly distributed throughout society. Political, social, and religious views, as well as social conduct (and its consequences), are linked to variables such as age, race/ethnicity, gender, and socioeconomic status. An examination of criminal offenders and their victims reveals the social characteristics of these individuals. The following profile of criminal law violators in the United States is based primarily on street criminals, and more specifically those offenders arrested for crimes.

OFFENDERS

GENDER

Worldwide, men commit more crimes than women (Sutherland & Cressey, 1970). In 1992, 81 percent of those arrested in the United States were males. Men not only commit more street crimes than women (murder, robbery, burglary); they also have a "virtual monopoly" on the commission of organized, corporate, and political crime (Beirne & Messerschmidt, 1991). However, the incidence of female criminality may be changing somewhat, as indicated by recent crime statistics. While the number of men arrested in the United States between 1981 and 1990 increased by 27.4 percent, the number of women arrested during that same period went up 48.4 percent. This recent increase in female criminality has been referred to as "the shady side of liberation" (Steffensmeier & Allan, 1991) and is attributed to women now having greater opportunities to commit crime as a result of leaving home and entering the labor force. Criminologist Freda Adler and her colleagues (1991, p. 44) note, "To embezzle, one needs to be in a position of trust and control of funds. To get in a bar fight, one needs to go to a bar. To be an inside trader on Wall Street, one needs to be on the inside."

However, not everyone agrees with this interpretation. Critics note that the sharpest rise in American female criminality has been among those women least affected by the liberation movement: poor females, women of color, and adolescents under age 18. For example, although women account for approximately 40 percent of all arrests for embezzlement each year, most of these thefts are for under $150, hardly the sum of money a middle-class female accountant would steal. Margaret Andersen (1993) argues that escalating female arrest statistics over the past 20 years may reflect an increase in the detection of female crime and not a rise in the actual number of crimes themselves. She notes that as a result of changing views of women, brought about in part by the feminist movement, police may be more likely to arrest women for criminal activity. Also, the greater willingness of the business community to prosecute offenses such as shoplifting, writing bad checks, and credit card fraud—the types of crimes women commit—would also contribute to the rise in female arrest rates (Steffensmeier in Andersen, 1993).

AGE

Crime has always been a predominantly youthful activity in the United States. In 1992, individuals under 25 accounted for 45 percent of all those arrested for violent crime and 60 percent of property crime arrestees. After age 24, arrest rates decline sharply and continue falling until they are negligible for individuals 65 and over.

Some youthful crimes, such as petty theft, drinking, experimenting with drugs, and crimes resulting from drug-induced altered states of consciousness, may be a result of "growing up" (Jolin & Gibbons, 1987). However, by the mid- to late-twenties, "aging out" (Siegel, 1989) contributes to a significant reduction in criminal activity. Young adults have legitimate access to sex and alcohol as well as the money needed to purchase many of the things they desire. Responsibilities to family members and employers, coupled with increased penalties (offenders are no longer treated as juvenile offenders), make crime less attractive. Those who choose to remain criminally active now have access to "less risky, more lucrative types of crime, such as gambling, fraud, and employee theft" (Steffensmeier & Allan, 1991).

RACE AND SOCIAL CLASS

Of those Americans arrested in 1992 for all crimes, 68 percent were White and 30 percent were Black. Fifty-four percent of those arrested for murder and 61.2 percent of the people arrested for robbery were African Americans. These figures are significant in light of the fact that African Americans comprise approximately 13 percent of the United States population.

Some researchers argue that high Black arrest and incarceration rates are indicative of racially biased police, prosecutors, and judges and a criminal justice system that chooses to measure crime by focusing on law-violating acts committed by the poor: so-called street crime. Criminologist Samuel Walker (1989) points out that the focus on street crime reveals a bias against crimes committed by *all* lower-class people, not just Blacks. Walker notes that "people commit the crimes that are available to them" (p. 25), and crimes like armed robbery are dealt with harshly by the United States justice system. If police started investigating political and corporate violations of the law, they would find equally high rates of crime in the upper classes, and "the wealthy might even be convicted and punished more than the poor" (Pepinsky & Jesilow, 1984, p. 81).

However, it may be that index crimes receive the most attention from the police and the most severe punishment because society regards them as the most serious transgressions, especially since these crimes have become so much more violent. Although Charles Tittle's 1978 review of 35 studies that examined the crime/class relation found only a weak relation between the two variables, John Braithwaite (1981) looked at over 200 studies of social class and crime and concluded that lower-class youths did have higher rates of criminal behavior.

VICTIMS

The 1991 data on victimization in the United States (see Table 9.2) reveal a pattern that has been fairly consistent over a number of years. Crime victims in the United States are more often men than women and younger people rather than elderly individuals. Although large metropolitan areas have the highest rates of crime in the United States (as in most nations of the world), crime rates are not evenly distributed within these areas. Residents of inner cities have considerably higher rates of victimization than people who live in suburbs, and rural populations are the least victimized. Poor people, in general, and African Americans, in particular, are most likely to be victims of violent crimes. In fact, individuals with incomes of less than $7,500 are two-and-a-half times more likely to be victims of violent crimes than are people with incomes of $50,000 or more (Shim et al., 1988). However, the most affluent families in U.S. society have the highest victimization rates for theft. We also know that, with the exception of robbery, violent crimes and a significant amount of property crimes are *intraracial* activities. This means that Black offenders prey on Black victims, and White offenders disproportionately victimize White individuals. A cursory review of these associations indicates that young, poor, unemployed, urban (inner-city) Black males are most likely to be victims of crime—especially violent crime.

Millions of crime victims fail to report offenses to authorities each year. Peter Finn (1986) argues that among other things, this failure to notify police is a function of people's

TABLE 9.2 Victimization Rates, United States: 1991 (victimizations per 1,000 persons age 12 or older)

	Total	Crimes of Violence					Crimes of Theft
		Total*	Robbery	Assault			
				Total	Aggravated	Simple	
Sex							
Male	105.1	40.3	7.8	32.4	11.5	20.9	64.8
Female	80.4	22.9	3.5	17.9	4.4	13.4	57.5
Age							
12–15	163.9	62.7	10.0	51.6	12.9	38.7	101.2
16–19	185.1	91.1	8.3	79.2	25.5	53.8	94.1
20–24	189.4	74.6	13.9	59.0	23.0	36.0	114.8
25–34	106.3	34.9	7.2	26.6	8.3	18.3	71.4
35–49	75.5	20.0	4.0	15.4	3.9	11.4	55.6
50–64	45.0	9.6	1.8	7.6	2.4	5.2	35.4
65 or older	23.2	3.8	1.9	1.8	.9	.9	19.5
Race							
White	90.9	29.6	4.4	24.3	7.4	16.9	61.4
Black	105.6	44.4	13.5	30.4	11.1	19.3	61.1
Other	80.2	28.1	7.4	20.5	8.2	12.3	52.0
Ethnicity							
Hispanic	95.6	36.2	10.0	25.2	11.8	13.4	59.4
Non-Hispanic	91.9	30.8	5.2	24.8	7.5	17.3	61.2
Family income							
Less than $7,500	121.5	59.4	9.6	48.0	19.6	28.4	62.1
$7,500–$9,999	102.9	42.1	7.9	34.2	9.5	24.7	60.8
$10,000–$14,999	103.4	43.1	7.6	33.9	9.8	24.1	60.2
$15,000–$24,999	88.3	30.9	5.0	24.8	7.5	17.4	57.4
$25,000–$29,999	88.8	31.9	6.0	25.6	8.3	17.3	56.9
$30,000–$49,999	85.4	25.0	3.7	20.5	6.3	14.2	60.4
$50,000 or more	85.7	19.9	3.3	16.2	3.9	12.3	65.8
Residence							
Central city	118.9	43.7	11.5	30.7	10.8	19.9	75.2
Suburban	87.6	26.4	3.9	22.0	6.5	15.5	61.2
Nonmetropolitan areas	69.4	24.9	1.5	22.7	6.5	16.1	44.4

SOURCE: Bureau of Justice Statistics, U.S. Department of Justice, *Bulletin: Criminal Victimization* (Washington, DC: U.S. Government Printing Office, 1991), p. 6.

*Includes data on rape not shown separately.

dread of getting involved. Crime victims may be embarrassed by the incident and/or not want to relive a traumatic experience by telling their stories repeatedly to police officers, prosecutors, and juries. In addition, many individuals fear cross-examination by the defendant's attorney. Poor people are especially concerned about losing wages for time spent in court.

Victims may also believe that even if they cooperate with authorities, their cases will be postponed indefinitely or dismissed (Finn, 1986). And even if the offender is caught and punished, there is little if any chance of recovering property and money. Ultimately, people may fear they will be victimized a second time if the perpetrator is not convicted or if the individual is released from prison. A victim's failure to notify authorities significantly reduces the chances that an offender will be apprehended and convicted, providing the perpetrator both freedom and increased confidence to engage in additional criminal acts.

Most states have established programs to compensate victims of violent crimes, provided these individuals have reported the incidents and cooperated with authorities. Victims may receive compensation for unreimbursed medical expenses, funeral expenses, loss of wages, and payments to dependents of deceased victims. A few states also contribute funds for psychotherapy (Finn, 1986). These programs not only provide assistance when crime victims experience severe emotional distress and physical injury, but through victim cooperation with police, they also increase the likelihood that offenders will be apprehended and convicted.

CRIME AND UNEMPLOYMENT

Over the past 30 years, social scientists have spent a great deal of time and effort examining the relationship between unemployment (especially urban unemployment) and crime. From a common-sense point of view, we would expect to find a positive relationship between these two variables: As unemployment goes up, rates of crime rise, as well.

One researcher has concluded that a single percentage point increase in unemployment in the United States accounted for almost a 4 percent increase in the nation's homicides and a 6 percent rise in robberies. J. Harvey Brenner (in Currie, 1985) has argued that this escalation in crime is not only a response to the direct loss of income but also a result of increased drug and/or alcohol use, both of which are related to property and violent crime. In addition, unemployment leads to dislocation, as people move across town or across the country looking for work. This movement disrupts family ties and informal mechanisms of social control, freeing those inclined to engage in criminal behavior.

However, other investigators have found a negative relationship between unemployment and crime (as unemployment goes up, crime goes down), and still other studies have concluded there is no relationship between unemployment and rates of urban crime. The inconsistency of these findings can be partially explained by the various statistical techniques used to interpret data as well as the level of analysis (unemployment and crime rates from urban neighborhoods to the entire nation) examined by the researchers.

In addition, the work of some particularly creative investigators has indicated that the relationship between unemployment and crime is more complex then previously imagined. For example, unemployment could simultaneously increase the deviant motivation that leads to criminal activity and also decrease the opportunity to commit crimes (Cantor & Land, 1985). So even though the number of muggers may go up as people lose their jobs, the number of potential victims will decline as individuals with less disposable income spend more time at home. Similarly, residential burglaries could decline, as people stay home, discouraging burglars who wish to avoid confrontations with their victims. A latent (unintended) consequence of layoffs and job cutbacks may be *target hardening.* In this case, a house or apartment—the target of burglars—becomes harder to safely penetrate because people are at home and not at work. Rates of juvenile crime could also decline, as unemployed adults have more time to supervise the activities of their children (Currie, 1985).

However, after examining the results of 53 unemployment/crime studies, Theodore Chiricos (1987, p. 202) concludes that the relationship between these two variables regarding property crimes in the 1970s "remains essentially positive, frequently significant, and not inconsequential." These findings are important, inasmuch as almost 90 percent of street crimes consist of property offenses. Chiricos argues (p. 203) that "while the relationship between unemployment and crime rates is far from perfect, it is sufficient to put jobs back on the agenda for dealing with crime." If Chiricos is correct, creating jobs will be far more effective in reducing urban crime rates than funneling limited resources into a criminal justice system that often does little more than pick up the pieces after crimes have been committed.

EXPLANATIONS OF CRIME AND VIOLENCE

FUNCTIONALISM AND CRIME

After reading a crime story in the newspaper or watching the report of a particularly gruesome criminal act on the nightly news, people often ask, Why? Psychologists and psychiatrists would attempt to discover what internal factors (personality maladjustment or hormonal imbalance, for example) were responsible for the deviant behavior. Sociologists, however, are less concerned about Randy Smith's personal reasons for embezzling money from the First National Bank than they are about why people like Smith (White, middle class, middle aged, married, well-educated) so often (disproportionately) commit the crime of embezzlement. Whereas psychologists search for *internal* causes of crime, sociologists examine those social forces that are *external* to individuals and, in a sense, push them into criminal behavior.

Writing in the functionalist tradition, sociologist Robert Merton (1968) argued that a person's location or position in the system of stratification and the social pressures that impinge on that individual are responsible for a significant amount of crime in societies like the United States. For Merton, all societies socialize their members to aspire to a number of culturally defined and accepted *goals,* as well as teach people how to attain these goals by a variety of acceptable *means* of behavior. However, in societies of the so-called American type, two problems arise that lead to high rates of criminal behavior. First, much more emphasis is placed on being successful (attaining the goals) than on how this success is achieved. To use an old sports cliché, "Winning isn't the most important thing; it's the *only* thing." Second, because of high rates of unemployment, inadequate school systems, and racial/ethnic discrimination, the opportunity structure or means to succeed for many people in the lower classes is blocked. Merton referred to this goals/means imbalance in the social structure and the pressure it exerts on people to engage in various types of deviant and criminal behavior as *anomie.*

As a result of one or both of these factors, many people engage in *innovative* (or criminal) behavior to achieve the culturally approved goal of having money and material success in life. For Merton, a good deal of street crime (burglary, robbery, larceny) committed by lower-class individuals is innovative behavior. This behavior is a reaction to external forces (culturally defined success goals coupled with a blocked opportunity structure). Some occupational and corporate crime can also be explained from this perspective. Although these offenders may be quite well off financially, they want even more money and material possessions. They live in a society that socializes people into believing that "more is better," a society that has no clear-cut definition of how much wealth is enough.

The great French sociologist Emile Durkheim (1939; original 1895) argued that crime is normal because it is impossible to find or realistically imagine a society that does not have criminal behavior. He used the word *normal* in terms of statistical normalcy—that is, crime is found in all human societies. For Durkheim, crime is normal because it is impossible for all members of society to reach agreement on what the rules of society should be. Anything less than total agreement means that the behavior of one group of people will be considered deviant by the standards of another group. Public drunkenness, reckless driving, and fighting, considered manly by a particular youth subculture, constitute dangerous, law-violating behavior from the perspective of the larger society. Also, no government can possibly enforce all its laws and regulations. Even under repressive regimes like Nazi Germany and the former Soviet Union, people committed a wide range of criminal acts. Finally, crime is inevitable because "man is a normative creature" (Nisbet, 1974, p. 216), continually dividing up the social world into that which is acceptable and that which is not. Behavior deemed unacceptable becomes criminal, and those who violate society's laws are punished and often treated with contempt.

CONFLICT SOCIOLOGY AND CRIME

Because both physical and social resources (wealth, status, and power) are in short supply (and therefore in demand), conflict is a fact of life in virtually every society. Groups struggle to acquire these resources, and the winners of this contest are in a position to dominate the losers (Williams & McShane, 1988). Law (or more accurately, the ability to make the law) is one of the valued resources people struggle to control. Those individuals who have control over or make laws "are best able to promote their own ideas and interests against others" (Turk, 1975–1976, p. 280). Law, therefore, is a crucial societal mechanism that allows people in power to control the lives of those with less power to a great extent. Behavior that is threatening or offensive to those in power can be criminalized.

All conflict theorists would agree on the points outlined above. However, the world of conflict sociology is quite diverse. Minimally, we could divide these theorists into two groups: non-Marxist conflict theorists and Marxist conflict theorists. From a non-Marxist perspective, "crime is considered to be the normal actions of normal people who have insufficient power to control the criminalization process" (Vold, 1979, p. 313). Earlier in this century, Catholic immigrants, many of whom consumed alcohol as part of their lifestyle, lost a power struggle to rural, Protestant nativists that resulted in the prohibition of the manufacture, distribution, and consumption of alcohol. Similarly, the Marijuana Tax Act of 1937 criminalized the actions of many poor, powerless, migrant Mexican farm workers in the West and Southwest who smoked marijuana (Thio, 1988).

Societies are comprised of numerous groups in conflict over a variety of issues, with each group attempting to maximize its wealth, power, and status as well as perpetuate its particular world view and way of life. From this perspective, the behavior of *both* lawmakers and lawbreakers is considered normal. Those who make the law are working in their own self-interest: to maintain, if not enhance, their position of control and moral superiority in society. Those who violate the law see a hitherto normal component of their culture become criminalized.

According to Karl Marx and Friedrich Engels, crime is the end result of a capitalist economic system that produces a war of "all against all." Individuals socialized to believe that material possessions and wealth are the most important things in life (Engels, 1845, p. 248) victimize each other in a competitive, consumer-oriented society. To maximize political control and enhance their wealth, members of the ruling class engage in criminal acts of "domination and repression," such as corporate crimes and crimes of government (e.g., Watergate). In their effort to survive in an oppressive society, the proletariat commit crimes of "accommodation and resistance" (Quinney, 1977, p. 34). Predatory crimes like robbery and burglary are the result of chronic unemployment and poverty, while personal crimes such as assault and rape are born of frustration, the brutalization of workers by their superiors, and abominable living conditions. Marx and Engels predicted that in a communist society, property crimes would cease because "everyone receives what he needs to satisfy his natural and spiritual urges" (Engels, 1845, p. 249). In a communist state, incidents of rule-violating behavior would be rare events, and the criminal justice system that Marx saw as an anachronism of capitalism would simply cease to exist.

Despite Marx's prediction that crime would almost completely disappear in a communist society, crime is still very much evident following the Communist Revolution in China. In fact, some of the most flagrant and brutal violations of basic human rights have been carried out by the criminal justice system in the name of the state. (See "Focus on China" later in this chapter.) While the breakdown of communism in Eastern Europe has led to a rise in crime, the previously low crime rate was due more to the repressive control of government than to the universal satisfaction of the people.

Non-Marxist conflict sociologists agree that society can never be entirely free of crime because all societies experience conflict and the resulting criminalization of the behavior of those who lose this struggle. Marxist conflict theorists, on the other hand, contend that just as the class struggle will end with the demise of capitalism, so, too, will criminal behavior, as societies are transformed into truly classless democratic states. Since the former "communist" countries of Eastern Europe were, in reality, totalitarian states comprised of an elite class of "haves" and a large mass of "have-nots," Marxists are still waiting for a classless, crime-free socialist society to emerge.

DIFFERENTIAL ASSOCIATION

While functionalist and conflict theories look at crime from a macro perspective—that is, they examine the structure and values of the larger society and how these factors exert pressures on individuals that produce criminal behavior—the noted American criminologist Edwin Sutherland has offered a *process* theory of crime (Sutherland & Cressey, 1970, pp. 75–78). In other words, Sutherland's nine-point theory outlined the specific manner or "process by which an individual comes to engage in criminal behavior" (p. 75). The following is a recapitulation of the theory of **differential association**, first proposed in 1939.

Although psychological and medical theories popular in the first 30 to 40 years of the twentieth century saw crime as the result of biological and/or mental defects in the individual, Sutherland argued that criminal behavior is learned. As such, it is not transmitted from parents to their children through genetic coding, nor does criminal behavior occur spontaneously, invented by the individual on the spur of the moment. Rather, criminal behavior is learned in interaction with other people within intimate personal groups. Sutherland did not believe that movies and newspapers (and now we could add television) play a very important part in generating criminal behavior.

People learn techniques for committing crime, as well as "the specific direction of motives, drives, rationalizations, and attitudes," from others. This means that individuals not only learn the methods and techniques of how to commit a crime; they also learn and internalize a set of attitudes that permits them to rationalize this behavior to themselves and others. If an individual is surrounded by people who define laws as unimportant and encourage the violation of these laws and he or she is exposed to relatively few people who consistently communicate the message that laws must be obeyed, the person will become delinquent or criminal. "This is the principle of differential association" (Sutherland & Cressey, 1970, p. 75).

Differential association has been sharply criticized (and dismissed) as nothing more than a "bad apple" explanation of crime; someone who associates with criminals will quite naturally engage in criminal behavior. However, Sutherland never meant that associating with criminals would automatically lead one to crime and a criminal lifestyle (Williams & McShane, 1988). It was the sum of the contents of the communications (favorable or not favorable to violation of the law) and the circumstances in which these communications were learned that were important. For example, children with delinquent associations (friends) would *not* engage in law-violating behavior if they received more definitions favorable to obeying the law from others, especially those with whom they have strong emotional ties, such as parents, brothers, and sisters. Conversely, children who associate with nondelinquents but who are told by their parents that it is acceptable to cheat on income taxes and to steal things from work would be likely to engage in law-violating behavior.

Grounded in the psychological principles of learning theory, differential association remains one of the most important, enduring theories of criminal behavior. Perhaps the idea that criminal behavior is learned behavior may strike some as less than earth shattering today, but it was a radical departure from the widely accepted biological and Freudian perspectives of 60 years ago.

TELEVISION AND VIOLENCE

The typical 16-year-old American has witnessed some 16,000 murders on television in addition to tens of thousands of other violent acts. Is it possible that viewing these incidents on a daily basis contributes to the growing number of violent crimes that are committed in the United States every year? As its name clearly implies, **social learning theory** holds that all social behavior—including aggressive behavior, in this instance—is learned (Brewer & Crano, 1994).

While criminal behavior can be learned from individuals and groups, as Sutherland contends, a growing number of studies show that some forms of criminal violence can also be learned from watching television. Social psychologist Leonard Eron (in Sweeney, 1992a, p. 6), who has conducted research on the media violence/aggressive behavior relationship for 35 years, told a Senate committee, "There can no longer be any doubt that heavy exposure to televised violence is one of the causes of aggressive behavior, crime, and violence in society." Commenting on this same causal relation, researcher Arnold P. Goldstein (in Raspberry, 1994) stated, "There's just no question of the effect of television. Literally hundreds of studies all point to this conclusion. The only people who seriously question the link—like the tobacco industry questioning the link between cigarette smoking and cancer—are the TV people themselves, and even some of them are coming around."

Goldstein (in Raspberry, 1994) argues that watching violence on television has three principal effects: the *aggression effect,* the *victim effect,* and the *bystander effect.* The aggression effect includes the imitation of violence, sometimes referred to as the *copycat syndrome.* Almost 200 studies involving 244,000 viewers indicate that a substantial number of viewers become more aggressive after watching television shows that contain violence. Research indicates that younger children—who cannot make the distinction between reality and fantasy—are more likely to be affected than older ones, and boys are more influenced than girls. As differential association theory would predict, violent behavior on the part of viewers increases when violence on the program is justified and/or rewarded in the script as well as when violence appears to result in little pain (and a rapid recovery) on the part of the victim.

The victim effect results in an increase in the level of fear regarding the world in general on the part of viewers. The bystander effect leads to heightened feelings of callousness and indifference to actual violence (Raspberry, 1994); viewers become desensitized to violent acts and to the subsequent pain and suffering of victims. The implications of these latter two effects are significant. People who have a steady diet of television violence could become even more fearful of becoming victims of violent crime than the actual situation warrants, causing them undue emotional discomfort. Concerning the bystander effect, individuals may eventually resign themselves to life in a violent society and harbor the mistaken view that they can do nothing about this situation.

If television violence contributes to violent, antisocial behavior, how can this situation by rectified? One possible approach is self-regulation on the part of the broadcast industry—that is, for stations to reduce if not completely eliminate violence from those programs and times when children and adolescents are most likely to be watching. Under pressure from Congress, the major networks and cable channels have agreed to a system of monitoring television programs and a rating system similar to that used by the motion picture industry.

A second alternative is government-mandated, strict regulation concerning the broadcast of violence; similar regulations are in place in Belgium, France, and England. Since this type of censorship would meet strong resistance from the U.S. television industry as well as other groups in society, it is not likely to become policy any time in the near future.

A third alternative is the installation of a "V" (for *violence*) microchip that could be installed in new television sets (for an additional cost of $5), which would allow parents to block the reception of violent programs or entire stations at all times or during blocks of time when children are not supervised by adults. The main problem with this approach is that parents would have to scan pages of program listings to determine which shows or time periods they should block (Kiernan, 1993).

A SUBCULTURE OF VIOLENCE

The geography of violent crime indicates that criminal violence is not randomly distributed in physical space. For example, the South has long had the highest rates of homicide

CRIME AND JUSTICE IN CHINA
Verdict First, Trial Second

Despite the predictions of Marxists that crime would cease to exist in communist societies, criminal behavior has hardly disappeared in the years following the Communist Revolution in China. In fact, some of the most flagrant and brutal violations of basic human rights have been carried out by the criminal justice system in the name of the state.

In the late 1980s, rates of crime in China increased and were reported to be out of control in some areas of the country (Cheung, 1988). The overall crime rate jumped 30 percent from 1988 to 1989, including substantial increases in some violent crimes (robbery: 68 percent; murder: 15 percent). A national survey conducted in 1989 revealed that the threat of crime was second only to inflation as the greatest concern of urban residents in China (in Scobell, 1990). Activity among organized criminal syndicates, secret societies, and criminal gangs is also on the rise. Organized deviant behavior is taken seriously by Chinese officials because it represents a potential threat to the authority of the central government (Cheung, 1990).

A transient population, estimated to be as high as 50 million people, is often blamed for much of the country's crime increase, especially in China's largest cities. Poor living conditions and high rates of inflation have fueled discontent, large-scale protests, riots at sporting events, mass looting, and attacks on government officials and property (Cheung, 1988).

Smuggling operations funnel drugs, antiques, guns, and ammunition out of China, while hard-to-get items such as televisions, refrigerators, VCRs, cigarettes, luxury automobiles, and car parts clandestinely make their way into the country. The tremendous amount of money to be made in these activities has attracted and corrupted officials at the highest levels of Chinese society. There is even speculation that members of the People's Liberation Army are involved in these illegal operations (Lau, 1990).

The combination of marriage customs and poverty in some areas of China has resulted in an extremely lucrative criminal enterprise: selling women. With promises of a higher standard of living, desperately poor, semiliterate and illiterate peasant women are enticed to leave their villages by "people peddlers" who sell them to men in regions of China where "arranged marriages, dowries and putting a price on a bride are deeply rooted in tradition" ("People Peddlars," 1989). This form of criminal activity is especially difficult to control, inasmuch as the peddlers are often thought of (even by local officials) as "long-distance matchmakers."

JUSTICE FOR THE STATE OR FOR THE PEOPLE?

In 1979, the Fifth National People's Congress adopted codes of criminal law and criminal procedure. In criminal cases, trials are to be conducted by a judge and two citizen jurors. However, unlike the Western legal tradition, in which defense attorneys have an adversarial relationship with the prosecution (state), defense lawyers in China are supposed to place the interests of the "socialist cause and the people" before those of their clients (Scobell, 1990, p. 511). Comparing legal systems in the United States and his country, one Chinese defense attorney stated, "I represent the facts and the law, not the client. In our society the lawyer works for the state. In yours he works for the client" (Folsum & Minan, 1986, p. 232).

In a system of justice where the burden of proof lies with the accused to prove his or her innocence (Scobell, 1990, p. 509), defense attorneys are nothing more than agents of the state in uniform. One of the first things that people arrested in China see upon entering a cell is a prominently displayed sign that states: "Lenience to those who confess, severity to those who resist" (Asia Watch Committee, 1990, p. 41). Individuals who proclaim their innocence are accused of having a bad attitude. Failure to admit one's transgressions is viewed as further proof of guilt. Officials in pretrial detention centers do not hesitate to torture people accused of crimes if confessions are not forthcoming. Inmates are routinely beaten and shocked with cattle prods to sensitive parts of the body, including the face (Asia Watch Committee, 1990). In light of these procedures and the philosophy of justice regarding the accused, it is hardly surprising that one study concluded only 2.2 percent of defendants successfully had charges against them dropped (in Scobell, 1990).

Criminal trials are little more than exercises in formality, since verdicts are normally decided before courtroom proceedings even begin. Acknowledged by Chinese officials, this system of justice is referred to as "verdict first, trial second" (Asia Watch Committee, 1990, p. 42). The legal code and procedural laws in China have little if anything to do with safeguarding individual rights. Rather, they exist to protect the power structure of the ruling Communist party (Michael, 1988).

Toward the end of protecting the state, Chinese authorities have implemented the death penalty with increased frequency in the years following the rule of Chairman Mao, who stressed that capital punishment was to be used primarily against counterrevolutionaries. Scobell (1990) "conservatively estimates" that between 1980 and 1990, 10,000 to 20,000 people were executed in China.

PRISONS AS LABOR CAMPS

Under intense pressure to pay their own way and generate foreign currency, Chinese prison administrators are turning their facilities into forced labor camps. At the same time, U.S. buyers in search of cheaper goods (in a less-than-robust economy) are purchasing as many as 80 different products, ranging from machinery to textiles, that are made by many of the 12 to 16 million inmates (including hundreds of thousands of political prisoners) in China's approximately 3,000 prison labor camps (Barnathan, 1991; Wu in Barnathan, 1991).

Inmate laborers may be forced to stay in prison factories even after they are officially set free. One student activist involved in the failed democracy movement reported being beaten with fists and leather belts and being shocked by electric batons for failing to meet his production quota. Barnatham reported evidence that businesspeople from Hong Kong, Japan, and Taiwan had invested in China's prison factories. One prison official stated, "Foreign companies provide us with technology, equipment, and managerial knowhow" (Barnathan, 1991, p. 53). While there is no evidence that U.S. companies are currently involved in these practices, the federal government continues to give the Chinese preferred nation trade status. This virtually ensures that some prisonmade goods from Chinese gulags have penetrated the American market.

JUSTICE AS POLITICAL OPPRESSION

In a society where verdicts are handed down before trials begin, it is hardly surprising that people are arrested, detained, and tortured for their political and/or religious beliefs and practices. Following the unsuccessful democracy movement centered in Tiananmen Square in Beijing in 1989, Chinese authorities arrested between 10,000 and 30,000 people, and at least 40 officially announced executions of prodemocracy demonstrators were carried out. Former Central Intelligence Agency Director William Webster noted that, once the government crackdown against demonstrators began, "probably thousands of people have been killed" (Asia Watch Committee, 1990, p. 8). Students, workers, and others who did not play a major role in the democracy movement were reportedly sent to labor camps for "reeducation through labour" for up to 4 years without having been charged or convicted of crimes (*Amnesty International Report,* 1991). In late 1989 and early 1990, over 30 Catholic priests, bishops, and church members were sentenced to 3 years of labor reeducation for belonging to an underground church.

According to the human rights organization Asia Watch, the criminal justice system in China has operated at the whim of the central government since Mao took power in 1949. However, after the short-lived democracy movement in the spring of 1989, the nation's police, courts, and prisons have been "direct instruments of wholesale political oppression" (Asia Watch Committee, 1990, p. 34). From this perspective, China's worst criminals are not roaming the streets of its cities; rather, they are government officials who arbitrarily detain, torture, and execute political prisoners while denying them rights of due process. China's most heinous crimes are the systematic violations of due process, freedom of expression, freedom of movement, freedom of association, and freedom of peaceable assembly.

Speaking of the "verdict first, trial second" policy and the thousands of imprisoned supporters of the democracy movement awaiting trial, Asia Watch stated, "There is simply no rule of law in China worth mentioning, and no justice can be expected" (Asia Watch Committee, 1990, p. 43). In all probability, only a successful revolution will end human rights abuses and bring about a criminal justice system that is in fact just. Another failed democracy movement could result in repression, punishment, and torture in China on a massive scale, as well as end any hope for reform or change well into the next century.

in the United States, and large cities have higher rates of violent crimes than smaller cities and rural areas. One explanation for these findings is that a subculture of violence exists in these locales, with a set of values and norms that both supports and encourages violent behavior. These violence-supporting norms may be so strong that in some situations, nonviolence is forbidden (Kennedy & Baron, 1993). People who choose not to follow these subcultural norms are subject to criticism and ridicule.

Origins of the southern subculture of violence have been explained by the effects of that region's defeat and destruction in the Civil War—that is, political and economic exploitation of the region at the hands of the North gave rise to a high tolerance for interpersonal violence. Christopher Ellison (1991) notes that the subculture of southern violence does not support random types of street crimes like muggings and armed robberies

that victimize innocent, undeserving people; rather, the values of this region condone violence in "certain culturally defined situations," such as when confronted with unwarranted aggression, when a family member has been injured, or when the "good name" of women has been threatened. In other words, violence is condoned—if not demanded—in those situations when a person's honor or that of a loved one must be defended, when an individual is believed to have the right to retaliate against an aggressor, or when vengeance is believed to be clearly appropriate (Ellison, 1991). Some would dismiss the southern subculture of violence as little more than an enduring myth, but recent research lends support to this perspective (Ellison, 1991; Messner, 1983).

Whereas a subcultural theory for the South's high rate of homicide has long been debated, few people would question the urban subculture-of-violence interpretation as at least a partial explanation for high rates of violence in U.S. urban areas, especially the inner cities. According to one variation of this perspective, high rates of violent behavior in urban ghettos (including Black-on-Black crime) are rooted in a unique violence-permeated, social-historical experience that has included the brutalization of African Americans by slavery, mob lynchings, beatings by Ku Klux Klan members and corrupt police officials, and the like. As Charles Silberman (1978, p. 167) argues, "Violence is something black Americans learned in this country."

Taken to the extreme, this subculture of violence embraced by many young African American males has turned into urban warfare, with nationwide casualties each year in the thousands. As expressed through such means as rap music, this "oppositional culture" (Anderson, in Morganthau, 1993) has engendered a lifestyle that routinely engages in violence, much of which, from an outsider's point of view, is random and apparently pointless. In his book *Seductions of Crime,* sociologist Jack Katz (1988) argues both eloquently and convincingly that many of these crimes are in reality manifestations of a subculture that values power and freedom and whose members want to appear frightening and out of control to others.

VIOLENCE AND CRIME

A 1991 Senate Judiciary Committee report noted that the United States is "the most violent and self-destructive nation on earth" ("U.S. Leads World," 1991). The committee stated, "When viewed from the national perspective, these crime rates are sobering; when viewed from an international perspective, they are truly embarrassing." An examination of summary statistics over a 20-year period reveals just how fast the rate (number of crimes per 100,000 people) of violent crimes (murder, robbery, rape, and aggravated assault) has increased. Whereas the population of the United States went up 22 percent from 1972 to 1992, the number of violent crimes known to police during this same period jumped almost 90 percent (see Figure 9.1). In this section, we will look at the crimes of murder and robbery as well as examine the role of firearms in criminal violence.

MURDER

Comparisons of murder and nonnegligent manslaughter (the willful killing of one human being by another) statistics indicate that the murder rate in the United States is twice as high as that in Northern Ireland (with its ongoing civil war), nine times greater than that in England, and eleven times as high as that in relatively peaceful Japan. As Figure 9.2 indicates, this contrast is even more startling if we examine homicide statistics for males

FIGURE 9.1 Violent Crime in the United States

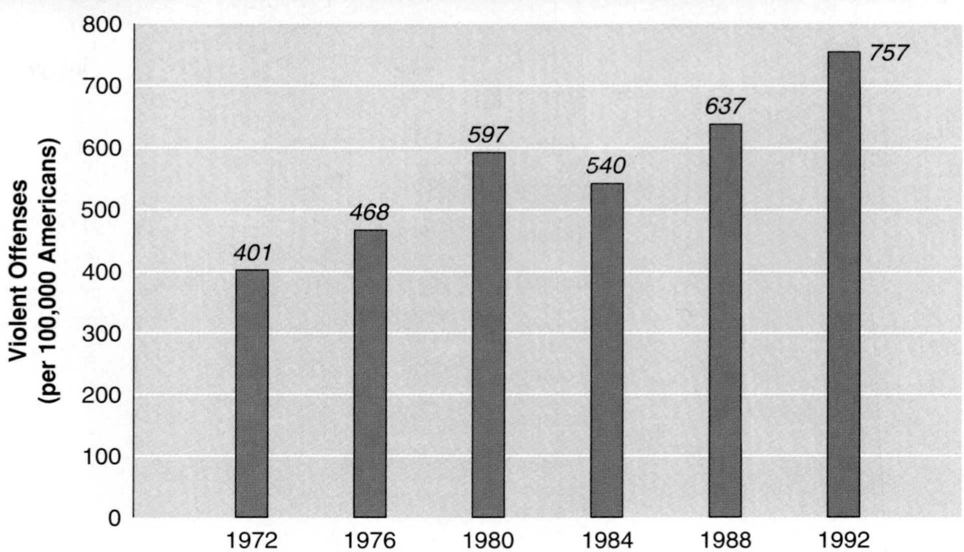

Source: Data from U.S. Department of Justice, Federal Bureau of Investigation, *Uniform Crime Reports: Crime in the United States* (1991, 1992).

between 15 and 24 years of age. For this population, the U.S. homicide rate is 73 times as high as that of Austria. In the United States, the number of homicides decreased from 22,500 in 1981 to 18,690 in 1984, only to hit an all-time high of 24,703 in 1991. If emergency medical procedures had remained at their 1950s' level of sophistication, the current murder rate in the United States would be more than three times higher.

An examination of Uniform Crime Reports data from 1992 and previous years reveals the following characteristics about murder in the United States:

1. In approximately 50 percent of all homicides, the victim and the offender are related to or acquainted with one another.
2. In more than 4 of 5 murders, both the offender and the victim are males. In 1992, 9 out of 10 female victims were murdered by males.
3. Murder is overwhelmingly an intraracial crime. In 1992, 94 percent of Black victims were slain by Black offenders, and 83 percent of White victims were victims of White assailants.
4. Although they comprised only 13 percent of the population in 1992, 1 out of 2 murder victims was Black. The lifetime risk of being a homicide victim is 1 out of 30 for Black males, 1 out of 132 for Black females, 1 out of 179 for White males, and 1 out of 495 for White females (*Report to the Nation on Crime and Justice,* 1988). Black males in the United States are 16.5 times more likely to be murdered than White females.
5. Homicide is the second-leading cause of death for individuals between the ages of 15 and 34.
6. Peak periods for homicide are the summer months, December, and weekends—times when routine activities bring people together (Messner & Tardiff, 1985).

FIGURE 9.2 Homicide and Young Males (homicides per 100,000 population for males 15–24 years of age, 1986 or 1987)

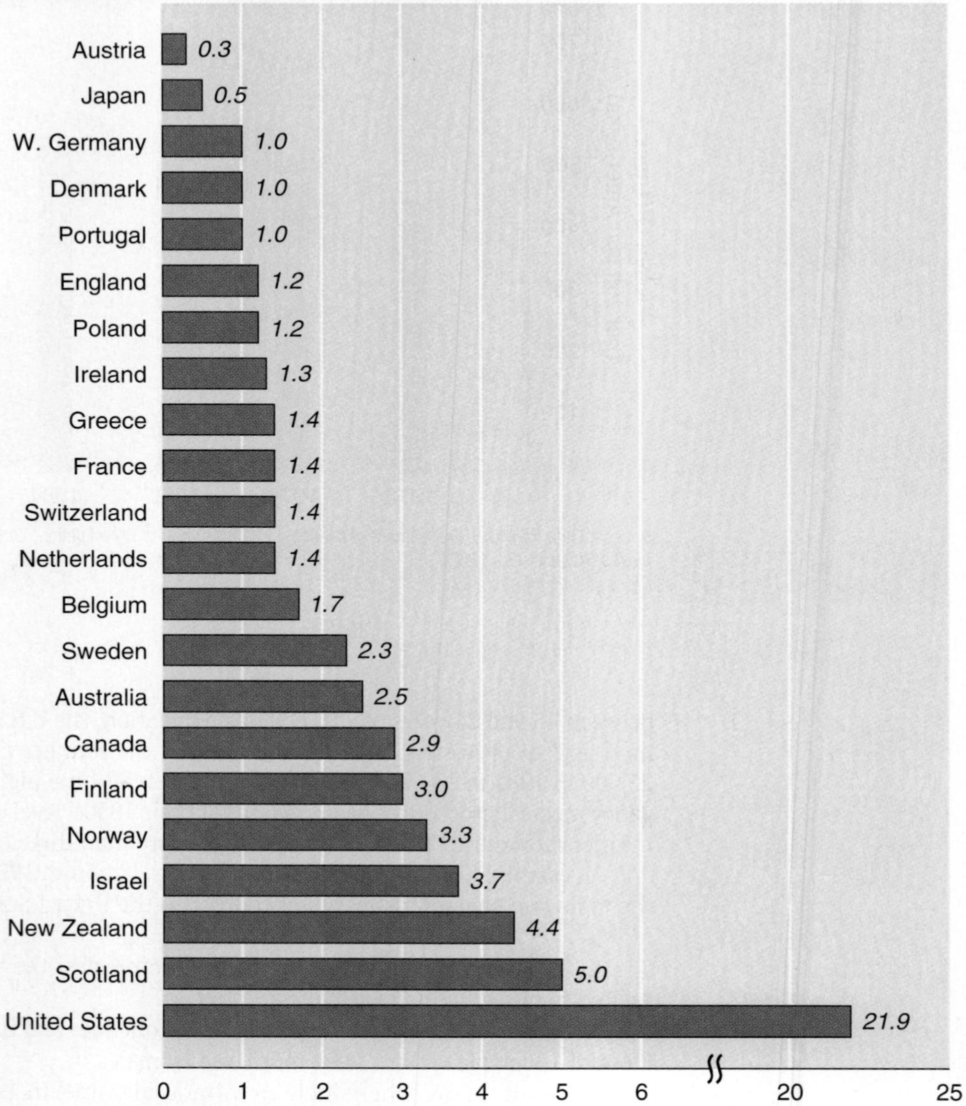

Austria	0.3
Japan	0.5
W. Germany	1.0
Denmark	1.0
Portugal	1.0
England	1.2
Poland	1.2
Ireland	1.3
Greece	1.4
France	1.4
Switzerland	1.4
Netherlands	1.4
Belgium	1.7
Sweden	2.3
Australia	2.5
Canada	2.9
Finland	3.0
Norway	3.3
Israel	3.7
New Zealand	4.4
Scotland	5.0
United States	21.9

0 1 2 3 4 5 6 20 25

Source: From *Criminology,* 1991, by F. Adler, G. O. W. Mueller, and W. S. Laufer, New York: McGraw-Hill. Copyright 1991 by McGraw-Hill Publishing Company. Reprinted with permission of McGraw-Hill Publishing Company.

Note: Data from National Center for Health Statistics, World Health Organization, and various country reports.

7. Murder in the United States is disproportionately a big-city crime. The murder rate in large cities is approximately twice as high as the rates in smaller cities and rural areas. In 1990, over 25 percent of all murders occurred in seven major cities: New York, Los Angeles, Chicago, Detroit, Houston, Philadelphia, and Washington, D.C. (Siegel, 1992). New York City alone accounted for almost 10 percent of the nation's murders.

ROBBERY

Robbery involves taking something of value from an individual by force, by the threat of force, or by placing the victim in a state of fear. Overall robbery rates, including armed robbery, peaked in 1980, declined steadily until 1985, and then began to rise again, reaching a rate of 272 per 100,000 population in 1991. Robbery rates in metropolitan areas of 50,000 or more were over four-and-a-half times as high as rates in smaller cities in 1992 and approximately 20 times as high as rates in rural regions of the United States.

Robbery is a young man's crime: Over 60 percent of those arrested for robbery in 1990 were under 25, and 92 percent were males. Surveys indicate that one in three victims was injured in completed robberies, and one in ten was injured seriously enough to require treatment in an emergency room or hospital (*Report to the Nation on Crime and Justice,* 1988).

Evidence suggests that most robbers in the United States and Canada are poor and uneducated, often have a drug or alcohol dependency problem, engage in little planning, and are typically unconcerned about the consequences of their crimes (Gabor et al., 1987). Target selection of these opportunist robbers is usually based on chance or the situation the offender finds himself in (Gabor et al., 1987). For example, one convicted robber recounting his crime stated, "It was a Sunday. I didn't know where to get some money. I had a gun but no bullets. . . . I saw a convenience store. On Sundays, you don't have much choice. I didn't look at the risk." Another noted, "I hit the first bank I ran into because I didn't have much time to look around."

Average robbery losses in 1992 were $402 from each convenience store and $3,325 from each bank victimized. In the past few years, the number of bank robberies in the United States has increased dramatically, hitting an all-time high of approximately 9,000 in 1990. Los Angeles alone accounted for over 2,000 of these crimes. Observers note that the Los Angeles area has an especially large number of banks that stay open for extended hours, and robbers can more easily make their escapes in freeway traffic (Kaplan, 1991).

Robbery rates have been affected by financial and technological changes in U.S. society. For example, the growing use and sophistication of burglar alarms means that homes, offices, and warehouses are harder to penetrate. A modern credit-card economy has resulted in a significant reduction in the number of cash transactions and fewer safes filled with money at the end of the day. Safecracking and other forms of commercial burglary have given way to armed robbery (Letkeman, 1973). A latent (unintended) consequence of technological change in society is that to some extent, usually nonconfrontational property crimes are being replaced by a crime of violence—robbery.

GUNS AND GUN CONTROL

During our decade-long involvement in the Vietnam War, more people were killed in the United States with guns than lost their lives fighting in the jungles of Southeast Asia (Block, 1989). Of the 24,700 murder victims in 1991, 57 percent were cut down by firearms. Two-thirds of the police officers killed in the line of duty were shot with handguns. In 1992, handguns were used to murder 33 people in Britain, 36 in Sweden, 97 in Switzerland, 128 in Canada, 60 in Japan, and 13,220 in the United States (Herbert, 1994).

Proponents of gun control argue that this degree of firearm-induced carnage—not found in any comparable modern, industrial, democratic society—could be sharply reduced through enactment and enforcement of legislation. For example, if handguns were not readily available, many attempted murders would end as aggravated assaults; assailants would be forced to rely on less deadly weapons (Block, 1989).

According to the *substitution hypothesis,* gun assaults are three to five times more likely to end in fatalities than attacks with knives, the next most dangerous weapons (Zimring, 1986). Gun-control advocates argue that having a firearm for self-protection gives people a false sense of security and that robbers and rapists almost always have the advantage of surprise and speed, which neutralizes even a well-armed person. In fact, "It is absolutely clear that the handgun in your house is more likely to kill you or a member of your family than to save your life" (Zimring & Hawkins, 1989).

Opponents of almost any form of government control over firearms and ammunition (including the powerful National Rifle Association) note that the 20,000 gun laws that exist at the local, state, and federal levels have done little if anything to reduce gun-related criminal violence. With some of the nation's strictest gun-control laws, New York City also has a very high rate of gun-related violent crime. Control advocates counter by noting that 90 percent of the firearms seized in that city used in the commission of a crime were purchased in other states. Even the most stringent gun-control laws will be largely ineffective if weapons can be purchased by simply driving across state lines.

With as many as 40 to 60 million handguns (the weapon most targeted by gun-control advocates) owned by private citizens, any mechanism for regulating the manufacture and sale of these weapons may well be a case of too little, too late. James Wright (1991) notes that even if handguns were made scarce to the point that a single weapon would escalate in price from $200 to $1,000, many criminals would pay that price, just as thousands of individuals will part with hundreds of dollars to purchase small amounts of cocaine or heroin. And if gun money is a problem, one out of every two homes in the country has a gun that can be stolen.

For years, the National Rifle Association (NRA), which reported a membership of 3.4 million people in 1993, and its allies have had their way regarding gun-control laws. This lobby—which some people consider to be the best organized and most powerful in the United States—has long been successful in blocking gun-control legislation at the state and national levels and in watering down to ineffectiveness bills they could not halt. However, in recent years, the organization Handgun Control has attracted tens of thousands of members (the organization claimed 400,000 members in 1994) and experienced some success countering the NRA. In addition, many police officers and police chiefs, angered over NRA opposition to banning armor-piercing "cop killer" bullets, have come out in favor of some form of gun control. The NRA suffered a setback in November 1993 when Congress passed the Brady Bill, legislation requiring a five-business-day waiting period before purchase of a gun. During this period, a background check is conducted to determine if the potential buyer is a convicted felon; that status would disqualify him or her from legally buying firearms. In May 1994, the NRA suffered another defeat when the House of Representatives passed (the vote was 216 to 214) and President Clinton signed legislation that banned the sale of 19 different types of assault-style weapons in the United States.

PROPERTY AND OCCUPATIONAL CRIMES

Most people rely on the media (especially newspapers, television, and radio) for information about their society, including news about crime and the criminal justice system. Unfortunately, some of this information is distorted or just plain wrong.

A study in New Orleans found that 13 percent of the crimes known to police over a given period were the violent offenses of murder, robbery, rape, and aggravated assault. However, the city's three television networks devoted approximately 83 percent of their

FIGURE 9.3 Property Crimes and Crimes of Violence as Percentages of Total Crimes

Of the 8 index crimes reported by the FBI for the years 1982 through 1991, between 10 and 13 percent were violent offenses and the remainder were property crimes.

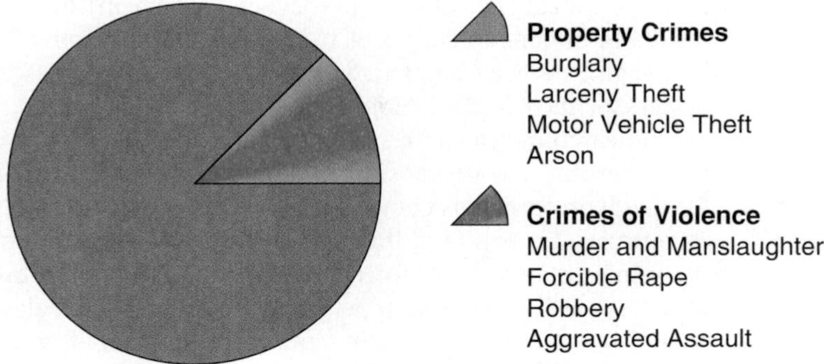

SOURCE: Adapted from U.S. Department of Justice, Federal Bureau of Investigation, *Uniform Crime Reports: Crime in the United States 1991* (Washington, DC: U.S. Government Printing Office, 1992).

crime coverage to these criminal acts, while in local newspapers, 51 percent of crime stories covered these forms of criminal violence (Sheley & Ashkins, 1981).

It is probably safe to assume that this overemphasis on violent crime takes place in the media all across the United States, leading to distortions about crime in general. In fact, property and corporate crimes are much more pervasive and cause more damage than violent crimes (see Figure 9.3). For example, in the 1970s, a congressional committee found that monetary losses from street crimes such as burglary and robbery amounted to "less than 5 percent of the estimated losses from corporate crime" (Coleman, 1989, p. 7). Nor are people aware that, according to some estimates, the number of injuries and deaths resulting from corporate crimes are far more numerous than the amount of human suffering and loss of life that result from street crimes of violence, such as aggravated assault and gang-related murders. In this section, we will examine briefly some property and occupational crimes in the United States.

PROPERTY CRIME

Burglary is the unlawful entry of a structure to commit a felony or a theft. In 1992, almost 3 million burglaries (approximately 21 percent of all index crimes) were known to U.S. police. Victims of this type of crime lost an estimated $3.8 billion, with an average loss of $1,278. Roughly two-thirds of burglaries reported to authorities are residential crimes, with the remaining one-third involving commercial structures (stores, offices, and warehouses).

Arrest statistics indicate that burglary, like robbery, is predominantly a youthful male activity; only 9 percent of those apprehended for this offense in 1992 were female. Thirty-four percent of those arrested were under 18 years of age, 32 percent were between 18 and 24, and 35 percent were 25 and older. Teenage burglars tend to operate in gangs and commit daytime crimes within 2 miles of their homes (Feeney, 1983).

In 1992, 55 percent of the almost 14.5 million index crimes known to police were in the *larceny-theft* category. These crimes include shoplifting, bicycle theft, pocket-picking, thefts from motor vehicles, thefts of motor vehicle parts and accessories, and the like. The latter two motor vehicle–related offenses accounted for 37 percent of all larceny thefts in 1992. The other high-incidence crime in this category is shoplifting, which results in billions of dollars of stolen merchandise annually. One study concluded that each consumer pays an extra $100 annually for purchases to partially compensate store owners for their losses ("More Than Sticky Fingers," 1988).

Research indicates that 10 to 15 percent of shoplifters are professionals and that 85 to 90 percent can be considered amateurs (Cameron 1964; Farrell & Ferrara, 1985). Although professionals comprise only a small percent of the shoplifting population, they account for 50 percent of the monetary losses from this crime. Shoplifting is one of the few crimes that is not (numerically speaking) dominated by males; a number of studies indicate that the majority of perpetrators are young females (Meier, 1983). Investigators have also found that adolescent females tend to shoplift in groups, whereas older women are typically solitary thieves.

Motor vehicle theft is defined as the attempted or completed theft of automobiles, trucks, buses, motorcycles, and so on. This is one of the fastest-growing crimes in the United States: Between 1949 and 1990, the motor vehicle theft rate (thefts per 100,000 population) jumped from 108 to 658—a sixfold increase. During 1990, approximately 1 of every 120 registered motor vehicles in the United States was stolen. The total monetary loss resulting from these crimes exceeded $8 billion and increased the cost of auto insurance premiums approximately 10 percent (O'Connell, 1992).

While cars are occasionally stolen for "joyriding" and short-term transportation use, an overwhelming number of auto thefts in the United States are committed for profit.

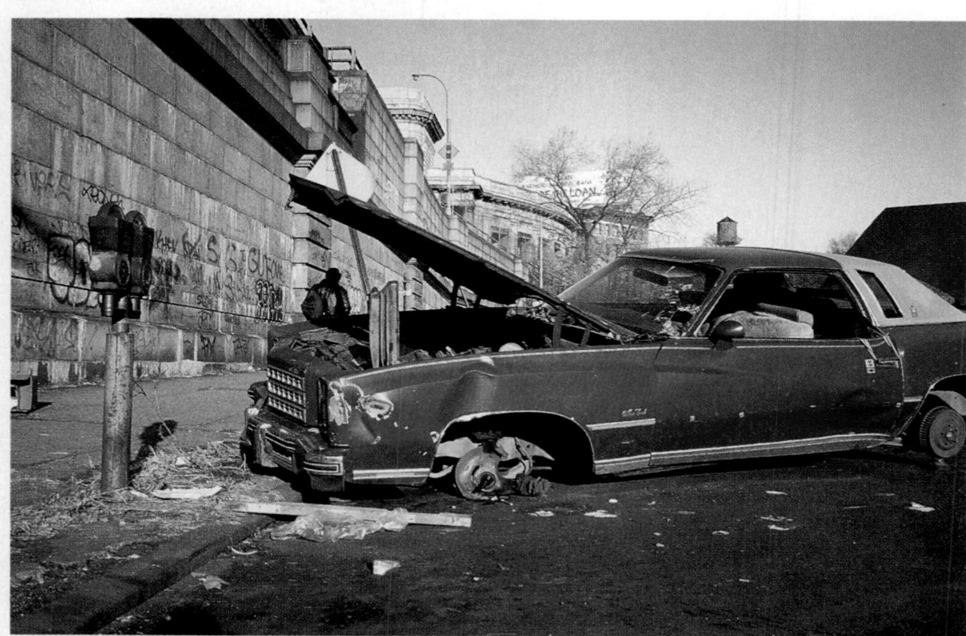

Approximately 1 of every 120 cars in the United States is stolen each year. Many are stripped of their most valuable components and then abandoned. The billions of dollars lost by insurance companies as a result of motor vehicle theft is passed along to consumers in terms of higher insurance premiums.

Amateur thieves tend to strip cars of radios, tires, and easily sold parts and abandon them in parking lots or little-used streets and roads. Professionals, on the other hand, take stolen cars to "chop shops," where they are disassembled. Parts with vehicle identification numbers (VINs) are discarded, whereas nontraceable parts are sold to body shops at bargain prices (McCaghy, 1980). Pros working the lucrative "buy back" scheme strip a car completely and discard the frame, which is eventually recovered by police. Declared a total loss by the insurance company, the car frame, now no longer considered stolen goods, is eventually sold to a salvage company. At this point, the organized car thieves buy the frame, reassemble the car, and sell it.

OCCUPATIONAL CRIME

Criminologist Gary S. Green (1990, pp. 12–13) defines *occupational crime* as "any act punishable by law which is committed through opportunity created in the course of an occupation that is legal." According to Green, there are four principal types of occupational crime: organizational, state authority, professional, and individual.

False and misleading advertising, price-fixing, bid-rigging, failing to provide safe working conditions for employees, as well as promoting and selling unsafe products are all examples of *organizational crime.* Many of these corporate law violations threaten the nation's health and safety. According to one estimate, each year, corporate crime in the United States results in 20 million serious injuries, including as many as 30,000 deaths (Schrager & Short, 1978). This figure is significantly higher than the number of homicides recorded by the UCR annually.

In 1971, the A. H. Robbins company began promoting the Dalkon Shield as a safe and effective birth control device. However, this intrauterine device (IUD) is alleged to have killed at least 18 women in the United States and injured tens of thousands of others worldwide. Hundreds of women who conceived while having a Dalkon Shield implanted in their body had premature babies with severe birth defects including cerebral palsy, mental retardation, and blindness (Green, 1990). Other women adversely affected by this device will never be able to bear children. To minimize their losses after the Dalkon Shield was withdrawn from the U.S. market in 1974, the manufacturer began selling it in Third World nations (Simon & Eitzen, 1993).

Organizational crimes against the environment, as aptly noted by Gilbert Geis (in Green, 1990, p. 135), result in the "compulsory consumption of violence" on the part of the public. That is, whereas people may be able to distance themselves from street predators through home and auto alarm systems, in most instances, they can do little if anything to protect themselves from the harmful effects of environmental crimes. The Rockwell International Corporation pleaded guilty to illegally disposing radioactive waste near the Rocky Flats nuclear weapons site near Denver. Company employees dumped highly toxic and radioactive waste in streams that flowed through the industrial complex and then falsified records submitted to state and federal health officials (Abramson & Takahashi, 1992).

State authority occupational crimes include police brutality, civil rights violations, police officers and politicians taking bribes, as well as genocide and torture on the part of government employees and government agencies. Posing as Arab businessmen in 1978, FBI agents conducted a "sting" operation and bribed a number of U.S. congressmen, with some individuals accepting as much as $100,000 in illegal payoffs (Green, 1990). These so-called ABSCAM transactions were videotaped and viewed by the entire nation as well as the jurors who convicted the offenders.

Professional occupational crimes are committed by highly trained individuals, such as health care practitioners (physicians, dentists, chiropractors, veterinarians, and psychologists) and attorneys. Some physicians perform unnecessary surgery and treatment, file fraudulent medical insurance claims, and engage in fee-splitting with other health care professionals. Some clinical psychologists and therapists have sexual relations with their patients (a crime in a number of states), who are especially vulnerable because of emotional problems.

Individual occupational crimes include theft by employees, income tax evasion, and consumer fraud. Some physicians, lawyers, and university professors pad their expense accounts or charge for work never performed, while some supermarket clerks and cashiers sell a $20 item, ring up $15 on the register, and pocket the rest. Employee theft, ranging from taking extra-long lunch hours to stealing ("borrowing") company equipment and merchandise, costs businesses (and eventually consumers, who absorb most of the loss) between $5 billion and $10 billion annually (Hagan, 1991).

Individuals and organizations involved in a wide range of health frauds bilk the public for as much as $27 billion a year ("Top 10 Health Frauds," 1989). Not only is one out of ten people harmed by the side effects of bogus cures for cancer, arthritis, AIDS, obesity, and sexual problems, but these individuals are steered away from legitimate medicines and treatments. Perpetrators of these health frauds prey on people's fear of disease, suffering, and death.

ORGANIZED CRIME IN THE UNITED STATES

Most people are familiar with the hard-core, often brutal crime figures depicted in Mario Puzo's novel *The Godfather* and a series of three movies with the same title. According to Jay S. Albanese (1989), this characterization of highly structured criminal associations is one of three versions of organized crime (OC) in the United States today: (1) the nationwide conspiracy model, (2) the local, ethnic group model, and (3) the enterprise model.

In his book *Theft of a Nation* (1969), an extensive revision of a report he prepared for the President's 1967 Crime Commission, criminologist Donald Cressey argued there was a nationwide alliance of at least 24 "tightly knit" crime "families" operating in the United States. Controlled by a commission of the rulers of the most powerful families, members of the Mafia, or Cosa Nostra ("our thing"), are all Italians and Sicilians or of Italian and Sicilian descent. With approximately 900 members and 9,000 associates, five of these families operate in the New York City area, where they take in over $1 *billion* annually in profits (Cook, 1991) from a variety of illegal activities, especially gambling, loansharking, and drug dealing.

These crime families are feudal, patriarchal organizations that can be traced back to Sicily a thousand years ago, when they were established to protect members from foreign conquerors. The primary strength of these families is that they are part of an organization that exists independently of any specific members (Cressey, 1969). In other words, if a member dies or is sent to prison, his position is filled by another individual. OC families are more than a collection of family members bound together by personal characteristics; they are hierarchical structures comprised of enduring statuses.

The local, ethnic group model of OC posits that "bonds of kinship—not crime or some network of conspiracy is what ties some Italian crime families together" (Ianni & Reuss-Ianni, 1972, p. 151). Anthropologist Francis Ianni lived with a crime family for two years and concluded that these groups "are structured by action rather than by a series of statuses" (p. 153). Leadership positions down to "middle management" are assigned on the basis of kinship, and the transfer of money does not take place through formal channels but is "part of the close kin-organization of the family" (p. 154). OC families, therefore, are loosely organized at the local level, often comprised of individuals who share a common ethnic heritage (Albanese, 1991).

According to the enterprise model, OC and legitimate businesses both exist for the same reason—to make money. However, the latter cannot legally meet the demands that millions of people have for drugs, gambling, prostitution, and the like, whereas "small, flexible organizations of criminals" attempt to meet these consumer cravings by moving into the illegal marketplace when opportunities present themselves (Albanese, 1989, p. 98). Hardly limited to those of Italian and Sicilian extraction, these subterranean businesspeople come from a variety of racial and ethnic backgrounds. The illegal business associations and transactions of these criminals are not confined to members of their own group.

Albanese (1991, p. 217) argues that "serious empirical investigation" supports the enterprise model. These criminal associations are a local rather than a national phenomenon, and family ties are of little importance in the illegal marketplace. If they do exist, some Italian crime families have been significantly weakened by a decade of aggressive police investigations, numerous arrests, and successful prosecutions of high-ranking members. The director of the New York State Organized Crime Task Force believes that crime families in the greater New York City area could be reduced to street gangs in the next 10 years (Raab, 1991).

Over the past 10 to 20 years, the nature of OC in the United States has changed significantly enough to warrant the inclusion of a fourth model. We are witnessing the proliferation of ethnic groups (often first-generation immigrants) involved in illegal activities that have strong ties with their homelands. Hong Kong–based Chinese syndicates fearful of losing their wealth, influence, and power when control of the island is returned to China in 1997 are moving to the United States. Cuban, Colombian, Nigerian, Israeli, and Jamaican gangs, among others, are engaged in a variety of criminal activities ranging from drug trafficking and bringing women into the country for prostitution to credit card fraud. Speaking of the new ethnic crime groups, a Drug Enforcement Agency agent said, "They keep very tight control of their people. . . . We have seen cases where people have been killed on the suspicion they might be talking to the police" (Seamonds, 1988). Implicated in hundreds of homicides across the United States, Jamaican posses (pronounced "passes") are especially well armed and violent.

Although the structure, distribution, and precise activities of OC groups in the United States have been a matter of debate, we can be quite sure of at least one thing: These organizations, in one form or another, will remain a menacing and dangerous component of contemporary society. Americans have been involved in counterfeiting, smuggling, prostitution, racketeering, corruption, and influence peddling since before the Revolution (Lupsha, 1989). To that list, we can add a long history of illegal gambling, usury, drug use, and gun running. As long as people desire prohibited goods and services, organizations will exist to supply them.

ORGANIZED CRIME—THE GLOBAL DIMENSION

If the existence of organized, sometimes highly complex crime groups could be linked to some particular societal structure or sociohistorical experience, we would have a more precise understanding of this phenomenon, and, armed with this knowledge, law enforcement officials would be better able to combat these organizations. However, criminal organizations have flourished in centuries-old feudal societies as well as modern nations, in some relatively poor developing countries and the world's wealthiest states, and in both capitalist and communist economies.

One of the world's oldest continually existing criminal organizations is the Japanese *yakuza* (literally "gangster," "gambler," or "good for nothing"). This organization can be traced back to the Tokugawa Shogunate (1603–1867), when members engaged in a wide variety of illegal activities, including gambling, vice, extortion, and blackmail. Japanese police believe that there are 3,300 *yakuza* gangs nationwide with approximately 90,000 members; the largest—*Yamaguchi-gumi*—has 26,000 individuals in 944 groups. Collectively, these gangs have an annual revenue of up to $50 billion. As a result of their criminal activity at all levels of Japanese society, police estimate that one-third of inmates in Japanese prisons are *yakuza*.

While we tend to think of organized crime as part of the underworld, the *yakuza* have an air of respectability in Japan. Gang members have business cards denoting their affiliation and rank and work out of plush, expensive offices. When a godfatherlike figure was installed as the head of the *Yamaguchi-gumi* organization, the ceremony was videotaped and cassettes were widely distributed. Some have speculated that criminal gangs have their own representatives in parliament. Former Prime Minister Noboru Takeshita, elected in 1987, has been suspected of having ties to organized crime groups ("Gangster Story," 1992; "Japan's Gangsters," 1990). Recently, the parliament passed legislation aimed at controlling *yakuza* ("Cracking Down," 1992).

Organized criminals in the developing nation of Thailand have brought between 20,000 and 30,000 girls and women into their country from neighboring Burma and forced them

Saichi, a yakuza *gang member in Japan, shows his hands.* Yubitsume *is the ritual act within the* yakuza *of slicing off a finger joint for making an error. Saichi has made four errors and lost four finger joints.*

into prostitution. The parents of these mostly poor, rural women are told by criminals posing as job recruiting agents that their daughters will have steady, respectable work in Thailand. The transport of these females from Burma to Thailand poses few problems after border guards and police are paid off. However, instead of laboring in factories or as maids, the young girls and women are forced to join the ranks of an estimated 800,000 to 2,000,000 prostitutes working in brothels all over the country. They typically work 10 to 18 hours a day and service between 5 and 15 clients daily. After a fire swept through a brothel in the capital city of Bangkok, a number of charred female bodies were found literally chained to beds. Fearful of contracting the HIV virus from older prostitutes, many men who frequent Thailand's brothels prefer young girls. Unfortunately, because of the frequency of sexual contact, all these females are at risk of becoming HIV positive. One study found that between 50 and 70 percent of these girls and women tested positive for the AIDS-producing virus ("Daily News," 1994; Spadd, 1994).

Before he was gunned down by authorities in December 1993, multibillionaire Pablo Escobar was the head of a Colombia-based international "narcoterrorist" organization that distributed cocaine throughout Europe and the United States. He organized smugglers and dealers into the drug-based criminal equivalent of a multinational corporation (Watson, 1993). Escobar's private army of over 1,000 gunmen killed anybody who threatened his organization's highly lucrative drug dealings, including rival gang members, prosecutors, judges, supreme court justices, politicians, journalists, and approximately 400 policemen. Government officials also believe he was responsible for blowing up a Colombian airliner that claimed the lives of 107 people (Watson, 1993). Rich, powerful, and violence prone, drug cartels have corrupted and destabilized Bolivian and Colombian governments (Adler et al., 1991). Escobar's death appears to have shifted control of a sizeable portion (an estimated 80 percent) of the world's cocaine trade from his crumbling organization based in the city of Medellin to a rival and especially violent cartel operating out of Cali, Colombia. One of the Cali-based druglords reportedly favors cutting up his victims (which have included at least 100 Indian peasants) with a chainsaw (Wilkinson, 1994a).

Perhaps more like outlaw governments than criminal gangs, drug warlords in Burma command a significant amount of territory in the region of the country bordering China, Laos, and Thailand. Collectively, these drug warlords control approximately 60 percent of the world's output of opium, a substance used in the production of heroin. One of the most successful and powerful of these warlords has an army of 18,000 to 20,000 men equipped with automatic weapons, rocket launchers, anti-aircraft guns, and their own munitions factories. These drug-financed organized crime groups or armies are so strong that even the Burmese government—one of the world's most repressive regimes—has been unable to subdue them (Lintner, 1994; Lintner & Mai, 1994).

The collapse of communism in the former Soviet Union and Eastern European countries has ushered in a tidal wave of organized criminal activity. Whereas crime groups were held in check prior to the political and economic transitions that occurred in these countries, the collapse of oppressive governments and a rebirth of the profit motive have combined to form a "devastating mixture" (Elliot, 1993). The situation is especially bad in politically volatile Russia, where groups of heavily armed former athletes and military veterans (many with combat experience in Afghanistan) are weakening the local economy. A high-ranking police official noted that in order to survive, "Every business in Russia has to deal with the mafia" (in Elliot, 1993). According to one local businessman, retail enterprises in Moscow pay up to 30 percent of their gross incomes to the various gangs that have proliferated in the post-Communist era (Costello, 1994).

After a particularly gruesome weekend in June 1994, when Moscow police recorded almost a dozen bombings and eight execution-style "contract killings," Russian President Boris Yeltsin decided that drastic action was needed to rid the nation of "criminal filth." Yeltsin's get-tough policy was initially welcomed by a populace that believes widespread criminal activity is one of the nation's most serious problems. However, resistance from people across the political spectrum mounted when it was learned that law enforcement authorities now had the power to detain individuals and search homes, offices, and cars almost at will, even if there were no evidence that a crime had been committed (Specter, 1994).

Russian crime groups are involved in stealing cars throughout Europe as well as running some of the biggest prostitution rings on the continent. As is the case in Burma, Russian women are often tricked by gang members who promise opportunities abroad. In an economy that has seen tens of thousands of jobs disappear and inflation increase at over 35 percent per month in 1993, some women desperate for employment knowingly consent to becoming prostitutes. Working in countries stretching from Sweden to China, these women are provided with fraudulent identity documents. These documents are often confiscated when the woman's ability to generate sufficient profit for the organization declines and she is left to fend for herself. A Czech police officer noted that fear of gang members who may beat or even kill them keeps Russian prostitutes in his country from appealing to the authorities for help.

Despite U.S. Senator John Kerry's concern that organized crime is "the new communism, the new monolithic threat" (in Elliot, 1993, p. 22), there is no evidence for a worldwide organized crime conspiracy, no "Crime International" board of directors. This may be the only bright spot in a world (especially Europe and Asia) that is experiencing a significant increase in organized criminal activity.

THE CRIMINAL JUSTICE SYSTEM

Every modern society has an institutionalized, formal mechanism of social control that it utilizes to apprehend, try, and punish those individuals found guilty of violating criminal laws. The effectiveness of the various components of what in the United States is referred to as the criminal justice system (CJS)—comprised of the police, the courts, and the prisons—as well as how these units are viewed by citizens in different countries depend on the overall structure of society and a nation's social history.

For example, as a result of wide-scale, institutionalized corruption and brutality that have existed for decades in law enforcement agencies across the country, police in Mexico are hated by a significant portion of the population. One observer noted that people are very fearful of extortion, robbery, torture, and even murder: "That's what happens *after* the police arrive" (Oster, 1989, p. 166). In Japan, police have been accused of routinely abusing suspects during interrogation sessions by depriving them of sleep, feeding arrestees meager rations, and not permitting them to use the toilet for long periods of time. However, the police in Japan are viewed quite favorably by the majority of the populace, who believe these practices are a small price to pay for living in a society with one of the lowest crime rates (especially for violent crime) in the world.

The evolution of crime and justice in United States has produced a multifaceted CJS (existing at the city, county, state, and federal levels) that is a system in name only. Rather than resembling some highly integrated, well-oiled machine, the various components and levels of this gigantic system are often at odds with one another. For example, police and prosecuting attorneys may have very different perceptions of what constitutes a "good bust." And while police officers want to see those individuals arrested for violating criminal laws vigorously prosecuted, district attorneys know that if they cannot establish the legal guilt of the accused, they are wasting the precious resources of an overburdened judicial system. In addition, police officers may have little if any respect for judges they believe routinely hand out probation to criminals who belong in jail. Acutely aware of prison overcrowding, judges in some jurisdictions realize they can only incarcerate individuals convicted of committing the most violent crimes. Each year in the United States, a relatively small number of people are arrested *and* convicted for committing violent crimes. Some criminologists think that unless the certainty of being caught and punished for these acts goes up significantly, rates of violent crime in the United States will remain high.

Criminal justice in the United States is very expensive, costing over $60 billion in 1993. Approximately 48 percent of CJS expenditures go for police protection, 22 percent for the courts' legal services and public defenders, and almost all the remaining 30 percent is earmarked for corrections. With high rates of crime, the greatest per capita prison population in the world (see Table 9.3), and the demands of a public that views crime as one of the nation's most serious social problems, practitioners in the CJS may end up competing against each other for limited tax dollars. In 1992, San Diego city officials decided to pump money into the construction of jails rather than hire more police officers. Although they would have undoubtedly liked to have both more police and more jails, fiscal realities being what they were, these officials had to make a painful decision that was not very popular with the police. In this section, we will discuss problems with the CJS in the United States.

TABLE 9.3 Incarceration Rates Worldwide: 1990–1991

Country	Rate of Incarceration (per 100,000 population)
United States	455
South Africa	311
Venezuela	177
Canada	111
China	111
Australia	79
Denmark	71
Albania	55
Ireland	44
Japan	42
India	34

SOURCE: FBI and Bureau of Justice Statistics.

THE POLICE

According to criminologist Jerome Skolnick (1975), the nation's almost 555,000 police officers (1992) are involved in a major struggle—that is, the struggle to maintain order in a democratic society. One of the fundamental problems with policing in the United States (as in other democratic societies) is protecting society without violating individual rights. Inasmuch as law and order are frequently in opposition to one another, the police have been assigned an impossible task. To the extent that police follow procedural laws that protect the rights of individuals, such as laws of search and seizure, they may not be able to maintain order and vice versa. As Skolnick (1975, p. 7) noted, "Law is not merely an instrument of order, but may frequently be its adversary." In totalitarian societies where procedural laws exist in name only (see "Focus on China"), police can maintain order and control crime without having to worry about making lawful searches and arrests. However, in societies of this type, the price of crime-free streets is unrestricted intrusion by police into the lives of citizens.

Even in a democratic society like the United States, the police have a great deal of power. In their everyday dealings with the general public and with those suspected of committing crimes, police officers have the ability or discretion to act in a number of different ways. **Discretion** may be defined as the freedom and authority to make decisions and choose a course of action from a number of alternatives. A policy of discretion assumes that the officers on the scene are best able to decide how to handle the situation (Wintham & Gladis, 1989). Most experts believe that discretion will always be an integral component of police activity because it is impossible to construct a set of rules and laws that specify what an officer should do in each and every situation (Daudistel et al., 1979).

However, police discretion may lead to discriminatory behavior and/or preferential treatment. After reviewing studies of police decision making, Siegel (1989, p. 441) notes that "the effect of offender's class, race, and sexual characteristics may be diminishing in magnitude, but it continues to influence police discretion." For example, a report by an oversight board in Chicago alleged that between 1973 and 1983, police in that city engaged in systematic torture and abuse of suspects. The abuse included electric shocks, beatings, suffocation, and psychological torture. These activities were reported to have occurred in a poor, predominantly Black neighborhood; victims alleged that shocks were administered by wires and clips to their penises, testicles, and earlobes (E. Harrison, 1992).

The police, on the other hand, feel that they are only doing their job. According to Van Maanen (1978), many police officers in the United States believe that "they are perpetually engaged in a struggle with those who would disobey, disrupt, do harm, agitate, or otherwise upset the just order of the regime. And that as policemen they and they alone are the most capable of sensing right from wrong; determining who is and who is not respectable." It follows from this perspective that police tend to order their world into two camps: those who are "for us" and those who are "against us." Van Maanen (1978) offers a typology of citizens who fall into the "against us" category: (1) "suspicious persons," those whom the police have reason to believe have committed serious crimes, (2) "assholes," those people who will not listen to police and do what they are told to do in given situations, and (3) "know nothings," those individuals who are in neither of the first two categories.

A veteran police officer characterized his job this way:

> I guess what our job really boils down to is not letting the assholes take over the city. Now I'm not talking about your regular crooks. . . . What I'm talking about are those shitheads out to prove they can push everybody around. . . . They're the ones

> who make it tough on the decent people out there. You take the majority of what we do and it's nothing but asshole control. (Van Maanen, 1978, p. 221)

"Assholes" are treated harshly and are often the recipients of physical attacks or "street justice" when the police believe this is the only way to establish control over these individuals. These attacks (as well as the alleged incidents of abuse in Chicago) would be an example of what Skolnick (1975, p. 71) calls *unauthorized discretion*—that is, discretionary behavior an officer engages in illegally or improperly.

Except when an individual is arrested at the scene of a crime or a suspect is clearly identified, a relatively small number of criminal transgressions are solved by police. In most robberies and property crimes, for example, little if any physical evidence will be obtained that will prove useful to the crime lab. And in the vast majority of burglaries and auto thefts, there are no witnesses. When available, eyewitness accounts are often vague and unreliable, and in many cases, witnesses refuse to cooperate with investigating officers. Overworked officers across the United States routinely shelve tens of thousands of criminal investigations (typically grand theft and burglary) each month because of a lack of time (Serrano, 1989a). As a result of worker shortages, detectives in San Diego rarely visit the homes of burglary victims. Most individuals simply get a postcard from police informing them that unless they can supply officers with leads regarding their case, the investigation will be dropped (Serrano, 1989b).

THE COURTS

One of the most enduring images of the U.S. legal system is the criminal trial. Through books and movies, we have all been introduced to the fundamental courtroom procedures and the principal characters in the trial. The prosecutor, representing the state, and the defense attorney, as counsel for the accused, square off in a battle of wits and legal expertise as they present evidence and question and cross-examine witnesses. Out of this adversarial process, the truth emerges and the defendant is rightfully acquitted or convicted. Justice is served, and the criminal courts are shown once again to function as they were intended to.

However, the disposition of criminal cases through hotly contested Perry Mason–type courtroom trials is more fiction than fact. In the overwhelming majority of real-world cases, the question of guilt or innocence is not even contested. The President's Commission on Law Enforcement and Administration of Justice (1967) estimated that guilty pleas account for 90 percent of all convictions and as many as 95 percent of misdemeanor (less serious) convictions.

These guilty pleas are the result of **plea bargaining,** which may be defined as the defendant's agreement to plead guilty to a criminal charge with the reasonable expectation of receiving some consideration from the state. A good deal of misunderstanding surrounds the term *bargain.* It is supposed to convey a sense of compromise. That is, both parties—the defendant and the state—agree to give up something in exchange for something. Theoretically, both parties gain *and* lose in the process.

By pleading guilty to one or more charges, the defendant forfeits his or her right to a jury trial and the chance to be acquitted. However, by pleading guilty to a *lesser* charge, the individual could reduce the amount of time to be spent in prison (his or her gain). Upon acceptance of the plea bargain, the state gains a conviction and some measure of control (fine, probation, imprisonment) over the now-convicted criminal. On the

other hand, by not taking the case to trial (and winning), the state may lose a good deal of control.

For the plea bargaining process to run smoothly and efficiently, public prosecutors must have substantial discretionary power. The millions of criminal cases that must be processed annually in the United States demand that district attorneys wheel and deal, or our "assemblyline" system of justice will come to a screeching halt. Because prosecutors have the authority to offer and accept or reject any given deal (typically without any formal guidelines), the possibility exists that variables such as race/ethnicity, gender, and social class may enter into the final bargain. Just as police have considerable leeway regarding whom they choose to arrest, prosecutors establish the terms of the bargain to be offered and what kind of deal they will ultimately accept.

The other figure with considerable discretionary authority in the criminal court is the judge, who often decides (within prescribed limits) on the severity of the sentence. Sentencing practices have undergone particular scrutiny due to the fact that African Americans, who comprise approximately 13 percent of the population, accounted for 47 percent of state prison inmates in 1991. A study by Sentencing Project (an organization that promotes prison alternatives) stated, "If we continue to pursue the policies of the 1980s in the 1990s, we can expect that black males may truly become 'the endangered species' that many have predicted" (in Ostrow, 1991).

However, other studies indicate that the more blatant effects of racial and occupational discrimination on sentencing have decreased over the past 20 years. For example, Martha Myers (1988) examined the social backgrounds of judges in Georgia and their sentencing behaviors. She found that although Baptist and Fundamentalist judges were more punitive in sentencing, they were no more likely than other judges to discriminate against poor and/or Black offenders. While discrimination on the basis of race and class may be declining in the *direct* impact they have on punishment, these variables still may affect sentencing outcomes *indirectly* in that non-Whites and poor people are less likely to make bail, have competent legal representation, and take full advantage of plea bargaining (Siegel, 1989).

THE PRISONS

In 1792, a portion of the Walnut Street Jail in Philadelphia was converted into one of the nation's first prisons, with 36 solitary confinement cells constructed for serious offenders. However, the plan to rehabilitate prisoners in a rigidly controlled one-man, one-cell environment had to be abandoned because of lack of funds (Reed, 1983). Two hundred years later, these same problems plague the American penal system on a scale the founders of the Walnut Street Jail could never have imagined.

In 1966, approximately 200,000 people were behind bars in the United States. By 1982, that figure approached 400,000, and in 1993, there were 925,000 prisoners in state and federal correctional facilities. In less than 30 years, the inmate population of the United States had increased almost fivefold. One of every 280 Americans was in a state or federal prison, and another 450,000 were behind bars in local jails. Given the cost of $23,500 to keep one inmate incarcerated for one year, it is not difficult to comprehend the incredibly high cost of crime in U.S. society, over and above the money lost due to injuries incurred as a result of criminal behavior. Because of this unprecedented growth in the prison population, 38 states had overcrowded facilities, and the nation's correc-

A man convicted of assaulting a young girl is publicly flogged in Karachi, Pakistan; he was taken to the hospital after fainting from the 30 lashes he received. An estimated 15,000 people witnessed the event. Is public flogging an effective way of deterring this man (as well as those individuals who watched and heard of this administration of punishment) from committing future crimes, or is it nothing more than an anachronistic, barbarian form of punishment?

tional system as a whole was 17 percent above capacity in 1988. In 1993, California's prisons operated at 185 percent of their designed capacity.

There will be an even greater problem of prison overcrowding as a result of the "three strikes and you're out" law, under which individuals convicted of a third violent offense would spend the rest of their lives behind bars. Such legislation was recently passed in California and Washington, and similar laws are being considered by at least 30 other states and the federal government, as well. A study by the California Department of Corrections concluded that the state would have to build 20 additional prisons by the year 2000 and spend $2 billion a year to pay for those habitual felons imprisoned for life. California's prison population—already the largest in the country—would add 109,000 inmates by the year 2000 (Morain, 1994).

As prison populations surpass capacity, the ability of officials to maintain order is seriously diminished. Space normally used for recreation and education must be converted to dormitories, and prisoners live two or more to a cell. Overcrowding often leads to violence, with the strongest, most aggressive inmates dominating weaker prisoners. In the violent world of men denied their freedom, weaker inmates are punished doubly for their crimes. In addition to the sentences they are serving, these individuals are subject to harsh treatment and physical attacks at the hands of their fellow inmates. Lack of recreational outlets can also increase tension between inmates and guards, resulting in low morale, high staff turnover, and a further erosion of the administration's ability to manage and control prisoners (Blumstein, 1988).

According to Alfred Blumstein (1988), there are only three solutions to the overcrowding problem. The first is simply to construct more facilities. However, the cost of incarcerating hundreds of thousands of additional inmates over the next 10 to 20 years would be in the tens of billions of dollars.

The impact of crime as well as attempts to control this behavior through the criminal justice system and the population in general produce ramifications that are felt throughout society.

- While the annual monetary loss resulting from criminal behavior (hundreds of billions of dollars) can be crudely estimated, the physical pain and mental anguish endured by crime victims is incalculable. Debilitating injuries can cut short careers and keep people from earning a living. These individuals become a double loss for society, inasmuch as they have to be cared for and subsidized by tax-supported welfare institutions (in some cases, for the rest of their lives). Victims of especially violent crimes (rape, for example) can live in fear and carry the psychological scars of their experience for many years. With little if any mechanism for generating additional income, elderly victims of frauds may worry so much about their financial situation and ability to care for themselves that they become seriously ill. The prolonged care (both physical and mental) that some crime victims may require can strain family relationships. After a period of time, even loved ones may tire of caring for crime victims and begin to resent them. The unraveling of family ties can lead to alcohol and drug abuse, marital separation, and divorce.
- The nation's poor are especially hard hit by crime. Not only are lower-class individuals more likely to be victims of street crimes, but a $500 loss suffered by someone with an income of $10,000 is much more devastating than the same financial setback

A partial solution to the staggering cost of constructing new correctional institutions may be the privatization of prisons to some degree. Proponents of this approach also believe private enterprise can reduce the cost of running prisons by as much as 25 percent. They argue that privately owned prisons, free of cumbersome and costly government bureaucracies and union contracts, are more efficient than public prisons (Dilulio, 1988; Fitzgerald, 1991). Opponents claim that cost-cutting estimates of privatization are exaggerated, inasmuch as states will have to create regulatory agencies to oversee this new corrections industry (Bowditch & Everett, 1991). Critics also wonder how many cost-cutting measures will come at the expense of humane and effective treatment in bottom-line, profit-oriented organizations. Poorly paid, undereducated, unprofessional guards will be nothing more than correctional versions of "rent-a-cops" in the private security industry (Dilulio, 1988).

A second solution is the "front-door" approach. Advocates of this perspective argue that only hard-core, violent offenders should be imprisoned. The difficulty here, as Blumstein (1988) notes, is to come up with a variety of punitive and rehabilitative strategies for less serious offenders that will satisfy the criminal justice system and the public. The traditional methods of controlling people outside of prisons are probation and parole.

experienced by a person who earns $50,000 a year. John Dilulio (1989, p. 35) argues that "the truly disadvantaged" members of our society are consistently victimized by the "truly deviant" both directly (murders, muggings, creating a climate of fear, etc.) and indirectly (discouraging local economic development and providing bad role models for children). Store owners and manufacturers have no reason to expand or relocate their businesses to high-crime neighborhoods. This makes it much more difficult for teenagers and other inner-city residents without transportation to secure employment and escape from the vicious cycle of poverty that exists in urban America.

- Every dollar pumped into the criminal justice system is one less dollar that can be spent on an array of badly needed social services such as education, health care, day-care centers, shelters for women who have been abused, drug rehabilitation centers, and vocational training programs. If these services are to be provided, taxes will have to be increased, and everybody in society will end up paying the cost in one way or another.
- When those in positions of trust and power engage in criminal and marginally legal behavior, it sends a powerful message to young people that almost anything is tolerated in the quest for success. To the extent that so-called elite deviants receive preferential treatment by the CJS, the belief on the part of many lower-class individuals that there are two systems of justice in the United States—one for the rich and one for the poor—is only reinforced. This breeds not only disrespect for the law (which can lead to more crime) but also outright contempt for the CJS and other institutions in society.
- Guns used to combat criminals are also used for different purposes. A child or adolescent commits suicide with a gun every six hours in the United States, and over 90 percent of the people who attempt suicide with a gun are successful (Herbert, 1994).

In 1990, probation and parole agencies supervised more than 3.2 *million* Americans; officers often have case loads in excess of 200 individuals. Supervisory personnel can have little impact on and/or control over convicted offenders they see an average of only 10 to 12 minutes a week.

The final solution to prison overcrowding is the "back-door" approach—a device long used by parole boards to regulate prison populations. Board members release a select number of prisoners who have served an appropriate minimum but less than the maximum sentence. However, with the movement toward presumptive sentencing, which weakens the discretionary power of parole boards, this has become a less viable option (Blumstein, 1988).

Although the number of people incarcerated in the United States has increased significantly since 1980, the crime rate in general has remained high, with rates of violent crime increasing 32.7 percent between 1982 and 1991. To some individuals, this is proof that incarceration is no solution to the crime problem. However, other people are of the opinion that if tens of thousands of criminals (many of them habitual offenders) had not been jailed during this period, rates of both property and violent crime would have been much higher.

SUMMARY

1. The *Uniform Crime Report* published by the FBI provides detailed information on selected property and violent crimes known to police. *Victimization surveys* are samples of people over 12 years of age who are asked how many times in the past six months they have been victims of particular crimes. *Self-report studies* are measures of individuals' self-professed involvement in various types of criminal behavior.
2. Rates of criminal activity have increased in modernizing countries for all offenses, especially drug-related crimes, property crimes, and prostitution.
3. Worldwide, men commit more crimes than women. In the United States as in most nations, crime is predominantly a youthful activity. Whereas Blacks comprise roughly 13 percent of the population, they comprised 30 percent of all those arrested in 1992. Some people believe this is the result of a CJS that concentrates on crimes committed by poor people. There is no clear-cut relationship between crime and unemployment.
4. For functionalist sociologist Emile Durkheim, crime is a normal occurrence in every society because it is impossible for all members of society to reach agreement on what the rules of conduct should be. Conflict theorists contend that the most powerful groups in society pass laws that reflect their own interests and use these laws to control people who have other interests. Some of the behavior that these other groups consider normal—taking certain drugs, for example—has been criminalized. According to the theory of *differential association,* individuals learn the techniques, motives, drives, and rationalizations for committing crimes through interaction with other people.
5. There is now a significant body of research indicating that heavy exposure to television violence is one of the causes of crime and violence in U.S. society. According to the subculture-of-violence perspective, some groups of people have a set of values and norms that supports and encourages violent crime.
6. While the population of the United States went up 40 percent between 1960 and 1991, the number of violent crimes increased 300 percent. The murder rate in the United States is significantly higher than those of other comparable modern societies. Robbery rates are much higher in large metropolitan areas than in smaller cities and rural areas of the country.
7. Hand guns are involved in a significant number of violent crimes in this country. Gun-control advocates note that strictly regulating the sale of these weapons could reduce the homicide rate as well as the rates of other violent crimes. Opponents of gun control argue that no matter how strict these regulations may be, criminals will always find ways to obtain firearms.
8. While the media focus on crimes of violence, property crimes such as burglary and larceny theft account for the bulk of crimes known to police in the United States.
9. *Organizational, state authority, professional,* and *individual* crimes are considered occupational crimes—those offenses punishable by law that are committed by way of opportunities created in the course of an occupation.
10. Organized crime (OC) is a major problem in a growing number of countries in the world. There are three explanations regarding the origin and structure of OC in the United States: (a) the nationwide conspiracy model, (b) the local, ethnic model, and (c) the enterprise model.

11 The criminal justice system (CJS) is comprised of the police, the courts, and the prisons. In the United States, the police have the difficult job of providing order within the confines of procedural laws (laws of search and seizure, for example). Plea bargaining, which is much more common than the criminal trial in the United States, may be defined as the defendant's agreement to plead guilty to a criminal charge with the reasonable expectation of receiving some consideration from the state. With 925,000 people in state and federal correctional facilities, the United States has a greater percentage of its population incarcerated than any other nation.

CHAPTER TEN

FAMILY DISORGANIZATION AND SEXUALITY
Crisis in the Home

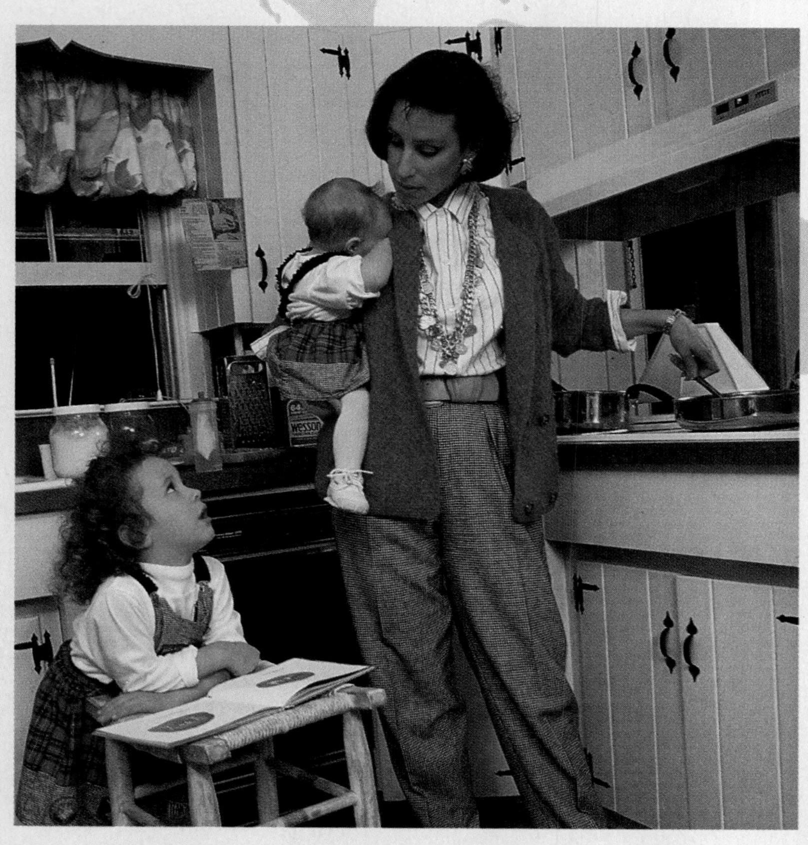

Anthropologist Serena Nanda (1991, p. 225) maintains that every society must solve three basic problems: "the regulation of sexual access between males and females, the division of labor between males and females, and the need to assign responsibility for childcare." The practice of marriage is the way societies typically regulate the exchange of products and services between men and women and solve these fundamental problems. Marriage is the socially approved sexual union between a man and a woman, presumed to be permanent and recognized as such by the couple and other members of society. Although marriage and the family are common to all human groups, family structure, customs of mate selection and residence, marriage forms, and patterns of authority and descent vary considerably across cultures and across time.

In the United States and other modern states, the family has changed dramatically over the past 200 years. Some of these changes were prompted or affected by the Industrial Revolution, although the relationship between Western modernization and the family is much more complicated than simply cause (industrialization) and effect (family) (Goode, 1963). Old customs, such as arranged marriages and staying together for the sake of the children, that had endured for hundreds if not thousands of years began to erode. Modified by powerful economic, political, cultural, and religious forces, the family in these countries is now characterized by "less marriage, more divorce, fewer children, more women working for pay, more sexual tolerance and cohabitation" (Tepperson & Wilson, 1993).

Living intimately with someone who is not a legal spouse—*cohabitation*—has increased significantly in rich nations (especially Sweden, Norway, Finland, and Denmark), where it is viewed by many people as an alternative preferable to marriage. This living arrangement gives individuals the advantages of marriage without the binding obligations of such a union (Tepperson & Wilson, 1993). It also makes the dissolution of a relationship much easier and less expensive than a divorce. By establishing a comprehensive social welfare system (see "Focus on Sweden") that provides extensive medical and educational benefits (among others), people feel free to have children without marrying. The economic opportunities and success of women in what are arguably the world's most egalitarian societies means that Scandinavian women are less financially dependent on men, a condition that contributes to both a low rate of marriage and a high rate of divorce.

Although divorce is less frequent in traditional societies, most human groups permit their members to dissolve marriages. In some societies, getting a divorce is a long and drawn-out affair, but in others, it can take no more than a few minutes to end a marriage. Among the Muslims who reside in Guider, Cameroon, divorce is controlled by men (women are not permitted to initiate this procedure) who must only state "I divorce you" three times before two witnesses (Schultz & Lavenda, 1990).

Although neither divorce laws nor customs in modern nations are as conducive to ending a marriage as they are among the Guider, the trend (especially in the post–World War II era) has definitely been toward making divorces easier to obtain. As a result of no-fault divorce laws first introduced in some American states in the 1960s, couples need only state that they are incompatible in order to terminate their marriage. Gone are the days when one or both parties had to demonstrate mental or physical cruelty or present evidence of an adulterous spouse to end the relationship.

In this chapter, we will see how economic forces associated with the postindustrial society have affected the structure and functioning of families. We will also examine some of the problems associated with divorce, especially as it affects children. In addition, a significant portion of our discussion will be devoted to domestic violence, as we try to understand why love and brutality are so often intertwined and why the usual source of our greatest joy (the family) is, for millions of people, the locus of their greatest sorrow. Finally, we will examine an alternative family arrangement—gay marriages—and the arguments on both sides of the issue regarding raising children in homosexual unions.

QUESTIONS TO CONSIDER

1. How have post–World War II economic changes in the United States affected the family?
2. What are the major characteristics of single-parent families?
3. What are some of the most common problems faced by two-paycheck families?
4. What is the difference between *normal violence* and *abusive violence* as they relate to child abuse? What are the major forms and consequences of child abuse?
5. What are the major causes of wife abuse? Why do so many battered women remain in abusive relationships?
6. What is the *battered wife syndrome* and how does this syndrome relate to the abuse and death of husbands at the hands of their wives?
7. What are the major forms of abuse of the elderly?
8. Why has the U.S. divorce rate increased significantly in the post–World War II era? What are the major social correlates of divorce? What are the consequences of divorce for children?

9. What are the principal arguments for and against homosexual marriages?
10. Are children who are raised by homosexual parents more likely to become homosexuals themselves than children who are raised by heterosexual parents?

THE IMPACT OF WORK AND THE ECONOMY ON FAMILY LIFE

As a consequence of the Industrial Revolution that began in the early 1800s, powerful economic forces transformed the American family from a unit in which husbands and wives ran a farm, shop, or small business *together* to a money-based, urban, manufacturing society that found spouses separated for most of the day (in those days, he at work in a factory, and she at home). The beginnings of a new gender-based division of labor had been established. Almost 200 years later, equally powerful economic currents are radically altering the American family, as the nation moves into the postindustrial era.

Whereas 40 percent of American jobs were service sector related and 60 percent were manufacturing based in 1959, by 1985, three out of four people were employed in service-oriented jobs, with only one out of four involved in the production of goods (Newman, 1988). As American business and industry made the transition from a labor-intensive manufacturing society to an information- and communications-intensive society, millions of high-paying production jobs were lost. Jobs also disappeared as corporate leaders in search of increased profits relocated to Third World countries with abundant supplies of cheap labor. Between 1981 and 1986, almost 10 percent of the civilian labor force—some 11 million people—became displaced workers. In addition, a significant number of individuals who remained employed were downwardly mobile, taking pay cuts of up to 50 percent (Newman, 1988). This dramatic economic change was to have a profound impact on the structure and behavior of the family.

UNEMPLOYMENT AND POVERTY

Social, political, and/or economic change rarely (if ever) affects everyone in a society to the same degree, and the economic upheaval of the past 25 to 30 years was no exception. The impact these alterations had on people's lives were far from uniform; rather, they were filtered through variables such as race, ethnicity, gender, age, residence (rural or urban), and social class. For example, while the average annual income of the poorest one-fifth of the population *decreased* by 13 percent in the 1980s to $9,190, the average yearly income of the richest one-fifth of American society *increased* by 9.2 percent to $79,000 (Roark, 1992).

Racial and ethnic minorities concentrated in big-city auto, steel, and rubber industries were hit especially hard by the economic restructuring of society (Baca Zinn, 1989). One study found that half of Black males employed in the manufacturing sector of five Great Lakes cities lost their jobs between 1979 and 1984. African American male production workers also had the highest rate of job loss in the nation as a whole (Hill & Negrey in Baca Zinn, 1989). This loss of income is compounded by the fact that upon termination, Blacks, Latinos, and women of every race and ethnic background have longer periods of unemployment than White males.

As noted in the above-mentioned studies, with the shift from a manufacturing- to a service-oriented economy, a significant number of relatively well-paying jobs held by men have simply vanished. As a result of this downward trend in male earning potential, by 1987, 34 percent of young White men ages 20 to 34 and 56 percent of young Black men did not earn enough money to support a family. Young men with a high school education or less are apt to be downwardly mobile and to face prolonged periods of unemployment in a service-dominated economy that requires a better-educated workforce (Wilkie, 1991). Inadequate financial resources and an uncertain future not only affect a couple's decision to marry; they are also important factors in the steady rise of married women's employment over the past 20 years.

Patricia Voydanoff (1990, p. 1102) argues that the transition to a postindustrial economy has created "problems in the performance of the worker-earner role" for a significant portion of the population. She states that "economic distress" in individuals and families has three major components:

- *Employment instability* includes periods of unemployment, duration of unemployment, downward mobility, inability of youths to gain entry-level positions, and forced early retirement.
- *Employment uncertainty* is a psychological factor referring to a person's assessment of future work prospects and the amount of time he or she is likely to be without a job. Employed individuals are often worried about the possibility of layoffs and cuts in salary.
- *Economic deprivation* is another subjective factor concerning a person's inability to meet current financial needs and the loss of monetary resources over a period of time.

A significant body of research documents that unemployment is associated with depression, anxiety, psychophysiological distress, and admission to mental hospitals. Unemployed blue-collar and white-collar husbands tend to receive less support from their wives and to report more arguments than men who are working. It is quite clear that unemployment can have significant negative consequences on husband/wife as well as parent/child relationships. A minimum level of income and job stability, therefore, is imperative for family stability and cohesion (Voydanoff, 1991).

The inescapable conclusion to be drawn from this and other studies is that children and Black Americans have been hit the hardest and therefore suffered the most as a consequence of this ongoing transition to a postindustrial economy. Because children depend on parents to meet their psychological and material needs, they are especially vulnerable to any economic changes that adversely affect their fathers and mothers. Official poverty rates for children decreased significantly in the 1960s, remained stable during the 1970s, and increased sharply in the 1980s (Eggebeen & Lichter, 1991). African American children were hit hardest during this period, enduring between two and three times as much poverty as White boys and girls. Evidence suggests that the sons and daughters of unemployed fathers are more likely to get sick (including contracting infectious diseases) and be ill for longer periods of time than are children from families where fathers are working (Margolis & Farran, 1981).

Children of families experiencing severe and prolonged economic hardships often attend inferior schools that are understaffed, that have poor physical facilities and equipment and outdated books, and that are located in poor neighborhoods. A poor learning environment means that students typically learn less and become bored with school. Lower educational attainment usually translates into less occupational and economic success as adults. This escalates the likelihood that family poverty (and all the problems associated with it) will continue from one generation to the next (Eggebeen & Lichter, 1991). A study of juveniles and adults in 150 U.S. cities found that high rates of Black unemployment were related to high rates of violent crimes in these urban areas. Sampson (1987) argues that as the availability of jobs for Black men decreases, the number of families headed by single Black women increases. "Family disruption," in turn, results in higher rates of robbery and murder, especially among adolescents.

Sociologist Maxine Baca Zinn (1989) suggests that in the 1980s, a number of old ideas regarding the relationships among poverty, race, and family were resurrected. Grounded in the culture-of-poverty thesis made famous in the 1960s, these perspectives view poverty as the result of a deficient culture (low aspirations, excessive masculinity, and the acceptance of female-headed families), disintegration of the traditional family (weak, female-headed families cause poverty), and a welfare system that discourages work and encourages people to have more children. In other words, according to this view, poor people have no one to blame for their misery but themselves.

However, as plausible and intuitively appealing as these explanations may appear (especially to political conservatives), they are not supported by data. To the contrary, as the work of sociologist William Julius Wilson (1987) strongly indicates, family disruption and related problems in Black America are not the *cause* of poverty; rather, these conditions are the *consequence* of chronic unemployment and poverty. (This topic is discussed in more depth in Chapter Six.)

President Clinton's pronouncement to the effect that welfare benefits should be a second chance for people, not a way of life, has been well received by many who are anxious to cut billions of dollars from government assistance programs. However, in a country that typically has an official unemployment rate of between 6 and 10 percent, where will hundreds of thousands of poor people—even those with new skills attained through job training programs—be able to find work? Any major cuts in benefits to impoverished families without an immediately available alternative (decent-paying jobs) to compensate for this reduction or elimination of funds can only result in an even more desperate situation for people in the underclass.

SINGLE-PARENT FAMILIES

For most of the history of the United States—when life expectancy was less than 50 years—one-parent families were the result of a death of a spouse, typically the husband. In more recent years, however, single-parent families are the product of a high divorce rate and children born out of wedlock.

Babies born out of wedlock are especially problematic for society, inasmuch as a significant number of these infants are born to poorly educated, poverty-stricken, lower-class mothers who do not have the financial ability to properly care for them (Benokraitis, 1993). These children contribute to the growing ranks of often desperately poor individuals who will have difficulty escaping a lifetime of poverty. Between 1970 and 1984, the number of infants born in the United States to never-married mothers increased 500 percent (Norton & Glick, 1986), while the number of children living with both parents declined from 87.7 percent in 1960 to 72.7 percent in 1988. Black Americans were especially affected by this change in family composition. Whereas 78 percent of White children resided with both parents, only 38.6 percent of Black youngsters lived with both their mothers and their fathers ("Something Happened," 1991).

The following is a summation of the major characteristics associated with single-parent families having at least one child under 18 years of age (Dornbusch & Gray, 1988; Eggebeen & Lichter, 1991; Norton & Glick, 1986):

- Approximately 9 out of 10 single-parent families are headed by women, a figure that has remained constant over the past 20 years.
- African Americans account for just under 13 percent of the U.S. population, but about one-third of all mother/child families are headed by Black women.
- By 1990, 51 percent of all Black children lived with only their mothers, compared with 16 percent of White children (see Table 10.1).
- The average age of mothers in single-parent households declined from 37.2 years in 1970 to 34.6 years in 1984. This age reduction was partially a result of the significant increase in young, never-married mothers, with almost 40 percent of births to women 20 years of age or younger (Wilson & Neckerman, 1987).

Single parents have lower levels of education than married parents; lone mothers or fathers have less than a high school education in almost three out of ten cases. The relatively low educational achievement of single parents contributes to their poor economic status. In 1985, the mean income for single mothers was $10,694, less than half the annual earnings of single fathers. Approximately two-thirds of these women were employed, and of the one-third who did not have jobs and had to rely on public assistance, 94 percent lived below the poverty level. The fact that one out of four divorced mothers never receives a cent of court-ordered child support from her ex-husband also contributes to the poor economic plight of these women. And of those divorced fathers who do support their children financially, only half end up paying what the courts mandated (Nazario, 1991). If the $34 *billion* that "deadbeat dads" owe in uncollected child support each year could be collected, "the economic security of America's children would be vastly improved" (Skocpol & Wilson, 1994).

Recently, a number of states have had some success in collecting delinquent child-support payments by reporting names of "deadbeat" parents to credit bureaus ("Credit Reporting," 1994). Similarly, the state of Maine has begun to confiscate driver's and professional licenses of parents who have fallen at least 90 days behind in paying child support. The Maine program has worked so well that President Clinton included a requirement that all states institute similar policies in his 1994 $9.3 billion welfare reform proposal ("Maine Yanks the Licenses," 1994).

Single parents and their children are significantly affected by their typically low socioeconomic status and the dynamics of their lifestyle. Severe financial problems (including loss of a job) in a family with two wage earners is much less likely to result in homelessness than similar problems in a single-parent family. It is hardly surprising that the two most important factors in the loss of one's dwelling are the high cost of housing and family poverty (Wood et al., 1990). To make matters worse, over 1 million low-cost, single-occupancy units were lost in the 1980s under the Reagan administration, as federal housing assistance was slashed from $29 billion in 1980 to $8 billion in 1986. As of 1994, there was a 10-year wait for public housing, and shelters for homeless families were filled beyond capacity (Bearak, 1994). Comprising 34 percent of those individuals without shelter nationwide, mother-only families are the fastest-growing segment of the homeless population (Bassuk, 1991).

Research shows that single parents give children more control over their own behavior regarding choice of friends and clothes, spending money, and the hours they come and go. When compared to children from two-parent families, youths living with only their

TABLE 10.1 Living Arrangements of U.S. Children: 1960–1990

Living Arrangement	Distribution (percent)			
	1960	1970	1980	1990
All Races				
Children under 18	100.0	100.0	100.0	100.0
Living with:				
two parents	87.7	85.2	76.7	72.5
one parent	9.1	11.9	19.7	24.7
mother only	8.0	10.8	18.0	21.6
father only	1.1	1.1	1.7	3.1
other relatives	2.5	2.2	3.1	2.2
nonrelatives only	0.7	0.7	0.6	0.5
Black[1]				
Children under 18	100.0	100.0	100.0	100.0
Living with:				
two parents	67.0	58.5	42.2	37.7
one parent	21.9	31.8	45.8	54.8
mother only	19.9	29.5	43.9	51.2
father only	2.0	2.3	1.0	3.5
other relatives	9.6	8.7	10.7	6.5
nonrelatives only	1.5	1.0	1.3	1.0
Hispanic[2]				
Children under 18	NA	100.0	100.0	100.0
Living with:				
two parents	NA	77.7	75.4	66.8
one parent	NA	NA	21.1	30.0
mother only	NA	NA	19.6	27.1
father only	NA	NA	1.5	2.9
other relatives	NA	NA	3.4	2.5
nonrelatives only	NA	NA	0.1	0.8

SOURCE: U.S. Bureau of the Census.

NOTES: Data exclude persons under 18 who are maintaining households or family groups.

NA = Not available.

[1]Black and other races (1960).

[2]Persons of Hispanic origin may be of any race.

mothers or fathers engage in more rule-violating, deviant behavior, such as truancy, running away from home, and conduct that results in arrest and contact with the juvenile justice system. This relationship between family structure and deviance on the part of children occurs in all social classes (summarized in Dornbusch & Gray, 1988).

One study found that children from single-parent families in their first year of schooling had lower grades than new students from two-parent households. Of particular interest was the discovery that teachers tended to believe that students from one-parent families would not perform as well as the other students. Teachers were under the false impression (as indicated in this research) that single parents were not as willing to work with their children as were individuals in dual-parent families (Epstein, 1984, in Dornbusch & Gray, 1988).

The implications of this study are potentially significant and far reaching. Perhaps most (if not all) of the differences in achievement and grades between children from single- and two-parent families is the result of a self-fulfilling prophecy on the part of instructors—that is, children performed to the level of their teachers' expectations. Inasmuch as teachers can have such a tremendous influence on children (especially in the first few years of school), students' self-concept may be impaired to the extent that they eventually do perform at lower levels. To the extent that this scenario occurs in schools across the United States, students from disadvantaged backgrounds will have an even more difficult time breaking the cycle of poverty.

A survey of young adults between 19 and 34 years of age found that individuals raised by one parent (primarily mothers) had lower levels of educational, occupational, and economic achievement. Women raised in single-parent families were more likely to have their first child at a younger age and be separated or divorced than women raised in two-parent homes. Mueller and Cooper (1986) speculated that children raised by both parents had not only economic advantages but also nonfinancial benefits such as guidance and advice, role modeling, and learning practical life skills (p. 174).

As noted in the previous section, family disruption in the lower classes is directly related to loss of urban industrial jobs. This factor has contributed significantly to the creation of single-parent families, particularly in Black America. In addition, the pool of marriageable young Black men—that is, individuals with incomes sufficient to support a family—has been further reduced by high rates of mortality and incarceration (Wilson & Neckerman, 1987).

TWO-PAYCHECK FAMILIES

While millions of single parents struggle to make ends meet on one paycheck, the majority of American families (over 60 percent) are comprised of two working adults. These individuals have an advantage over single earners in their ability to buy a home, save for their children's education, and purchase some of the items they desire. However, dual-paycheck families may find that as much as 68 percent of their second income is eaten up in babysitting and child-care expenses (Hanson & Odoms, 1991). In addition to paying more in taxes as a result of moving to a higher income bracket, working couples cope with different schedules, job-related demands, household maintenance, and their responsibilities as parents.

A distinction can be made between *dual-income couples* who both work in other than professional and managerial occupations and *dual-career couples* who work as professionals (accountants or attorneys, for example) or in managerial capacities. These latter individuals have "positions" (as opposed to "jobs") that require extensive training, long-term commitment, and ongoing professional growth (Benokraitis, 1993). Dual-income and dual-career couples face at least one common difficulty: how to establish a household division of labor as it relates to raising a family (if they have children), doing the shopping, preparing meals, and so on.

Herein lies the difficulty. Norms of fairness would suggest that if both husband and wife are employed full time, they should be equally responsible for doing household chores and looking after the children. However, as a result of a 200-year-old traditional patriarchal family structure in the United States (husband/father/breadwinner and wife/mother/homemaker), a significant number of men expect their wives to work full time *and* take care of the house and kids. These husbands will help only if and when they are so inclined. Under these circumstances, marriages can certainly be strained, as wives resent doing more than their share of housework and husbands resent being "forced" to do household chores. One study of 600 divorcing couples found that "neglect of home and children" was second only to "mental cruelty" as the reason cited by women for wanting to end their marriages (Levinger in Hochschild, 1989).

In an interesting example of longitudinal research, Hochschild (1989) studied 52 couples over an 8-year period as they wrestled with household responsibilities and the demands of full-time jobs. He discovered that, on average, women worked 15 more hours each week on home-related chores than men, a figure that translates to an extra month of 24-hour days over the course of a year. In only 20 percent of the families did men and women share work equally. Seventy percent of the husbands did between one-third and one-half as much work as their spouses. The remaining 10 percent did less than one-third, with some husbands refusing to do anything at all in the home. Men also tended to do one job at a time—that is, they either watched the children *or* cooked dinner. Women were much more likely to do both chores simultaneously.

Problems faced by dual-worker couples can be compounded when husbands and wives work different shifts. *Split-shift parenting* means that after working a full day, employed parents return home to put in another long stint as primary caregivers. These individuals "are like single-parents, but with two incomes" (McEnroe, 1991, p. 52). Since they do not spend a substantial amount of time together, couples in this work/household arrangement do not even have the benefit of the mutual support system that most normal dual-worker couples have. As of 1985, one of every five mothers and one of every six fathers with children under 14 worked evenings or nights or had a job with rotating shifts (McEnroe, 1991).

Dual-career couples face a potentially difficult decision (and ensuing problems) when either the husband or wife is faced with the prospect of being relocated to another city. The so-called trailing spouse may resent having to leave a good job, while the husband or wife initiating the career-related move may feel guilty over uprooting the entire family. The problem is likely to be even more acute when the following spouse cannot find a position on a par with the one he or she just left or when he or she has difficulty securing any form of employment. Research in this area has identified work-related relocation as one of life's most stress-producing situations, "similar in its effects to the death of a loved one or to a divorce" (Bureau of National Affairs, 1986, p. 17).

One solution to this problem is a *commuter* or *long-distance marriage,* in which spouses set up separate households and live apart for days, weeks, or even months at a time. Even though both individuals are able to pursue career goals under such an arrangement, a common complaint about long-term separation from family and friends is lack of emotional support and loneliness (Groves & Horm-Wingred, 1991). After couples who may have been in a commuter marriage for months or years start living together anew, they are likely to face readjustment problems. Because they became more independent while apart, once together again, these individuals may have trouble compromising and taking each other's views into consideration when making decisions. Given the realities of companies expanding and relocating to different parts of the country and people being reluctant to leave their positions in a less than booming economy, more and more couples are likely to experience this form of marital arrangement.

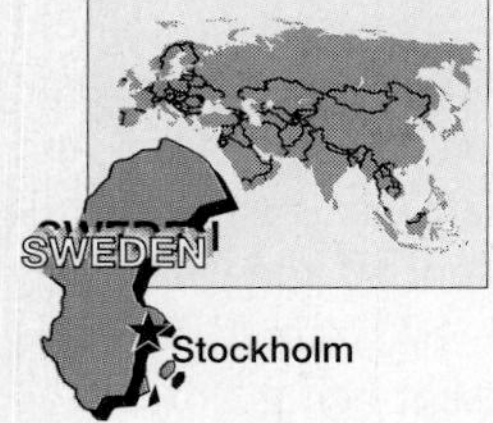

SOCIAL CHANGE IN A WELFARE STATE
Transformation or Destruction of the Swedish Family?

Perhaps no other nation has attempted to provide more benefits for its citizens—especially at the family level—than Sweden. This Scandinavian nation has an extensive government-subsidized day-care system paid for by parents on a sliding scale contingent on their income. In addition, the government provides child-care benefits for children up to age 6 whose parents are employed. Children between the ages of 7 and 12 are cared for in after-school "leisure centers" ("Progress," 1989). In addition to subsidized child care, the state provides free education from kindergarten through the university level (Adams & Winston, 1980; Popenoe, 1988; "Progress," 1989).

With a history of government-assisted family-support programs going back some 60 years, one would expect to find strong, vibrant families and few family-related social problems in Sweden. However, sociologist David Popenoe (1991a, p. 68), who has closely examined Swedish society, argues that the traditional family in that country is a "waning social institution." According to Popenoe (1988, 1991a), society's most basic institution has declined faster in Sweden than in any other Western industrialized country.

Marriage rates decreased sharply beginning in the mid-1960s, registering a 40 percent drop in 8 years. A decline of this magnitude in this duration has not occurred "anywhere else or at any other time" (Trost in Popenoe, 1988, p. 169). By the late 1980s, this unprecedented 25-year period of declining marriage rates began to level off ("Stork's Return," 1991). Not only are Swedish marriage rates lower than those in any other industrialized country, but the average age at matrimony may well be the highest. Although a significant number of people have decided against making legal commitments to each other, they are still living together. Rather than marry, many Swedes have opted for nonmarital cohabitation, with some individuals moving routinely from one relationship to another (*serial monogamy*). A significant consequence of these consensual unions is children born to unmarried parents. More than half of all Swedish babies are born out of wedlock. In the United States, by comparison, 22 percent of infants are born to unwed mothers.

Not only are there fewer marriages in Sweden, but both marriages and consensual unions are dissolving at a rate that may well be higher than that of any other Western nation. As a result, Sweden has both the smallest average household size (approximately 2.2 persons) and the largest percentage of adults living alone (about 20 per-

Is this young Swedish couple married, or are these individuals residing in nonmarital cohabitation? As a result of the high number of people living in consensual unions, over half of all children in Sweden are born out of wedlock.

cent) in the world. As a consequence of extensive economic assistance for the elderly, including pensions, a municipal housing allowance, complete medical coverage, and day-care treatment while residing at home or at medical centers, there is little reliance on family members for support ("Progress," 1989). Consequently, Sweden "has the world's lowest percentage of households with extended families" (Popenoe, 1991a, p. 68).

Financial support by the state has undermined the economic dependence of children on their parents as well as husbands and wives on each other. Inasmuch as all parents (regardless of their marital status) receive economic assistance for child care (health benefits, education, etc.), there is less financial incentive for couples to remain married or for people living together to continue doing so for the sake of the children. In addition, there is no reason for married couples to stay together for tax reasons, as the state abolished joint tax returns in the 1970s. While these fiscal policies may prevent some children from becoming prisoners of unhappy marriages held together by little more than financial obligations, others can too easily end up being raised in single-parent families.

With guaranteed part-time employment and tuition paid for by the government, children are less economically dependent on their parents. As a result, parental influence and control over the nation's youth has eroded. Parental authority was further diminished by a 1979 statute dubbed the "antispanking bill." The new law stated that children "should not be subjected to physical punishment or other humiliating treatment" (Popenoe, 1988, p. 199). Rates of juvenile delinquency in Sweden increased sharply during the most recent period of legislative policies aimed at the family and are now among the highest in Northern Europe. However, unlike a good deal of criminal behavior committed by young people in the United States, juvenile offenses in Sweden are typically minor and seldom violent. While it is difficult to pinpoint the specific causes of youthful transgressions in Sweden, the reduction of control parents have over their children is probably an important contributing factor.

Popenoe (1991a) argues that *familism* as a cultural value has diminished in Sweden. "Familism refers to the belief in a strong sense of family identification and loyalty, mutual assistance among family members, and a concern for the perpetuation of the family unit: the subordination of the interests and personality of individual family members to the interests and welfare of the family group" (p. 68). The well-being of individuals, therefore, and not the well-being of families, is of primary importance in modern Swedish society. It's not that family values are unimportant in Swedish society; rather, these values have taken a back seat to the more recent ideals of social equality and individual rights.

According to Popenoe (1988, 1991a), Swedish family decline is directly related to the domestic policies of the welfare state. More than 50 years of programs designed to promote the happiness and physical well-being of husbands and wives, parents and their children, has seriously undermined traditional family life. From a sociological perspective, the destruction of traditional family relationships and values are latent consequences of government social policies. By meeting so many of their economic needs, the state has unwittingly cut fundamental bonds that hold families together. As a result, family cohesion has been reduced to the emotional attachments members have for each other. And as any family therapist can attest, bonds of love and affection are all too easily broken by the pressures of daily life in modern societies.

Another important factor in the transformation of Swedish families has been the changing role of women. While American feminists were struggling for equality grounded in an ideal of gender *sameness,* Swedish women were striving for economic equality benefits based on gender *differences* (Popenoe, 1988). From this latter perspective, the biological fact that females get pregnant, carry a fetus to term, and give birth means women cannot be treated *exactly* the same as men in society. For example, in Sweden, this struggle brought about 9 months of parental leave at almost full salary and 60 days of paid leave to care for a sick child up to 12 years of age. Swedish women, who earn about 88 percent of what Swedish men do (in the United States, the comparable figure is about 71 percent), have also been quite successful in their campaign for financial parity.

The combination of social benefits directed at mothers and pregnant women, near income equality, and the world's highest percentage of working-age women in the marketplace (77 percent) has resulted in an unprecedented level of economic well-being for Swedish women. However, one could argue that monetary success and economic security have contributed to high rates of divorce in Sweden. With less fear for their financial well-being or that of their children, women are in a much better position to go it alone should their marriages fail.

The large number of dual-income families in Sweden means that children are raised to a great extent by staff members in day-care centers. A 1975 government study revealed that at least half the children in day-care facilities spent 9 or more hours a day away from their parents, while 20 percent of those cared for by state employees were separated from family members for 10 or more hours each working day (Adams & Winston, 1980). No matter how professional and well meaning, care given by employees may lack the "human touch" that can only be given by parents, siblings, and relatives. Although psychologists, social workers, and home helpers are proficient at attending to the specialized needs of children, who is to look out for the "whole person" (Popenoe, 1988, p. 206)?

If David Popenoe and others are correct, the family in Sweden has been the victim rather than the benefactor of

government-sponsored welfare programs. And although the overburdened and increasingly debt-ridden Swedish government has slashed social expenditures by $20 billion and introduced small fees for medical services (Marshall, 1994), the damage to the nation's families will not be quickly undone.

Our brief examination of the state/family relation in Sweden calls for an answer to some fundamental questions: *Can* a comprehensive welfare system help produce healthy, well-adjusted, contributing members of society? To what extent *should* the state provide benefits for its citizens?

By way of comparison, the United States has the least developed family-oriented social and economic benefit programs of any modern industrial state. The United States also has high rates of divorce, separation, desertion, latchkey children, homelessness, and babies born out of wedlock. At the other end of the welfare continuum, Sweden has even higher rates of divorce, rising juvenile crime, 50 percent of its children born to unwed mothers, and a decline in familism as a cultural value. It may well be that too much of a good thing (the welfare state) is just as bad as a paucity of state-sponsored benefits.

Perhaps the major difference between the United States and Sweden regarding family-oriented social policies is rooted in the basic values of these two societies. Although the effectiveness of some welfare programs can be called into question, Swedes realize that their government is attempting to improve the quality of life of the society as a whole. More accurately, the Swedish welfare program is a system whereby people take care of each other. While politicians develop and government bureaucracies administer benefits programs, the tremendous amount of money needed to finance an all-encompassing welfare system comes from income tax rates up to 50 percent for the majority of taxpayers as well as a value-added tax of 23.36 percent on almost all goods and services (American Embassy, Stockholm, 1991).

In the United States, on the other hand, the family has been allowed to fend for itself to a much greater extent. Help in solving everyday problems, it is commonly believed, should come primarily from friends, relatives, and private organizations (churches, for example). Americans have also convinced themselves that rugged individualism has been a major ingredient in the American success story and that this ethos will be severely diminished by a helping hand (especially the government's) that helps too much. What's more, the very notion of a welfare state smacks of socialism, an ideology that politicians in the United States have successfully labeled as un-American, if not downright evil. As a result of these values and policies, the United States will arguably never have the type and scope of family-oriented welfare system found in Sweden.

FAMILY VIOLENCE

Violence in the family is not a new phenomenon. Gelles and Pedrick-Cornell (1990, p. 27) note that "the history of Western society is one in which children have been subjected to unspeakable cruelties." The same could be said for women. In ancient Rome, men had almost unlimited power over the lives of their children and wives. Husbands could chastise, divorce, even kill their wives for adultery, public drunkenness, and attending public games (Gelles & Pedrick-Cornell, 1990). During the Middle Ages, women could be burned alive for talking back to a priest, stealing, prostitution, scolding and nagging, masturbating, and homosexual behavior (Straus & Gelles, 1986).

The often-heard expression "rule of thumb" dates back to the eighteenth century, when English common law stated that a man had the legal right to physically discipline his wife as long as the stick used in the beating was no thicker than his thumb. In male-dominated societies where physical punishment was the prevailing method for maintaining law, order, and respect for authority, it is hardly surprising that men would resort to violence for the purpose of disciplining their wives and children (*Domestic Violence,* 1987). A tragic irony of this situation is that victims of domestic violence are typically socialized to believe they deserve to be abused, having no one to blame for their suffering but themselves. It follows that physical suffering and mental anguish are often compounded by self-hatred.

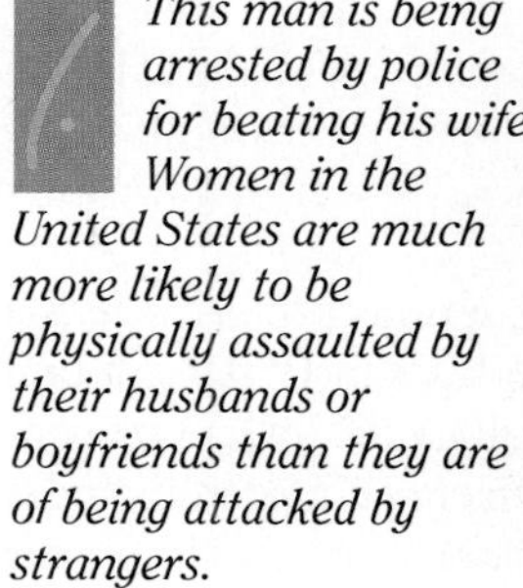

This man is being arrested by police for beating his wife. Women in the United States are much more likely to be physically assaulted by their husbands or boyfriends than they are of being attacked by strangers.

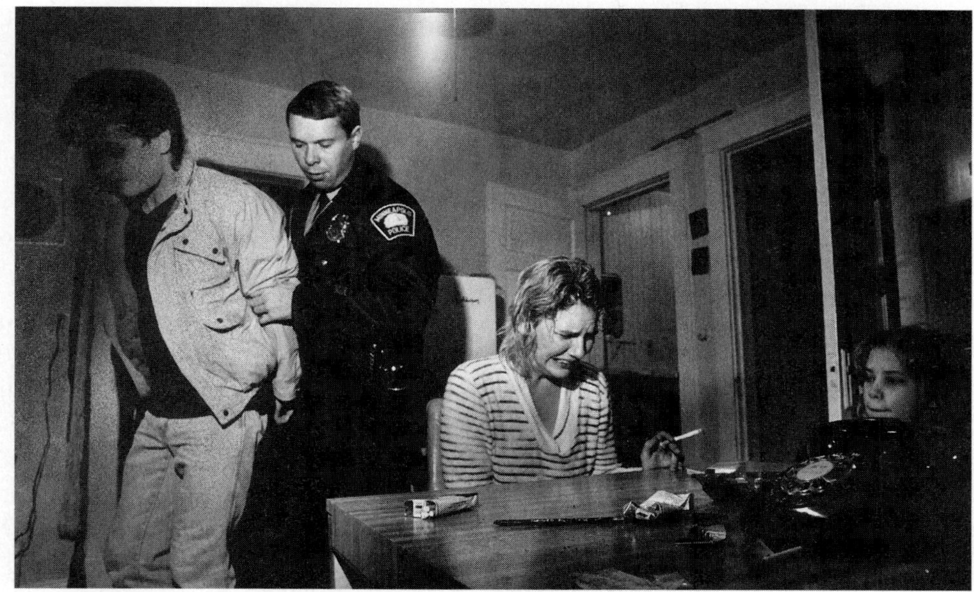

While domestic violence has existed in societies throughout the world for thousands of years, this behavior (at least in the United States) has only been considered a social problem since the early 1960s. It is generally believed that child abuse became an issue of national scope and concern as a consequence of research published in 1962 by C. H. Kempe and his colleagues entitled "The Battered-Child Syndrome." As a result of this article and the interest it triggered, investigative hearings into child abuse were called at both the state and federal levels, and by 1968, legislation requiring the reporting of child abuse to official agencies was passed in all 50 states (*Domestic Violence,* 1987).

Perhaps as an outgrowth of both the crusade against child abuse and the women's movement, wife abuse was identified as a major social problem in the 1970s. And in the 1980s, violence against the elderly became a concern. This discovery of family violence and the ensuing definition of this behavior as problematic is an excellent example of how social problems are created and evolve. No behavior, regardless of how destructive it may be to society, will be addressed until it has been labeled a problem and generated both a groundswell of public concern and the mobilization of resources.

CHILD ABUSE

As a result of media coverage, the general public tends to think of child abuse primarily in terms of violence and physical punishment. Numerous researchers define ***violence*** as "an act carried out with the intention or perceived intention of causing physical pain or injury to another person" (Gelles & Pedrick-Cornell, 1990, p. 22). A distinction is often made between *normal violence* and *abusive violence.* The former consist of the slaps, pushes, shoves, and spankings that people generally consider part of raising children or interacting with one's husband or wife. Abusive violence is significantly more serious and consists of punching, kicking, biting, choking, beating, stabbing, shooting, or attempting to stab or shoot (Gelles & Pedrick-Cornell, 1990).

Because so much domestic violence never comes to the attention of the police, school officials, or child protection services, estimates of the extent of child abuse in the United States vary from several hundred thousand cases to 3 million cases annually (Conte, 1991). As Gelles (1978, p. 582) notes, most of the projections concerning the incidence of child abuse are "educated guesses."

In addition to abusive violence, neglect and sexual abuse are serious problems in the overall mistreatment of children. A review of 546,000 child abuse cases in 19 states found that 59 percent of the cases were neglect, 28 percent were physical abuse, and 13 percent were sexual abuse (U.S. Congress, 1987, in Little, 1989). The neglect of children includes such behaviors as inadequate physical and medical care, emotional cruelty, improper supervision, unlawfully keeping children out of school, exploiting children financially, and exposing children to immoral and/or criminal influence (Meier, 1964).

National surveys designed to determine the rate of child abuse and neglect have yielded contradictory findings. One survey found that the rate of abuse *reported to authorities* had increased from 9.8 cases per 1,000 children in 1980 to 16.3 cases per 1,000 in 1986—a jump of 66 percent in only 6 years. During this time, reports of physical abuse increased by 58 percent, and reports of sexual abuse more than tripled. According to the results of another study, based on parents' self-reports of child abuse, very severe violence against children declined from 36 cases per 1,000 children in 1975 to 19 per 1,000 in 1985—a decrease of 47 percent in 10 years (Straus & Gelles, 1986).

Explanations for the significantly different findings of these studies include:

1. The continued reluctance of parents to report abusive behavior increasingly viewed as deviant and illegal by the larger society
2. Expanded publicity about child abuse
3. Reductions in family violence as a result of prevention and treatment programs
4. The improving economy
5. The changing structure of the American family—a rise in the average age at first marriage as well as the average age for having a first child and a decline in the number of children per family, which translates to fewer unwanted children (Gelles & Conte, 1990; Straus & Gelles, 1986)

PHYSICAL ABUSE

Research indicates that mothers are somewhat more likely to physically abuse their children than are fathers. The explanation usually given for this finding is that mothers spend considerably more time with their offspring. It also appears that boys have a higher rate of being physically abused than girls. Some investigators argue that, being more aggressive, boys commit more punishable offenses than girls and that U.S. society tolerates physical punishment of boys as a method of toughening them up (Gelles, 1978). It is believed or rationalized that this behavior prepares boys for their roles as adult males in an aggressive, competitive, often violent society.

While gender is a significant factor in child abuse, biological relationship is also an important component. Psychologist Martin Daly (in Pringle, 1989) states that the "stepparent versus genetic parent is apparently the single most powerful predictor of abuse risk that anybody has discovered." A child living with a stepparent is 100 times more likely to be murdered than a child living with two biological parents. It appears that biological kinship offers some protection against child abuse.

Although research examining the relationship between age and abuse is somewhat contradictory, younger children appear to be more likely to be abused than their older siblings. A number of studies have found that the period between three months and three years is a particularly dangerous time in a child's life (Fontana, 1973; Galdston, 1965). Younger children cry more and therefore interfere with the activities of adults to a greater degree. Lacking sophisticated cognitive skills, these children are less likely to respond favorably when their parents attempt to talk and reason with them.

In addition to very young children, the following types of children are likely to be physically abused: children born out of wedlock, premature infants, children who are malformed or mentally retarded, twins, children who are unattractive, demanding children, and infants born during a mother's depressive illness (Gelles & Pedrick-Cornell, 1990; Tower, 1989).

SEXUAL ABUSE

In a review of studies of sexual abuse, Peters et al. (1986) found the number of females sexually abused ranged from 6 to 62 percent, whereas the number of boys sexually abused varied from 3 to 31 percent. Some of the tremendous variation in findings within gender categories can be attributed to methodological and definitional differences between studies. There is also a reporting discrepancy.

Although girls are more likely to report sexual abuse (Gelles & Conte, 1990), some research shows that boys may be just as vulnerable to this form of maltreatment (Tower, 1989). For example, attempting to avoid the label of "sissy," abused boys may be reluctant to inform their parents or school officials that they have been sexually molested. Also, parents appear to be less inquisitive when their sons exhibit unusual behavior—in this case, the type of behavior resulting from sexual abuse.

The average age of abused children is between 8 and 12, although actual rates of teenage abuse may be much higher than official statistics indicate. Adolescents who fear stigmatization or restriction of privileges (Tower, 1989) may be reluctant to report incidents of sexual abuse to parents and/or teachers.

Research in this area has focused on two types of abuse: *incest* (family sexual abuse) and *pedophilia* ("love of children"). In single-parent, female-headed households, girls are especially vulnerable to their mothers' boyfriends, and if the mother should marry, to the new husband and his male friends (Tower, 1989). Sexually abused girls are more likely to have mothers who are employed outside the home or who are disabled or ill (Finkelhor & Baron, 1986). Boys are typically victimized outside the family by male offenders whose primary sexual orientation is toward children. These individuals are emotionally fixated in adolescence and were often abused themselves as children.

CONSEQUENCES OF ABUSE

Regarding the impact of abuse on children, psychologist Robert Emery (1989) argues there are no specific behavioral or emotional reactions that characterize young victims. He also notes that "being a victim of violence may not be the principal factor responsible for many of the psychological difficulties that have been found among abused children" (p. 324). Other elements of the child's overall psychological environment can be more damaging than physical abuse.

Emery's argument notwithstanding, a review of the literature yields a number of problems associated with child abuse, including increased aggression, troubled peer relations, lower performance on cognitive tasks, increased rates of delinquency, adult criminal behavior, and violent criminal behavior (Emery, 1989; Widom, 1989). Inasmuch as underreporting is a significant problem in the study of child abuse, available data are incomplete and inconclusive. Usually, only the most extreme cases are discovered by or reported to police and/or child protection services. It follows, therefore, that the effects of child abuse known to health care professionals and researchers may not be typical of the total population of abused children.

There is some evidence that female victims of sexual abuse run an increased risk of becoming prostitutes (Simons & Whitbeck, 1991). To escape an abusive parent or sibling, girls may run away from home and drift into drug abuse and various forms of delinquent and criminal behavior, including prostitution. This latter activity can be a way of making money while living on the streets. Because repeated sexual abuse in the home can lead to emotional distancing during sex, these girls may have already learned this coping device routinely used by prostitutes. In addition, some investigators speculate that early sexual abuse may lead to prostitution by reinforcing a girl's or woman's feelings of herself as a debased sex object (James & Meyerding in Simons & Whitbeck, 1991).

Concerning physical abuse, numerous studies have documented that while parents commonly use physical punishment as a mechanism for controlling the aggressive behavior of children, the latent (unintended) consequence of this punishment is to increase the incidence of aggression. In addition, violent behavior in youths is quite likely to carry over to adulthood, with tragic consequences for the children of abuse victims. Virtually every study on this subject has found that abused children are more likely to be abusive parents than are individuals who were not abused during their formative years (Gelles & Pedrick-Cornell, 1990). After reviewing some of this research, Kaufman and Zigler (1987) concluded that approximately one-third of those physically abused, sexually abused, or neglected during childhood will similarly mistreat their children.

In a test of the violence-breeds-violence or cycle-of-violence hypothesis, Cathy Widom (1989) found that when variables such as age, sex, and race were held constant, neglected and physically abused children had significantly higher arrest rates for violent crimes than a control group of individuals who did not experience abuse and neglect. It is important to keep in mind that abused children do not automatically or inevitably engage in criminal behavior. Rather, these children have a greater probability than nonabused boys and girls of becoming criminally active.

Research by Murray Strauss (1991) supports and extends the cycle-of-violence perspective. He argues that although corporal punishment and the physical abuse of children "may produce conformity in the immediate situation, in the longer run it tends to increase the probability of deviance, including delinquency in adolescence and violent crime inside and outside the family as an adult" (p. 133). According to this *cultural spillover theory,* violence from one sphere of life produces violence in other spheres of interaction.

The sight of a badly beaten two-year-old inevitably raises the question, How could anybody possibly do that to a helpless child? Answers typically focus on the mental health of the perpetrator: That person must be sick. However, Robert Emery (1989, p. 322) states that "if anything conclusive can be said about child abuse research . . . it is that the psychopathological model does not apply to the great majority of abusive parents." In other words, no so-called abusive personality has been identified. A wide variety of factors are related to child abuse, such as having been abused as a child, situational stress, lack of childrearing knowledge, and not understanding children's motives for misbehaving. Parental stress resulting from unemployment, problems at work, serious illness, and death of a loved one also contributes to higher rates of violence for both mothers and fathers (Straus & Kantor, 1987). Just as economic factors affect the overall health of the family, economic strains are linked specifically to increased incidence of child abuse.

Once again, it is evident that the welfare of the nation's children is contingent to some extent on external factors, such as the types of available jobs, pay scales within jobs, political decisions concerning the amount and duration of unemployment compensation, and job training and retraining programs.

BATTERED WOMEN

In June 1994, Americans were shocked and fascinated by the murders of Nicole Brown Simpson and a male friend, allegedly at the hand of O. J. Simpson, Nicole's former husband and the father of her two young children. In the weeks following the murders, details released about the case included accounts of domestic violence: a series of calls by Nicole to 911, the last one as recently as October 1993, and O. J.'s arrest for assault in 1989, to which he pleaded "no contest."

Although the Simpson case is spectacular in terms of the publicity it has attracted, in fact, it is typical in terms of the pattern of domestic violence it shows. The abusive husband was treated leniently by the law enforcement and judicial systems, despite recurring violent behavior, and he even denied that a problem existed, claiming that such incidents are normal between men and women. The battered wife also denied the seriousness of the situation, refusing to press charges against her husband despite making desperate calls for help to the police. According to some accounts, the couple was considering reconciliation.

Domestic violence is the leading cause of death and injury to women in the United States, causing more physical (and probably emotional) harm than the number of motor vehicle accidents, rapes, and muggings combined. As many as 6 *million* women are physically abused by their boyfriends and husbands each year (Brody, 1992). Wife abuse is an especially serious problem. In 1989, more U.S. women were beaten by their husbands than were married (Public Concern Foundation, 1991). There can be little doubt that in households across the country, "the marriage license is a hitting license" (Straus, Gelles, & Steinmetz, 1980).

Like physically abused children, battered women are slapped, punched, kicked, burned, stabbed, and occasionally shot. They often require medical attention and overnight hospitalization. In New York state, 25 to 40 percent of emergency room admissions of women are domestic-violence related (Digirolamo, 1991). One study found that the psychological consequences of continued abuse can be very serious and, in the long run, may be even more detrimental to a woman's well-being than the physical punishment she suffers. Women who have been abused have higher levels of headaches, nervousness, and depression and lower self-esteem (Gelles & Straus, 1988). A study in Hartford, Connecticut, discovered that approximately 28 percent of physically abused women attempted suicide at one time, and about 15 percent were eventually committed to state mental institutions. Thirty-four percent of these women became addicted to alcohol and other drugs (in *Domestic Violence,* 1987).

Another aspect of violence against women, albeit one that is frequently overlooked, is forced marital sex. A survey of 304 abused women in 10 Minnesota shelters for battered women revealed that 36 percent of the women had been raped by their husbands or cohabitating partners (Spector in Finkelhor & Yllo, 1982). In some instances, forced marital sex is another aspect of general physical abuse that women endure; in other relationships, forced sex is a product of specific sexual conflicts typically regarding the frequency and type of sexual activity.

CAUSES OF WIFE ABUSE

The number of children in a family seems to be related to wife abuse. Straus and his colleagues (1980) found that childless couples had low rates of violence, and in couples with six or more children, wife abuse was nonexistent. The researchers suggested that as the number of children increases (to a point), so, too, does the stress on the parents. Having more children also reduces the amount of privacy a couple has as well as the opportunities and time they have to communicate. Perhaps in large families (six or more children), the stress is alleviated significantly as the older children take an especially active role in caring for their younger siblings. Length of marriage is also a factor in wife abuse. A study in Kentucky found that women married from one to three years were especially at risk of being physically abused. After the initial year of marriage (or "extended honeymoon"), many young couples become quite belligerent (*Domestic Violence,* 1987).

Many studies have found that the majority of husbands who beat their wives use and abuse alcohol and other drugs. This association has given rise to the "demon rum" explanation of domestic violence (Gelles & Pedrick-Cornell, 1990). According to this perspective, alcohol and drugs serve as disinhibitors. This theory assumes that men are naturally violent and socialized to control their impulses. However, under the influence of alcohol or drugs, their ability to keep these tendencies in check is weakened.

As appealing as this common-sense explanation may be, there is little evidence to support a cause-and-effect relationship between taking drugs and abusing one's wife. Rather, men who want to physically harm their wives use alcohol and drugs as an excuse. They use these drugs to rationalize their violent behavior to themselves and to others. "It wasn't me beating my wife, it was the drugs." "I was drunk and didn't know what I was doing." As Gelles and Pedrick-Cornell (1990, p. 18) point out, "Violent spouses and parents learn that, if they do not want to be held responsible for their violence, they should drink before they hit or at least say they were drunk." Abusers use the "demon rum" explanation to shift the blame from their own willful behavior to a substance many people believe is *the* cause of domestic violence.

Data from numerous studies have documented that spousal abuse, like other forms of family violence, is more prevalent in the lower classes. Experts in this field tend to agree that the employment status of men is an important causal factor in this relationship. As Gelles and Pedrick-Cornell (1990, p. 75) note, "Being unemployed is devastating to men in our society." A significant component of the traditional role of being a man (specifically, a husband and father) is to be able to provide for one's family. This is especially important in a status-conscious, consumer-oriented society like ours, where self-worth can be linked to material wealth and the esteem (or lack thereof) derived from one's occupation and socioeconomic status.

However, wife abuse is not limited to lower-class men. Because of their economic and social standing, middle- and upper-class husbands have more success in keeping police and other authorities at a distance, thus keeping their cases from becoming official statistics. In addition, the wives of these men may be less likely to report incidents of abuse when they occur. A Denver study found that, in spite of being abused, women wanted to protect their husbands' positions or their acquired social status, were too embarrassed by the event to report it, or believed the police could do little if anything to rectify the situation (*Domestic Violence,* 1987).

WHY DO WOMEN STAY IN ABUSIVE RELATIONSHIPS?

The reluctance if not downright refusal on the part of many women (regardless of their socioeconomic standing) to report incidents of physical abuse to authorities and their inclination to stay in abusive relationships lead many people to believe that women who are abused provoke their husbands to violence and/or must enjoy being abused (Gelles & Pedrick-Cornell, 1990). This blame-the-victim attitude holds women responsible, at least in part, for their suffering.

Researchers have explored this aspect of domestic violence and discovered a number of reasons why women stay in abusive relationships (Buel in Brody, 1992; Gelles, 1976; Strube & Barbour 1983; Truninger, 1971):

1. Many nonworking married women are economically dependent on their husbands and lack the education, skills, or confidence to find secure employment. Even if some employment were available, money earned at low-paying work would be insufficient to pay for babysitting or day care.
2. The more committed a woman is to her boyfriend or husband and the relationship, the more likely she is to tolerate abuse.
3. Women often cling to the belief that abusive partners will change.
4. Women fear they will have no place to go: The overwhelming number of shelters for battered women will not accept children.
5. Many women feel that because their husbands control family finances and can hire good lawyers, they (the women) will be on the short end of an eventual divorce settlement and lose custody of their children.
6. Leaving an abusive relationship is no guarantee that the violence will end; to the contrary, it often triggers more serious, sometimes fatal abuse. Women have been stalked by their husbands and beaten in or near shelters. However, most battered women find these facilities to be much-needed safe havens where they are protected, at least temporarily, from their abusive partners. Shelters provide support groups and other services to battered women in addition to letting them know that they are not alone in their misery or their struggle to lead lives free from abuse (Strong & DeVault, 1992).

Perhaps the only thing worse than enduring sexual and/or physical abuse is experiencing these degrading acts in an environment one does not understand, often totally cut off from the support of family and friends. Sociologist Eileen Moran (in Hays, 1993) explains how some Asian women, newly arrived in the United States, find themselves trapped in abusive relationships—trapped by a lack of understanding of how institutions in this country function and constrained by the values and practices of their native cultures. These women are often fearful of authorities in general or may not believe they have a legitimate right to ask for help. Also, a number of Asian women speak little if any English, and those who do make contact with shelters may have problems adjusting to the food or may encounter other cultural differences that are overwhelming during this time of crisis. Some of these women are abused not only by their husbands but by the men's parents, as well (Moran in Hays, 1993). To make her predicament even more difficult, a South Asian woman is apt to believe that publicly complaining about her situation will shame and dishonor the family name, something that would be even more unbearable than the abuse she is suffering.

SOCIETAL RESPONSES TO WIFE ABUSE

If, as we have seen, so many women find themselves trapped in abusive relationships, what can be done to reduce their pain and misery? For many people, there is only one viable solution: The state, in the form of the criminal justice system, must intervene on behalf of the woman. An experiment in Minneapolis concluded that when police arrested and confined an abusive husband in jail for one night, there was only a one in ten chance he would be arrested for the same offense at a future date. In those instances where husbands were told by officers to temporarily leave the house or the police acted to mediate the dispute between spouses, slightly fewer than one in five husbands repeated their violence (Sherman, 1985). Research in California also found that arresting abusive males substantially reduced the number of new assaults on women (Berk & Newton, 1985).

As a result of these studies and others, laws in 15 states and Washington, D.C., now require arrests in all cases of domestic assault and battery. However, later research in Milwaukee found that whereas employed men arrested for spousal assault had a 16 percent lower rate of abuse toward their wives in the following year, unemployed men arrested for the same crime were 44 percent *more* likely to assault their wives in the year after being released from jail. Criminologist Lawrence Sherman notes that "mandatory arrest laws in criminal violence may cause more violence against women in the long run" (in Coleman, 1991).

Traditionally in U.S. society, the courts have been less than sympathetic to the plight of battered women, either choosing to steer clear of domestic disputes or siding outright with husbands accused of assaulting their wives. One can understand why a district attorney would be reluctant to bring a wife abuse case in a courtroom with a judge who stated:

> Even if the woman shows up in my court with visible injuries I don't really have any way of knowing who's responsible or who I should kick out of the house. Yes, he may have beaten her, but nagging and a sharp tongue can be just as bad. Maybe she used her sharp tongue so often that she provoked him to hit her. (in *Domestic Violence,* 1987, p. 97)

Fortunately, the last 20 to 25 years have seen a change of attitudes in many judges and other criminal justice officials. Another judge told the accused, "If you think the courts can't punish you for assaulting your wife you are sadly mistaken."

Mandatory arrest often leads to court-ordered counseling of abusive men. Some 200 social agencies across the United States now provide male-led group treatment (Gottlieb, 1993), and abusive men are also being helped by marriage and family therapists in private practice. One component of treatment is to teach wife abusers how to control their anger. However, research has shown that anger control will not reduce abusive behavior in at least one subset of violent men. Psychologist Neil Jacobson (in Schrof, 1994) has found that one in five wife batterers is so in control of his emotions that during the beatings, his heart rate drops to a very composed 35 to 40 beats a minute. Jacobson notes, "This group of batterers is no more likely to be helped by therapists than are serial killers" (p. 68).

In an attempt to deal with the majority of wife abusers, who can be helped by some form of intervention, sociologist and family therapist Lewis Yablonsky (1994) offers a unique strategy: Rather than remove the abused woman from the home (which is what most current programs do), Yablonsky would have male batterers removed and placed in shelters.

> First offenders who assault their spouses would be placed, by court order, in the live-in facility for a six-month period. They would work their usual job during the day, and attend mandatory group therapy sessions to deal with their deviant behavior every evening and weekends. Their paychecks would, by court order, go to their wife and children. In the first three months of their six-month sentence they would not be allowed to have any contact with their family. In the last three months, their wives, if interested in reconciliation, would attend a weekly session with their husbands. If the husband broke any rules of the program, he would be subject to a six-month to one-year prison sentence. (p. B6)

Rather than further punish the wife (and often the abused children, as well) by removing her from the home and further disrupting her life, this program has the advantage of taking the offending husband away from his victims. But because he is able to keep his job, the husband is both permitted and directed to meet his financial obligations to his family. More importantly, being placed in a shelter with other abusive husbands, having his freedom restricted, and being required to attend therapy sessions forces the abusive husband to deal with his behavior and its consequences for him and his family.

BATTERED MEN

In a male-dominated, macho society that has produced tough-guy folk heroes like John Wayne and Sylvester Stallone and a long list of strong "love-'em-and-leave-'em" movie stars, it may be difficult to understand and accept the findings of some researchers that men have slightly higher rates of being physically abused than women (Saunders, 1986; Straus & Gelles, 1986; Straus et al., 1980). On the other hand, sociologist Mildred Daley Pagelow (1994) argues that data from public agencies such as the Department of Justice indicate that 95 percent of victims of domestic violence are females. But regardless of the rates of husband and wife victimization, the circumstances surrounding violent incidents of this nature and the consequences of these acts are very different.

Because men are, on average, bigger, stronger, and more aggressive than women, they are less likely to be seriously injured in incidents of domestic violence. Also, men can use their physical advantages to escape household confrontations before they are more seriously hurt. Even though abused men as a whole do not suffer as much physically as abused women, this aspect of family violence is quite serious.

In an attempt to refute what they believe is the exaggerated "pseudo-issue of the 'battered husband syndrome'" (Pagelow, 1994), critics claim that much of the violence on the part of wives against husbands is retaliatory in nature—that is, women (often fearful for their lives) eventually defend themselves after prolonged abuse at the hands of their mates. In 1993, the entire United States and much of the world followed the story of Lorena Bobbitt, the woman who cut off her husband's penis (and was later acquitted of "malicious wounding"), claiming that he had repeatedly physically and sexually abused her. Women trapped in abusive relationships who strike out against their husbands complete the cycle of domestic violence, often with tragic results (as in the Bobbitt case) for all concerned.

Although men generally deliver the last and most damaging blow in domestic confrontations (Eshleman, 1994), this is not always the case. Between 800 and 1,000 abusive husbands are killed by their wives each year (Baum, 1991). Approximately two-thirds of these women will be convicted of murder and spend considerable time (for some, life sentences) in prison. Twenty-five percent of the women tried for killing their partners are acquitted as a result of a legal strategy that has been called the **battered wife syndrome.** This defense is based on the months or typically years of often brutal and sadistic physical abuse a woman has suffered at the hands of her boyfriend or husband. The killing is viewed as an act of self-defense. In 1991, amidst a good deal of controversy, the governors of three states pardoned a number of women who were imprisoned for assaulting or killing their abusive partners.

One of the reasons why thousands of women will be convicted for retaliatory acts of violence is that in 37 states, judges are not required to hear evidence of spousal abuse during the women's trials. From a conflict perspective, this is the final act of violence against women in a male-dominated society.

ABUSE OF THE ELDERLY

Few among us look forward to growing old, if for no other reason than the onset of more aches and pains, as well as the increased risk of contracting life-threatening diseases. Also, advanced age is held in something less than high esteem in youth-oriented nations like the United States. One need only watch a few television programs and commercials or flip through the pages of popular magazines to see that almost every aspect of contemporary society (work, recreation, social relations) is geared toward young and middle-aged people. However, for many individuals, becoming a senior citizen means more than being out of step with the main currents of American society; the final stage of life turns into a period of unnecessary suffering and abuse. Because so many people from this segment of the population (especially those 80 years of age and older) are physically and mentally impaired, they are often defenseless targets of abuse.

As is the case with other forms of domestic violence, accurate data regarding the incidence and distribution of abuse in the elderly population are lacking. Annual estimates of elder abuse range from 140,000 (Shapiro, 1992) to 2.5 million cases per year (Pedrick-Cornell & Gelles, 1982). This discrepancy can be explained in part by different reporting methods. The low estimate corresponds to the number of cases reported to authorities; asking elderly people if they have been abused in some manner during the previous 12 months generates more reports of abuse.

Another important factor is the definition of abuse used by researchers. Some investigators limit elder abuse to physical harm, while other students of this problem include a number of categories of mistreatment. Richard Douglass (1983) considers four types of abuse against the elderly:

1. *Passive neglect* occurs when an aged, dependent person is denied essential food, clothing, and medical attention because of the ineptitude or inability of his or her caregiver.
2. *Active neglect* occurs when elderly dependent people are intentionally denied the necessities of life.
3. *Emotional abuse* occurs when the elderly are called names, threatened, insulted, frightened, or intimidated.
4. *Physical abuse* occurs when the aged are harmed physically (including being physically restrained) or sexually molested. Giving people excessive doses of medication to keep them manageable or asleep would be included in this category.

Other researchers include *financial exploitation* and *violation of rights* as types of abuse against people who are elderly (Lau & Kosberg, 1979). For example, the elderly are sometimes forced out of their residences and into nursing homes.

Research has found that elderly Americans and Canadians are abused by family and nonfamily members in a variety of circumstances. Very old women are especially at risk, often abused by their middle-aged daughters. Mentally and physically impaired seniors are more likely to be victimized than aged people who are in better health (Pedrick-Cornell & Gelles, 1982). For some elderly women, physical abuse is a continuation of the battering at the hands of their husbands that has occurred for much if not most of their married lives. This situation can become even more severe when husbands suffer from Alzheimer's disease or other age-related neurological illnesses (Brady, 1991).

Some cases of violence against the elderly may be delayed retaliation for child abuse. A 40-year-old woman physically abused her complaining, bedridden father, whom she said repeatedly raped her when she was a child (Brady, 1991). Steinmetz (in *Domestic Violence,* 1987) discovered that 1 out of 2 individuals mistreated as children physically abused their elderly parents, in contrast to only 1 of 400 individuals not abused as children. In these situations, who is the victim and who is the offender?

People who are aged are also sometimes swindled by relatives. Middle-aged children and other relatives may take money from older people to support expensive drug habits (Shapiro, 1992). Like individuals of any age, the elderly may be reluctant to notify authorities when they have been conned for fear of looking foolish. In addition, they may be embarrassed to tell police that the culprits are their own children. Also, elderly victims may be psychologically and physically dependent on the individuals who took money from them.

Modern medicine and the changing demographic profiles of industrial states explain in large measure how elder abuse became a problem and why this problem will almost inevitably become worse in the future. In 1900, the average American could expect to live to age 47; life expectancy today is approximately 75. Unable to find and/or afford quality medical care in nursing homes, many middle-aged people will have to care for aged parents in their homes. This situation can certainly produce stress on the part of caregivers, a condition highly correlated with elder abuse. Susan Steinmetz (in *Domestic Violence,* 1987, p. 133), one of the foremost experts on domestic violence, stated, "The bottom line is that if you increase the stress on family members without adding supports to help them cope with it, you increase the likelihood of violence because a person and a family can only handle so much."

Short of a comprehensive health plan providing some level of support for a rapidly aging population, millions of senior citizens in the United States will find the latter stage of life to be anything but the "golden years." Declining mental and physical health will likely be accompanied by all manner of abuse. However, as important as physical resources may be in dealing with this problem, a major shift in attitudes toward the elderly must also occur. We must learn to treat these individuals with the dignity and respect they deserve.

A CROSS-CULTURAL PERSPECTIVE

In their review of the available data, family abuse researchers Gelles and Pedrick-Cornell (1990, pp. 29–30) report, "Family violence is most common in Western, industrialized, developed nations such as Great Britain, Germany, and France." A major exception to this finding is Scandinavia. The widespread use of contraceptives, free abortions, and good day-care systems partially explains the low rates of child abuse in these nations. In developing countries, family violence seems to be tied to the disorganization that occurs as a result of modernization (Gelles & Pedrick-Cornell, 1990). Rural-to-urban migration, separation from the extended family, job searches, and changing occupations can produce stress and confusion that are manifested in family violence.

In addition to statistics gathered by police and social welfare agencies in modern and developing nations, research by anthropologists has revealed that family violence occurs in smaller and more traditional societies, as well. To better understand the scope and various manifestations of this problem, David Levinson (1989) examined the available literature on family violence in 90 peasant groups representative of every cultural region in the world. He discovered that one or more forms of this behavior existed in all but 15 of the societies sampled.

Examples of infant/child/adolescent–directed violence include infanticide, child slavery, child prostitution, mutilation for begging (i.e., mutilating children in the hope of eliciting sympathy and donations from strangers), forced homosexual relations, painful initiation rights (scarification, whipping, bloodletting, forced vomiting), and the gang rape of girls. As a result of numerous social, cultural, and economic factors, men are valued more highly than women in most societies; the tragic consequences of such favoritism are often fatal to females beginning at a very early age.

In India, a young mother makes a poisonous mixture of herbs and castor oil and forces it down her newborn daughter's throat. The baby bleeds from the nose and dies soon afterward (Dahlburg, 1994). When asked why she would do such a thing, the woman replied, "Instead of her suffering the way I do, I thought it better to get rid of her" (p. A1). However, most of the deaths of Indian baby girls by their mothers are not gender-related mercy killings. Instead, these killings occur because women are considered financial liabilities. Not only are females considered less economically productive than males; their dowry—the money and property a girl's parents must bring to her husband's household at marriage—can equal up to 15 years of a family's income. One government official noted, "To the father of a child, a girl is a net outflow" (in Dahlburg, 1994). Although the number of female infants killed each year in India is unknown, one study found that during a recent 3-year period, 500 newborn females were killed in 16 villages (in Dahlburg, 1994).

At the other end of the life spectrum, the elderly are usually treated with respect and cared for by family members in small peasant societies. Levinson (1989) speculates that older individuals are treated well in these more traditional groups because they are sources of vital information valued by younger people. Nevertheless, there are exceptions to this general finding. In 12 percent of the societies examined, elderly people must give up their property; in 21 percent, some older individuals are not permitted to live with the main social group; and in another 21 percent of these communities, the aged are sometimes killed.

The most disturbing finding of this research is that adult women are most likely to be victims of family violence and adult men are most likely to be the perpetrators of this behavior. It is hardly surprising, therefore, that more than any other family members, these women are apt to suffer "severe and debilitating injuries" (Levinson, 1989, p. 81). In some of these groups, women are subject to being beaten, raped, killed, or forced to commit suicide by their husbands and/or other members of society. From the point of view of those who inflict punishment on adult females, women should be and deserve to be beaten for one or more of the following reasons:

1. Punishment for adultery or because the husband suspects that his wife has not remained faithful to him.
2. Punishment for cause—that is, a husband may beat his wife as a result of her failure to perform some specific duties or treat him with proper respect.
3. Punishment at will—meaning that a husband may beat his wife for any reason or no reason at all. The essence of this form of violent discipline is contained in an old Serbian saying: "Beat a woman and a horse every three days" (Levinson, 1989, p. 9).

No doubt these same justifications for battering women are used by men in modern industrial societies, as well. Levinson discovered that wife beating is most likely to occur in those societies "in which husbands have the economic and ultimate decision making power in the household" (1989, p. 82) as well as those in which adults routinely resolve their differences by resorting to violence. Conversely, societies with low levels of this form of violence (or none at all) are characterized by economic equality between the sexes, equal access to divorce for both men and women, and outside intervention in domestic disputes (Bernard in Levinson, 1989).

DIVORCE

In modern societies, divorce is usually thought of as an unfortunate if not tragic occurrence for all concerned. The once-strong emotional bond between husband and wife disintegrates and is formally cut by the state, with each former partner now faced with the challenge of starting a new life. Lacking the emotional maturity and sophistication of adults to deal with the family breakup, children (especially young children) are thrust into a new way of life (perhaps with parents who are now outwardly hostile to each other) for which they are hardly prepared. The potential negative consequences of marital dissolution on children are the primary reasons why societies are concerned about increasing divorce rates (Eshleman, 1994). In accord with this popular sentiment, social scientists have long maintained that the two-parent family structure is necessary for "normal child development" (Demo & Acock, 1988, p. 619).

Although divorce is permitted in most societies (including primitive societies, where rates are often very high), the incidence of marital dissolution differs from one country

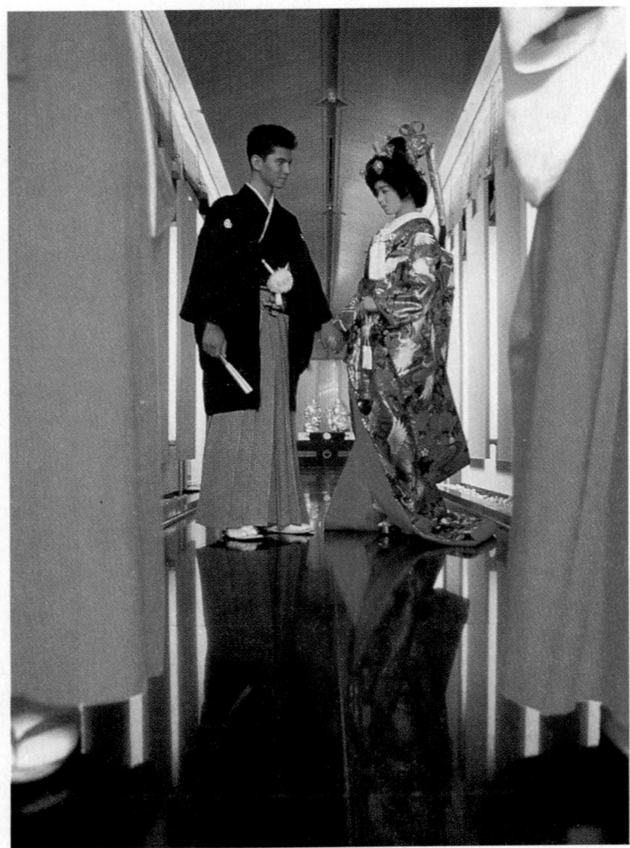

This young Japanese couple, attired in traditional outfits for ceremonial purposes, are about to be married. For a number of social, cultural, and economic reasons, the Japanese are less likely to divorce than people in other modern, capitalist societies.

TABLE 10.2 Divorce Rates in Selected Countries: 1990

Country	Divorce Rate*
Chile	0.46
Italy	0.48
Mexico	0.63
Iran	0.69
Syria	0.69
Portugal	0.93
Poland	1.11
Japan	1.27
Israel	1.29
France	1.87
Austria	2.11
Sweden	2.26
Norway	2.40
Australia	2.49
Hungary	2.70
Cuba	3.51
Ukraine	3.71
Puerto Rico	3.80
United States	4.70
Maldives	7.93

SOURCE: *Demographic Yearbook 1991,* Statistical Division, Department for Economic and Social Information and Policy Analysis, United Nations, New York, pp. 508–510.

*Divorce rates are the number of final divorce decrees granted under civic law per 1,000 midyear population.

to another (Goode, 1964). Evidence has documented (see Table 10.2) that economic development and the overall modernization process are accompanied by increasing divorce rates (Nimkoff, 1965); rates of marital dissolution are especially high in the advanced stages of socioeconomic development (Trent & South, 1989).

One exception to this trend is Japan, where the divorce rate in 1990 was approximately 25 percent of that of the United States, even after a decade-long increase. Japanese couples stay married longer than people in most economically advanced nations for a number of reasons:

1. In a group-oriented society that strongly discourages nonconforming behavior, many people think it is disgraceful for a woman to divorce, a belief that is fostered by the mass media.
2. Japanese people routinely poke fun at single women over the age of 25, making it that much more difficult for divorced women (usually older than 25) to remarry.

TABLE 10.3 Marriages and Divorces in the United States: 1960–1992

Year	Marriages		Divorces and Annulments	
	Number[1]	Rate[2]	Number[1]	Rate[2]
1960	1,523	8.5	393	2.2
1965	1,800	9.3	479	2.5
1970	2,159	10.6	708	3.5
1975	2,153	10.0	1,036	4.8
1980	2,390	10.6	1,189	5.2
1985	2,413	10.1	1,190	5.0
1990	2,448	9.8	1,175	4.7
1992	2,362	9.2	1,215	4.7

SOURCE: Department of Health and Human Services, National Center for Health Statistics.

[1] x 1,000.
[2] Per 1,000 population.

3. Because of wage discrimination against women in general and older women in particular, it is difficult for divorced women to earn an adequate living.

Divorce rates in the United States have increased significantly as the country has progressed economically in the post–World War II era, having more than doubled between 1960 and 1992 (see Table 10.3). According to one estimate, at current rates, as many as 6 out of 10 marriages will end in separation or divorce (Martin & Bumpass, 1989). Again, economic development and the overall modernization process are strongly associated with increasing rates of divorce (Cherlin, 1990; Goode, 1964; Trent & South, 1989).

A steady rise in the number of working women has affected divorce rates in a number of ways. The changing status of women (especially economic) means that they are no longer as financially dependent on men as they have been in the past and have the economic resources to leave bad marriages. (However, Benokraitis [1993] makes the point that although Sweden has a greater percentage of women in the workforce than does the United States, it has a lower divorce rate.) The self-esteem gained from a successful job or career gives many women the confidence to extricate themselves from less than satisfying relationships. Also, the workplace affords women the opportunity to meet men and form attachments that may undermine the marital bond.

Divorce has been made easier by the removal of both formal and informal sanctions against it. Given the decline in the power and influence of religion, divorce is no longer associated with sin, evil, and personality maladjustment. As Bellah et al. (1985, p. 90) note, "Divorce as a solution to an unhappy marriage, even a marriage with young children, is far more acceptable today than ever before." With the acceptance of divorce as a fact of modern life, individuals contemplating marital dissolution are less likely to be pressured by their friends to stay married. A 1962 survey of young adult American women found that 51 percent agreed with the statement that "divorce is usually the best solution when a couple can't seem to work out their marriage problems" (in Cherlin, 1990). When the same women were interviewed in 1977, 80 percent agreed with the statement. The unprecedented number of divorces in the post–World War II period means that divorce "feeds upon itself" to a large extent (Popenoe, 1991b, p. 51). As fewer people and sanctions oppose marital dissolutions and more potential mates become available (other divorced individuals), divorce has become increasingly normal.

Beginning in approximately 1960, a number of states adopted no-fault divorce laws. As a result, divorces could be obtained on grounds of irreconcilable differences or irretrievable breakdown. It was no longer necessary to demonstrate that one's spouse was at fault for a marriage to be terminated. Some states have streamlined their divorce laws to the extent that no-fault is the only grounds for dissolving a marriage (Rice, 1990). To reduce the high rate of divorce in the United States, it has been argued that the courts should return to the pre-no-fault era. It has also been suggested that parents with children under age 16 not be permitted to divorce.

Commitment to the institution of marriage has also been weakened in modern societies that emphasize individual happiness, self-fulfillment, and personal growth. Andrew Cherlin (1990, p. 152) concludes, "With an increase in affluence, the emphasis shifts from survival to satisfaction, from being to having; an ideology stressing personal fulfillment becomes dominant." In other words, when our basic physiological needs of food, clothing, and shelter have been satisfied, we begin to be preoccupied with becoming fulfilled and self-actualized. The quest for individual happiness is now the paramount goal in life for millions of people. If a union with one's spouse is not the vehicle by which this happiness can be obtained, the marriage may be terminated. And while people may continue to wed with the romantic notion of being together "till death do you part," the reality of the situation is that the marriage can be dissolved if either partner does not achieve his or her desired level of happiness and fulfillment.

A comparison of first-marriage cohorts in the United States between 1965 and 1974 and 1974 and 1984 revealed that the number of couples cohabitating before they were legally joined increased from 11 percent to 44 percent. Couples who live together before marrying have a greater likelihood of divorcing than individuals who do not live together prior to marriage. Similar results were found in Canada and Sweden (Thompson & Collela, 1992).

DEMOGRAPHIC FACTORS

The probability of marital breakup is not randomly distributed throughout society; rather, it is correlated with a number of demographic factors (Benokraitis, 1993; Eshleman, 1994; Glenn & Supancic, 1984; Kammeyer, 1987).

AGE

Couples who marry prior to age 18 have an especially high rate of divorce, often due to emotional immaturity. Young people may also be pressured into divorce by parents and relatives who opposed the marriage. Beyond the ages of 26 for men and 23 for women, age at marriage has little association with divorce.

SOCIOECONOMIC CLASS

Although divorce has been increasing in every stratum of society, there is an inverse relationship between socioeconomic class and marital dissolution in the United States: The lower the income, the higher the divorce rate. One possible explanation for this relationship is that people in the middle and upper classes have more years of formal education than individuals in the lower classes and may be more inclined to pursue careers. Both of these factors are associated with delaying marriage beyond the early to late twenties. People at the bottom of the socioeconomic ladder tend to marry much earlier, which in itself places stress on the marriage. Then they often have problems meeting their financial obligations, which in turn can become a significant source of tension between husbands and wives. Eshleman (1994) comments that even though working-class couples are able to meet day-to-day living expenses, they may become frustrated by their inability to afford new cars, clothes, and other items desired in a consumer-oriented society. One solution to this problem is to divorce and go it alone; another is to end the marriage and find a more economically successful partner.

RACE

Since 1960, Blacks have had a divorce rate approximately twice as high as that of Whites, with racial differences in marital dissolution existing at all income, educational, and occupational levels. These findings have been explained in part by higher rates of Black teenage and premarital pregnancies. Women whose first birth is out of wedlock are more likely to separate than those whose initial birth is after marriage. Another explanation points to the disproportionate number of African Americans who are poor. As noted earlier, the frustration and tension resulting from a chronic shortage of money places a tremendous strain on individuals and often leads to divorce.

RELIGIOUS AFFILIATION AND ATTENDANCE

Marital dissolution is slightly higher for Protestants than for Catholics; Jews have a lower divorce rate than either of the others. The divorce rate for White males who never attend religious services is three times higher than that for those who go to services at least twice a month. A similar although not as significant difference was found for White female religious service attenders and nonattenders.

ECONOMIC CONSEQUENCES

One need not be a social scientist to realize that divorce can result in both short- and long-term psychological, social, and economic suffering for all concerned. These hardships, coupled with the fact that divorce is widespread in modern societies, make this a social problem of major proportions.

Marital dissolution affects every member of the family, but the impact of divorce is not experienced uniformly. As Lenore Weitzman (1990, p. 179) notes, "Divorce has radically different economic consequences for men and women." For example, when income is compared to needs (living expenses), divorced men on average experience an *increase* in their standard of living, while divorced women (and their children) experience a 73 percent *decrease*.

Inasmuch as only one in seven separated or divorced women receives alimony payments, women find themselves in the difficult position of having to provide for themselves and their children on less than 50 percent of predivorce combined family income. Of the women awarded child support, two out of four receive less than they are entitled to, and one out of two (approximately 1.2 million women nationwide) collect nothing at all ("Almost 5 Million Women," 1991). In 1989, the average mother received $2,995 for child support for one or more children; this is not a significant amount of money, considering expenses for food, clothing, school, health care, transportation, and recreation. Typically, alimony and other forms of supplementary income cover only half the cost raising a child (Weitzman, 1990).

Weitzman argues that the economic consequences of divorce have contributed to the sharp rise in female poverty in the United States. Even with full-time employment, one out of three single women with children cannot live above the poverty level. If such conditions persist, a two-tier society may develop in the not too distant future. The first tier will be comprised primarily of men (and the women and children who live with them), and the second tier will be made up of the former wives of these men and their children (Weitzman, 1990).

EFFECTS ON CHILDREN

Over 1 million divorces affecting children occur each year, a threefold increase since 1960. Half of all American children will see their parents divorce, and one out of ten will experience three marital breakups (Sweet, 1990). According to projections, 38 percent of White children and 75 percent of Black children born to married parents will see their parents divorce before they turn 16.

Tens of thousands of other children will reside in intact families characterized by a high degree of parental conflict (Grych & Fincham, 1990). While the conventional wisdom resulting from this observation would suggest that children will be negatively affected by the breakup of the family, social scientists are interested in determining what aspects of a child's personality and behavior will be influenced by a divorce and what features of the entire parental conflict, divorce, and postdivorce family structure are responsible for these changes. There are three primary explanations of the negative consequences divorce has on children's lives (Amato & Keith, 1991).

According to the *parental absence* perspective, children of divorced parents have problems because they spend some portion of their childhood with one parent instead of two. They have less parental attention, help, and supervision. A lack of parental support can result in poor academic performance and low self-esteem as well as antisocial behavior. Lack of parental role models can produce improper and/or inadequate learning of skills needed for success in the outside world.

The *economic disadvantage* explanation focuses on the economic liabilities of being raised in a single-income family. A paucity of economic resources may threaten a child's nutrition and health as well as deprive him or her of educational toys, books, private lessons, computers, trips, and other goods and services that are linked to academic and later occupational success.

Those holding a *family conflict* view feel that parental tension and conflict before and during the separation cause most of the problems children experience. According to this explanation, "Children of divorce exhibit problems not because of the change in family structure, but because of the accompanying conflict" (Amato & Keith, 1991, p. 27). In their review of research conducted on the relationships among divorce, family composition, and children's well-being, Demo and Acock (1988) found that adolescents are not so much affected by family structure (single-parent or intact family) as they are by parental discord. Younger children, however, suffer "temporary deleterious effects when their parents divorce" (p. 639).

In an effort to determine which of these perspectives has the most explanatory power, sociologists Paul Amato and Bruce Keith (1991) examined 92 studies of parental divorce and child well-being based on data from over 13,000 children. To begin, they determined that children from divorced families had a lower level of well-being than did children from continuously intact families. However, the size of the overall negative effect on children was weak rather than strong. Whereas the parental absence and economic disadvantage explanations were only modestly supported by the data, the family conflict perspective was strongly supported. The authors concluded that because no one explanation accounted for the full range of findings from these studies, all three perspectives are needed for a complete understanding of how divorce affects children.

The negative consequences of witnessing their parents' divorce may be a disruptive force in the lives of children long after the marital dissolution. Psychologist Judith Wallerstein (1992) kept track of 60 families for as long as 15 years after their divorce. She reported that one-third of the children were adapting quite well to their new living situations five years after family breakup but that 37 percent had not recovered from the dissolution and suffered a variety of behavioral problems. The remaining children were doing well in some areas and not so well in other aspects of their lives. Ten years after the divorce, 41 percent of the children (now young men and women) were anxious, underachieving, self-deprecating individuals.

It was at this period that Wallerstein discovered the "sleeper effect"—delayed adjustment problems that plagued 66 percent of the 19- to 23-year-old women in her study. These women were anxious and fearful in their relations with men regarding commitment, love, and sex. Some were afraid of betrayal by unfaithful partners. Amato and Booth (1991) support Wallerstein's observations, reporting that most studies have found that children of divorced parents have lower psychological well-being as adults than children raised in intact families. Children of divorced parents are also more likely to have their marriages fail, as parental divorce is associated with marital problems and divorce proneness.

Returning to the previous research, Wallerstein (1992) found evidence of a psychological syndrome she called the "overburdened child." Because 25 percent of divorced women and 20 percent of divorced men had failed to get their lives back together as long as 10 years after the marital dissolution, they could not effectively raise their children. As a result, the overburdened child was forced to raise himself or herself to a large extent. (For instance, a six-year-old girl made her meals, dressed herself, and put herself to bed.) In addition, these children became caretakers for their mothers or fathers, "holding the parent together psychologically." These children faced the double burden of fending for themselves at an age when they require substantial nurturing, as well as looking after a struggling, inept guardian.

The divorce of a middle-aged couple can also be an unsettling experience for their young adult children. One researcher interviewed 50 college students (ages 18 to 26) with recently divorced parents and found that most were cynical and preoccupied with thoughts of death, disease, and crippling disabilities. With few exceptions, these individuals feared they were destined to make the same mistakes in relationships that their parents did. These fears were typically reinforced by the parents themselves (Cain, 1990).

If the findings of these studies are accurate reflections of the problems adult children of divorce encounter, the sheer number of individuals who experience the breakup of their families means that millions of people will carry the troubling psychological baggage of that episode and its aftermath with them for many years. Since there is no significant reversal of the nation's high divorce rate in sight, we can expect that the effects of divorce will impact individual lives and even society as a whole for years to come—in what ways and to what degree remain to be seen.

GAY FAMILIES

As a result of gay activism, favorable court rulings, gay rights legislation, and a more tolerant public, homosexuals have made strides toward the overall acceptance of their lifestyle that were unthinkable only a generation ago. However, in what has been referred to as the "last great civil rights movement" (S. Harris, 1991), many gay men and women are still fighting for the right to legally marry. While a number of cities allow domestic partnerships that give gay couples some benefits, such as health coverage and sick leave, many people in the gay community want more. Legislation recognizing gay marriages would not only be an important symbolic victory; it would give homosexual couples access to the tax breaks, Social Security benefits for surviving spouses and dependents, comprehensive family health plans, and financial discounts now available exclusively to married heterosexuals (Rebeck, 1990).

According to the National Center for Lesbian Rights, there are more than 2 million gay mothers and fathers in the United States. While most of their children are from earlier heterosexual relationships, between 5,000 and 10,000 lesbians have given birth after "coming out"—that is, making public their sexual preference and lifestyle (Seligmann, 1990). Although most medical doctors will not artificially inseminate single females, some health centers cater to the desires of lesbian women to become mothers. Other lesbian couples have successfully adopted children.

Advocates of homosexual marriages (Hartinger, 1991, p. 683) argue that society has a good deal to gain from committed relationships, both heterosexual and homosexual, and that "gay marriages wouldn't weaken the family; they would *strengthen* it." Permitting homosexuals to marry could also reduce promiscuity and the incidence of sexually transmitted diseases, including AIDS. Children raised in loving, intact families would not be subject to the problems faced by children in single-parent households.

Brent Hartinger (1991) argues that a review of 35 studies on homosexual parents found that parents' sexual preference has no effect on the sexual orientation of children. In other words, children raised by gay parents are no more likely to become homosexuals than children raised in heterosexual families. Children raised by gay parents may also

This lesbian couple share an intimate moment while feeding their child. A number of homosexual women have given birth after being artificially inseminated; other lesbian couples have adopted children. Some people see same-sex marriages as further proof that the traditional American family is declining. Others see these unions as a necessary alternative that permits people with a different sexual orientation to enjoy family life.

be more sensitive to the struggles and persecution of a minority group and reach adulthood with a more strongly defined sense of social justice (Clay, 1991).

An increasing body of research seems to support the theory that sexual preference is a function of biology and not choice. If this is the case, the argument of gay marriage opponents is considerably weakened. These individuals claim that gay marriage (and homosexuality in general) is unnatural, typically grounding their position in religious doctrine. They believe that because homosexual behavior is a matter of choice, proponents of this lifestyle have willfully embarked upon a path of sin and ungodly conduct. Dennis O'Brien (1991, p. 684), who does not believe that homosexuals should be accorded the legal right to marry, states that American democracy "rests on a powerful set of assumptions about human nature and society." He feels strongly that homosexual marriages do not harmonize with these values. As support for this position, O'Brien cites the 1879 Supreme Court ruling that religious freedom did not allow Mormons the right to engage in polygamy (multiple marriage partners), a custom that is not condoned by American society; thus, homosexual marriages could be considered illegal for this same reason.

However, values, like so many other aspects of culture, are subject to change. Once-cherished beliefs that kept women subservient to men, kept slaves in the fields, and kept women out of voting booths and the political arena have been radically altered or have disappeared altogether. Just as these values have changed, so, too, have attitudes regarding homosexuality. This is especially evident in the arts, where Broadway shows about AIDS and homosexuality (such as *Angels in America*) have been well received.

O'Brien also states that heterosexual relationships are the way societies perpetuate themselves, insuring the survival of the group from one generation to the next. Legitimating gay marriages would undermine the reproductive capacity of a nation. Advocates of gay marriages point out that only 10 percent of the population is homosexual and that this small percentage of people hardly poses a threat to the perpetuation of society. And if homosexuality is a function of biological factors to any significant degree, that 10 percent will remain constant (Hartinger, 1991).

There are two contradictory trends regarding heterosexual Americans' views and behavior toward homosexuality and homosexuals. Passage of domestic partnership laws in a number of cities indicates a more tolerant attitude toward gays and lesbians. And when California governor Pete Wilson vetoed a bill in 1991 that would have outlawed job discrimination against gays, a *Los Angeles Times* poll indicated that 46 percent of that state's residents opposed Wilson's action (S. Harris, 1991). Support for gay rights in other states not as socially liberal as California (on some issues) would probably be much less. On the other hand, incidents of gay bashing have increased in many parts of the nation, as members of the homosexual community have been accused of spreading the virus that causes AIDS. These assaults have helped fuel the growth of militant homosexual organizations such as Queer Nation.

If gay marriages are to become a reality in the United States, legislation will have to be passed at the state as opposed to the federal level. Although the law was not changed, Hawaii's supreme court ruled in 1993 that the existing prohibition against same-sex marriages may violate the state constitution. This decision could have more far-reaching implications. If Hawaii (or any other state) would eventually legalize homosexual marriages, these unions would have to be recognized in every other state, a policy that has always existed concerning heterosexual unions. Would every state matter of factly follow this policy? What would be the consequences for people legally married in one state but not recognized as such in the state they currently reside in regarding a multitude of issues, including divorce and child custody?

Like a stone tossed into calm waters, family turmoil has a ripple effect that can produce problems for people in many other aspects of their lives and for society as a whole. Consider the following:

- An unhappy marriage may lead to extramarital affairs that not only enhance the chances of divorce but also increase the possibility of contracting and spreading sexually transmitted diseases, including AIDS. Kinsey et al. (1953) found that by age 40, 50 percent of American males and 26 percent of females had had at least one extramarital sexual encounter. One might argue that in the current, more sexually liberal environment, these figures would be even higher. There is also evidence that divorced individuals commit suicide in greater numbers than either married or widowed people (Danigelis & Pope, 1979) and that shifts in the rate of divorce have a significant impact on suicide rates in the United States (Wasserman, 1984).
- As previously noted, abused children often become aggressive and are more likely to be abusive parents themselves. This perpetuation of violence from one generation to the next is especially difficult to break in families who do not seek out or will not permit intervention on the part of mental health professionals and the criminal justice system. Some research has found that abused children can become passive and withdrawn (Wilson & Herrnstein, 1985), which may prove detrimental in

SUMMARY

1 The transition to a postindustrial economy has created problems for workers that have led to distress on the part of individuals and families. People who are unemployed are continually worried about losing their jobs and are likely to be depressed and anxious. It appears that a minimum level of income and job security is necessary for family stability and cohesion.

2 Approximately one out of four American families is a single-parent family; roughly 90 percent of these units are headed by women. In 1990, 51 percent of all Black children lived with only their mothers, as compared with 16 percent of White children. A significant number of these women live below the poverty line because of poor education, poor job skills, and "deadbeat dads" who pay little if any child support.

3 Dual-paycheck families routinely have problems regarding the division of household and childrearing responsibilities. Studies have shown that women typically do more work at home than their husbands and may grow resentful as a result of this inequitable practice.

4 Family violence has existed in societies throughout the world for thousands of years, although this behavior has only been considered a social problem for a relatively short period of time. *Normal violence,* which consists of slapping, pushing, and shoving, can be contrasted with *abusive violence,* such as punching, choking, beating, stabbing, and shooting. Whereas the former is generally considered part of childrearing practice and daily interaction, the latter is dangerous (often fatal) and illegal.

5 The major forms of child abuse are physical abuse, sexual abuse, and neglect. Mothers are somewhat more likely to be physically abusive than are fathers, and boys are more likely to be so punished than girls. Young children (under three years of age) are at greater risk of physical abuse than older children. It appears

establishing and maintaining relations with other people later in life.

- Passage of the controversial "three strikes and you're out" legislation, which would put individuals found guilty of committing three violent crimes in prison for life, might result in some women failing to call the police when abused. Knowing that their already twice-convicted husbands could be incarcerated for life, these women—who want the beatings to stop but do not want to lose their mates—may feel that they cannot ask for police intervention. They might also be very fearful of in-laws, many of whom would hold them responsible for the sentencing of their loved ones. Knowing the consequences of a guilty verdict, when these offenders came to trial, would juries be willing to convict, even if they did believe the defendants had in fact committed the assaults? A life sentence for wife battering might be beyond people's norms of fairness, thereby reducing the chances of guilty verdicts under these circumstances.
- It can be argued that the African American family is undergoing the most widespread change since their ancestors were forcibly removed from their lands of origin and enslaved in the New World. This largely economically motivated transformation has hit Black children especially hard. By 1990, half were residing in single-parent, female-headed families, and half were living in poverty. To the extent that these conditions are associated with problems such as crime, violence, drug abuse, and poor school performance, these children (and in the next 15 to 20 years, their children) will find it extremely difficult to move into the middle class. Urban ghettos are likely to become even more violent as people become increasingly desperate and forlorn.

that girls are more vulnerable to sexual abuse than boys, especially at the hands of stepfathers or their mothers' boyfriends.

6 As many as 6 million women are battered by their boyfriends and husbands each year in the United States. Many women stay in abusive relationships because they are economically dependent on their husbands, are committed to the relationship, and/or believe the abusive partner will change. Other women have no place to go or are fearful of losing their children if they divorce abusive husbands. Men are also subject to abuse at the hands of their wives or girlfriends. However, because men are usually bigger and stronger than their mates, they are less likely to be seriously injured. Much of the violence against men is retaliatory in nature—that is, women defending themselves after prolonged abuse by their husbands.

7 Although divorce occurs in most societies, the rates of marital dissolution vary greatly. The rate of divorce in the United States is among the highest in the world, as a result of an erosion of the stigma associated with being divorced, the proliferation of no-fault divorce laws, and a shift in emphasis on the part of many people from marriage and long-term commitment to personal growth and happiness. Divorce can result in severe emotional and economic problems for children and adults. However, the breakup of a marriage in which parents have been fighting (sometimes physically) for an extended period of time can benefit children.

8 Many homosexuals are fighting for the right to legally marry and raise children. Marriage would accord them the benefits (health care, for example) now accorded only heterosexual couples. Many studies have concluded that children raised by homosexual parents are no more likely to become homosexual themselves than children raised by heterosexual parents.

CHAPTER ELEVEN

DRUGS, ALCOHOL, AND GAMBLING
Taking a Chance

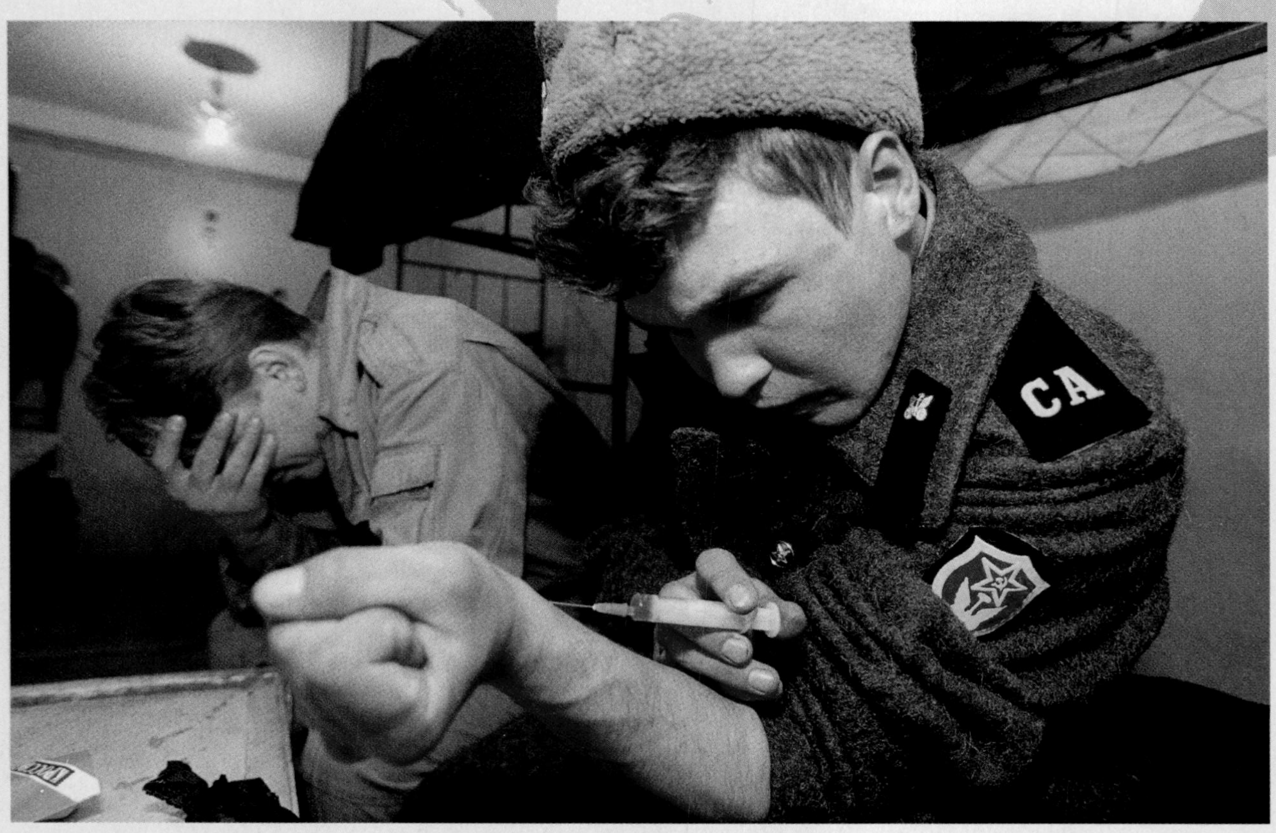

The ingestion of drugs is a cultural universal—that is, these substances are used to some extent in all human societies. Because this pattern of behavior is so pervasive and firmly entrenched in many societies, it will be extremely difficult, if not impossible, to completely eradicate. Some researchers are of the opinion that the so-called war on drugs cannot be won because the use of mind-altering substances is an inescapable part of our biological existence—a drive as basic as those of hunger, thirst, and sex (Siegel in Beaty, 1989). From this perspective, drug abusers are individuals who cannot control this drive—that is, they want to experience the transitory psychological and/or physiological advantages of a drug-induced state of well-being as often as possible.

Regardless of whether the pervasive use of drugs is grounded in some physiological/psychological need we inherit as a component of our humanity or whether drug taking is learned in much the same way that we become involved in any other form of behavior, the ingestion of mind-altering substances is closely associated with a wide range of human activities, including religious practices, the treatment of pain and disease, the enjoyment of food, and the enhancement of sexual pleasure, as well as to improve physical performance on the job, on the battlefield, and/or on the playing field (Weil & Rosen, 1983).

Concerning the improvement of physical performance, for centuries, poor South American Indians doing hard manual labor for up to 14 hours a day high in the Andes Mountains have relied on the mild stimulation of chewing coca leaves with low cocaine content (Inciardi, 1986). On the other side of the world, in modern, fast-paced Japan, many workers endure equally long days by taking "awakening medicine," one of the street names for methamphetamines. Japanese police estimate that there are between 200,000 and 600,000 speed addicts in the country.

Although drugs have been integrated into many aspects of virtually every society at one time or another, social groups typically put limits or restrictions on what drugs can be used as well as when, where, and under what circumstances. Herein lies a fundamental component of the "drug problem." Emile Durkheim argued that as moral animals, human beings classify all activities as "acceptable" or "unacceptable." A major consequence of this moralizing is the designation of drug taking as deviant behavior that is almost always subject to some sanction or penalty.

Certainly one of the contributing factors to the use of illicit (illegal) drugs and alcohol in the United States is the proliferation of mixed messages regarding these substances by the government, the entertainment industry, advertisers, and parents to children. To begin, the legal and commercially very lucrative drugs tobacco and alcohol are factors in the deaths each year of approximately 425,000 and 150,000 people, respectively. These are staggering figures in their own right and even more bewildering when compared to the relatively small number of people (10,000) who die annually as a result of ingesting illegal drugs.

While intermittent public service announcements on television warn of the dangers of illegal drugs ("This is your brain on drugs": scrambled eggs in a frying pan), we are constantly bombarded with the sights and sounds of young, happy, healthy, successful, and sexy people who are smoking, drinking, and partying their way through life. For every "Just say no" pronouncement on the airwaves, hundreds if not thousands of commercials are saying "yes, yes" to alcohol and cigarettes. It is hardly surprising, therefore, that Joe Camel is more recognizable to many schoolchildren in the United States than are photos of some former presidents. With his likeness (cigarette in mouth) increasingly evident on the sides of urban buses and billboards in many other countries, Joe Camel will soon be known to children across the globe.

The federal government also plays both sides of the street, so to speak, concerning its drug policy. Each year, approximately $12 billion is spent at the national level (much more is allocated by local and state governments) to fight the war on drugs, yet in 1989, the federal government allocated a price support of $55 billion to the tobacco industry (Duke & Gross, 1993; *Agricultural Statistics,* 1993).

In this chapter, we look at various aspects of alcohol and drug use as well as another form of behavior that some people think is one of fastest-growing social problems in the United States (also legitimated by the government to a great extent): gambling. We will examine the growth and distribution of these forms of behavior along with the social characteristics of those who drink alcohol, use illegal drugs, and gamble. Possible solutions to the negative consequences of these actions will also be discussed. First, we will examine drug and alcohol abuse.

QUESTIONS TO CONSIDER

1. Under what circumstances did numerous drugs routinely used in the United States become illegal?
2. What are the basic characteristics of drug dependence?
3. In recent years, has the use of illegal drugs increased or decreased in the United States?
4. What are *anabolic steroids,* and why have these drugs become so popular with young males? Why are these substances so dangerous?
5. What is the relationship between drug use and crime? Drug use and AIDS?

6. What are the major arguments for and against the legalization of drugs in the United States?
7. What are the principal social correlates of alcohol use and abuse? What health problems are associated with alcohol use and abuse?
8. What can be done to prevent people from driving while intoxicated?
9. What is the *disease model* of alcohol abuse? How do sociologists explain vastly different rates of alcohol use and abuse from one social group to another?
10. Under what circumstances do some people become pathological gamblers? What is the relationship between gambling and crime? How and why do some governments encourage people to gamble? What is the future of gambling in the United States?

UNDERSTANDING THE PROBLEM OF DRUG AND ALCOHOL ABUSE

HISTORY OF THE PROBLEM IN AMERICA

Americans have had a love affair with the car ever since the initial Model T came rolling off the assembly line almost 100 years ago. However, this romance with the automobile is nothing more than a mild infatuation when compared to the passion we have demonstrated for consuming a wide variety of drugs ever since the first shipload of European settlers came to North America. Many of these people continued the British tradition of hearty drinking in taverns. These establishments were required by law to keep a certain amount of liquor on the premises, and workmen often received part of their wages in the form of rum (Rush in McKim, 1986). In 1827, the American Temperance Society pushed for a moderate, or "tempered," use of alcohol in the United States. By 1855, 13 states had moved to control alcohol consumption to the extreme and passed prohibition laws, although by 1868, 9 had repealed these statutes.

With the implementation of the Prohibition Amendment in 1920, the "noble experiment" began—an experiment that proved to be a costly failure and came to an end in 1933. The proliferation of "bathtub gin," speakeasies (illegal saloons), bootlegging, smuggling, and organized crime was indicative of the resolve on the part of millions of people to have their "demon alcohol," no matter what the law said or what the authorities attempted to do (Kerr, 1991). If there was ever any doubt, the period of Prohibition clearly demonstrated that drinking is a deeply embedded cultural tradition in this country, with a broad base of appeal and support.

A drug that dates back some 6,000 years, marijuana (*cannabis sativa*) was probably introduced into the United States by Mexican farm laborers working in the southwestern part of the country. Although Mexican field hands were welcomed initially, in the tough economic times of the 1930s, they came to be viewed as surplus labor in states experiencing high unemployment. Organizations with names such as *Allied Patriotic Societies* and *Key Men of America*, as well as local criminal justice officials, put pressure on the federal government to do something about (preferably send back home) now-unwanted Mexican citizens working in the United States—a group of people who were increasingly associated with the recently discovered evils of marijuana (Musto, 1987).

It was during this period that Harry J. Anslinger, the head of the Bureau of Narcotics—a man Inciardi (1986, p. 21) portrays as part "Neanderthal ultraright-wing conservative" and part "astute government bureaucrat who viewed the marijuana issue as a mechanism for elevating himself and the Bureau of Narcotics to national prominence"—made his move. As a result of Anslinger's crusade against the evils of this latest drug of concern, the Marijuana Tax Act of 1937 came into existence. This act did not outlaw cannabis per se, but growing, distributing, buying, selling, and using that substance were regulated and effectively curtailed by stiff taxes. Within 5 years, the price of a marijuana cigarette increased in cost between 600 and 1,200 percent.

Marijuana use escalated in the 1950s; it was the first drug to be associated with the youthful rebellion in the "psychedelic sixties" (Ray & Ksir, 1987). By the 1990s, marijuana was the most commonly used illegal drug in the United States. Approximately one-half of all nonlegal drug episodes were associated with this substance (Goode, 1991b). Partly as a result of this wide-scale use, 11 states (which comprised one-third of the U.S. population) decriminalized the possession of small amounts of marijuana between 1973 and 1978 in what may be described as a short-lived reform movement (DiChiara & Galliher, 1994; Goode, 1991a). **Decriminalization** refers to reducing the penalty for committing a criminal act while not legalizing it (Siegel, 1992). Alaska repealed its decriminalization law by way of a referendum in 1990.

At the same time the temperance movement was agitating for control of alcohol consumption, other crusaders were focusing on heroin. This drug was outlawed before alcohol with the passage of the Harrison Act (legislation that regulated all drug transactions) in 1914. After years of use as a harmless cure-all substance, heroin was now thought of as "the most threatening drug in history" (Inciardi, 1986, p. 97). As an increasing number of individuals were arrested for ingesting this now-controlled substance, its use was linked to various urban problems, especially crime. Heroin was also associated with less than desirable "foreigners and alien subgroups" living in urban America (Musto, 1987, p. 65). The stigma of using heroin (and other drugs) resulting from the Harrison Act, coupled with the public's association of drugs and crime, led to the image—that is still with us in large measure—of the drug user as a degenerate and dangerous fiend.

Cocaine was another popular curative used in the late nineteenth century to treat a wide variety of physical problems and emotional difficulties. First bottled in 1894, Coca-Cola ("the real thing") contained coca until it was removed in 1903 after a government report criticized the drug-laced beverage as being habit forming. By 1908, 40 different soft drinks commercially available in the United States contained coca. Also regulated by the Harrison Act, cocaine (like heroin) was beginning to be associated with the lower classes and criminal elements in the 1920s.

From the 1930s to the 1960s, cocaine use declined significantly and was limited primarily to jazz musicians and people with deviant and/or marginal occupations and lifestyles (Abadinsky, 1989). However, in the late 1960s and early 1970s, cocaine resurfaced in mainstream America as a result of two policy decisions by the federal government (Inciardi, 1986). The first was the decision to reduce the legal production of amphetamine-type drugs and place more stringent controls on commonly abused sedatives. The second was funding of the World Bank project to construct the Pan American Highway, which effectively linked the heretofore remote coca-producing regions of Peru to major cities. Cocaine quickly filled the demand created by the government's sudden get-tough policy with amphetamines and has become one of the most popular illegal substances used in the United States.

The illegality and high cost of many mind-altering substances may account for the use of inhalants, a particularly dangerous category of drugs favored by individuals under

This young Chilean boy is inhaling the mind-altering contents of aerosol products such as paints and cleaners that he sprayed into a plastic bag, a practice called "huffing" in the United States. The toxic properties of these chemicals can lead to brain damage and death.

18 years of age. These mind-altering, toxic chemicals are found in everyday household products such as paint, turpentine, model airplane glue, lighter fluid, and a wide variety of cleaning products, often dispensed in aerosol cans. Users spray the contents of these products into plastic bags and then inhale the fumes, a process called "huffing." Because of the toxicity of these chemicals, huffing is estimated to result in more brain damage than the effects of all other drugs combined. In addition, as many as 1,200 people die each year from inhaling poisonous fumes in this manner ("Huffing," 1994). Because these products are legal and inexpensive and can be purchased by individuals of any age, it is very difficult to control the use of inhalants.

As this brief history reveals, many drugs that were routinely used in this country by large numbers of people were eventually controlled and/or made illegal. The process of criminalizing drug consumption often involves linking a particular unsavory element of society to a particular drug. However, if drug use ever was limited to a few identifiable groups in this country, that is no longer the case today. The same can be said for drug addiction, which Witters et al. (1992) characterize as an "equal-opportunity" affliction—a condition found among all races, ethnic groups, religions, and social classes. There can be little doubt that as a nation, we will continue to use both legal and illegal drugs at high, albeit fluctuating rates. The question to be answered is how problematic this consumption will be for individual users (and abusers) and the larger society.

DEFINING DEPENDENCE

DEPENDENCE

We know that people use and abuse drugs for a variety of reasons: because they do not have enough money or have too much; because they are attempting to escape painful sit-

uations or are seeking adventure; because they are wildly overjoyed or horribly depressed; because they are bored and frustrated; because they have too much to do (Bryjak, 1990). For whatever reasons people initially take up the use of illicit drugs, the ingestion of these substances can lead to *drug dependence* (formerly called *drug addiction*), a condition that has three basic characteristics (Goode, 1991a):

1. The user continues to ingest the drug over an extended period of time.
2. The user may find it difficult (if not impossible) to quit, taking drastic measures (stealing, dropping out of school or work, abandoning family and friends) to continue using the drug.
3. If the user stops ingesting the substance, he or she may experience painful physical symptoms as well as severe mental distress. These characteristics are virtually identical in *alcohol dependency,* or *alcoholism* (Schuckit in Goode, 1991a).

By the time habitual drug and/or alcohol abusers (some people are hooked on two or more drugs—"polydrug" abusers) experience the pains of withdrawal, they have developed a tolerance for the substance in question—that is, their bodies have gradually adjusted to the level of the drug ingested. When tolerance to a particular substance develops, the user must increase the amount of the drug taken to achieve the same feeling that was previously experienced with a lesser quantity of the drug.

Users may realize they are drug dependent when their bodies react adversely (sometimes violently) upon cessation or withdrawal of drug taking. This adverse reaction is often called a **withdrawal syndrome** or **abstinence syndrome.** The negative effects brought about by discontinuing drug use disappear once the substance is ingested again. Usually, the higher the dosage of the drug being taken, the more severe the withdrawal symptoms experienced. As might be expected, these symptoms vary from drug to drug. Withdrawing from narcotics, for example, can be a very unpleasant ordeal, with long-time users suffering from stomach cramps, diarrhea, nausea, vomiting, and involuntary twitching in the arms and legs (McKim, 1986; Ray & Ksir, 1987; Stephens, 1992).

SEX DIFFERENCES IN DEPENDENCE

The general explanations of drug use and abuse are thought to apply equally to both sexes; however, it has been suggested that the process of drug dependence may be somewhat different for males and females (Pohl & Boyd, 1992). This contention is based on biological differences between men and women and differences between the sexes concerning psychological development and personality structure.

As a result of the socialization process, women in American society (and most others) experience the family/social environment in a manner quite dissimilar to that of men. Women are socialized into a mode of "attachment and emotional dependence"—that is, they are encouraged to make and maintain lifelong attachments and to believe in the importance of mutual interdependence; they are taught to be caring and nurturing. If such a significant portion of women's self-concept is contingent on maintaining successful relationships, when these attachments are threatened, become weaker, or simply fall apart, women might abuse illicit drugs and alcohol as a form of self-medication. Pohl and Boyd (1992) note that "being female" may lead to some forms of drug dependency and suggest the following antecedents to "female addiction":

- Lowered self-esteem
- Past history of sexual abuse
- Family history of substance abuse

- Genetic predispositions
- Gynecological problems
- Poverty

While these factors are also associated with male addiction (with the exception of gynecological problems), they are more likely to be causal factors in female addiction. Regarding gynecological factors, in a study of female heroin addicts, it was not clear if these problems were somehow responsible for the women's addiction or if these problems were the result of their chemical dependency (Anderson, 1981).

DRUG USE AND ABUSE

INTERNATIONAL TRENDS

A report by the World Health Organization (WHO) states that drug use is a growing problem in both developed and developing nations (Okie, 1992). Along with the United States, Japan and Sweden have had "largescale epidemics of amphetamine abuse" (Witters et al., 1992, p. 250), and one observer notes that in some neighborhoods of Zurich, Switzerland, large numbers of drug users congregate in "listless sprawls" on "filthy blood-splattered sidewalks" (Guskind, 1992). In Poland and other Eastern European countries currently undergoing rapid economic and political change, rates of drug use have increased dramatically.

South American drug dealers have moved into Nicaragua and are trying to establish a cocaine market in that country by selling this substance at one-tenth its price in Europe and the rest of Central America. As is the case in other developing nations, drug use in Nicaragua has been attributed to a large, poorly educated, "marginalized" population suffering high rates of unemployment (Barahona, 1992).

Until recently, the only drugs abused in much of Africa were marijuana and alcohol (Okie, 1992). However, this may be changing since Nigeria, Zaire, and Zimbabwe have become major transit points for global drug traffickers because of having large international airports. No doubt some of these drugs will remain in Africa as the more affluent urban middle and upper classes (as well as a significant portion of poor people who reside in cities) will be targeted as drug customers. Because relatively low-paid officials (such as customs officers) are easily corrupted by wealthy drug traffickers (Kraft, 1994), it is highly probable that drugs will become easily available in many African nations.

U.S. TRENDS

Drug use in the United States peaked in 1985, when some 37 million people acknowledged using an illegal substance. By 1988, that number had plummeted to 28 million and remained low until 1992, when slight increases in marijuana and LSD use were reported by eighth-graders and college students (see Table 11.1 for percentages of illicit drug use). In 1992, approximately 1.3 million individuals reported using cocaine at least once in the past month, and over 22.6 million people said they had ingested that drug at some time during their lives. The corresponding numbers for hallucinogens such as LSD and PCP are 525,000 and almost 16.5 million, respectively. (See Figure 11.1, "Categories of Drugs," for a description of these and other psychoactive substances.)

TABLE 11.1 Illicit Drug Use among Americans (by sex and age groups for total population)

Age	Observed Estimate		
	Ever Used	Used Past Year	Used Past Month
12–17	*16.5%*	*11.7%*	*6.1%*
Male	16.3	11.0	5.7
Female	16.6	12.5	6.5
18–25	*51.7*	*26.4*	*13.0*
Male	53.3	30.4	16.7
Female	50.0	22.6	9.5
26–34	*60.8*	*18.3*	*10.1*
Male	66.1	22.3	12.6
Female	55.5	14.4	7.6
35+	*28.0*	*5.1*	*2.2*
Male	34.1	6.7	3.2
Female	22.7	3.7	1.4
Total	*36.2*	*11.1*	*5.5*
Male	41.0	13.4	7.1
Female	31.7	9.0	4.1

SOURCE:: *1992 National Household Survey on Drug Abuse,* Substance Abuse and Mental Health Services Administration, U.S. Department of Health and Human Services.

NOTE: Any illicit drug use includes use of one or more of the following: marijuana, nonmedical use of psychotherapeutics, inhalants, cocaine, hallucinogens, and heroin.

INCREASE IN MARIJUANA USE

A 1993 nationwide survey of 50,000 junior and senior high school students revealed a marked increase in marijuana use (and smaller gains in the use of other drugs) among high school students. One of the researchers noted, "We have the unenviable role of informing the country that drug use is making a comeback, that the epidemic could be re-emerging" (Johnston in Treaster, 1994).

This increase in the use of marijuana on the part of teenagers is significant because for some of these young people, "pot" will become a "gateway" drug—that is, a relatively mild or "soft" mind-altering substance that will lead to the ingestion of more powerful drugs (Witters et al., 1992). Substance abuse expert Herbert Kleber (in Treaster, 1994) notes, "If you used marijuana less than 10 times the likelihood of using cocaine was practically nil. But if you used marijuana more than 100 times, or twice a week for a year, the likelihood of using cocaine went up to 70 percent."

THE "CRACK" CRAZE

Cocaine has been around for decades, but an especially potent derivative of this substance—*"crack"*—is relatively new. This drug has caught the attention of the media, the American public, and law enforcement officials (especially in major cities). Smoked

FIGURE 11.1 Categories of Drugs

A useful mechanism for classifying psychoactive substances—those drugs that have a significant impact on the central nervous system—categorizes these drugs according to both their chemical structure and physiological effect. Sociologist Richard Stephens (1992, pp. 10–11) offers the following fivefold typology:

1. Narcotics

Narcotics act to depress the central nervous system. Morphine, opium, and codeine are derived directly from the opium poppy. Heroin is a semisynthetic narcotic that is chemically processed from opium. A major problem with narcotics is that they produce physical dependence. Depressants are also more dangerous than most other drugs because in high doses, they can interfere with vital brain functions and lead to death.

2. Generalized Depressants

This category of drugs is comprised of sedative/hypnotic substances such as secobarbital (Seconal), pentobarbital (Nembutal), and methaqualone (Quaalude). These depressants, along with so-called minor tranquilizers such as diazepoxide (Librium) and diazepam (Valium), are used in medicines to induce a calm, relaxed state and sleep. Combining alcohol with depressants can be dangerous because their effects are additive: An amount of alcohol *or* a dose of a depressant that some people are used to and can tolerate physiologically can result in a coma and death when combined (Weil & Rosen, 1983).

3. Hallucinogens

With an active ingredient of tetrahydrocannabinol (THC), marijuana is considered a mild hallucinogen. Mescaline, which is derived from the peyote cactus, is still used by North American Indians as part of their rituals in the Native American Church. One of the most powerful drugs in this category is LSD. Hallucinogens are popular with some people because their use is thought to be related to profound insights into oneself and the world. People under the influence of phencyclidine (PCP) are likely to experience changes and distortions of body image as well as rapid and sudden mood changes, including laughing, crying, delusional thoughts, and repetitive behavior.

4. Stimulants

Stimulants make people feel more alert and energetic by activating and exciting the nervous system. Amphetamines can suppress hunger, making them popular with people concerned about losing and/or maintaining their weight (Weil & Rosen, 1983). Cocaine and its derivatives (including "crack") are two of the most popular stimulants used today and are thought to be at the forefront of a host of drug-related problems—including drug dependence—in the United States.

5. Mood Modifiers

Mood modifiers include the so-called major tranquilizers, such as Thorazine and Elavil, that are generally used to treat in-patients with severe psychosis and other serious psychiatric problems. They are not typically used as recreational drugs.

SOURCE: Based on "Psychoactive Drug Use in the United States Today" by Richard C. Stephens, in *Drugs, Crime, and Social Policy* (pp. 1–31), edited by T. Mieczkowski, 1992, Boston: Allyn and Bacon; and *Chocolate to Morphine: Understanding Mind-Active Drugs* by A. Weil and W. Rosen, 1983, Boston: Houghton Mifflin.

"crack" cocaine produces a very rapid, very intense high that lasts between 15 and 30 minutes. The "equally intense feelings of depression and cravings" (Johnson et al., 1992) explain why individuals who are psychologically dependent on this drug may consume as many as 40 doses in a 24-hour period. Because this substance is also an appetite sup-

pressant, heavy "crack" users can lose 30 percent or more of their normal body weight (Mieczkowski, 1992).

PUMPING UP WITH ANABOLIC STEROIDS

Developed in the 1930s, anabolic steroids are synthetic derivatives of the male hormone testosterone. Although some practitioners in the sports community remain skeptical about the effects of steroids, most experts are of the opinion that these drugs (taken orally or by injection) can lead to rapid gains in body weight, muscle mass, and endurance. Some individuals have added as much as 100 pounds to their frames in only 14 months. However, there are no studies indicating that steroid users can enhance athletic performance—that is, increase ability, skill, or cardiovascular capability (National Institute on Drug Abuse, 1991). Most steroid users "stack" these drugs—that is, they take two or more types of steroids in megadoses, sometimes in combination with other drugs (such as stimulants, depressants, pain killers) and other hormones (Schrof, 1992).

The demonstrated side effects of steroid use are alarming. Male users can suffer shrinking testicles, low sperm count, impotence, baldness, development of femalelike breasts, an enlarged prostate, severe acne, and a yellowing of the skin and eyes. Females who use these drugs experience masculinizing effects, including a deepening of the voice, hair growth on the body and face, and breast reduction. Women may also stop menstruating or have irregular periods. Both sexes are subject to high blood pressure, liver damage, cancer, and a host of other physical problems (National Institute on Drug Abuse, 1991; Schrof, 1992). Psychologically, users can undergo depression, increased aggression, and mood swings that can become homicidal in intensity. These periods of pronounced fury have been called "roid rages." Heavy users may become psychologically dependent on steroids and have a difficult time cutting back on or completely stopping the use of these substances.

Although physiologically and psychologically damaging, anabolic steroids do not carry the stigma associated with cocaine, heroin, or even marijuana. The latter are illegal, feared, and despised because they produce mental states ranging from mild euphoria to ecstasy. However, anabolic steroids do not produce a high, nor are they ends in themselves. Rather, they are means to the most important goal in American society—success—in this case, success on the athletic field. Because these drugs have been used toward that end, parents and coaches who would normally do anything they could to prevent adolescents from becoming involved with mind-altering drugs often tolerate or even encourage steroid use.

CONSEQUENCES OF DRUG USE AND ABUSE

DRUGS AND DOMESTIC CRIME

For many people (including numerous practitioners in the criminal justice system), the association between drugs and crime is a simple, straightforward cause-and-effect relationship: Drug use causes crime. Although that is certainly a possibility, it is only one of four feasible relationships between these variables (Wilson & Herrnstein, 1985).

To begin, the relationship between drugs and crime may be *spurious,* meaning there is no causal connection at all. Second, *direct causality* (drug use causes crime) has two derivatives. The pharmacological effects of drugs may produce behavioral changes, such as increased impulsivity and/or higher levels of aggression, that result in the commission of crime. Also, the prohibitive cost of illegal drugs may cause people to engage in criminal activity to support their drug taking (especially if they are physically and/or psychologically dependent on these substances). The drug/crime relationship may be *conditionally causal*—that is, drug use may cause criminal behavior, providing some other conditions exist. Drug use may result in criminal behavior among adolescent males only when they are in the company (and experience the peer pressure) of other young males. Last, drug use and criminal behavior may be the result of some *common cause*—that is, one or more factors (one's personality or extreme poverty) are responsible for both these occurrences (drug use and crime).

Whatever the reason, numerous studies have discovered a strong association between drug use and criminal behavior. A survey conducted in 24 major cities by the National Institute of Justice/Drug Use Forecasting Program (1992) of men being booked at a police station shortly after being arrested found that between 40 percent (Omaha) and 85 percent (Philadelphia) tested positive for illegal drugs (see Figure 11.2). In 14 of these cities, 60 percent or more of those arrested had used a prohibited substance. For women, the range was between 44 percent (San Antonio) and 85 percent (Manhattan in New York City). In 15 of 21 cities surveyed, 60 percent or more of those women arrested tested positive for illegal drugs. Another national survey found that almost one-third of inmates incarcerated in state prisons were under the influence of an illegal drug or had consumed a significant amount of alcohol just prior to committing the crime for which they were convicted (in Gropper, 1985).

James Inciardi (1986) interviewed 1,002 heroin and other drug users between 1978 and 1981, including a group of 573 Miami narcotics users. In one 12-month period, this latter group committed a remarkable 215,000 crimes. Not counting the 129,000 crimes that were drug sales and so-called victimless crimes (for example, prostitution and gambling), this group of 573 narcotics users committed almost 6,000 robberies and assaults, approximately 6,700 burglaries, almost 900 vehicle thefts, and 81,000 other crimes of shoplifting, larceny, and fraud.

A good deal of research on the relationship between drug use and crime has focused on the uses of heroin and cocaine (Gentry, 1991). It appears that poor, inner-city heroin addicts and heavy users of cocaine were criminally active *prior* to their addiction. However, heavy use and addiction can dramatically increase both the frequency of criminal behavior and the seriousness of these offenses (Gentry, 1991).

DRUG USE AND AIDS

The "tiny blood transfusion" that occurs when needles and syringes are shared by people who inject drugs is an ever-increasing mechanism for the transmission of the virus that causes AIDS in the United States and at least 50 other countries (Des Jarlais & Friedman, 1994, p. 82). In the United States, approximately one-third of all people with HIV (some 113,000 individuals) contracted the virus by injecting themselves with illicit drugs. In some urban areas—including European and Asian cities (see Table 11.2)—40 percent or more of those individuals who inject themselves with these substances are HIV positive—that is, they have the virus that causes AIDS. Once established in the drug-injecting community, AIDS can spread quickly to other groups of people through sexual contact and pregnancy (Des Jarlais & Friedman, 1994). A deadly combination of this form of drug ingestion and prostitution has given the city of Santos, Brazil, the dubious distinction of being the AIDS capital of South America (Black et al., 1992).

Inasmuch as the sale of needles and syringes is regulated by law and injecting drug users want to avoid carrying their equipment around with them, if possible, these individuals frequent "shooting galleries"—places where they rent, use, and then return needles and syringes. Payment for this service is typically made in cash or in drugs. Drug-injecting equipment is used by one customer after another until the needles become dull and/or clotted with dried blood and must be discarded (Des Jarlais & Friedman, 1994).

One study of 50 Mexican American males and their female sexual partners (total 100 subjects) found that even though most of the 27 women who also injected drugs understood how HIV is transmitted, they continued to share needles (Parra, 1993). In addition, almost 90 percent of the women knew that their male partners were injecting drugs, and only a small percentage of men and women in this group reported using condoms.

FIGURE 11.2 Drug Use by Male and Female Booked Arrestees

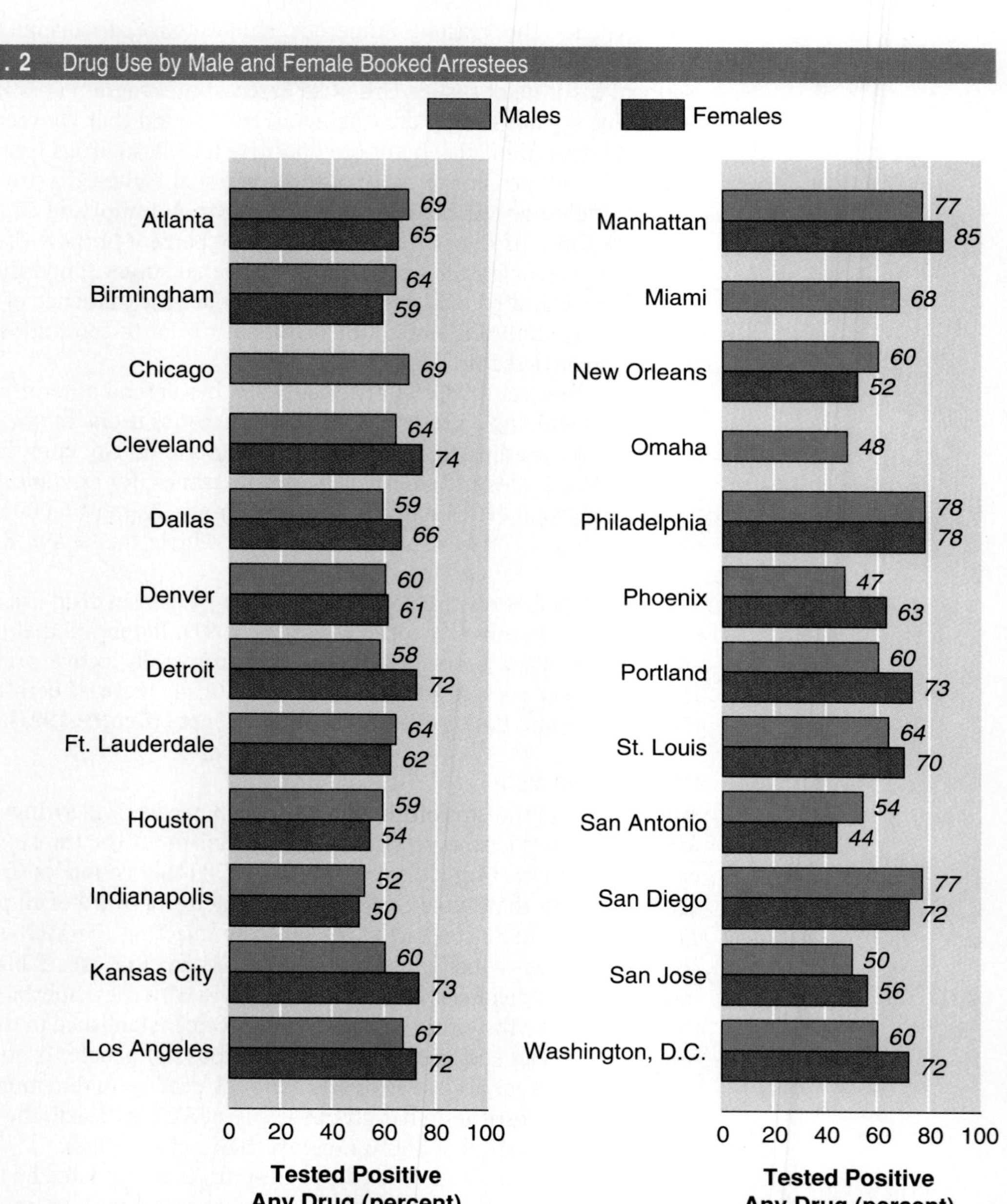

SOURCE: From *Drug Use Forecasting 1992 Annual Report,* Drug Use Forecasting Program, National Institute of Justice.

NOTE: Positive by urinalysis, January through December 1992. Drugs tested for include cocaine, opiates, PCP, marijuana, amphetamines, methadone, methaqualone, benzodiazepines, barbiturates, and propoxyphene.

TABLE 11.2 Drug Users with HIV Infection (in percent)

City	Country	1978	'79	'80	'81	'82	'83	'84	'85	'86	'87	'88	'89	'90	'91
Amsterdam	Netherlands									33	31	31	34		
Bangkok	Thailand										1	43			
Berlin	Germany								31	49	49	45			
Bilbao	Spain							42	42		44	45	27	30	
Bologna	Italy		0	0	9	7.5	39	37							
Detroit	United States								13		16		16		
Edinburgh	Scotland					0	14	42	37						
Geneva	Switzerland				7		27		52						
Hamburg	Germany								0	23	16	13			
London	England								5	6	4	5			
Manipur	India									0	0	0		54	
Milan	Italy				11	28	61	67	69	73					
New York City	United States	9	26	38		50		57		55				50	
Padua	Italy						20	28	65	50					
Rio de Janeiro	Brazil									4				20	37
Rome	Italy								34	42	33	31	32		
San Francisco	United States									7	12	12	11		
—	Sardinia	0	0	0	1	10	18	32	43	57					
Tours	France					0	0	15	17						
Vienna	Austria									7	12	30	28	24	

SOURCE: From "AIDS and the Use of Ingested Drugs" by Don C. Des Jarlais and Samuel R. Friedman.

NOTE: Figures come from myriad sources, including hospital records, stored blood samples, and treatment programs. The information is incomplete because studies were not undertaken every year.

DRUG USE AND THE LAW

Regardless of how successful the ongoing "war on drugs" may eventually be in the United States, we can be quite sure of one thing: There will always be people who abuse illegal (and legal) mind-altering substances. Therefore, some form of intervention/treatment/therapy is needed to help these individuals (including those who have not been arrested) break their drug habituation. Although people's views regarding how much federal and state money should be spent on what kinds of drug treatment programs differ substantially, virtually everybody agrees on the need for these programs. However, there is anything but a consensus regarding the possible legalization of some, if not all, of the currently illicit drugs in this country.

THE DEBATE OVER LEGALIZATION

A number of commentators have outlined the benefits to millions of individuals and to society as a whole that would result from the legalization of drugs (Nadelmann, 1992; Ostrowski, 1990; Stephens, 1992). One of the most frequently cited advantages of such a policy would be the reduction of crime. Drug legalization would wipe out the over 1 million arrests made for substance-related offenses (mostly for possession and use of drugs) in the United States in 1991 (7.1 percent of total arrests) and allow police to concentrate on other criminal offenders. Police currently spend so much time pursuing drug dealers and users that in some parts of the country, property crimes like burglary have been effectively decriminalized.

In addition, organized crime would be deprived of its major source of income—illegal drug-generated money—which is used to finance and spread other forms of criminal activity (prostitution for example) and buy into and therefore partially control legitimate businesses. Violent crimes associated with dealers and gangs fighting over drugs and territory would also likely decline drastically if drugs were legalized. Of Washington, D.C.'s 438 homicides in 1989, some 60 to 80 percent were thought to be drug related (Dennis, 1990). Just as people no longer engage in gun battles over the production and distribution of alcohol, they would also stop killing each other over freely available and much more affordable drugs. Fewer police officers would be killed and millions of inner-city residents across the country would no longer have to live in a constant state of fear for themselves and their children.

Taking the above-mentioned factors into consideration, James Ostrowski (1990) estimates that society as a whole suffers what amounts to a triple monetary loss as a result of current U.S. drug laws and policies. Taxpayers spend some $10 billion annually at all levels of the criminal justice system (police, courts, and prisons) to deal with the drug problem. As much as $80 billion (tax free) a year goes to organized crime groups in this and other countries, and victims of criminals looking for drug money lose an additional $7.5 billion annually.

Proponents of legalization argue that a successful reduction of the drug supply could in fact exacerbate many of the problems related to the abuse and distribution of illegal substances. For example, if seizures by customs agents were successful in reducing the supply of drugs coming into the United States and the demand for these drugs remained constant, the street price for substances like heroin and cocaine would likely increase. This price escalation would in turn lead to higher rates of street crime. According to one estimate, a price increase of 10 percent in the cost of illegal drugs is associated with a 1.1 percent rise in the crime rate (Winick, 1992).

Another response to a diminishing supply of illegal substances would be an increase in the number of users and abusers who would turn to so-called *designer drugs,* which are illicit drugs made in clandestine laboratories. These substances are often much more powerful than existing drugs, and because they are crudely prepared, they may contain toxic impurities (Witters, Venturelli, & Hanson, 1992).

Opponents of legalization argue that in a nation that already has millions of people addicted to alcohol, having untold millions more addicted to heroin, cocaine, and amphetamines would be disastrous. Former "drug czar" in the Bush administration William Bennett (1990, pp. 50–51) stated, "If you're in favor of drugs being sold in stores like aspirin, you're in favor of boom times for drug users and drug addicts. With legalization, drug use will go way up." If this scenario did in fact come to pass, how would the daily lives of people in homes, schools, factories, and offices across the country be affected? What impact would all this have on "socially productive activities"? (Stephens, 1992). Would a latent consequence of legalization be a serious erosion of the work ethic, as Americans further embrace an attitude of "Don't worry, be happy"? In addition, how much credibility would the government have if it both endorsed the sale of drugs and made money (tax revenues) off these substances and at the same time attempted to convince people (especially children) that drugs like heroin are dangerous and should be avoided?

Proponents of legalization argue that the fear of a resultant tremendous increase in the number of users and abusers of drugs has been greatly exaggerated. To begin, they note that opinion polls consistently indicate that only a small number of people (as low as 1 percent) who currently abstain from these substances would start using them upon legalization. Second, states that decriminalized marijuana in the 1970s did not experience an upsurge in users coming from neighboring states where cannabis was still illegal. Finally, extensive decriminalization of a number of drugs in Holland did not result in a marked increase in usage (Dennis, 1990; "Bring Drugs Within the Law," 1993).

While issues concerning the legalization of drugs will continue to be hotly debated, it does not appear that removing one or more widely used mind-altering substances from the illegal side of the ledger will transpire in the near future. If nothing else, this highly volatile topic is just the type of politically charged issue that most officeholders (and their eventual challengers come election time) would just as soon avoid. In the meantime, the government will continue to pursue what Charles Winick (1992) refers to as the "liberal hard-line" approach. This strategy is liberal in that drug abusers are encouraged to seek treatment and end their involvement with illegal drugs and hard-line to the extent that the bulk of government funds are earmarked to combat the drug problem through the vigorous enforcement of existing drug laws.

SINGAPORE: DRUGS AND THE DEATH PENALTY

There is no debate over legalization in Singapore, a nation with some of the harshest drug laws in the world. Police in this city-state that rests at the tip of the Malaysian peninsula can stop anybody, anytime without a warrant and make him or her take a drug test. Individuals who test positive will spend between 3 months and 3 years in a drug rehabilitation center (Wallace, 1994b). Anyone apprehended by police with more than half an ounce of heroin or cocaine is considered a drug trafficker and executed if found guilty by a single presiding judge. (Singapore abolished the jury system in 1969.) Of the 47 individuals hanged by the state between 1989 and 1993, 22 were drug traffickers (Wallace, 1994b).

The government is also considering caning, or flogging, to deter drug users in light of the fact that the number of hard-core addicts known to officials increased from 2,288 in 1990 to 2,992 in 1993. In this procedure, a martial arts expert strikes the offender's bare buttocks with a 4-foot rattan cane. Recipients of this punishment usually pass out from the intense pain by the third or fourth blow; they also lose a great deal of blood (Wallace, 1994b).

THE DUTCH COMPROMISE

At the other end of the continuum of public policy and drug use is what might be best described as the "Dutch compromise." After drug use in the Netherlands increased from a very low rate in the mid-1960s to a serious "health and public order problem in urban areas" in the mid-1970s, a commission formed to investigate this situation reached two general conclusions (van Vliet, 1990):

1. Inasmuch as drug use in some form is found in virtually every human society, any attempt to completely eradicate this behavior is an "unrealistic option."
2. Since all drugs are not equally dangerous when consumed, the risk criterion of each substance should be taken into consideration when policy decisions are made.

On the basis of this reasoning, Dutch officials attempted to segment the drug market in their country. The Opium Act of 1976 made a distinction between drugs that presented society with an "unacceptable risk" (heroin, cocaine, LSD, and amphetamines) and less dangerous "cannabis products" (marijuana and hashish). Punishment associated with the former drugs was significantly increased, and penalties for use of the latter substances were basically eliminated (van Vliet, 1990).

While heroin-using penalties remained stiff, the government also instituted a harm-reduction program (that is, reducing the harm addicts do to themselves) aimed at habitual users who were unwilling or unable to kick their drug habit. Confidential, nonjudgmental outreach strategies were implemented to help addicts otherwise beyond normal treatment facilities. Drug counselors seek out addicts, who tend to congregate in certain

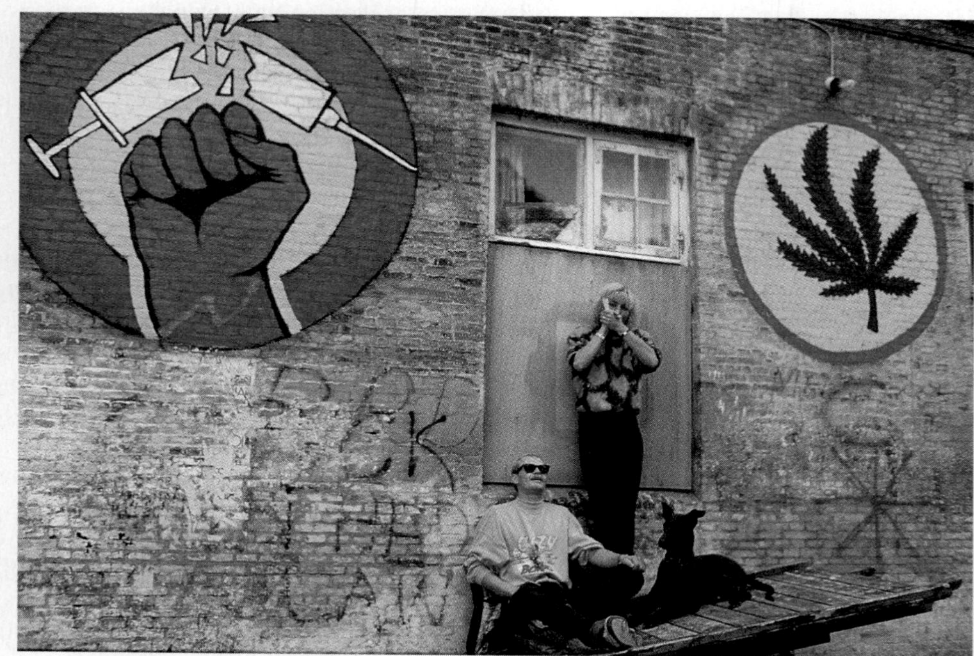

Whereas marijuana and hashish (symbolized by the leafy figure on the right) can be purchased legally in Amsterdam's coffee shops, drugs such as heroin and cocaine (symbolized by the hypodermic needle on the left) are illegal, as the government in the Netherlands considers them to pose an "unacceptable risk."

parts of the city, to give them methadone (a heroin substitute) and sterile needles. As a result of this strategy, an estimated 60 to 80 percent of heroin users are known to officials (Duke & Gross, 1993; van Vliet, 1990).

High-quality hashish and marijuana are legally sold in over 300 coffee shops in Amsterdam. These substances are often on the menu. Many such establishments also dispense information about the dangers of using both hard and soft drugs.

Since these laws were implemented, the number of cocaine and heroin users in the Netherlands has decreased (Duke & Gross, 1993); the number of soft-drug users stood at about 2 percent of the total population in 1990. (In the United States, 4.2 percent of the population admitted having used marijuana sometime in the past month in 1992.) According to some observers, young people in the Netherlands are "increasingly indifferent toward marijuana" (Duke & Gross, 1993), and those who do ingest these drugs are not necessarily considered deviant by nonusers.

ALCOHOL USE AND ABUSE

According to the National Institute of Alcohol Abuse and Alcoholism (NIAAA), the per capita consumption of beer, spirits (liquor), and wine increased slightly (1 percent) in the 1950s, jumped dramatically in the 1960s (21.3 percent), rose moderately in the 1970s (9.1 percent), and *decreased* in the 1980s (12 percent). However, there has been no such decrease among college students. The recent decline among the general public has been attributed to several factors, including an aging population, increased taxes on alcoholic beverages, stricter penalties for drunk driving, and antidrinking groups (especially in minority communities) countering the alcohol industry's attempt to convince more people to drink ("Substance Abuse," 1993). Like virtually any other form of behavior, the consumption of alcoholic beverages is not randomly distributed throughout the population. Rather, it is correlated with a number of social characteristics.

SOCIAL CHARACTERISTICS OF USERS AND ABUSERS

AGE

Young people consume more alcohol than older individuals, and the onset of drinking in the United States occurs at an early age. A 1987 survey of 11,400 students from 224 schools (34 private and 190 public) in 20 states found that 75.9 percent of eighth-graders and 87.3 percent of tenth-graders had consumed alcohol sometime in their lives. Researchers discovered that not only were more tenth-graders drinking than their younger classmates, but the tenth-graders were also drinking more frequently (Windle, 1991).

A 1994 report on the alcohol consumption of college students, conducted by Columbia University's Center for Addiction and Substance Abuse, discovered a startling increase in "binge" drinking (which is downing five or more cans of beer or glasses of wine in a single sitting), especially among women. The percentage of college women who sometimes consume enough beer, wine, or spirits to get drunk increased from 10 percent in 1977 to 35 percent in 1993 (Eaton, 1994). The report stated that as many as one of every three college students qualifies as an alcohol abuser. College students in the United States spend more money per year on alcohol ($5.5 billlion) than they do on books and all other nonalcoholic beverages combined. The report also found that 40 percent of students with academic problems drink excessively and that alcohol is a factor in 28 percent of dropout cases (Eaton, 1994).

TABLE 11.3 Alcohol Use among Americans (by sex and age groups for total population)

Age	Observed Estimate		
	Ever Used	Used Past Year	Used Past Month
12–17	*39.3%*	*32.6%*	*15.7%*
Male	41.6	33.7	16.9
Female	37.0	31.4	14.5
18–25	*86.3*	*77.7*	*59.2*
Male	87.7	79.8	65.6
Female	85.0	75.6	53.0
26–34	*91.7*	*79.0*	*61.2*
Male	93.4	83.6	70.0
Female	90.0	74.5	52.8
35+	*87.0*	*62.6*	*46.5*
Male	93.8	69.0	56.1
Female	81.0	57.0	38.0
Total	83.0	64.7	47.8
Male	87.3	69.5	55.9
Female	79.0	60.2	40.4

SOURCE: *1992 National Household Survey on Drug Abuse,* Substance Abuse and Mental Health Services Administration, U.S. Department of Health and Human Services.

The Columbia researchers discovered that some 90 percent of all campus rapes involve drinking alcohol on the part of the perpetrator, the victim, or both (Eaton, 1994). A 1993 survey of college students by the National Institute on Drug Abuse (NIDA) reported that 18 percent of respondents told investigators they took advantage of someone sexually or had been victimized sexually as a consequence of their drinking (Pelton, 1994). These figures lend support to the high estimate of so-called date rape among college students in this country. The probability that people will drink (both men and women) stays relatively high until middle age and then decreases (see Table 11.3).

Numerous studies have found that elderly Americans are less likely to drink at all, drink heavily, or become problem drinkers than younger individuals (in Akers, 1992). Although alcohol abuse among the elderly is lower than in other age brackets, it may be a more serious problem than previously recognized and has the potential to become an even greater health and social hazard as the millions of baby boomers begin aging. Even though a 75-year-old man is likely to drink less than a 45-year-old man, this fact probably has less to do with age than with what demographers call *cohort effects.* Whereas the older man in this example grew up during the Great Depression and Prohibition, the younger man came of age in the 1960s and 1970s, when people were drinking a great deal and experimenting with a host of illegal drugs. If Americans under 50 years of age continue to drink at their current high levels of consumption, in the next 15 to 40 years, we could witness a tremendous increase in alcohol-related problems among the elderly (National Institute on Alcohol Abuse and Alcoholism, 1988). The number of people over 65 years of age in the United States will increase from 33 million in 1992 to 58.8 million in the year 2025.

SEX

Although gender differences in alcohol consumption have been declining in all age groupings, males drink more than females do. In school-age children (see Table 11.3), this difference is minimal. Typically, men drink more frequently than women, consume more alcohol than women, and are more likely to be heavy drinkers (Clinard & Meier, 1992). While as a group, women consume less alcohol than men and have fewer alcohol-related problems, among the heaviest drinkers, women have just as many drinking-related difficulties (if not more) as men (National Institute on Alcohol Abuse and Alcoholism, 1990). Single, separated, and divorced women who don't work are more likely to be heavy drinkers and to experience alcohol-related problems than women who are married, widowed, and/or work outside the home. These findings indicate that role deprivation—the loss or exclusion of women from roles such as wife, mother, and worker—may put women at greater risk for abusing alcohol (National Institute on Alcohol Abuse and Alcoholism, 1990). For a number of physiological reasons, women become intoxicated after drinking smaller amounts of alcohol than men. In addition, chronic alcohol abuse on the part of women results in death rates from 50 to 100 percent higher than those of male alcoholics.

Female alcoholics may encounter barriers to treatment that males are much less likely to find problematic. For example, because fewer women than men are employed full time, many women do not have access to employer-paid alcoholism treatment. In addition, women with young children may fear that if they are identified and labeled as alcoholics, the authorities may move to take those children away from them (National Institute on Alcohol Abuse and Alcoholism, 1990).

SOCIAL CLASS

Contrary to what many people think, individuals in the lower classes are *less* likely to drink than men and women in the middle and upper classes. In other words, people who are more highly educated and fully employed are more likely to consume alcohol than people who are less educated and more apt to be unemployed (Akers, 1992).

RACE, ETHNICITY, RELIGION, AND REGION

A greater percentage of White males and females consume alcohol in the United States than do Black men and women, although the *proportion* of problem drinkers in both races is about the same. Young African Americans are more likely to abstain from drinking than White youths, indicating that Blacks begin drinking heavily and have alcohol-related problems somewhat later in life than Whites (in Akers, 1992; Clinard & Meier, 1992). Latino males have high rates of alcohol use (including heavy drinking), and Latino females have a high rate of abstention. Edwin Lemert (1982) reports that drinking patterns of Native Americans differ from one nation to another, ranging from mainly abstainers to very heavy drinkers. When compared to the general population, a relatively small percentage of Native Americans drink, although the rate of problem drinking among users is much greater than that of the larger population. Both Irish and Italian Americans drink frequently (and often heavily), but the former have high rates of alcoholism (to be discussed later) whereas the latter do not.

Catholics, Jews, and liberal Protestants are more likely to drink than conservative and fundamentalist Protestants and Mormons. A disproportionate number of nondrinking Protestants explains in part why alcohol consumption is lower in the South than in any other region of the country. However, southern drinkers as a whole consume more alcohol than drinkers from any other part of the country (Clinard & Meier, 1992). It appears that Southerners fall into the extreme categories of abstainers or heavy drinkers. Finally, rates of drinking are higher in urban and suburban America than they are in small towns and rural parts of the country.

CONSEQUENCES OF ALCOHOL USE AND ABUSE

GENERAL HEALTH PROBLEMS

Consumed in moderation, alcohol has little if any negative health effect on most people. To the contrary, it has even been suggested that one or two (maximum) drinks a day may even be beneficial to an individual's mental and physical well-being (National Institute on Alcohol Abuse and Alcoholism, 1992b). However, even moderate drinking carries some health risks (such as strokes caused by bleeding, harmful interaction with over 100 medications), and heavy drinking carries the risk of serious health problems. A large enough dose of alcohol in a short period of time can be fatal. (College students in the United States and Japan have died after consuming as much as a quart of liquor in one to two hours.) Inasmuch as people have different levels of susceptibility to the physiological effects of alcohol, the impact of ingesting the same number of drinks can differ significantly from individual to individual (Clinard & Meier, 1992).

The physical malady associated with heavy drinking in the minds of most people is *cirrhosis* of the liver, a condition found in 8 percent of chronic drinkers and only 1 percent of the nonalcoholic population (McKim, 1986). As a result of excessive scarring from chronic drinking, the liver cannot function effectively. If the consumption of alcohol is not curtailed, cirrhosis can lead to death. Liver damage can also lead to a weakened immune system, leaving the body susceptible to a number of infections. The excessive use of alcohol is also related to cancers of the mouth, throat, and liver, those parts of the body that are directly exposed to spirits as they are ingested. People who smoke and drink are even more likely to contract cancer because alcohol appears to facilitate the cancer-causing properties of tobacco.

Other physical problems associated with heavy drinking include degeneration of the heart muscle, or *alcoholic cardiomyopathy* (sometimes called cirrhosis of the heart), diseases of the digestive system, respiratory disorders (including pneumonia), blood abnormalities, central nervous system maladies, malnutrition, blackouts, and in men, atrophy of the testicles, reduced sperm production, and impotence (Clinard & Meier, 1992; McKim, 1986; Ray & Ksir, 1987).

FETAL ALCOHOL SYNDROME

Since the mid-1980s, a good deal of attention has been focused on *fetal alcohol syndrome* (FAS)—the permanent mental and physical damage done to a developing fetus by a woman who drinks when she is pregnant. According to some estimates, FAS is the leading cause of mental retardation in this country, with as many as 1 out of every 10 retarded Americans being afflicted with this syndrome. Children of women who are "binge drinkers" (who consume a number of drinks at one sitting) appear to be particularly at risk, although only 1 in 3 babies of alcoholic women will exhibit full-blown FAS (Rosenthal, 1991).

Some observers are of the opinion that the risk of FAS-related abnormalities has been exaggerated. They point to countries such as Italy and France, where adults (including pregnant women) routinely consume alcohol with their meals, and they note that rates of FAS are no higher in these societies (Chafetz in Peele, 1991). Alcohol researcher Stanton Peele argues that the much higher rates of mental and physical abnormalities experienced by the children of low-income minority women are more likely the result of smoking, malnutrition, and poor health care. If Peele is correct, FAS has become a kind of medical scapegoat for physical and mental problems that are essentially class based (poverty, malnutrition, and inadequate health care).

ALCOHOL AND AIDS

There are at least two possible connections—one physiological, the other more psychological—between the consumption of alcohol and the virus that causes AIDS. Alcohol can suppress the activities of certain immune system cells; this could increase the vulnerability of those individuals exposed to HIV. Also, among those people already infected with HIV, alcohol-induced immunosuppression might add to HIV-induced immunosuppression and speed up the physiological processes that lead to AIDS (National Institute on Alcohol Abuse and Alcoholism, 1992a, p. 1).

Regarding the psychological dimension, a number of researchers have reported finding an association between alcohol use and high-risk sexual behavior. One study of heterosexual men and women found that individuals who combine drinking with sexual activity were less likely to use condoms during intercourse, and a survey of teenagers in Massachusetts reached the same conclusion. Approximately 60 percent of women who contract sexually transmitted diseases (including AIDS) were under the influence of alcohol when they had intercourse (Eaton, 1994). A study of homosexual men found that even moderate drinking was associated with high-risk (unprotected) sexual behavior (in National Institute on Alcohol Abuse and Alcoholism, 1992c, pp. 2–3).

DRUNK DRIVING

Of the more than 120 million licensed drivers in the United States, almost 100 million drink alcohol to one degree or another (Clinard & Meier, 1992). It has been estimated that as many as 5 percent of drivers on the road at any one time may be legally drunk; that figure approaches 10 percent on weekends. A driver with a blood alcohol level (BAL) of 0.15 (8 to 10 drinks) is 18 times more likely to be involved in a traffic accident than a non-drinking driver (Jacobs, 1986). It is hardly surprising, therefore, that as many as 25,000 people are killed annually in the United States in drinking-related motor vehicle accidents. Tens of thousands more are injured each year in these mishaps.

Even though over 2 million arrests are made annually for drunk driving, more arrests than for any other category for which statistics are compiled (Jacobs, 1986), the probability of being apprehended by law enforcement officials for this offense has been estimated at only 1 in 2,000 (Ross, 1984). Organizations like Mothers Against Drunk Driving (MADD), Remove Intoxicated Drivers (RID), and Students Against Driving Drunk (SADD) have been working to reduce the number of drunk drivers on the road by educating the public to the dangers of operating a motor vehicle while intoxicated and by pressuring state and local governments to step up enforcement of drunk-driving laws and to increase the penalties for drunk driving.

While these groups have been quite successful in their efforts to convince the public that drunk driving is deviant behavior, they have discovered that many jurisdictions do not have the money to allocate officers and other resources to this problem on a permanent basis (Collins & Frey, 1992). This means that although the *severity* of punishment

in some states for drunk driving may be high (fines of a thousand dollars or more, 200-plus hours of community service, suspension of driving privileges for three to six months, and jail time for repeat offenders), these penalties will have only a limited deterrent effect if the *certainty* of punishment remains low.

Because the overwhelming number of persons arrested for drunk driving are young males, the federal government has in past years threatened to withhold highway funds to those states that do not raise the minimum legal age for the possession and consumption of alcohol from 18 to 21 years. However, research by Linda Mooney and her colleagues (1992) on young people in one state where the legal drinking age was 18 (Louisiana) and another with a minimum age requirement of 21 (North Carolina) discovered little evidence to support the assumption that raising the drinking age to 21 will lower the rate of possession and consumption of alcohol by the target population—that is, people between the ages of 18 and 20. To the contrary, the researchers found that greater quantities of alcohol were consumed by the target population (18- to 20-year-olds) in North Carolina (with a minimum drinking age of 21) than in Louisiana (with a minimum drinking age of 18). The authors suggest that the illegality of alcohol for 18- to 20-year-olds in North Carolina may well enhance its desirability (the "forbidden fruit" hypothesis). "Because of its illegality, alcohol consumption becomes a way to protest or gain peer status, or it simply may be more desirable because of the risk involved" (Mooney et al., 1992, p. 64). If even a small percentage of these young people drive after drinking, the likelihood of alcohol-related traffic accidents will increase.

H. Laurence Ross (in Sykes & Cullen, 1992), one of the foremost researchers in the area of drinking and driving, notes that in the United States, there is no alternative to transportation by automobile in many areas. He also points out that this is a society that equates the consumption of alcohol with the good life. We might add that millions of individuals (perhaps the majority of people) would be loath to give up their cars even if public transportation were available. If the certainty of being apprehended and punished for drunk driving will never be very high because of the tremendous costs involved and if educating people to the dangers of this activity will only be partially effective, perhaps the only remaining viable alternative is to introduce *informal* mechanisms of intervention and social control to those situations where intoxicated individuals are about to drive. Using a self-administered questionnaire, researchers discovered that 83 percent of respondents (out of a sample of 195) had attempted to prevent a friend, relative, or even a stranger from driving after that individual had consumed alcohol (Collins & Frey, 1992). Not only did these people spend a significant amount of time and energy during these interventions, but in the majority of cases (81 percent), their efforts were successful.

ALCOHOL AND VIOLENCE

The association between the use of alcohol and numerous crimes of violence has been well documented. A survey of victims of violent crimes (rape, robbery, and assault) reported that 21 percent of the offenders were thought to be under the influence of alcohol at the time of the offense (*Drugs and Crime Facts,* 1991). Over one-third of prison inmates consumed alcoholic beverages every day during the year they committed their crimes (U.S. Department of Justice, 1988). One researcher found that alcohol was involved in two-thirds of the 588 homicide cases he examined (Wolfgang, 1966).

Criminologists Marshall Clinard and Robert Meier (1992) note that it is unclear what role (if any) drinking plays in the commission of these offenses. "There is no direct 'causal' relationship between alcohol use and violent crimes, and alcohol does not inevitably lead to aggression" (p. 250). If drunkenness and alcoholism were primarily responsible for much of the violence in society, rates of homicide, rape, and aggravated assault would be significantly higher than past and present levels.

CAUSES OF PROBLEM DRINKING

That problem drinking often runs in families has been known for hundreds of years. In more recent times, patterns of intergenerational alcohol abuse have been verified by careful, systematic observation. These observations—both folk and scientific—lead to the inevitable question: Does an individual become a problem drinker because of some physiological predisposition to alcohol use and abuse inherited from his or her parents, or does an individual *learn* through the socialization process to both drink and abuse alcohol within the context of the home environment (National Institute on Alcohol Abuse and Alcoholism, 1992d)?

THE DISEASE MODEL

As many as 9 out of 10 Americans believe that alcoholism is a disease (Kohn, 1991), a view that is held in a modified version by the NIAAA. "Substantial evidence indicates that genetic factors play a significant role in the development of at least some forms of alcoholism" (National Institute on Alcohol Abuse and Alcoholism, 1992c, p. 1).

Genetic susceptibility to problem drinking may operate in at least two ways:

1. Genes may play a *direct* role in the development of alcoholism by affecting in some manner how the body metabolizes alcohol.
2. Genes may have an *indirect* contribution on heavy drinking inasmuch as they influence an individual's personality or temperament in such a way that he or she becomes "vulnerable to alcoholism" (National Institute on Alcohol Abuse and Alcoholism, 1992d).

While the director of the NIAAA argues that progress has been made in understanding the genetic "vulnerability to alcoholism," he also notes that "it is probable that environmental influences will be at least as important, and possibly more important, than genetic influences" (Gordis, 1992, p. 3).

Although the idea that alcoholism and drunkenness are biologically based diseases can be traced to the early nineteenth century in the United States, this perspective was given new life with the founding of Alcoholics Anonymous (AA)—now a worldwide organization that has grown significantly in size and influence over the years—by two reformed heavy drinkers in 1935. The alcoholism-as-disease argument, as subscribed to by AA, is as follows (Fingarette, 1988; Peele, 1989):

- Alcoholism is a specific physiological disease to which some people are vulnerable.
- If people susceptible to this disease start using alcohol at some point during their lives, they will inevitably progress to a stage of uncontrollable drinking.
- The disease exists in and of itself and cannot be traced to sociocultural factors including childrearing practices and social class.
- Because the disease is incurable, complete abstention from alcohol is the only hope people have for sobriety.
- People can hold this disease in check (not drink) by belonging to support groups organized by and for those individuals who share the same physiological condition.

The alcoholism-as-disease model and the self-proclaimed success of groups like AA in helping individuals to control their problem drinking have been sharply criticized by many scientists and social commentators for a variety of reasons. Behavioral geneticist

Robert Plomin (in Kohn, 1991, p. 32) notes that although AA wants people to accept their view that alcoholism is a genetic disease, the evidence needed to support this contention "isn't all that convincing." Even researchers who believe that some forms of problem drinking have a biological basis note that alcohol abuse is more than simply a genetic disease. Regarding the genes-cause-alcoholism approach, one psychologist working in this field noted, "The public has been sold a bill of goods" (McGue in Kohn, 1991, p. 34).

Heavy drinkers who accept the fundamental premise (as put forth by AA) that people who cannot control their drinking suffer from a biological disease may become discouraged by this dismal diagnosis and never attempt to stop. Others may internalize the label "alcoholic" and drink even more. Still others may reject treatment if they come to believe that lifelong abstinence is the only possible remedy for heavy drinking (Fingarette, 1988).

Because AA has long been reluctant to publish statistics regarding the social and physical characteristics of individuals who attend meetings or the organization's overall success and failure rates, it is virtually impossible to know what impact (especially over the long term) their philosophy and group support programs have had on people. In addition, successful treatment of people with drinking problems may be more a function of individual characteristics than of any specific alcohol-reduction strategy. For example, an examination of other treatment programs indicated that well-educated middle- and upper-class White problem drinkers who were employed, married, and middle aged or older had twice the improvement rate of heavy drinkers from the lowest socioeconomic classes (Peele, 1989).

SOCIOLOGICAL INTERPRETATIONS

From a sociological perspective, alcohol use (and most of the abuse) as well as the variety of behavior associated with this activity are viewed as a form of learned behavior—learned in accordance with group values and, to a lesser extent, the values of the larger society of which the individual is a member. The fact that Catholics, Jews, and liberal Protestants drink more than fundamentalist Protestants and Mormons reflects the specific values of these groups and not the genetic makeup of their members. If the religious values of Joseph Smith (1805–1844) and other early leaders of the Church of Jesus Christ of Latter Day Saints had been radically different, Mormons today might have one of the highest rates of alcohol-related physical and social problems instead of one of the lowest. Mormons learn from an early age that they must abstain from alcohol, whereas children raised in other groups internalize a very different message.

These latter individuals eventually come to believe that not only is social drinking acceptable, but heavy drinking (especially on the part of males) and related conduct such as fighting and aggressive sexual behavior will be tolerated and may even be demanded in some situations. In Russia, for example, drinking is associated with manhood (see "Focus on Russia" in this chapter). Because patterns of alcohol use (including chronic drinking) reflect cultural and ethnic values, these values and the resulting alcohol-related behavior can also be changed.

CONTROLLING THE PROBLEM: CROSS-CULTURAL STRATEGIES

Strategies for reducing alcohol consumption focus on two very different groups of people: (1) heavy drinkers and (2) social drinkers and abstainers. Heavy drinkers account for only a relatively small percentage of all alcohol consumers, but they represent a significant portion of those people with alcohol-related problems. Because of their often long

AN OLD PROBLEM IN A NEW COMMONWEALTH
Gorbachev, Home-Brew, and Alcoholism

According to legend, a tenth-century Russian leader rejected Islam in favor of Christianity for his people because the former prohibited the use of alcohol whereas the latter did not. Grand Prince Vladimir I reputedly said, "It is Russia's joy to drink; we cannot do without it" (in Gray, 1993, p. 26). Regardless of the veracity of this story, there can be little doubt that Russians as a group (as well as other ethnic groups in the region) are heavy drinkers with an affinity for alcohol.

More recently, a Soviet medical specialist summed up his fellow citizens' love of alcohol in the following manner (in Connor, 1972, pp. 39–40): "People drink when they meet, when they take leave of each other; to quiet their hunger when they are hungry, to stimulate their appetite when they are satisfied. They drink to get warm when it is cold, to cool off when it is hot. They drink when they are drowsy, to wake up, and when they are wakeful, to bring sleep."

Although it is impossible to obtain a completely accurate figure on alcohol consumption in the new Commonwealth (as it would be in any country), statistics indicate that between 1955 and 1984, Soviet citizens increased their intake of alcoholic beverages approximately 240 percent. Even though the annual 1984 intake was 15.5 liters per person (lower than in Britain or France), Russians typically engage in prolonged drinking bouts in which they consume vodka and other powerful spirits that are roughly 40 percent absolute alcohol ("Veni, Vidi, Vodka," 1989).

One result of this volume and pattern of alcohol consumption is a large population with drinking problems: 5 million alcoholics are registered with the Russian Ministry of Health (out of a population of 280 million), and another 20 million people report being alcohol dependent. According to official estimates, 60 percent of the country's alcoholics are under 30 years of age (Darialova, 1991; "Veni, Vidi, Vodka," 1989), insuring that drinking-related problems will in all likelihood plague the Commonwealth for at least 40 more years.

While life expectancy has increased over recent years in virtually every modern industrial state and in most developing nations, in the former Soviet Union, it decreased for men, from 66 years in 1965 to 62 years in 1984. Experts agree that alcohol is the primary cause of this life-span reduction. Studies by researchers outside the Commonwealth suggest that alcohol abuse within those states is the third most common cause of death behind heart disease and cancer.

According to Russian experts, heavy alcohol consumption is a major factor in various forms of criminal behavior. "About two-thirds of all intentional homicides; three-fourths of all serious bodily injuries, assaults, and robberies; more than one-half of all thefts of personal property; and more than two-fifths of all traffic violations are committed under the influence of alcohol" (Yakovlev, 1979). The association between drunkenness and homicide appears to be greater in the Commonwealth than in other countries that compile such statistics. One Russian

Public drunkenness and alcohol abuse are serious problems in Russia. People can be found stumbling around in an alcoholic stupor or passed out "dead drunk" in public places at any time of the day or night.

observer argues that up to 40 percent of all divorces and the mistreatment of thousands of children are alcohol related (in Connor, 1972).

In an effort to reduce the many negative consequences of alcohol use and abuse, former Soviet President Mikhail Gorbachev launched a nationwide antialcohol campaign in the mid-1980s. The production of vodka and other drinks was reduced, and the price of spirits was increased by 15 to 25 percent in 1985 and another 25 percent in 1986. The number of state stores selling alcohol was cut by 55 percent in less than a year, and their hours of operation were limited to between 2 P.M. and 5 P.M. Government officials also launched a campaign to destroy vineyards in wine-producing states ("Veni, Vidi, Vodka," 1989).

Gorbachev's strategy yielded significant dividends, and the nation's health improved rapidly. Crime dropped 25 percent and rates of absenteeism declined 33 percent. Unfortunately, these successes were short lived. The latent consequences (that is, the unanticipated and/or unintended results) of Gorbachev's antialcohol campaign turned out to be more of a threat to Soviet society than the initial alcohol-related problems he was attempting to solve.

To begin, the production of "home brew" (illegally distilled spirits), a long-standing Russian tradition (especially in rural areas), increased dramatically. Demand for ingredients needed in the distillation process resulted in rationing, shortages, and thefts of certain products (especially sugar) in many parts of the country. In 1987, authorities reported that 242,000 tons of sugar were stolen. While the theft of home-brew ingredients from already poorly stocked state stores was something the government could ill afford, the most severe economic blow was the loss of 13 percent of the former Soviet Union's *total* revenue derived from liquor taxes. One Russian economist stated that the three most serious blows to the Gorbachev regime (prior to 1989) were Chernobyl (the nuclear disaster), the fall of oil prices, and the antialcohol campaign ("Veni, Vidi, Vodka," 1989).

Perhaps the most tragic results of the mid-1980's alcohol reduction program were the losses of life and the often irreparable damage done to people's health as a result of consuming alcohol substitutes. To satisfy their thirst for vodka and other liquors, people began drinking cologne, after-shave, toothpaste, glues of all types, nail polish, window-cleaning fluid, disinfectants, antifreeze, brake fluid, insecticides, cockroach poison, hair lotion, cough medicine, and cattle-growth stimulators ("Veni, Vidi, Vodka," 1989). People spread shoe polish on bread; when the alcohol in the mixture was absorbed, they scraped off the dried residue and ate the bread. Even the quality of paint declined as a result of people stealing the alcohol needed to manufacture it. In short, former Soviet citizens consumed almost everything and anything that contained alcohol. In one year, 40,000 people were poisoned by drinking alcohol surrogates; 11,000 of them died. One Moscow official stated that the cost of caring for these poison victims was "colossal" ("Veni, Vidi, Vodka," 1989).

The hostility of the Soviet people, coupled with the Central Committee's criticism of the antialcohol campaign in 1987, caused Gorbachev to retreat from his stringent control policies. In 1989, legal alcohol production was increased and hours of operation at state liquor stores were extended. By the middle of 1989, sales were up dramatically, and the state was once again receiving a significant portion of its annual revenue from alcohol taxes ("Veni, Vidi, Vodka," 1989).

Explanations for high rates of alcohol consumption and alcoholism in the Commonwealth are rooted in that nation's culture and the structure of the former Soviet society. Sociologist Walter D. Connor (1972) offers the following interpretations:

1. Young men are socialized at an early age into a culture that equates drinking with masculinity. Males who refrain from drinking or who consume alcohol in moderation are "considered something less than real men" (p. 40). Drinking (which often results in drunkenness) is a demonstration of attributes considered essential to manliness.
2. Alcohol consumption is such an integral part of the Russian culture that the social pressure to drink is very intense. Individuals who abstain are viewed as "stupid" in their choice to forego one of life's pleasures. Connor reports a study that found 42 percent of people undergoing treatment for alcohol problems resumed drinking because friends and relatives convinced them to do so. Heavy social drinking and drunkenness are not only tolerated; they are often encouraged.
3. The volume of alcohol produced in the Commonwealth along with the number of state outlets means that vodka and other alcoholic beverages are accessible to the bulk of the population. Prior to Gorbachev's nationwide antialcohol campaign, there were 238,000 state liquor stores.
4. Boredom and frustration in a society with a scarcity of consumer goods and a highly inefficient government also contribute to the use and abuse of alcohol. One Soviet official stated, "The main reason for two decades of hard drinking was that people got tired of lies, stupidity and having nothing useful to do" ("Veni, Vidi, Vodka," 1989). Physical isolation and extreme weather conditions in many remote towns and villages may lead residents to conclude that there is little to do but drink. For example, one far northern village (population 3,000) receives 120,000 bottles of vodka

annually, which translates to approximately 60 bottles per adult per year (Quinn-Judge, 1990).

Regarding the treatment of alcoholism, Russian specialists have, for the most part, eschewed the medical model that views individuals with alcohol disorders as sick. Rather, the alcoholic is considered a normal person who has overindulged for a prolonged period of time and developed a serious drinking problem (Connor, 1972). However, in 1987, Alcoholics Anonymous opened a chapter in Moscow, and, with the help of American practitioners, a number of counseling and rehabilitation centers were established ("Veni, Vidi, Vodka," 1989). The two hospitals in the Russian capital that deal with alcoholics are overcrowded and, by local standards, expensive (Gutterman, 1994).

Because of the link between alcohol and crime in the old Soviet Union, a number of medical treatment programs were mandated for "socially dangerous alcoholics" (Yakovlev, 1979, p. 103). Alcoholics who have committed dangerous criminal acts are not viewed as blameworthy, nor are they considered criminally responsible for their acts. Instead, these individuals are sent by the courts to mental institutions. Other alcoholic offenders are remanded to medical institutions with special medical and labor programs. Termination of this treatment is at the discretion of the institution. A third category of treatment is for noncriminal chronic alcoholics and drug abusers. This mandatory program consists of medical treatment and labor reeducation (Yakovlev, 1979). At their peak, these treatment and labor centers held almost 100,000 offenders; that number was reduced to 28,000 in March 1994, reflecting the more liberal attitudes of the post-Soviet era (Gutterman, 1994).

It appears that in the post-Soviet era, people are drinking at least as much as they did in the days of communism, and if anything, alcohol-related problems are increasing. In 1992, one-third of the 2.7 million crimes recorded by Russian police were alcohol related (Gray, 1993). A former policeman believes that since the transition to a more democratic, capitalist state, problem drinking has increased. "Under communism many people were afraid that they would lose their party cards if they were found drunk in public. But life has become harder now and more people are drinking, either to forget about things for a while or because they are afraid of what will happen tomorrow" (in Gray, 1993, p. 26). If this observation is correct, the hardships that tens of millions of people are experiencing as Russia undergoes a particularly difficult and unpredictable societal transformation will generate an ever-increasing number of alcohol-related problems.

Just as the Indian caste system survived the implementation of political, religious, and economic philosophies imposed on the indigenous people by outsiders, alcohol use and abuse in many of the former Soviet republics are deeply rooted in these nations' social life and traditions and are likely to endure, regardless of prevailing political and economic conditions.

involvement in and commitment to an alcohol-related lifestyle, these individuals are the most difficult people to reach or influence with anti- or controlled-drinking strategies. On the other hand, social drinkers (those individuals whose lives are not significantly affected by their consumption of alcohol) are more likely to be persuaded to maintain their responsible drinking, and abstainers may be convinced to maintain their nondrinking behavior. Following are a number of strategies aimed at reducing the consumption of alcohol around the world (Fingarette, 1988; Peele, 1989).

USING LEGISLATION TO REDUCE ALCOHOL CONSUMPTION

The quantity of alcohol consumed could be diminished by raising the state and/or federal tax on each bottle of beer, wine, and spirits sold. This strategy, which has resulted in a sharp decline in cigarette smoking in Canada and the Scandinavian countries (where cigarettes are taxed at a rate of up to $3.90 *per pack*), could prove to be just as effective in retarding the sale of alcoholic beverages. This policy might prove to be especially useful in controlling problem drinking on the part of teenagers and young adults, who could only afford to buy more limited quantities of beer at a cost, for example, of $10 a six-pack. Money generated from this "sin tax" could be used for alcohol awareness programs at the elementary and high school levels and to fund government-sponsored treatment programs for heavy drinkers.

A related strategy would be to reduce the easy access to alcoholic beverages that currently exists in many parts of the United States. For example, in some states, beer, wine, and spirits can be purchased in liquor stores, supermarkets, convenience stores, drugstores, and gas stations. Limiting sales to state-licensed liquor stores, a policy that exists in most of Canada, would presumably force people to make an extra effort to purchase alcoholic beverages.

The alcohol industry spends over 1 billion dollars a year encouraging Americans to drink. Much of this advertising is aimed at teenagers, who consume more than 1 billion bottles and cans of beer a year. Breweries have been accused of selling not beer but an alcohol-consuming lifestyle that is associated with relaxation, fun, fantasy, romance, sex, sports, adventure, and risk taking ("Alcohol and the Soft Sell," 1994; Hacker in Roan, 1994). The beer industry denies these allegations, noting that it "does not advertise to customers who cannot, by law, consume their products" (Becker in Cimons, 1991). The Sensible Advertising and Family Education Act (SAFE Act), introduced in the Senate in 1994, would require all alcohol beverage advertisements to include a health warning. The federal government could also prohibit the alcohol industry from advertising on television, just as it did with the tobacco industry in 1970.

INDIVIDUAL TREATMENT STRATEGIES

Various types of alcohol treatment strategies have been implemented over the years in an effort to get problems drinkers to completely stop or significantly curtail their alcohol consumption. The two most effective treatments have been aversion therapy and therapy that helps individuals deal with the negative emotions that lead to problem drinking (Miler & Hester in Peele, 1989).

Aversion therapy includes such techniques as administering chemicals that lead to vomiting after the ingestion of alcohol and giving patients electric shocks after they drink. A somewhat less physically painful and equally effective offshoot of this strategy, called *covert sensitization,* involves associating nauseating images with alcohol use.

Controlled-drinking therapy, common in Britain, Scandinavia, and some southern European countries, teaches problem drinkers to moderate their intake of alcohol. In other words, these individuals learn how to consume relatively small quantities of alcohol and then stop drinking before this behavior results in any difficulties for themselves or others. This strategy has been almost completely rejected in the United States, where the alcohol treatment industry is of the opinion that abstinence is the only solution to problem drinking. Peele (1989, p. 201) argues that this is unfortunate inasmuch as *"not a single comparative study"* has found that abstinence is any more effective in treating alcoholism than controlled-drinking therapy (emphasis in the original).

Recent evidence suggests that people with alcohol problems may be able to drink moderately after taking an opiate antagonist called *nalmefene* that blocks the brain's pleasurable response to drinking without any negative side effects (Monroe, 1993). Researchers were optimistic in the wake of an initial experiment involving only 14 problem drinkers. All the subjects reported that months after having stopped taking the drug, they were drinking less or had stopped drinking completely.

GAMBLING

SCOPE OF THE PROBLEM

Gambling is a cultural universal. There are no historical periods or societies in which the wagering of money or other valuables on the outcome of some event or sport was absent.

Gambling was prevalent in ancient Egypt and Greece as well as the Roman Empire, where people bet heavily on the outcome of chariot races and gladiators who fought to the death (Ragland, 1991). In the American colonies, patriots anxious to rid themselves of English rule sold lottery tickets to finance the Revolutionary War. Lotteries were also instrumental in the founding of some of the nation's most prestigious universities: Harvard, Yale, and Princeton (Bayer, 1990). Gambling has always been popular in the United States, a country where people have never been shy about risking their money in the hopes of quick financial gain. Government-regulated lotteries, betting on horseraces, and casino gambling are found in most European countries as well as in many Asian nations. In addition, various forms of illegal gambling are found in almost all modern societies.

Since so much money is wagered illegally in the United States and people may be less than forthright when questioned about their gambling activity, we have little more than wide-ranging estimates of the amount of money that changes hands as a result of gambling each year. One expert reports that each year, approximately $240 billion is wagered legally *and* illegally in the United States and that this figure increases by about 10 percent annually (Christiansen in Welles, 1989). Another investigator notes that in 1989, "the gross legal gaming handle" (that is, the amount of money wagered) was $246.9 billion (Lesieur, 1992, p. 43). If this latter figure is accurate, the amount of illegal betting (which most experts believe to be far greater than the amount of legal betting) could push the total of legal *and* illegal betting to a figure in the neighborhood of $1 trillion. The illegal profits earned annually in the United States from gambling are second only to money earned by organized crime as a result of the sale of drugs.

PATHOLOGICAL GAMBLERS

Similarly, we do not have accurate figures on the number of people who wager on a regular basis or on how many of these individuals are problem gamblers. A 1988 study commissioned by the National Institute of Mental Health concluded that as many as 4.2 million adult Americans may be addicted to gambling (Berliner, 1991). In 1980, pathological gambling became a legitimate or official social problem when it was certified as a mental disorder by the American Psychiatric Association (Greene, 1982). Although the overwhelming majority of people who gamble never go beyond the *social phase*—occasionally buying lottery tickets, playing cards, and making small sports wagers with friends—pathological gamblers progress through three stages of the so-called disease (Ciarrocchi in Gammon, 1986).

After a *big win* (the first stage) that nets half a year's salary or more, people come to believe that gambling is the key to their financial success. Both gambling episodes and the amount of money wagered increase, and the individual is well on his or her way to the *losing phase.* By this time, pathological gamblers are motivated by their need for action as well as their desire to win. For these individuals, the process of picking a horse, anticipating, and then watching a race generates a high that is comparable to the pleasure experienced from taking mind-altering drugs. Chasing and being part of the action provides a powerful rush of thrills and excitement. It is not unusual for gamblers to go without food, sleep, and even using the bathroom during these periods. Because gamblers experience a euphoric state of mind, researchers in a number of countries report withdrawallike symptoms when pathological gamblers attempt to stop betting (Lesieur, 1992). Rapidly sliding into the *desperation phase,* the gambler becomes irrational, almost delusional, and out of control. The individual is consumed by betting and incurs enormous financial losses as relationships with family, friends, and employers disintegrate.

The consequences of pathological gambling not only take their toll on the gambler, but they also affect his or her entire familial, social, and occupational network as well as the larger society. Henry R. Lesieur (1992, pp. 45–48) has outlined the not-always obvious costs of this behavior.

INDIVIDUAL AND FAMILY PROBLEMS

Chronic gamblers suffer from a wide range of physical and mental problems, including depression, insomnia, intestinal disorders, and stress-related diseases. According to one study, the typical pathological gambler not only destroys his or her own life but also disrupts the lives of between 10 and 17 other people, many of whom are family members (Politzer in Greene, 1982). The families of these individuals may be in a continual state of debt; in extreme cases, utilities are shut off, automobiles and furniture are repossessed, and mortgages are foreclosed. To make matters worse, family members are harassed by bill collectors. Spouses grow resentful as family resources are depleted. Children feel lonely, guilty, abandoned, and rejected by parents whose gambling occupies all their time. One study found that children of pathological gamblers are more likely to be abused than children of the general population.

THE WORKPLACE

Not only do compulsive gamblers miss an inordinate number of workdays, but people preoccupied with making the next bet and burdened with heavy financial losses do not make productive employees. Pathological gamblers may also be bookmakers (people who accept bets), engaging in this illegal activity from their legitimate places of business. Lesieur argues that the less work-related supervision the gambler has (typically in management positions and the professions), the freer the individual is to engage in gambling activities in the workplace.

GAMBLING AND CRIME

Because pathological gambling invariably results in losses of substantial amounts of money, individuals who find themselves with mounting debts often turn to crime. A psychiatrist who works with gamblers found that "two out of three compulsive gamblers have committed some illegal activity as a way to pay off debts or get more money to continue gambling" (Rosenthal in Berliner, 1991, p. B1). As much as 40 percent of the nation's white-collar crime may be related to gambling. Drug users may spend hundreds of dollars a day to support their habit, but gamblers can lose tens of thousands of dollars in a single weekend. Researchers have found that compulsive gamblers are often involved in check forgery, armed robbery, fencing stolen goods, tax evasion, burglary, pimping, prostitution, and selling drugs. In addition, pathological gamblers engage in an estimated $1.3 billion worth of insurance fraud each year.

THE GOVERNMENT, BIG BUSINESS, AND GAMBLING

Most people would be surprised, to say the least, if they saw government-financed commercials on television and advertisements in local newspapers advocating drug and alcohol use. While the typical politician would regard any such policy as abhorrent, many of these same individuals have no qualms about convincing as many people as possible to buy lottery tickets. In 1964, New Hampshire became the first state to have a legal, government-controlled and -sponsored lottery. New York and New Jersey followed suit in 1970, and by 1994, 39 states and the District of Columbia had lotteries. In 23 states, people can bet on dice games and roulette wheels. Taken collectively, state-run lotteries in 1990 were the nation's twenty-fourth largest business, recording over $20 billion in total sales (Karcher, 1992).

These states decided that one way to generate revenue was to capitalize on people's desire to strike it rich. Those individuals reluctant to wager were enticed to place bets by slick, sometimes controversial ad campaigns. In the nation's capital, for example, one advertisement featured a picture of Martin Luther King, Jr., with the slogan, "His vision lives on—Honor the dream—DC Lottery" ("Rien ne va Plus," 1990). Government officials discovered that they could effectively counter a good deal of antigambling criticism by linking the buying of lottery tickets to well-known, influential symbols and individuals (like Dr. King), continually reminding people that the proceeds of their wagers are used for socially desirable ends, such as education.

State lotteries have been criticized for a number of reasons. First, even though they offer jackpots as high as $100 million, lottery officials fail to adequately inform the betting public that the chances of winning are as high as 17 *million* to 1. Some economists believe that if state lotteries were regulated by the Federal Trade Commission, they would be put out of business for consumer fraud ("Rien ne va Plus," 1990).

Lottery-type wagering is also contributing to a tremendous rise in gambling on the part of teenagers. The lottery may serve as an initial or "gateway" gambling activity that leads to other forms of wagering. A survey of 2,700 adolescents in four states found that approximately half gambled once a year and that 5 percent could be classified as pathological gamblers (in Levine, 1990). In 1992, approximately 280,000 teenagers were denied entrance to casinos in Atlantic City, New Jersey, and another 29,000 were expelled from these gambling establishments when their real ages were determined (Holmstrom, 1994b).

Lottery advertisements are primarily aimed at lower- and working-class Americans (the "selling of hope" as Goodman [1994] calls it), who spend a greater percentage of their income on these games than do more affluent individuals. Lottery winners are depicted as rolling in money (sometimes literally) and living carefree lives of luxury. A lottery commercial in Massachusetts shows a milkman driving an expensive new sports car to his mansionlike home after winning the jackpot. One study found that the poorest third of households accounted for more than 50 percent of weekly lottery tickets sold (in Bayer, 1990).

With lottery jackpots sometimes exceeding $100 million, Americans will wait in long lines to buy tickets. Are state-sponsored lotteries a desirable way of generating funds to help pay for everything from basic city services to public schools? Or are governments contributing to the nation's social problems by encouraging people to wager money that many of them cannot afford and perhaps even helping them become compulsive gamblers?

Although the use and abuse of alcohol and illegal drugs costs U.S. citizens dearly in terms of drunk-driving accidents, drug-related street crime, and money spent on law enforcement, the overall impact of these substances is much greater than most people realize. Consider the following consequences of our polydrug-using society:

- The abuse of alcohol and illegal drugs costs the business community between $144 and $160 billion each year—approximately half the cost of the nation's annual outlay for defense. These costs result from a decline in productivity, poor-quality workmanship, industrial accidents and fires, tardiness, absenteeism, medical treatment for substance abusers, and the premature death of these individuals. Bell South estimates that 65 percent of its health care costs are directly related to substance abuse. General Motors states that substance abusers work on average only 140 out of 240 workdays a year and cost the company $1 billion annually. Much of this loss is passed on to consumers, who pay an additional $400 per vehicle for GM's employee drug problem (Rice et al., 1991; Stutman, 1990). No doubt, consumers pay for drug abuse on almost every product and service they use to the amount of perhaps thousands of dollars a year per family.
- Between 1986 and early 1990, at least 100,000 babies were born to drug-abusing mothers (Kraar, 1990). The medical expenses for prolonged intensive care for these infants run into the billions of dollars annually. Some of the most seriously affected "crack babies" may require comprehensive medical treatment for years and never grow up to be productive members of society. What chance will they have to thrive in a society where even some of the brightest, best-educated people are only marginally successful in the economic marketplace? And no dollar amount can calculate the human suffering endured by these children and their families.
- Because they have tremendous power over desperate people with tremendous amounts of money (often in the form of cash), law enforcement officials at all levels, in every region of the country have been corrupted by drug dealers and traffickers (Ostrowski, 1990). Police officers, FBI agents, Drug Enforcement Agency agents, coast guard officers, prison guards, customs inspectors, prosecutors, and judges have all compromised their duties and principles and given in to the temptation of often significant amounts of money. These officials have something to sell that is an integral part of the success of both local and international drugs distributors—that is, "the non-enforcement of the law" (Wisotsky, 1990a).
- Numerous observers are of the opinion that the fear, panic, and loathing of drugs in this country have

Economist Paul Mason (in Francis, 1994, p. 11) notes that lotteries "give legislators an excuse to raise tax revenues by preying on the vices of the public, and particularly on those with less education and lower incomes." This amounts to a regressive tax on the poor, who may not even see an equitable portion of their wagers pumped back into the local community. In Detroit, the purchase of lottery tickets by predominantly local residents accounted for $104 million of Michigan's school aid fund. However, only $80 million of that money was returned to city schools; the remaining $24 million ended up in more affluent suburban schools ("Rien ne va Plus," 1990).

Some businesses and corporations either directly or indirectly contribute to gambling in this country. When a television sportscaster was asked whether his detailed presentation of point spreads on National Football League games on Sunday afternoons promoted gambling, he stated, "Oh definitely. I think gambling is great fun" (Underwood, 1986). Almost every major newspaper in the country publishes point spreads for football

whipped up a kind of drug hysteria that is slowly but surely eroding some fundamental rights of citizens. Urine testing in the workplace, roadblocks, routine strip searches, school locker searches without cause, and forfeiture of property because of minuscule amounts of drugs (the "zero tolerance" policy) are all occurring in this country (often with the blessing of the public) in the name of fighting the drug war (Ostrowski, 1990).

- Conflict theorists would argue that the war on drugs provides a made-to-order pretext for the government to extend its control over the lower classes. Under sentencing laws enacted by Congress, every gram of crack cocaine is considered the equivalent of 100 grams of powder cocaine (Newton, 1992). As a result of this policy, poor, crack-using African Americans are serving relatively long prison sentences while Whites apprehended with much larger amounts of powder cocaine are treated much more leniently. One study found that 90 percent of all federal-level crack defendants are Black, and many of these people are serving up to 5 years in prison for possessing as little as 5 grams of crack (Newton, 1992). Critics contend that even if crack cocaine is more psychologically addicting than powder cocaine, the tremendous disparity in sentencing is not justified.
- In depressed areas of American cities, successful drug dealers with all the material trappings associated with affluent businesspeople have become role models for local youth. These illegal entrepreneurs are an all too obvious reminder that making it in the drug business "is not a remote fantasy like winning the lottery, but a plausible, accessible option for the masses" (Wisotsky, 1990a). In many inner cities, where up to 40 percent of the residents live below the poverty level and one of every two teenagers is unemployed, drugs dealers with flashy cars and stylish clothes provide a stark contrast to the realities of an economic situation that shows few if any signs of improving.
- In South America, intervention in the form of U.S. military personnel battling local drug lords, the spraying of illicit crops, and economic sanctions against cocaine-exporting countries only fuels existing anti-Yankee sentiment. South Americans are more likely to see the drug problem in the United States as "demand-side" and not "supply-side" driven. They feel the United States should clean up its own house before placing the blame as well as the responsibility for solving the problem on its neighbors. Most people in the United States may not care if South Americans are dissatisfied with our drug policies; nonetheless, these policies may have to be reexamined as countries in this part of the world become potentially larger consumers of American exports.

The ever-changing political, social, and economic conditions in the United States and other nations will both influence and be influenced by this country's appetite for drugs.

and basketball games as well as injury reports on players, information that is only of use to gamblers. Some newspaper sports pages also carry advice columns on how to bet. Editors readily defend this policy, saying they are providing a service for their readers (Underwood, 1986). Some horseracing tracks now have automatic banking machines so that bettors can obtain cash advances on their credit cards.

THE FUTURE OF GAMBLING

It appears that the number of people who gamble, the amount of money they wager, and gambling-related social problems will increase in the coming years for at least two reasons. To begin, technological innovations that gave gambling such a boost in the post–World War II era will continue, making it that much easier for people to wager on games of chance. As a result of more and more sporting events being broadcast on television, betting on football and basketball games may be even more popular that wagering on horses. As one bookmaker noted, "It used to be that 85 percent of my customers made bets on horses. Now it's just the opposite—90 percent of their bets are on team sports" (Underwood, 1986).

Americans may soon be able to buy lottery tickets and play bingo over the telephone, using "900 numbers" that are typically quite expensive. Video lottery terminals (VLTs) may be part of the consumer landscape in the near future, as these machines will be found everywhere from convenience stores and supermarkets to neighborhood bars (Karcher, 1992). These measures should reduce long lines when jackpots get into the tens of millions of dollars and should permit people to bet almost anyplace they go during the course of the day. Video poker games are one of the most popular, lucrative (from the casinos' point of view), and addictive forms of gambling to hit Las Vegas and Atlantic City in years; gamblers often sit in front of these machines for hours at a time.

The explosion of lotteries has contributed to what sociologist Vicki Apt (in Welles, 1989) refers to as the "de-skilling" of gambling. Horseplayers and other sports bettors have to expend some time and effort by way of deciding what horse or team they are going to wager on, but it takes no ability whatsoever to buy a lottery ticket. Nonskill games like the lottery have proven to be very effective in recruiting millions of people to gamble. Whereas individuals who wager on skill-intensive games, such as sports betting, are enticed by the action, people who participate in non- or low-skill games are motivated by the hope of winning huge jackpots (Welles, 1989).

Finally, gambling in the United States will increase as long as local and state governments view this activity as a viable source of revenue. Riverboat gambling began anew on the Mississippi River in 1991, as boats departed from river towns in Iowa. Not to be shortchanged, other states along the nation's longest river may soon have their own gambling boats. Deadwood, South Dakota, legalized casino gambling; some Colorado towns have slot machines; and Vermont considered legalizing video poker machines. Florida is considering building casinos on beaches, and the Louisiana legislature has approved a bill for a giant casino to be built in New Orleans that officials hope will bring the state $100 million a year ("Faites vos Jeux: Louisiana," 1992). A number of cities have legal card parlors where people can play poker for money; the house charges gamblers a fee (by the half hour or hour) to sit in on a game.

Slightly more than half the nation's 280 Indian reservations now have some form of casino gambling that collectively generates almost as much money each year ($1.4 billion) as Native Americans receive annually from the Bureau of Indian Affairs ("Bugsy and the Indians," 1992). A specialist in wagering laws notes that gambling-generated income has been "the biggest economic advance for the Indians in three centuries" (Rose in "Bugsy and the Indians," 1992, p. 28). With unemployment rates in Native American communities as high as 50 percent, many Native Americans view the profits from legalized gambling on reservations as a partial solution to their money-related problems.

No doubt, there is some saturation point at which the number of lottery games and other forms of gambling will exceed the demand of players and potential players. However, until that point is reached, local and state governments appear willing to enhance their coffers with proceeds from gambling, regardless of the social problems that result from such a policy.

SUMMARY

1 Mind-altering substances are used to some extent in all human societies. Americans have consumed alcohol in significant quantities since the colonial period. In the past 100 years, marijuana, cocaine, heroin, and many other drugs have been popular with a sizeable segment of the population. Legal and illegal drugs are used by people of every racial and ethnic group and social class.

2 Drug use is a growing problem in the developing world and former Iron Curtain countries such as Poland and the Czech Republic. As these countries become more affluent, we can expect their rates of drug use to increase.

3 For whatever reason people initially take drugs, the ingestion of these substances can lead to *drug dependence,* a condition wherein drugs are used over a long period of time, the user may find it difficult to quit, and cessation of use can lead to painful physical symptoms and/or severe mental distress. The process of drug dependence may be somewhat different for men and women.

4 In the United States, approximately one-third of all people with AIDS contracted the disease by injecting themselves with illicit drugs. In some European and Asian cities, more than 40 percent of the intravenous drug–using population is HIV positive.

5 Drugs can be a *direct cause* of crime (behavioral changes lead to crime), can *conditionally cause* crime (peer pressure from drug-using friends results in criminal behavior), or can be a *common cause* of crime (both drug use and crime are caused by poverty).

6 People who favor legalizing drugs believe that crime rates would decrease substantially as a result of this action and that the criminal justice system would have more time and resources to allocate to controlling other forms of criminal behavior. Opponents argue that legalization would only create more addicts and drug-related behavioral problems.

7 Overall alcohol consumption has decreased in the United States as a result of an aging population, increased taxes on alcoholic beverages, and antidrinking groups that have successfully convinced many people to reduce their intake of this substance.

8 Drinking alcohol (even in moderation) is associated with numerous health-related problems. A number of researchers have reported finding a connection between alcohol and high-risk sexual behavior, such as not using condoms during intercourse, for both heterosexuals and homosexuals.

9 According to the *disease* model, some unknown number of people become alcoholics because they inherit a gene that metabolizes alcohol in a particular and harmful manner or they inherit some aspect of their personality that makes them psychologically vulnerable to alcoholism. From a sociological perspective, alcohol consumption, as well as the resulting behavior, is learned behavior. The values a particular group of people has regarding the use of alcohol will determine the rate of heavy and problem drinking in that group.

10 Gambling is also a cultural universal, with some form of wagering found in all societies. As much as $240 billion is wagered in the United States legally and illegally each year. Pathological gambling can lead to severe problems in the family and the workplace. Many people also turn to criminal behavior to pay off gambling debts. Most states have legal lotteries, and a growing number of states have legalized casino betting toward the end of generating a portion of the funds needed to pay for everything from more police to new schools and social programs.

HEALTH AND HEALTH CARE
Paying the Price

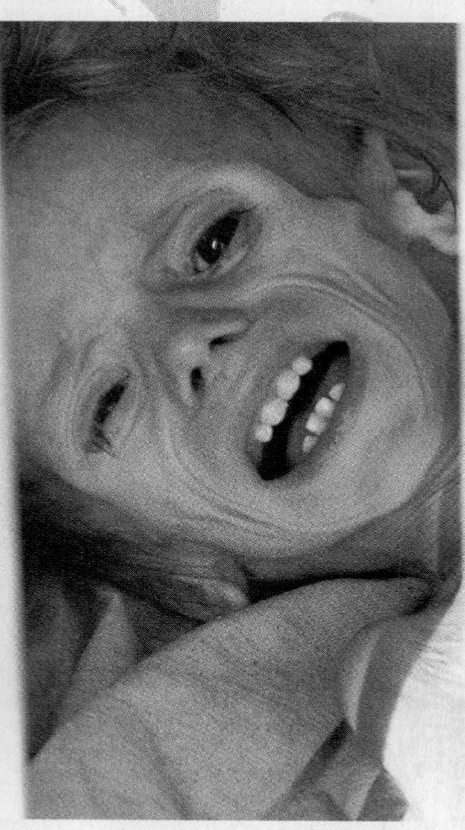
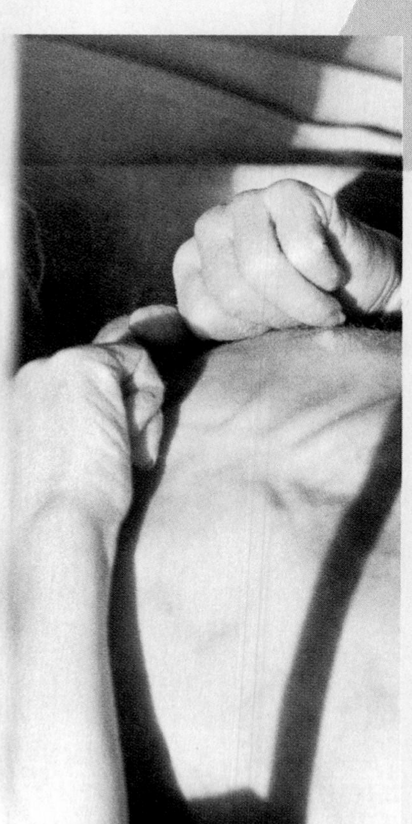

Living in a country blessed with an abundance of both money and skilled medical practitioners, hundreds of thousands of people in the United States spend tens of millions of dollars each year on elective cosmetic surgery. For prices ranging from a few hundred dollars to many thousands of dollars, these individuals take advantage of the marvels of modern medical science to have just about every imaginable part of their bodies augmented, reduced, firmed, stretched, smoothed, lifted, tucked, or in some other way sculpted to perfection. Unwanted fat is sucked out, unwanted blemishes or tattoos sanded off, and desired eyelid or other coloration stenciled in by trained professionals, ready and eager to help make their patients all that they can be. As even a quick skimming of the telephone directory or of nearly any upscale magazine's advertisements will verify, cosmetic surgery has become a high-growth industry in this society. With a little bit of imagination and the proper bank balance, no one has to remain shackled to a body that does not meet prevailing standards of physical beauty.

Meanwhile, in developing countries such as India, Thailand, China, and the Philippines, which are not quite so blessed with an abundance of medical practitioners or high per capita incomes, people are also lining up for elective surgery. However, in this case, their alterations are being undertaken for the enhancement of other people's bodies rather than their own. They are selling body parts to keep themselves and their families alive. Lured by offers of up to three years' income, thousands of poverty-stricken people have become commercial donors of skin patches, kidneys, and other organs. Once harvested, these organs and tissues will be utilized by the more affluent members of the global society to restore or repair their own flawed chassis.

This thriving trade in human body parts has been condemned by a few physicians in these nations as "immoral, ethically objectionable and socially degrading" (Colabawallah in Wallace, 1992). However much they may share this sentiment, those on the donating end of the exchange nonetheless recognize the fact that moral outrage over their own exploitation is a luxury they cannot afford. "It's not easy money, it's a matter of survival for me. We just can't survive on the money I make" (Kumar in Wallace, 1992). In the quest for physical survival, people who can least afford to become ill often must risk their health to subsidize others whose financial health exceeds their physical well-being.

In this final chapter, we examine a series of problems related to illness, health, and health care. Like education, income, and power, access to good health and good health care is a valuable and valued resource that is distributed unequally among and within societal populations around the world. For some fortunate individuals, "Live long and prosper" is not just a wish but a reality. For many less fortunate people, "Get sick and die" is not just a curse but a grim fact of life.

QUESTIONS TO CONSIDER

1. In what sense is the psychological model of health a multidimensional concept?
2. Why are infant mortality rates so much higher and longevity rates so much lower in developing countries?
3. How do cultural factors influence women's health in developing countries?
4. What are the leading causes of death in developed countries?
5. What is the *epidemiological transition?*
6. What are the major at-risk population groups with regard to the AIDS epidemic?
7. Why do the World Health Organization and other international agencies regard tobacco smoking as a global epidemic?
8. Why is it highly unlikely that the governments of countries such as the United States will ban the use of tobacco products in the near future?
9. What particular factors have contributed to the exceptionally high costs of health care in the United States?
10. Which specific population groups in the United States are most likely to lack health insurance?
11. What is a *managed competition* health care plan?
12. What is the *Hawaii plan* of health care?

MEASURING HEALTH AND ILLNESS

In our examination of health and health care problems, we will look at patterns of health and sickness exhibited by people in the United States and in many other societies. However, analyzing these patterns within and across countries often is not as simple as you might expect. Like other concepts, *health* and *illness* have important subjective, as well as objective, dimensions. As medical sociologist David Mechanic (1992, p. 798) observes, "The definition of illness and disability is the 'rope' in a tug of war in which competing parties seek determinations in their own interest." To a large extent, answers to questions about the presence or absence of good health and of good health care in a particular society depend on prevailing conceptions of health and illness in that society.

Sociologist David E. Stull (1992) has identified three major models employed in different times and different places to conceptualize health. These models involve physical definitions, social definitions, or the subjective evaluation of health.

THE MEDICAL MODEL

The medical, or physical, model of health defines *health* as the absence of disease, as determined by some combination of self-reports by patients, observations by medical personnel, and medical tests. These diseases may be either acute (that is, of sudden onset and short duration, such as appendicitis) or chronic (that is, frequently occurring or of long duration, such as recurring ear infections in some children or arthritis in some older adults).

From this perspective, measuring health is a matter of counting the number or percentage of individuals in a given society who are disease free. Conversely, illness is measured by calculating the number or percentage of individuals in a given society infected with a particular disease—for example, the tuberculosis (TB) rate in the United States, or a comparison of TB rates in New Zealand and China. Health care efforts revolve around curing diseases or illnesses affecting individuals and preventing their spread to other population members, as well as promoting behavior changes that might lessen individuals' likelihood of developing specific diseases (for example, encouraging a low-fat diet to lower the risk of a coronary attack).

THE FUNCTIONAL MODEL

Sociologist Talcott Parsons's analysis of health and sickness (1951) was the foundation for the social, or functional, model of health. From this perspective, *health* refers to the ability of individuals to function socially—that is, to perform appropriate and expected social roles. By way of contrast, *illness* is shown by individuals' inability to carry out their normal roles. This particular conception of health translates into a measurement of illness through an examination of various indicators of people's fulfillment of role obligations—for example, work and school absenteeism numbers and rates. As is the case with the medical model, from the functional perspective, good health care involves curative and preventive measures aimed primarily at individual population members within the larger societal setting.

THE PSYCHOLOGICAL MODEL

The psychological, or multidimensional, model defines health on the basis of people's subjective evaluations of their own state of being. In this approach, the measurement of health and illness involves asking members of a particular population to assess and rate their life situations. Their responses are likely to reflect psychological and social well-being, as well as physical health considerations.

In contrast to the medical and functional models, which focus exclusively or largely on the individual, the psychological model also places a good deal of emphasis on societal structural factors that affect people's overall state of being. For example, the World

Health Organization (WHO), whose "Health for All by the Year 2000" campaign has been its major organizing force since 1977, sees health as a state of complete physical, mental, and social well-being rather than merely as the absence of physical disease or infirmity. Consequently, WHO's efforts have been aimed at identifying and assessing the various economic, social, and environmental factors that shape people's individual and collective sense of well-being (World Health Organization, 1993). The International Human Suffering Index (HSI), compiled by the former Population Crisis Committee (recall our discussions of the HSI in Chapter Three and Chapter Six), also examines social and economic factors such as political freedom, civil rights, education, and communications technology as they affect humans' life situations throughout the developed and developing worlds. The ultimate health care goal of these organizations is to bring about changes in these structural conditions, thereby promoting the physical, social, and mental well-being of societal populations now living in distress.

HEALTH, ILLNESS, AND DEATH IN DEVELOPING COUNTRIES

In 1991, a child born in Afghanistan or Angola could expect to live less than 45 years on average—that is, assuming that child managed to make it through its first year. The odds of an infant in either of those two countries surviving to the age of 1 were less than 1 in 7. By way of contrast, a child born in Japan or Switzerland that same year on average had at least a 99.5 percent chance of surviving its first year and could look forward to living more than 79 years. In the least developed countries, mortality rates for children under age 5 are 11 times higher than those in the developed world (198 deaths per 1,000 live

TABLE 12.1 Infant Mortality and Life Expectancy, Selected Countries: 1991

Country	Infant Mortality Rate (per 1,000 births)	Expectation of Life at Birth (years)
Afghanistan	164	43.5
Angola	151	44.3
Sierra Leone	151	44.8
Guinea	144	42.8
Central African Republic	138	47.1
Chad	134	39.8
Japan	4	79.2
Switzerland	5	79.1
Austria	5	77.3
France	6	77.8
Italy	6	78.1
United States	10	75.7

SOURCE: U.S. Bureau of the Census, *World Population Profile: 1991.*

births compared to 18). Acute respiratory infections and diarrhea were responsible for over half of all childhood deaths worldwide in 1990 (World Health Organization, 1992).

Table 12.1 demonstrates the tremendous disparities in infant mortality and longevity rates between some of the most developed and some of the least developed societies in the world at the beginning of the 1990s. These startling variations point to the very divergent health and health care experiences of the respective populations of these two different worlds.

PRIMARY HEALTH RESOURCES

One way of measuring the different health and illness patterns of developed and developing countries is in terms of primary health resources. As defined by the World Health Organization (1993), these factors include access of the general population to safe drinking water, sanitation facilities, and basic health services; prenatal, birth, and infant care for women and their children; immunization against major diseases, especially for children; an adequate supply of trained medical personnel; and adequate public funding of health services and health education.

Figure 12.1, which has been compiled from data collected by the United Nations Development Program, shows some of the large differences between developing and developed countries for three of these resources as of 1990. As might be expected, the pattern is one of nearly universal access to primary health factors for the populations of developed societies and little or no access for large segments of the populations of developing societies. In the developing world, significant numbers of people cannot even count on such fundamental health resources as safe drinking water, human waste disposal facilities, and reasonable access to basic health care services. Under these conditions, it is hardly surprising that death rates from infectious diseases are so high in many of these countries, especially in comparison to developed nations.

FIGURE 12.1 Populations with Access to Primary Health Variables: 1988–1990

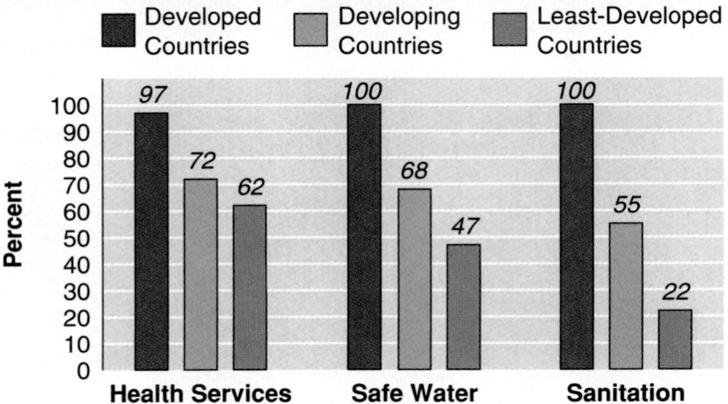

SOURCE: United Nations Development Program, *Human Development Report 1993.*

LEADING CAUSES AND PATTERNS OF DEATH

Figure 12.2 shows the leading causes of death in developing and in developed societies as of 1990. As the figure so graphically illustrates, the populations of poorer, developing countries are much more at risk of dying from communicable diseases than people in the developed world. Their lesser access to safe drinking water and human waste sanitation facilities, immunization, and disease-fighting drugs greatly increases their exposure to malaria, cholera, diphtheria, diarrhea, and other parasitic or infectious diseases. Of the 17.5 million people who died from these afflictions in 1990, 17 million came from developing countries. This number represents 44 percent of all the deaths in developing nations, whereas only 4 percent of all deaths in developed countries were the result of these communicable diseases.

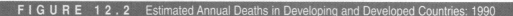

FIGURE 12.2 Estimated Annual Deaths in Developing and Developed Countries: 1990

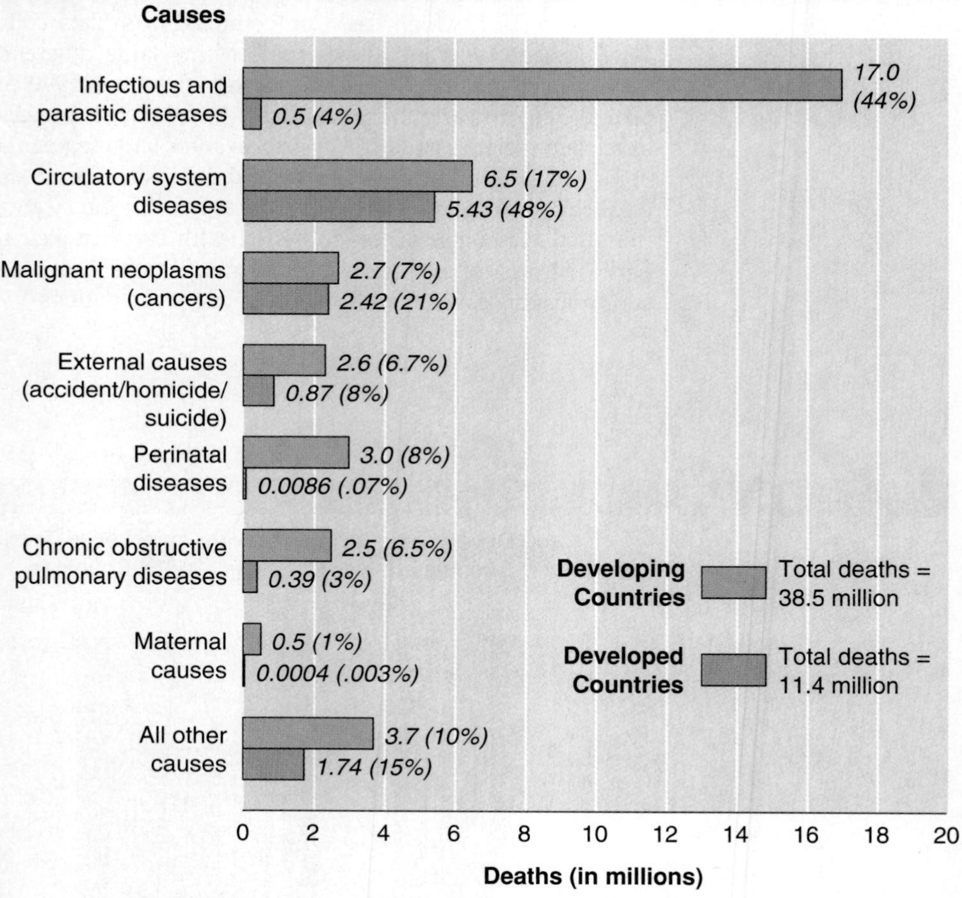

Source: World Health Organization, *Global Health Situation and Projections 1992.*

Note: Numbers in parentheses refer to the percentage of all deaths in the given type of society, developing or developed, resulting from the particular cause.

The members of developed nations are much more at risk of death from circulatory system (including heart and cerebrovascular) diseases and from cancers. Of the 11.4 million people who died in developed countries in 1990, nearly 69 percent (7.85 million) expired from these causes. Of the 38.5 million deaths that occurred in developing countries, only 24 percent resulted from the same sources. These particular diseases are associated with generally affluent but generally unhealthy lifestyles featuring too much fatty food, alcohol, smoking, and stress and too little physical exercise (Siegel et al., 1993). For many members of developed societies, the most serious life-threatening resource problem is not too little of a good thing but rather too much.

Unfortunately, the more prosperous population segments in advanced developing countries are currently experiencing a rise in circulatory system diseases and cancers as a result of the more affluent lifestyles made possible by economic development. At the same time, those population groups who remain outside the development loop (for example, the Indian peasants in Chiapas, Mexico, who were discussed in Chapter Six) are still subject to more traditional fatal diseases as their societies undergo what the World Health Organization (1993, p. A-28) has called an "epidemiological transition."

WOMEN'S HEALTH

The overall low levels of primary health resources and generally high mortality rates found in many developing countries often conceal the fact that health resources are distributed very unequally within particular populations. In general, residents of urban areas have higher rates of access to better health resources than their rural counterparts. And in both rural and urban areas, men and boys have far greater access to health-sustaining goods and facilities than women and girls. In large measure, these gender-based unequal health opportunity structures are responsible for the large number of females who are "missing" throughout the developing world.

Based on projections from female birth and longevity rates around the world, demographers estimate that there should be as many as 100 million more women and girls living in developing nations than there currently seem to be. In trying to explain this enormous discrepancy, researchers have looked to the ways in which traditional gender stereotypes have created what could be called "dual health markets" in most developing countries. Like the dual labor markets that allocate employment on the basis of majority or minority group status, these health markets allocate health resources on a males-first basis. Within the context of resource-poor environments, the result is a widespread pattern in which females frequently receive little or nothing.

For example, throughout much of North Africa, the Middle East, and South Asia, young boys are fed first at every meal and given the most nutritious foods available. This bias begins at birth, as many nursing mothers breastfeed their sons much longer than they do their daughters. Later, young girls eat only after their brothers have finished and have to make do with whatever food is left. As a result, most girls' nutritional needs go unmet, leading to undernourishment, chronic fatigue, and illness as they enter their reproductive years. These girls typically will experience a large number of pregnancies and (assuming they survive childbirth) will be expected to carry out demanding mothering roles with their children while still doing unpaid work in farming or other agricultural activities. The net result is greater fatigue, malnourishment, and severe health problems for the vast majority of women (Jacobson, 1993). If and when women in developing countries do have access to prenatal, childbirth, or reproductive health care, that care typically is "less than adequate" (Mensch, 1993, p. 246). As we saw in our discussion of sex and gender issues in Chapter Eight, illnesses

and diseases related to women's particular reproductive health needs remain major causes of female mortality in the developing world.

HEALTH AND ECONOMIC DEVELOPMENT

Obviously, gender is only one factor affecting health and health care in developing nations. Data from international agencies, including the World Health Organization and the United Nations Development Program, indicate that as a country's gross national product and other indicators of economic development increase, so also does the number of health care services and health care providers. Economic development also brings about environmental and structural alterations. The improvement of drinking water and sanitation facilities, health education, and a general upgrading and more equitable distribution of economic resources all have positive impacts on societal health. Consequently, increasing the level of economic development in developing countries is an important priority in improving the overall standard of living in these nations. However, a government's commitment to providing health care for its people may be more important than economic factors alone. For example, whereas life expectancy increased by 9 years between 1960 and 1985 in Mexico, a relatively economically advanced Latin American society, during that same period, people were living 10 to 15 years longer in much poorer Cuba and in war-torn Nicaragua. The increase in Cuba was especially noteworthy, inasmuch as people in that country already had a significantly longer life expectancy than people in many other countries throughout Latin America (Najman, 1989).

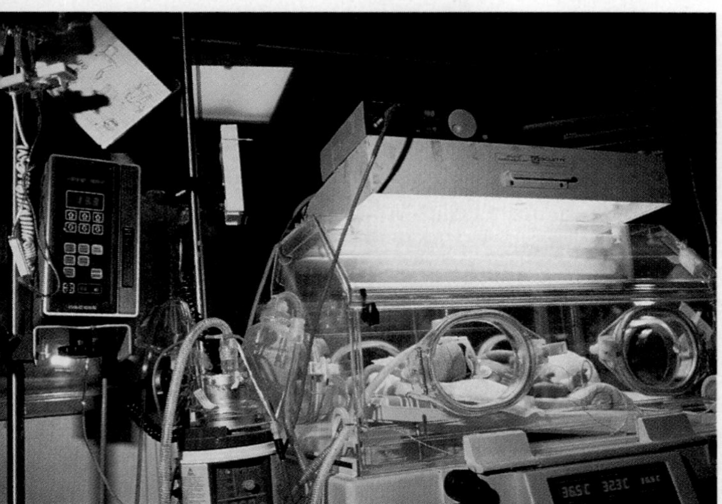

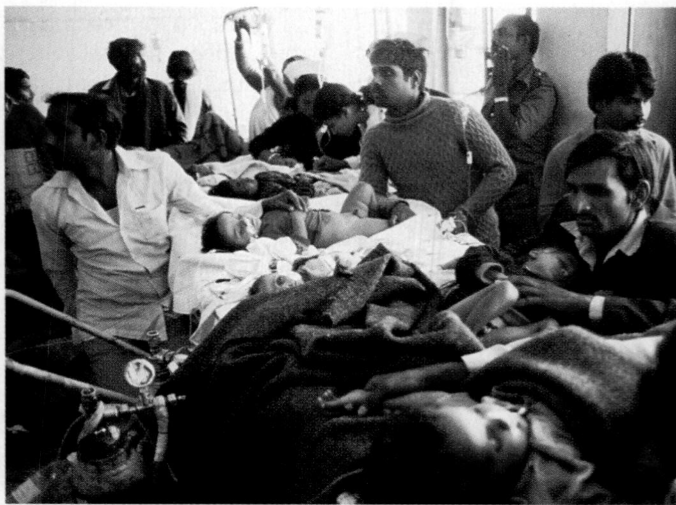

Economic disparities between developed and developing countries "trickle down" into very different health and health care patterns for even their youngest members. Many children in the United States and other affluent societies, who have access to sophisticated neonatal and infant treatment facilities, have much brighter survival prospects than most Indian children, who must depend on clinics that have too few resources and too many patients.

As a result of stagnating economies and a limited number of institutions of higher learning, many developing countries have so few physicians that medical care is unobtainable for the bulk of the population. Geographic residence is also related to the availability of professional health care. In many developing countries, as many as 60 to 70 percent of all physicians live in the national capital, leaving the rest of the country "obviously medically starved" (Roemer, 1993, p. 328). For example, in Mexico, there is 1 physician for every 400 individuals in Mexico City, but only 1 physician for every 20,000 to 35,000 people in the outlying rural districts of the country. The World Health Organization (1993) has identified this maldistribution of medical personnel as the major health care problem at the global level.

Despite continuing problems, current figures represent real improvements in the situation of many developing countries since 1960. Those improvements have been hailed by the World Health Organization as a sign that significant progress is being made in improving the health of the global population. However, this progress has not been shared evenly among the developing nations. The situation of the world's least developed countries, or LDCs (a group composed primarily of African, South Asian, and Southeast Asian nations), has actually worsened in comparison to that of other developing countries during this time period (United Nations Development Program, 1993; World Health Organization, 1993).

As we saw in our earlier discussions of population problems and global inequality in Chapters Three and Six, the LDCs have fallen considerably behind the rest of the world in terms of the social, physical, and economic well-being of their populations and seem likely to drop even farther behind in the near future. Minimal economic development and maximum abject poverty are the chief characteristics of these countries. Until such time as they can achieve real economic progress or gain commitments for significant and sustained economic aid from their more affluent global neighbors, political leaders in the LDCs will continue to regard public health resources and facilities as luxury items. The ongoing health problems faced by the populations of the world's least developed societies are just one indicator of their losing struggle for survival.

SOCIETAL RESPONSES TO PREVENTABLE DEATH AND ILLNESS

Careful analysis of the data in Figure 12.2 also reveals that a large number of the deaths that occur across the globe each year are preventable. These deaths don't have to happen, and many wouldn't happen if both developing societies and developed societies would institute a series of changes in their respective environments and in the lifestyles of their respective members.

In the case of developing countries, prevention of many deaths is beyond the abilities of individuals but within the capacities of the society. Changes needed to lower preventable deaths would primarily involve the kinds of environmental and structural alterations associated with economic development. The ultimate solution to developing nations' existing mortality problems thus entails completing the modernization processes they have already begun. The major impediment to these changes, of course, is the enormous sums of money required to complete economic development: money that developing countries don't have and that developed countries are unwilling or unable to give.

With regard to developed nations, measures to prevent deaths would entail changing current conditions that continue to create and inflict various forms of harmful pollution on their members. (Recall our discussion of economic development and environmental problems in Chapter Four.) However, changes in these societies' established fossil fuel– and chemical-based economies could represent a version of "killing the goose that lays the golden eggs." Therefore, such changes are likely to be opposed by those population segments that benefit the most from the status quo.

To a significant extent, death-preventive efforts in both developing and developed countries must also focus on changing people's specific behaviors that, with or without their knowledge, are killing them. Like many larger structural changes, these attempts are also likely to be resisted strongly by the targeted individuals, who possibly would interpret them as unfair infringements on their personal freedoms. Two important examples that illustrate the great difficulties in implementing lifestyle change policies are the AIDS epidemic and smoking, which we will examine in some detail. In both cases, societies have tried to address health-destroying, life-threatening diseases through a mixture of programs, ranging from educating people to alter their lifestyles voluntarily to forcing individuals to change their behaviors through a system of legally sanctioned punishments.

AIDS: LOOKING FOR SOLUTIONS TO A GLOBAL EPIDEMIC

AIDS (acquired immune deficiency syndrome) is a communicable disease contracted by one individual from another either directly through sexual activity or indirectly by contact with infected blood (usually through a transfusion or intravenous drug use). Pregnant women who are infected can also transmit the disease to their babies.

Although there is some dissension from this view, the prevailing belief is that AIDS is caused by the human immunodeficiency virus (HIV), which is constantly showing new strains. As of September 1993, an estimated 339,000 people in the United States had contracted the AIDS virus. People with AIDS fall into the following categories (Cox, 1992, p. 23):

1. Sexually active homosexual and bisexual men	58 percent
2. Intravenous drug users	23 percent
3. Homosexual and bisexual men who are also intravenous drug users	6 percent
4. Heterosexual men and women	6 percent
5. People receiving blood transfusions	2 percent
6. Hemophiliacs	1 percent
7. Undetermined/other	4 percent

GLOBAL PATTERNS

People who are infected with HIV typically die within two years after the onset of AIDS symptoms, and the mortality rate for this disease is almost 100 percent (Cox, 1992). Worldwide, nearly 160 countries have reported a total of 2.6 million AIDS cases and an estimated 13 million more people infected with HIV, at a rate of about 5,000 new cases a day. Harvard University researcher Dr. Jonathan Mann predicts that this "global epidemic" could claim 25 million lives by the beginning of the next century, with another 120 million people becoming HIV positive (in Haney, 1992). Another Harvard researcher (Haseltine in "Next Century Could See," 1992) projects that more than 1 billion people will be infected by the end of the next few decades.

Three major patterns of HIV transmission appear to exist in the world today (Cox, 1992):

1. In North America and Western Europe, the most heavily afflicted populations are homosexual men and intravenous drug users. Because AIDS cases in these countries were limited almost exclusively to the homosexual community during the early 1980s, AIDS was often called the "gay plague." Some religious groups saw the disease as divine retribution for immoral behavior, and these moral undertones have continued to shape some communities' responses to the epidemic (Findlay, 1991; Shipp & Navarro, 1991). From 8 to 10 of every 11 people with AIDS in these countries are males. However, with the spread of AIDS in the heterosexual community and among intravenous drug users, women are now the fastest-growing subgroup of afflicted persons in the United States. Most new AIDS cases in women, according to the Centers for Disease Control, are the result of heterosexual contact (Cimons, 1993). AIDS has also hit some racial and ethnic minorities especially hard in the United States. As of mid-1993, Latinos (16.7 percent) and African Americans (30 percent) accounted for nearly half of all reported AIDS cases in the country. This high level of incidence within the African American community, in particular, has led a growing number of Blacks to view AIDS as part of a White genocidal conspiracy against them (Clark, 1992). It has also become a growing issue for African American political leaders, who are concerned about cuts in funding of AIDS research and the apparent slowness with which White leaders have been responding to the AIDS crisis (Gruson, 1992). More recently, AIDS has spread rapidly among the teenage population, apparently due to the lack of sex education curricula in many public schools and teens' widespread belief in their own immortality (France, 1992). In one notorious and widely reported incident, several female members of a San Antonio teen gang proved their "toughness" by having sex with male gang members known to have the HIV virus ("Teen Girls Prove," 1993).

2. In sub–Saharan African countries and some Caribbean nations, both HIV and AIDS are spreading rapidly, primarily through heterosexual intercourse, which now accounts for approximately 80 percent of the infections in Africa. Because of the manner in which the disease is transmitted, AIDS is the leading cause of death among young adults, especially women, in many cities. By the end of the decade, an estimated 15 million people will be dying of AIDS, millions of children will become orphans because of AIDS, and millions more children will be infected by their mothers during pregnancy (Brown, 1990; Kraft, 1992). In countries such as Zaire, which do not have the facilities for testing blood donations, transfusion of infected blood has also become a major cause of AIDS ("Zaire Capital on Brink," 1991). The crushing poverty in most of these African nations has prevented the establishment of any extensive health programs directed to the AIDS crisis (Brown, 1992).

3. The final pattern of HIV/AIDS transmission includes Asia, Eastern Europe, North Africa, and most of the Pacific countries. In the next six to eight years, India could surpass sub–Saharan Africa as the world region hardest hit by the AIDS epidemic. To date, the cities of Bombay and Madras have most of India's AIDS cases. The disease is spread by prostitutes, and as many as one in three women who work the streets are infected. According to some reports, AIDS is being transmitted to a large extent by many of India's 4 million truck drivers, who frequent the thousands of highway brothels all over the country. To a lesser extent, intravenous drug users and small rural blood banks that reuse needles and unsterilized equipment also are contributing to the spread of AIDS on the Indian subcontinent (Drogin, 1992).

SOCIETAL RESPONSES

The particular circumstances under which AIDS is transmitted have made it extremely difficult to formulate effective societal policies for halting its spread. As we have already noted, gay men and intravenous drug users are two of the largest at-risk groups in devel-

oped countries such as the United States. Both of these population segments have been condemned as immoral by many conservative religious groups, who have been slow to define the AIDS epidemic as a health problem rather than a morality issue. These groups are vehemently opposed to public education campaigns that focus on safe sex either for gays or for the young heterosexuals (especially women) who now constitute one of the fastest-growing AIDS populations. The solutions to the AIDS problem proposed by conservative religious groups have most often involved attempts to convince homosexuals and drug users to renounce their evil ways and return to the straight and narrow and to convince adolescents to remain completely celibate. However well intended, these attempts have not been extraordinarily successful to date. Other religious-based opposition to safe-sex campaigns has come from more moderate groups such as the Roman Catholic Church, which condemns both homosexuality and the use of condoms by heterosexuals, even if that use is for the purpose of disease prevention rather than pregnancy prevention.

In the developing countries of Africa, where AIDS infection among women has skyrocketed, the primary source of opposition to effective societywide preventive programs has been prevailing cultural beliefs and social practices that continue to subjugate women. Eighty percent of all women with AIDS live in Africa, where, as Kraft (1992, p. 12) notes, "Women have little power in the boardroom and even less in the bedroom." Long-standing traditions have made women completely subordinate to men, so that they have no say in their marital sexual relations. In Africa, husbands infected by prostitutes or through casual extramarital sex have spread AIDS to their wives and children, causing millions of children and monogamous married women to come down with the disease. Inasmuch as they are completely dependent on their husbands for financial support, women who fear infections nonetheless cannot refuse their husbands sex, out of fear of being abandoned or punished for not fulfilling their marital obligations. In this case, women's low social status is literally killing them. "You cannot have a heterosexual AIDS epidemic in which women have power or close to equality" (Williams in Kraft, 1992, p. 14), but in Africa and many other developing areas of the world, women have nothing close to equality.

Other governments around the world have responded to the spread of AIDS in their countries in a variety of ways. Extreme positions regarding official intervention at the national level in this crisis can be found in Cuba and Japan.

Cuba may be the only country in the world to halt the spread of AIDS. Everyone in that country who tests positive for the disease (and virtually everyone old enough to have sex is tested) is quarantined in one of the nation's seven sanitariums. People so confined receive the wages they were earning before they became infected, regardless of whether they can work. As a result of this strict confinement policy, Cuba's rate of HIV infection is approximately one one-hundredth that of the United States and is actually decreasing (Burkett, 1991).

Whereas Cuba's government has enacted very stringent programs to control the spread of AIDS, until late 1992, the Japanese all but ignored the disease. In fact, one of the wealthiest nations on Earth claimed it did not have enough money to sponsor television commercials or pay for AIDS awareness posters (Paxton, 1992). However, the government of Japan is now trying to make up for lost time by airing TV documentaries and public service announcements, warning people that casual sex is risky and asking them to be tolerant of people with AIDS. Widespread prejudice against those afflicted with the disease is one of the reasons individuals are reluctant to be tested for the HIV virus or, for that matter, even to talk about AIDS. Some Japanese believe that AIDS is a foreigners' disease and/or a sign of an evil, sinful life in a previous incarnation. The founder of one volunteer AIDS action group stated that "many believe people who are HIV-positive, drug users and homosexuals should be exterminated from society" (Minami in Kurtenbach, 1992, p. A4). As a result of the stigma and fear associated with the disease, fewer than half of all Japanese hospitals knowingly accept AIDS patients for treatment. It is exactly this type of response that has allowed AIDS to become a global, rather than simply an international, killer.

SMOKING: THE POLITICS OF BANNING BEHAVIORS

The World Health Organization (1993, p. A-30) has called smoking an "epidemic" and estimates that about 3 million people will die worldwide each year from tobacco use during the 1990s. That figure is projected to rise dramatically to about 12.5 million deaths annually within the next four decades unless significant global efforts are made to curb smoking (*Universal Almanac 1993,* p. 352).

Some countries such as Singapore have adopted tough, punishment-centered approaches involving fines of up to $3,000 to reduce or eliminate their populations' smoking ("Singapore Gets Tough," 1993). In the United States, the campaign against smoking has been fueled by the results of a first-of-its-kind, government-sponsored study, which in 1993 concluded that tobacco is the single largest killer of people in this country today. This exhaustive examination of the 2,148,000 deaths recorded nationwide in 1990 claimed that cigarette smoking was the primary contributing factor in 400,000 cases (19 percent of the total)—more deaths than were caused by alcohol, illicit drugs, firearms, unsafe sex, motor vehicle accidents, disease-causing germs, and toxic environmental agents combined (Stolberg, 1993). The February 1994 Surgeon General's report on smoking placed that figure even higher, at 419,000 deaths (Lamb, 1994).

These two reports were the latest in a long series of studies that, in 1964, led the U.S. Surgeon General to require that hazard warnings be printed on all cigarette packages and in all cigarette advertising and, in the 1970s, to ban cigarette advertising on television entirely. Government regulations helped reduce the smoking rate from 42 percent of the population to 25 percent between the mid-1960s and the late 1980s. However, in 1990, there were still an estimated 45.8 million smokers in the United States, whose habit cost the country from $60 to $100 billion per year in medical bills, higher insurance premiums, lost productivity, and various ventilation, cleaning, and maintenance costs (*Universal Almanac 1993,* p. 215).

THE ANTISMOKING MOVEMENT

Organized opposition to smoking, which has been present in the United States in some form since the early 1960s, was given a boost by the 1986 Surgeon General's report. In that report, then-Surgeon General C. Everett Koop called smoking "the chief, single, avoidable cause of death in our society and the most important public health issue of our time" (Koop in Siegel et al., 1993, p. 181). As a result of increasing government attention to the health risks of smoking, some states began to institute educational programs to alert their populations to the dangers of tobacco use. In many instances, such as in California, these programs were financed through tax increases on cigarettes and other tobacco products. California's program, the largest and most aggressive in the country, has also been the most successful in terms of getting people to give up smoking. According to assessment studies carried out by the University of California, the $599 million campaign resulted in a 28 percent decrease in the number of smokers throughout the state over a 5-year period, a rate more than three times higher than the national average during the same time period ("Smoking Down 28%," 1994).

Antismoking sentiments and groups were strengthened even further by a 1993 Environmental Protection Agency report that indicated that so-called secondhand or passive smoke from cigarettes is responsible for as many as 3,000 lung cancer deaths among nonsmokers and from 150,000 to 300,000 cases of bronchitis and pneumonia among infants and children nationwide each year (Environmental Protection Agency, 1993). This evidence that the harmful effects of smoking are not confined to smokers alone led groups to mobilize on behalf of placing restrictions on smoking in public buildings. As of mid-1994, a large and growing number of individual communities had passed a variety of ordinances limiting or prohibiting smoking altogether in restaurants, offices, airports, bus and train stations, and other facilities used by the public. At the same time, strict laws in Minnesota, Maryland, Washington, and other states placed additional curbs on smoking in public.

Once immune to regulatory efforts, the tobacco industry's political clout was beginning to erode: "Tobacco has been king of the mountain. Now, everyone is rushing the mountain at once, and tobacco doesn't look so big anymore" (Daynard in Roberts & Watson, 1994a, p. 34). Tobacco companies also found themselves facing a growing number of lawsuits from surviving families of smokers who died of lung cancer or other smoking-related diseases. In May 1994, the family of a nonsmoker who allegedly contracted lung cancer through the secondhand smoke of customers in his barber shop also filed a $650 million wrongful death suit against 18 U.S. tobacco companies, opening up a whole new avenue of legal worries and expenses for the tobacco industry (Carter, 1994).

TOBACCO INDUSTRY RESPONSES

As restrictive local and state laws have steadily multiplied and the number of adult smokers has steadily declined, tobacco companies have responded with several policies that have proved highly controversial and inflammatory.

First, in an apparent attempt to recruit new customers, tobacco advertising has begun to focus on groups that, in the past, had been underrepresented among the ranks of smokers—namely, women and adolescents. Beginning years ago with a highly successful "You've come a long way, baby" campaign that remains an effective pitch, cigarette manufacturers have increased both the number of brands of "women's" cigarettes and the number of dollars spent on their advertising. The result, according to studies, has been a dramatic increase in the number of girls and women who have begun smoking. Living in a culture in which they are judged largely by physical appearance, many of these young women are susceptible to advertising that preys upon their self-doubts. One health specialist charges that "the tobacco industry exploits and reinforces these vulnerabilities by linking smoking to fashion, where unnaturally slim models epitomize beauty" (Kaufman in Dalton, 1994).

However, adolescent boys have also been singled out for cigarette advertising, most notably through the persona of Joe Camel, a cartoon creature that has been enormously successful in significantly increasing its namesake brand's share of the under-18 smoking market (Cowley, 1991). Survey reports indicate that each year, about 1 million teenagers begin smoking, starting at the average age of 14.5 years. Of the 3.1 million teenagers who currently smoke, 57 percent claim to have tried to stop but without success (Roberts & Watson, 1994b).

Despite tobacco companies' denials that they were targeting adolescents, they were accused by Surgeon General Jocelyn Elders of preying on adolescent insecurities and desires for independence from adults to convince young people that, by smoking, "they're slim, they're sexy, they're sociable, they're sophisticated, and successful. . . . [As a result], the teen-ager gets an image, the tobacco companies get an addict" (Elders quoted in

As members of developed societies have become more conscious of the health consequences of smoking and cut back on their own consumption, tobacco companies have focused their marketing efforts increasingly on people in developing countries. China now has the largest number of smokers in the world, thanks to aggressive campaigns that splash images of cowboys and other Western icons in cities and towns and on the sides of buses.

"Elders Rips Tobacco Ads," 1994). Elders called on the Federal Trade Commission to ban the Joe Camel (and a new Josephine Camel) character from all future advertising. For its part, the Food and Drug Administration (FDA) asked Congress for authorization to regulate the sales of tobacco products, under the claim that the nicotine found in tobacco is a drug, which falls under FDA responsibilities (Hilts, 1994). Tobacco industry officials responded by claiming that nicotine is not addictive and angrily denied charges that they deliberately manipulated nicotine levels in an effort to keep smokers addicted to their products ("Nicotine Not Addictive," 1994).

Second, as the U.S. market has become more and more hostile, tobacco companies have begun to increase their exports abroad, especially to Asian countries. For example, although smoking rates in Japan have declined somewhat in the past few years, as of 1993, 60 percent of all Japanese men still smoked ("Sixty Percent of Japanese Men," 1993). In China, cigarette smoking has increased dramatically over the past decade. That country now has the largest number of smokers in the world (300 million, or one-quarter of China's entire population), and foreign cigarette manufacturers have been eager to tap this booming market. Chinese smokers currently purchase about 1.6 trillion cigarettes each year, and that number has been growing steadily (Tefft, 1994). Cigarette smoking also increased in Pakistan by 200 percent and in India by 400 percent between 1970 and 1980. Cigarettes sold in these countries have up to twice as much tar and nicotine as those consumed in the developed world (Najman, 1989).

Until 1993, tobacco companies' $6.2 billion export trade was supported by the U.S. federal government, which challenged health-related laws in foreign countries as violations of U.S. trade laws. However, with the Clinton administration's distinct antismoking stance, this policy was rescinded (Roberts & Watson, 1994a). Nonetheless, U.S. tobacco export revenues have grown at a rate of over 6 percent a year, in spite of protests that this trade represents one more example of the "dumping" of hazardous materials on unsuspecting developing countries.

THE FUTURE OF U.S. TOBACCO

Given the current antismoking climate in the United States, short of a complete ban on tobacco, the most likely policy will involve increased government regulation on cigarettes and other tobacco products. The Fairness in Tobacco and Nicotine Regulation Act of 1993 introduced in Congress would put the manufacture, sale, labeling, advertising, and promotion of tobacco products under the regulatory authority of the FDA without banning the products themselves (Durbin & Synar, 1993). Although the bill certainly represents significant restrictions on the carte blanche currently enjoyed by the tobacco industry, it likely would go a long way in addressing antismoking groups' concerns about adolescent smoking and other issues, while addressing industry concerns about its economic future, as well. Each side would get less than it wants, but each would get something. In the real world of social problem resolution, compromises of this type are about as good as things get.

HEALTH CARE USA: A SYSTEM IN CRISIS

The overall physical wellness and longevity of a population are directly related to the level of medical technology and the number of trained health care professionals in the given society. They are also shaped by the level of access different population segments have to the health care system. In this regard, like the classic spaghetti Western movie of the same name, the health care system in the United States could be described as a composite of *The Good, the Bad, and the Ugly.* And in the view of many critics, in recent years, the bad and the ugly have begun to far outweigh the good.

THE GOOD: HIGH-QUALITY HEALTH CARE

When it is working well, the U.S. health care system is capable of dramatic accomplishments. Over the past century, overall life expectancy has increased by nearly 60 percent, from 47 years to 75 years. In the space of only 10 years, from 1979 to 1989, deaths from heart disease, the leading cause of death in the country, declined by 30 percent (*Universal Almanac 1993,* p. 206). Polio and other infectious diseases have been controlled, and body organs are now transplanted almost routinely. New drugs have eased the anguish of people suffering from a variety of emotional and mental disorders (*Health Care Crisis,* 1992). Sophisticated treatment in emergency rooms has saved the lives of tens of thousands of people who in previous times would have died from their wounds or injuries. Thirty years ago, there was one intensive care burn unit for every 30 million people in the United States; today, there is a burn treatment center for every 1 million Americans. In short, the overall societal investment in health care over the years "has extended the lives of millions of people and it has improved the quality of life of millions more" (*Health Care Crisis,* 1992, p. 14).

THE BAD: SPIRALLING COSTS

The bad or down side of health care in the United States is the phenomenal cost of running this sprawling, often disjointed system. In 1960, Americans paid an average of $143 each, or a total of $27.1 billion, for health care services. As of 1990, that figure had exploded to $666.2 billion, or $2,566 each, a per capita increase of nearly 1,800 percent

TABLE 12.2 U.S. National Health Care Expenditures: 1960–1990

Year	Total (in billions of dollars)	Per Capita (in dollars)	Percent of Year GNP
1960	27.1	143	5.3
1965	41.6	204	5.9
1970	74.4	346	7.3
1975	132.9	592	8.3
1980	250.1	1,063	9.2
1985	422.6	1,710	10.5
1990	666.2	2,566	12.2

SOURCE: U.S. Health Care Financing Administration, *Health Care Financing Review,* Fall 1991.

(see Table 12.2). For the next two years, health spending increased by over $86 billion annually. In 1992, the country as a whole spent $839 billion—approximately 14 percent of the entire U.S. gross domestic product—for its health care and was moving rapidly toward the $1 trillion mark ("Health Care Reform," 1993). From all outward appearances, the system is running out of control as a result of the joint effects of a number of cost-increasing factors.

In contrast to the health care systems of most other industrialized societies, that found in the United States is based on a free-market, entrepreneurial model with very little government intervention (Roemer, 1991). Health care is regarded as a product that, like other commodities and services, is made available for purchase to those who can afford it. By way of contrast, in virtually all other developed countries, health care is defined as a basic right of all citizens, and access to the health care system is provided through government programs and policies. It is this free-market view of health care in the United States that, according to critics, is largely responsible for the exponential increases in health care costs each year. The following is a list of the major reasons for the high costs of health care in this country (*Brokaw Report,* 1992; Coleman, 1992; *Health Care Crisis,* 1992; Rosenblatt, 1993; Sedgwick, 1992; "Wasted Health Dollars," 1992; Welch, 1992):

1. Hospital costs are by far the largest single component of health care spending in the United States (see Figure 12.3). Of the $585 billion total national expenditures for personal health care in 1990, $256 billion, or 44 percent, went to hospitals (Siegel et al., 1993). As for-profit organizations whose operating expenses are often high, hospitals often charge exorbitant prices for treatment. In one typical case, a Florida woman hospitalized for 69 days was charged $78,575 for her stay. Items on the bill included $300 per day for a bed in a double room, $7 for a four-inch adhesive bandage strip, and $2.85 for each aspirin tablet she was given. Common cotton swabs cost the patient nearly $100.

2. Technologically based medical advances are a major contributing factor to rising health care expenses. The cost of developing and utilizing procedures such as open-heart surgery, organ transplants, and magnetic resonance imaging (MRI)—a device that can see inside bodily organs—is staggering. The approximately 5 million MRI scans per-

FIGURE 12.3 Distribution of U.S. National Health Care Expenditures: 1990

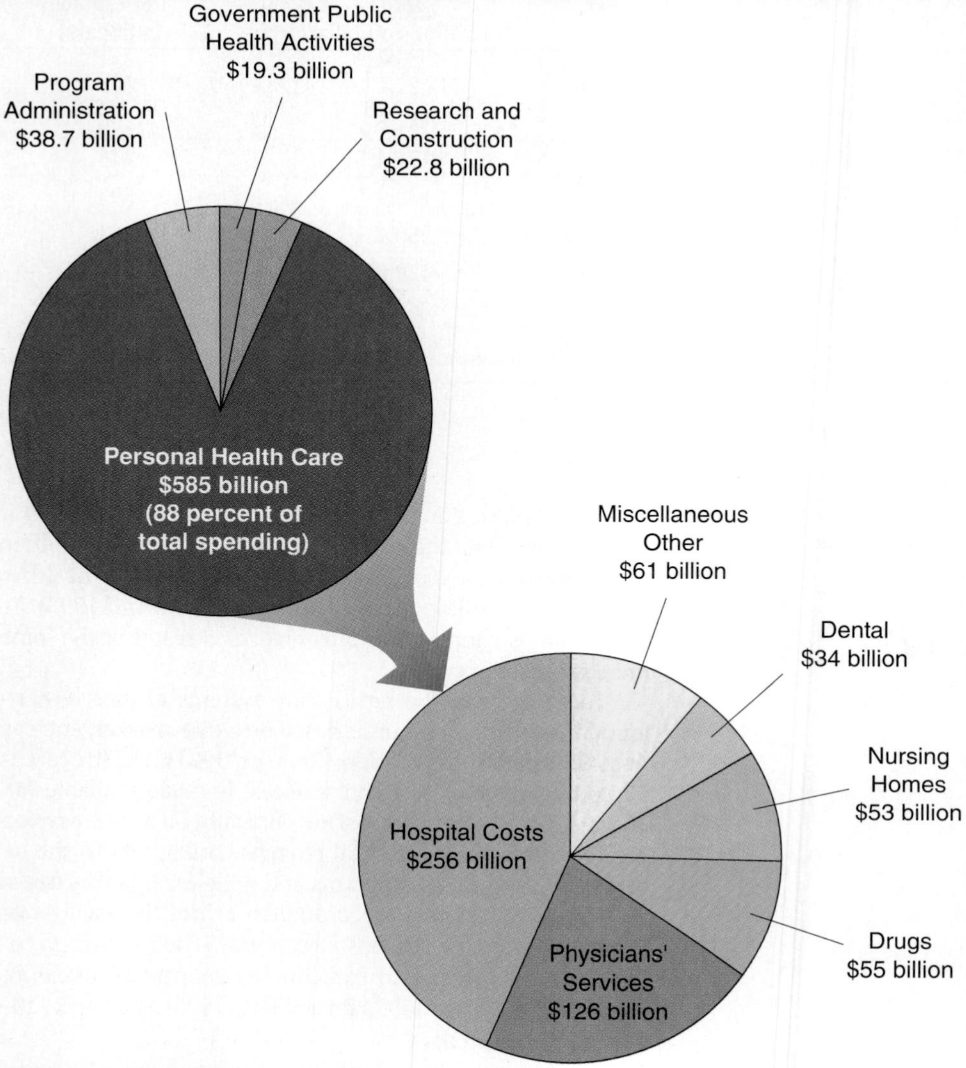

SOURCE: Compiled from data in *Health Care Financing Review,* Fall 1991, U.S. Health Care Financing Administration.

formed in 1990 at a cost ranging from $600 to $1,000 each added $5 billion to the nation's health care bill. Even when these procedures are used efficiently and appropriately (evidence indicates that many are not), they are very expensive.

3. Of the total annual national health care bill, about 20 percent (more than $165 billion) is spent for administrative costs and claims handling. The different requirements, policies, and forms of the country's more than 1,500 third-party payers (primarily, private health insurers) generate a great deal of operating costs for hospitals and for physicians (Jacobs et al., 1994).

4. In some cities, two or more hospitals compete for the area's health care dollars and, in so doing, provide duplicate services, have redundant technologies, and end up with too many hospital beds. Of the approximately 927,000 hospital beds in this country, only 63 percent are being used at any given time. Consumers ultimately pay for the installation and maintenance of facilities and equipment regardless of whether they are actually utilized.

5. Approximately 25 percent of all U.S. physicians are general practitioners, whereas the remaining 75 percent specialize in some particular form of medicine such as cardiology or obstetrics. The cost of training many of these physicians is funded by taxpayers through Medicare and Medicaid reimbursements to teaching hospitals and later through higher fees charged to patients (Gorman, 1992). As a result of this move toward greater specialization, in many areas of the country, including some large cities, there are not enough generalist physicians to provide basic health care services for local populations.

6. Physicians' incomes increased 43 percent from 1984 to 1992. Whereas family practice doctors earn a relatively modest $111,500 a year, on average, cardiologists make $205,000. In 1987, physicians in the United States earned 5.4 times more than the average worker. In Germany, that figure was 4.2; in Canada, 3.7; and in France, Japan, and the United Kingdom, 2.4. Some health care experts argue that physicians' salaries represent only a small part of overall health costs. Others claim that physicians' incomes account for 15 to 20 percent of total medical expenses in the United States.

7. A number of studies have concluded that between 20 and 30 percent of all medical procedures performed each year may be unnecessary. A report by the Rand Corporation (in *Health Care Crisis,* 1992) stated that 14 percent of heart bypass operations were "inappropriate" and another 30 percent were "questionable." Because they see physicians more frequently than younger individuals, elderly people are especially prone to unnecessary treatment, or "medical overload." These excess procedures may be a result of the fee-for-service nature of most health care, in which providers are paid for each treatment or service performed, rather than a flat or fixed fee. Since their income levels are a direct consequence of their activity level, physicians have a powerful incentive to maximize their treatment of patients.

8. The number of medical malpractice suits filed against hospitals and physicians has doubled over the past 10 years. The average monetary award in cases found in favor of plaintiffs has reached $300,000. Annual malpractice insurance premiums for the average physician now are over $15,000, whereas practitioners in high-risk specialties such as obstetrics pay over $150,000 annually. Like other businesspeople, physicians make up for their increased operating costs by raising their fees. To lessen their chances of being sued, many physicians order more expensive diagnostic tests on their patients, and the costs of these procedures are borne by health care consumers. Time, money, and resources are squandered as a result of hospitals and physicians practicing "defensive medicine."

9. A demographic factor that certainly has contributed to the high cost of health care in the United States, and will continue to do so well into the next century, is the aging, or "graying," of the U.S. population. Older individuals need more health care than younger people (they filled 40 percent of the nation's hospital beds in 1992), and the cost of caring for an elderly and longer-living society will increase significantly as the large group of baby boomers, who will begin turning 65 in the year 2011, require more medical attention and care in nursing homes.

10. According to the U.S. Government General Accounting Office, approximately 10 percent of the nation's health care bill (that is, over $80 billion annually) is the result of outright fraud. With millions of claims filed each year, there is more than ample opportunity for physicians, laboratories, and hospitals to extract money illegally from public

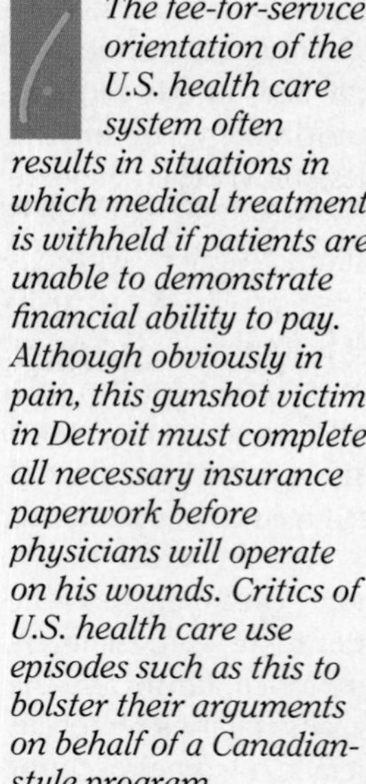

The fee-for-service orientation of the U.S. health care system often results in situations in which medical treatment is withheld if patients are unable to demonstrate financial ability to pay. Although obviously in pain, this gunshot victim in Detroit must complete all necessary insurance paperwork before physicians will operate on his wounds. Critics of U.S. health care use episodes such as this to bolster their arguments on behalf of a Canadian-style program.

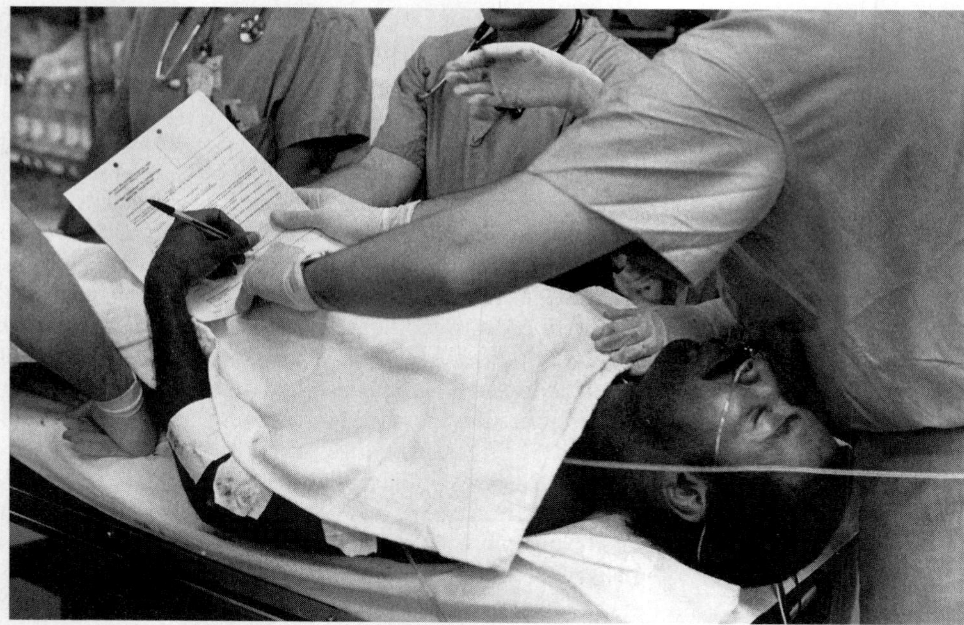

and private insurance providers. Physicians sometimes charge for services never rendered, falsify reimbursement codes to collect more funds than permitted by insurance companies and government agencies, and submit inflated bills for medical supplies. The justice system is so overwhelmed by health care–related fraud cases that federal prosecutors do not even bother pursuing suspected violations unless the monetary value exceeds $100,000.

Carl Shramm argues (in *Brokaw Report,* 1992) that too many physicians practicing specialized medicine (the number has doubled over the past 25 years) has contributed to escalating health care costs. However, as in the case of many developing countries, even with the rising numbers of practicing physicians, many rural and urban areas of the United States currently lack adequate professional medical care. For example, in 1988, affluent Beverly Hills, California, had one internist for every 566 people. Its significantly poorer Los Angeles County neighbor, Compton, had one internist for every 19,422 people. Whereas poor Americans are not getting enough medical care, wealthy Americans may be getting too much.

THE UGLY: UNEQUAL ACCESS TO HEALTH CARE

In spite of the fact that both national and per capita health expenditures in the United States are the highest of any industrialized nation, our health care system delivers less "bang for the buck" than that of any other country. In 1990, the United States ranked first among 18 Organization for Economic Cooperation and Development (OECD) countries in health care spending but last in terms of the proportion of its people protected by public health insurance. In contrast to an average of 96 percent population eligibility in the other 17 nations, in this society, only 40 percent of the population was eligible for hospital care under public insurance (Sivard, 1993, p. 41). This constitutes the "ugly" dimension of our current health care system.

According to the U.S. Census Bureau's Current Population Survey of March 1993, 38.9 million American people lacked health insurance coverage in 1992, an increase of over 2 million from the 1991 level ("38.9 Million Lack," 1993). Whereas most individuals over age 65 were covered by some form of insurance (largely, Medicare), young adults between the ages of 18 and 35 were much more likely to lack health coverage: Nearly 29 percent in the 18 to 24 cohort and nearly 21 percent in the 25 to 35 age cohort were without health insurance (U.S. Bureau of the Census, 1993b). Over 56 percent of the uninsured were working adults; the remainder were made up of nonworking adults (nearly 18 percent) and children (25 percent). More than half of all uninsured individuals (53 percent) lived in families with annual incomes under $20,000 (Coolidge, 1994). Another 20 million individuals of all ages are underinsured, which means that a serious medical problem would wipe them out financially.

At present, government or public health insurance provides coverage for about 40 percent of the U.S. population, primarily through the Medicare program for individuals over age 65 and the Medicaid program for individuals who meet specified no- or low-income criteria. However, neither program provides 100 percent coverage for its members. In 1992, nearly 68 percent of all people covered under Medicare also held supplemental private health insurance (U.S. Bureau of the Census, 1993b). However, poverty-level individuals and families on Medicaid simply cannot afford the cost of supplemental private health insurance. Their access to health care services is limited to the extent to which Medicaid will cover their bills (on average, about 75 percent of medical expenses).

Nearly 10 million children, primarily from low-income families that do not qualify for Medicaid benefits, are included among the uninsured population (Coolidge, 1994). A member of the Children's Defense Fund notes, "Children have definitely borne the brunt of the breakdown in our [health] care system" (Rosenbaum in Spiegel, 1992, p. A1). Because their families cannot afford or have no access to medical benefits, these children are 50 percent more likely to have health problems than children from families that do have coverage. Nonexistent or inferior health care benefits for so many children is a major reason why, of the 24 industrial countries that comprise the OECD, the United States ranks twenty-first in infant mortality and sixteenth and seventeenth, respectively, in male and female life expectancy.

Women in their midforties and older are more likely than men in the same age group to be without health insurance. These women often work at part-time jobs that provide no coverage or see their husband-dependent health insurance terminated as a result of being divorced or widowed. Black and Latino women in this age group are even more likely than White women to lack medical coverage (Barringer, 1992a).

Although a large number of people now are covered by the government's Medicaid program, many physicians will not treat them because the plan pays only about 70 percent of their medical expenses, leaving physicians left to dun individual patients for the remaining fees. These people are often forced to search for physicians who will treat them when they become ill or disabled. Because so many Americans (57 percent) are dependent on work-related health insurance plans, when they lose their jobs, they also lose their health care coverage. They are exposed to the full economic consequences of illness or accident at the very moment they are most vulnerable financially. In describing this situation, one critic notes, "No other industrialized country visits upon persons unfortunate enough to lose their jobs the added hardship of also losing health insurance for themselves and their families" (Reinhardt in *Health Care Crisis,* 1992, p. 27).

TACKLING THE U.S. HEALTH CARE PROBLEM

In September 1990, the U.S. Department of Health and Human Services released its report *Healthy People 2000.* Building on its ongoing work in identifying important dimensions and current deficiencies in U.S. public health, the report outlined three broad national health objectives, with specific target goals, for the coming decade:

1. Increasing the span of healthy life (that is, the average number of illness-free years) for Americans
2. Reducing existing health disparities among Americans
3. Achieving access to preventive health services for all Americans (U.S. Department of Health and Human Services, 1992a, p. 6)

Most observers agree that significant changes in the present U.S. health care system are necessary for these lofty objectives to have any realistic chance of success. However, both the experts and the general public are widely divided over the question of just what sorts of changes will be required to make the goal of good health and good health care for all a reality. Proposals have ranged from a complete restructuring of U.S. health care to revisions of existing program components.

RESTRUCTURING PROPOSALS

With so many individuals at risk as a result of nonexistent or poor medical coverage, the question that more people are asking is how to provide universal access to medical treatment while simultaneously holding down medical costs. Increasing attention is being paid to the health care systems of countries such as France, Germany, and Japan, which provide health care coverage for all population members at costs considerably lower than those in the United States (Maremont et al., 1992). The Canadian single-payer system, in particular, has been cited as the most likely model for the restructuring of U.S. health care.

THE CLINTON PLAN

Acting on the basis of public surveys taken during the 1992 presidential campaign and during his first year in office that indicated widespread concern and dissatisfaction with the state of U.S. health care, in 1993, President Clinton sent Congress a comprehensive health care reform bill. The main component of the Clinton plan is a national health insurance program that would be paid for through taxes on employers and on employees. The United States is one of only two industrialized countries in the world (the other is South Africa) without some type of national insurance to provide health care access to all its citizens, even though polls indicate that a majority of Americans are in favor of such a system (Anderson, 1992).

Under the Clinton proposal of managed competition, a series of regional health alliances serving as go-betweens for consumers and health service providers would negotiate a variety of health care packages at agreed-upon costs. The individual businesses that formed the memberships of these alliances would contribute up to 80 percent of the average cost of participation in the national insurance program, and individual employees would pay the remaining premium costs of the particular health care package they selected. Individuals also would be responsible for a copayment for each physician, hospital visit, or prescription, up to a specified annual limit (Fritz, 1993). This insurance

NORTHERN DISCLOSURE
The Canadian Health Care System

When health care reform talk in the United States turns to ideas for replacing the current private enterprise system with a more public-directed approach, the model that typically comes to mind is that of Canada. Canada's national health insurance system is not the first of its kind, nor the largest: Both Germany and Japan have government-run systems that are larger, older, or both (Roemer, 1991). However, for reasons having as much to do with geographic and cultural proximity as anything else (that is, Canada is very close to the United States, rather than thousands of miles away, and its people are in many ways more like Americans than they are different), it is the Canadian health care system that U.S. reformers envision as the prototype or starting point for what our own health care might one day become (Siegel et al., 1993).

The current Canadian national health care structure had its origins in the western prairie province of Saskatchewan in the years immediately following World War II. The Social Democratic Party that then controlled the provincial government introduced a hospital insurance plan in 1947 and expanded that plan to include all forms of medical care in the early 1960s. This socialized medicine approach initially was strongly opposed by Saskatchewan's physicians and private health insurers, but their resistance was overcome by a combination of a tough, hard-ball government stance and growing general public support for the change. Based on its inquiry into the Saskatchewan program, the Canadian federal government passed the 1966 Medical Care Act that created a virtually identical program at the national level (Adams, 1993; M. W. Walsh, 1993).

The essence of what Canadians call their Medicare system is its single-payer feature. All expenses for covered medical services and treatments are paid for by the government, rather than by individuals or by private insurers. Within each of the country's ten provinces and two territories, payments are made by the respective provincial or territorial government, using a combination of funds contributed by the federal government and monies raised by the province or territory itself. These government revenues come from a variety of sources, including income taxes, payroll taxes, and sales taxes. Canadian taxes, on average, are significantly higher than comparable taxes in the United States.

It has been this fact, as much as any other, that has led many U.S. politicians to reject any kind of government-sponsored national health insurance system. As we discussed in our overview of social problems in Chapter One, societal responses to problems often are decided as much on their political viability as on their technical merit. No politician facing reelection would willingly go on record as supporting a tax increase unless the mandate from the voting public were overwhelming, and public support for a tax-supported national health insurance program in the United States has not yet reached the "overwhelming" point (Hasson, 1994a).

In addition to paying for all health care expenses, in the Canadian system, the government also sets and regulates health care costs, specifying acceptable physician and hospital fees and monitoring these fees on a continuing basis. At the start of each fiscal year, hospitals are given "global budgets" to provide agreed-upon services during the year. However, each hospital is also given complete control over the day-to-day allocation of its resources and is subject to review by local community boards, rather than by the federal or provincial government (Beatty, 1993). For their part, individual Canadians are given complete freedom to select whatever physician or hospital best suits their needs and preferences. There is no list of preferred or mandated health care providers, as is often the case with health maintenance organizations or other collective health programs in the United States (Fulton, 1993). This freedom of individual choice appears to be one factor contributing to the high level of Canadians' overall satisfaction with their country's health care system.

Since 1983, a series of national and provincial surveys have documented the fact that anywhere from 75 percent to 90 percent of the Canadian population perceive their health care as being "good" or better. These same polls also show that a major fear of many people in the United States—the likely cataclysmic economic impact of a major illness—simply isn't present in Canada. According to many of its supporters, this elimination of the possibility of financial ruin ranks as one of the most significant and enduring accomplishments of Canada's 30-plus-year nationalized health insurance system (McKinnon, 1993). For national and per capita costs far lower than those in the United States, virtually all Canadians have been guaranteed access to health-restoring curative medicine and health-maintaining preventive medicine. However, the Canadian system is not without its drawbacks.

To the extent that demand for services exceeds available funding, individual patients often have to wait—sometimes, for weeks or months—for some procedures such as hip-replacement or gall bladder operations (Symonds, 1992). And in recent years, as the Canadian economy has faced the same recessionary forces as its southern neighbor, the federal government has cut its health insurance funding to the provinces from 50 percent to 30 percent, placing provincial governments in the position of either having to cut back services or to increase taxes. For example, Ontario physicians had their pay for every medical procedure cut by nearly 5 percent, and in December 1993, Toronto hospitals were closed to all but emergency cases for almost three weeks (Hasson, 1994b). Like U.S. health care, the Canadian system is characterized by wide variations in medical treatment from one region to another and, within a given region, from one hospital to another. For example, one 1994 study found that some Ontario hospitals performed surgery at rates 350 percent higher than others, whereas other hospitals seemingly prescribed drugs to elderly patients at unprecedented rates (Brown, 1994). Finally, recent audits indicate a significant increase in health care fraud. In Ontario, the most heavily populated province, an estimated $47 million to $473 million has been lost through false health cards, overbilling, and claims filed by nonresidents, adding to what is already a financially strapped system ("Canada Plans Crackdown," 1994).

Regardless of its apparent advantages over the present U.S. health care system, it is unlikely that Canadian-style national health insurance could be implemented in this society in the near future. The Canadian system originated at a time when that country's physicians did not have the enormous political clout currently enjoyed by the American Medical Association in the United States. Additionally, the provincial governments that gave birth to publicly funded health insurance were more socialistic in nature than most U.S. state governments and certainly much more so than the U.S. federal government. Finally, cultural differences between the two countries' populations make Canadians much more egalitarian than their U.S. counterparts. In responding to criticism that his country's health system forced everyone to settle for the same level of health care, one Canadian official observed, "It never struck me that anybody would feel it was appropriate to buy better service or that someone could jump line as a result of having money. In Canada, we believe deeply that . . . equality in terms of service for health care is a human entitlement. It's not something that comes to you as a result of your ability to earn money" (Beatty, 1993, p. 31). As long as a majority of Americans express different beliefs, national health insurance for all remains only a very remote possibility.

would be "portable" in that it would not be tied to individuals' current jobs. Workers who changed jobs would take their coverage with them to their new places of employment. For its part, the government would finance its extension of Medicare and Medicaid insurance benefits to people who are elderly, poor, or unemployed largely through increased taxes on cigarettes and other tobacco products. To help keep overall costs under control, the amount that insurance premiums could be raised would be limited by the government (Chen, 1994).

As might be expected with any plan of similar proportions, the Clinton proposal has met with a great deal of resistance. A number of generally conservative groups—including big business, the American Medical Association, health insurance companies, and the "religious right"—have voiced their opposition to what they see as further government intrusion into their personal rights and liberties (in the case of businesses, the AMA, and the insurance companies) and to public subsidizing of abortion and birth control (in the case of the "religious right") (Bayer, 1994; Briggs, 1994; Dillin, 1994b; Uchitelle, 1994). On the other hand, the plan has also been opposed by liberal population segments—including immigrants' advocacy groups, community hospitals, and even some members of so-called Generation X (those in the "twenty-something" age cohort)—because of its exclusion of undocumented immigrants from health coverage and its shifting of increasing financial burdens onto younger members of the population (Feldmann, 1993c; Karl, 1993; Tolchin, 1993).

Much of the opposition has been centered around the uncertainties of the Clinton plan's economic costs (Marks, 1993b; Risen, 1993b), but some observers claim this public concern is merely a smokescreen to conceal its true (and hidden) political basis: "Many vested interests in America would rather debate the issue than do anything about it. . . .

In a $750 billion a year industry, a lot of interests are served by the status quo, and many would prefer infinite sharpening of the fine points to major alterations of the status quo" (Vladeck, 1992). Whatever the actual source of opposition, as of late 1994, the Clinton plan had yet to be approved by the Congress, whose different members had introduced at least a half-dozen alternative health care proposals reflecting their own beliefs and concerns (Appel, 1994). Well before the end of the first year after its introduction, the timetable for the Clinton health care reform plan had fallen behind by more than a year.

THE STATE PLANS: WHAT CAN CLINTON LEARN?

Whereas the fate of a national health insurance plan remains in doubt, at least one state already has hands-on experience with universal health care coverage. In 1974, Hawaii introduced a health care plan based on mandatory health insurance coverage by employers for all employees working at least 20 hours a week and on expanded Medicaid coverage for people who are unemployed or poor. After going through several revisions, the plan now covers about 98 percent of all Hawaiian residents. The Hawaii plan provides only basic health coverage benefits through Kaiser and Blue Cross, but its strong emphasis on preventive care has reduced the state's infant mortality rate to one of the nation's lowest and increased its average life expectancy to one of the nation's highest (Siegel et al., 1993). Although employers at times complain about the costs to them, there is a high level of overall satisfaction with the program from consumers, who are guaranteed some degree of health coverage, regardless of their financial and employment situations. As Hawaii's director of health has stated, "We have all the health problems of the rest of the states. What makes us different is that we decided to do something about the health care problem" (Lewis in *Health Care Crisis,* 1992, p. 37).

Other states have not been so successful in their attempts to do something about their health care problems. In 1992, Vermont introduced a comprehensive health care reform bill containing many of the features of the Clinton plan. Under the direction of the Vermont Health Care Authority, the program was to have guaranteed access to health insurance for all state residents by 1995. The program initially succeeded in setting budgets for hospitals and in cutting administrative costs by standardizing insurance claims forms, but final passage of the bill was stalled by questions of how the changes would be financed. Proponents' claims that "health care is about to take its rightful place next to food, shelter, and clothing" as a basic and universal right in Vermont (Wright in Marks, 1993a) proved premature. In June 1994, the state legislature defeated the proposal on the basis of its projected costs and its likely consequences for businesses already struggling in a recessionary climate.

A second highly controversial and radical state plan that also was ultimately rejected was that proposed by Oregon in 1991. The intent of the Oregon plan was to extend Medicaid and private health insurance to large numbers of people then excluded from access to health care but at the price of eliminating coverage for "some medical procedures widely accepted as beneficial" (Strosberg, 1992, p. 3). This rationing-of-health-services feature proved unacceptable to the federal government, which, as the provider of Medicaid, had final approval over the plan. In 1992, then-President Bush rejected the proposal on the basis that it violated the 1990 Americans with Disabilities Act by, in effect, placing a secondary value on the lives of Oregonians with physical disabilities (Siegel et al., 1993).

The fact that two of three attempted state-level universal health insurance plans failed should be cause for some concern to advocates of national health insurance. However, the fact that at least one state-level plan has been working well for over 20 years should be cause for some optimism, especially if some of the conditions that contributed

The consequences of poor health and poor health care have spread across individual societies and across the global society, as well. To the extent that individuals' and populations' levels of physical, psychological, and social well-being affect nearly every aspect of their lives, so also do the effects of their lack of well-being.

- As we saw in Chapter Eight, women's potential contributions to their home countries' economic and social advancement often are stymied by traditional gender stereotypes that keep women from developing and utilizing their talents. This problem of the loss of valuable human resources is compounded by the higher levels and greater severity of female health problems in developing countries, where women receive little or no medical treatment.
- Women in developed societies such as the United States are also subject to unequal health care treatment. Much of the medical research conducted to test new treatments has excluded women entirely, thus placing them at risk from drugs developed without regard for their possible interactive effects on female hormones (Roan, 1992). In addition, some studies have indicated that health care costs for women are significantly higher than those for men of comparable age (Schwinn, 1994).
- In the United States, according to reports, the higher observed disease, illness, and death rates for African Americans is a direct result of the lack of health insurance coverage for many members of this population segment. This widespread exclusion of African Americans from health care treatment has been described by critics as a type of "medical apartheid," reflective of continuing racism in U.S. society (Brooks et al., 1991).
- Although a growing number of people, representing many different segments of U.S. society, would like to see tobacco products banned entirely for health reasons, it seems very unlikely that such a drastic policy will be enacted in the foreseeable future. For better or worse, tobacco is a major industry that occupies a significant place in the U.S. economy. In 1993, for example, in addition to the $6.2 billion in tobacco exports, homegrown smokers spent an estimated

to the success of the Hawaii plan can be replicated at the national level. It is not clear, though, that this is the case.

According to Siegel and his associates (1993), the Hawaii plan was introduced at a time in which the incumbent president (Richard Nixon) was not opposed to the idea of universal health care coverage. In this respect, at least, President Clinton can be regarded as a positive factor. However, a significant portion of Hawaii's success can be attributed to its high level of unionization and relative isolation from the other states, making it difficult for disgruntled businesses to relocate elsewhere in order to avoid picking up the costs of the health care plan. This particular circumstance obviously wouldn't hold for the nation at large, where unions have steadily declined and unhappy employers could exercise the option of relocating to Mexico or to some other foreign country if they were unhappy about footing too much of the health insurance bill. Additionally, Hawaii's small population size and low levels of unemployment also have assisted in the success of its health plan. These are two conditions that, again, wouldn't apply at the national level, where both the population size and the unemployment rate are much greater. Two features of the Hawaii plan that could be applied at the national level, however, are its emphasis on providing coverage for basic health services and its strong focus on preventive health care. Both of these features aid significantly in keeping overall costs down. If

$42 billion for cigarettes, generating $11 billion in federal, state, and local taxes. Approximately 681,000 jobs are tied directly to tobacco, including over 136,000 farmers in 23 states. Tobacco currently is the sixth-largest cash crop in the country (Lamb, 1994). Even assuming the necessary political support, eliminating this powerhouse industry would be tantamount to driving a knife into the country's wallet. The economic repercussions would be catastrophic, especially in an era of recession, increasing unemployment, and occupational structural changes. Furthermore, any prohibition of smoking and tobacco product use would likely result in the creation of a black market in illegal cigarettes and problems of increasing crime similar to those resulting from the prohibition of alcohol in the 1920s (Eisenberg, 1994).

- Although most of the over-65 population of the United States are covered through Medicare and many lower-income people are covered through Medicaid, those individuals who lack supplemental private health insurance must make copayments for health care services, including prescriptions. In the United States, prices for drugs are on average 60 percent higher than prices in Britain and many other countries, including Mexico (Fritz, 1994; Lipman, 1994). These prices place an additional burden on people already in precarious financial straits. The nearly 39 million Americans with no health insurance whatever must pay the physical and emotional consequences of being unable to afford what may be life-sustaining pharmaceuticals.
- At present, most Americans with private health insurance receive this coverage as part of their employment compensation. However, for the most part, these health care benefits are tied to the job. If individuals lose their jobs or change jobs, the coverage ceases. As more and more jobs have been permanently lost and others have been downgraded to part-time status as a result of the occupational structural changes discussed in Chapter Six, millions of additional people have lost their health coverage. Many other individuals who may not be especially satisfied with their present jobs are constrained from making employment changes for fear of losing health coverage benefits. "This means that individual workers lose their freedom to change jobs, while the American labor market loses the flexibility that has been so important to its success" (Siegel et al., 1993, p. 17).

they could be instituted at the societal level, the Clinton plan (or something like it) conceivably could work.

REVISIONIST PROPOSALS

Short of substantial restructuring of the current health care system, a number of proposals and plans already in operation have attempted to extend health care access and to reduce health care costs through revisions of specific facets of that system. The most widespread and successful of these efforts has been the *health maintenance organization* (HMO).

HMOs are group medical practices organized to provide full coverage for subscribers' health needs at preestablished prices (Siegel et al., 1993). The number of Americans enrolled in HMOs increased by over 600 percent in less than 20 years, from 5.98 million in 1976 to 36 million in 1992 (Jacobs et al., 1994). As of 1992, 555 HMOs were in operation throughout the United States, primarily in the western states. About 65 percent of these were *individual practice associations,* in which the HMO contracts with individual physicians or medical groups who provide services to HMO members in the providers' own offices. However, nearly half of all HMO members belong to group plans, in which a group of physicians contract with the HMO to provide care. Kaiser Permanente, the nation's largest HMO, has its own hospitals and medical offices throughout California, Hawaii, other western states, and in the Northeast.

An alternative to the health maintenance organization is the *preferred provider organization* (PPO). PPOs are medical groups that offer discounted service costs to health insurers, who, in return, refer their members to the PPO for treatment. In 1990, approximately 65 million people, about 26 percent of the U.S. population, had the PPO option, primarily through their participation in Blue Cross and Blue Shield insurance programs (Siegel et al., 1993).

Although both the PPOs and the HMOs have been moderately successful in keeping health costs under some control, they have done little or nothing to extend health care access to those who remain outside the health coverage loop. That particular problem is one that continues to confront tens of millions of Americans each day.

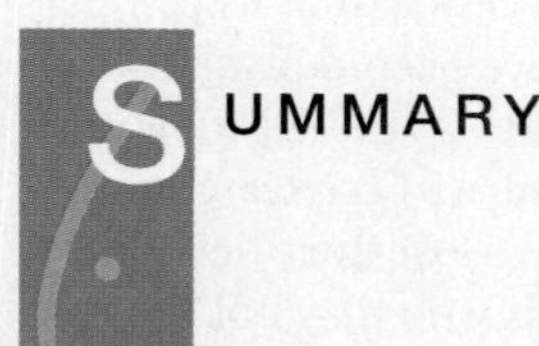

SUMMARY

1. Health can be conceptualized from medical, functional, or psychological perspectives. The medical model defines health as an absence of illness or disease, whereas the functional model defines health in terms of individuals' abilities to perform their assigned roles. The psychological model of health emphasizes physical, psychological, and social well-being in measuring the health of individuals.
2. Because they often lack access to primary health resources such as safe drinking water, sanitation, and basic health services, the populations of developing countries have much higher infant mortality rates and much lower life expectancies than members of developed nations. Traditional gender beliefs and practices also create particular health problems for women in developing societies.
3. People in developed societies tend to die from cardiovascular diseases and cancers, whereas individuals in developing countries are much more prone to death from infectious and parasitic diseases. As some developing nations have attained higher levels of economic development, the more affluent segments of their populations have begun to die more frequently from cardiovascular and cancer-related causes.
4. To a large extent, many of the leading causes of human mortality are preventable. This is especially the case with AIDS and with smoking. Although AIDS has been referred to as a "gay plague," the disease has spread to the heterosexual population as well, placing many population groups at risk. Informational and preventive campaigns designed to halt the spread of AIDS have often been unsuccessful because of the moral undertones surrounding this disease in developed countries and the subordinate position of women in many developing countries, especially in Africa.
5. Although many government reports have linked smoking with lung cancer and other diseases, hundreds of millions of people around the world continue to smoke, especially in developing countries in Asia. Public education programs and restrictive state and federal legislation have decreased the numbers of smokers in U.S. society, but it is unlikely that a complete ban on smoking will be instituted in the United States or in other societies in the near future.

6 Although at times, health care services in the United States may be among the best in the world, health care costs in this country are much higher than those found in any other industrialized society. As an entrepreneurial free-market system, health care in the United States is subject to a variety of cost-increasing forces that would not be found in not-for-profit health systems. A combination of overspecialized medical personnel, expensive medical technology, high administrative costs, and widespread fraud, among other factors, has made the already high costs of health care increase well beyond those of any other developed society in the world.

7 In addition to the exorbitant costs of many health care services, the U.S. system is also characterized by the lowest rate of health insurance coverage of any industrialized nation. Recent reports indicate that as many as 38.9 million individuals, many of them children and members of racial or ethnic minorities, have no health coverage at all, and another 20 million people are underinsured.

8 Taking a cue from other industrial nations, in 1993, President Clinton introduced a managed health care plan to Congress that would in effect create national health insurance. The Clinton plan has met with stiff resistance from established medical and insurance groups as well as from members of some religious groups, who are opposed to its intrusion into free-market health principles or its public funding of birth control and abortion. A number of alternative proposals introduced by different Congressional representatives make it unlikely that a national health insurance program will be implemented in the immediate future.

9 Hawaii has been in the forefront of state-level efforts to institute universal health care coverage. The Hawaii plan has been in effect for over 20 years and now covers about 98 percent of the state's population through employer- and employee-funded mandatory insurance. Other state-level programs introduced in Vermont and in Oregon have been rejected on the basis either of their projected costs or their proposal to ration health care services among various population segments.

10 In the absence of a national health insurance program, health maintenance organizations and preferred provider organizations have helped hold down medical costs for their millions of subscribers. However, they have done little to provide access to health care services for the millions of other Americans currently cut off from any sort of public or private insurance.

EPILOGUE
Slouching toward the Millennium

If you have managed to make it through the last 12 chapters without becoming fatally depressed, you should treat yourself to some sort of reward—you deserve it. For as bad as things might seem when we examine the dimensions of any single social problem facing the modern world, they can look infinitely worse when we consider the entire set of problems now confronting humanity. As we have tried to emphasize throughout this book, social problems do not exist in isolation from one another. Rather, they are connected in complex cause-and-effect patterns, so that they build on and reinforce one another.

For example, rapid population growth in many developing countries places tremendous strains on local environmental resources; as these resources are used up, already-poor populations are plunged even deeper into poverty. In turn, this increasing poverty leads people to exploit their environments even further in the interest of short-term survival, thus creating both long-term environmental destruction and long-term poverty. As both environmental and economic resources dwindle, genocidal conflicts may erupt among different population segments struggling to maintain their own existence; people's attempts to escape these struggles can create international hostilities, as waves of refugees stream across national borders and place staggering burdens on their host societies. This vicious circle can be broken only by attacking all its individual elements—rapid population growth, poverty, and environmental destruction—simultaneously, but the enormous costs of such a massive undertaking put it beyond the reach of most developing societies. In the absence of necessary funding, the problems continue to worsen.

However, it would be both inaccurate and unfair to leave you with the impression that things are completely hopeless, that the whole world is doomed. Instead, we would like to leave you with the thought that although real solutions to social problems can at times appear impossible, they have been attained in the past and can be in the future.

Concerned people can and will make a difference in dealing with social problems, as they already have on so many occasions.

For example, in the early part of this century, the massive problems found in Chicago and other large cities seemed beyond salvation. But while the pioneer social theorists of the Chicago school were formulating their ecological models of urban change and decay, a group of social activists were making significant strides in addressing the problems generated by those processes. Led by Jane Addams (1860–1935), these sociologists-turned-social workers labored to improve conditions in the city's worst slums by creating and operating Hull House, a settlement house to meet neighborhood residents' physical, educational, economic, and social needs. Based on Addams's vision of a society "in which all individuals, regardless of gender, ethnicity, race, or economic status, would have the opportunity fully to express and to develop their talents, interests, and ambitions" (Lagemann, 1985, p. 2), Hull House offered newly arrived immigrants and people who were poor such essential services as a medical dispensary, low-cost hot meals, a day-care nursery, a savings bank, and both basic and advanced education classes. Hull House was so successful that it became the model for many other settlement houses across the United States that helped ease the pain and suffering of countless urban dwellers. Addams was also deeply involved in feminist, pacifist, and racial civil rights movements, ultimately holding executive offices in such groups as the National American Woman Suffrage Association, the National Association for the Advancement of Colored People, the American Union Against Militarism, the Woman's Peace Party, and the Women's International League for Peace and Freedom. For her efforts on behalf of peace and equality, Jane Addams was awarded the Nobel Peace Prize in 1931 (Robinson, 1991).

Addams's vision did not end with her death. More recently, it seems, that vision has grown and been shared by many people in many different countries. As we saw in Chapter Two, global military spending has declined steadily since the end of the Cold War. Between 1987 and 1994, the nations of the world collectively reduced their military expenditures by $933 billion. According to some estimates, an additional $459 billion will be trimmed from the world's military budget by the turn of the century (Knickerbocker & Grier, 1994). This trillion dollar (as of 1995) cutback represents an enormous savings of both money and human resources, as well as a slowdown in the number of weapons of mass destruction.

In the future, a much larger chunk of this so-called peace dividend conceivably could be used to address some of humankind's most pressing problems, such as widespread starvation, misery, and death in sub–Saharan Africa and the increasing deterioration of the planet's ecosystem. For example, reforestation programs sponsored by the United Nations and the World Bank could benefit significantly from an infusion of fresh money. Under the auspices of these programs, the People's Republic of China (PRC) has already planted 70 million acres of trees, and the former Soviet Union has reforested another 55 million acres. These large-scale replantings, along with smaller-scale efforts in Japan, Brazil, the United States, India, and Indonesia, are countering—to some extent—the destructive effects of air pollution, acid rain, and the loss of valuable topsoil. In China, reforestation has not only resulted in the sustained growth of woodlands but also provides the raw materials needed for paper and wood products. This industry, in turn, provides jobs for a growing number of people in the PRC (Langan, 1994).

At the 1994 International Conference on Population and Development (ICPD), held in Cairo, delegates approved 80 percent of the organization's "Program of Action," which included issues such as "universal access to family planning; economic, social, and political empowerment for women; education for women and girls; [and] respect for the fundamental rights of women to decide for themselves the size and spacing of their families"

("Eighty Percent of Action Plan Approved," 1994). This emphasis on the rights of girls and women is of crucial importance, inasmuch as elevating the status of females is considered *the* most effective method of lowering fertility rates in the developing world. The Secretary General of ICPD stated that the level of agreement reached at the Cairo meetings was "a landmark of decision making" ("Eighty Percent of Action Plan Approved," 1994). Additionally, in 1994, 63 countries also signed a "Statement of Population Stabilization" calling for the advancement of family planning, maternal health, and child health consistent with each country's culture and aspirations. Three of the signatories—China, India, and Bangladesh—represent approximately 40 percent of the world's total population ("Sixty-Three Leaders Endorse Stabilization," 1994).

The return of democracy to much of Eastern Europe has been some of the most encouraging news over the past decade. It is also a perfect example of how the determination of people to alter the conditions under which they live can bring about fundamental social, political, and economic changes in even the most difficult of circumstances. After a failed anticommunist revolution in Hungary in 1956 and an unsuccessful drive toward liberalization in Czechoslovakia in 1968, the Eastern European governments attempted a kind of tradeoff with their citizens. If the people would remain politically inert—that is, if they agreed to accept passively the dictates of the totalitarian regimes under which they lived—they could expect to see their material and economic well-being improve (Nagorski, 1993).

However, in the case of Poland, by 1970, a failed economic program resulted in sudden and substantial price hikes on food and other basic commodities. Workers' demonstrations against these increases in several cities were brutally suppressed by government forces—50 people were killed. Similar demonstrations were crushed in 1976. In 1980, a union started in the Lenin Shipyards in the city of Gdansk was begrudgingly recognized by the Polish government. Led by an electrician named Lech Walesa, *Solidarnosc* ("Solidarity") marked the beginning of the end of Soviet-style communism in Poland and in much of Eastern Europe. After another decade of struggle and sacrifice on the part of millions of Poles, the communists were swept out of power. In the first democratic elections in Poland in over 50 years, Solidarity candidates won 99 out of 100 seats in the Senate. People in other Eastern European countries soon followed suit, and the once seemingly invincible and impregnable stranglehold that totalitarian regimes held over tens of millions of people was broken.

The example of Eastern Europe should offer us great hope for the future. If only a small portion of the energy, determination, and courage shown by these individuals during an extraordinarily difficult period could be replicated by people (including political leaders) in other nations, we would have a good start toward solving many of the world's most serious problems. Over 2,500 years ago, legendary Chinese philosopher Lao-tzu is said to have noted, "A journey of a thousand miles must begin with a single step," an observation repeated by communist leader Mao Zedong on the eve of his army's long march across China to eventual victory. On the long journey toward solving contemporary social problems, several important steps already have been taken.

GLOSSARY

acid rain Heavily acidic moisture, resulting from nitrogen and sulfur gases in the atmosphere, that falls as rain, causing destruction of forests, lakes, and other ecosystem elements.

apartheid The political and economic policy that mandated racial segregation in South Africa, discriminating against people of non-European heritage.

assimilation The process by which minority ethnic and racial groups are absorbed or incorporated into the mainstream sociocultural system, eventually losing their distinctive cultural and physical identities.

battered wife syndrome A criminal defense sometimes used by women accused of killing their allegedly abusive husbands or boyfriends; in short, the defense argues that the killing was an act of self-defense, based on the months or typically years of often brutal and sadistic physical abuse the woman has suffered at the hands of her partner.

blocked opportunity The theory of urban riots that systematic discrimination, resulting in a very limited or nonexistent economic structure, is the cause of minimal economic success and produces the frustration and aggression among poor, inner-city residents that sporadically results in collective violence.

bourgeoisie According to Marxist theory, the social class that owns private property in industrialized societies.

comparable worth The principle calling for equal pay for jobs that, while different, are of substantially equal difficulty and importance.

concentration effects The overall debilitating psychological, cultural, social, and economic effects of living in an impoverished neighborhood.

cultural assimilation The process by which a minority group adopts the cultural and behavioral patterns of the majority group and gives up its own established patterns.

cultural lag According to sociologist William Ogburn, the process whereby one component of a society changes faster than another related component of that society; in modern societies, material culture (especially technology) typically changes faster than associated values, norms, and laws.

culture of poverty A self-perpetuating and self-defeating world view among people who are poor that helps insure they will remain so, even across generations; in general, values and attitudes emphasize immediate gratification and living for the moment rather than delaying gratification and working for the future.

de facto discrimination Discriminatory actions that exist and are accepted as common practice but that are not supported by law.

de jure discrimination Discriminatory actions that are supported or required by law.

decriminalization Reducing the penalty for committing a criminal act while not legalizing the act; for example, in some states, the penalty for possessing a small amount of marijuana (typically defined as a quantity for personal use) has been substantially lowered.

demand-side management (DSM) A variety of strategies designed to reduce energy consumption in a given society.

demographic transition A theory that explains population changes in the modern world; namely, the birth and death rates of a society will change (which will determine its rate of growth) as it passes through four stages; the theory was originally developed by Warren Thompson in 1929 and further developed by Frank Notestien in 1945.

desalination The process of removing salt and other substances from seawater or mineral-rich water.

desertification The process through which once arable land is literally turned into desert as a result of deforestation, overgrazing, and harmful agricultural practices.

developed, or northern, countries The more economically developed and politically democratic nations in the northern hemisphere of the contemporary world.

developing, or southern, countries The contemporary nations disproportionately located in the southern hemisphere currently undergoing societal modernization.

differential association The theory of criminologist Edwin Sutherland that if definitions favorable to violations of the law are in excess of definitions unfavorable to violations of the law, the individual will engage in criminal behavior.

discretion (police) The freedom and authority police officers have to make decisions as well as to choose courses of action from a number of alternatives; *unauthorized discretion* refers to the discretionary behavior an officer engages in illegally or improperly.

discrimination Unfair or unequal treatment of members of some specific group.

dual labor market An occupational structure divided into an upper tier of high-paying, high-prestige jobs and a bottom tier of low-paying, low-prestige jobs.

emigration The process of leaving one country for the purpose of taking up permanent residence in another country.

enforcement terrorism A form of violence used by revolutionary groups to gain the support of local people as well as to keep these individuals from cooperating with the government in power.

entrepreneurial immigrants Individuals who come to the United States and start their own businesses.

ethnic group People who possess a distinctive, shared culture and a sense of common identity or "peoplehood" based on that culture.

frustration-aggression theory The theory of urban riots that frustrations resulting from low social, economic, and political status experienced by poor, inner-city residents periodically erupt in a deadly, destructive rampage of collective violence.

gender An individual's classification as "girl" or "boy," "woman" or "man," based on her or his physiological, psychological, and sociocultural characteristics.

gender assignment The process by which individuals are defined, typically at birth, as being either "female" or "male."

gender roles Specific social roles assigned to individuals on the basis of sex.

gender socialization The social learning process through which individuals acquire and internalize the proper role of "female" or "male," as defined by their culture.

gender stereotypes Categorical portrayals of all members of a given sex as being alike in terms of basic nature and specific attributes.

gender stratification Hierarchies of social inequality based on sex.

genocide Deliberate and systematic destruction of a racial, ethnic, political, or religious group, in whole or significant part, by killing its members or imposing conditions detrimental to their survival.

gentrification The return of middle- and upper-class people to deteriorating inner-city neighborhoods.

"glass ceiling" In business, the set of invisible and informal barriers that effectively keep women out of companies' highest-level positions.

Green Revolution The introduction of new crops (such as short, stiff-stemmed wheat) and new technologies (including double-cropping and intensive use of fertilizers) that lead to greater crop yields; began in Mexico in the 1950s and has been most successful in a select few Indian states.

human capital factors Resources that people bring with them to the labor market that make them more or less successful in finding jobs, such as education, interest, and aptitude.

immigration The process of entering one country from another country for the purpose of taking up permanent residence.

indigenous peoples Groups whose ancestors were the original inhabitants of lands that were later colonized, settled, or invaded by others.

institutionalized discrimination A discriminatory pattern in which what was once a system of formal subjugation of minorities evolves into an informal system and is

maintained by established practices that discriminate covertly and perhaps unintentionally.

interdependence Relationships among societal components such that events taking place in any component both affect and are affected by events in other components.

labeling theory of deviance The theory that deviance is the result of a social process that defines certain phenomena and people as deviant and also establishes an official response to such deviance.

low-intensity conflicts (LICs) Armed conflicts that usually occur in less-developed countries and typically involve an army of the state fighting guerrillas, terrorists, or civilians; characterized by small-arms fighting, skirmishes, bombings, ambushes, and massacres.

majority group A recognizable group of people who dominate economic, political, and educational institutions and can structure most societal activities to their best advantage.

minority group A recognizable group of people whose nonvalued cultural or physical traits (and thus lack of effective power) block them from obtaining control over important societal institutions.

misemployment Work that is illegal or not economically productive, such as burglary, prostitution, and begging.

multiculturalism, or pluralism The retention, rather than the blending, of racial and ethnic group identities within a given society; true pluralism also entails a sharing of political power by different groups.

new-wave immigrants People from Central, Southern, and Eastern Europe as well as Asia and other non-European countries who immigrated to the United States in the late nineteenth and early twentieth centuries.

nonrenewable resources Materials such as coal, oil, and natural gas that exist in fixed supplies and cannot be replaced.

objectivistic view Any social theory that focuses on factual or objective conditions in explaining human social patterns.

old-wave immigrants People from Northern and Western Europe who immigrated to the United States in the early and mid-nineteenth century.

ozone layer The portion of the atmosphere that protects the earth's surface against excessive ultraviolet (UV) radiation from the sun.

perpetual resources Materials such as water and solar energy that constantly replenish themselves despite the level of human usage.

physical assimilation The blending of physical traits of majority groups and minority groups through biological reproduction.

plea bargaining An arrangement in which the defendant agrees to plead guilty to a criminal charge with the reasonable expectation of receiving some consideration (in the form of a more lenient sentence) from the state.

pluralism See **multiculturalism.**

political economy In modern societies, the close, symbiotic relationship between political and economic institutions.

political refugees People who leave their native countries and come to the United States because of ideological and political differences with the existing power structure or because of the economic hardships created by the policies of that same government.

political terrorism A form of unconventional warfare waged against national governments that is unrestrained by humanitarian concerns.

posttraumatic stress disorder (PTSD) Behavioral and/or psychological problems (such as anxiety, depression, anger, and violence) that result from experiencing one or more incidents of overwhelming terror; a significant number of U.S. combat veterans have manifested some symptoms of PTSD.

prejudice An irrational, negative feeling or belief about members of a certain group based on presumed characteristics of that group.

primary deviance According to labeling theorists, occasional and random acts of deviance committed by nearly everyone at some time or other.

professional immigrants Highly educated and highly skilled people (for example, doctors and business managers) who come to the United States to enhance their economic positions and further their careers.

proletariat According to Marxist theory, the laboring class in industrialized societies.

"pull" factors Socioeconomic characteristics that draw migrants to a given geographical location, including increased opportunity for employment and better living conditions.

"push" factors Socioeconomic characteristics that drive migrants from a particular geographic location, including limited or nonexistent economic opportunity and racial, religious, and political persecution.

race A classification of human beings based on genetic characteristics.

relations of production According to Marxist theory, an individual's standing with regard to the economic mode of production; the basic division was between those who owned private property and those who did not.

renewable resources Materials such as food grains and forest products that can be recreated or replaced within a relatively short time through human intervention.

residue management A series of environmentally sound agricultural techniques that include planting new crops in the decomposing residue of the previous year's harvest, rotating crops, and using environmentally friendly herbicides.

riffraff theory The theory of urban riots that rioters are irresponsible, emotionally disturbed individuals, many of whom have histories of violent, criminal behavior.

secondary deviance According to labeling theorists, acts of deviance committed as a result of being labeled deviant.

sex An individual's classification as "female" or "male" based on anatomical, chromosomal, and gonadal differences.

sexual harassment Any unwelcome tactile, visual, or verbal communication of a sexual nature.

social disorganization The theoretical model that argues that problems in a given society are the result of a disturbance in the state of balance and harmony that normally exists within and among the structural components of society.

social learning theory The theory that all social behavior, including aggressive behavior, is learned.

social pathology The theoretical model that argues that problems in a given society are the result of deliberate or inadvertent actions of morally evil or misguided individuals within that society.

social problems Conditions arising from the operation of the social order that are perceived as unacceptable by an influential segment of the population and that become the targets of attempted corrective social action.

societal substructure According to Marxist theory, the economic system that conditions and shapes all other important social and cultural arrangements in any society.

solid wastes A catch-all term referring to paper, glass, metals, wood, vegetation clippings, and other leftover materials created through residential or business activities.

state terrorism A form of violence used by a government against its own people with the goal of terrifying them into submission.

stereotypes Oversimplified and categorical beliefs that all members of some particular group are assumed to possess specific traits that distinguish them from all members of other groups.

structural assimilation The successful entrance of minority group members into secondary and primary group relationships with members of the majority group.

subjectivistic view Any social theory that focuses on people's subjective perceptions and interpretations of objective phenomena in explaining human social patterns.

total fertility rate (TFR) The average number of children born to a woman in a given society if current age-specific birth rates remain constant.

underemployment The underutilization of labor, which takes a number of forms: short-term seasonal work, such as construction and harvesting crops; makeshift work, such as picking through garbage and selling salvageable items; and working for reduced wages during economic slowdowns.

withdrawal syndrome or abstinence syndrome The adverse reaction that occurs when prolonged use of one or more drugs is terminated; psychological effects include intense craving for the drug, and physiological symptoms may include nausea and vomiting.

zero-sum game According to conflict theorists, any situation of scarce or limited resources in which gains made by one person or group come at the expense of other persons or groups; a "win-lose" situation.

BIBLIOGRAPHY

A

Abandinsky, H. (1989). *Drug abuse.* Chicago: Nelson-Hall.

Abandinsky, H. (1990). *Organized crime.* Chicago: Nelson-Hall.

Abramson, R., & Takahashi, D. (1992, March 26). Rockwell agrees to $18.5-million fine. *Los Angeles Times.*

Abu-Lughod, J L. (1991). *Changing cities.* New York: HarperCollins.

Aburdene, P., & Naisbitt, J. (1992). *Megatrends for women.* New York: Villard Books.

Acid rain from 3 nations destroys a Polish forest. (1991, September 11). *Journal of Commerce,* p. 5b.

Acid rain's high cost to Europe. (1991, September 28). *New Scientist,* p. 16.

Action alert: International news. (1993, January–February). *Ms.,* pp. 12–13.

Adams, C. T., & Winston, K. T. (1980). *Mothers at work—Public policies in the United States, Sweden, and China.* New York: Longman.

Adams, J. (1991, May). The real lessons of the Gulf War. *Atlantic,* pp. 36–50.

Adams, O. (1993). Understanding the health care system that works. In A. Bennett & O. Adams (Eds.), *Looking north for health* (pp. 113–141). San Francisco: Jossey-Bass.

Adler, F., Mueller, G. O. W., & Laufer, W. S. (1991). *Criminology.* New York: McGraw-Hill.

Agricultural Statistics. (1993). Stabilization and price support programs (ch. 11). Washington, DC: U.S. Department of Agriculture.

Ahmed, B., & Smith, S. K. (1992). How changes in components of growth affect the population aging of states. *Journal of Gerontology, 47*(1), 27–37.

Akers, R. L. (1992). Alcohol. In E. F. Borgatta & M. L. Borgatta (Eds.), *Encyclopedia of sociology, vol. 1* (pp. 42–47). New York: Macmillan.

Alba, R. D. (1992). Ethnicity. In E. F. Borgatta & M. L. Borgatta (Eds.), *Encyclopedia of sociology, vol. 1* (pp. 575–584). New York: Macmillan.

Albanese, J. S. (1989). *Organized crime in America.* Cincinnati: Anderson.

Albanese, J. S. (1991). Organized crime: The mafia mystique. In J. F. Sheley (Ed.), *Criminology* (pp. 201–218). Belmont, CA: Wadsworth.

Albini, J. (1992). The distribution of drugs: Models of criminal organization and their integration. In T. Meiczkowki (Ed.), *Drugs, crime, and social policy: Research, issues, and concerns* (pp. 79–108). Boston: Allyn and Bacon.

Alcohol and the soft sell. (1994, February 17). *Christian Science Monitor.*

Almost 5 million women shortchanged on child support. (1991, October 11). *San Diego Union.*

Amato, P. R., & Booth, A. (1991). Consequences of parental divorce and marital unhappiness for adult well being. *Social Forces, 69*(3), 895–914.

Amato, P. R., & Keith, B. (1991). Parental divorce and the well-being of children. *Psychological Bulletin* (110), 26–46.

Amato, P R., & Zuo, J. (1992). Rural poverty, urban poverty, and psychological well-being. *Sociological Quarterly, 33*(7), 229–240.

America in the 21st century. (1989). Washington, DC: Population Reference Bureau.

America's cities. (1992, May 9). *The Economist,* pp. 21–24.

American Embassy, Stockholm. (1991). *1991 national trade data bank market reports.*

Amnesty International report. (1991). London: Amnesty International Publications.

Andersen, M. (1981). Personalized nursing: An intervention model for drug dependent women in an emergency room. *Focus on Women: Journal of Addictions and Health, 1*(4), 217–226.

Andersen, M. L. (1993). *Thinking about women—Sociological perspectives on sex and gender.* New York: Macmillan.

Anderson, P. (1992, May 17). Survey indicates public support for national health insurance. *San Diego Union-Tribune.*

Andreski, S. (1964). Limited resources causes war. In D. L. Bender & B. Leone (Eds.), *War and nature—Opposing viewpoints* (pp. 64–68). St. Paul: Greenhaven.

Anglin, M. D., & Speckart, G. (1988). Narcotics use and crime: A multisample, multimethod analysis. *Criminology, 26*(2), 197–233.

Anti-choice protestor found guilty of murdering Florida abortion provider. (1994, March 11). *Reproductive Freedom News, 3*(5), 8.

Apocalypse right now? (1994, January/February). *Psychology Today,* pp. 27–31.

Appel, A. (1994, April 21). Health-care reform bills bounce left and right in halls of Congress. *Christian Science Monitor.*

Armstrong, S. (1993a, April 6). California melting pot boils over as illegal immigrants enter state. *Christian Science Monitor.*

Armstrong, S. (1993b, May 7). California debates whether smog regulations foul business climate. *Christian Science Monitor.*

Asch, S. E. (1951). Effects of group pressure upon the modifications and distortions of judgments. In H. Guetzkow (Ed.), *Groups, leadership, and men.* Pittsburgh: Carnegie.

Asia Watch Committee. (1990). *Punishment season—Human rights in China after martial law.* New York: Asia Watch Committee.

Associated Press. (1993, June 28). Brazil's child prostitutes increase. *San Diego Union-Tribune.*

Austerity triggers riots in Nigeria. (1989, July–August). *Africa Report,* pp. 10–11.

Auto cheats buy from dealers, sell as private citizens. (1991, October 15). *Los Angeles Times.*

Awasthi, D. (1992, June). Drinking filth. *India Today, 30,* 20.

B

Baca Zinn, M. (1989). Family, race, and poverty in the eighties. *Journal of Women and Culture in Society, 14*(4), 856–874.

Bader, E. J. (1988, May/June). The connection between population control and women's status. *Utne Reader,* p. 89.

Baer, L. S. (1978). *Let the patient decide: A doctor's advice to older persons.* Philadelphia: Westminster Press.

Bahr, H. M., Chadwick, B. A., & Strauss, J. H. (1979). *American ethnicity.* Lexington, MA: D. C. Heath.

Baker, M. A., White Berheide, C., Ross Greckel, F., Carstarphen Gugin, L., Lipetz, M. J., & Texler Segal, M. (1980). *Women today: A multidisciplinary approach to women's studies.* Monterey, CA: Brooks/Cole.

Ball, J., Shaffer, J. W., & Nurco, D. N. (1983). Day to day criminality of heroin addicts in Baltimore—A study in continuity of offense rates. *Drug and Alcohol Dependence, 12,* 119–142.

Balling, R. C., Jr. (1992, May 17). Evidence waning for "global warming." *San Diego Union-Tribune.*

Bando, M. S. (1986). *Japanese women yesterday and today.* Tokyo: Foreign Press Center/Japan.

Banerjee, R. (1992, June 30). Life beside the tracks. *India Today,* p. 13.

Banfield, E. C. (1970). *The unheavenly city: The nature of our urban crisis.* Boston: Little, Brown.

Banks, A. S. (Ed). (1993). Burundi. *Political handbook of the world: 1993* (pp. 118–121). Binghamton, NY: CSA Publications, State University of New York.

Banner, L. W. (1984). *Women in modern America: A brief history.* San Diego: Harcourt Brace Jovanovich.

Barahona, E. (1992, November). Getting high in Nicaragua. *World Press Review,* p. 51.

Barberis, M. (1993, May). Lithuania. *Population Today,* p. 11.

Barbour, J. (1991, October 13). World has 30 million lost who seek a place to call home. *San Diego Union.*

Barfield, C. (1994, April 3). Poverty to prosperity. *San Diego Union-Tribune.*

Barnaby, F. (1992, January). Nuclear countdown. *New Statesman,* pp. 14–16.

Barnathan, J. (1991, December 30). It's time to put the screws to China's gulag economy. *Business Week,* pp. 52–53.

Barnet, R. J. (1982). *The roots of war.* New York: Althenium.

Barnet, R. J. (1983). Modern Bureaucracies Cause War. In D. L. Bender & B. Leone (Eds.), *War and human nature* (pp. 50–54). St. Paul: Greenhaven.

Baron, L. (1992, September). Beyond the green revolution: Singin' the population blues. *ZPG Reporter, 24*(6), 1–4.

Barringer, F. (1992a, May 7). Middle-aged women lack health insurance more often than men. *Los Angeles Times,*.

Barringer, F. (1992b, November 10). For new elderly, woes fall hardest on women. *San Diego Union-Tribune.*

Barry, C. (1992, May 19). Women's group a first in Russia. *Christian Science Monitor.*

Bassuk, E. L. (1991, December). Homeless families. *Scientific American,* pp. 66–74.

Battersby, J. (1993a, May 19). South African women seek unity to promote cause of equal rights. *Christian Science Monitor.*

Battersby, J. (1993b, December 7). Multiracial body assumes seat of power in South Africa. *Christian Science Monitor.*

Battersby, J. (1993c, December 15). South Africa reels from racial attack. *Christian Science Monitor.*

Baum, G. (1991, April 15). Should these women have gone free? *Los Angeles Times.*

Baum, G. (1992, December 29). Knocking at the door. *Los Angeles Times.*

Baumann, M. (1994, May 26). Chemical-weapon use is reported. *USA Today.*

Bayer, A. (1990, January). Are lotteries a ripoff? *Consumer Research Magazine,* pp. 11–16.

Bayer, A. (1992, April 30). Women are poised for political surge into seats of House, Senate. *San Diego Union-Tribune.*

Bayer, A. (1994, March 11). Religious right calls Clinton's health plan dead wrong. *San Diego Union-Tribune.*

Bearak, B. (1994, February 27). A turf war for urban squatters. *Los Angeles Times.*

Beatty, P. (1993). A comparison of our two systems. In A. Bennett & O. Adams (Eds.), *Looking north for health* (pp. 28–39). San Francisco: Jossey-Bass.

Beaty, J. (1989, August 21). Do humans need to get high? *Time,* p. 58.

Becker, H. (1963). *Outsiders: Studies in the sociology of deviance.* New York: Free Press.

Beers, D. (1992, February 9). A biting controversy. *Los Angeles Times Magazine,* pp. 22–44.

Begley, S., with Hager, M. (1991, November 4). Bring back the ozone layer! *Newsweek,* p. 49.

Beirne P., & Messershmidt, J. (1991). *Criminology.* San Diego: Harcourt Brace Jovanovich.

Bell, D. (1973). *The coming of post-industrial society.* New York: Basic Books.

Bell, D. (1976). *The post-industrial society: A venture in social forecasting.* New York: Basic Books.

Bellah, R. S., Madsen, R., Sullivan, W. M., Swidler, A., & Tipton, S. M. (1985). *Habits of the heart—Individualism and commitment in American life.* New York: Harper & Row.

Belsie, L. (1992, April 30). Primaries suggest 1992 may be "year of the woman." *Christian Science Monitor.*

Belsie, L. (1993, September 13). Rise of part-time work in industrialized nations could signal slow recovery. *Christian Science Monitor.*

Bencivenga, J. (1992, March 4). Cities said to lose political clout. *Christian Science Monitor.*

Benjamin, L. (1991). *The black elite: Facing the color line in the twilight of the twentieth century.* Chicago: Nelson-Hall.

Bennett, W. J. (1990). Drugs damage American society. In N. Bernards (Ed.), *Drugs—Opposing viewpoints* (pp. 47–53). San Diego: Greenhaven.

Benokraitis, N. V. (1993). *Marriage and families.* Englewood Cliffs, NJ: Prentice Hall.

Berger, P. L., & Luckmann, T. (1966). *The social construction of reality: A treatise in the sociology of knowledge.* Garden City, NY: Doubleday.

Bergeson, A. (1980). Cycles of formal colonial rule. In T. K. Hopkins & I. Wallerstein (Eds.), *Processes of the world system* (pp. 119-126). Beverly Hills, CA: Sage.

Berk, R. A., & Newton, P. J. (1985, April). Does arrest really deter wife battery? An effort to replicate the findings of the Minneapolis spouse abuse experiment. *American Sociological Review, 50,* 253–262.

Berkowitz, L. (1968). The study of urban violence: Some implications of laboratory studies of frustration and aggression. In L. H. Motti & D. R. Bowen (Eds.), *Riots and rebellion: Civil disobedience in the urban community.* Beverly Hills, CA: Sage.

Berliner, U. (1991, December 15). Compulsive gambling takes heavy toll. *San Diego Union.*

Bernard, J. (1981). *The female world.* New York: Free Press.

Bernard, J. (1986). The good provider role: Its rise and fall. In A. R. Skolnick & J. Skolnick (Eds.), *Family in transition.* Boston: Little, Brown.

Berry, W. (1991, November). What the Gulf War taught us. *The Progressive,* pp. 26–29.

Bharadwaj, L. K. (1992). Human ecology and the environment. In E. F. Borgatta & M. L. Borgatta (Eds.), *Encyclopedia of sociology, vol. 2* (pp. 848–867). New York: Macmillan.

Bhatia, J. (1988, July 14). Only tinsel dreams for Bombay's battered urchins. *Far Eastern Economic Review,* pp. 45–46.

Bhatia, J. (1989, March 30). New-fangled New Delhi. *Far Eastern Economic Review,* pp. 40–41.

Bielby, W. T., & Baron, J. N. (1984). A woman's place is with other women. In B. F. Reskin (Ed.), *Sex segregation in the workplace: Trends, explanations, remedies* (pp. 27–55). Washington, DC: National Academy Press.

Bingham, M. Wall, & Gross, S. Hill. (1987). *Women in Japan.* St. Louis Park, MN: Glenhurst Publications.

Bior, H. (1992, May 27). Experts see water desalination as crucial to Middle East peace. *Christian Science Monitor.*

Black, R. F., Collins, S., & Boroughs, D. L. (1992, July 27). Shooing up the future. *U.S. News and World Report,* pp. 55–56.

Bleviss, D. L., & Walzer, P. (1991). Energy for motor vehicles. In G. R. Davis (Ed.), *Energy for planet earth: Readings from Scientific American magazine* (pp. 48–58). New York: Freeman.

Block, I. (1989). Gun control would reduce crime. In W. Dudley (Ed.), *Crime and criminals—Opposing viewpoints* (pp. 192–199). San Diego: Greenhaven.

Blumstein, A. (1988). Prison crowding. *Crime file study guide.* Washington, DC: National Institute of Justice.

Bogert, C. (1992, November 2). Get out the Geiger counters. *Newsweek,* pp. 64–65.

Bokhari, F. (1993, October 25). Pakistan's profitable First Women's Bank carves new niche. *Christian Science Monitor.*

Bokhari, F. (1994, January 4). Poverty and illegal traders strip Pakistan of protective trees. *Christian Science Monitor.*

Bonacich, E. (1992). Class and race. In E. F. Borgatta & M. L. Borgatta (Eds.), *Encyclopedia of sociology, vol. 1* (pp. 204–208). New York: Macmillan.

Bonfante, J., & Painton, P. (1992, May 18). This land is your land . . . This land is my land. *Time,* pp. 28–33.

Boulard, G. (1993, March 17). Combating environmental racism. *Christian Science Monitor.*

Bowditch, C., & Everett, R. S. (1991). Private prisons are not more efficient than public prisons. In S. L. Tipp (Ed.), *America's prisons—Opposing viewpoints.* San Diego: Greenhaven Press.

Bowring, R., & Kornicki, P. (1993). *Cambridge encyclopedia of Japan.* New York: Cambridge University Press.

Boxall, B. (1993, June 29). Tougher for girls from the word "go." *Los Angeles Times.*

Boyden, J. (1993). *Families: Celebration and hope in a world of change.* New York: Gaia Books.

Brady, D. (1991, August 19). A hidden terror. *MacLean's,* p. 36.

Brady, J. (1983, October). Arson, urban economy, and organized crime—The case of Boston. *Social Problems, 31,* 1–27.

Braithwaite, J. (1981). The myth of social class and criminality reconsidered. *American Journal of Sociology, 46,* 36–47.

Braun, G. (1991, November 15). "Career suicide" of bias cases told. *San Diego Union.*

Bremmer, P. (1988, May). Terrorism: Myth and realities. *Department of State Bulletin, 88,* 61–64.

Brenner, S.-O., & Starrin, B. (1988). Unemployment and health in Sweden: Public issues and private troubles. *The Society for the Psychological Study for Social Issues, 44*(4), 125–140.

Brewer, M. B., & Crano, W. D. (1994). *Social psychology.* Minneapolis-St. Paul: West.

Briggs, D. (1994, February 13). Anti-abortion forces take aim at health plan. *San Diego Union-Tribune.*

Bring drug laws within the law. (1993, May 15). *The Economist,* pp. 13–14.

Brinkley, J. (1993, December 9). Practice of "female circumcision" has arrived in U.S., many suspect. *San Diego Union-Tribune.*

Brinton, M. C. (1988). The social-institutional bases of gender stratification: Japan as an illustrative case. *American Journal of Sociology 94*(2), 300–334.

Brinton, M. C. (1989, August). Gender stratification in contemporary urban Japan. *American Sociological Review 54,* 549–564.

Broad, P. (1991). Reminiscences of Pery Broad. In J. Racwicz. *KL Auschwitz seen by the SS.* Warsaw: Impression Publishers.

Broad, W. J. (1992, February 5). Defining those new plowshares those old swords will make. *New York Times.*

Brody, J. E. (1992, March 25). Domestic violence is the greatest risk to U.S. women. *San Diego Union-Tribune.*

Brokaw Report. (1992, December 30). The American health care system. NBC News Special Report.

Bromley, R., & Gerry, C. (1979). Who are the casual poor? In R. Bromley & C. Gerry (Eds.), *Casual work and poverty in third world cities* (pp. 3–23). Chichester, England: John Wiley and Sons.

Brooke, J. (1993, May 14). Brazilian state leads way in saving children. *New York Times.*

Brooks, D. D., Smith, D. R., & Anderson, R. J. (1991, November 20). Medical apartheid: An American perspective. *Journal of the American Medical Association, 266*(19), 2746–2749.

Brooks, N. R. (1993, June 30). Gender pay gap found at highest corporate levels. *Los Angeles Times.*

Brown, B. (1994, May 29). U.S. study of Ontario health care uncovers wide variations in treatment. *Buffalo News.*

Brown, L. R. (1991, November/December). The environmental crisis: A humanist call for action. *The Humanist,* pp. 26–30.

Brown, L. R., & Jacobson, J. (1987, May/June). The future of urbanization around the world. *Utne Reader,* pp. 42–43.

Brown, L. R., Flavin, C., & Kane, H., eds. (1992). *Vital signs 1992—The trends that are shaping our future.* New York: W. W. Norton.

Brown, P. (1990, November 17). Africa's growing AIDS crisis. *New Scientist,* pp. 38–41.

Brown, P. (1992, January 4). Poverty holds up Africa's fight against AIDS. *New Scientist,* p. 3.

Brownmiller, S. (1975). *Against our will: Men, women and rape.* New York: Simon and Schuster.

Brownmiller, S. (1993, January 4). Making female bodies the battlefield. *Newsweek,* p. 37.

Brownstein, R. (1994, May 15). 4 decades later, legacy of Brown vs. Topeka is cloudy. *Los Angeles Times.*

Bruner, K. (1993a, October 7). Brazil economy struggling after president's first year. *Christian Science Monitor.*

Bruner, K. (1993b, November 30). Brazil's corruption scandal widens, delaying fiscal reforms. *Christian Science Monitor.*

Bruner, K. (1993c, August 31). Mystery trails deaths in Brazil. *Christian Science Monitor.*

Bryjak, G. J. (1982–1983, Winter). India's urban catastrophe. *Journal of the Institute for Socioeconomic Studies, VII,* pp. 77–90.

Bryjak, G. J. (1984, March). India's cities in crisis. *USA Today—Society for the Advancement of Education, 112,* 18–22.

Bryjak, G. J. (1990, July). Reducing demand is our only hope. *USA Today—The Magazine of the American Scene,* pp. 20–22.

Bryjak, G. J. (1991, December 11). Steroids' risky link to the American dream. *San Diego Tribune.*

Bryne, J. M. (1988). Probation. *Crime file study guide.* Washington, DC: National Institute of Justice.

Brzezinski, Z. (1993, March). Power and morality. *World Monitor,* pp. 22–28.

Buckley, W. E., Yesalis, C. E., Friedl, K. E., Anderson., W. A., Streit, A. L., & Wright, J. E. (1988, December 16). Estimated prevalence of anabolic steroid use among male high school seniors. *Journal of the American Medical Association, 260*(23), 3441–3446.

Budansky, S. (1992a, March 16). The nuclear epidemic. *U.S. News and World Report*, pp. 40–44.

Budansky, S. (1992b, April 27). Mopping up after the Cold War. *U.S. News and World Report*, pp. 10–11.

Budansky, S., & Auster, B. (1991, October 14). Missions implausible. *U.S. News and World Report,* pp. 24–31.

Bugsy and the Indians. (1992, March 21). *The Economist,* pp. 27–28.

Burden, D. S. (1986). Single parents and the work setting: The impact of multiple jobs and home-life responsibilities. *Family Relations, 35,* 37–43.

Bureau of Justice Statistics. (1988). *Report to the nation on crime and justice.* Washington, DC: U.S. Department of Justice.

Bureau of Justice Statistics. (1991). *Bulletin: Criminal victimization.* Washington, DC: U.S. Department of Justice.

Bureau of Justice Statistics. (1992). *National update.* Washington, DC: U.S. Department of Justice.

Bureau of National Affairs. (1986). *Work and family—A changing dynamic.* Washington, DC.

Burkett, E. (1991, December 8). Cuba has put lock on AIDS. *San Diego Union.*

Burundi, Rwanda presidents die when their plane crashes. (1994, April 7). *San Diego Union-Tribune.*

Bustelo, C. (1992, February). The "international sickness" of sexual harassment. *World Press Review,* p. 24.

C

Cain, B. S. (1990, February 18). The price they pay—Older children and divorce. *New York Times Magazine,* pp. 28–55.

Cameron, M. O. (1964). *The booster and the snitch.* New York: Free Press.

Canada plans crackdown on health-care fraud. (1994, May 25). *San Diego Union-Tribune.*

Canada's north to be split up. (1992, May 6). *San Diego Union-Tribune.*

Cantor, D., & Land, K. C. (1985, June). Unemployment and crime rates in the post–World War II United States: A theoretical and empirical analysis. *American Sociological Review, 50,* 317–332.

Caplan, N. S., & Paige, J. M. (1968, August). A study of ghetto rioters. *Scientific American, 219,* 15–21.

Carter, J. (1990, March 26). What we can expect from the peace dividend. *Fortune,* p. 145.

Carter, J. (1994, May 14). Tobacco companies sued in death of nonsmoker. *San Diego Union-Tribune.*

Carvel, J. (1994, March 30). Microwaves could disarm deadly mines. *San Diego Union-Tribune.*

Chandler, A. D. (1970). *The papers of Dwight David Eisenhower—The war years: IV.* Baltimore: Johns Hopkins Press.

Charles, D. (1990, October 13). Counting the cost of the Cold War cleanup. *New Scientist,* p. 11.

Chatterjee, P. (1993, June 30). Bhutanese refugees carry tales of torture, harassment. *Christian Science Monitor.*

Chen, E. (1994, April 3). Key facets of Clinton's health plan still intact. *Los Angeles Times.*

Chengappa, R. (1988). India's urban chaos. *World Press Review,* p. 57.

Cherlin, A. (1990). Recent changes in American fertility, marriage, and divorce. *Annals of the American Academy of Political and Social Sciences, 510,* 145–154.

Cherry, K. (1987). *Womansword: What Japanese words say about women.* Tokyo: Kodansha International.

Cheung, T. M. (1988, November 3). Crackdown on crime. *Far Eastern Economic Review,* p. 23.

Cheung, T. M. (1990, July 26). Exemplary justice. *Far Eastern Economic Review,* pp. 23–24.

China won't put curb on pollution. (1992, May 31). *San Diego Union-Tribune.*

Chiricos, T. G. (1987, April). Rates of crime and unemployment: An analysis of aggregate research evidence. *Social Problems, 34*(2), 187–212.

Chirot, D. (1977). *Social change in the twentieth century.* New York: Harcourt Brace Jovanovich.
Chown, S. M. (1977). Morale, careers and personal potentials. In J. E. Birren & K. W. Schaie (Eds.), *Handbook of the psychology of aging* (pp. 672–691). New York: Van Nostrand Reinhold.
Christensen, A. S. (1988). Sex discrimination and the law. In A. H. Stromberg & S. Harkess (Eds.), *Women working* (pp. 329–347). Mountain View, CA: Mayfield.
Chubin, S. & Tripp, C. (1988). *Iran and Iraq at war.* Boulder, CO: Westview.
Chung, D. K. (1993, November 22–28). Talking trash. *Japan Times Weekly International Edition.*
Church, G. J. (1993a, March 15). A case of dumb luck. *Time,* pp. 26–30.
Church, G. J. (1993b, November 22). Jobs in an age of insecurity. *Time,* pp. 32–39.
Cimons, M. (1991, November 5). Liquor, beer ads aimed at youths attacked. *Los Angeles Times.*
Cimons, M. (1993, July 23). Sex seen as source of most new AIDS cases in women. *Los Angeles Times.*
Clark, C. (1992, May 31). Many blacks see AIDS virus as white conspiracy. *San Diego Union-Tribune.*
Clay, J. W. (1991, April). Respecting and supporting gay and lesbian parents. *Education Digest,* pp. 51–52.
Clayton, M. (1992, July 3). Canada's natives exercise new clout on national scene. *Christian Science Monitor.*
Cleeland, N. (1991, March 9). Gasping in smoggy Mexico City—Oxygen kiosk may prove helpful. *San Diego Union.*
Clinard, M. B., & Meier, R. F. (1992). *Sociology of deviant behavior.* Fort Worth: Harcourt Brace Jovanovich College Publishers.
Cockburn, A. (1992, August 17). Crisis is over and the banks won big. *Los Angeles Times.*
Cohen, J. E. (1992, November). How many people can earth hold? *Discovery,* pp. 114–119.
Cohen, L. E., & Felson, M. (1979). Social change and crime rate trends: A routine activities approach. *American Sociological Review* (44), 588–608.
Cohen, L. R. (1991, May/June). Sexual harassment and the law. *Society,* pp. 8–13.
Cohen, S. (1992, September 13). Black factory workers face sagging economy, low wages—and racism. *Los Angeles Times.*
Coleman, B. C. (1992, September 2). Growth of medical specialties questioned. *San Diego Union-Tribune.*
Coleman, D. (1991, November 27). Do arrests increase the rates of repeated domestic violence? *New York Times.*
Coleman, J. W. (1989). *The criminal elite: The sociology of white collar crime.* New York: St. Martin's Press.
Coles, R. (1983). The need for scapegoats causes war. In D. L. Bender & B. Leone (Eds.), *War and human nature* (pp. 59–63). St. Paul: Greenhaven.
Colhoun, J. (1992, April 22). Census fails to quash report on Iraqi deaths. *The Guardian,* p. 5.
Collins, M. D., & Frey, J. H. (1992). Drunken driving and informal social control: The case of peer intervention. *Deviant Behavior, 13,* 73–87.
Collins, R. (1975). *Conflict sociology: Toward an explanatory science.* New York: Academic Press.
Collins, R. (1979). *The credential society: An historical sociology of education and stratification.* New York: Academic Press.
Commission on Cities. (1988). Race and poverty in the United States and what should be done. In F. R. Harris & R. W. Wilkins (Eds.), *Quiet riots: Race and poverty in the United States.* New York: Pantheon.
Conklin, J. E. (1992). *Criminology.* New York: Macmillan.
Connor, W. D. (1972). *Deviance in Soviet society—Crime, delinquency and alcoholism.* New York: Columbia University Press.
Conot, R. (1992, May 17). An urban plan that would more than pay for itself. *Los Angeles Times.*
Conte, J. R. (1991). Child abuse. *New Grolier electronic encyclopedia.* Chicago: Grolier.
Conway, M. M. (1991). *Political participation in the United States* (2nd ed.). Washington, DC: Congressional Quarterly.
Cook, J. (1991, October 21). But where are the don's yachts? *Forbes,* pp. 121–126.
Coolidge, S. D. (1994, January 28). Who doesn't have health insurance? *Christian Science Monitor.*

Copeland, P. (1991, December 25). Peace researcher logs fewer wars in '91, but more deaths. *San Diego Union.*
Corcoran, E. (1992, March). Disarming developments. *Scientific American,* p. 110.
Cose, E. (1993). *The rage of a privileged class.* New York: HarperCollins.
Costa, M. (1991). *Abortion: A reference handbook.* Santa Barbara, CA: ABC-CLIO.
Costello, D. R. (1994, February). Moscow, summer 1993. *Canisius College Chronicle,* pp. 4–6.
Coughlin, E. K. (1994, January 5). The emergence of the "global city." *Chronicle of Higher Education,* pp. A8–9.
Court, J. (1988). Sex and violence: A ripple effect. In N. M. Malmuth and E. Donnerstein (Eds.), *Pornography and sexual aggression.* New York: Academic Press.
Courtney, H. (1993, October/November). Energy and population. *ZPG Reporter, 25*(5), 1, 4.
Cowen, R. C. (1992, June 9). Global warming study remains educated guess. *Christian Science Monitor.*
Cowley, G. (1991, December 23). I'd toddle a mile for a Camel. *Newsweek,* p. 70.
Cox, F. D. (1992). *AIDS booklet.* Dubuque, IA: Wm. C. Brown.
Cracking down on the "yakuza." (1992, May). *World Press Review,* p. 48.
Crawford, R. (1991, May). Pioneers' prognosis. *Far Eastern Economic Review, 9,* 62.
Credit reporting spurs child support payments. (1994, June 30). *San Diego Union-Tribune.*
Cressey, D. R. (1969). *Theft of a nation.* New York: Harper & Row.
Crime. (1988). Wylie, TX: Information Plus Publishers.
Critchfield, R. (1990, October). Grain man. *World Monitor,* pp. 43–51.
Critchfield, R. (1992, July 24). Sowing success, reaping guns. *World Monitor,* pp. 24–30.
Crompton, R., & Mann, M., eds. (1986). *Gender and stratification.* Cambridge: Polity Press.
Crowell, M. T. (1991, September 30). Facing up to elder care. *San Diego Tribune.*
Curbing chemical warfare. (1992, September 10). *Christian Science Monitor.*
Currie, E. (1985). *Confronting crime—An American challenge.* New York: Pantheon.
Cylke, F. K., Jr. (1993). *The environment.* New York: HarperCollins.

D

Dahlburg, J. T. (1992, September 2). The atom sows crop of sadness. *Los Angeles Times.*
Dahlburg, J. T. (1993, June 6). Tracking the Russian connection. *Los Angeles Times.*
Dahlburg, J. T. (1994, February 2). The fight to save India's baby girls. *Los Angeles Times.*
Dahrendorf, R. (1959). *Class and class conflict in industrial society.* Stanford, CA: Stanford University Press.
Daily news. (1994, January 31). National Public Radio.
Daimon, S. (1993, August 9– 15). Takako Doi set to become first woman House Speaker. *Japan Times Weekly International Edition.*
Dalton, R. (1994, February 23). UCSD research links girls' smoking, ads. *San Diego Union-Tribune.*
Daly, J. (1992, January 20). Going for broke. *MacLean's,* pp. 34–35.
Damage done by cattle-raising. (1993, January 15). *Washington Spectator,* 19(2), 1–3.
Dammann, P. (1992, August). St. Petersburg's street kids. *World Press Review,* p. 50.
Danigelis, N., & Pope, W. (1979, June). Durkheim's theory of suicide as applied to the family: An empirical test. *Social Forces, 108,* 1081–1086.
Darialova, N. (1991, February 18). Vodka: The opiate of the masses. *Forbes,* pp. 96–98.
Daudistel, H., Sanders, W. B., & Luckenbill, D. F. (1979). *Criminal justice—Situations and decisions.* New York: Holt, Rinehart and Winston.
Davidson, G., & Neale, J. N. (1994). *Abnormal psychology.* New York: Wiley.
Davies, J. C. (1962, February). A theory of revolution. *American Sociological Review, 27,* 5–19.
Davis, K., & Moore, W. E. (1945). Some principles of stratification. *American Sociological Review 10*(2), 242–249.
Dean, P. (1994, March 1). The global village's ultimate fetish. *Los Angeles Times.*
Death and destruction spread. (1992, May 11). *Los Angeles Times.*

Deaux, K. (1992). Sex differences. In E. F. Borgatta & M. L. Borgatta (Eds.), *Encyclopedia of sociology, vol. 3* (pp. 1749–1753). New York: Macmillan.

Demo, D. H., & Acock, A. C. (1988, August). The impact of divorce on children. *Journal of Marriage and the Family,* pp. 619–648.

Dennis, R. J. (1990, November). The economics of legalizing drugs. *Atlantic Monthly,* pp. 126–132.

DePalma, A. (1994, January 21). Rebellion in Mexico is putting the heat on Salinas. *New York Times.*

Des Jarlais, D. C., & Friedman, S. R. (1994, February). AIDS and the use of injected drugs. *Scientific American,* pp. 82–88.

Despite political gains, fewer Hispanics occupy high elected offices. (1991, January 6). *San Diego Union.*

Deyo, T. (1991, September/October). Employer-assisted housing: Strategies for revitalizing communities. *Journal of Housing, 45,* 227–234.

Diamond, L. (1988). *Class, ethnicity and democracy in Nigeria.* Syracuse, NY: Syracuse University Press.

DiChiara, A., & Galliher, J. F. (1994, February). Dissonance and contradictions in the origins of marijuana decriminalization. *Law and Society Review,* pp. 41–77.

Diegmueller, K. (1989, July/August). Middle America priced out of house and home. *Current,* pp. 16–21.

Digirolamo, K. (1991, November 6). Learning what to do about domestic violence. *New York Times.*

Dillin, J. (1993a, June 18). As "good" jobs become "bad" jobs, Congress takes a closer look. *Christian Science Monitor.*

Dillin, J. (1993b, October 10). US work force hit hard as manufacturing jobs flee. *Christian Science Monitor.*

Dillin, J. (1994a, February 11). Washington moves to curb illegal immigrants. *Christian Science Monitor.*

Dillin, J. (1994b, February 14). Businesses line up against Clinton plan; public is still divided. *Christian Science Monitor.*

Dilulio, J. J. (1988). Private prisons. *Crime file study guide.* Washington, DC: National Institute of Justice.

Dilulio, J. J. (1989, Summer). The impact of inner city crime. *The Public Interest,* pp. 28–46.

Disaster looms for Bombay. (1990, August 9). *Nature,* p. 498.

do Rosario, L. (1992, February). Tokyo pushes its limits. *World Press Review,* p. 51.

Dogan, M., & Kasarda, J. D. (1988). Introduction—How giant cities will grow and multiply. In M. Dogan & J. D. Kasarda (Eds.), *A world of giant cities—The metropolis era: vol. 1* (pp. 12–29). Newbury Park, CA: Sage.

Dolan, M. (1992, March 24). Global warming creates a climate of uncertainty. *Los Angeles Times.*

Domestic violence. (1987). Plano, TX: Information Aids.

Dornbusch, S. M., & Gray, K. D. (1988). Single-Parent Families. In S. M. Dornbusch & M. H. Strober (Eds.), *Feminism: Children and the new families.* New York: Guilford.

Douglass, R. L. (1983, July). Domestic neglect and abuse of the elderly: Implications for research and service. *Family Relations,* pp. 393–402.

Drew, K. (1993, June 8). Romanian economic reforms move slowly. *Christian Science Monitor.*

Drogin, B. (1991, May 23). The misery that is Bangladesh. *Los Angeles Times.*

Drogin, B. (1992, November 26). Bombay—Epicenter of disaster. *Los Angeles Times.*

Drogin, B. (1993, November 9). Apartheid's sad lesson for pupils. *Los Angeles Times.*

Drug and crime facts. (1991). Rockville, MD: Drug and Crime Data Center and Clearinghouse.

Duany, A. (1989, May/June). Granny flats: Another idea for creating affordable housing and strengthening community ties. *Utne Reader,* p. 72.

Dudley, W. (1990). Introduction. In W. Dudley (Ed.), *Immigration—Opposing viewpoints* (pp. 13–14). San Diego: Greenhaven.

Duerksen, S., & Cleeland, N. (1994, March 21). Rx for violence. *San Diego Union-Tribune.*

Duke, S. B., & Gross, A. C. (1993). *America's longest war: Rethinking our tragic crusade against drugs.* New York: G. P. Putnam's Sons.

Dunn, A. (1994, May 19). Asian-American study reveals hidden poverty. *San Diego Union-Tribune.*

Durbin, R., & Synar, M. (1993, September 14). FDA should regulate tobacco. *Christian Science Monitor.*

Durkheim, E. (1938). *The rules of the sociological method.* New York: Macmillan.

Durning, A. B. (1989, November). *Poverty and the environment: Reversing the downward spiral.* Worldwatch Paper 92.

Durr, F. (1971). *The urban economy.* Scranton, PA: Intext Educational Publishers.

Dworkin, R. (1993, June 10). Feminism and abortion. *New York Review of Books,* pp. 27–29.

Dye, T. R. (1990). *Who's running America?: The Bush era* (5th ed.). Englewood Cliffs, NJ: Prentice Hall.

Dyer, G. (1985). *War.* New York: Crown.

E

Eaton, W. J. (1993, October 5). U.S. poverty total rises to 3-decade high. *Los Angeles Times.*

Eaton, W. J. (1994, June 8). College binge drinking soars, study finds. *Los Angeles Times.*

Eccles, J. S. (1987). Adolescence: Gateway to gender role transcendence. In D. B. Carter (Ed.), *Current conceptions of sex roles and sex typing* (pp. 225–242). New York: Praeger.

Eggebeen, D. J., & Lichter, D. T. (1991, December). Race, family structure and changing poverty among American children. *American Sociological Review, 56,* 801–817.

Ehrenreich, B. (1990). The war on drugs is necessary. In N. Bernards (Ed.), *War on drugs—Opposing viewpoints* (pp. 23–28). San Diego: Greenhaven.

Ehrenreich, B. (1994, January 24). Feminism confronts Bobbittry. *Time,* p. 74.

Eighty percent of action plan approved. (1994, May/June). *Popline,* p. 3. E

Eisenberg, I. (1994, April 6). Cigarette taxes and black markets. *San Diego Union-Tribune.*

Eitzen, D. S., & Baca Zinn, M. (1991). *In conflict and order: Understanding society* (5th ed.). Boston: Allyn and Bacon.

Elders rips tobacco ads, calls smoking an addiction of teens. (1994, February 25). *San Diego Union-Tribune.*

Elkin, V. (1993, January/February). Home-grown farming success. *World Watch, 6*(1), 7–9.

Ellickson, R. C. (1990). The homelessness muddle. *The Public Interest, 99,* 45–60.

Elliot, M. (1993, December 13). Global mafia. *Newsweek,* pp. 22–28.

Ellison, C. G. (1991). An eye for an eye? A note on the southern subculture of violence thesis. *Social Forces, 69*(4), 1223–1239.

Elmer-Dewitt, P. (1992, February 17). How do you patch a hole in the sky that could be as big as Alaska? *Time,* pp. 64–68.

Elson, J. (1992, March 30). Passions over pornography. *Time,* pp. 52–53.

Emery, R. E. (1989). Family violence. *American Psychologist, 44*(2), 321–328.

Enemies negotiate U.N. control of Rwanda airport. (1994, May 19). *Los Angeles Times.*

Energy Information Administration. (1993). *Annual energy outlook 1993.* Washington, DC: U.S. Department of Energy.

Engels, F. (1845, 1875). The condition of the working class in England. In *Karl Marx and Frederick Engels: Selected works, vol. 4* (pp. 295–583). New York: International Publishers.

England, P., & Farkas, G. (1986). *Households, employment and gender.* New York: Aldine.

England, P., Farkas, G., Stanek Kilbourne, B., & Dou, T. (1988). Explaining occupational sex segregation and wages: Findings from a model with fixed effects. *American Sociological Review, 53,* 544–558.

Entwisle, B., & Coles, C. M. (1990). Demographic surveys and Nigerian women. *Signs: Journal of Women in Culture and Society, 15*(21), 259–284.

Environmental Protection Agency. (1993). *Respiratory health effects of passive smoking: Lung cancer and other disorders.* Washington, DC: Environmental Protection Agency.

Environmental refugees: A growing problem. (1993, March/April). *Popline,* p. 3.

Eshleman, J. R. (1994). *The family—An introduction* (7th ed.). Boston: Allyn and Bacon.

Esipisu, M. (1994, January 1). In Africa, democratic hopes falter as despair rises, western aid falls. *San Diego Union-Tribune.*

Espada, M. (1992, March 11). Putting Columbus in his place. *Christian Science Monitor.*

Europe's new flags. (1992, February 24). *U.S. News & World Report,* pp. 44–45.

Evans, S. M., & Nelson, B. J. (1989). *Wage justice: comparable worth and the paradox of technocratic reform.* Chicago: University of Chicago Press.

F-15 sale: Wrong new world order. (1992, March 8). *New York Times.*

Fagot, B. I., Hagan, R., Driver Leingach, M., & Kronsberg, S. (1985). Differential reactions to assertive and communicative acts of toddler boys and girls. *Child Development, 56,* 1499–1505.

Faites vos jeux: Louisiana. (1992, June 20). *The Economist,* p. A28.

Farewell, welfare. (1993, October 23). *The Economist,* pp. 67–68.

Faris, R. E. L. (1967). *Chicago Sociology—1920–1932.* Chicago: University of Chicago Press.

Farkas, G., Grobe, R. P., Sheehan, D., & Shuan, Y. (1990). Cultural resources and school success: Gender, ethnicity, and poverty groups within an urban school district. *American Sociological Review 55,* 127–142.

Farrell, K. L., & Ferrara, J. A. (1985). *Shoplifting: The antishoplifting guidebook.* New York: Praeger.

Fava, S. F. (1991). Suburbs. *Academic American encyclopedia* (elec. ed.). Danbury, CT: Grolier.

Federal cost of running welfare soars. (1994b, January 3). *Los Angeles Times.*

Feeney, F. (1983). Burglary. In S. H. Kadish (Ed.), *Encyclopedia of crime and justice, vol. 1* (pp. 129–132). New York: Free Press.

Feldmann, L. (1993a, July 26). Belt tightening forces higher education to restructure. *Christian Science Monitor.*

Feldmann, L. (1993b, July 30). Congress's female caucus grapples with diversity. *Christian Science Monitor.*

Feldmann, L. (1993c, October 15). White House plan: No green card, no health coverage. *Christian Science Monitor.*

Feldmann, L. (1993d, November 9). Water, water everywhere, but not enough to drink. *Christian Science Monitor.*

Ferree, M. Marx, & Hess, B. B. (1991). The new feminist movement: Visions and revisions. In L. Kramer (Ed.), *The sociology of gender: A text-reader* (pp. 367–381). New York: St. Martin's.

Ferrell, D. (1992, September 9). Off Palos Verdes, a DDT dumping ground lingers. *Los Angeles Times.*

Fertility choices vital in raising status of women. (1992, January/February). *Popline, 14,* 1.

Fewster, S., & Gorton, T. (1987). *Japan: From shogun to superstate.* New York: St. Martin's.

Fifty-one percent of rape victims are girls under 18, Justice Department reports. (1994, June 23). *Los Angeles Times.*

Findlay, S. (1991, June 17). AIDS: The second decade. *U.S. News & World Report,* pp. 20–22.

Fineman, M. (1991, November 29). Growing pollution clouds future of famed Taj Mahal. *Los Angeles Times.*

Fineman, M. (1992, August 10). Post-traumatic stress leads to anxiety, violence in Kuwait. *Los Angeles Times.*

Fingarette, H. (1988). *Heavy drinking—The myth of alcoholism as a disease.* Berkeley: University of California Press.

Finkelhor, D., & Baron, L. (1986). High-risk children. In D. Finkelhor (Ed.), *Sourcebook on child sexual abuse* (pp. 60–88). Beverly Hills, CA: Sage.

Finkelhor, D., & Yllo, K. (1982). Forced sex in marriage: A preliminary research report. *Crime and Delinquency, 28,* 459–478.

Finn, P. (1986). Victims. In *Crime file study guide.* Washington, DC: National Institute of Justice.

Fiske, E. B. (1992, May 12). For many, a void after high school. *Christian Science Monitor.*

Fitzgerald, R. (1991). Private prisons are more efficient than public prisons. In S. L. Tipp (Ed.), *America's prisons—Opposing viewpoints.* San Diego: Greenhaven Press.

Flavin, C., & Kane, H. (1993, November–December). Coal use levels off. *World Watch, 6*(6), 40.

Flavin, C., & Lenssen, N. (1994). Reshaping the power industry. In L. Starke (Ed.), *State of the world 1994* (pp. 61–80). New York: W. W. Norton.

Fogel, C. (1993, August 2). Break the toxic waste habit. *Christian Science Monitor.*

Folsum, R. H., & Minan, J. H. (1986). *Law in the People's Republic of China.* Oceanside, NY: Professional Coursebook Series.

Fontana, V. (1973). *Somewhere a child is crying: Maltreatment—Causes and prevention.* New York: Macmillan.

Fornara, P. (1989, May/June). Home sharing as a housing alternative. *Utne Reader,* p. 71.

Fornos, W. (1987). *Losing people, gaining ground: A blueprint for stabilizing world population.* Ephrata, PA: Science Press.

Fornos, W. (1991a). *Population institute letter.* Washington, DC: Population Institute.

Fornos, W. (1991b, November/December). Children of the streets: A global tragedy. *Popline,* p. 3.

Forty percent of women find sexual harassment at work, poll says. (1991, October 11). *San Diego Union.*

Foster, C. (1993a, June 9). Australian farmers, miners fight land claim. *Christian Science Monitor.*

Foster, C. (1993b, December 23). Australia grants Aborigines right to claim native title. *Christian Science Monitor.*

Frammolino, R. (1993, November 20). A new generation of rebels. *Los Angeles Times.*

France, K. (1992, July/August). AIDS explodes among teens. *Utne Reader,* pp. 30–31.

Francis, D. R. (1993a, September 3). US workers' wages continue to erode. *Christian Science Monitor.*

Francis, D. R. (1993b, December 31). Rising health costs limit other programs. *Christian Science Monitor.*

Francis, D. R. (1994, March 10). States may not find jackpot in gambling. *Christian Science Monitor.*

Frankel, B. (1993, June 8). Reality dashes refugees' dreams. *USA Today.*

Freud, S. (1961). *Civilization and its discontents.* New York: W. W. Norton.

Frey, W. H. (1993, April). U.S. elderly population becoming more concentrated. *Population Today—News, Numbers, and Analysis, 21*(4), 6–9.

Frieden, B. J. (1989, Fall). The downtown job puzzle. *The Public Interest,* pp. 71–86.

Friedman, T. L. (1994a, March 14). World's big economies turn to the jobs issue. *New York Times.*

Friedman, T. L. (1994b, March 16). Accent on education as talks on jobs end. *New York Times.*

Fritz, M. (1992, September 21). Neo-Nazism attracts a new lost generation. *San Diego Union-Tribune.*

Fritz, S. (1992, June 30). Ruling pleases neither side; both vow to continue fight. *Los Angeles Times.*

Fritz, S. (1993, September 26). Prospects of reform hit home. *Los Angeles Times.*

Fritz, S. (1994, January 30). Prescription drug pricing hurting the poor, elderly. *Los Angeles Times.*

Fulton, J. (1993). *Canada's health care system: Bordering on the possible.* New York: Faulkner & Gray.

Fussell, P. (1992). *Wartime—Understanding and behavior in the Second World War.* New York: Oxford University Press.

G

Gabor, T., Baril, M., Cusson, M., Elie, D., LeBlanc, M., & Normandeau, A. (1987). *Armed robbery—Cops, robbers, and victims.* Springfield, IL: Charles Thomas.

Galbraith, J. K. (1991, October 19). Address to the National Press Club. National Public Radio.

Galdston, R. (1965). Observations of children who have been physically abused by their parents. *American Journal of Psychiatry, 122*(4), 440–443.

Gallup, G., Jr. (1991). *The Gallup poll—Public opinion 1990.* Wilmington, DE: Scholarly Resources.

Games, S. (1993, August 15). The asylum-seeker: Persecuted and unwanted in Europe. *Los Angeles Times.*

Gammon, C. (1986, March 10). Tales of self-destruction. *Sports Illustrated,* pp. 64–77.

Gangster story: Japan. (1992, December 5). *The Economist,* p. 33.

Gardels, N., & Snell, M. B. (1989, April 23). Breathing fecal dust in Mexico City. *Los Angeles Times,* Book Review, p. 16.

Gardner, M. (1992, May 26). Senior women in poverty. *Christian Science Monitor.*

Gardner, M. (1994, February 24). Child care—A double standard. *Christian Science Monitor.*

Garfinkel, H. (1956). Conditions of a successful degradation ceremony. *American Journal of Sociology 61,* 420–424.

Garst, R. D. (1991). Nigeria. *The academic American encyclopedia* (elec. ed.). Danbury, CT: Grolier.

Gascoyne, S. (1993, March 23). Toxic-waste cleanup is a burning issue. *Christian Science Monitor.*

Gee, thanks, boss—What a lucky break. (1992, January 27). *Business Week,* p. 41.

Geist, C. D., & Nachbar, J. (1983). *The popular culture reader* (3rd ed.). Bowling Green, OH: Popular Press.

Gelles, R. J. (1976, November). Abused wives: Why do they stay? *Journal of Marriage and the Family,* pp. 659–668.

Gelles, R. J. (1978, October). Violence toward children in the United States. *American Journal of Orthopsychiatry 48*(4), 580–592.

Gelles, R. J. (1987). The cost of family violence. *Public Health Reports, 102,* 638–651.

Gelles, R. J., & Conte, J. R. (1990, November). Domestic violence and sexual abuse of children: A review of research in the eighties. *Journal of Marriage and the Family, 52,* 1045–1058.

Gelles, R. J., & Pedrick-Cornell, C. (1990). *Intimate violence in families.* Newbury Park, CA: Sage.

Gelles, R. J., & Straus, M. A. (1988). *Intimate violence.* New York: Simon and Schuster.

Genovese, F. C. (1991, January). Affordable housing. *Journal of Economics and Sociology, 50,* 41–42.

Gentry, C. S. (1991). Drugs and crime. In J. F. Sheley (Ed.), *Criminology—A contemporary handbook* (pp. 423–440). Belmont, CA: Wadsworth.

George, V. (1988). *Wealth, poverty and starvation: A world perspective.* New York: St. Martin's Press.

Germani, C. (1992a, July 27). Planning to go for a dip in ocean? Think again, says pollution study. *Christian Science Monitor.*

Germani, C. (1992b, September 29). Anthropologist Leakey warns of "sixth extinction." *Christian Science Monitor.*

Gershen, M. (1983). Mylai was not a war crime. In D. L. Bender & B. Leone (Eds.), *War and human nature: Opposing viewpoints* (pp. 130–135). St. Paul: Greenhaven.

Gerstenzang, J., & Marshall, T. (1994, April 11). 10,000 die in Rwanda; many foreigners escape. *Los Angeles Times.*

Gilbert, A. (1988). The housing of the urban poor. In A. Gilbert & J. Gugler (Eds.), *Cities, poverty, and development—Urbanization in the third world* (pp. 81–115). London: Oxford University Press.

Gilbert, N. (1983). *Capitalism and the welfare state—Dilemmas of social benevolence.* New Haven: Yale University Press.

Gillam, J. (1993, November 29). Latino caucus gains clout in legislature as population shifts. *Los Angeles Times.*

Glasser, R., & Pardue, S. (1993, May 18). A troubled energy source. *Christian Science Monitor.*

Glenn, N. D., & Supancic, M. (1984, August). The social and demographic correlates of divorce and separation in the United States: An update and reconsideration. *Journal of Marriage and the Family,* pp. 563–575.

Global unemployment called worst since 1930s. (1994, April 9). *San Diego Union-Tribune.*

Goldberg, C. (1993, July 25). Flaring Siberia gas: Torches light way to eco-disaster. *Los Angeles Times.*

Goldberg, C. (1994, March 12). Women a potent anti-Yeltsin force in Russia. *Los Angeles Times.*

Golden, A. (1994, January 5). Hate, neglect provided fuel for rebellion. *San Diego Union-Tribune.*

Goldstein, S. (1994, May 26). Russian "mafia" soon may pose global nuclear threat. *Buffalo News.*

Gongren, G. (1986). Adjudication and penalty of juvenile delinquency in China. Unpublished manuscript.

Goode, E. (1991a). *Deviant behavior.* Englewood Cliffs, NJ: Prentice Hall.

Goode, E. (1991b). Drug abuse. *The academic American encyclopedia* (elec. ed.). Danbury, CT: Grolier.

Goode, E. (1992). *Collective behavior.* Fort Worth: Saunders College Publishing.

Goode, W. J. (1963). *World revolution and family patterns.* New York: Free Press.

Goode, W. J. (1964). *The family.* Englewood Cliffs, NJ: Prentice Hall.

Goodgame, D. (1993, February 22). Welfare for the well-off. *Time,* pp. 36–38.

Goodman, E. (1992, May 4). Women are fed up. *Los Angeles Times.*

Goodman, R. (1994, March 22). Interview on The Dice Are Loaded. The Discovery Channel.

Gordis, E. (1992, October). The genetics of alcoholism—A commentary. *Alcohol alert,* p. 3. National Institute on Alcohol Abuse and Alcoholism.

Gordon, M. M. (1964). *Assimilation in American life.* New York: Oxford University Press.

Gorman, C. (1992, September 14). Is health care too specialized? *Time,* p. 56.

Gorodetzky, C. W. (1991). Marijuana. *The academic American encyclopedia* (elec. ed.). Danbury, CT: Grolier.

Gorriti, G. A. (1989, July). How to fight the drug war. *Atlantic Monthly,* pp. 70–76.

Gottlieb, A. (1993, November 5). Whose shocking crime? *New York Times.*

Gould, S. J. (1981). *The mismeasure of man.* New York: Norton.

Graham, O. L., Jr., & Beck, R. (1992, May 19). To help inner city, cut flow of immigrants. *Los Angeles Times.*

Graven, K. (1990, March 21). Sex harassment at the office stirs up Japan. *Wall Street Journal.*

Gray, M. (1993, May 17). Drowning their sorrows: Troubled Russians are hitting the bottle. *MacLean's,* p. 26.

Gray, P. (1991, July 8). Whose America? *Time,* pp. 12–17.

Green, G. S. (1990). *Occupational crime.* Chicago: Nelson-Hall.

Green, P. (1993, December 29). Argentina squeezes its middle class. *Christian Science Monitor.*

Green, P., & Bartal, D. (1992, April 13). Turning a sea into toxic soup. *U.S. News & World Report,* p. 47.

Greene, J. (1982, September). The gambling trap. *Psychology Today,* pp. 50–55.

Greenhouse, S. (1993, May 20). New tally of world's economies catapults China into third place. *New York Times.*

Greenhouse, S. (1994, February 3). State Dept. finds widespread abuse of world's women. *New York Times.*

Greenstone, D. J. (1991). Culture, rationality, and the underclass. In C. Jencks & P. E. Peterson (Eds.), *The urban underclass.* Washington, DC: Brookings Institute.

Greenwald, J. (1991, September 9). Permanent pink slips. *Time,* pp. 54–56.

Greenwald, J. (1993a, October 18). Here comes the sun. *Time,* pp. 84–85.

Greenwald, J. (1993b, November 22). Bellboys with B.A.s. *Time,* pp. 36–37.

Greider, W. (1989, May/June). Gimme shelter: Even middle-class Americans now feel housing crisis. *Utne Reader,* pp. 60–63.

Grier, P. (1993, July 30). World demographic shifts signal resource crunch. *Christian Science Monitor.*

Grier, P. (1994, May 11). Nationalist trend threatens world borders. *Christian Science Monitor.*

Griffin, S. (1973). *Rape: The all-American crime.* Andover, MA: Warner Modular Publications.

Grigsby, J. S. (1991, April). Paths for future population aging. *Gerontologist, 31*(2), 195–203.

Grigsby, W. G., & Wilson, A. (1991). Housing. *Academic American encyclopedia* (elec. ed.). Danbury, CT: Grolier.

Gropper, B. A. (1985, February). Probing the links between drugs and crime. *National Institute of Justice—Research in brief.* Washington, DC: U.S. Department of Justice.

Gross, G. (1994, March 24). Assassination in Tijuana. *San Diego Union-Tribune.*

Grossfeld, S. (1993, July 25). Wasting away: America's losing battle against hunger. *Boston Globe.*

Groves, M., & Horm-Wingred, D. M. (1991, July). Commuter marriages: Personal, family, and career issues. *Sociology and Social Research,* pp. 212–217.

Gruson, L. (1992, March 9). Black politicians discover AIDS issue. *New York Times.*

Grych, J. H., & Fincham, F. D. (1990). Marital conflict and children's adjustment: A cognitive-contextual framework. *Psychological Bulletin, 108*(2), 267–290.

Gugler, J. (1988a). Overurbanization reconsidered. In J. Gugler (Ed.), *The urbanization of the third world.* London: Oxford University Press.

Gugler, J. (1988b). Urban ways of life. In A. Gilbert & J. Gugler (Eds.), *Cities, poverty, and development—Urbanization in the third world* (pp. 116–133). London: Oxford University Press.

Gurr, T. (1968). Urban disorder: Perspectives from the comparison study of civil strife. In L. H. Motti & D. R. Bowen (Eds.), *Riots and rebellion: Civil disobedience in the urban community.* Beverly Hills, CA: Sage.

Gusfield, J. (1963). *Symbolic crusade: States, politics and the American temperance movement.* Urbana: University of Illinois Press.

Guskind, R. (1992, October 10). Needle Park's gone, addicts aren't. *National Journal,* p. 2315.

Gutterman, S. (1994, July 2). Changes in Russia bring freedom but no aid to detained alcoholics. *Los Angeles Times.*

H

Hacker, H. (1951). Women as a minority group. *Social Forces, 30,* 60–69.

Hacker, H. (1974). Women as a minority group: 20 years later. In F. Denmark (Ed.), *Who discriminates against women?* (pp. 124–134). Beverly Hills, CA: Sage.

Hackett, G., & Barry, J. (1989, December 25). The myth of the "peace dividend." *Newsweek,* p. 51.

Hagan, F. E. (1991). *Introduction to criminology—Theories, methods, and criminal behavior.* Chicago: Nelson-Hall.

Hager, M., with Harlan, B., Mason, M., & Murr, A. (1991, April 29). Dances with garbage. *Newsweek,* p. 36.

Halverson, G. (1994, January 13). Merger rush sweeps the US, with more expected in '94. *Christian Science Monitor.*

Handlin, O. (1951). *The uprooted.* New York: Grosset and Dunlap.

Haney, D. Q. (1992, June 4). Explosive, disastrous AIDS spread predicted. *San Diego Union-Tribune.*

Hanson, S. L., & Odoms, T. (1991, August). The economic costs and rewards of two-earner, two parent families. *Journal of Marriage and the Family,* pp. 622–634.

Hardin, G. (1990). Immigrants harm the U.S. economy. In W. Dudley (Ed.), *Immigration—Opposing viewpoints* (pp. 85–89). San Diego: Greenhaven.

Harris, M. (1991, August). Fraud. *Money,* pp. 75–91.

Harris, R. (1994, August 3). Brazil bemoans its homeless children. *Los Angeles Times.*

Harris, S. (1991, December 11). Gay militancy—The last great civil rights movement? *Los Angeles Times.*

Harrison, E. (1992, February 8). Chicago police used torture, report alleges. *Los Angeles Times.*

Harrison, P. (1992, May/June). Slower population growth stimulates economic growth. *Popline,* p. 1.

Harrower, M. (1976, July). Were Hitler's henchmen mad? *Psychology Today.*

Hartinger, B. (1991, November). A case for gay marriages. *Commonweal, 22,* 681–683.

Hasson, J. (1994a, April 28). Canadian system gets mixed reviews there. *USA Today.*

Hasson, J. (1994b, April 28). Single-payer system picks up momentum. *USA Today.*

Haupt, A., & Kane, T. T. (1991). *Population handbook.* Washington, DC: Population Reference Bureau.

Havemann, J. (1993, July 3). The trade secrets of Denmark. *Los Angeles Times.*

Havemann, J., & Kempster, N. (1993, July 6). The case of the disappearing worker: What's gone wrong? *Los Angeles Times.*

Hays, C. L. (1993, December 6). Enduring violence in a new home. *New York Times.*

Health care crisis: Containing costs, expanding coverage. (1992). New York: McGraw-Hill.

Health care reform: Tough, but stay with it. (1993, January 6). *Los Angeles Times.*

Health-care costs. (1993, January 5). *USA Today.*

Hearn, L. (1992, June 30). Roe survives hard blow by split Supreme Court. *San Diego Union-Tribune.*

Heilbroner, R. L. (1980). *An inquiry into the human prospect.* New York: W. W. Norton.

Henderson, H. (1987, May/June). Crabgrass frontier: The suburbanizaton of America. *Utne Reader,* pp. 45–50.

Henneberger, M. (1994, February 6). Pot surges back, but it's a whole new world. *New York Times.*

Henshaw, S. K. (1990, March/April). Induced abortion: A world review, 1990. *Family Planning Perspectives, 22*(2), 76–89.

Herbert, B. (1994, March 2). Deadly data on handguns. *New York Times.*

Hershey, S. (1993, April). France faces societal aging. *Population Today—News, Numbers, and Analysis, 21*(4), 4.

Hessle, S. (1989, March/April). Families falling apart: A report from social services. *Child Welfare, LXVIII*(2), 209–213.

Hickey, E. W. (1991). *Serial murderers and their victims.* Pacific Grove, CA: Brooks/Cole.

Hilts, P. J. (1994, February 26). FDA claims authority to ban cigarette sales. *San Diego Union-Tribune.*

Hiltzik, M. (1992, March 25). Somalia conflict toll put at 14,000. *Los Angeles Times.*

Hirao, S. (1993, February 8–14). Korean residents fight prejudice, promote rights. *Japan Times Weekly International Edition.*

Hispanics more often hurt on job. (1992, February 18). *San Diego Union-Tribune.*

Hochschild, A. (1989). *The second shift—Working parents and the revolution at home.* New York: Viking Penguin.

Holloway, D. (1993, June 10). The politics of catastrophe (book review). *New York Review.*

Holmes, R. M., & De Burger, J. (1988). *Serial murder.* Newbury Park, CA: Sage.

Holmes, S. A. (1994, March 3). Survey finds minorities resent one another almost as much as they do whites. *New York Times.*

Holmstrom, D. (1993a, June 16). Ecuador Indians fight for forests. *Christian Science Monitor.*

Holmstrom, D. (1993b, September 7). Mississippi flooding leaves a toxic legacy: Pollution in Gulf of Mexico. *Christian Science Monitor.*

Holmstrom, D. (1994a, January 13). Violent crime is down—But not in public schools. *Christian Science Monitor.*

Holmstrom, D. (1994b, February 17). Casino gambling surges in the U.S., tempting more teenagers. *Christian Science Monitor.*

Holstein, J. A., & Miller, G. (Eds.). (1993). *Reconsidering social constructionism: Debates in social problems theory.* Hawthorne, NY: Aldine de Gruyter.

Homeless women: Life on the street is deadly. (1992, March 16). *Christian Science Monitor.*

Homelessness grows in rich and poor countries of Europe. (1992, February 15). *San Diego Union-Tribune.*

Hoppenstand, G. (1992). Yellow devil doctors and opium dens: The yellow peril stereotype in mass media entertainment. In J. Nachbar & K. Lause (Eds.), *Popular culture: An introductory text.* Bowling Green, OH: Popular Press.

Hopper, C. B., & Moore, J. (1991, April). Women in motorcycle gangs. *Harper's,* pp. 28–29.

Hornblower, M. (1993, June 21). The skin trade. *Time,* pp. 45–51.

Horowitz, R. (1990). Sociological perspectives on gangs: Conflicting definitions and concepts. In C. R. Huff (Ed.), *Gangs in America.* Newbury Park, CA: Sage.

Hospital care found worst for poor blacks. (1994, April 20). *San Diego Union-Tribune.*

Hottelet, R. C. (1992, March 20). Ethnic masses are more restless. *Christian Science Monitor.*

Howard, J. R. (1974). *The cutting edge: Social movement and social change in America.* Philadelphia: Lippincott.

Hser, Y., Anglin, M. D., & Chou, C. (1992). Narcotics use and crime among addicted women: Longitudinal patterns and effects of social interventions. In T. Mieczkowski (Ed.), *Drugs, crime, and social policy: Research, issues, and concerns* (pp. 197–221). Boston: Allyn and Bacon.

Huffing. (1994, March 4). *ABC News 20/20.*

Huggett, C. (1991, July 29–August 4). Scientist warns that acid rain threatens Japan's forests. *Japan Times Weekly International Edition.*

Human suffering index. (1992). Washington, DC: Population Crisis Committee.

Hunt, K. (1993, July 11). Death and life in a company town. *Los Angeles Times Magazine.*

Hurd, M. D. (1992, September). Book review—The economics of population aging: The "graying" of Australia, Japan, and the United States. *Journal of Economic Literature, 30*(3), 1529–1531.

Ianni, F. A. J., & Reuss-Ianni, E. (1972). *A family business: Kinship and social control in organized crime.* New York: New American Library.
If nation's economy is to recover, cities need more aid, mayors say. (1992, January 22). *Buffalo News.*
If you can think of something even beastlier, do it. (1988, March 26). *The Economist,* pp. 53–54.
Ignelzi, R. J. (1992, February 24). Boomers may draw "social insecurity." *San Diego Union-Tribune.*
In the state courts. (1994, March 11). *Reproductive Freedom News,* 3(5), 3–4.
Inciardi, J. A. (1983). Arson. In S. H. Kadish (Ed.), *Encyclopedia of crime and justice, vol. 1* (pp. 76–80). New York: Free Press.
Inciardi, J. A. (1986). *The war on drugs: Heroin, cocaine, and public policy.* Palo Alto, CA: Mayfield.
Inciardi, J. A. (1987). *Criminal justice.* San Diego: Harcourt Brace Jovanovich.
Inciardi, J. A. (1992). *The war on drugs II.* Mountain View, CA: Mayfield.
India's greatest religious divide. (1989, June 3). *The Economist,* p. 40.
Indian peasants in southern Mexico state storm 4 cities, towns; casualties reported. (1994, January 2). *Los Angeles Times.*
Ingwerson, M. (1992, June 23). The great income-mobility debate. *Christian Science Monitor.*
Ingwerson, M. (1994, February 25). US capital's next storm: A shower of pink slips. *Christian Science Monitor.*
Inman, B. (1990, August 2). Apartment rental costs soaring. *Rancho Santa Fe Times.*
International Planned Parenthood Federation: 500 million women denied family planning. (1992, November–December). *Popline,* p. 3.

J

Jacklin, C. N. (1989). Female and male: Issues of gender. *American Psychologist, 44*(2), 127–133.
Jackson, K. T. (1985). *Crabgrass frontier: The suburbanization of the United States.* New York: Oxford University Press.
Jackson, P. G. (1988, February). Assessing the validity of official data on arson. *Criminology, 26,* 191–195.
Jacob, J. E. (1992, February 16). Black America, in deep economic crisis, needs a Marshall Plan. *San Diego Union-Tribune.*
Jacobs, J. (1977). *Stateville—The penitentiary in mass society.* Chicago: University of Chicago Press.
Jacobs, J. B. (1986). Drinking and crime. *Crime file study guide.* National Institute of Justice.
Jacobs, N. R., Siegel, M. A., & Foster, C. D. (Eds.). (1994). *Into the third century: A profile of America.* Wylie, TX: Information Plus.
Jacobson, J. L. (1988, November). *Environmental refugees: A yardstick of habitability* (Worldwatch Paper 86). Washington, DC: Worldwatch Institute.
Jacobson, J. L. (1993). Women's health: The price of poverty. In M. Koblinsky, J. Timyan, & J. Gay (Eds.), *The health of women: A global perspective* (pp. 3–31). Boulder, CO: Westview Press.
Jaggar, A. M. (1983). *Feminist politics and human nature.* Totowa, NJ: Rowman and Allanheld.
Japan battles to keep a lid on its trash. (1992, June 15–21). *Japan Times Weekly International Edition.*
Japan's gangsters: Honourable mob. (1990, January 27). *The Economist,* pp. 19–22.
Jarvis, M., & Radovicz, E. (1992, May/June). Brazilian street children. *Society,* pp. 65–69.
Jenkins, B. (1992). Terrorism. In E. F. Borgatta (Ed.), *Encyclopedia of sociology.* New York: Maxwell Macmillan.

Johnson, P. M. (1992, May 27). Recognition of north-south dependency is solution to environmental challenges. *Christian Science Monitor.*

Johnson, P., Hamid, A., & Sanabria, H. (1992). Emerging models of crack distribution. In T. Mieczkowski (Ed.), *Drugs, crime, and social policy: Research, issues, and concerns* (pp. 56–78). Boston: Allyn and Bacon.

Johnson, S. (1992). Rape: The conservative backlash. *Ms—The World of Women, II*(5), 88–89.

Johnson, S. (1993, January 2). Impact of immigrants is focus of concern, studies. *San Diego Union-Tribune.*

Johnston, O. (1991, April 9). Bulk of Americans living longer, but Blacks are not. *Los Angeles Times.*

Jolin, A., & Gibbons, D. (1987). Age patterns in criminal involvement. *International Journal of Offender Therapy and Comparative Criminology, 31,* 237–260.

Jones, B. C. (1994, May 7). Diploma now the great divider. *San Diego Union-Tribune.*

Jones, C. (1992, February 27). Latin-Japanese workers feel cool welcome. *Christian Science Monitor.*

Jones, C. (1993a, April 29). Ethnic Vietnamese flee Cambodia, but a wary Hanoi mutes protest. *Christian Science Monitor.*

Jones, C. (1993b, September 27). East Asia's economic model is no miracle, study shows. *Christian Science Monitor.*

Joseph, P. (1990, Spring). Political changes after the Cold War. *Dissent,* pp. 145–148.

K

Kabala, S. J. (1991, November). The environmental morass in Eastern Europe. *Current History,* pp. 384–389.

Kahana, Y. (1992, May 27). Experience in Israel's Negev demonstrates advantages of drip-irrigation method. *Christian Science Monitor.*

Kammeyer, K. C. (1987). *Marriage and the family: A foundation for personal decisions.* Boston: Allyn and Bacon.

Kane, H. (1992a). Third world debt persists. In L. Starke (Ed.), *Vital signs 1992—The trends that are shaping our future* (pp. 68–69). New York: W. W. Norton.

Kane, H. (1992b). Infant mortality declining. In L. Starke (Ed.), *Vital signs 1992—The trends that are shaping our future* (pp. 78–79). New York: W. W. Norton.

Kang, K. C. (1993, September 16). A village cries out for help. *Los Angeles Times.*

Kaplan, D. A. (1991, December 9). The bank robbery boom. *Newsweek,* pp. 62–63.

Kaplan, D. A. (1994, January 24). Bobbitt fever: Why America can't seem to get enough. *Newsweek,* pp. 52–55.

Kaplan, R. D. (1994, February). The coming anarchy. *Atlantic Monthly,* pp. 44–76.

Karcher, A. J. (1992, May/June). State lotteries. *Society,* pp. 51–56.

Karl, J. (1993, October 8). Clinton's health-care plan and the "generation gap." *Christian Science Monitor.*

Kaslow, A. (1992, July 16). U.S. mayors make case for action on urban needs. *Christian Science Monitor.*

Kaslow, A. (1994, February 4). Clinton launches effort to retrain jobless instead of keeping them on the dole. *Christian Science Monitor.*

Kasten, B., & Lieberman, J. L. (1992, May 19). Enterprise zones: "Greenlining" for growth. *Christian Science Monitor.*

Kastillas, J., & Rubinson, R. (1990). Cultural capital, student achievement, and educational reproduction: The case of Greece. *American Sociological Review, 55,* 270–279.

Katz, J. (1988). *Seductions of crime.* New York: Basic Books.

Katz, J. (1991, December 8). Gang killings in L.A. top a record 700. *Los Angeles Times.*

Katz, M. (1993, October 26). U.S. pushes Ukraine to scrap nukes. *USA Today International Edition.*

Kaufman, J., & Zigler, E. (1987, April). Do abused children become abusive parents? *American Journal of Orthopsychiatry, 57*(2), 186–192.

Kaye, T. (1988, May/June). The birth dearth: Conservatives conceive a population crisis. *Utne Reader,* pp. 91–93.

Kaylor, R. (1984, July 9). Calcutta: A city "of ruthless hates, passionate loves." *U.S. News and World Report,* pp. 45–46.

Kelley, S. (1994, February 14). Editorial cartoon. *San Diego Union-Tribune.*

Kempe, C. H., Silverman, F. N., Steele, B. F., Droegemueller, W., & Silver, H. K. (1962). The battered-child syndrome. *Journal of the American Medical Association,* (181), 17–24.

Kempton, M. (1991, November 7). The back of the bus. *New York Review of Books,* p. 52.

Kennedy, J. (1991). Native peoples in the United States and Canada. In M. J. Cohen & R. A. Hoehn (Eds.), *Hunger 1992: Second annual report on the state of world hunger* (pp. 155–157). Washington, DC: Bread for the World Institute on Hunger and Development.

Kennedy, L. W., & Baron, S. W. (1993). Routine activities and a subculture of violence. *Journal of Research in Crime and Delinquency, 30*(1), 88–112.

Kennedy, P. (1993). *Preparing for the 21st century.* New York: Random House.

Kerr, K. A. (1991). Prohibition. *The academic American encyclopedia* (elec. ed.). Danbury, CT: Grolier.

Key to posttraumatic stress lies in brain chemistry, scientist find. (1990, June 12). *New York Times.*

Keyfitz, N. (1992, January/February). Consumerism and the new poor. *Society, 29,* 42–47.

Kiahla, P. (1989, May 22). "Violence is nice honestly." *MacLean's,* pp. 40–41.

Kiernan, V. (1993, August 14). A chip to veto violence on television. *New Scientist,* p. 5.

Kim, M. (1989). Gender bias in compensation structures: A case study of its historical basis and persistence. *Journal of Social Issues, 45*(4), 39–50.

Kinsey, A. C., Pomeroy, W. B., & Martin, C. E. (1948). *Sexual behavior in the human male.* Philadelphia: Saunders.

Kinsey, A. C., Pomeroy, W. B., Martin, C. E., & Gebhard, P. H. (1953). *Sexual behavior in the human female.* Philadelphia: Saunders.

Kirk, D. (1988, February 22). Guns and pencils. *New Republic,* pp. 102–103.

Kirp, D. L., Yodof, M. G., & Strong Franks, M. (1986). *Gender justice.* Chicago: University of Chicago Press.

Kiser, E. (1992). War. In E. F. Borgatta & M. L. Borgatta (Eds.), *Encyclopedia of sociology, vol. 3* (pp. 2243–2247). New York: Maxwell Macmillan.

Klare, M. (1990, May). Wars in the 1990s—Growing fire power in the Third World. *Bulletin of the Atomic Scientists,* pp. 9–13.

Klare, M. (1992, April). Is peace possible? *The Progressive,* pp. 19–21.

Knickerbocker, B. (1992a, April 8). Cost of nuclear waste cleanup in the billions. *Christian Science Monitor.*

Knickerbocker, B. (1992b, September 3). Toxics release and the right to know. *Christian Science Monitor.*

Knickerbocker, B. (1993a, November 9). Behind standoff on water rights: A century of policy and habit. *Christian Science Monitor.*

Knickerbocker, B. (1993b, November 15). Ban on dumping nuclear waste at sea. *Christian Science Monitor.*

Knickerbocker, B. (1994a, February 8). Refining the Clean Water Act may not be easy for Clinton. *Christian Science Monitor.*

Knickerbocker, B. (1994b, March 4). US joins global effort by curbing some but not all exports of waste. *Christian Science Monitor.*

Knickerbocker, B., & Grier, P. (1994, June 8). UN urges humanitarian use of "peace dividend." *Christian Science Monitor.* E

Koeppel, B. (1986). For rent, cheap, no heat. In J. M. Elliot (Ed.), *Urban society.* Guilford, CT: Dushkin.

Kohn, A. (1991, October 6). Hitting the bottle. *Los Angeles Times Magazine,* pp. 32–34.

Korn, D. (1992, March 13). Genocide of the Kurds. *Christian Science Monitor.*

Kornblum, W., & Julian, J. (1992). *Social problems.* Englewood Cliffs, NJ: Prentice Hall.

Kottak, C. (1994). *Cultural anthropology* (6th ed.). New York: McGraw-Hill.

Kozol, J. (1992). *Savage inequalities: Children in America's schools.* New York: Harper Perennial.

Kraar, L. (1990). The demand for drugs must be cut. In N. Bernards (Ed.), *War on drugs—Opposing viewpoints* (pp. 200–206). San Diego: Greenhaven.

Kraft, S. (1992, March 1). Africa's death sentence. *Los Angeles Times Magazine,* pp. 12–16, 36.

Kraft, S. (1994, February 17). A gaping gateway for drugs. *Los Angeles Times.*

Kramer, R. (1986). The third wave. *Wilson Quarterly,* (10), 110–129.

Krauthammer, C. (1992, March 23). Do we really need a new enemy? *Time,* p. 76.

Kuper, L. (1992). Genocide. In E. F. Borgatta & M. L. Borgatta (Eds.), *Encyclopedia of sociology, vol. 2* (pp. 757–762). New York: Maxwell Macmillan.

Kurdeck, L. A. (1991). The relations between reported well-being and divorce history, availability of a proximate adult and gender. *Journal of Marriage and the Family, 53,* 71–78.

Kurtenbach, E. (1992, January 3). Poet's admission, growing list of cases force Japanese to acknowledge AIDS. *Buffalo News.*

Kuttner, R. (1989, May/June). Fresh ideas on affordable housing. *Utne Reader,* pp. 73–75.

L

Lacayo, R. (1994, January 10). Unraveling the safety net. *Time,* pp. 25–27.

LaFranchi, H. (1993a, June 21). New French laws placate demands for "zero immigration." *Christian Science Monitor.*

LaFranchi, H. (1993b, November 10). Europe's future on the line in response to job crisis. *Christian Science Monitor.*

La Freniere, P., Stryer, F. F., & Gauthier, R. (1984). The emergence of same-sex affiliative preferences among preschool peers: A developmental/ethological perspective. *Child Development, 55,* 1958–1965.

Lagemann, E. C. (1985). *Jane Addams on education.* New York: Teachers College Press, Columbia University.

Lamb, D. (1987). *The Arabs—Journeys beyond the mirage.* New York: Vintage Books.

Lamb, D. (1994, April 3). Farmers reap desolate harvest on Tobacco Road. *Los Angeles Times.*

Langan, F. (1994, June 8). Forest plantations in China receive Canada funding. *Christian Science Monitor.* E

Laquer, W. (1987). *The age of terrorism.* Boston: Little, Brown.

Larmer, B. (1991, December 1). Life under the ozone hole. *Newsweek,* p. 43.

Larson, C. J. (1973). *Major themes in sociological theory.* New York: David McKay.

Last of Kuwait's 732 oil wells torched by Iraq is extinguished. (1991, November 7). *San Diego Union,* p. A15.

Lau, E. (1990, May 24). Cadres and criminals. *Far Eastern Economic Review,* pp. 10–11.

Lau, E., & Kosberg, J. (1979). Abuse of the elderly by informal care providers. *Aging* (299), 10–15.

Lauer, R. H., & Lauer, J. C. (1991, July). The long-term relational consequences of problematic family backgrounds. *Human Relations,* pp. 286–290.

Lauter, D., & Silverstein, S. (1991, October 8). When sex talk goes too far. *Los Angeles Times.*

Leacock, E. B. (1971). Introduction. In E. B. Leacock (Ed.), *The culture of poverty.* New York: Simon and Schuster.

Leakey, R. E. (1983). Aggression is not an instinct. In D. L. Bender & B. Leone (Eds.), *War and human nature* (pp. 22–25). St. Paul: Greenhaven.

Leary, W. E. (1993, January 12). U.S. must consider AIDS as race issue, panel says. *San Diego Union-Tribune.*

Lee, J. (1992, April 25). Ex-"comfort girls" end silence on war crimes. *Los Angeles Times.*

Lee, R. W., III (1990). Economic aid could not stop drug production. In N. Bernards (Ed.), *War on drugs—Opposing viewpoints* (pp. 182–189). San Diego: Greenhaven.

Leeman, S. (1992, December 25). Racial intolerance rises in Britain, with more minorities targeted in attacks. *San Diego Union-Tribune.*

Leerhsen, C. (1991, May 6). The second battleground. *Newsweek,* pp. 60–61.

Lemert, E. M. (1982). Drinking among American Indians. E. L. Gomberg, H. R. White, & J. A. Carpenter (Eds.), *Alcohol, science, and society revisited* (pp. 80–95). Ann Arbor: University of Michigan Press.

Lemonick, M. D. (1992, February 17). The ozone vanishes. *Time,* pp. 60–63.

Lemonick, M. D. (1993, November 15). Toxins on tap. *Time,* pp. 85–87.

Lenski, G. (1966). *Power and privilege: A theory of social stratification.* New York: McGraw-Hill.

Lenski, G. E., & Lenski, J. (1991). *Human societies: An introduction to macrosociology* (6th ed.). New York: McGraw-Hill.

Lenssen, N. (1991, December). *Nuclear waste: The problem that won't go away.* Worldwatch Paper 106.

Lenssen, N. (1993). Providing energy in developing countries. In L. Starke (Ed.), *State of the World 1993* (pp. 101–119). New York: W. W. Norton.

Lesieur, H. R. (1992, May/June). Compulsive gambling. *Society,* pp. 43–50.

Let them eat guns. (1991, November 2). *The Economist,* p. 61.

Letkeman, P. (1973). *Crime as work.* Englewood Cliffs, NJ: Prentice Hall.

Levine, A. (1990, June 18). Playing the adolescent odds. *U.S. News and World Report,* p. 51.

Levine, B. (1993, July 4). Skipping school. *Los Angeles Times.*

Levine, S. B. (1980). The rise of American boarding schools and the development of a national upper class. *Social Problems 28*(1), 63–94.

Levins, H. (1994, May 30). Rising "warrior class" called threat to U.S. *San Diego Union-Tribune.*

Levinson, D. (1989). *Family violence in cross cultural perspective.* Newbury Park, CA: Sage.

Levy, J. R. (1993, October 25). Firm finds green solution to nuclear contamination. *Christian Science Monitor.*

Lewis, F. (1992, April 26). Women first must pierce glass walls. *San Diego Union-Tribune.*

Lewis, G. J. (1982). *Human migration—A geographical perspective.* New York: St. Martin's Press.

Lewis, H. (1971). Culture of poverty? What does it matter? In E. B. Leacock (Ed.), *The culture of poverty.* New York: Simon and Schuster.

Lewis, O. (1961). *The children of Sanchez.* New York: Random House.

Lewis, R. L. (1991). Race riots. The academic American encyclopedia (elec. ed.). Danbury, CT: Grolier.

Lide, V. (1990, July/August). The perils of pollution. *China Business Review,* pp. 32–37.

Life on EZ street. (1993, June 30). *Los Angeles Times.*

Link, B. G., & Dohrenwend, B. (1989). The epidemiology of mental disorders. In. H. Freeman & S. Levine (eds.), *The handbook of medical sociology* (pp. 102–127). Englewood Cliffs, NJ: Prentice Hall.

Lintner, B. (1990, June 28). Roads from Mandalay. *Far Eastern Economic Review,* p. 27.

Lintner, B. (1994, January 20). Pusher with a cause. *Far Eastern Economic Review,* pp. 24–26.

Lintner, B., & Mai, C. (1994, January 20). Opium war. *Far Eastern Economic Review,* pp. 22–24.

Lipman, L. (1994, February 3). Bitter pill: Medicines cost more in the U.S. *San Diego Union-Tribune.*

Lloyd, P. (1982). *A third world proletariat?* London: George Allen and Unwin.

Logan, C. H. (1991). Private prisons are just. In S. L. Tipp (Ed.), *America's prisons—Opposing viewpoints.* San Diego: Greenhaven Press.

Logan, J. R., & Molotch, H. L. (1987). *Urban fortunes—The political economy of place.* Berkeley: University of California Press.

Long, W. R. (1992, March 8). Argentina struggles to cut huge bureaucracy. *Los Angeles Times.*

Long, W. R. (1993a, November 13). Something's rotten in Rio: Police corruption. *Los Angeles Times.*

Long, W. R. (1993b, December 18). Latin America records more economic growth. *Los Angeles Times.*

Long, W. R. (1993c, December 18). Scandal frazzles Brazil's congress. *Los Angeles Times.*

Long, W. R. (1993d, August 30). Amazon murder mystery. *Los Angeles Times.*

Long, W. R. (1994, March 1). Latin American producers put pedals to metal. *Los Angeles Times.*

Look at Native Americans across the USA. (1994, April 28). *USA Today.*

Lopez, G. (1990, May). Why generals wage war on the people. *Bulletin of the Atomic Scientists,* pp. 30–33.

Lorber, J. (1992). Gender. In E. F. Borgatta & M. L. Borgatta (Eds.), *Encyclopedia of sociology, vol. 2* (pp. 748–754). New York: Macmillan.

Lorber, J., & Farrell, S. A. (Eds.). (1991). *The social construction of gender.* Newbury Park, CA: Sage.

Lorch, D. (1994, May 8). Rwanda refugees survive in filth. *San Diego Union-Tribune.*

Lowe, M. D. (1992a). Shaping cities. In *State of the world 1992* (pp. 119–137). New York: W. W. Norton.

Lowe, M. D. (1992b, July/August). Reclaiming cities for people. *World Watch,* pp. 19–25.

Lundman, R. J. (1980). *Police and policing—An introduction.* New York: Holt, Rinehart and Winston.

Lupsha, P. A. (1989). Organized crime. In W. G. Bailey (Ed.), *Encyclopedia of police science* (pp. 375–380). New York: Garland.

Lyman, M. D. (1987). *Narcotics and crime control.* Springfield, IL: Charles C. Thomas.

M

MacFarquhar, E., with Seter, J., Lawrence, S. V., Knight, R., & Schrof, J. M. (1994, March 28). The war against women. *U.S. News & World Report,* pp. 42–48.

MacKinnon, C. (1993, July/August). Turning rape into pornography: Postmodern genocide. *Ms.,* pp. 24–30.

MacLachlan, S. L. (1993, October 22). African-American women chip away at "concrete" ceiling. *Christian Science Monitor.*

MacLeod, A. (1992a, April 22). Europe harnesses the wind. *Christian Science Monitor.*

MacLeod, A. (1992b, September 9). Germans grapple with hatred. *Christian Science Monitor.*

MacLeod, A. (1993, September 13). Nuclear recycling faces environmental challenge in Britain. *Christian Science Monitor.*

Maddison, A., & Associates. (1992). The political economy of poverty, equity, and growth: Brazil and Mexico. New York: Oxford University Press.

Magagnini, S. (1992, November 22). Prejudice remains strong against Japanese underclass. *San Diego Union-Tribune.*

Maharaj, D. (1991, November 3). Retirees often fall prey when con artists call. *Los Angeles Times.*

Maine yanks the licenses of eight "deadbeat dads." (1994, June 28). *San Diego Union-Tribune.*

Makombe, K. (1992, November). Desperate and on the street. *World Press Review,* pp. 26–27.

Marcuse, E. (1989, March). An equality of terror. *World Press Review,* pp. 17–18.

Maremont, M., with Shares, G. E., Toy, S., & Garland, S. B. (1992, March 9). Can Europe help cure America's health care mess? *Business Week,* pp. 52–54.

Marger, M. N. (1987). *Elites and masses: An introduction to political sociology* (2nd ed.). Belmont, CA: Wadsworth.

Margolis, L. H., & Farran, D. C. (1981). Unemployment and children. *International Journal of Mental Health, 13,* pp. 107–124.

Margolis, M. (1993, August 3). Social critic crusades against Brazil hunger. *Los Angeles Times.*

Marin, R. (1988, May/June). How we help and harm the homeless. *Utne Reader,* pp. 36–47.

Marks, A. (1993a, September 21). Vermont aims to pioneer health-care reform plan. *Christian Science Monitor.*

Marks, A. (1993b, November 3). Clinton team defends costs of health plan. *Christian Science Monitor.*

Marshall, T. (1994, February 15). The welfare costs that are dragging down Europe. *Los Angeles Times.*

Marshall, W. L. (1988). The use of sexually explicit stimuli by rapists, child molesters and non-offenders. *Journal of Sex Research, 25,* 267–288.

Martin, T. C., & Bumpass, L. L. (1989). Recent trends in marital disruption. *Demography, 6,* 37.

Marx, K. (1967, original 1867). *Capital.* F. Engels (Ed.). New York: International Publishers.

Marx, K., & Engels, F. (1955, original 1848). *The communist manifesto.* S. H. Beer (Ed.). New York: Appleton-Century-Crofts.

Maugh, T. S. (1991, December 15). Survey of identical twins links biological factors with being gay. *Los Angeles Times.*

Maugh, T. H., III, & Zamichow, N. (1991, August 30). Study ties part of brain to men's sexual orientation. *Los Angeles Times.*

McCaghy, C. H. (1980). *Crime in American society.* New York: Macmillan.

McCaghy, C. H., Giordano, P. C., & Henson, T. K. (1977). Auto theft—Offender and offense characteristics. *Criminology, 15*(3), 367–385.

McCamant, K., & Durrett, C. (1989, May/June). Good housekeeping: Cohousing can reincorporate community into the American dream. *Utne Reader,* pp. 68–72.

McCord, C., & Freeman, H. P. (1990). Excess mortality in Harlem. *New England Journal of Medicine, 322*(3), 173–177.

McDonnell, P. J. (1993, November 9). Mexico's resentment rises along with border barriers. *Los Angeles Times.*

McEnroe, J. (1991, February). Split-shift parenting. *American Journal of Demographics,* pp. 50–52.

McFalls, J. A. (1991). *Population: A lively introduction.* Washington, DC: Population Reference Bureau.

McKim, W. A. (1986). *Drugs and behavior—An introduction to behavioral pharmacology.* Englewood Cliffs, NJ: Prentice Hall.

McKinnon, I. (1993). Voices from the polls: Consensus and satisfaction from Canadian patients and taxpayers. In A. Bennett & O. Adams (Eds.), *Looking north for health* (pp. 61–67). San Francisco: Jossey-Bass.

McLemore, S. D. (1994). *Racial and ethnic relations in America.* Boston: Allyn and Bacon.

McLeod, B. (1986, July). The Oriental express. *Psychology Today 20,* 48–52.

McNair, L. J. (1983). War is kill or be killed. In D. L. Bender & B. Leone (Eds.), *War and human nature* (pp. 108–111). St. Paul: Greenhaven.

Mechanic, D. (1992). Health and illness behavior. In E. F. Borgatta & M. L. Borgatta (Eds.), *Encyclopedia of sociology, vol. 2* (pp. 795–800). New York: Macmillan.

Mehren, E. (1993, October 21). Number of children living in poverty continues to rise. *Los Angeles Times.*

Meier, E. G. (1964). Child neglect. In N. E. Cohen (Ed.), *Social work and social problems.* New York: National Association of Social Workers.

Meier, R. F. (1983). Shoplifting. In S. H. Kadish (Ed.), *Encyclopedia of crime and justice, vol. 4* (pp. 1497–1502). New York: Free Press.

Meisler, S. (1993, July 7). Migration viewed as "human crisis." *Los Angeles Times.*

Melady, T. P. (1974). *Burundi: The tragic years.* Maryknoll, NY: Orbis Books.

Mellor, J. W. (1991). Green revolution reduces hunger in India. In *Hunger 1992—Second annual report on the state of world hunger* (pp. 42–48). Washington, DC: Bread for the World Institute on Hunger and Development.

Mensch, B. (1993). Quality of care: A neglected dimension. In M. Koblinsky, J. Timyan, & J. Gay (Eds.), *The health of women: A global perspective* (pp. 235–253). Boulder, CO: Westview.

Merrill, J. (1992, July). Building a new urban order. *ZPG Reporter*, p. 1.

Merton, R. K. (1968). *Social theory and social structure* (enlarged ed.). New York: Free Press.

Messner, S. F. (1983). Regional and racial effects on the urban homicide rate: The subculture of violence revisited. *American Journal of Sociology, 88*(5), 997–1007.

Messner, S., & Tardiff, K. (1985). The social ecology of urban homicide: An application of the routine activities approach. *Criminology, 23*(2), 241–267.

Methvin, E. H. (1992, June 18). How to hold a riot. *National Review,* pp. 32–35.

Meyer, M. (1992, November 9). Los Angeles 2010: A Latino subcontinent. *Newsweek,* pp. 32–34.

Michael, F. (1988). Law: A tool of power. In Y. Wu, F. Michael, J. F. Copper, T. Lee, M. H. Chang, & A. J. Gregor (Eds.), *Human rights in the People's Republic of China* (pp. 33–55). Boulder and London: Westview Press.

Michaels, J. (1992a, February 27). Dekasegi drawn by promise of jobs. *Christian Science Monitor.*

Michaels, J. (1992b, June 19). Rape trial highlights Brazilian native rights. *Christian Science Monitor.*

Michaels, M. (1993, August 9). Rio's dead end kids. *Time,* pp. 36–37.

Michels, R. (1966, original 1915). *Political parties.* New York: Free Press.

Mieczkowski, T. (1992). Some observations on the scope of crack use and distribution. In T. Mieczkowski (Ed.), *Drugs, crime, and social policy: Research, issues, and concerns.* Boston: Allyn and Bacon.

Milgram, S. (1963). Behavioral study of obedience. *Journal of Abnormal and Social Psychology, 67,* 371–378.

Milgram, S. (1965, February). Some conditions of obedience and disobedience. *Human Relations, 18,* 57–76.

Miller, H., McDonald, W., & Cramer, J. A. (1978). *Plea bargaining in the United States.* National Institute of Law Enforcement and Criminal Justice. Washington, DC: Government Printing Office.

Miller, M. (1992, March 31). Mexico confronts Cortes—Again. *Los Angeles Times.*

Millman, J. (1992, May 10). Weapons for the masses. *Los Angeles Times Magazine,* pp. 19–21.

Mills, C. W. (1956). *The power elite.* London: Oxford University Press.

Mirror on the U.S. (1992, March). *World Press Review,* pp. 42–43.

Moffett, G. D. (1992a, July 8). Fertility rates decline in third-world nation. *Christian Science Monitor.*

Moffett, G. M. (1992b, July 8). Population programs seek outside funds. *Christian Science Monitor.*

Monroe, L. R. (1993, June 1). An alternative to alcohol? *Buffalo News.*

Montagu, A. (1976). *The nature of human aggression.* New York: Oxford University Press.

Montalbano, W. D. (1991, October 1). A global pursuit of happiness. *Los Angeles Times.*

Montalbano, W. D. (1993, November 13). No longer a step behind in Turkey. *Los Angeles Times.*

Montalbano, W. D. (1994, June 24). Italians' baby boom goes bust. *Los Angeles Times.*

Mooney, L. A., Gramling, R., & Forsyth, C. (1992). Legal drinking age and alcohol consumption. *Deviant Behavior, 13,* 59–71.

Moore, M. (1992, March). Cold war victory. *Bulletin of the Atomic Scientists,* p. 2.

Morain, D. (1994, March 1). Costs to soar under "3 strikes" plan, study says. *Los Angeles Times.*

Morales, E. (1989). *Cocaine—White gold rush in Peru.* Tucson: University of Arizona Press.

More than sticky fingers. (1988, November). *Psychology Today,* p. 10.

More thyroid cancer reported in children from Chernobyl area. (1992, September 3). *San Diego Union-Tribune.*

Morello, C. (1992, May 23). For Mediterranean nations, sea of pollution woes is deep as ever. *San Diego Union-Tribune.*

Morgan, S. (1993, August 28). Minorities outraged at burden of toxics. *San Diego Union-Tribune.*

Morganthau, T. (1988, March 28). The drug gangs. *Newsweek,* pp. 20–32.

Morganthau, T. (1993, November 29). The new frontier for civil rights. *Newsweek,* pp. 65–66.

Morning news. (1991, October 22). National Public Radio.

Morning news. (1992, May 5). Discussion of enterprise zones. National Public Radio.

Morning news. (1994, March 20). National Public Radio.

Mouat, L. (1993, June 9). Indigenous people press for rights. *Christian Science Monitor.*

Mouat, L. (1994, January 18). UN is forced to rethink peacekeeping missions. *Christian Science Monitor.*

Mount Fuji ravaged by pollution. (1992, February 3–9). *Japan Times Weekly International Edition.*

Much of Russia's water of substandard quality. (1994, July 3). *St. Paul Pioneer Press.*

Muehlenhard, C. L., & Linton, M. A. (1987). Date rape and sexual aggression in dating situations: Incidence and risk factors. *Journal of Counseling Psychology, 34*(2), 186–196.

Mueller, D. P., & Cooper, P. W. (1986). Children of single parent families: How they fare as young adults. *Family Relations, 35,* 169–176.

Muello, P. (1993, July 24). Did police massacre 7 Brazilian urchins? *San Diego Union-Tribune.*

Mukherjee, S., & Singh, A. M. (1981). Hierarchical and symbiotic relationships among the urban poor: A report on pavement dwellers in Calcutta. In United Nations report *The residential circumstances of the poor in developing countries* (pp. 135–163). New York: Praeger.

Murakami, A. (1992a, May 18–24). Sexual harassment verdict viewed as landmark ruling. *Japan Times Weekly International Edition.*

Murakami, A. (1992b, August 10–16). Politics loses some of its "Madonna" touch. *Japan Times Weekly International Edition.*

Murkowski, F. (1993, May 11). Russia has to clean up nuclear weapons dumped in sea. *Christian Science Monitor.*

Murphy, K. (1992, May 26). There's no housing in Cairo at all; people live in tombs! *Los Angeles Times.*

Mushrooming ragtag armies worry Pentagon. (1994, June 5). *Buffalo News.*

Musto, D. (1987). *The American disease—Origins of narcotic control.* New York: Oxford University Press.

Myers, D. C. (1990). *Social psychology.* New York: McGraw-Hill.

Myers, M. (1988). Social background and the sentencing behavior of judges. *Criminology, 26*(4), 649–658.

N

Naciri, M. (1989, Winter). Urban systems and developing strategies. *Daedalus—Journal of the American Academy of Arts and Sciences,* pp. 159–178.

Nadelmann, J. D. (1992). Drug prohibition in the United States: Costs, consequences. In T. Mieczkowski (Ed.), *Drugs, crime, and social policy: Research, issues, and concerns* (pp. 299–322). Boston: Allyn and Bacon.

Nadle, M. (1992, May). For men only? No! *World Monitor,* pp. 44–49.

Nagorski, A. (1993). *The birth of freedom: Shaping lives and societies in the new Eastern Europe.* New York: Simon and Schuster. E

Nagpaul, H. (1988). India's giant cities. In M. Dogan & J. D. Kasarda (Eds.), *A world of giant cities—The metropolis era: vol. 1* (pp. 252–290). Newbury Park, CA: Sage.

Najman, J. M. (1989). Health care in developing countries. In H. E. Freeman & S. Levine (Eds.), *Handbook of medical sociology* (pp. 332–346). Englewood Cliffs, NJ: Prentice Hall.

Naked planet. (1992, April 5). *Los Angeles Times Magazine,* pp. 16– 20, 51–52.

Nanda, S. (1991). *Cultural anthropology.* 4th ed. New York: Van Nostrand.

Nasar, S. (1992, April 21). Fed report gives new data on gains by richest in 80's. *New York Times.*

National Advisory Commission on Civil Disorders. (1968). *Report of the National Advisory Commission on Civil Disorders.* Washington, DC: Government Printing Office.

National Institute of Justice. (1992, June). *Drug use forecasting.* Washington, DC: U.S. Department of Justice.

National Institute on Alcohol Abuse and Alcoholism. (1988, October). Alcohol and aging. *Alcohol Alert* (2).

National Institute on Alcohol Abuse and Alcoholism. (1990, October). Alcohol and women. *Alcohol Alert* (10), PH 290.

National Institute on Alcohol Abuse and Alcoholism. (1992a, January). Alcohol and AIDS. *Alcohol Alert* (15), PH 311.

National Institute on Alcohol Abuse and Alcoholism. (1992b, April). Moderate drinking. *Alcohol Alert* (16), PH 315.

National Institute on Alcohol Abuse and Alcoholism. (1992c, October). NIAA's genetic research. *Alcohol Alert,* PH 328S.

National Institute on Alcohol Abuse and Alcoholism. (1992d, October). The genetics of alcoholism. *Alcohol Alert,* PH 328.

National Institute on Drug Abuse. (1991). *Anabolic steroids—A threat to body and mind.* Research Report Series. Washington, DC: U.S. Department of Health and Human Services.

Natividad, L. (1992, June 14). A scary, powerful word: Unite. *San Diego Union-Tribune.*

Nauss, D. W. (1994a, March 1). Auto makers drive for new world markets. *Los Angeles Times.*

Nauss, D. W. (1994b, March 1). The pressure mounts to recycle used vehicles. *Los Angeles Times.*

Navarrette, R., Jr. (1992, April 12). Life in the academic fast track. *Los Angeles Times.*

Nayar, R. (1990, October). Revenge of the gazelles. *New Statesmen and Society,* pp. 18–21.
Nazario, T. (1991, March). When your ex won't pay. *Parents,* pp. 63–67.
Neier, A. (1992). *Human Rights Watch News Letter.*
Nelan, B. W. (1992, October 26). Strike against racism. *Time,* p. 61.
Nelan, B. W. (1993, June 21). Fighting off doomsday. *Time,* pp. 36–38.
Nelson, H. D. (1982). *Nigeria—a country study.* Washington, DC: U.S. Government Printing Office.
Neumanin, L. (1991, October 20). Aung San Suu Kyi's lonely war. *San Diego Union.*
New horrors in a long-running show. (1988, April 4). *U.S. News and World Report,* pp. 11–12.
New study casts doubt on global warming. (1994, March 7). *Christian Science Monitor.*
Newman, K. S. (1988). *Falling from grace: The experience of downward mobility in the American middle class.* New York: Vintage Books.
Newton, J. (1992, November 11). Harsher crack sentences criticized as racial inequity. *Los Angeles Times.*
Next century could see one-fifth world infected, says expert. (1992, December 16). *San Diego Union-Tribune.*
Nicotine not addictive, industry tells Congress. (1994, April 15). *San Diego Union-Tribune.*
Nimkoff, M. F. (1965). *Comparative family structure.* New York: Houghton Mifflin.
Nisbet, R. (1974). *The sociology of Emile Durkheim.* New York: Oxford University Press.
Nixon, W. (1992, May/June). The population problem is not just about people. *Utne Reader,* p. 44.
Nolan, J. (1991, Fall). The politics of proliferation. *Issues in Science and Technology,* pp. 63–69.
Norton, A. J., & Glick, P. C. (1986). One parent families: A social and economic profile. *Family Relations, 35,* 9–17.
Norval, G. D., & Supancic, M. (1984, August). The social and demographic correlates of divorce and separation in the United States: An update and reconsideration. *Journal of Marriage and the Family,* pp. 563–575.
Nullis, C. (1992, June 27). Contraceptive use increases, WHO finds in report on health. *Los Angeles Times.*
Numbers game. (1993, Fall). *Time,* pp. 53–54.

O

O'Ballance, E. (1988). *The gulf war.* London: Brassey's Defence Publishers.
O'Brien, D. (1991, November). Against gay marriages—I. *Commonwealth, 22,* 684–685.
O'Connell, J. (1992). San Diego still tops in free wheeling car theft. *San Diego Union-Tribune.*
O'Dougherty, L. (1989). *Central Americans in Mexico City: Uprooted and silenced.* Washington, DC: Center for Immigration Policy and Refugee Assistance, Georgetown University.
O'Hare, W. P. (1992, December). America's minorities—The demographics of diversity. *Population Bulletin, 47*(4).
Oakes, J. (1985). *Keeping track: How schools structure inequality.* New Haven, CT: Yale University Press.
Ogburn, W. F. (1950). *Social change.* New York: Viking Press.
Ogburn, W. F. (1957). Cultural lag as theory. *Sociology and Social Research, 41,* 167–174.
Ogose, S. (1993, November 15–21). Polluted ground water and sinking land are the price of progress. *Japan Times Weekly International Edition.*
Oka, T. (1993, December 10). Ethnic ghettos or integration: An immigration dilemma. *Christian Science Monitor.*
Okie, S. (1992). World health report cites growth in drug abuse. In *Ourselves and others: The Washington Post sociology companion* (pp. 177–178). Boston: Allyn and Bacon.
Olen, H. (1991, October 22). Most states now ban marital rape. *Los Angeles Times.*
One-fourth of humanity live in poverty. (1993, September–October). *Popline,* p. 3.
Organized export of prostitutes from CIS is flourishing. (1993, June 2). *Current Digest of the Post-Soviet Press,* pp. 17–18.
Orwell, G. (1949). *1984.* New York: Harcourt Brace.
Oster, P. (1989). *The Mexicans: A personal portrait of a people.* New York: Harper & Row.

Ostrow, R. J. (1991, January 5). U.S. imprisons black men at 4 times S. Africa rate. *Los Angeles Times.*

Ostrowski, J. (1990, July). Has the time come to legalize drugs? *USA Today—The Magazine of the American Scene,* pp. 27–30.

Our African future. (1990, February). *American Demographics,* p. 9.

P

Pagelow, M. D. (1994, July 3). "Battered men" syndrome is a myth. *Los Angeles Times.*

Parra, E. O. (1993, October 6). AIDS-related risk behavior, knowledge, and beliefs among women and their Mexican American sexual partners who used intravenous drugs. *Journal of the American Medical Association, 270,* 1533.

Parrillo, V. N. (1994). *Strangers to these shores* (4th ed.). New York: Macmillan.

Parrish, M. (1992, September 20). America's poisons on the move. *Los Angeles Times.*

Parsons, T. (1951). *The social system.* New York: Free Press.

Parsons, T. (1954). *Essays in sociological theory.* New York: Free Press.

Parsons, T., & Bales, R. F. (1955). *Family, socialization, and interaction processes.* New York: Free Press.

Pasternak, J. (1993, November 9). Integration, Rockford style: Schools divided by race. *Los Angeles Times.*

Paterno, S. (1991, April 14). A legacy of violence. *Los Angeles Times.*

Paxton, M. (1992, March 30–April 5). Low awareness in Japan—Still "nothing to do with me." *Japan Times Weekly International Edition.*

Paz, O. (1994, January 7). A warning to all of Mexico that reforms are urgent. *Los Angeles Times.*

Pearce, D. (1978, Winter/Spring). The feminization of poverty: Women, work, and welfare. *Urban and Social Change Review,* pp. 28–36.

Pearce, D. (1990). The feminization of poverty. *Journal for Peace and Justice Studies, 2*(1), 1–20.

Pearson, J. (1988, September 26). How Iraq's radical leader is turning into a pragmatist. *Business Week,* p. 69.

Pederson, R. (1993, March 31). Young girls targeted as sex objects. *San Diego Union-Tribune.*

Pedrick-Cornell, C., & Gelles, R. J. (1982, July). Elder abuse: The status of current knowledge. *Family Relations,* pp. 457–465.

Peele, S. (1989). *The diseasing of America—Addiction treatment out of control.* Lexington, MA: D. C. Heath.

Peele, S. (1991). Drinking during pregnancy may not cause fetal alcohol syndrome. In C. P. Cozic & K. Swisher (Eds.), *Chemical dependency—Opposing viewpoints* (pp. 112–118). San Diego: Greenhaven.

Pelton, T. (1994, April 3). College students buck the trend, keep drinking. *San Diego Union-Tribune.*

People peddlars. (1989, February 23). *Far Eastern Economic Review,* pp. 41–42.

Pepinsky, H. E., & Jesilow, P. (1984). *Myths that cause crime.* Cabin John, MD: Seven Locks Press.

Perlmutter, P. (1992, April 10). Divided we fall: Group rights in America. *Christian Science Monitor.*

Pesce, C., & Blais, J. (1992, April 23). Statistics in survey staggering. *USA Today.*

Peters, S. D., Wyatt, G. E., & Finkelhor, D. (1986). Prevalence. In D. Finkelhor (Ed.), *A sourcebook of child sexual abuse* (pp. 15–39). Beverly Hills, CA: Sage.

Peterson, J. (1987, March). The feminization of poverty. *Journal of Economic Issues, 21,* 329–337.

Peterson, P. E. (1991–1992). The urban underclass and poverty paradox. *Political Science Quarterly, 106*(4), 617–637.

Peterson, S. (1993a, May 6). Thousands are displaced by Zaire's ethnic violence. *Christian Science Monitor.*

Peterson, S. (1993b, November 5). A small girl's silence tells story of Burundi's crisis. *Christian Science Monitor.*

Pfohl, S. J. (1985). *Images of deviance and social control.* New York: McGraw-Hill.

Phillips, K. (1993). *Boiling point: Republicans, Democrats and the decline of middle-class prosperity.* New York: Random House. 6

Pohl, J., & Boyd, C. (1992). Female addiction: A concept analysis. In T. Mieczkowski (Ed.), *Drugs, crime, and social policy: Research, issues, and concerns* (pp. 138–152). Boston: Allyn and Bacon.

Poland, J. R. (1989). Detectives. In. W. G. Bailey (Ed.), *Encyclopedia of police science* (pp. 142–145). New York: Garland.

Pollack, J. (1992, August 18). Spain's falling arches. *Los Angeles Times.*

Pope, H. G., & Katz, D. L. (1988). Affective and psychotic symptoms associated with anabolic steroid use. *American Journal of Psychiatry, 145*(4), 487–490.

Pope, V. (1992, April 13). Poisoning Russia's river of plenty. *U.S. News and World Report,* pp. 49–51.

Popenoe, D. (1988). *Disturbing the nest—Family change and decline in modern societies.* New York: Aldine De Gruyter.

Popenoe, D. (1991a). Family decline in the Swedish welfare state. *The Public Interest,* (102), Winter, 65–77.

Popenoe, D. (1991b, May). Breakup of the family: Can we reverse the trend? *USA Today Magazine—Society for the Advancement of Higher Education,* pp. 50–53.

Population Action International. (1992). *International human suffering index.* Washington, DC: Population Action International.

Population and the environment: The challenges ahead. (1991). New York: United Nations Population Fund.

Population Crisis Committee. (1991). *Access to affordable contraception—1991 report on world progress toward population stabilization.*

Portes, A., & Rumbaut, R. G. (1990). *Immigrant America: A portrait.* Berkeley: University of California Press.

Portes, A., & Stepick, A. (1993). City on the edge: The transformation of Miami. Berkeley: University of California Press.

Posey, C. (1992, March). Nuclear world order. *Omni,* pp. 41–88.

Post, T. (1993, January 4). A pattern of rape. *Newsweek,* pp. 32–36.

Postel, S. (1993a). Facing water scarcity. In L. Starke (Ed.), *State of the world 1993* (pp. 22–41). New York: W. W. Norton.

Postel, S. (1993b, July/August). The politics of water. *World Watch, 6*(4), 10–18.

Postel, S. (1994). Carrying capacity: Earth's bottom line. In L. Starke (Ed.), *State of the world 1994* (pp. 3–21). New York: W. W. Norton.

Powell, B. (1992, May 8). Down but not out. *Newsweek,* pp. 52–53.

Power, J. (1991, June 7). World gets more to eat, Africa gets less than ever. *Los Angeles Times.*

Power, J. (1992, February 18). Forgotten women. *San Diego Union-Tribune.*

Pregnancy risk high in developing world. (1992, September/October). *Popline,* p. 4.

President's Commission on Law Enforcement and the Administration of Justice. (1967). *Task force report: The courts.* Washington, DC: Government Printing Office.

Press, R. M. (1993a, September 27). Tribal clashes in Kenya continue. *Christian Science Monitor.*

Press, R. M. (1993b, September 29). Burundi's ethnic strife rekindles. *Christian Science Monitor.*

Press, R. M. (1993c, October 22). Military coup in Burundi dissolves new democracy. *Christian Science Monitor.*

Press, R. M. (1993d, October 26). Refugee flight threatens to spread fighting in region. *Christian Science Monitor.*

Press, R. M. (1993e, October 26). UN peacekeepers aim to contain strife, protect the displaced. *Christian Science Monitor.*

Press, R. M. (1993f, November 2). Burundi army learns democracy has roots. *Christian Science Monitor.*

Press, R. M. (1993g, November 29). Conditions worsen for refugees fleeing Burundi's ethnic upheaval. *Christian Science Monitor.*

Press, R. M. (1993h, February 18). Eritrea's women fighters face difficult transition. *Christian Science Monitor.*

Pressac, J. (1993). *The crematoria of Auschwitz: Machinery of mass murder.* New York: CNRS Editions.

Pringle, H. (1989, December). The Hansel and Gretel syndrome. *Omni,* pp. 38–39.

Pritchard, C. (1994, June). The land where eggs cost $9 each. *U.S. News and World Report.*

Privat, P. (1992, June 29). Down and out in Europe. *Newsweek,* p. 32.

Progress. (1989, Fall). *Social Policy,* pp. 75–76.

Protest by fire. (1990, October 8). *Time,* p. 61.

Public Concern Foundation. (1991, December). *Newsletter,* p. 3.

Q

Quinn, J. F. (1987). Sex roles and hedonism among members of outlaw motorcycle clubs. *Deviant Behavior 8,* 47–63.

Quinn-Judge, P. (1990, December 21). Absolute hell. *New Republic,* p. 12–13.

Quinney, R. (1977). *Class, state, and crime—On the theory and practice of criminal justice.* New York: David McKay.

R

Raab, S. (1991, October 21). U.S. says mob is drying up in New York. *New York Times.*

Racism shadows German unity anniversary. (1992, October 4). *San Diego Union-Tribune.*

Ragland, F. (1991). Gambling. *The academic American encyclopedia* (elec. ed.). Danbury, CT: Grolier.

Randall, L. (1992, August 17). Women candidates abound in '92. *Christian Science Monitor.*

Randall, T. (1991, January 23/30). Domestic violence: The role of alcohol—In reply. *Journal of the American Medical Association, 265*(4), 460–461.

Rape rate in America far higher than figured. (1992, April 24). *San Diego Union-Tribune.*

Raskin, A. (1992, August 2). Lazy, crazy or just like us? *Los Angeles Times Book Review,* p. 1.

Raspberry, W. (1994, February 6). TV violence begets real violence. *San Diego Union-Tribune.*

Ray, O., & Ksir, C. (1987). *Drugs, society, and human behavior.* St. Louis: Times Mirror/Mosby.

Rebeck, G. (1990, September/October). Gay families begin to win recognition. *Utne Reader,* p. 34.

Rebels slaughter 300 civilians in Liberia. (1993, June 7). *Buffalo News.*

Reckless, W. C. (1967). *The crime problem.* New York: Appleton-Century-Crofts.

Reddy, A. K. N., & Goldemberg, J. (1991). Energy for the developing world. In G. R. Davis (Ed.), *Energy for planet earth: Readings from Scientific American magazine* (pp. 60– 71). New York: Freeman.

Reed, J. (1983). Prisons. In S. H. Kadish (Ed.), *The encyclopedia of crime and justice, vol. 3* (pp. 1197–1207). New York: Free Press.

Reed, M. (1993, December 4). Mental illness rises among the jobless. *Los Angeles Times.*

Reese, S. (1992, March 17). "Boomerang generation" returning to the nest. *San Diego Union-Tribune.*

Reeves, D., & Cohen, M. J. (1991a). Introduction. In *Hunger 1992—Second annual report on the state of world hunger* (pp. 7–10). Washington, DC: Bread for the World Institute on Hunger and Development.

Reeves, D., & Cohen, M. J. (1991b). Equity, Ecology, and Alternative Agricultural Technologies. In *Hunger 1992—Second annual report on the state of world hunger* (pp. 44–47). Washington, DC: Bread for the World Institute on Hunger and Development.

Remnick, D. (1992). The vast landscape of want: Poverty in the USSR. In *Ourselves and others: The Washington Post sociology companion* (pp. 110–116). Boston: Allyn and Bacon.

Renner, M. (1988, June). Rethinking the role of the automobile. Worldwatch Paper 84.

Renner, M. (1990). Converting to a peaceful economy. In L. Starke (Ed.), *State of the world 1990* (pp. 154–172). New York: W. W. Norton.

Renner, M. (1992). Nuclear arsenal shrinking. In L. Starke (Ed.), *The trends that are shaping our future* (pp. 80–87). New York: W. W. Norton.

Renner, M. (1993). Preparing for peace. In L. Starke (Ed.), *State of the world 1993* (pp. 139–157). New York: W. W. Norton.

Renzetti, C. M., & Curran, D. J. (1992). *Women, men, and society* (2nd ed.). Boston: Allyn and Bacon.

Report on progress towards population stabilization. (1990). Washington, DC: Population Crisis Committee.

Report to the nation on crime and justice. (1988). Washington, DC: U.S. Department of Justice.

Reserved contempt. (1990, September 15). *The Economist,* p. 41.

Revolution on the farm. (1992, June 29). *Time,* pp. 54–56.

Rice, D. P., Kelman, S. K., & Miller, L. S. (1991, May/June). Estimates of economic costs of alcohol and drug abuse and mental illness, 1985 and 1988. *Public Health Reports, 106*(3), 280–292.

Rice, P. F. (1990). *Intimate relationships, marriages and families.* Mountain View, CA: Mayfield.

Richardson, L. (1988). *The dynamics of sex and gender: A sociological perspective* (3rd ed.). New York: Harper & Row.

Rien ne va plus. (1990, December 15). *The Economist,* pp. 23–24.

Rifkin, J. (1992, March/April). Beyond beef. *Utne Reader,* pp. 96–109.

Risen, J. (1993a, September 3). Lifting workers out of poverty proves difficult. *Los Angeles Times.*

Risen, J. (1993b, September 12). Health package fails math test, critics charge. *Los Angeles Times.*

Ritter, J. (1994, May 26). Stalemate over gulf war biological weapons. *USA Today.*

Roan, S. (1992, June 9). Working on a cure for unequal medicine. *Los Angeles Times.*

Roan, S. (1994, February 22). Under the influence. *Los Angeles Times.*

Roark, A. C. (1992, December 17). U.N. calls many child deaths preventable. *Los Angeles Times.*

Robbins, C. (1992, March 16). The x factor in the proliferation game. *U.S. News and World Report,* pp. 44–51.

Roberts, S. V., & Watson, T. (1994a, April 19). Should cigarettes be outlawed? *U.S. News & World Report,* pp. 32–38.

Roberts, S. V., & Watson, T. (1994b, April 19). Teens on tobacco. *U.S. News & World Report,* pp. 38, 43.

Robinson, J. (1991). Jane Addams. *The new Grolier electronic encyclopedia.* Danbury, CT: Grolier. E

Roemer, M. I. (1991). *National health systems of the world, volume 1: The countries.* New York: Oxford University Press.

Roemer, M. I. (1993). *National health systems of the world, volume 2: The issues.* New York: Oxford University Press.

Rohr, D. (1992, June 1). Too much, too fast. *Newsweek,* pp. 34–35.

Roman, S. (1992). The treatment of drug addiction: An overview. In T. Mieczkowski (Ed.), *Drugs, crime, and social policy: Research, issues, and concerns* (pp. 222–249). Boston: Allyn and Bacon.

Romero, E. (1992, March 20). Mexico swamped by the rising tide of its own pollution. *San Diego Union-Tribune.*

Roodman, D. M. (1993, November–December). Power brokers: Managing demand for electricity. *World Watch, 6*(6), 22–29.

Roos, P. A. (1985). *Gender and work: A comparative analysis of industrial societies.* Albany: State University of New York Press.

Root, A. (1988, May/June). European governments want more white babies. *Utne Reader,* p. 92.

Rosenbaum, J. L. (1989, January). Family dysfunction and female delinquency. *Crime and Delinquency, 35*(1), 31–44.

Rosenblatt, R. A. (1992, November 10). Old age means new problems, report warns. *Los Angeles Times.*

Rosenblatt, R. A. (1993, January 3). Government waste rampant, GAO says. *Los Angeles Times.*

Rosenblatt, R. A. (1994, March 30). Survey finds sharp rise in working poor. *Los Angeles Times.*

Rosenthal, E. (1991). Drinking during pregnancy causes fetal alcohol syndrome. In C. P. Cozic & K. Swisher (Eds.), *Chemical dependency—Opposing viewpoints* (pp. 105–112). San Diego: Greenhaven.

Ross, A. (1990, May). Do-it-yourself weaponry. *Bulletin of Atomic Scientists,* pp. 20–22.

Ross, E. (1993, November 18). Changes to Vermont's system mandate work for recipients. *Christian Science Monitor.*

Ross, E. A. (1922). *The social trend.* New York: Century Company.

Ross, E. A. (1931). *Civic sociology: A textbook in social and civic problems for young Americans.* Yonkers-on-Hudson, NY: World Book Company.

Ross, H. L. (1984). Social control through deterrence: Drinking and driving laws. In R. Turner & J. Short (Eds.), *Annual review of sociology* (pp. 21–35). Palo Alto, CA: Annual Reviews.

Rossi, A. (1984). Gender and parenthood. *American Sociological Review, 49,* 1–49.

Rotella, S. (1992, March 29). Toxic burner heats debate in Tijuana, S.D. *Los Angeles Times.*

Ruggles, P. (1990). *Drawing the line: Alternative poverty measures and their implication for public policy.* Washington, DC: Urban Institute.

Ruggles, P. (1992, Spring). Measuring poverty. *Focus, 14*(1), 1–5.

Rumbaitis-del Rio, C. (1994, March). Not a drop to drink. *BALANCE data* (31).

Running dry. (1993, May). *World Monitor,* pp. 10–11.

Russell, J. W. (1994). *After the fifth sun: Class and race in North America.* Englewood Cliffs, NJ: Prentice Hall.

Russia's anti-drink campaign. (1988, December 23). *The Economist,* pp. 50–54.

Russia's Kola peninsula called "dirtiest place on the globe." (1994, March 28). *San Diego Union-Tribune.*

Ryan, W. (1976). *Blaming the victim* (rev. ed.). New York: Random House.

S

Sachdev, P. (Ed.). (1988). *International handbook on abortion.* New York: Greenwood.

Sadik, N. (1991). Foreword. In *Population and the environment: The challenges ahead* (pp. 3–4). New York: United Nations Population Fund.

Salholz, E., Clift, E., Springer, K., & Johnson, P. (1990, February 9). Women under assault. *Newsweek,* p. 60.

Sampson, R. J. (1987, September). Urban black violence: The effect of male joblessness and family disruption. *American Journal of Sociology 2,* 348–342.

Sanders, W. B. (1980). *Rape and women's identity.* Beverly Hills, CA: Sage.

Sanders, W. B. (1983). *Criminology.* Reading, MA: Addison-Wesley.

Sassen, S. (1991). *The global city: New York, London, Tokyo.* Princeton, NJ: Princeton University Press.

Satchell, M. (1991, May 6). Poisoning the border. *U.S. News and World Report,* pp. 33–41.

Satchell, M. (1992, May 4). A whiff of discrimination? *U.S News and World Report,* pp. 34–35.

Satchell, M. (1994, March 7). Deadly trade in toxics. *U.S. News and World Report,* pp. 64–68.

Sattaur, O. (1989, May). India's troubled waters. *New Scientist, 27,* 46–51.

Saunders, D. G. (1986). When battered women use violence: Husband abuse or self defense. *Violence and Victims, 1,* 47–60.

Savage, D. G. (1990, March 2). Asians, Latinos surge in U.S. growth rates. *Los Angeles Times.*

Sawa, T. (1992, November 16–22). A frugal, caring Japan could be environmental pioneer. *Japan Times Weekly International Edition.*

Schaefer, R. T. (1990). *Racial and ethnic groups* (4th ed.). Glenview, IL: Scott, Foresman/Little, Brown Higher Education.

Scherer, R. (1993, December 27). Asia leads the world in economic growth. *Christian Science Monitor.*

Schlesinger, A., Jr. (1991, July 8). The cult of ethnicity, good and bad. *Time,* p. 21.

Schneider, B. (1991, July/August). The first nuclear civil war. *Defense and Diplomacy,* pp. 7–14.

Schneider, K. (1991, December 2). Deep-sea bottom eyed for dumping. *San Diego Union.*

Schoenberger, K. (1990, October 30). In Japan's worst slum, angry underclass feels a nation's prejudice. *Los Angeles Times.*

Scholand, M. (1993, November–December). Building for the future. *World Watch, 6*(6), 36–38.

Schrager, L., & Short, J. (1978). Toward a sociology of organization crime. *Social Problems, 25,* 415–425.

Schrof, J. M. (1992, June 1). Pumped up. *U.S. News and World Report,* pp. 55–63.

Schrof, J. M. (1994, February 21). A lens on matrimony. *U.S. News and World Report,* pp. 66–68.

Schultz, E. A., & Lavenda, R. H. (1990). *Contemporary anthropology—A perspective on the human condition.* St. Paul: West.

Schur, E. M. (1979). *Interpreting deviance—A sociological perspective.* New York: Harper and Row.

Schwartz, J. (1987, May 11). A "superminority" tops out. *Newsweek,* pp. 48–49.

Schwinn, E. (1994, March 10). Equality found ailing in cost of health care for men, women. *San Diego Union-Tribune.*

Scobell, A. (1990, September). The death penalty in post-Mao China. *The China Quarterly, 123,* 503–521.

Scott, D. C. (1992a, April 16). Guatemalans prepare to go home. *Christian Science Monitor.*

Scott, D. C. (1992b, July 8). Mexican men get the message about limiting family size. *Christian Science Monitor.*

Scott, D. C. (1994, January 10). Uprising may have economic and political repercussions. *Christian Science Monitor.*

Scott, G. (1993, February 22). I can't cry anymore. *Time,* p. 51.

Scott, W. (1990, August). PTSD in DSM-III: A case in the politics of diagnosis and disease. *Social Problems, 37*(3), 294–310.

Seager, J., & Olson, A. (1986). *Women in the world: An international atlas.* New York: Simon and Schuster.

Seamonds, J. (1988, January 18). Ethnic gangs and organized crime. *U.S. News and World Report,* pp. 31–34.

Sedgwick, J. (1992, December). The health care crisis. *Self,* pp. 154–159, 173.

Seligmann, J. (1990). Variations on a theme. *Newsweek,* Special Issue, Winter/Spring, 38–46.

Serrano, R. A. (1989a, February 12). Police blame explosion in crime, population for drop in service. *Los Angeles Times.*

Serrano, R. A. (1989b, February 12). Most victims get a post card, not an officer. *Los Angeles Times.*

Serrill, M. S. (1993, June 21). Defiling the children. *Time,* pp. 53–55.

Sexual harassment a problem around world, report indicates. (1992, December 5). *San Diego Union-Tribune.*

Shapiro, J. P. (1992, January 13). The elderly are not children. *U.S. News and World Report,* pp. 26–27.

Shapiro, L. (1990, May 28). Guns and dolls. *Newsweek,* pp. 56–65.

Shaw, D. (1990, December 11). Asian-Americans chafe against stereotype of "model citizen." *Los Angeles Times.*

Shear, J. (1990, September 3). The dream out of reach for Japanese. *Insight,* pp. 8–17.

Sheley, J. F., & Ashkins, C. D. (1981). Crime, crime news, and crime views. *Public Opinion Quarterly, 45*(492), 506.

Shelley, L. (1980, February). The geography of Soviet criminality. *American Sociological Review, 45,* 111–122.

Shelley, L. (1981). *Crime and modernization—The impact of industrialization and urbanization.* Carbondale, IL: Southern Illinois University Press.

Sherman, L. (1985). Domestic violence. *Crime file study guide.* Washington, DC: National Institute of Justice.

Shim, K. H., et al. (1988). *Criminal victimization in the United States–1986.* Washington, D C.: U.S. Department of Justice, Bureau of Justice Statistics.

Shipp, E. R., & Navarro, M. (1991, November 18). Reluctantly, black churches confront AIDS. *New York Times.*

Shogren, E. (1993, August 20). Welfare recipients, experts criticize the system. *Los Angeles Times.*

Shrivastava, R. S. (1992. Crime and control in comparative perspectives: The case of India. In H. Heiland, L. I. Shelley, & H. Katoh (Eds.), *Crime and control in comparative perspectives.* Berlin: Walter de Gruyter.

Side effects of the U.S. "peace dividend." (1992, March 21). *Science & Society,* p. 191.

Siegel, L. J. (1989). *Criminology.* St. Paul: West.

Siegel, L. J. (1992). *Criminology—theories, patterns and typologies.* St Paul: West.

Siegel, M. A., Landes, A., & Foster, C. D. (Eds.). (1993). *Health: A concern for every American.* Wylie, TX: Information Plus.

Silberman, C. E. (1978). *Criminal violence, criminal justice.* New York: Vintage Books.

Silk, L., & Kono, T. (1994, January 16). Sayonara, Japan Inc. *San Diego Union-Tribune.*

Simon, D. R., & Eitzen, D. S. (1993). *Elite deviance* (4th ed.). Boston: Allyn and Bacon.

Simon, J. L. (1991, Winter). The case for greatly increased immigration. *The Public Interest* (102), 89–103.

Simon, J. S. (1990). Immigration helps the U.S. economy. In W. Dudley (Ed.), *Immigration—Opposing viewpoints* (pp. 80–84). San Diego: Greenhaven.

Simon, S. (1992, June 12). Survey finds anti-Semitism on rise in ex-Soviet lands. *Los Angeles Times.*

Simons, R. L., & Whitbeck, L. B. (1991, September). Sexual abuse as a precursor to prostitution and victimization among adolescent and adult homeless women. *Journal of Family Stress,* 12(3), pp. 361–379.

Simpson, V. L. (1992, November 11). Anti-Semitism, racial strife plague Europe. *San Diego Union-Tribune.*

Singapore gets tough on smoking. (1993, May 31). *San Diego Union-Tribune.*

Singer, R. (1988). Sentencing. *Crime file study guide.* Washington, DC: National Institute of Justice.

Sivard, R. L. (1991). *World military and social expenditures—1991.* Washington, DC: World Priorities.

Sivard, R. L. (1993). *World military and social expenditures—1993.* Washington, DC: World Priorities.

Sixty Minutes. (1991, December 22). Hussein and Hussein. CBS News.

Sixty percent of Japanese men smoke, survey finds. (1993, June 7–13). *Japan Times Weekly International Edition.*

Sixty-three leaders endorse stabilization. (1994, May/June). *Popline,* p. 4. E

Skocpol, T., & Wilson, W. J. (1994, February 13). New welfare goals: Jobs and parenting. *Los Angeles Times.*

Skolnick, J. H. (1975). *Justice without trial—Law enforcement in democratic society.* New York: John Wiley and Sons.

Skolnick, J. H., & Currie, E. (1994). *Crisis in American institutions* (9th ed.). New York: HarperCollins.

Sloane, W. (1993, November 9). Russia women's bloc plans for elections. *Christian Science Monitor.*

Smoking down 28 percent in California over 5 years; campaign credited. (1994, March 22). *San Diego Union-Tribune.*

Smolowe, J. (1988, August 22). Return of the silent killer. *Time,* pp. 46–49.

Sneider, D. (1992a, February 24). Caucasus dispute rages despite peace efforts. *Christian Science Monitor.*

Sneider, D. (1992b, June 22). Russians cope with arc of crises. *Christian Science Monitor.*

Snell, B. C. (1994). American ground transport. In J. H. Skolnick & E. Currie (Eds.), *Crisis in American institutions* (9th ed.), (pp. 276–289). New York: HarperCollins.

Sobo, E. (1990, September). Crooning for contraception in Nigeria. *The Progressive,* pp. 26–28.

Something happened. (1991, October 26). *The Economist,* pp. 6–7.

Sommer, M. (1992, February 19). Who will pay for peace? *Christian Science Monitor.*

Sommer, M. (1993, August 18). Struggling to cut the half-life of Moscow's nuclear mess. *Christian Science Monitor.*

Sontag, D. (1993, October 18). New immigrants test nation's heartland. *New York Times.*

Spadd, E. (1994, January 31). Thai police blamed in illicit sex trade. *Christian Science Monitor.*

Spaid, E. L. (1993a, June 2). Sexual harassment found in U.S. schools. *Christian Science Monitor.*

Spaid, E. L. (1993b, June 9). Women claim place on agenda at UN human rights meeting. *Christian Science Monitor.*

Spaid, E. L. (1993c, October 5). Past pollution still fouls many of today's waterways. *Christian Science Monitor.*

Spanier, G. B., & Thompson, L. (1984). *Parting—The aftermath of separation and divorce.* Beverly Hills, CA: Sage.

Spates, J., & Macionis, J. (1987). *Sociology of cities.* New York: St. Martin's Press.

Speaking of: Water. (1993, December 14). *Los Angeles Times.*

Specter, M. (1994, June 19). Russia's outrage swells over crime decree. *San Diego Union-Tribune.*

Spector, M., & Kitsuse, J. I. (1987). *Constructing social problems.* Hawthorne, NY: Aldine de Gruyter.

Spiegel, C. (1992, June 23). Uninsured children pay price. *Los Angeles Times.*

Spilerman, S. (1976, October). Structural characteristics of cities and the severity of racial disorders. *American Sociological Review, 41,* 771–793.

Stammer, L. B. (1992a, March 25). Study finds serious harm to 10 percent of world's best soil. *Los Angeles Times.*

Stammer, L. B. (1992b, June 29). 20 firms assailed for ozone depletion. *Los Angeles Times.*

Stanglin, D. (1992, April 13). Toxic wasteland. *U.S. News and World Report,* pp. 40–49.

Steele, C. M. (1992, April). Race and the schooling of Black Americans. *Atlantic Monthly,* pp. 68–78.

Steffensmeier, D., & Allan, E. (1991). Gender, age, and crime. In J. P. Sheley (Ed.), *Criminology.* Belmont, CA: Wadsworth.

Stephens, R. C. (1992). Psychoactive drug use in the United States today: A critical overview. In T. Mieczkowski (Ed.), *Drugs, crime, and social policy: Research, issues, and concerns* (pp. 1–31). Boston: Allyn and Bacon.

Stern, M. (1994, February 3). U.S. rips Mexico's Chiapas abuses. *San Diego Union-Tribune.*

Stevens, W. K. (1992, June 7). Summit: Can world unite against a peril all can see? *San Diego Union-Tribune.*

Stief, T. M. (1993, October). Infant deaths fall but remain high for Blacks. *Population Today,* p. 5.

Stolberg, S. (1993, November 10). Mortality study finds tobacco is no. 1 culprit. *Los Angeles Times.*

Stoner, M. R. (1991, December 24). Homelessness and AIDS: An L.A. secret. *Los Angeles Times.*

Stork's return. (1991, April 13). *The Economist,* p. 47.

Storr, A. (1968). *Human aggression.* Riverside, NJ: Atheneum.

Stover, E., & McGrath, R. (1992, Spring). Calling for an international ban on a crippling scourge—Land mines. *Human Rights Watch, 10*(2), 6–7.

Straus, M. A., & Gelles, R. J. (1986, August). Societal change and change in family violence from 1975 to 1985 as revealed by two national surveys. *Journal of Marriage and the Family,* pp. 465–479.

Straus, M. A., & Kantor, G. K. (1987). Stress and child abuse. In R. E. Helper & R. S. Kempe (Eds.), *The battered child* (pp. 42–59). Chicago: University of Chicago Press.

Straus, M. A., Gelles, R. J., & Steinmetz, S. K. (1980). *Behind closed doors.* Garden City, NY: Anchor.

Strauss, M. (1991). Discipline and deviance: Physical punishment of children and violence and other crimes in adulthood. *Social Problems, 38,* 133–154.

Strobel, F. R. (1993). *Upward dreams, downward mobility: The economic decline of the American middle class.* Lantham, MD: Rowman & Littlefield.

Strong, B., & DeVault, C. (1992). *The marriage and family experience* (5th ed.). St. Paul: West.

Strosberg, M. A. (1992). Introduction. In M. A. Strosberg, J. M. Wiener, R. Baker, with I. A. Fein (Eds.), *Rationing America's medical care: The Oregon plan and beyond* (pp. 3–11). Washington, DC: Brookings Institute.

Strube, M. J., & Barbour, L. S. (1983, November). The decision to leave an abusive relationship: Economic dependence and psychological commitment. *Journal of Marriage and the Family,* pp. 785–793.

Stull, D. E. (1992). Health and the life course. In E. F. Borgatta & M. L. Borgatta (Eds.), *Encyclopedia of sociology, vol. 2* (pp. 800–803). New York: Macmillan.

Stutman, R. M. (1990, July). Can we stop drugs in the workplace? *USA Today—The Magazine of the American Scene.,* pp. 18–20.

Stutsman, R. (1992, February). Bearing the burden. *ZPG Reporter, 24*(1), 1–4.

Substance abuse. (1993). In J. W. Wright (Ed.), *The universal almanac.* Kansas City: Andrews & McMeel.

Sugio, N. (1991, April 1–7). Government moves to revise waste law. *Japan Times Weekly International Edition.*

Sugio, N. (1992, April 27–May 3). Developing countries told to pay for conservation. *Japan Times Weekly International Edition.*

Sumner, W. G. (1883). *What social classes owe each other.* New York: Harper and Brothers.

Sutherland, E. H., & Cressey, D. R. (1970). *Criminology.* Philadelphia: Lippincott.

Suzuki, M. (1992). Environmental groups in Japan lack national cohesion. In *Speaking out: vol. 3, Realistic approaches to environmental issues* (pp. 26–29). Tokyo: Toyota Motor Corporation.

Swearingen, W. D. (1988, October). Geopolitical origins of the Iran-Iraq war. *Geopolitical Review, 78,* 405–416.

Sweeney, L. (1992a, April 7). Researcher links violence on TV with aggression. *Christian Science Monitor.*

Sweeney, L. (1992b, September 1). School bus surveillance increases. *Christian Science Monitor.*

Sweet, R. W. (1990, November/December). Missing children: Found facts. *NIJ Reports—The Bimonthly Journal of the National Institute of Justice,* pp. 15–18.

Switzerland. (1992). *Universal almanac* (p. 464). Kansas City: Andrews & McMeel.

Sykes, G. M., & Cullen, F. T. (1992). *Criminology.* Fort Worth: Harcourt Brace Jovanovich.

Symonds, W. C. (1992, March 9). It's not perfect, but it sure works. *Business Week,* p. 54.

T

Talbott, S. (1990, August 20). Sorry to see the Cold War go. *Time,* p. 56.

Tamayo Lott, J. (1993, January). Do United States racial/ethnic categories still fit? *Population Today,* pp. 6–7, 9.

Tavris, C., & Offir, C. (1977). The longest war. In C. Tavris & C. Offir (Eds.), *The longest war.* New York: Harcourt Brace Jovanovich.

Taylor, C. S. (1990). Gang imperialism. In C. R. Huff (Ed.), *Gangs in America.* Newbury Park, CA: Sage.

Teen girls prove they're "tough" by having sex with HIV carriers. (1993, April 27). *San Diego Union-Tribune.*

Tefft, S. (1994, May 25). Tobacco companies see huge market in China. *Christian Science Monitor.*

Tempest, R. (1993, November 17). Get rich and succeed, Chinese party urges. *Los Angeles Times.*

Tempest, R. (1994, March 1). The last frontier for sales. *Los Angeles Times.*

Tepperson, L., & Wilson, S. J. (1993). Who are your next of kin? An overview of trends. In L. Tepperson & S. J. Wilson (Eds.), *Next of kin* (pp. 1–20). Englewood Cliffs, NJ: Prentice Hall.

Testing awareness of the Holocaust. (1993, May 5). *Christian Century,* p. 481.

Thick, hazy air threatens 23 million in U.S. (1994, April 30). *San Diego Union-Tribune.*

Thio, A. (1988). *Deviant behavior.* New York: Harper & Row.

Thirty-eight million, nine hundred thousand lack health insurance. (1993, December 15). *San Diego Union-Tribune.*

Thomas, W. I., with Swain Thomas, D. (1928). *The child in America.* New York: Knopf.

Thompson, D. (1992, January 13). Breezing into the future. *Time,* pp. 48–49.

Thompson, E., & Collela, U. (1992). Cohabitation and marital stability. *Journal of Marriage and the Family, 54,* 259–267.

Thompson, M. (1994, April 11). Well, maybe a nuke or two. *Time,* p. 58.

Threats to earth, air and water. (1992, October 15). *Washington Spectator, 18*(19), 1–3.

Tienda, M., & Stier, H. (1991). Joblessness and shiftlessness: Labor force activity in Chicago's inner city. In C. Jencks & P. E. Peterson (Eds.), *The urban underclass.* Washington, DC: Brookings Institute.

Time running out at power plant. (1994, March 28). *San Diego Union-Tribune.*

Timmerman, K. R. (1992). *The death lobby.* New York: Houghton Mifflin.

Tinbergen, N. (1968, June 28). On war and peace in animals and man. *Science, 160,* 1411–1418.

Tittle, C. R., Villemez, W. J., & Smith, D. A. (1978). The myth of social class and criminality: An empirical assessment of the empirical evidence. *American Sociological Review, 43,* 643–656.

To some, elitism is feminists' folly. (1992, February 15). *San Diego Union-Tribune.*

Toch, T., with Wright, A. (1993, August 2). Public schooling's opportunity gap. *U.S. News & World Report,* p. 45.

Today on the planet. (1992, May 26). *Los Angeles Times.*

Tolchin, M. (1993, August 29). Medical plan's exclusion of migrants is questioned. *San Diego Union-Tribune.*

Top 10 censored stories of 1991. (1992, May/June). *Utne Reader,* pp. 86–91.

Top 10 health frauds. (1989, October 29). *FDA Consumer,* pp. 28–31.

Toufexis, A. (1988, August 1). The dirty seas. *Time,* pp. 44–50.

Toufexis, A. (1990, October 22). From the asylum to anarchy. *Time,* pp. 58–59.

Tower, C. C. (1989). *Understanding child abuse and neglect.* Boston: Allyn and Bacon.

Toynbee, A. (1983). Mylai was a war crime. In D. L. Bender & B. Leone (Eds.), *War and human nature: Opposing viewpoints* (pp. 125–129). St. Paul: Greenhaven.

Treaster, J. B. (1994, February 1). Survey finds marijuana use is up in high schools. *New York Times.*

Trent, K., & South, S. J. (1989). Structural determinants of the divorce rate: A cross cultural analysis. *Journal of Marriage and the Family, 51,* 391–404.

Trieman, D. J., & Roos, P. A. (1983). Sex and earnings in industrial society: A nine-nation comparison. *American Journal of Sociology, 89,* 612–650.

Trumbull, M. (1994, February 18). Up for reinvention: Job retraining. *Christian Science Monitor.*

Truninger, E. (1971). Marital violence: The legal solutions. *Hastings Law Review, 23,* 259–276.

Tucker, W. T. (1991). New housing regulations cause homelessness. *The Public Interest* (102), 78–88.

Tumin, M. (1953, August). Some principles of stratification: A critical analysis. *American Sociological Review, XVIII*(4), 387–394.

Tuohy, W. (1993, January 20). Crime knows no boundaries. *Los Angeles Times.*

Turk, A. (1975–1976). Law as a weapon in social conflict. *Social Problems, 23,* 276–291.

Turning off the gas. (1989, October 20). *Commonweal,* pp. 548–549.

Tyson, J. L. (1992, May 27). Three Gorges Dam in China threatens fish and fishermen. *Christian Science Monitor.*

Tyson, J. L. (1993, November 29). Mandatory sentences lead to surge of women in prison. *Christian Science Monitor.*

Tyson, J. L. (1994, May 5). More US Blacks favor going a separate way. *Christian Science Monitor.*

Tyson, J. L., & Tyson, A. S. (1992, August 5). Restless migrants stream to cities. *Christian Science Monitor.*

U

Uchitelle, L. (1994, May 17). Top executives veto president's plan. *San Diego Union-Tribune.*

Underwood, J. (1986, March 10). The biggest game in town. *Sports Illustrated,* pp. 30–56.

Uniform Crime Reports. (1990). *Crime in the United States.* Washington, DC: U.S. Department of Justice.

United Nations. (1991). *The world's women 1970–1990: Trends and statistics.* New York: United Nations.

United Nations Department for Economic and Social Information and Policy Analysis. (1991). *Demographic yearbook 1991.* New York: United Nations.

United Nations Development Program. (1993). *Human development report 1993.* New York: Oxford University Press.

United States Bureau of the Census. (1990). *Household wealth and asset ownership: 1988.* Current Population Reports, Series P70-22. Washington, DC: U.S. Government Printing Office.

United States Bureau of the Census. (1991). *Statistical abstract of the United States.* Washington, DC: U.S. Department of Commerce.

United States Bureau of the Census. (1992a). *Income, poverty, and wealth in the United States: A chart book.* Current Population Reports, Series P60-179. Washington, DC: U.S. Government Printing Office.

United States Bureau of the Census. (1992b). *Studies in the distribution of income.* Current Population Reports, Series P60-183. Washington, DC: U.S. Government Printing Office.

United States Bureau of the Census. (1993a). *Statistical abstract of the United States, 1993.* Washington, DC: U.S. Government Printing Office.

United States Bureau of the Census. (1993b). *Money income of households, families, and persons in the United States: 1992.* Current Population Reports, Series P60–184. Washington, DC: U.S. Government Printing Office.

United States Bureau of the Census. (1993c). *Poverty in the United States: 1992.* Current Population Reports, Series P60-185. Washington, DC: Government Printing Office.

United States Congress, Select Committee on Children, Youth and Families. (1987). Abused children in America: Victims of official neglect. In Craig B. Little (Ed.), *Deviance and control—Theory, research, and social policy* (1989). Itasca, IL: F. E. Peacock.

United States Department of Agriculture. (1993). Stabilization and price support programs. In *Agricultural statistics* (chapter XI). Washington, DC: U.S. Department of Agriculture.

United States Department of Health and Human Services. (1992a). *Healthy people 2000: National health promotion and disease prevention objectives.* Boston: Jones and Bartlett.

United States Department of Health and Human Services. (1992b). *1992 national household survey on drug abuse.* Washington, DC: U.S. Government Printing Office.

United States Department of Justice. (1988). *Report to the nation on crime and justice* (2nd ed.). Washington, DC: U.S. Government Printing Office.

United States Department of Justice. (1991). *Bulletin: Criminal victimization.* Washington, DC: U.S. Government Printing Office.

United States Health Care Financing Administration. (1991, Fall). *Health care financing review.* Washington, DC: U.S. Government Printing Office.

United States leads world in violent crimes. (1991, March 13). *San Diego Union.*

Universal Almanac 1993. (1992). Kansas City: Andrews and McMeel.

Useem, M., & Karabel, J. (1986). Pathways to corporate management. *American Sociological Review, 51*(2), 184–200.

V

Valentine, M. (1992, Spring). Population and the earth summit. *In Context,* pp. 18–19.

van Creveld, M. (1991). *The transformation of war.* New York: Free Press.

Van Maanen, J. B. (1978). The asshole. In P. K. Manning & J. Van Maanen (Eds.), *Policing—A view from the street.* Santa Monica, CA: Goodyear.

van Vliet, H. J. (1990, Spring). The uneasy decriminalization: A perspective on Dutch drug policy. *Hofstra Law Review,* pp. 717–750.

Van Voorst, B. (1992, November 9). A thousand points of blight. *Time,* pp. 68–69.

Vasquez, J. M. (1983, September 15). Mexico City—Strangling on growth. *Los Angeles Times.*

Vast acceleration of family planning use vital for development. (1991, May–June). *Popline,* p. 1.

Veni, vidi, vodka. (1989, December 23). *The Economist,* pp. 50–54.

Vigil, J. D. (1988). *Barrio gangs: Street life and identity in southern California.* Austin: University of Texas Press.

Vigil, J. D., & Long, J. M. (1990). Emic and etic perspectives on gang culture. In C. R. Huff (Ed.), *Gangs in America.* Newbury Park, CA: Sage.

Vistica, G. (1992a, February 20). Navy launches attack on sexual harassment. *San Diego Union-Tribune.*

Vistica, G. (1992b, December 27). Dead in the water. *San Diego Union-Tribune.*

Vladeck, B. C. (1992, February 4). A classic clash of political values. *New York Times.*

Vold, G. B. (1979). *Theoretical criminology.* New York: Oxford University Press.

Voydanoff, P. (1990, November). Economic distress and family relations: A review of the eighties. *Journal of Marriage and the Family, 52,* 1099–1115.

W

Wade, R. C. (1972). Violence in the cities: A historical view. In K. T. Jackson & S. K. Schultz (Eds.), *Cities in American history.* New York: Knopf.

Walker, L. E. A. (1986). Psychological causes of family violence. In M. Lystad (Ed.), *Violence in the home: Interdisciplinary perspectives.* New York: Brunner/Mazel.

Walker, S. (1989). *Sense and nonsense about crime—A policy guide.* Pacific Grove, CA: Brooks/Cole.

Walker, S. L. (1994, April 22). Critics fume at mayor of world smog capital. *San Diego Union-Tribune.*

Wallace, C. P. (1992, August 27). For sale: The poor's body parts. *Los Angeles Times.*

Wallace, C. P. (1994a, March 23). Asia tires of being the toxic waste dumping ground for rest of world. *Los Angeles Times.*

Wallace, C. P. (1994b, April 1). Singapore: What price justice? *Los Angeles Times.*

Wallerstein, I. (1974). *The modern world system: Capitalist agriculture and the origins of the European world-economy in the sixteenth century.* New York: Academic Press.

Wallerstein, I. (1979). *The capitalist world-economy.* New York: Cambridge University Press.

Wallerstein, I. (1984). *The politics of the world-economy: The states, the movements, and the civilizations.* Cambridge, UK: Cambridge University Press.

Wallerstein, J. S. (1992). Children of divorce—Wounds that won't heal. In O. Pocs (Ed.), *Marriage and the family 92/93.* Guilford, CT: Dushkin.

Walsh, J. (1993, Fall). The perils of success. *Time,* pp. 55–56.

Walsh, M. W. (1993, October 4). Canadian doctors fought reform. *Los Angeles Times.*

Walters, L. S. (1993, October 4). Progress on education found to be inadequate. *Christian Science Monitor.*

Wandi, J. (1990, July 9). Problems of China's aging population viewed. *Beijing Review, 15,* 30.

Warr, M. (1985, February). Fear of rape among urban women. *Social Forces, 32,* 238–250.

Warshaw, S. (1988). *Japan emerges.* Berkeley, CA: Diablo Press.

Wasserman, I. M. (1984, November). A longitudinal analysis of the linkage between suicide, unemployment, and marital dissolution. *Journal of Marriage and the Family,* pp. 853–859.

Waste and the environment. (1993, May 29). *The Economist,* pp. 3–18.

Wasted health dollars. (1992, July). *Consumer Reports,* pp. 435–448.

Watanabe, T. (1992a, January 14). When life on the job is literally killing you. *Los Angeles Times.*

Watanabe, T. (1992b, August 17). Japan Inc. no friend to women. *Los Angeles Times.*

Waters, T. (1990, April). Ecoglasnost. *Discover,* pp. 51–53.

Watson, R. (1992, February 17). The devil's work. *Newsweek,* pp. 30–31.

Watson, R. (1993, December 13). Death on the spot. *Newsweek,* pp. 18–21.

Watson, R., with Warner, M. G., Waller, D., Nordland, R., & Breslau, K. (1992, August 17). Ethnic cleansing. *Newsweek,* pp. 16–20.

Weber, M. (1978, original 1921). *Economy and society.* G. Roth and C. Wittich (Eds.). Berkeley: University of California Press.

Weil, A., & Rosen, W. (1983). *Chocolate to morphine—Understanding mind-active drugs.* Boston: Houghton Mifflin.

Weiner, M. (1978). *Sons of the soil—Migration and ethnic conflict in India.* Princeton, NJ: Princeton University Press.

Weinstein, W. (1976). *Historical dictionary of Burundi.* Metuchen, NJ: Scarecrow Press.

Weis, L. (Ed.). (1988). *Class, race, and gender in American education.* Albany: State University of New York Press.

Weitzman, L. J. (1990). The economic consequences of divorce. In W. Feigelman (Ed.), *Readings on social problems.* New York: Holt, Rinehart and Winston.

Welch, W. M. (1992, May 7). Runaway fraud reported in health-care system. *San Diego Union-Tribune.*

Welles, C. (1989, April 24). America's gambling fever. *Business Week,* pp. 112–117.

West, D. J., & Farrington, D. P. (1973). *Who becomes delinquent?* London: Heinemann Educational Books.

Wetherall, W. (1993, January 25–31). Ethnic Ainu seek official recognition. *Japan Times Weekly International Edition.*

While Mexico's people live in the north, its water is in the south. (1992, May 27). *Christian Science Monitor.*

White, G. L., Richardson, G. E., Grosshans, O. R., Perkins, F. J., & Murdock, R. T. (1987, August/September). Preventing steroid abuse in youth: The health educator's role. *Health Education,* pp. 32–35.

Whitman, D. (1991, October 21). What keeps the poor poor? *U.S. News and World Report,* pp. 42–44.

Widom, C. S. (1989, April). The cycle of violence. *Science, 244,* 160–166.

Wilkens, J. (1992, December 27). Gantlet of change. *San Diego Union-Tribune.*

Wilkens, J., & Hearn, L. (1992, December 27). Employers act on, head off complaints. *San Diego Union-Tribune.*

Wilkie, J. R. (1991, February). The decline in men's labor force participation and income and the changing structure of family economic support. *Journal of Marriage and the Family, 53,* 111–122.

Wilkinson, P. (1986). Terrorism versus liberal democracy: The problem of response. In W. Gutteridge (Ed.), *Contemporary terrorism.* New York: Facts on File.

Wilkinson, T. (1994a, February 12). Colombia's new era of traffickers. *Los Angeles Times.*

Wilkinson, T. (1994b, June 16). Gangs find fresh turf in Salvador. *Los Angeles Times.*

Williams, D. (1993, January 5). Women taking new roles amid Somalia chaos. *Los Angeles Times.*

Williams, F. P., III, & McShane, M. D. (1988). *Criminological theory.* Englewood Cliffs, NJ: Prentice Hall.

Williamson, J. B., Munley, A., & Evans, L. (1980). *Aging and society.* New York: Holt, Rinehart and Winston.

Wilson, J. Q. (1968). *Varieties of police behavior.* Cambridge, MA: Harvard University Press.

Wilson, J. Q., & Herrnstein, R. J. (1985). *Crime and human nature.* New York: Simon and Schuster.

Wilson, W. J. (1987). *The truly disadvantaged: The inner city, the underclass and public policy.* Chicago: University of Chicago Press.

Wilson, W. J. (1991–1992). Another look at the truly disadvantaged. *Political Science Quarterly, 106*(4), 639–656.

Wilson, W. J. (1992, May 6). Imagine life without a future. *Los Angeles Times.*

Wilson, W. J., & Neckerman, K. (1987). Poverty and family structure: The widening gap between evidence and public policy issues. In W. J. Wilson (Ed.), *The truly disadvantaged—The inner city, the underclass, and public policy.* Chicago: University of Chicago Press.

Windle, M. (1991). Alcohol use and abuse: Some findings from the National Adolescent Student Health Survey. *Alcohol World—Health and Research, 15*(1), 5–11.

Winick, C. (1992). Drug abuse. In E. F. Borgatta & M. L. Borgatta (Eds.), *Encyclopedia of sociology, vol. 1* (pp. 516–519). New York: Maxwell Macmillan.

Winokur, J. (1987). *The portable curmudgeon.* New York: New American Library.

Winsberg, M. D. (1993, October). America's foreign born. *Population Today,* p. 4.

Wintham, D. C., & Gladis, S. D. (1989). Two models of discretion. In W. G. Bailey (Ed.), *Encyclopedia of police science* (pp. 153–156). New York: Garland.

Wisotsky, S. (1990a). *Beyond the war on drugs—Overcoming a failed public policy.* Buffalo: Prometheus.

Wisotsky, S. (1990b). The war on drugs violates civil liberties. In N. Bernards (Ed.), *War on drugs—Opposing viewpoints* (pp. 59–66). San Diego: Greenhaven.

Witkin, G. (1991, April 8). Kids who kill. *U.S. News and World Report,* pp. 26–32.

Witteman, P. (1991, February 11). Lost in America. *Time,* pp. 76–77.

Witters, W., Venturelli, P., & Hanson, G. (1992). *Drugs and society.* Boston: Jones and Bartlett.

Wolf, E. C. (1986, October). *Beyond the green revolution: New approaches for third world agriculture* (Worldwatch Paper 73). Washington, DC: Worldwatch Institute.

Wolfgang, M. (1966). *Patterns in criminal homicide.* New York: Wiley.

Women in double jeopardy of sexual abuse during police custody in Pakistan. (1992, Fall). *Human Rights Watch,* p. 4.

Wood, D. B. (1992, May 27). Long drought heightens struggle over movement of water in California. *Christian Science Monitor.*

Wood, D. B. (1993, November 10). New study fuels California debate over immigration. *Christian Science Monitor.*

Wood, D., Valdez, B., Hayashi, T., & Stein, A. (1990). Homelessness and housed families in Los Angeles: A study comparing demographic, economic, and family function characteristics. *American Journal of Public Health, 80*(9), 1049–1952.

World access to birth control. (1992). Washington, DC: Population Crisis Committee.

World Development Report. (1992). *Development and the environment.* New York: Oxford University Press.

World grows by 97 million people a year. (1992, April 30). *San Diego Union-Tribune.*

World Health Organization. (1992). *Global health situation and projections.* Geneva: World Health Organization.

World Health Organization. (1993). *World health statistics annual: 1992.* Geneva: World Health Organization.

Wright, E. O. (1985). *Classes.* New York: McGraw-Hill.

Wright, J. (Ed.). (1992). Marijuana. *The universal almanac 1993* (p. 213). Kansas City: Andrews & McMeel.

Wright, J. D. (1991). Guns and crime. In J. S. Sheley (Ed.), *Criminology.* Belmont, CA: Wadsworth.

Wright, R. (1992, March 3). Global alliances shifting from political to economic. *Los Angeles Times.*

Wright, R. (1994, June 14). Rich-poor gap widens around the globe. *Los Angeles Times.*

Y

Yablonsky, L. (1994, July 1). Family violence. *Los Angeles Times.*

Yakovlev, A. M. (1979). Criminological foundation of the criminal process. In M. Cherif Bassiouni & V. M. Savatski (Eds.), *The criminal justice system of the USSR* (pp. 103–129). Springfield, IL: Charles R. Thomas.

Yanagashita, M. (1993, May). Slow growth will turn to decline of the Japanese population. *Population Today—News, Numbers, and Analysis, 21*(5), 4–5.

Yarbo, S. (1992, May 4). Ecuador to grant Indians title to rain forest lands. *Christian Science Monitor.*

Yates, R. E. (1990, April 8). Japan's violent young rebels "fight back." *San Diego Union.*

Yenkin, J. (1993, June 16). Child hunger said to affect 12 million. *Buffalo News.*

Yoshino, I. R., & Murakoshi, S. (1983). Burakumin. In *Kodansha encyclopedia of Japan, vol. 1* (pp. 216–217). Tokyo: Kodansha.

Z

Zaire capital on brink of AIDS disaster. (1991, November 4). *San Diego Tribune.*

Zhongyu, X. (1986). On the education and redemption of juvenile delinquents in China. Unpublished manuscript.

Zimring, F. E. (1986). Gun control. *National Institute of Criminal Justice—Crime file study guide.* Washington, DC: U.S. Department of Justice.

Zimring, F. E., & Hawkins, G. (1989). Gun control would not reduce crime. In W. Dudley (Ed.), *Crime and criminals—Opposing viewpoints* (pp. 213–217). San Diego: Greenhaven.

NAME INDEX

SUBJECT INDEX

Note: The letter "B" after a page number indicates that the topic is addressed in a "Focus On" box on that page.

A

B

D

F

G

O

P

R

S

U

PHOTO CREDITS

p. xviii: © Steve McCurry/© Magnum; p. 4: The Bettmann Archive; p. 12: John Duricka/AP Wide World (left) & Jeff Speed/JB Pictures (right); p. 19: Francisco Conde/Impact Visuals; p. 24: Robel/JB Pictures; p. 29: Paul Miller/Black Star; p. 35: The Bettmann Archive (left) & Marleen Daniels/Gamma Liaison (right); p. 51: ABC/Ajansi/Gamma Liaison; p. 62: Gianni Giansanti/Sygma; p. 66: John Trotter/JB Pictures; p. 75: © Steve McCurry/© Magnum; p. 79: Owen Franken/Sygma; p. 82: Krasner/Trebitz/Gamma Liaison; p. 96: Gustavo Gilabert/JB Pictures; p. 104: © Steve McCurry/© Magnum; p. 108: Stehane Compoint/Sygma; p. 118: Vincent Heloup/Figaro/Gamma Liaison; p. 124: John Nordell/JB Pictures; p. 130: Alexis Duclos/Gamma Liaison; p. 139: Alon Reininger/Woodfin Camp & Associates; p. 142: Kulish/L.A. Daily News/Sygma; p. 147: Julio Etchart/Reportage/Impact Visuals; p. 155: Pierre Perrin/GLMR/Gamma Liaison; p. 162: Harvey Finkle/Impact Visuals; p. 168: Joel Sartore/JB Pictures (left) & Kamal Kishore/Reuters/Bettmann (right); p. 183: Steve Rubin/JB Pictures; p. 185: Gustavo Gilabert/JB Pictures; p. 194: M. A. Bridges/Sygma; p. 198: Peter Charlesworth/JB Pictures (left) & Baldev/Sygma (right); p. 212: James Nubile/JB Pictures; p. 220: John Gibbins/Reuters/Bettmann; p. 224: Stephen Jaffe/JB Pictures; p. 229: Jose Azel/Contact/Woodfin Camp & Associates; p. 238: Paul Chesley Photographers/Aspen; p. 245: PhotoCall-Dublin/Sygma; p. 247: Francis Apesteguy/Gamma Liaison; p. 252: Alon Reininger/Contact/Woodfin Camp & Associates; p. 258: Timothy Ross/JB Pictures; p. 276: Michele Bartran/JB Pictures; p. 280: © Alberto Venzago/© Magnum; p. 287: AP Wide World; p. 292: Rob Nelson/Black Star; p. 302: Joseph Rodriquez/Black Star; p. 305: Donna Ferrato/Domestic Abuse Awareness Project/Black Star; p. 317: Doug Kirkland/Sygma; p. 324: © Eugene Richards/© Magnum; p. 328: Viktor Korotayev/ GLMR/Gamma Liaison; p. 333: Steve Rubin/JB Pictures; p. 344: Romano Cagnoni/Black Star; p. 353: © G. Pinkhassov/© Magnum; p. 359: N. Palumbo/Gamma Liaison; p. 364: P. du Sighiti/Reuters/Bettmann; p. 372: Erica Lansner/Black Star (left) & Steve Rubin/JB Pictures (right); p. 379: © Raghu Rai/© Magnum; p. 384: © Leonard Freed/© Magnum.